PANCAVIMSA BRAHMANA
THE BRAHMANA OF TWENTY FIVE CHAPTERS

D1859792

PANCAVIMSA BRAHMANA

THE BRAHMANA OF TWENTY FIVE CHAPTERS

TRANSLATED BY

DR. W. CALAND

Emeritus Professor of Sanskrit in the University of Utrecht

GYAN

Published by

Gyan Publishing House
5, Ansari Road
Daryaganj, New Delhi-110002
Phone: 011-47034999, 9811692060
E-mail: books@gyanbooks.com

Distribution Network
gyanbooks.com
India, USA, Canada, UK, Australia, France

© Publisher

All rights reserved. No part of this work may be reproduced, stored, adapted, or transmitted in any form or by any means, electronic, mechanical, photocopying, micro-filming, recording or otherwise, or translated in any language, without the prior written permission of the copyright owner and the publisher.

ISBN : 978-81-212-1987-7 (PB)
First Published, 1931

2nd Impression 2021

Printed at: Gyan Press, Delhi.

The book is sold subject to the condition that it shall not, by way of trade or otherwise, be lent, resold, hired out, or otherwise circulated without the prior publisher's written consent.

Pancavimsa Brahmana
The Brahmana of Twenty Five Chapters
Translated by: Dr. W. Caland

PAÑCAVIṂŚA-BRĀHMAṆA

THE BRĀHMAṆA OF TWENTY FIVE CHAPTERS

TRANSLATED BY

DR. W. CALAND

Emeritus Professor of Sanskrit in the University of Utrecht

PRINTED AT THE BAPTIST MISSION PRESS
PUBLISHED BY THE ASIATIC SOCIETY OF BENGAL

CALCUTTA
1931

W. CALAND.

Born, den Briel, August 27th, 1859.

INTRODUCTION.

Chapter I. The Sāmavedic Texts.

It may be desirable to give as complete a descriptive list as possible of the books belonging to the Sāmaveda.

Three "Schools" or *śākhā*'s ("branches") are to be distinguished; that of the Kauthumas, that of the Rāṇāyanīyas and that of the Jaiminīyas. The last mentioned *śākhā* will be here passed in silence, as this Introduction only regards the Brāhmaṇa of the Kauthuma-Rāṇāyanīyas[1].

§1. Texts of the Kauthumas.

A. The gānas.

1. The grāmegeyagāna (or veyagāna) in 17 prapāṭhakas, each of which is divided in two halves; published in the great edition of the Sāmaveda (in 5 volumes) by Satyavrata Sāmaśrami, Calcutta 1874, in the Bibliotheca Indica: Vol. I, page 94—Vol. II, page 242. A valuable and very correct edition (more correct in some respects than the edition of Calcutta) has been procured by Kṛṣṇasvāmin Śrautin under the title: *Sāmavedasaṃhitāyāṃ Kauthumaśākhāyā Veyagānam*, Tiruvadi, 1889. This edition is printed in Grantha characters.

2. The araṇyegeyagāna (or āraṇyagāna) in 6 prapāṭhakas, each again divided in two halves: arkaparvan: I. a—II a; dvandvaparvan: II. b—III. b; vrataparvan: IV. a—V. b; śukriyaparvan: VI. To these the mahānāmnī's belong as an appendix. This gāna is contained in the edition of Calcutta Vol. II, pages 244–384, 387–518.

3. The ūhagāna in 7 parvans: daśarātra, saṃvatsara, ekāha, ahīna, sattra, prāyaścitta and kṣudra, divided over 23 prapāṭhakas, which again consist of two (only 9, 21 and 23 of three) halves. It is contained in the edition of Calcutta (*sparsim*): Vol. III, page 1—Vol. V, page 380, Vol. V, pages 602–673. An index is found in the Introduction to Vol. V, pages t-ghgh.

---

[1] With reference to the books of the Jaiminiyas, my Introduction to the edition of the Jaiminīya-saṃhitā, page 17 sqq. may be consulted.

4. The ūhyagāna in 7 parvans, designated in the same manner as in the ūhagāna, divided into 16 prapāṭhakas, each again divided into halves; published in the edition of Calcutta, Vol. V, pages 381–600.

B. The ārcikas.

1. *a.* The pūrvārcika in 6 prapāṭhakas: the collection of verses on which are composed the sāmans of the grāmegeyagāna, in the edition of Calcutta Vol. I, page 1—Vol. II, page 242; edited also by Benfey: "Die Hymnen des Sāmaveda," Leipsic 1848 and by Stevenson: "Saṃhitā of the Sāmaveda," London 1843.

1. *b.* The āraṇyakasaṃhitā in 5 daśati's, the verses on which the araṇyegeyagāna is (partly) composed, in the edition of Calcutta Vol. II, pages 244–384. Separately edited by Goldschmidt (Monatsber. der kgl. Akad. zu Berlin 1868, pages 229–248) and by Fortunatov.

2. The uttarārcika, the collection of verses to which belongs the ūhagāna, in 9 prapāṭhakas, each divided in two (the last four in three) halves; contained also in the editions of Benfey and Stevenson.

3. The collection of stobhas, in 2 prapāṭhakas, published in the edition of Calcutta Vol. II, pages 519–542.

C. The Brāhmaṇas.

1. The Pañcaviṃśa or Tāṇḍyamahābrāhmaṇa in 25 chapters (prapāṭhakas), published together with the commentary of Sāyaṇa (or rather Mādhava), in two volumes in the Bibliotheca Indica by Anandachandra Vedāntavāgīśa, 1870, 1874. For the text two MSS. of the University Library at Leyden were compared by me. Regarding this Brāhmaṇa see below, chapter III.

2. The Ṣaḍviṃśabrāhmaṇa in 5 adhyāyas; a kind of appendix to the preceding, reckoned as its 26th book. It has been edited uncritically by Jibananda Vidyasagara at Calcutta in 1881 under the title: "Daivatabramhana and Shadbingshabramhana of the Samaveda with the commentary of Sayanacharya." Its first prapāṭhaka has been separately edited, translated and annotated in German by Kurt Klemm ("Das Ṣaḍviṃçabrāhmaṇa mit Proben aus Sāyaṇa's Kommentar nebst einer Übersetzung," Gütersloh, 1894). Its latest part, that which treats of Omina and Portenta (the adbhutabrāhmaṇa) has been separate-

ly edited and translated by A. Weber under the title: "Zwei Vedische Texte über Omina and Portenta" (Abhandl. der Kgl. Akad. der Wiss. zu Berlin, 1858). The best edition of the complete text is "*Ṣaḍviṃśa-brāhmaṇam vijñāpanabhāṣyasahitam*: het Ṣaḍviṃśabrāhmaṇa van den Sāmaveda" etc., by H. F. Eelsingh, Leiden, Brill, 1908. The text clearly intends to supplement the Pañcaviṃśabrāhmaṇa, hence its desultory character. It treats of the Subrahmaṇyā formula, of the one-day-rites that are destined to injure (*abhicāra*) and other matters. This brāhmaṇa, at least partly, is presupposed by the Ārṣeyakalpa and the Sūtrakāras.

3. The Sāmavidhānabrāhmaṇa in 3 prapāṭhakas, edited with the commentary of Sāyaṇa by A. C. Burnell, London, 1873: by Satyavrata Sāmaśrami in the Journal "Uṣā," Calcutta, 1895. Under the title: "Das Sāmavidhānabrāhmaṇa, ein altindisches Handbuch der Zauberei" this book has been translated into German by Sten Konow, Halle/S., 1893. Its aim is to explain how by chanting various sāmans some end may be attained. It is probably older than one of the oldest dharmaśāstras, that of Gautama.

4. The Ārṣeyabrāhmaṇa in 3 prapāṭhakas, edited by A. C. Burnell: "The Ārṣeyabrāhmaṇa of the Sāmaveda, the Sanskrit text edited together with extracts from the commentary of Sāyaṇa," Mangalore, 1876. A somewhat better edition is that published in the Journal "Uṣā" by Satyavrata Sāmaśrami together with the whole commentary of Sāyaṇa, Calcutta, 1891-1892. This quasi-brāhmaṇa is, on the whole, nothing more than an *anukramaṇikā*, a mere list of the names of the sāmans occurring in the first two gānas.

5. The Devatādhyāyabrāhmaṇa in 3 khaṇḍas, edited by A. C. Burnell, Mangalore, 1873 and by Vidyāsāgara, see under No. 2; the title on the wrapper here is daivatabrāhmaṇa. It deals with the deities to which the sāmans are addressed.

6. The Upaniṣadbrāhmaṇa[1] comprising ten prapāṭhakas:

(*a*) The first two contain the mantras for the domestic or gṛhya rites. This book has been published more than once. The whole of it is given by Satyavrata Sāmaśrami under the title: "Mantrabrāhmaṇa," Calcutta 1890, with a commentary. The first prapāṭhaka

[1] There exists another reckoning, according to which the Vaṃśa is the 6th, the Saṃhitopaniṣad the 7th, and the Upaniṣad the 8th in the list of the brāhmaṇas.

has been edited separately by H. Stönner, Halle/S, 1901, together with a translation in German; the second prapāṭhaka has been edited and translated in German by H. Jörgensen, Darmstadt, 1911. Regarding other editions of this text see Stönner, page XV. Usually this part of the Upaniṣad is designated as Mantrabrāhmaṇa.

(*b*) The Upaniṣad proper: the Chāndogya-upaniṣad edited for the first time by Röer in the Bibliotheca Indica, 1850, in the Ānandāśrama series 1890 and by Böhtlingk with a German translation, Leipsic, 1889. It has been translated several times.

7. The Saṃhitopaniṣadbrāhmaṇa in 5 khaṇḍas, edited by A. C. Burnell with a commentary and index of words, at Mangalore, 1877. It treats of the effects of recitation, the relation of the sāman and the words on which it is chanted, the *dakṣiṇās* to be given to the religious teacher.

8. The Vaṃśabrāhmaṇa in 3 khaṇḍas, edited by A. Weber in Indische Studien, vol. IV, pages 371 sqq.; by A. C. Burnell, Mangalore, 1873; by Satyavrata Sāmaśrami in the Journal "Uṣā." 1892. It contains the lists of teachers of the Sāmaveda[1].

D. The Sūtras for Śrautapurpose.

1, 2. The Ārṣeyakalpa of Maśaka and the Kṣudrasūtra, edited by W. Caland under the title: "Der Ārṣeyakalpa des Samāveda," Leipsic, 1908. The Arṣeyakalpa or Maśakakalpasūtra describes in 11 adhyayas the gavāmayana, the ekāhas, the ahīnas and the sattras, closely following the Pañcaviṃśabrāhmaṇa. It is nothing more than a dry list of all the sāmans that are to be applied and the stomas that are to be adhibited. It is, then, younger than the Brāhmaṇa but older than the Sūtras of Lāṭyāyana-Drāhyāyaṇa. It must be prior even to the ritualistic authorities as Gautama, Dhānañjayya, Śāṇḍilya and others, whose divergent opinions are often quoted in the Sūtra.—The Kṣudrasūtra, which sometimes is quoted likewise as being composed by Maśaka, treats of the kāmya and prāyaścitta

[1] These Brāhmaṇas are mentioned partly in an older text, *viz.* the Chandogagṛhyapariśiṣṭa (I. 22), known to me only by two MSS., and attributed to Drāhyāyaṇa. I cite this passage, although it is very corrupt: *pañcaikaṃ* (this must mean *pañcaviṃśaṃ*) *ṣaḍviṃśaṃ sāmavidhānam ārṣeyaṃ daivataṃ saṃhitopaniṣadam catvāry upaniṣada ekaṃ vaṃśam ekaṃ tu. tataḥ paraṃ sūtrādīni....lakṣaṇāni ca śāstrāṇi ca....vācayitvā*, etc.

rites. Its arrangement and style are wholly different from that of the Ārṣeyakalpa proper. Whilst it is certain that the author of the Ārṣeyakalpa has not been acquainted with the uttarārcika, this cannot as yet be affirmed with equal certainty about the Kṣudrasūtra.

3. The Kalpānupadasūtra in 2 prapāṭhakas, each comprising 12 paṭalas. This book seems to be an appendix to the Ārṣeyakalpa (the Kalpasūtra) and the Kṣudrasūtra, which two works the author often cites without naming them; once we find mentioned the *māśakam*. As this Sūtra is known only from one single ms., and as this ms. is rather corrupt, the text is very difficult to understand.

4. The Upagranthasūtra in 4 prapāṭhakas. The text has been published in the Journal "Uṣā" by Satyavrata Sāmaśrami, Calcutta, 1897. It is attributed to Kātyāyana, see Sāyaṇa on Pañc. br. VII. 4. 8 and cp. Weber, "Vorlesungen über altind. Literaturgeschichte" 2, page 92, note. The first three prapāṭhakas are a kind of appendix to the Kṣudrasūtra and to those parts of the Brāhmaṇa to which this Sūtra refers. In the Upagranthasūtra the Kṣudrasūtra is referred to as Ārṣeyakalpa. The last prapāṭhaka is a separate work on the pratihāra parts of the sāmans.

5. The Anupadasūtra in 10 prapāṭhakas, a kind of running commentary on the Pañcaviṃśabrāhmaṇa. The text, in a rather bad state, is known to me from three MSS. It cites a great many Vedic authorities.

6. The Śrautasūtra of Lāṭyāyana in 10 prapāṭhakas, edited together with the commentary of Agnisvāmin, by Ānandachandra in the Bibliotheca Indica, Calcutta, 1872.

7. The Nidānasūtra in 10 prapāṭhakas, edited by Satyavrata Sāmaśrami in the Journal "Uṣā," Calcutta, 1896. Of this text A. Weber published the part on vedic metres (I. 1—7) in "Indische Studien," Vol. VIII, pages 83-125. The author of this book appears to have been Patañjali, see Sāyaṇa on Pañc. br. XIV. 5. 12: *tathā nirālambakamatā bhagavatā patañjalinoktam: saptame 'hany arkaḥ kṛtākṛto bhavaty abrāhmaṇavihitatvād iti.* This quotation is actually found (without, however, the word *arkaḥ*, which may have been inserted for the sake of clearness) in the Nidānasūtra (IV. 7). It is very remark-

able that of the Gautamīya pitṛmedha sūtra (on which see below §2.) the last chapter, beginning *tad apy aparapakṣe prāyaṇaṃ parijihīrṣitaṃ bhavati*, is said, in a grantha edition of this text, to belong to the Pātañjalanidānasūtra, being the 4th khaṇḍa of its 5th prapāṭhaka. We find, indeed, this whole chapter in our text of the Nidānasūtra, not, however, in V. 4, but in II. 6. From Burnell's Catalogue of a collection of Skt. MSS. (London, 1870) we gather (on page 55) that a certain prayogamuktāvali quotes among other authorities the Patañjalaśākhā. So the author of the Nidānasūtra seems to have been Patañjali. There are in this Sūtra some passages which run parallel to Lāṭyāyana-Drāhyāyaṇa, without agreeing literally with these passages. Moreover, our Sūtra contains one quotation from the Brāhmaṇa that is n o t to be traced in this text (III. 12: *atha pramamhiṣṭhīye vadati: hiṃsito 'nvīkṣeta yam icchet prasṛjyamānaṃ pratyeyād iti*). So our text may have belonged originally neither to the Kauthuma nor to the Rāṇāyanīya śākhā. Could it have been originally a book of the Bhāllaviśākhā? cp. Bṛhaddevatā V. 25 and Vasiṣṭha Dharmaśāstra I. 14. 15: *athāpi bhāllavino nidāne gāthām udāharanti*. Or were there two different Nidānasūtras? In either case now-a-days this Nidāna is reckoned among the Sūtras of the Kauthumas.

8. The U p a n i d ā n a s ū t r a in 2 paṭalas, known to me only from a South Indian edition in grantha characters (the title of the little book, in which this treatise and others are contained, runs: *pañcanadavāstavyena prayāgakulatilakena kṛṣṇasvāmiśrautisamākhyena sūriṇā samyak pariśodhya, pañcanadasthajyotirvilāsamudrākṣaraśālāyām mudritā vijante*). Even the title of this treatise is, up to now, unknown. It begins with the same words as the Nidānasūtra: *athātaś chandasāṃ vicayaṃ vyākhyāsyāmaḥ*, and it treats of the different metres, first in a general way, then especially for the two ārcikas (pūrva and āraṇyaka); the second paṭala begins: *atha rahasyachandāṃsi*; here *rahasya* is equal to *āraṇyaka*.

9. The **P a ñ c a v i d h a s ū t r a** in 2 prapāṭhakas, edited by R. Simon as 5th fasciculus of the "Indische Forschungen," Breslau, 1913. It describes in which manner a sāman must be divided in its parts: prastāva, (udgītha, upadrava), pratihāra and nidhana[1].

[1] On the separate prastāva-, pratihāra- and nidhanasūtras see R. Simon, Pañcavidhasūtra, Introd. page 6 and Burnell, Introd. to Ārṣ. br. pages xxv sqq.

10. The Ṛktantra in 5 prapāṭhakas, edited by A. C. Burnell, Mangalore, 1879; it is also found in the Grantha edition of the Grāmegeyagāna mentioned in § 1. a 1. It is a prātiśākhya, *i.e.*, a grammatical treatise which is intended to show how the padas must change in order to become the real hymnical text. According to Burnell (Catalogue of a collection of Sanskrit Manuscripts, London 1870, page 41) the last two prapāṭhakas are called Saṃjñāprakaraṇa; this is probably the same as the Saṃjñālakṣaṇa mentioned in the Caraṇavyūha.

11. The Sāmatantra in 13 prapāṭhakas. It begins *svaro nantyaḥ* and is printed (*disjectis membris!*) in the grantha edition of the Veyagāna. On this text see Burnell, Ārṣ. br. Introduction, page XXIV.

12. The Mātrālakṣaṇasūtra in 3 khaṇḍikas, published in the Grantha edition of the Veyagāna and in the collection of Sāmavedic treatises mentioned under No. 8, on pages 43–50; cp. also Burnell, a Catalogue, etc., page 43. It begins: *athāto hrasvadīrghaplutamātrāṇy akṣarāṇi vyākhyāsyāmaḥ.* It treats of the mātrās of the sounds.

13. The Stobhānusaṃhāra in 3 paṭalas, in śloka metre; printed in the collection of Sāmavedic treatises and beginning:

ādyantadarśanastobho vidhāgīteṣu sāmasu |
pāde pāde 'nusaṃhāryas sopāyo nidhane bhavet ||

See Burnell, Introduction to Saṃhitopanisadbrāhmaṇa, page XVI.

14. The Gāyatravidhānasūtra in 3 paṭalas, printed in the same collection, pages 50–54. I find this treatise nowhere mentioned. It treats of the way in which the gāyatra chant is to be applied at the out-of-door laud, (bahiṣpavamānastotra) etc.,

15. The Puṣpa or Phullasūtra in 10 prapāṭhakas, edited under the title Sāmaprātiśākhya in the journal "Uṣā" by Satyavrata Sāmaśrami, Calcutta, 1890 and by R. Simon with a very useful introduction and translation into German in the Abhandlungen der Bayer. Akad. der Wiss., 1e Klasse, XXIII. Band, III. Abt., München, 1909. This book contains principally the rules for adapting (*ūha*) the sāmans that are given by the grāmegeya- and araṇyegeyagānas on other verses than those to which they belong in these gānas.

E. The sūtras for gṛhya and smārta purpose.

1. The Gobhilīyagṛhyasūtra in 4 prapāṭhakas, edited by Chandrakānta Tarkālaṅkāra in the Bibliotheca Indica, Calcutta, 1890 and, together with a translation in German by F. Knauer, Dorpat, 1884. It describes the domestic rites in use amongst the Kauthumas[1]; the mantras are those contained in the Mantrabrāhmaṇa (see above, c 6).

2. The Karmapradīpa or Kātyāyanasmṛti in 3 prapāṭhakas, edited by Jibananda Vidyasagara in his Dharmaśāstrasaṃgraha, Calcutta, 1876, vol. II, page 603 sqq. The first prapāṭhaka has been separately edited and translated by F. Schrader, Halle a/d. S., 1889; the second by A. V. Staël Holstein, Halle a/d. S., 1900.

3. The Gṛhyāsaṃgraha in 2 prapāṭhakas, edited in the edition of Gobhila, by M. Bloomfield in the Journal of the German Or. Society, vol. XXXV and by Satyavrata Sāmaśrami in the Journal " Uṣā ", Calcutta, 1891.

4. Minor treatises as the Śrāddhakalpa, the Sandhyāsūtra, the Snānavidhi, all in the edition of Gobhila in the Bibliotheca Indica.

The Gobhilagṛhyakarmaprakāśikā gives a complete survey of the texts of the Kauthumas, which is repeated in the Introduction to my edition of the Jaiminīyasaṃhitā, page 13. Even now it is not possible to identify all the texts enumerated there.

§ 2. Texts of the Rāṇāyanīyas.

We have, as yet, no certainty about the question whether the Saṃhitā (*i.e.*, the gānas and the ārcikas) and the Pañcaviṃśa- and Ṣaḍviṃśa-brāhmaṇas of the Kauthumas were also in use with the Rāṇāyanīyas precisely in the same form as these books are known to us. But as it can be proved that the commentator of the Pañcaviṃśa-brāhmaṇa was a Rāṇāyanīya, and the same may be said about Varadarāja, who commented upon the Ārṣeyakalpa, it is probable that these texts at least were common property of the two śākhās. Further, it is certain that they had a different Śrautasūtra and Gṛhyasūtra, the Śrautasūtra being that of Drāhyāyaṇa,

[1] It is striking, that Hemādri in his Śrāddhakalpa, pages 1460, 1468, designates Gobhila as the Rāṇāyanīyasūtrakṛt and his Sūtra (page 1424) as the Rāṇāyanīyasūtra. In the Tarpana of the Kauthumas it is Rāṇāyani who comes first, see Gobhilagṛhyaprakāśikā, page 113.

edited (only partly) by J. N. Reuter with the excellent commentary of Dhanvin: "The Śrautasūtra of Drāhyāyaṇa with the commentary of Dhanvin," Part I, London 1904 (up to XI. 1, but the text was ready for printing up to XVI. 4; of the last unpublished part, Dr. Reuter was so kind as to send me the proof-pages). The Sūtra of Drāhyāyaṇa is nearly identical with that of Lāṭyāyana, the only difference is that Drāhyāyaṇa has a few sūtras more. The Rāṇāyanīyas have also a different G ṛ h y a s ū t r a, ascribed to K h ā d i r a, in 4 paṭalas. It has been edited (text and English translation) by H. Oldenberg in the Sacred Books of the East, Vol. XXIX, pages 371 sqq. An excellent edition has appeared in the Bibliotheca Saṃskrita No. 41 of the Mysore collection: "The Khādiragṛhyasūtra with the commentary of Rudraskanda", Mysore, 1913. The text is to be found also in a South Indian edition in Grantha characters. This Gṛhyasūtra is a mere recast and abbreviation of the Gobhilīyasūtra. One more text can with some probability be assigned to the Rāṇāyanīyas, *viz.*, the D r ā h y ā y a ṇ a g ṛ h y a p a r i ś i ṣ ṭ a, comprising apparently two prapāṭhakas. It is known to me in one complete manuscript, whilst the other contains the first prapāṭhaka and a part of the second. Whether the G a u t a m a p i t ṛ m e d h a s ū t r a, the G a u t a m a s m ṛ t i and the G a u t a m a d h a r m a ś ā s t r a belonged originally to a Gautamaśākhā of the Sāmaveda, is uncertain.

Chapter II. O n t h e i n t e r r e l a t i o n a n d t h e h i s t o r i c d e v e l o p m e n t o f t h e o l d e r S ā m a v e d i c t e x t s.

The Saṃhitā of the Sāmaveda, then, comprises:

1. Four song-books (grāmegeya- and araṇyegeyagāna, ūha- and ūhyagāna).

2. Three collections of verses: the text-books to these song-books; the verses agree on the whole with the verses of the Ṛksaṃhitā.

The songs, chaunts, sāmans of the gānas are based or composed on the verses. From a verse (a *ṛk*) a sāman is made by musical notation, by certain changes as stretching of vowels, and repetition of syllables, and by inserting different sounds and syllables, sometimes whole sentences or verses. These insertions are called *stobhas*.

The relation between the p ū r v ā r c i k a (and āraṇyakasaṃhitā) and uttarārcika on the one side and the first two gānas (grāme- and araṇyegeyas) on the other side, is clear: with each verse of the p ū r v ā r c i k a corresponds a single chant, a single sāman; each of these sāmans have a name, mostly derived from the name of that Ṛṣi who is said to have "seen" the sāman and these sāmans are collected in the first two song-books. The arrangement of the *yonis*, *i.e.*, the verses on which the sāmans are composed, in the pūrvārcika, is systematic: first come the verses addressed to Agni, then, those addressed to Indra, and then, those addressed to Soma pavamāna. Each group is subdivided according to their metres The u t t a r ā r c i k a, on the other hand, rests on a wholly different principle and has a different aim. In this part of the Saṃhitā single verses are not recorded, but its bulk consists of tristichs or pragāthas (*i.e.* two verses: 1. either a bṛhatī or a kakubh; 2. a satobṛhatī; in the praxis out of these two verses are made three, so that practically such a pragātha is equally a tristich.) We find likewise complexes of 4, 6, 7, 9 and 10 verses. The aim of this collection is purely practical: it contains the verses on which at the occasion of the several kinds of great sacrifices the lauds are chanted: on the whole, each first verse of such a tristich occurs in the pūrvārcika, this means that the melody (the sāman) which belongs to this verse in the pūrvārcika, is to be applied on the whole tristich of the uttarārcika. One example will make this clear. The first verse of the pragātha in the uttarārcika 1. 1. 13 (=vs. 35 of the continuous numeration), beginning *taṃ vo dasmam ṛtīṣaham*, is found in the pūrvārcika: 3. 1. 5. 4. (=vs. 236 of the continuous numeration). To this verse belong, according to the grāmegeyagāna, five melodies the last of which is the naudhasa (grām. VI. 1. 37, see Calcutta edition, Vol. I, page 487): On this melody, now, the two verses of the uttarārcika 35 and 36 (out of which by repetition three verses are made) must be chanted in the praxis of the Soma-sacrifice: as third pṛṣṭha-laud of the ordinary Agniṣṭoma; these three verses as used in the praxis are given in the ūhagāna I. 1. 6 (see Calcutta edition, Vol. III, page 93). But it is a fact that there is a great number of verses in the uttarārcika that have no correspondent verse in the pūrvārcika *e.g.*, the first 18 verses of the uttarārcika and many more. This is explained by the fact that these verses, which all belong to the morning service (the *prātaḥsavana*), are chanted on the gāyatra-melody which is composed on the well known verse addressed to Savitṛ: *tat savitur vareṇyam*, etc. This melody has been recorded in the devatādhyāyabrāhmaṇa; it is given as an appendix to the editions of the grāmegeyagāna (Ed. Calcutta, Vol. V, page 601). On the other hand, many *yonis* (and sāmans composed on these) are found in the pūrvārcika which have no correspondent verse (and chant) in the uttarārcika. This is explained by the fact, that sāmans are chanted not only at the great sacrifices of soma, but likewise on many other occasions: at the establishing of the sacred fires (the agnyādheya); at the foundation of the high altar of bricks (the agnicayana); at the pravargya ceremony and on other occasions. These sāmans were chanted as solo (*parisāman*), mostly by the Prastotṛ (Lāṭy. I. 5. 8 sqq., I. 6. 1 sqq., etc.).

About the ūhagāna and the ūhyagāna the following remarks may be made. Each of these gānas is divided in 7 parvans: 1. daśarātra, 2. saṃvatsara, 3 ekāha, 4. ahīna, 5. sattra, 6. prāyaścitta, 7. kṣudra. As to their aim, these two gānas precisely correspond with the uttarārcika, they serve the praxis of the soma-sacrifices: the ūhagāna runs parallel with the uttarārcika and the grāmegeya, the ūhyagāna with the āraṇyakasaṃhitā and the araṇyegeyagana The names themselves are clear: *ūhati* means "to adapt"; the ūhagana contains the melodies of the grāmegeya but adapting them and working them out so as they are to be chanted in the praxis; the ūhyagāna (which word is abbreviated from ūharahasyagāna, rahasya being another name for āraṇyaka), adapting the melodies of the araṇyegeyagāna to the verses on which they must be chanted in the praxis. It can be proved with certainty that these two gānas belong to the later strata of the Sāmavedic literature: that they are later than the grāme- and araṇyegeyagānas, later than the Pañcaviṃśabrāhmaṇa, later than the Ārṣeya- and Kṣudrakalpa, later than the sūtra of Lāṭyāyana-Drāhyāyaṇa, later even than the Puṣpasūtra. That they are later than and, even in their sequence, based on the Ārṣeyakalpa and the Kṣudrasūtra, can be proved. The Ārṣeyakalpa describes the gavāmayana, the ekāhas, the ahīnas and the sattras; all the sāmans to be used on these occasions occur in the 2nd—5th parvans of the ūha- and ūhyagānas in precisely the same sequence as in the Ārṣeyakalpa. For the chants of the ten-day-rite, which had been treated fully in the Brāhmaṇa, the ūha- and ūhyagānas lean on this text. The Kṣudrasūtra describes the prāyaścitta and kāmya rites: with these run parallel the last two parvans of the ūha and the ūhya. That both texts, Ārṣeyakalpa and Kṣudrasūtra, are prior to the ūha- and ūhyagānas, may be proved by one example from each. In the Ārṣeyakalpa IX.: 9. b. we read *auśanasyarkṣu vaiśvajyotiṣam antyam yat pra gāyateti*: "the closing chant is the vaiśvajyotiṣa, chanted on the verses of the auśana, as indicated by the words *pra gāyata*". The verses of the auśana are SV. I. 523=II.27 (28): *pra tu drava* etc.; on these must be chanted the vaiśvajyotiṣa belonging to SV I. 534 (*pra gāyata*). But, as there are likewise vaiśvajyotiṣa-melodies on other verses, the addition was necessary. Now, the ūhagāna XIX. 1. 7 (Sāmaveda, ed. Calcutta, Vol. III, page 82) gives the vaiśvajyotiṣa on these verses *pra tu drava*. If the author of the Ārṣeyakalpa had been acquainted with the ūhagāna, his indication: "(the vaiśvajyotiṣa) as indicated by the words *pra gāyata*" would have been wholly superfluous. To prove that the Kṣudrasūtra also is earlier than the ūhagāna, the following example may suffice. Kṣudrasūtra I. 6 (No. 30) we read: *annādyakāmasyendrā yāhi dhiyeṣita iti madhyamām tṛcasya prabhṛtim kṛtvā tāsu kāleyam, i.e.*, "for one who is desirous of obtaining food, he should take the middle verse of the tristich beginning: *indrā yāhi dhiyeṣitaḥ* as first and chant on these (so arranged) verses the kāleya." The tristich here mentioned is SV. II. 496–498, its middle verse is the one intended; on these verses, but arranged 497, 496, 498, he should chant the kāleya (grāmegeyagāna VI. 2. 7, ed. Calc. Vol. I, page 491, composed on SV. I. 237). Now, we find in the ūhagāna XXI. 2. 4 (ed. Calc. Vol. V, page 638) the chant precisely as the author of the Kṣudrasūtra had prescribed it. Had the author of the sūtra been acquainted with the ūhagāna, his indication "taking the middle verse at the beginning" would have been wholly superfluous. To prove that neither was the Sūtrakāra acquainted with the ūha- and ūhyagānas, the following proof may be adduced. In the Pañcaviṃśabrāhmaṇa it is prescribed at V. 4. 5-6 that the chanters at the mahāvrata-rite must chant the sāman called vasiṣṭhasya nihava over the cātvāla, and that this sāman must be chanted on a verse addressed to the "All-gods". As there are many verses addressed to this deity in the collection of the Sāmaveda, it is uncertain which verse is to be taken. The Sūtrakāra (Lāṭy. III. 9. 12, Drāhy. X. I. 11) makes the following precision, *viśve devā iti vasiṣṭhasya nihavam ūhet, i.e.*: "he should adapt the vasiṣṭhasya nihava to the verse SV. ār. saṃh. III. 9"; the sāman, composed on SV. I. 313: *asāvi devam*, is given by grāmegeyagāna VIII. 1. 36 (ed. Calc. Vol. I, page 629); the melody on the verse addressed to the "All-gods" is found in the ūhagāna IX. 3. 12 (ed.

Calc. Vol. V, page 602). It is not possible that the Sūtrakāra would have expressed himself as he does, if at his time the ūhagāna existed. Dhanvin, the commentator of Drāhyāyaṇa, remarks on this last mentioned passage: "*Is not the expression: 'he should adapt'* meaningless, as its (*i.e.* the sāman's) reading is known (*viz.* from the ūhagāna)? That is true, but they say:—"the ūha (*i.e.* the ūhagana) is made after the time of this expression (of the Sūtrakara's)" [1].—We have now to prove our assertion that even the Puṣpasūtra is older than ūha- and ūhyagānas, an assertion not accepted by all scholars [2]. The aim of this text, in my opinion, is to give the rules for adapting the sāmans, as they are handed down in the grāme- and araṇyegeyagānas, for practical use at the sacrifices. This is clearly proved by the last words of the part, which originally ended the text (VIII. 234): *evaṃ sarveṣām eṣa vikāravidhir, etena pradeśenohyaḥ sāmagaṇaḥ kalpayitavyaḥ.* Professor Simon, the learned editor and translator of the sūtra, renders these words as follows:—"Hiermit sind nun die Veränderungen in allen (sāmans) ordnungsgemäsz angeführt. Nach dieser Darlegung ist es möglich, die Gesammtheit der zum ūhagāna gehörenden Sāmans in der Praxis zu gebrauchen." According to my opinion, the last sentence should be translated: "by means of this indication (this set of rules) the group of sāmans (as they are handed down in the grāme- and araṇyegeyagānas) must be adapted (and) made ready (for practical purposes)." It is highly probable that amongst the Sāmavedic Brāhmins in early times certain rules were established and handed down by oral tradition for the adaptation (the ūha) of the sāmans in the grāme- and araṇyegeyagānas, that these rules were at last collected and arranged in a book (our Puṣpasūtra), and that afterwards for convenience's sake these rules were all brought into action; in this manner the two last books of songs, the two last gānas, arose. So, when we read in the Nidānasūtra (II. 1): *ṛṣikṛtaḥ svid ūhā 3 anṛṣikṛta iti vai khalv āhuḥ.... ṛṣikṛta ity aparam.* and in the Jaimininyāyamālāvistara (IX. 2. 1—2):

ūhagrantho 'pauruṣeyaḥ pauruṣeyo 'tha vāgrimaḥ |
vedasāmasamāna-tvād vidhisārthatvato 'ntimaḥ ||

---

[1] The text runs: *nanu ca ūhed iti vacanam anarthakam, tasyādhyānasiddhatvāt, satyam etad, vacanottarakālam ūhaḥ kṛta ity āhuḥ.*

[2] Regarding this controversy, see the author's criticism of Simon's Puṣpasūtra in "Deutsche Literaturzeitung" 1909, No 30; Simon's paper in the Journal of the German Or. Soc. vol. 63, page 731, and the author's paper ib. vol. 64, page 347.

the answer must be even as said in the last part of this śloka: "The ūhagāna is made by the Ṛṣi's, so far as it contains the melodies "seen" by them, but, on the other hand, it is made by men, so far as it has been adapted by men." With the fact, now, as it seems, clearly established that these last two gānas are of younger date, the Sāmavidhānabrāhmaṇa also harmonises, where sāmans are cited from these two gānas, but only of the first two.

The names of these gānas are now all clear. The grāmegeyagāna contains those sāmans that were studied in the community, the araṇyegeyagāna, on the other hand, hands down those sāmans that, because they were so very sacred, or, what is nearly the same, from a primitive standpoint, so very dangerous, were studied in the forest, outside the community (see especially the exhaustive paper of H. Oldenberg on Āraṇyaka in Nachrichten der kgl. Ges. der Wiss. zu Göttingen, Phil.-hist. kl. 1915, page 382 and for the Āraṇyaka texts of the Sāmaveda page 392 sqq.).

We now come to a very difficult question, and one which is of the highest importance not only for a true insight into the historic development of the older Sāmavedic texts, but also of great weight for the explanation of many a passage in the Brāhmaṇa and the kindred texts. This question is: "was the pūrvārcika or was the uttarārcika the older part?" Scholars are at variance. I myself maintained that the uttarārcika must be regarded as prior to the pūrvārcika, chiefly on the argument that a collection of verses on which the Sāmans had to be chanted (as is the uttarārcika) must have been *a priori* older than a collection of verses that served to register the melodies on which these verses had to be chanted (as is the pūrvārcika). Oldenberg, on the other hand, has made it appear that the pūrvārcika (together with the āraṇyaka part) was the older part, because this part only is mentioned in the vratas, and, moreover, the uttarārcika is nowhere quoted in the Sāmavidhānabrāhmaṇa. I add to this that even so late a work as the Atharvapariśiṣṭa mentions (46. 3, 6) as last verse of the Sāmaveda the last but one of the p ū r v ā r c i k a (*viz.* Sv. I. 584). Convinced by Oldenberg's strong arguments, I thereupon proposed to formulate the facts thus: that from the oldest times on the chanters must have had at their disposal a certain collection of tristichs and pragāthas, that served them at the soma-rites for chanting after their melodies; that this collection might have been the fore-runner of the uttarārcika as it is known to us now-a-days. Oldenberg himself, who wrote: "möglich ist es natürlich, dasz, als das Pūrvārcika redigiert wurde, ein Kanon der Agniṣṭoma-liturgien schon fixirt war," did not materially differ from my view.

The study of the Brāhmaṇas and the kindred texts has now suggested to me a hypothesis, that perhaps may throw light on this difficult question. To state it directly at the beginning of my argumentation, this is my hypothesis: the author of the Brāhmaṇa was not acquainted with our uttarārcika, it did not exist at his time, but the chanters drew the verses they wanted, directly from the Ṛksaṃhitā, and the uttarārcika was composed in later times, in order to have at hand, in the regular order of the sacrifices, the verses that were wanted.

The facts, on which this thesis is based, are the following.

1. It is expressly stated (see the translation of Pañcaviṃśa-brāhmana IV. 4. 1, sqq. with my notes) that in a certain case a great number of verses had to be taken directly from the Ṛksaṃhitā. That the word used here by the three sūtras: *daśatayīṣu* (Sāyaṇa periphrases *dāśatayyām*) means "in the ten books of the Ṛksaṃhitā," is proved by a sentence in the Nidānasūtra (II. 11, see note 4 on Pañc. br. VIII. 8. 26) *dāśatayenādhyāyena* as contrasted with ib. II. 2: *chāndasenādhyāyena*, which must signify: "a chapter of the Sāmavedasaṃhitā." This presupposes for the chanters the acquaintance with the Ṛksaṃhitā or at least with a part of it, from which their verses were to be taken directly.

2. The expression *saṃbhārya* to denote a complex of verses to be taken from different parts of the Veda occurs thrice in the Brāhmaṇa: XI. 1. 5, XVI. 5. 11 and XVIII. 8. 8. This expression is simply incomprehensible from a Sāmavedistic standpoint, because in the uttarārcika they are given as a whole, all after one another, but from a Ṛgvedistic standpoint they are truly *saṃbhārya's*.

3. From the passage in the Brāhmaṇa IV. 2. 19, where a jarābodhīya-sāman is mentioned, to be chanted on SV. I. 25 (=II. 733–735) it seems right to infer, that the uttarārcika was later than the Brāhmaṇa. If this is true, the Brāhmaṇa cannot but have taken his verses directly from the Ṛksaṃhitā. The compilator of the uttarārcika may have inserted this triplet, because it occurred in the Brāhmaṇa.

4. See also the notes on the Brāhmaṇa XI. 7. 3, XIV. 1. 9.

There can, however, be made several objections to this hypothesis.

In the first place, the verses as cited in the Brāhmaṇa diverge in not a few cases, more or less, from the reading presented in our Ṛksaṃhitā. But it is a fact that, when the author of the Brāhmaṇa quotes from the Ṛksaṃhitā in general, his citation mostly contains one or more corruptions (see the Brāhmaṇa I. 2. 9, I. 7. 6, IX. 2. 22, XXIV. 1. 9). In one case a change in a verse of the Ṛksaṃhitā can be proved to be caused by the ritual (see the note on XI. 5. 1). Elsewhere a divergence from the Ṛkverse may have been caused by its sāman-reading (see XIV. 6. 4). So the variants may be caused by slovenness, but in part they could be explained by the surmise that our Brāhmaṇa presupposes a recension of the Ṛksaṃhitā different from the one known to us (see note 1 on VI. 10. 14). That some verses are found in the ārcika but not in our Ṛksaṃhitā might be explained by the conjecture that our Ṛksaṃhitā once contained more verses than it now does in its present recension (see note 2 on VIII. 1. 1, note 1 (end) on XII. 13. 22). But I am not able to remove all the difficulties that seem to move against my hypothesis. I draw the reader's attention to the puzzle contained in VIII. 8. 26, SV. II. 62 as against ṚS. VIII. 98. 9 (here perhaps we might guess that the compiler of the uttarārcika changed the Ṛk-verse so as to bring it in accordance with the Brahmaṇa.) A weighty argument against the hypothesis might be drawn from XII. 1. 9, 10, XII. 7. 9, 10, XIII. 1. 10–12, XIII. 7. 8-9, where the terms pentastichs, decastichs and so on, are used. We may ask here: "how could we know which verses are intended, unless it were supposed that the uttarārcika existed at the time when the Brāhmaṇa was composed?" But perhaps the author of our Brāhmaṇa allowed here a free choice, whilst in later times the compiler of the uttarārcika fixed these verses probably in accordance with the Jaiminīyabrāhmaṇa, which, as far as I have ascertained, states by citing their opening words, which verses had to be employed. Another difficulty is presented by the passage XIII. 1. 1 as compared with *ib.* 5.

Although, then, all is far from certain, I suppose that now we may with some measure of probability propose the following development of the oldest Sāmavedic literature.

The chanters were acquainted with the Ṛksaṃhitā, at least with certain parts of it. From this text they took their verses [1] and on these

[1] Cp. Oldenberg in the Journal of the German Or. Soc., Vol. XXXVIII, page 441: "der Ṛigveda ist zugleich der älteste Sāmaveda," but read in the context this assertion is not equivalent to my hypothesis.

they chanted the lauds at the sacrifices of soma. In order to facilitate the study and memorization of this material, a double register was composed, one of the melodies and one of the verses, on which the melodies were chanted. The first register they arranged so, that each time only the first verse of a tristich or a pragātha was taken up, and this verse was considered as the bearer of the melody. To this collection were added sāmans of a different kind, that had to be chanted by a single Chanter at other occasions. In this manner two books of songs, two gānas, arose: the one to be studied inside the community: the grāmegeyagāna, and another to be studied in the forest, outside the community: the araṇyegeyagāna; this book comprised those sāmans that were the most holy (dangerous). Besides these song-books arose at the same time the second register: the ārcika (the later pūrvarcika) and the āraṇyaka. Thereupon a Brāhmaṇa originated. Based on this Brāhmaṇa the Ārṣeyakalpa was composed by Maśaka, who described minutely the sacrifices of soma, but omitted the ten-day-rite, because its detailed description was already given in the chapters 10-15 of the Brāhmaṇa. Based again on these two books the śrautasūtra was composed (that of Lāṭyāyana-Drāhyāyaṇa). Then only the uttarārcika was compiled, which contained the verses of the Ṛksaṃhitā, arranged in their regular order, so as they were to be used in the sacrifices. Now, if a Chanter knew by heart his two gānas and if he knew which verses ought to be adhibited in any rite, he could bring about all the changes that were necessary for adapting a melody to a given triplet or pragātha. These rules for adaptation were then fixed and systematically arranged in a special book: the Puṣpasūtra. But, in order to have at hand for immediate use the sāmans so as they were to be adapted according to the rules of the Puṣpasūtra, two more books were composed: the adapted song-books: 1. the ūhagāna and 2. the ūharahasyagāna (called by abbreviation uhyagāna). The first contains ready made for sacrificial use the sāmans in their regular order resting on the grāmegeyagāna, the second those that rest on the araṇyegeyagāna. This is according to my view the history of the oldest Sāmavedic texts[1].

---

1 The material on which rest for the greater part the above given considerations and conclusions is found in the paper of Oldenberg in the Journal of the German Or. Soc. (Vol. XXXVIII); in a paper: "De Wording van den Sāmaveda" (Versl. en Meded. der. Kon. Ak. v. Wetensch. Afd. Lett. 4e R., Deel IX); in my

Chapter III. On the Pañcaviṃśabrāhmaṇa

§1. The relation between the Pañcaviṃśabrāhmaṇa and the Jaiminīyabrāhmaṇa.

Some remarks must be made, at the beginning, about the Jaiminīyabrāhmaṇa.

The Vedic texts themselves and their commentaries contain a great number of citations drawn from a Śāṭyāyanibrāhmaṇa or a Śāṭyāyanakam [1], and it has been remarked that the great plurality of these citations occurs in the text known to us as the Jaiminīyabrāhmaṇa. But all the citations from the Śāṭyāyanaka are not found literally in the Jaiminīyabrāhmaṇa, and some of these have n o t at all been traced in it. It is, therefore, probable, that the two Brāhmaṇas, though, on the whole agreeing, were not wholly alike. Perhaps the original Śāṭyāyanaka, which is lost to us, was taken over by the Jaiminīyas, either a part or the whole of it and amplified with other passages.

Now, the Jaiminīya and the Tāṇḍyamahābrāhmaṇa have much material in common, which is to be expected *a priori*, as they treat of the same matter: the rite of the Sāman-chanter and his assistants. They both contain the description of the Gavāmayana (the sacrifice lasting a year long), the prototype (*prakṛti*) of a one-day-rite (ekāha), the detailed description of the ten-day-rite which has its place at the end of a sattra, the description of the various one-day-rites (ekāhas) and of the ahīnas (sacrifices of more than one and less than twelve days). Peculiar to the Pañcaviṃśabrāhmaṇa are the contents of the first three Chapters, for which see below, § 6. But, although the contents of the two Brāhmaṇas are, on the whole, similar, the two books differ widely with regard to their diction: the Jaiminīyabrāhmaṇa is much more prolix, whilst the Pañcaviṃśa gives only what is strictly necessary and often so sketchily that the myths or legends found in it are sometimes

---

Introduction to the Jaim. br. (Indische Forschungen 2. Heft, 1907, Breslau); in Oldenberg's review of this work in G. G. A. 1908, No. 9; in the author's review of Simon's Puṣpasūtra (D.L.Z. 1909, No. 30); in a short notice in the Journ. of the Germ. Or. Soc., Vol. LXII, page 347 and in a notice in the Vienna Journal (W. Z.K.M.), Vol. XXII, page 436.

[1] See on these citations my paper: "Over en uit het Jaiminīyabrāhmaṇa," in Versl. in Meded. der K. Ak. van Wetensch. 5e Reeks, Deel. I, page 5 sqq. The contents of this paper, which is written in Dutch and therefore inaccessible to many scholars, are here repeated in a somewhat abbreviated form.

hardly comprehensible. It is as if the author presupposes that these myths or legends are known to his readers. This may be caused either by the fact that there was current a certain cycle of legends and myths, or that the Pañcaviṃśa borrowed them from the other Brāhmaṇa: the Śāṭyāyani- or the Jaiminīyabrāhmaṇa. In the latter case, the Jaiminīya must be the older of the two. Now, are there any facts that may make this last possibility plausible?

An investigation of this matter must rest on two considerations: (1) on the linguistic facts and (2) on the ritualistic facts, *i.e.* the contents.

A. The linguistic facts.

In the Pañcaviṃśabrāhmaṇa we find constantly the locative of stems in *-n* with the case sign *-i*: *ātmani*, *carmaṇi*, *ahani*, *sāmani*; once only *ātman* in *ātman dhatte*, at the side of *ātmany adhatta* IV. 1. 15. In the Jaiminīya, on the other hand, the locatives in *-n* are preponderant; sporadically we find a form in *-i* (*rājani* II. 25, *carmaṇi* II. 405, *varṣmaṇi* II. 376).

In the Pañcaviṃśa we find without any exception as ending of the nom. plur. of stems in *-ī* the classical ending *-yaḥ*, whilst the Jaiminīya in this case has mostly the vedic ending *-īḥ*; compare *yāvatyaḥ*.. *tāvatyaḥ* of PBr. IV. 2. 7 with *tavatīḥ* of JBr. II. 377; *viṣṇumatyaḥ* XIII. 3. 1 as against *viṣṇuvatīḥ* III. 91; *pratnavatyaḥ* XI. 1. 2 against *pratnavatīḥ* II. 12; *puroḍāśinyaḥ* XXI. 10. 10 as against *puroḍāśinīḥ* II. 287; *āpriyaḥ* XV. 8. 1 against *āprīḥ*; *pravatyaḥ* XI. 5. 1 against *pravatīḥ* II. 16; *paṣṭhauhyo garbhiṇyaḥ* XVIII. 9. 21 as against *paṣṭhauhīḥ* II. 203, 204[1].

The accusative of stems in *-u* is *tanūm* in PBr. XII. 12. 3 as against the older vedic form *tanvam* of JBr. III. 82, 178.

Classical is the form *asthīni* of PBr. IX. 8. 1, 13 as against *asthāni* of JBr. I. 252, 345, 347.

---

[1] No criterium of posteriority or priority is provided by the regular occurrence of the ending *-yāḥ* of the gen. -abl. sing. from stems in *-ā*, *-ī*, in the PBr. as against the ending *-ai* (*-yai*) in JBr., see Acta Orientalia Vol. V, page 51. Nor, as far as I see, can a criterium of this kind be found in the occurrence of datives from stems in *-i*, such as *gatyai*, PBr. XI. 1. 15, *ariṣṭyai* XVI. 10. 10, *prabhūtyai* XI. 10. 19 as against the ending *-taye* which is regular in the JBr.—On *anuvyam* of PBr. X. 3.2 as against *anuyuvam* of the Jaim. br. cp. my Introduction to the edition of the Kāṇvīya Śatapathabrāhmaṇa, page 51.

In the PBr. we meet with *yuvām* (XXI. 1. 1), the classical nom. dual, whereas the JBr. presents throughout in such cases the older form in *-am*.

The vedic pronoun *tva* occurs several times in the JBr., and perhaps but once in PBr. (IV. 1. 2), though here it has become unrecognizable either through faulty sandhi or because the author of the Brāhmaṇa did not acknowledge this form, which perhaps had become obsolete in his time.

In some verbal forms the PBr. has the younger, classical forms, as against the vedic forms of the JBr.: *dugdhe* PBr. XII. 11. 18, *duhe* the JBr. more than once; *duhate* of PBr. is classic, *duhre* of JBr. (four times at least) is vedic.

The JBr. has, at least thrice, the adverb known thus far only from the Ṛksaṃhitā *oṣam*, whereas the PBr. uses the common *kṣipra*; cp. PBr. XII. 13. 23: *etābhir vā indro vṛtram ahan; kṣipraṃ vā etābhiḥ pāpmānaṃ hanti, kṣipraṃ vasīyān bhavati,* with JBr. I. 205: *etābhir vā indro vṛtram ahan..oṣam eva dviṣantaṃ bhrātṛvyaṃ hanty; oṣaṃ śriyam aśnute ya evaṃ veda.*

From the syntax one fact must be mentioned which, according to most scholars would be apt to prove definitely the priority of the Pañcaviṃśa to the Jaiminīyabrāhmaṇa, *viz.*, the use of tense for narrations; the first mentioned text using constantly the imperfect, the Jaiminīya promiscuously the imperfect and the perfect, though here also the imperfect prevails. But I am far from convinced that the use of the imperfect is with certainty to be regarded as pointing to an older stratum of language.

B. The ritualistic facts.

From the ritual two facts may be adduced which seem to prove that the Pañcaviṃśa is later than the Jaiminīya. In the description of the mahāvrata-rite we meet in more than one Brāhmaṇa a barbaric rite, based on animistic views, that an inhabitant of Magadha and a courtezan should copulate. This rite is ordained in the JBr. (II. 404), but it does n o t occur in the Pañcaviṃśa, whilst in the Śāṅkhāyanaśrautasūtra (XVII. 6. 2), which is one of the younger texts, it is expressly stated that practices of this kind are obsolete and must be disregarded. In the description of the Gosava the JBr. (II. 113, see "das Jaiminīyabrahmaṇa in Auswahl," No. 135) has some prescriptions that are most barbaric; these are n o t found in the Pañcaviṃśa (XIX. 13). Further, it is rather striking, that nowhere in the PBr. are the ekāha-rites, that may be used for *abhicāra*, mentioned, whilst the JBr. deals fully with them. Perhaps the author of the PBr. found these rites too barbaric. In one passage of the JBr. however (II 112, see 'Over en uit het Jaiminīyabrāhmaṇa page 26), a certain quasi-myth is laid in the mouth of a certain Tāṇḍya, and this quasi-myth is found in the PBr. (XX. 3. 2), though in not precisely the same words. The question is: can by this Tāṇḍya be meant the author, to whom our Pañcaviṃśabrāhmaṇa, which is called also Tāṇḍyamahābrāhmaṇa, is attributed? To me, at least, this conclusion does not seem urgent, for in the Śatapathabrāhmaṇa (VI. 1. 2 25) a Tāṇḍya likewise is mentioned, who is cited as an authority for a certain detail in the agnicayana, a matter alien to the department of the Chanters. Moreover, in the passage of the PBr. we note a certain inconsistency: where the JBr. has *īśāna deva*, *i.e.* Rudra, the PBr. has instead of this deity the *viśve devāḥ*, but the sāman by means of which Prajāpati through this deity seeks to retain the cattle, is in both texts the mārgīyava, the sāman that elsewhere in PBr. (XIV. 9. 12) is brought into connection with Rudra. Could it possibly be that the author of the PBr. had in his mind the passage found in our JBr. and that he took it over, replacing the god Rudra of whom he stood in awe, by another deity, but, inconsistently, retaining the sāman?

The conclusion at which I arrive, not, however, without some hesitation, is that the Jaiminīyabrāhmaṇa (or the Śāṭyāyanibrāhmaṇa, which must have been so closely related to it) must be older than the Pañcaviṃśabrāhmaṇa and that the author of the last mentioned work must have been acquainted with the Brāhmaṇa of the Jaiminīyas. However, we must always bear in mind that the whole of the JBr. has not yet been fully examined. Further proofs *pro* or *contra* could only be furnished by a thorough examination of this so bulky work, for which the time is not yet ripe.

§2. The Pañcaviṃśabrāhmaṇa and the vedic texts outside the Sāmaveda.

Some passages seem to prove convincingly that the author of our Brāhmaṇa has been acquainted either with the Kāṭhaka or with the Maitrāyaṇīsaṃhitā or with both. See the notes on XVIII. 6.9,10,27 and especially on XXIII. 16. 12.

Whether the ritual of the Kauthumas agrees more with that of the Aitareyins or with that of the Kauṣītakins is still a matter to be investigated.

Of the Sūtras it is certain that Āpastamba (with Hiraṇyakeśin) leans on our text, as well as does Kātyāyana in his śrautasūtra. These two texts have taken from the JBr. their description of the ekāhas and ahīnas. The arrangement of the gavāmayana, designated by Āpastamba (XXI. 16. 5) as *tāṇḍakam*, agrees with that of the Kauthumas (see their Ārṣeyakalpa).

§ 3. The Pañcaviṃśabrāhmaṇa and the Saṃhitā of the Kauthumas.

In two instances the Brāhmaṇa deviates from the Saṃhitā to which it is said to attach itself. We read (XI. 4. 4) the verse *indram gīrbhir havāmahe*, whereas the Ārcika (I. 236=II. 86) and the Ṛksaṃhitā (VII. 76. 5) read *indraṃ gīrbhir navāmahe*. The second instance is found XV. 1.1, where we meet with the reading *akrānt samudraḥ parame vidharman* as against the tradition of the Ārcika (I. 529=II. 603) and the Ṛksaṃhitā (IX. 97.40) *akrānt samudrah prathame vidharman*. In the last instance the Ārṣeyakalpa (see my edition, page 214) sides with the Brāhmaṇa; the first instance is uncontrollable in the Ārṣeyakalpa, because the variant does not occur in the first pada. The Nidānasūtra (see note 1 on XI. 4. 4) acknowledges these variants. I am at a loss to explain this fact satisfactorily. There seem to be two possibilities: either the Pañcaviṃśabrāhmaṇa refers to a Ṛksaṃhitā slightly different from the one known to us, or its author substitutes arbitrarily another reading to that of the Ārcika (or of the Ṛksaṃhitā), in order to facilitate his explanation.

All the chants, all the sāmans, mentioned in the Pañcaviṃśabrāhmaṇa occur in the two oldest gānas. But it is not always an easy task to identify them, because often more than one sāman goes under the same name. Therefore, we have to compare the ūha- and the ūhyagāna to state with certainty in such cases which sāman is meant by the author of the Brāhmaṇa. But if the present reader is not able to point out in every case the sāman intended by the Brāhmaṇa, this is partly his own fault, because the Brāhmaṇa (without the help of these gānas, which are proved to be later) itself contains some prescriptions that are of value to identify the sāmans. For instance we learn from XII. 11. 26, XIII. 5. 28, XIII. 11. 24, etc., that the pavamāna-lauds must end in a nidhana (*i.e.*

a sāman with a nidhana), that in other cases (see XIV. 11. 39, XV. 5. 37) these lauds must end in *iḍā* (*i.e.* a sāman with the word *iḍā* at the end). Another kind of criterium is that *jāmitvam* or "sameness" (on this see note 2 on VI. 2. 5) must be avoided. Thus for instance in the normal Agniṣṭoma the chants of the midday-pavamāna-laud are:

the āmahīyava ending in nidhana, being *nidhanavat*,
the raurava ending in *iḍā*, being *aiḍa*,
the yaudhājaya being *antarṇidhana* and *triṇidhana*,
the auśana being *svāra*.

Whenever three sāmans are chanted on one and the same tristich, the first must be *aiḍa*, the second *svāra*, the third *nidhanavat*. By noticing these and similar restrictions (as they are given for instance X. 6-12) it must be possible to identify the sāmans even without the help of the last two gānas. Sometimes the comparison of the Jaiminīya-brāhmaṇa helps us to state which sāman is meant, see *e.g.* the notes on IX. 2. 5 and IX. 2. 16.

§4. The Brāhmaṇa and the Ārṣeyakalpa.

Maśaka, the author of the Ārṣeyakalpa, starts his detailed description of all the verses and the sāmans, to be used at the different rites, with the prescriptions of the Brāhmaṇa; where this authority failed him, he had a free hand and partly perhaps took notice also of the data furnished by the Jaiminīyabrāhmaṇa. As the detailed description of the ten-day-rite was already contained in the Chapters VI—IX. 2 of the Brāhmaṇa, Maśaka omitted it. But, though Maśaka follows in the wake of the Brāhmaṇa, there are a few discrepancies to be noted. The Brāhmaṇa (IV. 6. 6) states expressly that as opening tristich for the viṣuvat-day must be taken the verses beginning *vāyo śukro ayāmi te* (SV. II. 978—980), but the Ārṣeyakalpa (II. s. a) takes a different tristich, perhaps because anuṣṭubh-verses in the out-of-doors-lauds seemed to him anomalous, cp. the Brāhmaṇa l. c. 8. A second case of disagreement between the Brāhmaṇa and the Ārṣeyakalpa is found PBr. IV. 2. 10 (see note 2 on IV. 2. 14), where for the brahman's ukthastotra the traikakubha is prescribed, whereas the Ārṣeyakalpa (I. 1. 6, end) gives the saubhara. I cannot account for this discrepancy, but it has been noted by the author of the Nidānasūtra, who gives a certain reason why the traikakubha is to be replaced by the saubhara; he regards these sāmans as optional. The third case is PBr XXI. 11. 3. b, where for the ahīna called "Vasiṣṭha's four-day-rite" the two janitrasāmans are ordained; this is passed over in silence by Maśaka (VII. 6). Here it is the Sūtrakāra, who remarks, that either these sāmans are optional, because the Ārṣeyakalpa does not prescribe them, or that they may be applied on the fourth day.

§ 5. The Brāhmaṇa and the Śrautasūtra.

With regard to the relation between the Brāhmaṇa and the Sutra of Lāṭyāyana there is one puzzle. The Brāhmaṇa (I.4. 1) contains a certain formula: *adhvanām adhvapate*, etc. About this formula the Sūtrakāra (Lāṭy. II. 3.1, Drāhy. IV. 3.1) remarks, that in case the Chanters apply the formulas of the Raurukins, they should address the sun with this formula. Now, according to the Sūtrakāra this formula is the first of a whole set. Here lies the puzzle! It is not probable that the Brāhmaṇa, when it gives this mantra *adhvanām adhvapate*, implies equally all those other formulas given by the Sūtrakāra after that which begins *adhvanām adhvapate*. This we must infer from the Jaiminīyabrāhmaṇa, where this same formula occurs and immediately after follows the *upasthāna* of the dhiṣṇyas with *samrāḍ asi*, etc., just as in the Pañcaviṃśabrāhmaṇa. Dhanvin in his commentary on Drāhyāyaṇa designates the *upasthāna* with the formulas *adhvanām adhvapate*, etc. as belonging to another śākhā: *śākhāntarīyam upasthānam*. How this is to be explained I fail to see. In Gobhilagṛhs. III. 2.7 a passage is quoted from a Raurukibrāhmaṇa, and Ruruki is enumerated among the ten *pravacanakartāraḥ*, which probably means: "composers of a Brāhmaṇa." [1]

§ 6 The composition of the Pañcaviṃśabrāhmaṇa.

The Brāhmaṇa proper, which begins with Chapter 4, is preceded by three Chapters, of which the first is certainly not a Brāhmaṇa but rather a kind of *yajussaṃhitā*, a collection of formulas in prose which are muttered by the Chanters on different occasions during the sacrifice of soma. For several reasons it seems probable, that this Chapter was composed later than the Brāhmaṇa, for, if this Chapter had originally formed a part of the Brāhmaṇa, it would not have been

[1] The ten are, according to the Gobhilagṛhyakarmaprakāśikā page 113: *śaṭhi, bhāllavi, kāllavi, tāṇḍya, vṛṣāṇakā, ruruki, śamabāhu, agastya, baṣkaśiras*, and *hūhū*.—The exact meaning of *pravacana* is not wholly certain, cp. Hillebrandt in Gött. Gel. Anz. 1903, page 948 and Winternitz in the Zeitschrift f. d. Kunde des Morgenl, vol. XVII, page 290 sqq.

necessary to repeat these mantras without abbreviation, as is the case with PBr. VI. 5.3 as compared with I. 2.4; VI. 6.16,17 as compared with I. 2.9; VI. 7.2 which is identical with I. 3.2 and VI. 7.6 which is the same as I. 3.1. Moreover, there is one yajus (I. 2.7) that occurs in the Brāhmaṇa itself (VI. 6.7) but with a variant: *punantu* instead of *sammṛjantu.* See also note 2 on VI. 6.17. One more fact may be adduced to prove that this *yajussaṃhitā* did not originally belong to the Brāhmaṇa. It has already been observed (see note 1 on page XIX) that the Pañcaviṃśabrāhmaṇa never uses the dative instead of the genitive-ablative form of stems ending in *ā, ī, ū*. Now, in the first Chapter (I. 5.10) we meet with the yajus: *dīkṣāyai varṇena prajāpatis tvā yunaktu.* If this mantra belonged to our śākhā, it would have run: *dīkṣāyā varṇena*, etc.

The reader's attention may be drawn to a curious reading in this first Chapter (I. 2.1) beginning: *yunaymi te pṛthivīm*, etc., not *yunajmi;* a verse taken from the Ṛksaṃhitā (III. 2.12) we find at I. 7.6 cited with the words: *samānam ayman paryeti*, not *ajman*. These are not misprints, as Bloonfield's concordance would make us believe, where the citations are given with *yunajmi* and *ajman*. That it was the original, though faulty reading of our text, is proved by the Leyden manuscript, by the citation in Lāṭy. I. 9.11 and by Sāyaṇa's commentary: *yunaymi yakāraś chandasārthaḥ, yunajmīty evaṃ śākhāntarapāṭhaḥ.* This other śākhā is then probably that of the Rāṇāyanīyas: the commentator of Maśaka, Varadarāja, who was a Rāṇāyanīya, cites the formula with *yunajmi.*

The second and third Chapter of our Brāhmaṇa describe the manner in which the various stomas are to be formed, see the introductory note on the translation of these Chapters. The Jaiminīya-brāhmaṇa has nothing corresponding to this description of the *viṣṭuti's*.

The rest of the Brāhmaṇa, the Brāhmaṇa proper, agrees in the main, as to its contents, with the Jaiminīya. In the treatment of the ten-day-period the PBr. differs from the JBr. In our Brāhmaṇa firstly the verses are explained which are applied in each part of the sacrifice (first of the bahiṣpavamāna, then of the ājyalauds, then of the midday pavamānalaud, then of the pṛṣṭhalauds, then of the ārbhavapavamānalaud, then of the yajñāyajñīya) and then the sāmans to be chanted on these verses are treated. The JBr., on other hand, treats firstly of the verse and, after each verse, of the sāman belonging to it.

§ 7. The name and author of the Brāhmaṇa.

There is in the Pañcaviṃśabrāhmaṇa itself not the least evidence that the name of its author was Tāṇḍya. The tradition which ascribes it to this sage is corroborated by such passages as the one quoted above (in § 1.b of this Chapter) from the Jaiminīyabrāhmaṇa: *tad u hovāca tāṇḍyaḥ*, and such as Āpastamba śrs. XXI. 16.5, 14 where our Brāhmaṇa is cited as *tāṇḍyakam*. That Tāṇḍya in later texts was considered as one of the composers of a Brāhmaṇa of the Sāmaveda has been noted above (note 1 on page XXIV). Laṭyāyana VII. 10.17 mentions a *purāṇaṃ tāṇḍam*, "an old Tāṇḍabrāhmaṇa"; this book, about which nothing can be said, must have been different from our Tāṇḍyabrāhmaṇa, because Lāṭyāyana, when citing this authority, simply uses the expression: 'the Brāhmaṇa.' Our Brāhmaṇa is designated by Agnisvāmin on Lāṭy. VI. 9.1, as *tāṇḍyapravacana*, by Sāyaṇa on ṚS. VII. 32.1 as *tāṇḍakam*. In the list given at the end of the Sāmavidhānabrāhmaṇa it is said that this Sāmavidhānabrāhmaṇa was handed down by Bādarāyaṇa to Taṇḍin and Śāṭyāyanin. Here then we have a slightly different name, which is found also in the plural *taṇḍinaḥ* to designate the adherents of this śākhā of the Sāmaveda. In the list of teachers of the Sāmaveda found in the Vaṃśabrāhmaṇa, we meet with Vicakṣaṇa Tāṇḍya.

§8. Linguistic peculiarities of the Pañcaviṃśabrāhmaṇa[1].

a. Phonologic and morphological peculiarities.

Of the accentuation which, according to Indian tradition, must have been of the same kind as that of the Śatapathabrāhmaṇa[2] there is no trace; the two Leyden manuscripts that have been compared by me for the constitution of the text, have no trace of any accent.

Sandhi.—We have already remarked that it is uncertain whether in *tāsāṃ tvevābruvan* (IV. 1. 2) we have to see a case of irregular sandhi (*tvā(h) eva abruvan*) or the words *tāsāṃ tu eva abruvan*, as Sāyaṇa does. Against the latter explanation the simple partitive genitive seems to plead, the first is made acceptable by the parallel passages from the other Brāhmaṇas.

---

[1] Cp. also Chapter III § 1. a.

[2] See page 9 of my Introduction to the Kāṇvīyabrāhmaṇa.

An instance of Ṛgvedic sandhi is found VIII. 9. 21: *vicicchidivām amanyata*, where the Leyden manuscript has the preferable reading *vicicchidivāṁ*. Noteworthy is the sandhi in *abhy u tu ṣuṇvanti* (V. 10. 6), cp. Wackernagel, Skt. gramm. Vol. I, § 207. *b*.

N o u n - i n f l e x i o n .—It has been remarked above (page XIX, note 1) that nowhere does the Pañcaviṃśabrāhmaṇa use the dative of stems in *ā*, *ī*, *ū* with a genitive-ablative function.

The dative of nouns on *ti* is never *taye*, but always (with one exception, occuring in a formula, IX. 4.6), *tyai*: *gatyai* XI. 1.5, *ariṣṭyai* XVI. 10.10, *prabhūtyai* XI. 10.19, *avaruddhyai* II. 5.4, *samaṣṭyai* II. 6.2, *astṛtyai* II. 10.5, etc.

For the locative of nouns in *n* cp. above page XIX.

Striking is the locative *jyotau* XVI. 10.2.

Note the nom. *paśuṣṭhā* (not °*ṣṭhāḥ*) XVIII. 6.26.

The instrumental of *ahan* is nowhere *ahobhiḥ* or *ahabhiḥ* but throughout (XV. 2.3, XV. 5.9, XV. 7.6, XVI. 10.3) *aharbhiḥ*.

Grammatically wrong is *vilomānaḥ*, adjective to *rātrayaḥ* XXIII. 19.11.

V e r b a l - f o r m s . Remarkable aorists are *adhinvīt* IV. 10.1, *ajyāsiṣṭām* XXI. 1.1 (also in JBr.) and *abhyartidhvam* VII 8.2; Böhtlingk (Petersb. Dict. "in kürzerer Fassung," Fasc. I, page 110) would correct *abhyarthidhvam*; he connects it apparently with *abhyarthayate*; we seem right in deriving it from *abhyrtīyate*.

Conjunctives are not rare. I noted *dhinvat*, *vṛścān*, *jayāt*, *stavātai*, *ucyātai*, *vyavān*, *ṛcchāt*, *duṣat*, *praṇayān* (IV. 10.1, VI. 5.12, VII. 2.2, VIII. 9.21, IX. 1.16, VII. 1.9, VII. 5.6, VIII. 2.10, VIII. 8.1).

Infinitives other than in *tum*: *nirmṛjaḥ* II. 2 3, *nirdahaḥ* II. 17.3, *pratiṣṭhāpam* XII 4.11, *praiṣam* XIV. 4.7. Probably handed down faulty is *nāśaknod utpatat* VII. 7.17 (in stead of *utpatam* ?). An infinitive with *a* privans is found X. 4.4: *asvaptum*, an inf. abl. is found XIX. 9.5: *apratiṣṭhātoḥ*.

b. S y n t a c t i c a l p e c u l i a r i t i e s .

C a s e s . Unheard of and strange is *alam* construed with the genitive instead of the dative: *yo 'laṃ prajāyāḥ san prajāṃ na vindate* XVIII. 5.9 This abnormal construction is probably to be explained in the following manner: our Brāhmaṇa is consistent in using the genitive of *ā*- and *ū*- stems, where many of the other Brāhmaṇas (especially the JBr.) use the dative. Our author seems to have a certain aversion for this case form in °*āyai* and substitutes here also the genitive. Equally striking and irregular is the dative dependent on *mīmāṃsate*: *tasmai jātāyāmīmāṁsanta* XII. 10.15, as against the usual locative which occurs XXIII. 4.2. Probably the locative in *tasmin nātiṣṭhetām* (VII. 6.11) has the same value as the dative. The genitive with *udbhinatti* XVI. 16.2 is noteworthy. That an accusative of object may be governed by a noun, appears from XI. 6.5: *anurūpa enam*; I found a similar construction in JBr. III. 111: *āgāmukā enam*. Whilst as a rule the other Brāhmaṇas construe *stauti*, *stuvanti* with the locative, our Brāhmaṇa uses the instrumental. Among the numerous instances I find only once the locative (*marutvatīṣu stuvanti*, IX. 7.2). Two instances of elliptic duals, although one of them occurs elsewhere as well, may be noted: *imau dvādaśau māsau* IV. 1.2 and *prajāpatiś ca vaṣaṭkāraś ca trayastriṁśau* VI. 2.5: "the eleventh and twelfth month," "Prajāpati and the Vaṣaṭ are the 32nd and 33rd."

T e n s e s o f t h e v e r b. That in the Pañcaviṃśabrāhmaṇa the imperfect tense is used for narration, has already been remarked (see Chapter III, § 1, a, end). Thrice the present tense seems to be used for narration IV 10. 7, XXIII. 1. 5, XXV. 3. 6. To the perfect forms usually with strong syllable of reduplication to denote a present tense (in the manner of the Greek perfect), which are mentioned by Delbrück in his Altind. Syntax, page 297, belong *ānaśe* (seven times), *dīdāya* X 5. 2, XIII. 11. 23, XV. 2. 3, *dādhāra* X. 5. 3, X. 3. 13, XXII. 28. 6, *bheje* XX. 16. 1, *upadadṛśe* (with the regular reduplication) XXV. 12. 5. Instead of the imperfect *amīmāṁsanta* XII. 10. 15, we would expect the present tense. The same can be said about *vyauchat* XVIII. 9. 8 as contrasted with the present tense of the Maitrāyaṇīsaṃhitā. On the contrary we expect instead of the present tense *sambharanti* of IV. 10. 7, the imperfect. A few times our author uses the aorist, which can be rendered by our present tense and which is so common in Maitr. Saṃh. (cp. Delbrück, Altind. Syntax, page 287), see VI. 9. 2, 3; VIII. 9. 7; XVI. 11, 2; XXII. 9. 5.

T h e u s e o f *ī ś v a r a*. Finally some remarks must be made about *īśvara*. It is used regularly II. 2. 3: *ślakṣṇeva tu vā īśvarā paśūn nirmṛjaḥ*, VII. 7. 5: *īśvaraṃ vai rathantaram udgātuś cakṣuḥ pramathitoḥ* and XVI. 15. 9: *īśvaro yajamāno 'pratiṣṭhātoḥ*. But in two passages, as has already been remarked by A. Weber (Indische

Studien, Vol. IX, page 279) we find abnormally *īśvarā*, refering not to a femininum: *sa īśvarā pāpīyān bhavitoḥ* IX. 10. 2; here the manuscript of Leyden reads as the printed text. The other passage is *īśvarermā bhavitoḥ* IV. 2. 10, *i.e.*, *īśvarā* (fem.!) *īrmā* (nom. pl. masc.) *bhavitoḥ*. We would be tempted to accept an irregular sandhi: *īśvarā(ḥ) īrmā bh.*, as the passage quoted by Sāyaṇa from the Śāṭyāyanibrāhmaṇa (which is identical with Jaim. br. II. 378) has: *īrma iva vā eṣā hotrāṇāṃ yad acchāvāko, yad acchāvākam anu saṃtiṣṭheterma iva tuṣṭuvānāḥ syur iti*. But that in Pañc. br. *īśvarā*, fem. sing., may be correct, though difficult to explain, is proved by the first passage cited (IX. 10. 2).

Chapter IV. The contents of the Brāhmaṇa.

General survey.

Chapter I. The collection of yajusformulae.

Chapter II and III. The *viṣṭutis*.

Chapter IV and V. The gavām ayana, the sacrifice lasting one year, the *prakṛti* of all the sattras.

Chapter VI—IX. 2. The jyotiṣṭoma, ukthya, atirātra, the *prakṛtis* of all the ekāhas and ahīnas.

Chapter IX 3—IX. 10. The somaprāyaścittas.

Chapters X–XV. The twelve-day-rite.

Chapters XVI–XIX. The one-day-rites.

Chapters XX–XXII. The ahīnas.

Chapters XXIII–XXV. The sattras.

Detailed table of contents.

a. The gavām ayana.

IV. 1. Introduction and general remarks.

IV. 2. The "proceeding" overnight-rite (*prāyaṇīya atirātra*).

IV. 3, 4 and 7. The brahman's chant during the year.

IV. 5. The svarasāman-days.

IV. 6. The viṣuvat or middle day.

IV. 8. 1–4. The go and āyus days.

IV. 8.5—IV. 9.23. The ten-day-rite, especially its tenth day with the mental laud.

IV. 10—V. 6. The mahāvrata.

V. 7—V. 8. The gaurīvita and other sāmans during the whole year.

V. 9. The time for the consecration (*dīkṣā*) introducing the years-rite.

V. 10. The years-rite with dismissed day-rites (*utsargiṇām ayana*).

b. The jyotiṣṭoma, ukthya, atirātra.

VI. 1-2. Origin of the sacrifice and its stomas.

VI. 3. The name agniṣṭoma, jyotiṣṭoma.

VI. 4. The special functions of the udgātṛ: the erection of the pillar of udumbara wood.

VI. 5—VI. 7.8. Continuation: the placing of the droṇakalaśa, of the pressing-stones, of the strainer; the *pravṛta* oblations.

Morning service.

VI. 7.9—VI. 8. The out-of-doors laud.

VI. 9—VI. 10. The verses of this laud (*kāmya*-verses).

VII. 1. The sāman on which this laud is chanted (gāyatra).

VII. 2. The ājya-lauds.

Midday service.

VII. 3-5. The midday pavamāna laud; its verses, (VII. 4), (metres) and sāmans (VII. 5).

VII. 6—VIII. 3. The pṛṣṭha lauds.

VII. 6-7. Rathantara and bṛhat (1).

VII. 8-9. Vāmadevya (2).

VII. 10. Naudhasa and śyaita (3).

VIII. 1-2. Variations on these (*kāmya*).

VIII. 3. Kāleya (4).

Afternoon and night service.

VIII. 4-5. The ārbhavapavamāna laud; its verses (metres) and sāmans.

VIII. 6-7. The agniṣṭoma laud.

VIII. 8-10. The three uktha lauds and their variations.

IX. 1-2. The night-rite: rātriparyāyas and twilight laud (*sandhi-stotra*).

IX. 3-10. The prāyaścittas (*e.g.* for *saṃsava* IX. 4; for *somātireka* IX. 7; for *dīkṣitamaraṇa* IX. 8).

c. The twelve day rite.

X. General remarks about the stomas, verses and chants; X. 6–12: the different characteristics of the first six days.

XI—XIII. P ṛ ṣ ṭ h y a s i x d a y p e r i o d o f t h e t w e l v e d a y r i t e.

XI. 1–5. First day.

XI. 1. Out-of-doors laud.
XI. 2. Ājya lauds.
XI. 3. Midday pavamāna laud.
XI. 4. Pṛṣṭha lauds.
XI. 5. Ārbhavapavāmana laud.

XI. 6–11. Second day.

XI. 6. Out-of-doors laud.
XI 7. Ājya lauds.
XI. 8 Midday pavamāna laud.
XI. 9. Pṛṣṭha lauds.
XI. 10. Ārbhavapavamāna laud.
XI. 11. Uktha lauds.

XII. 1–6. Third day.

XII. 1. Out-of-doors laud.
XII. 2. Ājya lauds.
XII. 3. Midday pavamāna laud.
XII. 4. Pṛṣṭha lauds.
XII. 5. Ārbhavapavāmana laud.
XII. 6. Uktha lauds.

XII. 7–13. Fourth day.

XII. 7. Out-of-doors laud.
XII. 8. Ājya lauds.
XII. 9. Midday pavamāna laud.
XII. 10. Pṛṣṭha lauds.
XII. 11. Ārbhavapavamāna laud.
XII. 12. Uktha lauds.
XII. 13. Ṣoḍaśin-laud.

XIII. 1–6. Fifth day.

XIII. 1. Out-of-doors laud.
XIII. 2. Ājya lauds.
XIII. 3. Midday pavamāna laud.
XIII. 4. Pṛṣṭha lauds.
XIII. 5. Ārbhavapavamāna laud.
XIII. 6. Uktha lauds.

XIII. 7–12. Sixth day.

XIII. 7. Out-of-doors laud.
XIII. 8. Ājya lauds.
XIII. 9. Midday pavamāna laud.
XIII. 10. Pṛṣṭha lauds.
XIII. 11. Ārbhavapavamāna laud.
XIII. 12. Uktha lauds.

XIV. 1—XV. 6. The three Chandoma days.

XIV. 1–6. First Chandoma day (7th day of the ten-day rite).

XIV. 1. Out-of-doors laud.
XIV. 2. Ājya lauds.
XIV. 3. Midday pavamāna laud.
XIV. 4. Pṛṣṭha laud.
XIV. 5. Ārbhavapavamāna laud.
XIV. 6. Uktha lauds.

XIV. 7–12. Second Chandoma day (8th day of the ten-day rite).

XIV. 7. Out-of-doors laud.
XIV. 8. Ājya lauds.
XIV. 9. Midday pavamāna laud.
XIV. 10. Pṛṣṭha lauds.
XIV. 11. Ārbhavapavamāna laud.
XIV. 12. Uktha lauds.

XV. 1–6. Third Chandoma day (9th day of the ten-day rite).

XV. 1. Out-of-doors laud.
XV. 2. Ājya lauds.
XV. 3. Midday pavamāna laud.

XV. 4. Pṛṣṭha lauds.
XV. 5. Ārbhavapavamāna laud.
XV. 6. Uktha lauds.

XV. 7–12. Tenth day

XV. 7. Out-of-doors laud.
XV. 8. Ājya lauds.
XV. 9. Mid-day pavamāna laud.
XV. 10. Pṛṣṭha lauds.
XV. 11. Ārbhavapavamāna laud.
XV. 12. Agniṣṭoma laud.

XVI—XIX. One-day rites (ekāhas).

XVI. 1. Jyotiṣṭoma.
XVI. 2. Goṣṭoma.
XVI. 3. Āyuṣṣṭoma.
XVI. 4. Abhijit.
XVI. 5, 6. Viśvajit.
XVI. 7. Sarvajit or Mahāvrata.
XVI. 8. First Sāhasra.
XVI. 9. Second Sāhasra.
XVI. 10. Third Sāhasra.
XVI. 11. Fourth Sāhasra.
XVI. 12. First Sādyaskra.
XVI. 13. Second Sādyaskra.
XVI. 14. Third Sādyaskra.
XVI. 15. Viśvajicchilpa.
XVI. 16. Ekatrika
XVII. 1. First Vrātyastoma.
XVII. 2. Second Vrātyastoma.
XVII. 3. Third Vrātyastoma.
XVII. 4. Fourth Vrātyastoma.
XVII. 5, 6. First Agniṣṭut.
XVII. 7 Second Agniṣṭut.
XVII. 8. Third Agniṣṭut.
XVII. 9. Fourth Agniṣṭut.
XVII. 10. Prajāpater apūrva.
XVII. 11. Bṛhaspatisava.

XVII. 12. Sarvasvāra.
XVII. 13, 14. Cāturmāsyas.
XVIII. 1. Upahavya.
XVIII. 2. Ṛtapeya.
XVIII. 3. Dūṇāśa.
XVIII. 4. Vaiśyastoma.
XVIII. 5. Tīvrasut.
XVIII. 6, 7. Vājapeya.
XVIII 8—11. Rajasūya.
XIX. 1. Rāj.
XIX. 2. Virāj.
XIX. 3. Aupaśada.
XIX. 4. Punastoma.
XIX. 5, 6. Two Catuṣṭomas.
XIX. 7. Udbhid, Valabhid.
XIX. 8, 9. Two Apacitis.
XIX. 10, 11. Two Agne stomas.
XIX. 12. Ṛṣabha.
XIX 13. Gosava.
XIX. 14. Marutstoma.
XIX. 15. Indrāgnyoḥ kulāya.
XIX. 16. Indrastoma.
XIX. 17. Indrāgnyo stoma.
XIX. 18, 19. Two Vighanas.

XX—XXII. *Ahīnas.*

XX. 1. Jyotiṣṭoma-atirātra.
XX. 2. Sarvastoma-atirātra
XX. 3. Aptoryāma.
XX. 4. Navasaptadaśa-atirātra.
XX. 5. Viṣuvat-atirātra.
XX. 6, 7. Go- and Āyus-atirātra.
XX. 8, 9. Viśvajit and Abhijit as atirātras
XX. 10. Four Ekastomas.
XX. 11. Angirasām two day rite.
XX. 12. Caitraratha's two day rite
XX. 13. Kapivana's two day rite.

XX. 14—XXI. 2 Garga's three day rite.
XXI. 3. Śabalī sacrifice.
XXI. 4. Three day rite of Horse sacrifice.
XXI. 5. Baida's three day rite.
XXI. 6. Chandomapavamāna three day rite.
XXI. 7. Antarvasu three day rite.
XXI. 8. Parāka three day rite.
XXI. 9. Atri's four day rite.
XXI. 10. Jamadagni's four day rite.
XXI. 11. Vasiṣṭha's four day rite.
XXI. 12. Viśvāmitra's four day rite.
XXI. 13. Abhyāsanga five day rite.
XXI. 14. Pañcaśāradīya five day rite.
XXI. 15. Vratamadhya five day rite.
XXII. 1. Six day rite of the Ṛtus.
XXII. 2. Six day rite for *āyuskāma*.
XXII. 3. Pṛṣṭhyāvalamba six day rite.
XXII. 4. Seven day rite of the Ṛṣis.
XXII. 5. Seven day rite of Prajāpati.
XXII. 6. Seven day rite for *paśukāma*.
XXII. 7. Seven day rite of Jamadagni.
XXII. 8. Seven day rite of Indra.
XXII. 9. Seven day rite of Janaka.
XXII. 10. Pṛṣṭhyastoma seven day rite.
XXII. 11. Eight day rite.
XXII. 12. Nine day rite of the Gods.
XXII. 13. Nine day rite for *paśukāma*.
XXII. 14. Trikakubh ten day rite.
XXII. 15. Kusurabinda ten day rite.
XXII. 16. Chandomavat ten day rite.
XXII. 17. Devapūḥ ten day rite.
XXII. 18. Pauṇḍarīka eleven day rite.

XXIII—XXV. Sattras.

XXIII. 1,.2. Two thirteen day sattras.
XXIII. 3–5. Three fourteen day sattras.
XXIII. 6–9. Four fifteen day sattras.
XXIII. 10. Sixteen day sattra.

XXIII.	11.	Seventeen day sattra.
XXIII.	12-13.	Two eighteen day sattras.
XXIII.	14.	Twenty day sattra.
XXIII.	15, 16.	Two twenty-one day sattras.
XXIII.	17, 18.	Twenty-two and twenty-three day sattra
XXIII.	19.	Twenty-four day sattras.
XXIII.	20-28.	Twenty-four—thirty-two day sattras.
XXIV.	1-3.	Three thirty-three day sattras.
XXIV.	4-10.	Thirty-four—forty day sattras.
XXIV.	11-17.	Seven forty-nine day sattra.
XXIV.	18.	Sixty-one day sattra.
XXIV	19.	Hundred day sattra.
XXIV.	20.	One year's sattra.
XXV.	1.	The ayana of the Ādityas.
XXV.	2.	The ayana of the Angiras.
XXV.	3.	The years sattra of Dṛti and Vātavat.
XXV.	4	The years sattra of the Kuṇḍapāyins.
XXV.	5.	The years sattra of the Tapaścits.
XXV.	6.	Twelve years sattra.
XXV.	7.	Sixty-six years sattra.
XXV.	8.	Hundred years sattra.
XXV.	9.	Agni's sahasrasārya.
XXV.	10-12.	Three sārasvata ayanas
XXV.	13.	Dārṣadvata ayana.
XXV.	14.	Turāyaṇa.
XXV.	15.	Sattra of the Serpents.
XXV.	16.	Three years sattra.
XXV.	17.	Thousand years sattra of Prajāpati.
XXV.	18.	Thousand years sattra of the Viśvasṛjs.

THE BRĀHMAṆA OF TWENTY FIVE CHAPTERS.

First Chapter.

(The Yajussaṃhitā.)

I. 1.

1. 'A great thing thou hast announced unto me, (a thing of) splendour thou hast announced unto me, (a thing of) glory thou hast announced unto me, (a thing of) honour thou hast announced unto me, enjoyment thou hast announced unto me, all thou hast announced unto me, let it succour me, let it enter into me, may I enjoy it '[1].

[1] Āp. śrs. X. 1. 4, except the words *kḷptiṃ me 'vocaḥ*, is identical; still more extensive is the formula according to Baudh. śrs. II. 9 : 38 15-19. The formula of the Jaiminīyas is different, see Jaim. śrs. I. 1 : 1. 2. This Yajus is muttered by the chosen priest, the Udgātṛ, when the Somapravāka, the person who announces the Soma-feast to the priests who are to function, has made his announcement, see Lāṭy. I. 1. 10, Drāhy. I. 1. 10, Caland-Henry, l' Agniṣṭoma, § 6.

2. 'Let the God go unto the God, let Soma go unto Soma, along the path of right'[1].

[1] Cp. Āp l. c. 6, Baudh. l. c. According to Lāṭy. I. 1. 20, 21, Drāhy. I. 1. 22, 23 these words are spoken by the Udgātṛ either on the day on which the Soma is brought or on the day which immediately precedes the Soma-feast proper, when he goes to the place of sacrifice, making, on leaving his home, first a few paces in northern direction, even if the place of sacrifice might be situated in any other direction than the north of his dwelling, cp. C (aland)-H (enry), § 31a. 'The God goes unto the God' is said, because the Udgātṛ is the earthly representant of the God Parjanya.'

3. Leaving behind what is amiss '[1].

[1] According to Lāṭy. I. 1. 22, Drāhy. I. 1. 24 he has to mutter these words after he has gone far (*dūraṃ vrajitvā*), *i.e.* after he has gone over a certain longer distance from his dwelling, because in this case it is possible that he might tread on some inauspicious place: *tadānīm aprayatadeśābhikramaṇādy avarjanīyaṃ syāt*, thus the commentator Dhanvin.

4. 'Badvan by name art thou, the way along which Soma goes; may I come unto Soma '[1].

[1] According to Lāṭy. I. 1. 24 and Drāhy. I. 1. 25, he has to mutter these words after he has taken the path which leads to the sacrificial ground. The meaning of

badvan is unknown. Āp. (X. 1. 5) has *padvā* and thus also one MS. of the text of Drāhyāyaṇa and the commentator on it. According to Sāyaṇa it is to be derived from the root *bad* : *sthairye* and means 'solid, firm'.

5. 'O ye Fathers, *bhūḥ*! O ye Fathers, *bhūḥ*! O ye Fathers, *bhūḥ*'[1].

[1] According to Lāṭy. I. 1. 24, Drāhy. I. l. c. this formula is to be muttered by the Udgātṛ when, being about to enter the mahāvedi, he treads on its northern border, whilst looking southward (towards the region of the deceased, the Fathers). Equally Āp. l. c. 7. The yajus is repeated thrice because the Fathers are threefold: father, grand-father and great-grand-father (Commentary).

6. 'O manly minded one! may I, lifting on high, look on thee that art lifting on high'[1].

[1] According to the Sūtrakāras (Lāṭy. I. 8. 1, Drāhy. II. 4, 1) the Chanters have to mutter this formula whilst the Adhvaryu erects the sacrificial post destined for the binding of the animal victim, cp. Schwab, das altindische Tieropfer § 43, C. H. § 106 f.

7. "Through clay soft (art thou), the ford of the Gods, the vedi art thou; do not hurt me"[1].

[1] The Sūtrakāras (Lāṭy. I. 9.2, Drāhy. III 1.2) ordain that, when the Hotṛ has finished his morning litany, the three Chanters have to enter the mahāvedi whilst muttering this formula, cp. C. H. § 124. Sāyaṇa seems to take *mṛdā* as an adjective of clay.'

8. "The head of Viṣṇu art thou, bestowing glory, bestow glory upon me"[1].

[1] Lāṭy. I. 9.8,9 and Drāhy. III. 1.8,9 prescribe that after the Adhvaryu who enters the havirdhāna-shed with the vasatīvarī-water, the Chanters enter this shed, having touched (with their right hand) the *rarāṭyā*. The *rarāṭyā* or *rarāṭī* is a kind of ornament made of grass, and fixed above the entrance of the havirdhāna (cp. C. H. § 125.0).

9. "For sap, for pith, for long life and for health"[1].

[1] This yajus they mutter (Lāṭy. l.c. 10, Drāhy. l.c. 10) whilst entering the hāvirdhāna-shed, cp. C. H. l.c.

I. 2.

1. "I yoke on thy behalf the earth together with Agni. I yoke the voice together with Sūrya. Yoked on thy behalf is the wind together with the intermediate region. Yoked are the three disunited ones of Sūrya"[1].

1 Cp. TS. III. 1. 6. b: *yunajmi te pṛthivīm jyotiṣā saha, yunajmi vāyum antarikṣeṇa te saha, yunajmi vācam saha sūryeṇa te, yunajmi tisro vipṛcaḥ sūryasya te.* The meaning of *vimṛj* and *vipṛc* is unknown. Sāyana (on TS.) refers to the three offering spoons juhū, upabhṛt, sruva. Sāyaṇa (on PB.) seems to read *vibhṛjaḥ* (*bharjane*). On the curious *yunaymi* cp. Introduction, Chapter III § 6.—According to Lāṭy. I. 9. 14 sqq., Drāhy. III. 1. 10 sqq. the Chanters extend, repeating this formula, their arms between the two shafts of the Soma cart and, without lifting their heals (*i.e.* standing on their level soles) touch with their hands the quantity of Soma which has been meted out for the morning pressing or, in case the Soma has not yet been divided, over the whole quantity of it. If they cannot reach the Soma, they must extend their hands only over the place and mutter the formula.

2. "On the seat of righteousness I sit down"[1].

1 According to the Sūtrakāras (Lāṭy. I. 9. 14-17, Drāhy. III. 1. 13-15 the Chanters should then pass on and sit down behind the right (the southern) havirdhāna-cart, muttering this formula. Here they should mutter the verses, on which afterwards the out-of-doors laud (the bahiṣpavamānastotra) will be chanted, cp. C. H. § 125. 0.

3. "The vessel of righteousness art thou"[1].

1 Muttering this formula the Chanters (Lāṭy. l. c. 20, Drāhy. l. c. 18) should lay hold of the droṇakalaśa, cp. C. H. § 130.

4. "Of the lord of the forest (*i.e.* of wood) art thou, of Bṛhaspati art thou, of Prajāpati art thou, the head of Prajāpati art thou, the "surviving" vessel[1] art thou; here I push myself forward for the sake of glory and spiritual lustre"[2].

1 See VI. 5. 1, where it is said that Prajāpati survived the cutting off of his head: the droṇakalaśa. 2 Muttering this formula, the Chanters push the droṇakalaśa forward, in an easterly direction.

5. "Ye children of Marut[1], dwellings of the Waters, summits of the mountains, swift falcons, through your voice lead Indra hither, through your noise expel disease. Yoked (as horses-joined) are ye, draw!"[2]

1 *maruto napātaḥ*, TBr. III. 7.9.1 (cp. Āp. XII. 3. 2) has *prayuto napātāraḥ*, which may be a corruption of *prayuto naptāraḥ*, cp. Jaim-br. I. 79: *prayuto napātaḥ*: *prayutaḥ* seems to be the genitive of a substantive *prayut*. 2 The Sūtrakāras (Lāṭy. I. 10.4, Drāhy. III. 2. 5) prescribe (following probably the ritual of the Jaiminīyas: *sammukhān grāvṇaḥ kṛtvābhimṛśati*, JBr. I. 79) that the Chanters, with this formula, touch the pressing stones after they have been put in order on the leather, cp. below note 3 on VI 6. 5.

6. "Here I push this[1] sacrificer on cattle (*i.e.* I make this sacrificer a possessor of cattle) and myself on cattle and spiritual lustre."[2]

[1] With regard to the text of Lāṭy. and Drāhy., where we read *imam* instead of *amum*, and Sāyaṇa's remark : *imam iti keṣām cit pāṭhaḥ*, I presume that our text is to be read, *idam aham imaṃ yajamānam*. [2] The Chanters, muttering this formula, push the droṇakalaśa forward on the pressing stones (Lāṭy. I. 10. 6, Drāhy. III. 2. 7).

7 'Let the Vasus wipe thee off with the Gāyatrī metre, let the Rudras wipe thee off with the Triṣṭubh metre, let the Ādityas wipe thee off with the Jagatī metre'[1].

[1] Cp. VI. 6.7 and Introduction Chapter III § 6.—According to Lāṭy. I. 10.18, Drāhy. II. 2.22 the Udgātṛ has to wipe off by means of the daśāpavitra, whilst muttering these formulas, the droṇakalaśa, first its lower part, then its middle and, lastly, its upper part.

8. 'The strainer, O Brahmaṇaspati, is stretched out; surpassing its members thou goest around it on all sides. No creature whose body has not been heated and who is raw, reaches it, but the cooked ones, who draw, have reached it'[1].

[1] On the meaning of the verse (cp. Ṛs. IX. 83.1), which is not entirely clear, cp. C.H. § 130. 5.—The verse accompanies the act of the Chanters, when they stretch the strainer on the droṇakalaśa, cp. C.H. § 130.

9. 'Let the clear Goddess Prayer go forward from us as a chariot well carpentered and swift; for my long life become thou strained, for my glory become thou strained. Of Earth and Sky the origin they know, let hear the waters that flow down. Sing thou, O Soma, here as Chanter, for my long life, for my spiritual lustre, for the weal of the sacrificer, for the reign of so and so'[1].

[1] In this quasi-yajus are contained two Ṛkverses VII. 34.1 and 2. The ablative *janitrāt* which is incomprehensible has been rendered as if (as in the Ṛs.) it were *janitram*.—These words are to be muttered by the Udgātṛ when the Soma is flowing in a continuous jet through the pavitra. (Lāṭy. I. 10.21, Drāhy. III. 2.29) cp. C. H. § 131.

I. 3.

1. 'Bekurā by name art thou, acceptable to the Gods. Obeisance to the voice, obeisance to the Lord of the Voice! O Goddess Voice, what from thy voice is the most sweet, therein place me. To Sarasvatī, *svāhā*!'

2. 'Let the Sun protect me from calamities from the side of heaven, the Wind from the side of the intermediate region, the Fire from the side of the earth, *svāhā*!'[1].

1 These two formulas accompany the oblations (Lāṭy. I. 11·9, Drāhy. III. 3. 17) which are offered by each of the Chanters successively as their *pravṛtahomas*, cp. C.H. § 134 c, page 170, and cp. VI. 7. 1-6.

3. 'What Soma-weapon of malignant ones shall go up to-day, let Varuṇa blow them away by means of the bow of Viṣūkuha'[1].

1 Cp. Āśv. śrs. V. 3.22, Ath. Saṃh. I. 20. 2.—The Sūtrakāras (Lāṭy. I. 11. 17, Drāhy. III. 3.26, and cp. C. H. § 134. c. end) prescribe that the Chanters on their way to the *āstāva* (the place, where the out-of-doors laud is about to be chanted) throw away, whilst muttering this formula, in a southerly direction from their left hand some blades of grass that they have previously taken.

4. 'With myself, with my progeny, with my cattle, thereby I pacify thought (and) speech'[1].

1 The pun is in the word *prasidāmi* which means also: 'I take my seat.'—Muttering this formula the Chanters take their seat on the *āstāva*, Lāṭy. I. 11. 18, Drāhy. III. 3. 27, C.H. § 134. d, page 173.

5. 'With Agni's brilliancy, with Indra's vigour, with Sūrya's splendour let Bṛhaspati yoke thee for the Gods, for out-breathing. Let Agni yoke the stoma with fervour, in order to convey the sacrifice, let Indra put vigour (into it). Let the wishes of the Sacrificer be efficacious'[1].

1 Muttering this formula the Udgātṛ, having received from the Prastotṛ a bundle of grass (the *prastara*) and stroking the calf of his right leg with it, 'yokes' (brings into action) the laud, the stotra, Lāṭy I. 12. 1 2, Drāhy. III. 4. 16–17, cp. C.H. § 134. f., page 175.

6. 'Food I shall make, food there will be[1], food I will create'[2].

1 Read *annaṃ bhaviṣyati* instead of *annaṃ praviṣyāmi*, cp. § 7. The yajus is much longer in JBr. I. 88.

2 Immediately afterwards the Udgātṛ mutters this formula, Lāṭy. l. c. 3, Drāhy. l. c. 3, C. H. l. c.

7. 'I have made food, food has come into existence, I have created food'[1].

1 This formula is to be muttered after the completion of the stotra, Lāṭy. l. c. 12, Drāhy. l. c. 26, C. H. § 134 h., page 181.

8. 'A falcon art thou with the Gāyatrī for metre. I hold on to thee, bring me safely across. May the laud of the laud come unto me. Joined with Indra may we win, may we enjoy progeny and life-sap'[1].

1 This yajus the Udgātṛ should cause the Sacrificer to mutter over the bundle of grass, Lāṭy. l. c. 13, Drāhy. l. c. 27.

9. 'With splendour, with milk, with heat have we united ourselves, with propitious thought, with insight, and with the true (essences) of mind, in order that I may speak to you what is most welcome. May I be Indra to your view, Sūrya to your eye, Vāta (wind) to your breathing, Soma to your smell, priesthood to your nobility'[1].

[1] With this formula are addressed, by the Udgātṛ, the persons who as spectators or assistant-chanters have attended to the laud, Lāṭy. l. c. 15, Drāhy. l. c. 29, C. H. l. c.—The last words must mean: may I become a purohita to you as far as you are kṣatriyas.

10. 'Obeisance to the Gandharva, whose words go in all directions. Lustre bestowing art thou, bring me unto lustre'[1].

[1] These words he addresses to the sun, Lāṭy. l. c. 16, Drāhy. l. c. 30, C. H. l. c.

I. 4.

1. 'O Lord of the paths, may well-being fall to my share on this path, that leadeth unto the gods'[1].

[1] According to the Sūtrakāras (Lāṭy. II. 3. 1, Drāhy. IV. 3. 1) this formula is to be addressed to Āditya, the Sun.—On this yajus see the remarks in the introduction, Chapter III § 5.

2-14. 'All-ruling Kṛśānu art thou.—Tutha art thou, nourishing the people.—The cloud art thou hurrying forward.—The intangible art thou, preparing the sacrificial gift.—The penetrating, forward bearing art thou.—The vehicle art thou, conveying the sacrificial gift.—The pleasant, the wise one art thou.—Tutha art thou, the omniscient.—Uśij art thou, the wise one.—Anghāri art thou, Bambhāri.—The one affording protection and worship art thou.—The clean one, the purifier art thou.—Thou art the one, whose law is the holy order, whose light is the Heaven.—The ocean art thou, encompassing all.—Ahi Budhnya art thou.—The one-footed Aja art thou.—Sagaras the Budhnya art thou.—The Kavya art thou, conveying the Kavya'[1].

[1] These formulas are addressed by the Chanters resp. to the āhavanīya-fire, the āstāva, the cātvāla, the śāmitra-fire, the āgnīdhrīya, the dhiṣṇya of the Hotṛ, of the Maitrāvaruna, of the Brāhmanācchaṃsin, of the Potṛ, of the Neṣṭṛ, of the Acchāvāka, to the mārjālīya, the pillar of udumbara wood, the seat of the Brahman, the old gārhapatya, the śālāmukhīya, the dakṣiṇāgni and the southern border of the mahāvedi, see Lāṭy. II. 2. 12—25, Drāhy. IV. 2. 3—16. and cp. C. H. § 142 (i), k, l, pages 193, 194.

15. 'Protect me, Fires, by means of your terrible edge, convey me! Obeisance to you! Do not hurt me'[1].

[1] According to the Sūtrakāras (Lāṭy. II. 2. 26, Drāhy. IV. 2. 17 and cp. C. H. page 194) the Chanters address with this formula all the localities (fires and hearths), that have been addressed already separately. I take *piprta* as imprt. to *piparti*; *anīka* reminds us of Agni as compared to a part of the arrow (at the upasad's).

I. 5.

1. 'The doors of the divine Order ye are, do not pinch me'[1].

[1] With the first half of this formula they touch the two western door-posts of the sadas and with the second half they enter the sadas. Lāṭy. II. 3.9. Drāhy. IV. 3. 10, cp. C. H. page 194.

2. 'Obeisance to the easterly seated friends, obeisance to the westerly seated ones'[1].

[1] Muttering this formula the Chanters take their seat to the north of the pillar of udumbara wood, Lāṭy. II. 3. 10, Drāhy. IV. 3. 11. cp. C. H. page 194.

3. 'A men-beholding falcon (art thou), with the eye of Agni I look at upon thee'[1].

[1] This formula is addressed to the Soma in the cup (*camasa*) by the Chanters, when looking upon it before drinking of it, Lāṭy. II. 5. 5, Drāhy. V. 1. 5, cp. C. H. § 147. d, page 219.

4. 'Of thee, o Soma, that art drunk by Indra, of thee that containest vigour, that hast the Gāyatrī for metre, that art accompanied by thy whole troop, that art invited, I partake, being accompanied by my whole troop and having been invited'[1].

[1] This formula is destined for the drinking of the Soma during the morning service, Lāṭy. Drāhy. ll. cc., cp. C. H. l. c.

5. 'Standing upright go up to the seven seers. Drunk by Indra, o Lord of the Word, mount to the seven Priests. Keep thy place, do not descend downward'[1].

[1] An exaggerated way of expressing the wish, that the Soma may not cause diarrhoea! The formula is muttered by the Chanters whilst, after having partaken of the Soma, they wipe their mouths, Lāṭy. l. c. 6, Drāhy. l. c. 6 and cp. C. H. l. c.

6. 'O Soma, enjoy thyself in my heart[1]; our father art thou, o august one! Do not hurt me'[2].

[1] As so often, 'heart' is equal to 'stomach'.

[2] Muttering this formula they touch their 'heart, Lāṭy. l. c, Drāhy l. c. 7, cp. C. H. l. c.

7. 'By our praises, o Soma, we strengthen thee, we that know the (right) words. Enter into us and be merciful'[1].

[1] The Chanters with this verse (Ṛs. I. 91. 11) touch their navel, Lāṭy. l. c., Drāhy. l. c. 8, cp. C. H. l. c.

8. 'Swell thou! Let manly power gather in thee from all sides, o Soma. Be thou in the gathering of strength'[1].

[1] With this verse (Ṛs. I. 91. 16) the Pratihartṛ performs the so-called *āpyāyana* rite, Lāṭy. l. c. 9, Drāhy. l. c. 10, cp. C. H. § 147. c.

9. 'Of thee, O Soma, that art drunk by the nearest, by the Ūrva (and) the Kāvya-fathers, of thee that art sweet, that art Nārāśaṃsa, that art accompanied by thy whole troop, that art invited, I partake, being accompanied by my whole troop and having been invited'[1].

[1] With this formula the Chanters partake of the Nārāśaṃsa-cups, twice during the morning service, with the word: 'nearest', twice at the midday service with the word 'Ūrva', once at the afternoon service with the word 'Kāvya', see Lāṭy. II. 5.14, Drāhy. V. 1. 18 and cp. C. H. §§ 153, 197, 236; cp. also Vaitānasūtra XIX. 20 with the note of the German translation of the author (page 53). —*ūrva* is the designation of the Pitaras at the midday service in the PBr. (but Sāyana has *aurva*) and the Jaiminīya texts, *aurva* in Lāṭy. and Drāhyāyaṇa. Difference of Śākhā?

10. 'With the colour of consecration, the form of ascetism, the greatness of mind, the power of speech, let Prajāpati yoke thee, for offspring and in-breathing'[1].

[1] According to Lāṭy. II. 5. 20, Drāhy. V. 1. 25 this yajus contains four formulas (1. *dīkṣāyai varṇena prajāpatis tvā yunaktu prajābhyo 'pānāya*; 2. *tapaso rūpeṇa p. t. y. prajābhyo 'pānāya*; 3. *manaso mahimnā*, etc.; 4. *vāco vibhūtyā..'pānāya*), each of which serves for 'yoking' (*i.e.* 'setting into action') the four *āvarti* lauds (*viz.* the four ājyas, the four pṛṣṭhas and the yajñāyajñīya stotra): all the stotras with the exception of the first in each savana: the pavamānastotras (bahiṣpavamāna, mādhyandinapavamāna and ārbhavapavamāna). For the first of these three is destined the formula PBr. I. 3. 5, for the second PBr. I. 5. 11, for the third PBr. I. 5. 14.—Cp. C. H. § 155 page 237.

11. 'Let Vāyu yoke the stoma with the mind, in order to convey the sacrifice, let Indra put vigour (into it); let the wishes of the Sacrificer be efficacious'[1].

[1] This is the formula (a variant of I. 3. 5) which is used for 'yoking' the midday-pavamāna laud, Lāṭy. II. 1, 2, Drāhy. IV. 1. 1, cp. C. H. § 178 a, page 279.

12. 'A male art thou with the Triṣṭubh for metre. I hold on to thee, bring me safely across. May the laud of the laud come unto me. Joined with Indra may we win. May we enjoy progeny and life-sap'[1].

[1] This formula, a variant of I. 3. 8 is destined to be muttered at the same occasion as the cited yajus, but during the midday-service, Lāṭy. II. 1. 5. Drāhy. IV. 1. 6, cp. C. H. § 178. c.

13. 'Of thee, o Soma, that art drunk by Indra, of thee that containest vigour, that hast the Triṣṭubh for metre, that art accompanied by thy whole troop, that art invited, I partake, being accompanied by my whole troop and having been invited'[1].

[1] This formula, a variant of I. 5. 4. is used at the midday-service at the same occasion, Lāṭy. II. 5. 5, Drāhy. V. 1. 5, cp. C. H. § 189. a.

14. 'Let Sūrya yoke the stoma with the word in order to convey the sacrifice; let Indra put vigour (into it); let the wishes of the Sacrificer be efficacious'[1].

[1] This formula, a variant again of I. 3. 5. b (cp. I. 5. 11), is used at the 'yoking' of the ārbhavapavamānalaud. Lāṭy. II. 1. 1, Drāhy. IV. 1. 1, cp. C. H. § 221. a.

15. 'Svara art thou, Gaya art thou, with the Jagatī for metre. I hold on to thee, bring me safely across. May the laud of the laud come unto me. Joined with Indra may we win, may we enjoy progeny and life-sap'[1].

[1] This formula, a variant of I. 3. 8 (cp. I. 5. 12), serves at the evening-service, Lāṭy. II. 1. 5, Drāhy. IV. 1. 6, cp. C. H. § 221. c.

16. "Of thee, o Soma, that art drunk by Indra, of thee that containest vigour, that hast the Jagatī for metre, that art accompanied by thy whole troop, that art invited, I partake, being accompanied by my whole troop and having been invited'[1].

[1] A variant to I. 5. 4 (cp. I. 5. 13), used as *bhakṣaṇamantra* during the third service.

17. 'Long life (hath been put) into my breath, breath into my mind, into the Ṛk verse that bestoweth long life[1].—My mind that hath gone unto Yama or hath not fled away, that, through King Soma we put again into ourselves'[2].

[1] Instead of the incomprehensible *āyupatnyām ṛci* we ought to read (cp. Jaim. br. I. 167 and Jaim. śrs. 19 : 23. 11 : *āyuṣmatyā ṛco mā chaitsi*) *āyuṣmatyām ṛci*.

[2] Muttering this formula the Chanters, one after another, look down upon the mess of boiled rice destined for Soma, Lāṭy. II. 10. 7, 8, Drāhy. VI. 2. 6, 7, cp. C. H. § 267. b, page 365.

18. My mind that hath gone far away unto Yama Vivasvat's son, make thou return it again unto me, that I may live and not die, and that I may be unhurt'[1].

[1] The tenth day of the twelve day rite being *ananuṣṭubha* (Baudh. śrs. XVI. 6: 252. 10), and PBr. I. 5. 17 being an Anuṣṭubh, the verse cited under I. 5. 17 is replaced on this day by the one given under I. 5. 18 (identical with Ṛs. X. 60. 10), which is a Paṅkti, thus according to the *eke* of Lāṭy. II. 10. 9, Drāhy. VI. 2. 9.

19. 'The endless (sharpness of) sight through which, forsooth, having spied around, he won the race, through which (he overcame) the falcon, the well-winged bird of prey[1], the (sharpness of) sight which they say is in Aditi, let the men-beholding Soma put that into me'[2].

[1] *yenāhyājim* may be *yenā hy ājim=yena hy ājim* or *yena ā hi....ajayad.* Jaim.: *yena hy ājim.*—About a race won by Soma through his farsightedness nothing is known, in the other Vedic texts it is Soma who is stolen by the eagle, no eagle is overcome by Soma.

[2] The formula accompanies the act of the Chanters when they smear on their eyes the butter from the Soma caru, Lāṭy. II. 10. 11, cp. C. H. § 237. b.

I. 6.

1. 'Let loose is the might of Indra. Of thee, o Soma, that hast been drunk by Indra, that containest vigour, that hast the Anuṣṭubh for metre, that art accompanied by the fallow (steeds), that art accompanied by thy whole troop, that hast been invited, I partake, being accompanied by my whole troop, having been invited'[1].

[1] According to Lāṭy. III. 1. 18. a and Drāhy. VII. 1. 17, this is the formula which is muttered by the Chanters before partaking of the ṣoḍaśin-graha at a sattra.

2. 'Of thee, o Soma, that hast been drunk by Indra, that containest vigour, that hast the Anuṣṭubh for metre, that art accompanied by thy whole troop, that hast been invited, I partake, being accompanied by my whole troop, having been invited'[1].

[1] This formula they mutter before partaking of the ṣoḍaśin-graha, in case the stotra has been sung on verses in which no mention is made of the bay (steeds), Lāṭy. l. c. b, Drāhy. l. c. 18.

3. 'Thou art the *stuta*, (*i.e.* the stotra completed) of the *stuta*, filled with strength, with milk. May the laud of the laud come unto

me, joined with Indra may we win, may we enjoy progeny and life-sap'[1].

[1] According to Lāṭy. II. 6. 12, Drāhy. V. 2. 19 (and cp. *e.g.* C. H. §155 s. f.) the Udgātṛ causes the Sacrificer to mutter this formula after each *āvarti*-stotra (*i.e.*) after all the lauds exc. the pavamāna lauds.

4. 'Of thou, o divine Soma, to whom has been offered with formulas, who hast been chanted in lauds, who hast been praised in verses, who hast been standing over the day, of the Soma-draught that giveth horses and cows, after thou hast been invited, I partake, having been invited'[1].

[1] This is the formula for partaking of the Soma after a twilight laud (*sandhistotra*), Lāṭy. III. 1. 27, Drāhy. VII. 1. 28.

5. 'On the place of sacred order, o divine Stoma, in the home of Viṣṇu I unyoke thee. O divine Stoma, thou hast reached this (moment of the sacrifice) without spilling[1], may we reach. a firm support'[2].

[1] If *anavakaram* may be taking as a gerund of *avakirati* with *a* privativum.

[2] According to the Sūtrakāras (Lāṭy. II. 11. 1, Drāhy. VI. 3. 4, cp. C. H. § 245) the Chanters 'unyoke' the Stoma whilst muttering this formula, at the end of the third service, after all the lauds have been chanted.

6. 'O Soma, come hither; follow me, o Soma, out of the sadas together with vigour'[1].

[1] Muttering this formula the Chanters, after the completion of the hāriyojana-oblations, leave the sadas by the western gate, Lāṭy. II. 11. 6, Drāhy. VI. 3. 12, cp. C. H. § 247. c.

7. 'Well thriving art thou, the best ray of light, the meeting place of the Gods, the sorcerer of the Gods[1]; by which manifestation thou quickenest the bráhman, thereby quicken me, thereby generate me; make me shine out'[2].

[1] *devānām yātuḥ*. Kāṭh. XXXVII. 14: 94. 13 it is narrated how the Gods saw the *devayātu* and the *brahmayātu*, who freed them from the Asuras.

[2] Immediately after the action mentioned in the note on the preceding §, the Chanters address with this formula the sun, or, if the sun has set, the gārhapatya-fire (*i.e.* the śālāmukhīya), Lāṭy. II. 11. 8, Drāhy. VI. 3. 14, cp. C. H l. c.

8. 'The flower of the Waters art thou, the sap of the plants, the offering most beloved to Indra, *svāha*'[1].

[1] Immediately after this they make two offerings into the āgnīdhrīya-fire, the first with this formula, the second with simple *svāhā*, Lāṭy. I. c. 9, Drāhy. I. c. 15, cp. C. H. l. c.

9. 'Of thee, o divine Soma, that art destined for the two fallow (steeds of Indra), of thee to whom has been offered with formulas, of thee that hast been chanted in lauds, that hast been praised in verses, of the Soma-draught that giveth horses and cows, after thou hast been invited, I partake, having been invited'[1].

[1] This is the formula with which the Chanters smell at the grains of which a part has been offered to Indra accompanied by the two fallow steeds, Lāṭy. II. 11, 12, Drāhy. VI. 3. 18, cp. C. H. § 247. d.

10. 'Of the guilt incurred by the Gods art thou the annulment. Of the guilt incurred by the Fathers art thou the annulment. Of the guilt incurred by men art thou the annulment. Of the guilt incurred by us art thou the annulment. Of the guilt we have incurred either by day or night thou art the annulment. Of the guilt we have incurred either sleeping or waking thou art the annulment. Of the guilt we have incurred either knowingly or unknowingly thou art the annulment. Of guilt after guilt thou art the annulment'[1].

[1] These formulas accompany the offering into the āhavanīya-fire of the eight chips of wood by the Chanters, Lāṭy. II. 11. 14, Drāhy. VI. 3. 20, cp. C. H. § 248. b.

11, 12. 'Of thee, o divine Soma, that hast been washed in water and pressed out by men—I take a draught full of sweetness'[1].

[1] The first half of this formula the Chanters mutter after having seated themselves around their cups, which have been filled with water and into which some stalks of dūrvā grass have been deposited, and after they have touched the contents of the cup. With the second half they smell at their hands, Lāṭy. II. 11.16-18, Drāhy. VI. 3.22-25, cp. C.H. § 249.

13. 'Hail to the waters, to the plants'[1].

[1] With this formula they pour the contents of each cup out in a northernly direction, Lāṭy. l.c. 19, Drāhy. l.c. 26, cp. C.H. l.c.

14. 'O Desire, turn the desire towards me'[1].

[1] This formula accompanies the act of turning the cup towards themselves, Lāṭy. l.c. 20, Drāhy. l.c. 27, cp. C.H. l.c.

15. 'Vigour art thou, vigour put into me'[1].

[1] With this formula they put their right hand on their breast, Lāty. l.c. 20 Drāhy. l.c. 28, cp. C.H. l.c.

16. 'O Breath, be awake in my Soma-draught'[1].

[1] They touch their eyes, ears and mouths muttering this formula, Lāty. l.c. 22 Drāhy. l.c. 29, cp. C.H. l.c.

17. 'Dadhikrāvan has been praised by me, the victorious, swift horse, that he may make our mouth fragrant, that he may prolong our life'[1].

[1] This verse is muttered by the Chanters immediately before they partake of the draught of the sour coagulated milk, the *dadhi*, Lāty. l.c. 23, Drāhy. l.c. 30, cp. C.H. § 250.

I. 7.

1. 'A horse thou art, a courser thou art, a charger thou art, a steed thou art, a prize-winner thou art, a runner thou art, a racer thou art, a stallion thou art'[1].

[1] If a chariot with horses should be given as sacrificial fee to the Udgātṛ or one of the other Chanters they should pronounce these names of the horse over the four or three or two horses; in case of four, first two over the right, then two over the left of the two horses that are put to the chariot proper, then two over the right side-horse, then two over the left side-horse, Lāty. II. 7. 20–27, Drāhy. V. 3. 23–31.

2. 'Follow the way of the Ādityas. Obeisance to you! Do not hurt me'[1].

[1] This formula he mutters (in the same case) whilst touching the forepart of the chariot, Lāty. II. 8. 1, Drāhy. V. 4. 1.

3. 'With the energy of Vāyu I accept thee, with the beauty of the stars I accept thee, with the lustre of Sūrya I accept thee'[1].

[1] With the first of these three formulas he accepts (he touches) those parts of the chariot that are made of leather, with the second those that are made of ebony, with the last those that are made of iron, copper or gold, Lāty. II. 8. 2–5, Drāhy. V. 4. 2.

4. 'The rathantara thou art; the vāmadevya thou art; the bṛhat thou art'[1].

[1] With the first formula he touches the right wheel, with the second the standing-place (the seat), with the third, the left wheel, Lāty. l. c. 6–8, Drāhy. l. c. 3–5.

5. 'The two curves, the two bows[1] on both sides of the chariot, which move forward along with the rushing wind, the far-darting one with keen senses, the winged one, may these fires, the promoters, bring us across'[2].

[1] Reading *āṅkā nyaṅkau* instead of *aṅkā nyaṅkū*; but the significance of these words seems early to have been lost.

[2] According to Lāṭy. II. 8.9, Drāhy. V. 4.6 he touches again the two wheels with this formula.

6. 'Vaiśvānara, as of old, ascended the firmament, on the ridge of heaven enjoying himself with the cheerful (Gods); producing, as of old, wealth for the creatures, watchful he accomplishes his course which is (day after day) the same'[1].

[1] Cp. Ṛs. III. 2. 12 which, however, differs slightly. Note *ayman*, on which cp. Introduction, Chapter III § 6.—According to Lāṭy. II. 8. 10, Drāhy. V. 4. 7 the Udgātṛ, to whom the chariot has been given, mounts it, muttering this formula.

7. 'O Gida, this is your chariot, this is, o Aśvins, your chariot, the unharmed, all-healing one'[1].

[1] When he has ascended the chariot, he mutters this formula, Lāṭy. l. c. 11, Drāhy. l. c. 10.

8. 'O Kṛśānu, draw on the left (reins)[1].

[1] With this formula he draws on the left reins, Lāṭy l. c. 12, Drāhy. l. c. 12.

9. 'O Dāsanu, ease off the right (ones)'[1].

[1] With this formula he eases off the right reins, Lāṭy. l. c 13, Drāhy. l. c. 13. —It is remarkable that the Sūtrakāras take as pratīka of these formulae *kṛśa* (not *kṛśāno*) and *dāsa* (not *dāsano*.)

I. 8.

1. 'At the impulse of the God Savitṛ I accept thee with the arms of the Aśvins, with the hands of Pūṣan'[1].

[1] The formula of acceptance of each fee should be preceded by these words, Lāṭy. II. 7. 13, Drāhy. V. 3. 14.

2. 'Let Varuṇa lead thee, o divine Dakṣiṇā: the horse to Varuṇa. Thereby may I obtain immortality, may life fall to the share of the giver, joy to me, the receiver'[1].

[1] These and the following formulas he mutters, when accepting the object indicated in the formula, Lāṭy. II. 7. 14, Drāhy. V. 3. 15.

3. 'Let Varuṇa lead thee, o divine Dakṣiṇā : the cow to Rudra. Thereby may I obtain immortality ; may life', etc. as above.

4. 'Let Varuṇa lead thee, o divine Dakṣiṇā : the he-goat to Agni. Thereby', etc.

5. 'Let Varuṇa lead thee, o divine Dakṣiṇā : the gold to Agni. Thereby', etc.

6. 'Let Varuṇa lead thee, o divine Dakṣiṇā : the she-goat to Agni and Soma. Thereby', etc.

7. 'The Lord of the food hath given of his food, of the pain-allaying, of the strengthening. Obeisance to the scorcher[1] of all people! O thou enjoying one, do not hurt me.

[1] Uncertain. Is the meaning of *kṣāma* 'digestion'? There is an *agni kṣāmavat*.

8. 'Let Varuṇa lead thee, o divine Dakṣiṇā : the ram to Tvaṣṭṛ. Thereby may I obtain,' etc. as above.

9. 'The women have cut thee (*viz.*, the fleece for the cloth), the industrious ones (*viz.*, the fingers of the women) have stretched (thee on the loom), the weaving females have woven (thee)'[1].

[1] This is the formula for the acceptance of a woven cloth, Lāṭy. II. 8. 23, Drāhy. V. 4. 23.

10. 'Let Varuṇa lead thee, o divine Dakṣiṇā : the garment to Bṛhaspati. Thereby may I obtain,' etc.

11. 'Let Varuṇa lead thee, o divine Dakṣiṇā : the non-living thing to the Āngirasa Uttāna. Thereby', etc.

12. 'Let Varuṇa lead thee, o divine Dakṣiṇā : the camel to Pūṣan. Thereby', etc.

13. 'Let Varuṇa lead thee, o divine Dakṣiṇā : the deer to Vāyu. Thereby', etc.

14. 'Let Varuṇa lead thee, o divine Dakṣiṇā : the man to Prajāpati, the elephant to Prajāpati, the boar to Prajāpati, the rice and barley to Prajāpati. Thereby', etc.

15. 'Let Varuṇa lead thee, o divine Dakṣiṇā : the sesamum and beans to Kṣetrapati. Thereby', etc.

16. 'Let Varuṇa lead thee, o divine Dakṣiṇā: the mule or the she-mule to Savitṛ. Thereby', etc.

17. 'Who hath given here to whom? Desire hath given to Desire. Desire is the giver, Desire is the receiver. Desire hath penetrated the Ocean. Through the mediation of Desire I accept thee. This to thee, O Desire!'[1].

[1] This formula, according to Lāṭy. II. 7. 18, Drāhy. V. 3. 19 is to be muttered after each formula of acceptance.

I. 9, 10.

The next two paragraphs of this first Chapter contain the so called Stomabhāga-formulas, *i.e.*, the formulas that are to be muttered by the Brahman priest if he be a Chandoga, a Sāmavedin. This priest (see Lāṭy. I. 12. 1, Drāhy. III. 4. 16), having been asked permission by the Prastotṛ with the words: 'O Brahman! we are going to chant, O Praśāstṛ?' gives his solemn permission (*prasava*) before each Stotra with a different formula. As a Soma feast comprises in its largest extension 33 stotras (cp. Dhanvin on Drāhy. XI. 3. 10), there are 33 Stomabhāga-formulas: 1. bahiṣpavamāna, 2–5. ājyas, 6. mādhyandina-pavamāna, 7–10. pṛṣṭhastotras, 11. ārbhavapavamāna, 12. yajñāyajñīya stotra, 13–15. ukthastotras, 16. ṣoḍaśistotra, 17–20. rātriprathama-paryāya, 21–24. rātrimadhyamaparyāya, 25–28. rātryuttamaparyāya, 29. sandhistotra, 30–33. atiriktastotras. For 1. serves the formula I. 9. 1; for 2–5 serve the formulas I. 9. 2-5; for 6. serves the formula I. 9. 6; for 7–10 serve the formulas I. 9. 7-10; for 11. serves the formula I. 9. 11; for 12. the formula I. 9. 12; for 13–15 serve the formulas I. 10. 1-3; for 16. serves the formula I. 10. 4; for 17–20. serve the formulas I. 10. 5-8; for 21–24. serves the formula I. 10. 9; for 25–28. the formula I. 10. 10; for 29. the formula I. 10. 11; for 30–33. serves the formula I. 10. 12.

1. 'A rein art thou, for the dominion thee; quicken the dominion; incited by Savitṛ chant ye for Bṛhaspati.'

2. 'The beginning art thou; for the law thee; quicken the law; incited by Savitṛ chant ye for Bṛhaspati.'

3. 'The following art thou, for the sky thee; quicken the sky; incited by Savitṛ chant ye for Bṛhaspati.'

4. 'The junction art thou; for the intermediate region thee; quicken the intermediate region; incited by Savitṛ chant ye for Bṛhaspati.

5. 'The Pratidhi art thou; for the earth thee; quicken the earth; incited by Savitṛ chant ye for Bṛhaspati.

6. 'The support art thou; for the rain thee; quicken the rain; incited by Savitṛ chant ye for Bṛhaspati.'

7. 'The *Prāva* art thou; for the day thee; quicken the day; incited by Savitṛ chant ye for Bṛhaspati.'

8. 'The *Anvā* art thou; for the night thee; quicken the night; incited by Savitṛ chant ye for Bṛhaspati.'

9. 'The Uśij art thou; for the Vasus thee; quicken the Vasus; incited by Savitṛ chant ye for Bṛhaspati.'

10. 'The Knowing one art thou; for the Rudras thee; quicken the Rudras; incited by Savitṛ chant ye for Bṛhaspati.'

11. 'The Flaming one art thou; for the Ādityas thee; quicken the Ādityas; incited by Savitṛ chant ye for Bṛhaspati.'

12. 'The force art thou; for the Fathers thee; quicken the Fathers; incited by Savitṛ chant ye for Bṛhaspati.'

I. 10.

1. 'The thread art thou; for progeniture thee; quicken the progeniture; incited by Savitṛ chant ye for Bṛhaspati.'

2. 'The rich one art thou; for the plants thee; quicken the plants; incited by Savitṛ chant ye for Bṛhaspati.'

3. 'The battle-winning art thou; for cattle thee; quicken the cattle; incited by Savitṛ chant ye for Bṛhaspati.'

4. 'The victorious one art thou, whose pressing-stones are yoked; for Indra thee; quicken Indra; incited by Savitṛ chant ye to Bṛhaspati.'

5. 'Over-lord art thou; for out-breathing thee; quicken the out-breathing; incited by Savitṛ chant ye for Bṛhaspati.

6. 'Bearer art thou; for in-breathing thee; quicken the in-breathing; incited by Savitṛ chant ye for Bṛhaspati.'

7. 'Saṃsarpa art thou, for sight thee; quicken the sight; incited by Savitṛ chant ye for Bṛhaspati.'

8. 'The strong one art thou; for the hearing thee; quicken the hearing; incited by Savitṛ chant ye for Bṛhaspati.'

9. 'The trivṛt art thou; for the trivṛt thee.—The savṛt are thou, for the savṛt thee.—The pravṛt art thou; for the pravṛt thee.—The anuvṛt art thou; for the anuvṛt thee. Incited by Savitṛ chant ye for Bṛhaspati'[1].

[1] Cp. Lāṭy. V. 11. 3, Drāhy. XV. 3. 3.

10. 'The niroka art thou; for the niroka thee.—The saṃroha art thou; for the saṃroha thee.—The praroha art thou; for the praroha thee.—The anuroha art thou; for the anuroha thee. Incited by Savitṛ chant ye for Bṛhaspati.'

11. 'Vasuka art thou; (for Vasuka thee).—Vasyaṣṭi art thou.—Veṣaśrī art thou.—Incited by Savitṛ chant ye for Bṛhaspati.'

12. 'Ākrama art thou; for Ākrama thee.—Saṃkrama art thou; for Saṃkrama thee.—Utkrama art thou; for Utkrama thee.—Utkrānti art thou; for Utkrānti thee. Incited by Savitṛ chant ye for Bṛhaspati.'

SECOND AND THIRD CHAPTER.

(The Viṣṭuti's.)

Introductory remarks. A stotra or "laud" is the chant of a certain number of stanzas (*ṛk*'s), put to melody, *i.e.*, chanted on or according to one of the numerous melodies or ways of chanting (*sāman*'s), which are recorded in the grāmegeyagāna or in the araṇyegeyagāna of the Sāmavedic texts. For instance, the yajñāyajñīyastotra is chanted on SV. II. 53, 54 according to the melody of grāmegeyagāna I. 2. 25, which is based on the verse SV. I. 35.

A stoma, on the contrary, designates the number of the chanted verses either during a whole day of the Soma-sacrifice or during a part of it.[1] The regular stomas are the *trivṛt*, the *pañcadaśa*, the *saptadaśa*, the *ekaviṃśa*, the *pañcaviṃśa*, the *triṇava*, the *trayastriṃśa*, the *catuścatvāriṃśa* and the *aṣṭācatvāriṃśa*, *i.e.*, the nine-versed, the fifteen-versed, the seventeen-versed stoma, etc.

[1] Sometimes the word *stoma* denotes simply: *yajña*: a sacrifice of Soma, as *e.g.* Marutstoma, Śunaskarṇastoma (elsewhere called *śunaskarṇayajña*), see XIX. 3. 2, XIX. 12. 2 etc.; see note on IV. 5, 7.

For the three pavamāna-lauds (the out-of-doors-laud, the midday-pavamāna-laud and the ārbhavāpavamāna-laud), which are the first ones of each *savana* (morning- midday- and afternoon-service) the Sāmavedic texts give each time the stanzas in full on which they are to be chanted, for instance the bahiṣpavamāna or out-of doors-laud of the normal catuṣṭoma agniṣṭoma is chanted on SV. II. 1-9 (Caland-Henry, l'Agniṣṭoma, § 134. g), the midday-pavamāna-laud on SV. II. 22-29 (C. H. § 178. b), the ārbhavapavamāna-laud on SV. II. 39-52 (C H. § 221. b).

For all the other lauds only *tṛcas* (*i.e.* complexes of three stanzas) or *pragāthas* (*i.e.*, complexes of two stanzas) are recorded in the Sāmavedic texts. A pragātha is turned into a tristich in the manner described in C. H. § 199. b, page 307. By repetition of these three stanzas the required number of stotra-verses is obtained. In which manner this repetition is to be made (*i.e.*, how a stoma is to be formed out of the three stanzas of a hymn) is explained in the two following Chapters of the Brāhmaṇa, which treat of the *viṣṭuti*'s : the different modes of getting out of a *tṛca* the number of verses required for the laud.

A *viṣṭuti* comprises always three rounds, three sections : *paryāya*'s, each of which should contain each stanza in different or equal numbers ; the first part (*viṣṭāva*) of a paryāya is called *tṛcabhāga*, the second *āvāpa* (*sthāna*), the third *paricarā* (*sc. ṛk*). In the second paryāya this order is changed and again in the third. Each of these "rounds," is introduced by the syllable *him* (*hum* in the chant). So, for example, of the first *viṣṭuti* (the *udyatī*, II. 1) the first paryāya consists of the thrice chanted first stanza introduced by the syllable *him*, the second paryāya consists of the thrice repeated second stanza equally introduced by *him*, and the third paryāya of the thrice chanted third stanza of the tristich, introduced by *him* So the schema is : *hum* 1. 1. 1 ; *hum* 2. 2. 2 ; *hum* 3. 3. 3. In which manner the Prastotṛ has to mark and control the stanzas chanted, is explained in C. H. § 155, page 237 and cp. § 142. o, page 195.

II. 1.

1. For three (verses) he[1] makes *him*, he (chants) the first (verse of the tristich thrice); for three (verses) he makes *him*, he (chants) the middle (one thrice); for three (verses) he makes *him*, he (chants) the last (one thrice). This is the 'ascending' viṣṭuti (or manner of getting

at the required number of verses for the laud) belonging to the nine-versed (laud).

[1] Properly the *hiṃkāra* is chanted unisono by all the chanters, here the singular seems to be used to indicate only the section.—The Chanters must previously agree as to the viṣṭuti they are going to use. The schema is *hum* 1. 1. 1; *hum* 2. 2. 2; *hum* 3. 3. 3. To the words *sa prathamayā* the verb *stute* or *stuvīta* is to be supplied; on the construction, see introduction, Chapter III, § 8.b.

2. It should be practised in chanting by an oldest son born of the oldest wife[1].

[1] Such a Yajamāna should cause the Chanters to use this viṣṭuti.

3. From the top he rises to the top[1]: it is a 'stepping-on viṣṭuti, used in order that he may step on (his younger brothers, *i.e.*, gain the ascendency over them), for by that (form) of the sacrifice which is 'stepping on' he prospers. Therefore this (viṣṭuti) is to be practised in chanting: for prospering.

[1] He rises higher than high, cp. the expression *bahor bhūyaḥ*.

4. It (this viṣṭuti) is a separation of good and bad (prosperity and adversity): with bad lot he parts who in chanting practises this (viṣṭuti). No one (no friendly power) that has returned (after having been expelled) is held off (is expelled); no one (no hostile power) that has been expelled, returns (in his realm) No bad one attains ascendency over him, who is better (more prosperous). No (hostile) tribe assails his tribe, they do not take the progeny (children or cattle) from each other; they content themselves with their own landed state. But Parjanya does not rain (on his lands), for the tristich is (equal to) these worlds (*viz.* earth, intermediate region, sky) and he separates these (worlds, being the tristich) by the *him*-sound.

5. This is the firmly supported viṣṭuti belonging to the nine-versed (laud); firm support gets he who in chanting practises this viṣṭuti.

II. 2.

1. For three (verses) he makes *him*, he chants them right off[1]; for three (verses) he makes *him*, he chants them right off; for three (verses) he makes *him*, he chants them right off. This is the 'returning' viṣṭuti belonging to the nine-versed laud.

[1] *i.e.* all three after another; *parācibhiḥ* means properly: 'moving thitherward, turning their back, going away, not returning.' The schema is *hum* 1. 2. 3; *hum* 1. 2. 3; *hum* 1. 2. 3.

2. A return[1] is reached by him who in chanting practises this (viṣṭuti). It is the uninterrupted viṣṭuti. The out-breathing, the in-breathing, the intermediate breathing are (equal to) the tristich[2], these (breathings, being the tristich) he makes continuous by the *him*-sound; he who practises this (viṣṭuti) lives his whole term of life and finds no premature death. Parjanya rains (on his lands), for the tristich is (equal to) these worlds, by means of the *him*-sound he unites them.

[1] *parivarta* must be a substantive, not a gerund as Sāyana and Böhtl.-Roth take it, cp. § 4 intra; it is probably the same word as *parivarta* from which *parivartini* of § 1 is derived; its precise meaning here and § 4 is not clear to me.

3. But being, as it were, slippery, this (viṣṭuti) could exterminate (his) cattle. This (viṣṭuti) is going hither and away[1]. He will be either better off or (at least) the same as he was (before), but he will not decline in welfare.

[1] *ācaparāca*, I fail to see the precise meaning of this expression.

4. The Bhāllavi's use to practise this (viṣṭuti). Therefore, when accepting, they do not fall forth from return[1].

[1] They obtain or retain 'return', whatever may be the meaning.

II. 3.

1 For three (verses) he makes *him*: he (chants) them right off; for three (verses) he makes *him*: the middle one (comes) first, the last one (comes) second, the first one (comes) last; for three (verses) he makes *him*: the last one (comes) first, the first one (comes) second, the middle one (comes) last[1]. This is the nest-like viṣṭuti belonging to the nine-versed laud.

[1] The schema is *hum* 1. 2. 3; *hum* 2. 3. 1; *hum* 3. 1. 2.

2. He who wishes for children or cattle should in chanting practise this (viṣṭuti); a nest (means) children, a nest (means) cattle, a nest even (comes into being).

3. This same (viṣṭuti) he should use for one born (long) after (his brothers), he comes at the head of these (other) children who come at the head (*i.e.* who by birth are the first).

4. This same (viṣṭuti) he should use for more Sacrificers[1]; in that all (the verses) occupy the first place, all the middle, all the last, he makes them (*viz.* the Sacrificers) all of equal participation, they do not push away each other, all become of equal mental strength.

[1] Probably at a sattra.

5. Parjanya will rain (on his lands), for the tristich is (equal) to these worlds (*viz.* earth, intermediate region, sky), these words (being the three verses of the tristich) he interlinks by means of the *him*-sound.

6. There is, however, a confusion of things (a mixture of good and bad, for one who uses this viṣṭuti).

7. There is a turning of things upside down: held off is the one who is returned (who seeks to return into his dominion from which he had been expelled), but he who has been held off, returns; the bad one obtains ascendancy over his better, a (hostile) tribe assails his tribe, they take away the offspring (the children, the cattle) from each other, they do not content themselves with their landed or state condition[1].

[1] Cp. II. 1. 4.

II. 4.

1. For five (verses) he makes *him*: he (chants) three (verses, *i.e.* thrice the first verse), then one (the second), then one (the third); for five (verses) he makes *him*: he (chants) one (*viz.* the first), then three (*i.e.* thrice the second verse), then one (the third verse); for five (verses) he makes *him*: he chants one (the first), then one (the second), then three (*viz.* thrice the third verse). This is the viṣṭuti belonging to the fifteen-versed laud containing five (verses) in each turn[1].

[1] The word *pañca* immediately before *pañcadaśasya* must be cancelled. The schema is *hum* 1. 1. 1. 2. 3; *hum* 1.2.2.2. 3; *hum* 1. 2. 3. 3. 3.

2. Fivefold is man[1], fivefold is cattle[2]; by means of this (viṣṭuti, which in each round comprises five verses) he obtains man and cattle. The fifteen-versed chant is a thunderbolt[3]. In that he divides (the verses) each in groups of five, he thereby divides (splits up, deranges) the thunderbolt: for the absence of evil result. This is the firmly supported viṣṭuti belonging to the fifteen-versed chant; firm support gets he who in chanting practises it.

[1] As consisting of hair, skin, flesh, bones and mark, Ait. br. II. 14.

[2] There are five paśus or animal victims: man, horse, bullock, ram, he-goat, Ath. S. XI. 2. 9.

[3] According to the Commentary because the pañcadaśa stoma and Indra are sprung forth from the breast of Prajāpati (see VI. 1. 8.) and the thunderbolt is connected with Indra.

II. 5.

1. For five (verses) he makes *him*: he (chants) three (*i.e.* the first verse thrice), then one (the second verse), then one (the third verse); for three (verses) he makes *him*: he (chants) them (these three verses) right off (in their order, without repetition); for seven (verses) he makes *him*: he (chants) one (the first), then three (*i.e.* thrice the second verse), then three (thrice the third verse)[1].

[1] The schema is *hum* 1. 1. 1. 2. 3; *hum* 1. 2. 3; *hum* 1. 2. 2. 2 3. 3. 3.

2. (This is) the (viṣṭuti) which is brought in accordance with three Stomas[1]. One desirous of spiritual lustre should in chanting practise it.

[1] Cp. II. 11. 2.

3. By the five (verses of the first round it is brought in accordance with) the fifteen-versed Stoma, by the three (verses of the second round, with) the nine-versed (Stoma), by the seven (verses of the third round, with) the seventeen-versed (Stoma).

4. The Stomas are strength, strength he thereby brings together (in bringing the three Stomas from different parts unto one point together), for the obtaining of spiritual lustre. In the possession of sharpness and spiritual lustre gets he who in chanting practises this (viṣṭuti).

II. 6.

1. For three (verses) he makes *him*: he (chants) the (verses of the whole tristich) right off (without any repetition); for five (verses) he makes *him*: he (chants) one (the first verse), then three (*viz.* thrice the second verse), then one (the third verse); for seven (verses) he makes *him*: he (chants) three (verses, *i.e.* thrice the first), then one (the second verse), then three (*i.e.* thrice the third verse). This is the ascending viṣṭuti belonging to the fifteenversed (chant)[1].

[1] The schema is *hum* 1. 2. 3; *hum* 1. 2. 2. 2. 3; *hum* 1. 1. 1. 2. 3. 3. 3.

2. By means of this (viṣṭuti) the Gods went to the world of heaven; one who wishes for the world of heaven should practise it, for reaching the world of heaven. After having practised it he does not fall forth from the world of heaven.

3. It is the 'stepping-on' viṣṭuti (used) in order that he may step on (his adversaries); by that (form) of the sacrifice which steps on, he prospers. Therefore this (viṣṭuti) is to be practised in chanting: for prospering.

II. 7.

1. For five (verses) he makes *him*: he (chants) three (verses, *i.e.* thrice the first verse), then one (the second), then one (the third); for five (verses) he makes *him*: he (chants) one (the first verse), then three (*i.e.* thrice the second verse), then one (the third verse); for seven (verses) he makes *him*: he (chants) one (the first verse), then three (*i.e.* thrice the second), then three (*i.e.* thrice the third verse). This is the viṣṭuti belonging to the seventeen-versed (chant), which contains ten (verses in the first two rounds taken together) and seven (in the last round)[1].

[1] Schema: *hum* 1. 1. 1. 2. 3; *hum* 1. 2. 2. 2. 3; *hum* 1. 2. 2. 2. 3. 3. 3.

2. By means of this (viṣṭuti) the Gods overcame the Asuras. He who in chanting practises this (viṣṭuti) overcomes his wicked rival.

3. It is the stepping on (viṣṭuti), (used) in order that he may step on (his adversaries); by means of that (form) of the sacrifice which steps on, he prospers; therefore this (viṣṭuti) is to be practised in chanting: for prospering.

4. It is the pregnant viṣṭuti[1]; children and cattle will be born unto him, who in chanting practises this (viṣṭuti).

[1] The pregnancy of this viṣṭuti is declared by the Commentator in the following manner. The first (read *prathameṣu* instead of *madhyameṣu*) *viṣṭāvas* (a *viṣṭāva* apparently is the designation of the verse of the tristich sung in different rounds) of this viṣṭuti contain three verses (*viz.* the first and each following *viṣṭāva* contains, read *ceti* instead of *veti*) one verse; this makes five (111, 1, 1). The last *viṣṭāvas* contain each (the first and the second) one, and the last contains three verses (3, 3, 333): equally five together. Between these two sets of five are enclosed seven verses (in each round) of the second verse (2, 222, 222). In that a greater number (of seven) in this manner is enclosed, this viṣṭuti is pregnant and, the middle of a pregnant woman being bigger, this viṣṭuti is designated as pregnant. But the same observation might be made equally about many other viṣṭutis.

5. The seventeen-versed (Stoma) is the peasantry[1], its embryo is the king; he thereby makes the king the embryo of the peasantry[2].

[1] The Vaiśya is connected with the *saptadaśa stoma*, cp. VI. 1. 10.

[2] By using this viṣṭuti the king (or Kṣatriya) will be surrounded by peasantry.

6. No one who has returned (into his realm) is expelled, no one who has been expelled, returns[1].

[1] So this viṣṭuti may conveniently be practised by a king who wishes to establish his reign and to keep away his rival, because he will be surrounded by his subjects.

7. The seventeenversed (Stoma) is food[1]. In that seven verses (the seven second verses) are in the middle and five (of the two others) around, food (being equal to the seventeenversed Stoma)[2] is put into the middle (*i.e.* into the stomach). Neither the Sacrificer nor his children (or his subjects) will suffer from hunger.

[1] Food is connected with the seventeenversed Stoma also ŚBr. VIII. 4. 4. 7

[2] According to the Commentator the stress is to be laid on 'seven,' because there are seven kinds of domesticated and seven kinds of wild plants.—Food (=seven) is brought into the middle of man (who is fivefold, II. 4. 2.) by the arrangement of the *viṣṭāva's*, see note on II. 7. 4.

8 Man is virāj-like[1], there are seven kinds of domestic animals[2]. In that the first verses (in the first two rounds) are ten in number and the last are seven (*viz.* in the third round), he makes the Sacrificer obtain firm footing among cattle.

[1] The virāj metre having verse-quarters of ten syllables (Ind. Studien Vol. VIII, page 58) and man possessing ten *prāṇas* (ŚBr. XI. 6. 3. 7.) or, according to others (TBr. I. 3. 7. 4.) nine *prāṇas*, to which the central one, the outlet of which is the navel, comes as tenth.

[2] Cow, horse, goat, sheep, man, donkey and camel (Baudh.).

9. This is the firmly supported viṣṭuti belonging to the seventeen-versed (Stoma). Firm footing obtains he who in chanting practises this (viṣṭuti).

II. 8.

1. This same viṣṭuti with transposition is the *saptaikamadhya* (viṣṭuti)[1].

[1] *Viz.* the (*daśa*)*saptā* viṣṭuti, which has in its last round one single verse in the middle. The viṣṭuti described in the preceding paragraph has in its last round

(*paryāya*): 1. 2. 2. 2. 3. 3. 3, the variant now mentioned has only one in the middle 1. 1. 1. 2. 3. 3. 3, the first and second *paryāya's* are the same in both.

2. The first (verse) is the place of priesthood, the middle one that of nobility, the last one that of peasantry; in that he gives the largest share (of stotriya-verses) to the first (verse) [1], thereby he brings strength and might in the priesthood and makes the nobility and peasantry subject to priesthood. A shining-out among the nobility as it were, falls to the share of him [2], who in chanting practises this (viṣṭuti).

[1] The first verse is used thrice in the first, once in the second, thrice in the last round, together seven times, whereas the second and third verses, that represent the *kṣatra* and the *viś*, are used in the three rounds only five times each.

[2] The same expression III. 9. 2.

3. This (viṣṭuti) is practised by the Trikharvas, therefore they, in contending for superiority, are not worsted.

II. 9.

1. For seven (verses) he makes *him*: he (chants) three (verses, *i.e.* thrice the first), then three (thrice the second), then one (the third verse); for three (verses) he makes *him*: he (chants) the (three verses) right off (*i.e.* without any repetition, in their regular order); for seven (verses) he makes *him*: he (chants) one (the first), then three (*i.e.* thrice the second verse), then three (*i.e.* thrice the third). This is the viṣṭuti that reposes on seven (*viz.* on the seven verses of the first round) [1].

[1] Schema: *hum* 1. 1. 1. 2. 2. 2. 3; *hum* 1. 2. 3; *hum* 1. 2. 2. 2. 3. 3. 3.

2. One who has a rival (whom he wishes to destroy) should practise it: just as one harrows with a harrow reposing on seven sharp-pointed (pins) [1], so he breaks to pieces his wicked rival.

[1] 'Or drawn by seven oxen' according to the Commentary.

3. This same (viṣṭuti) he should apply for a plurality of Sacrificers [1]. The first *him*-making (regards) the first (verse); in that he makes *him* with regard to this one for seven (verses), thereby it (this first verse) obtains seven (stotriya-verses); in that seven (verses) again (*i.e.* seven times the second verse in the three rounds, counted together) occur in the middle, thereby this one equally obtains seven (stotriya-verses); the last *him*-making (regards) the last verse; in that he makes *him*

with regard to this one for seven (verses), thereby it (this last verse) obtains seven (stotriya-verses)[2]. He makes them (the Sacrificers) equally participated, they do not push away each other, all become of equal strength.

[1] In case of a sattra.

[2] This paragraph, especially the accusative in *tāṃ saptabhyo hiṃkaroti*, is obscure to me.

4. This viṣṭuti is practised by the Ābhipratāriṇa's, therefore they are the mightiest of all their relations.

II 10.

1. The same viṣṭuti with transposition is the middleless *ubhayasaptaikamadhya* viṣṭuti[1].

[1] The viṣṭuti which in both, *viz.* in the first and last rounds has only one, single verse in the middle, in contrast to the viṣṭuti described in II. 8, where only one round is *saptaikamadhya*. As each *paryāya* has the second verse only once, this viṣṭuti is called 'middleless,' which means, according to the Commentator 'with thin middle.' The schema is: *hum* 1. 1 1. 2. 3. 3. 3; *hum* 1. 2. 3; *hum* 1. 1. 1. 2. 3. 3. 3.

2. This (viṣṭuti) should be practised by one born (long) after (his brothers). There is no room left for one born after; in that seven (verses) come first, seven last and three in the middle, man (*viz.* the word *puruṣa*) comprising three syllables, he thereby makes room for him in the middle and in this room he gets firm support.

3. This same (viṣṭuti) he should apply for one who is desirous of offspring; kept away[1] from the middle[2] is he who does not obtain offspring, he thereby[3] makes room for him in the middle and in accordance with this room (now occupied by him) children and cattle will be born unto him.

[1] If we are not justified in reading *saṃruddho* instead of *saṃrūḍho*, at least it is here used in this sense.

[2] Because one who has *prajā* is surrounded by it.

[3] *taṃ madhyataḥ* must stand for *tan* (=*tat*) *ma°*.

4. This same (viṣṭuti) he should apply for a noble, who is kept away by the people (his subjects, from his dominion). The seventeen-versed (Stoma) is the peasantry[1], its embryo is the king (=the noble) (he ought to be surrounded by his people); he thereby drives away the king

from his people[2]; kept off is the one who is returned (*viz.* who seeks to return to his dominion), but he who has been held off, returns.

[1] Cp. note 1 on II. 7. 5.

[2] We expect rather the contrary: he thereby forces the king amid his subjects (the king, a *puruṣa*, being *tryakṣara* and the middle round comprising three verses).

5. This same (viṣṭuti) he should apply for one against whom witchcraft is being exercised. The seventeenversed (Stoma) is Prajāpati[1]: he enters into the middle of Prajāpati, in order not to be struck down.

[1] For Prajāpati is seventeenfold; according to Ait. br. I. 1. 14 Prajāpati is the year, which is seventeenfold as consisting of twelve months and five seasons; T. S. I. 6. 11. 1 has a different explanation.

II. 11.

1. For five (verses) he makes *him*: he (chants) three verses (*i.e.* thrice the first verse), then one (the second), then one (the third); for three (verses) he makes *him*: he (chants) them right off; for nine (verses) he makes *him*: he (chants) three (verses: thrice the first), then three (thrice the second), then three (thrice the third)[1].

[1] Schema: *hum* 1. 1. 1. 2. 3; *hum* 1. 2. 3; *hum* 1. 1. 1. 2. 2. 2. 3. 3. 3.

2. (This is) the (viṣṭuti) which is brought in accordance with four Stomas[1]. One desirous of spiritual lustre should practise it in chanting; by the five verses (of the first round it is brought in accordance with) the fifteeenversed (chant), by the three (of the second round it is brought in accordance with) the nineversed (chant), by the nine (of the third round it is brought in accordance with) the thrice-nineversed (chant), by itself it is the seventeenversed (chant). The chants are strength, strength he thereby brings together from different sides into one point, in order that he may obtain spiritual lustre; in the possession of sharpness and spiritual lustre gets he who in chanting practises this (viṣṭuti).

[1] Cp. II. 5. 2.

II. 12.

1. For three (verses) he makes *him*: he (chants) them right oft; for five (verses) he makes *him*: he (chants) one (*i.e.* the first verse), then three (thrice the second verse), then one (the third verse); for nine (verses) he makes *him*: he (chants) three (verses, *viz.* thrice the first

verse), then three (thrice the second verse), then three (thrice the third verse). This is the ascending viṣṭuti belonging to the seventeen-versed (chant)[1].

[1] Schema: *hum* 1. 2. 3; *hum* 1. 2. 2. 2. 3; *hum* 1. 1. 1. 2. 2. 2. 3. 3. 3.

2. By means of this (viṣṭuti) the Gods went to the world of heaven; one who is desirous of getting to the world of heaven should in chanting practise it, so as to reach the world of heaven. He who has practised it in chanting falls not from the world of heaven. It is the getting-higher viṣṭuti, (used) in order that he may get higher. For by that (form) of the sacrifice which gets higher he prospers. Therefore this (viṣṭuti) is, in chanting, to be practised, in order that he may prosper.

II. 13.

1. For seven (verses) makes *him*: he (chants) three (verses: thrice the first), then three (thrice the second), then one (the third); for five (verses) he makes *him*: he (chants) one (the first), then three (thrice the second), then one (the third); for five (verses) he makes *him*: he (chants) one (the first verse), then one (the second), then three (thrice the third)[1]. (This is the viṣṭuti called:) 'the pair of bellows with its mouth directed downward.'

[1] Schema: *hum* 1. 1. 1. 2. 2. 2. 3; *hum* 1. 2. 2. 2. 3; *hum* 1. 2. 3. 3. 3.

2. He should apply this (viṣṭuti) (in the soma-sacrifice) of one whom he hates. Just as he (the blacksmith) would blow away with a pair of bellows, whose mouth is directed downward, so he blows away the cattle of the Sacrificer. (It is) the stepping-away viṣṭuti, by means of it the cattle of the Sacrificer steps away; he who in chanting practises this (viṣṭuti), fares worse.

II. 14.

1. For seven (verses) he makes *him*: he (chants) three (verses: thrice the first), then three (thrice the second), then one (the third); for seven (verse) he makes *him*: he (chants) one (the first verse), then three (thrice the second verse), then three (thrice the third verse); for seven (verses) he makes *him*: he (chants) three (verses: thrice the first verse), then one (the second), then three (thrice the third verse). (This is the viṣṭuti) belonging to the twenty-one-versed (chant), containing seven verses in each (turn)[1].

[1] Schema; *hum* 1. 1. 1. 2. 2. 2. 3; *hum* 1. 2. 2. 2. 3. 3. 3; *hum* 1. 1. 1. 2. 3. 3. 3.

2. There are seven kinds of domestic animals [1], these he gains by this (viṣṭuti), there are seven 'breaths' in the head [2], the organs of sense are the breaths, these he obtains by this (viṣṭuti).

[1] Cp. note 2 on II. 7. 8.

[2] Mouth, nose (dual), eyes, ears.

3. This is the firmly supported viṣṭuti belonging to the twenty-one-versed (stoma); he who in chanting practises it, gains a firm support.

II. 15.

1. For five (verses) he makes *him*: he (chants) three (verses: thrice the first verse), then one (the second), then one (the third); for seven (verses) he makes *him*: he (chants) one (the first), then three (thrice the second), then three (thrice the third); for nine (verses) he makes *him*: he (chants) three (verses: thrice the first verse), then three (thrice the second), then three (thrice the third verse). This is the ascending viṣṭuti belonging to the twenty-one-versed chant [1].

[1] Schema: *hum* 1. 1. 1. 2. 3; *hum* 1. 2. 2. 2. 3. 3. 3; *hum* 1. 1. 1. 2. 2. 2. 3. 3. 3.

2. By means of this (viṣṭuti) the Gods went to the world of heaven; one who is desirous of the world of heaven, should in chanting practise it, in order to obtain the world of heaven; he who in chanting has practised this (viṣṭuti) falls not from the world of heaven. It is the on-stepping viṣṭuti, (used) in order to step on; by that (form) of the sacrifice which steps on, he prospers; therefore this (viṣṭuti) should in chanting be practised, for prospering.

3. This (viṣṭuti) is of ninefold beginning (and) of ninefold termination, in that, (regarding the first point) the out-of-doors laud is ninefold [1] (*i.e.* nine-versed) and (regarding the second point) these nine (stotriya verses) are the last ones of the twenty-one-versed (chant) [2]. Ninefold are the vital airs (the *prāṇas*), it is the vital airs he thereby lays on both sides [3]; therefore that downward directed vital air has half the share of the upper vital airs. The whole (normal) term of life he reaches, he dies not before the (full term of) life, who in chanting practises this (viṣṭuti).

[1] According to the Commentary this viṣṭuti is usually applied on the last (yajñāyajñīya) laud of the regular agniṣṭoma sacrifice, which begins with the *trivṛt* or nine-versed out-of-doors laud (of 3 × 3 verses).

2 The last round (*paryāya*) of this viṣṭuti contains nine verses.

3 *Viz.* on both sides, above and below the navel, cp. Śat. Br. IX. 4. 3. 6: *nava vai prāṇāḥ sapta śirṣann avāñcau dvau* and above, note 1 on II. 7. 8. The function of the two downward directed *prāṇā's* (elsewhere taken as one single: *apāna* as opposed to *prāṇa*) is, to discharge the urine and the faeces; therefore, when this *prāṇa* is deficient, one dies of stangurine or constipation (*udavartākhyena rogeṇa*).

4. This (viṣṭuti) is practised in chanting by the Karadviṣ's, therefore these attain the full term of life.

II. 16.

1. For nine (verse) he makes *him*: he (chants) three (verses: thrice the first verse), then three (thrice the second), then three (thrice the third); for five (verses) he makes *him*: he (chants) one (verse, the first), then three (thrice the second), then one (the third); for seven (verses) he makes *him*: he (chants) three (verses: thrice the first), then one (the second), then three (thrice the third verse)[1]. (This viṣṭuti is called) 'the matching chant'[2].

1 Schema *hum* 1. 1. 1. 2. 2. 2. 3. 3. 3; *hum* 1. 2. 2. 2. 3; *hum* 1. 1. 1. 2. 3. 3. 3.

2 *pratiṣṭuti*, because, as it is set forth in the next §, it matches the other stomas.

2. By chanting the nine (verses of the first round) he matches the nine-versed (chant), by the five (of the second round he matches) the fifteen-versed (chant), by the seven of the third round he matches the seventeen-versed (chant); the twenty-one-versed chant is by itself present.

3. The chants that convey the sacrifice[1] are gratified by him in the last (agniṣṭoma) laud; just as he would gratify (*i.e.* quench the thirst of) the oxen or horses or mules that have carried (their burden), so he thereby gratifies in the last laud the chants. He who in chanting practises this (viṣṭuti) is gratified by (*i.e.* comes in possession of abundant) children and cattle.

1 *Viz.* the normal *catuṣṭoma agniṣṭoma*, commonly designated after its last stotra simply as agniṣṭoma. The four manners of chanting (stomas), mentioned in § 1, are used in this simplest form of Soma-feast, cp. C. H. page 503, last two lines.

4. This same (viṣṭuti) he should apply for one who is desirous of (obtaining) an office of house-chaplain (to a king or noble). The

nine-versed (chant) is priesthood[1], the twenty-one-versed one is nobility in that the twenty-one-versed (chant) begins with the nine-versed he sets down the priest hood before the nobility, he gets an office as chaplain and falls not from this office, who in chanting practises this (viṣṭuti).

[1] Because (see VI. 1. 6.) the *trivṛt stoma* and priesthood are both sprung from the mouth of Prajāpati.

[2] Why? According to VI. 1. 8 the *kṣatra* is equal to the *pañcadaśa stoma*.

[3] The out-of-doors laud is trivṛt.

5. This (viṣṭuti) is practised in chanting by the Prāvāhaṇi's; therefore they remain in the possession of the office of chaplain.

II. 17.

1. For nine (verses) he makes *him*: he (chants) three (verses: thrice the first verse), then three (thrice the second), then three (thrice the third); for three (verses) he makes *him*: he (chants) them right off; for nine (verses) he makes *him*: he (chants) three (verses: thrice the first verse), then three (thrice the second verse), then three (thrice the third verse)[1]. (This viṣṭuti is called) 'the lamp lighted on both sides'[2].

[1] Schema: *hum* 1. 1. 1. 2. 2. 2. 3. 3. 3; *hum* 1. 2. 3; *hum* 1. 1. 1. 2. 2. 2. 3. 3. 3.

[2] *sūrmī* 'a metal tube (?)' *jvalantī lohamayī sthūṇā*; on both sides of the lamp (the middle round) lights (the first and third rounds) are supplied. These surrounding *paryāyas* are *trivṛt* and Agni is often called *trivṛt*, e.g. T.S. V. 4. 7. 3; on *sūrmī* c.p. also note 4 on XV. 5. 20.

2. One desirous of spiritual lustre should in chanting practise it; the nine versed (*trivṛt*, thrice-threefold chant) is gleaming splendour[1], man (*i.e.* the word *puruṣa*) is trisyllabic; in that two nine-versed chants (*i.e.* two rounds, each of nine verses) are on both sides (*i.e.* before and after) and three (verses) are in the middle, the two ninefold ones heat him, just as he would heat gold, for (obtaining) gleaming splendour and spiritual lustre.

[1] Or 'fire,' Agni being equated with *trivṛt* and called *trivṛt*, cp. note 2 on preceding §.

3. Not conducive to cattle, however (is this viṣṭuti): it could burn up his cattle, and there is fear of leprosy, for, too much these two (ninefold rounds, which are equated to brightness) heat (or 'burn').

4. This same (viṣṭuti) he should apply for one who is calumniated; suffering from blemish (stain) is he who, suffers from ugly report; this ugly report, now, which is spread about him, is burnt up by the two ninefold (stomas): he who in chanting practises this (viṣṭuti) becomes of gleaming splendour.

Third Chapter.

(The viṣṭutis, continued.)

III. 1.

1. For nine (verses) he makes *him*: he (chants) three (verses: thrice the first verse), then five (five times the second verse), then one (the third); for nine (verses) he makes *him*: he (chants) one (verse, the first), then three (thrice the second verse), then five (five times the third verse); for nine (verses) he makes *him*: he (chants) five (verses: five times the first verse), then one (the second), then three (thrice the third verse)[1].

[1] Schema: *hum* 1. 1. 1. 2. 2. 2. 2. 2. 3; *hum* 1. 2. 2. 2. 3. 3. 3. 3. 3; *hum* 1. 1. 1. 1. 1. 2. 3. 3. 3.

2. The thrice-ninefold (or twenty-seven-versed) (chant) is a thunderbolt: he thereby splits up the thunderbolt[1], for the absence of evil result.

[1] *Viz.*, he splits up the weapon of his adversary, cp. II. 4 2.

3. Fixed[1] by five (verses) is this (viṣṭuti); the circulating[2] (verse) is one single, cattle is fivefold, the circulating (verse) is (equal to) the Sacrificer: in that he fixes[1] (this viṣṭuti) by five (verses) and in that there is one single circulating (verse), he thereby gives the Sacrificer firm support among cattle. This is the firmly supported viṣṭuti belonging to the thrice-nine-versed (chant). Firm support gets he who in chanting practises this (viṣṭuti).

[1] *pañcabhir vihitā, pañcabhir vidadhāti* (similarly III. 3. 2, III. 4. 3, III. 8. 3, III. 12. 3, III. 13. 3) seems to imply that over each round 5 verses are distributed.

[2] To *paricarā* the subst. *ṛk* must be supplied.—In this kind of stomas the *viṣṭāva*, which consists of the thrice chanted verse, is called the *tṛcabhāga*, the *viṣṭāva*, which consists of the five times chanted verse, is called the *āvāpasthāna* ('place of insertion,' because here are to be inserted the verses required for getting a higher number of verses, than indicated by any viṣṭuti of the Brāhmaṇa, or than

contained in the viṣṭutis which have been described in Chapter II of the Brāhmaṇa, these being considered as normal and *prakṛti* (?)); the *viṣṭāva*, which consists of one verse only, is called the *paricarā*. In the first round we have: *tṛcabhāga*, *avāpasthāna*, *paricarā*; in the second: *paricarā*, *tṛcabhāga*, *āvāpasthāna*; in the third: *āvāpasthāna*, *paricarā*, *tṛcabhāga*. The *paricarā* (=Sacrificer) and the *āvāpasthāna* (=cattle) are found in each round, and so it can be said *yajamānam eva tat paśuṣu pratiṣṭhāpayati*. (Is this the right interpretation? cp. also Lāṭy. VI. 5. 1. sqq.).

III. 2.

1. For seven (verses) he makes *him*: he (chants) three (verses: thrice the first verse), then three (thrice the second), then one (the third); for nine (verses) he makes *him*: he (chants) one (verse: the first), then three (thrice the second), then five (five times the third); for eleven (verses) he makes *him*: he (chants) five (verses: five times the first verse), then three (thrice the second verse), then three (thrice the third verse)[1]. (This is) the ascending viṣṭuti belonging to the thrice-nine-versed (chant).

[1] Schema: *hum* 1. 1. 1. 2. 2. 2. 3; *hum* 1. 2. 2. 2. 3. 3. 3. 3. 3; *hum* 1. 1. 1. 1. 1. 2. 2. 2. 3. 3. 3.

2. By means of this (viṣṭuti) the Gods went to the world of heaven; one who wishes for the world of heaven should in chanting practise it, so as to reach the world of heaven: having practised it, he does not fall from the world of heaven. It is the 'stepping-on' viṣṭuti, (used) in order to step on (his adversaries), for by that (form) of the sacrifice which steps on, he prospers. Therefore this (viṣṭuti) is in chanting to be practised: for prospering.

III. 3.

1. For eleven (verses) he makes *him*: he (chants) three (verses: thrice the first verse), then seven (seven times the second verse), then one (the third); for eleven (verses) he makes *him*: he (chants) one (verse: the first), then three (thrice the second verse), then seven (seven times the third verse); for eleven (verses) he makes *him*: he (chants) seven (verses: seven times the first verse), then one (the second), then three (thrice the third verse)[1].

[1] Schema: *hum* 1. 1. 1. 2. 2. 2. 2. 2. 2. 2. 3; *hum* 1. 2. 2. 2. 3. 3. 3. 3. 3. 3. 3: *hum* 1. 1. 1. 1. 1. 1. 1. 2. 3. 3. 3.

2. The thirty-three-versed (chant) is the end[1], the thirty-three-versed one forsooth is the highest of the chants. Fixed by seven (verses)[2]

is (this vistuti), the circulating verse is one single; seven are the kinds of domestic animals, the circulating (verse)[1] is (equal to) the Sacrificer. In that he fixes (this vistuti) by seven verses, and in that there is one single circulating (verse), he thereby gives finally (once for all) to the Sacrificer firm support among cattle. This is the firmly supported (vistuti) belonging to the thirty-three-versed (chant); firm support gets he who in chanting practises this (vistuti).

[1] *Viz.*, of the six-day sacrificial period: the *ṣaḍaha*

[2] Cp. note 1 on III. 1. 3.

III. 4.

1. For eleven (verses) he makes *him*: he (chants) three (verses: thrice the first verse), then five (five times the second verse), then three (thrice the third verse); for eleven (verses) he makes *him*: he (chants) three (verses: thrice the first verse), then three (thrice the second verse), then five (five times the third verse); for eleven (verses) he makes *him*: he (chants) five (verses: five times the first verse), then three (thrice the second verse), then three (thrice the third verse)[1]. (It is the vistuti) 'of nearer stair'[2].

[1] Schema: *hum* 1. 1. 1. 2. 2. 2. 2. 2. 3. 3. 3; *hum* 1. 1. 1. 2. 2. 2. 3. 3. 3. 3. 3; *hum* 1. 1. 1. 1. 1. 2. 2. 2. 3. 3. 3. (3. 5. 3, 3. 3. 5, 5. 3. 3).

[2] The same expression III. 13. 1. The transition from 3 to 5 and from 5 to 3 in the different *viṣṭāvas* is 'nearer' ('less') than in the preceding vistuti (of III. 3), where the *saṃkrama* is from 3 to 7 and from 7 to 1.

2. The thirty-three versed (chant) is the end. Just as one, who has climbed to the top of a big tree, advances from a 'nearer' stair, so he hereby, by the (vistuti) of 'nearer' stair, advances from the 'nearer' stair.

3. Fixed[1] by five (verses) is (this vistuti), the circulating (verses) are three in number, fivefold is cattle, man comprises his self (*ātman*), his children, his wife (and so makes up three, *viz.*, as much as in the number of the circulating verses). In that the circulating (verses) are three in number, he thereby gives to the Sacrificer firm support among cattle. Rich in cattle is he who in chanting practises this (vistuti).

[1] Cp. note 1 on III. 1. 3.

III. 5.

1. For nine (verses) he makes *him*: he (chants) three (verses: thrice the first verse), then five (five times the second verse), then one

(the third); for eleven (verses) he makes *him*: he (chants) one (the first verse), then three (thrice the second verse), then seven (seven times the third verse); for thirteen (verses) he makes *him*: he (chants) seven (verses: seven times the first verse), then three (thrice the second verse), then three (thrice the third verse)[1]. (It is) the ascending viṣṭuti belonging to the thirty-three-versed (chant).

[1] Schema: *hum* 1. 1. 1. 2. 2. 2. 2. 2. 3; *hum* 1. 2. 2. 2. 3. 3. 3. 3. 3. 3. 3; *hum* 1. 1. 1. 1. 1. 1. 1. 2. 2 2. 3. 3. 3. (3. 5. 1, 1. 3. 7, 7. 3. 3).

2. By means of this (viṣṭuti) the Gods went to the world of heaven; one desirous of (obtaining) the world of heaven, should in chanting practise it: in order to obtain the world of heaven. He who has practised it falls not from the world of heaven. From the top he ascends to the top[1]. (It is) the on-stepping viṣṭuti (used) in order to step on (his adversaries); by that (form) of the sacrifice which steps on, he prospers. Therefore this (viṣṭuti) should in chanting be practised, for prospering.

[1] Cp. note 1 on II. 1. 3.

III. 6.

1. For thirteen (verses) he makes *him*: he (chants) three (verses: the first verse thrice), then five (five times the second verse), then five (five times the third verse); for eleven (verses) he makes *him*: he (chants) five (verses: five times the first verse), then three (thrice the second verse), then three (thrice the third verse); for nine (verses) he makes *him*: he (chants) three (verses: thrice the first), then three (thrice the second), then three (thrice the third verse). (This is) the descending viṣṭuti belonging to the thirty-three-versed (chant).

Schema: *hum* 1. 1. 1. 2. 2. 2. 2. 2. 3. 3. 3. 3. 3. *hum* 1. 1. 1. 1. 1. 2. 2. 2. 3. 3. 3; *hum* 1. 1. 1. 2. 2. 2. 3. 3. 3. (3. 5. 5.=13; 5. 3. 3=11; 3. 3. 3=9.)

2. Just as one, having climbed up to the top of a big tree, would get down by taking hold of branch after branch, so he gets down into this world (*viz.*, the earth) by means of this (viṣṭuti), in order that he may get a firm support.

3. He begins[1] with the nine-versed (chant)[2] and concludes[1] with the nine-versed (chant)[3]. The breath is threefold ('the nine-versed chant is breath'), by breath he begins, turning again to breath he

concludes; his whole term of normal life lives he, he does not die before his natural term of life, who in chanting practises this (viṣṭuti).

1 *praiti* and *udeti* used as *prāyaṇa* and *udayana* of II. 15. 3.

2 According to the commentary on the first day of the six-day-sacrificial period, the *ṣaḍaha*.

3 The nine stotriya-verses of the last round in this stoma on the last, the sixth day of that period.

4. This (viṣṭuti) is practised in chanting by the Karadviṣ's, therefore they obtain the whole term of normal life.

III. 7.

1. For fifteen (verses) he makes *him*: he (chants) three (verses: thrice the first verse), then seven (seven times the second verse), then five (five times the third verse); for eleven (verses) he makes *him*: he (chants) five (verses: five times the first verse), then three (thrice the second verse), then three (thrice the third verse); for seven (verses) he makes *him*: he (chants) three (verses: thrice the first verse), then one (the second), then three (three times the third verse)[1].

1 Schema: *hum* 1. 1. 1. 2. 2. 2. 2. 2. 2. 2. 3. 3. 3. 3. 3; *hum* 1. 1. 1. 1. 1. 2. 2. 2. 3. 3. 3; *hum* 1. 1. 1. 2. 3. 3. 3 (3. 7. 5; 5. 3. 3; 3. 1. 3).

2. He who knows the thirty-three-versed (chant) as firmly established in the twenty-one-versed, gets a firm support. The twenty-one-versed (chant) is the firm support of the chants[1], in that these seven (stotriya-verses) are the last of the thirty-three-versed (chant)[2] and in that the viṣṭuti of the twenty-one-versed (chant) is divided in a sevenfold way[3], thereby he places the thirty-three-versed (chant) firmly into the twenty-one-versed. Firm support gets he who in chanting practises this (viṣṭuti).

1 Because it is the stoma of the *agniṣṭomastotra*, which is *sarvaprakṛti* (Comm.).

2 Just as the *ekaviṃśa* is the last chant of the normal *catuṣṭoma-agniṣṭoma* (the last round of the viṣṭuti here mentioned is 3. 1. 3).

3 Cp. II. 14. 1.

III. 8.

(Now follow the stomas of the Chandoma-days: the 7th, 8th and 9th of the ten-day sacrificial period).

1. For eight (verses) he makes *him*: he (chants) three (verses:

thrice the first verse), then four (four times the second verse), then one (the third verse); for eight (verses) he makes *him*: he (chants) one (verse, the first), then three (thrice the second verse), then four (four times the third verse); for eight (verses) he makes *him*: he (chants) four (verses: four times the first verse), then one (the second verse), then three (thrice the third verse)[1].

[1] Schema: *hum* 1. 1. 1. 2. 2. 2. 2 3; *hum* 1. 2. 2. 2. 3. 3. 3 3; *hum* 1. 1. 1. 1. 2. 3. 3. 3 (3. 4. 1; 1. 3. 4; 4. 1. 3).

2. The Chandoma (days) are cattle[1]; in that he makes *him* each time for eight (verses), cattle being eight-hoofed, he gains cattle hoof by hoof.

[1] Simply because of the greater number of verses.

3. Fixed[1] by four (verses) is (this viṣṭuti); the circulating (verse) is one single, cattle is four-footed, the circulating (verse) is the Sacrificer; in that he fixes (this viṣṭuti) by four (verses) and in that the circulating (verse) is one in number, he thereby gives to the Sacrificer a firm support among cattle. This is the firmly supported viṣṭuti belonging to the twenty-four-versed (chant); firmly supported is he who in chanting practises this (viṣṭuti).

[1] Cp. note 1 on III. 1. 3.

III. 9.

1. For fifteen (verses) he makes *him*: he (chants) three (verses: thrice the first verse), then eleven (eleven times the second verse), then one (the third verse); for fourteen (verses) he makes *him*: he (chants) one (verse, the first), then three (thrice the second verse), then ten (ten times the third verse); for fifteen (verses) he makes *him*: he (chants) eleven (verses, eleven times the first verse), then one (the second), then three (thrice the third verse)[1].

[1] Schema: *hum* 1. 1. 1. 2. 2. 2. 2. 2. 2. 2. 2. 2. 2. 2. 3; *hum* 1. 2. 2. 2. 3. 3. 3. 3. 3. 3. 3. 3. 3. 3; *hum* 1. 1. 1. 1. 1. 1. 1. 1. 1. 1. 1. 2. 3. 3. 3 (3. 11. 1=15; 1. 3. 10=14. 11. 1 3=15, together 44).

2. The first (verse of the tristich) is the place of priesthood, the second of nobility, the third of peasantry; in that the first two (verses) occur each fifteen times[1], but the last (the third verse) fourteen times[2], he thereby brings vigour and strength in priesthood as well as nobility, he thereby makes peasantry subject to priesthood as well as nobility.

A shining-out among nobility, as it were [3], falls to the share of him, who in chanting practises this (viṣṭuti).

[1] The first verse occurs thrice, once and eleven times in the first *viṣṭāva* of each round, the second verse occurs eleven times, thrice and once in the second *viṣṭāva* of each round.

[2] The third verse occurs once, ten times and thrice in the third *viṣṭāva* of each round.

[3] The same expression II. 8. 2.

3. The Chandoma (chants) (*viz.*, the chants of the Chandoma-days, of 24, 44 and 48 verses) are not really chants, for the chants (proper) are uneven (*i.e.*, of an uneven number of verses) [1], the metres are even (*i e.*, of an even number of syllables, gāyatrī of 24, triṣṭubh of 44, jagatī of 48, anuṣṭubh of 32, paṅkti of 40 syllables). In that this viṣṭuti of the forty-four-versed (chant) contains an uneven number [2] (of verses), they (the Chandoma-chants) become chants.

[1] The *trivṛt, pañcadaśa, saptadaśa, ekaviṃśa.*

[2] *Viz*, in the first and third round. Combine *yad eṣāyujinī* instead of *yad eṣā yujinī.*

4. This is the firmly supported viṣṭuti belonging to the forty-four-versed (chant). He who in chanting practises this (viṣṭuti) gets a firm support.

III. 10.

1. For fourteen (verses) he makes *him*: he (chants) three (verses: thrice the first verse), then ten (ten times the second verse), then one (the third); for fifteen (verses) he makes *him*: he (chants) one (the first verse), then three (thrice the second verse), then eleven (eleven times the third verse); for fifteen (verses) he makes *him*: he (chants) eleven verses (eleven times the first verse), then one (the second), then three (thrice the third verse) [1]. (This is) the middleless (viṣṭuti) [2].

[1] Schema: *hum* 1. 1. 1. 2. 2. 2. 2 2. 2. 2. 2. 2. 2. 3; *hum* 1. 2. 2. 2. 3. 3. 3. 3. 3. 3. 3. 3. 3. 3. 3; *hum*: 1. 1. 1. 1. 1. 1. 1. 1. 1. 1. 1. 2. 3. 3. 3 (3. 10. 1. 1. 3, 11, 11. 1. 3. together 44).

[2] *nirmadhya* 'devoid of middle,' *i.e.* 'with smaller middle': the first and third verses of the tristich occur in all the rounds in the first and third *viṣṭāva* together each fifteen times (3. 1. 11 and 1. 11. 3), the middle verse only fourteen times (10. 3. 1)

2. This world (the earth) can be said to exist and yonder world (the sky) can be said to exist, but the intermediate region is a hollow, as

it were. In that this viṣṭuti is middleless, he progenerates himself after (*i.e.* in accordance with) these worlds, children and cattle will multiply unto him who in chanting practises this (viṣṭuti.)[1].

[1] The three verses of the tristich are said to be in accordance with the nature of the three worlds: earth and sky are equal, in so far as they are visible, the first and the last verse (earth and sky) are also equal in number, but the second verse (the intermediate region) has a void.

III. 11.

1. For fifteen (verses) he makes *him*: he (chants) three (verses: thrice the first verse), then eleven (eleven times the second verse), then one (the third); for fifteen (verses) he makes *him*: he (chants) one (verse, the first), then three (thrice the second verse), then eleven (eleven times the third verse); for fourteen (verses) he makes *him*: he (chants) ten (verses: ten times the first verse), then one (the second), then three (thrice the third verse)[1]

[1] Schema: *hum* 1. 1. 1. 2. 2. 2. 2. 2. 2. 2 2. 2. 2. 2. 3; *hum* 1. 2. 2. 2. 3. 3. 3. 3. 3. 3. 3. 3. 3. 3. 3; *hum* 1. 1. 1. 1. 1. 1. 1. 1. 1. 1. 2. 3. 3. 3. (3. 11. 1=15; 1. 3. 11=15; 10. 1. 3=14).

2. For the ājya-lauds (of the Chandomadays) the first (viṣṭuti belonging to the forty-four-versed chant is destined, *viz.* III. 9), for the pṛṣṭha-lauds the second (*viz.* III. 10), for the uktha-lauds the third (*viz.* III. 11).

3*a*. The one destined for the ājya-lauds (the one described under III. 9) (is meant for the ājya-laud) of the Hotṛ (or first ājya-stotra); the one destined for the pṛṣtha-lauds (*viz.* III. 10) (is meant for the ājya-laud) of the Maitrāvaruṇa (or second ājyastotra), the one destined for the uktha-lauds (*viz.* III. 11) (is meant for the ājyastotra) of the Brāhmaṇācchaṃsin (or third ājyastotra); (for the ājya-laud) of the Acchāvāka (or fourth ājyastotra), the same (viṣṭuti is to be applied) as (for the ājya-laud) of the Hotṛ (*viz* III. 9).

3*b*. The one destined for the pṛṣtha-lauds (*viz.* III. 10) (is meant for the uktha-laud) of the Hotṛ; the one destined for the uktha-lauds (*viz.* III. 11) (is meant for the pṛṣṭha-laud) of the Maitrāvaruṇa; the one destined for the ājya-lauds (III. 9) (is meant for the pṛṣṭha-laud) of the Brāhmaṇācchaṃsin; (for the pṛṣṭha-laud) of the Acchāvāka the same (viṣṭuti is to be applied) as (for the pṛṣṭha-laud) of the Hotṛ (III. 10).

3c. The one destined for the uktha-lauds (III. 11) (is intended for the uktha-laud) of the Hotṛ[1]; the one destined for the ājya-lauds (III. 9) (is intended for the uktha-laud) of the Maitrāvaruṇa, the one destined for the pṛṣṭha-lauds (III. 10) (is intended for the uktha-laud) of the Brāhmaṇācchaṃsin; (for the uktha-laud) of the Acchāvāka the same (viṣṭuti is to be applied) as (for the uktha-laud) of the Hotṛ (III. 11).

3d. (In this manner) all (the viṣṭutis) are applied at the ājya-, at the pṛṣṭha- and at the uktha-lauds[1].

[1] Properly, there is no uktha for the Hotṛ, but obviously the author here means the agniṣṭomastotra. The expressions *hotur ājyam, maitrāvaruṇasyājyam,* etc. refer to those lauds to be chanted by the Chanters, which correspond with the successive recitations (*śastras*) of the Hotṛ, the Maitrāvaruṇa, the Brāhmaṇācchaṃsin and the Acchāvāka. An analogous case occurs in the Vaitānasūtra (XX. 13), where the expression *pra-ugastotra* is found (cp. the note of the author's translation into German).

4. The 'joining'[1] (viṣṭuti) is (equal to) cattle. In that this viṣṭuti follows along after a l l the services (*savanas*), he makes him prosper in regard to cattle after each savana; possessed of cattle becomes he who in chanting practises this (viṣṭuti).

[1] *samīṣanti* cp. Lāṭy VI. 2. 22.

III 12.

1. For sixteen (verses) he makes *him*: he (chants) three (verses: thrice the first verse), then twelve (twelve times the second verse), then one (the third); for sixteen (verses) he makes *him*: he (chants) one (the first verse), then three (thrice the second verse), then twelve (twelve times the third verse); for sixteen (verses) he makes *him*: he (chants) twelve (verses: twelve times the first verse), then one (the second), then three (thrice the third verse)[1].

[1] Schema: *hum* 1. 1. 1. 2. 2. 2. 2. 2. 2. 2. 2 2. 2. 2. 2. 3; *hum* 1. 2. 2. 2. 3. 3. 3. 3. 3. 3. 3. 3. 3. 3. 3. 3; *hum* 1. 1. 1. 1. 1. 1. 1. 1. 1. 1. 1. 1. 2. 3. 3. 3 (3, 12, 1; 1, 3, 12; 12, 1, 3, together 48).

2. The forty-eight-versed (chant) is the end. The Chandoma-(chants) are cattle; in that he makes *him* each time for sixteen verses, cattle consisting of sixteen parts[1], he gains the cattle part by part ('in sixteens').

[1] Four hoofs, four feet, head, neck, body and tail.

3. Fixed[1] by twelve (verses) is this (viṣṭuti); the circulating

(verse) is one single, the year has twelve months; the circulating (verse) is the Sacrificer; in that he fixes (this viṣṭuti) by twelve (verses) and in that the circulating verse is one in number, he thereby gives to the Sacrificer finally[2] (for good) a firm support in the year ('in the time'), in cattle. (This is) the firmly supported (viṣṭuti) belonging to the forty-eight-versed (chant). Firmly supported is he who in chanting practises this (viṣṭuti).

1 Cp. note 1 on III. 1. 3.

2 See the first words of the proceeding §.

III. 13.

1. For sixteen (verses) he makes *him*: he (chants) three (verses: thrice the first verse), then ten (ten times the second verse), then three (thrice the third verse); for sixteen (verses) he makes *him*: he (chants) three (verses: thrice the first verse), then three (thrice the second verse), then ten (ten times the third verse); for sixteen (verses) he makes *him:* he (chants) ten (verses: ten times the first verse), then three (thrice the second), then three (thrice the third)[1]. (This is the viṣṭuti) 'of nearer stair'[2].

1 Schema: *hum* 1. 1. 1 2. 2. 2. 2. 2. 2. 2. 2. 2. 2. 3. 3. 3; *hum* 1. 1. 1. 2. 2. 2. 3. 3 3. 3. 3. 3. 3. 3. 3. 3; *hum* 1. 1. 1. 1. 1. 1. 1. 1. 1. 1. 2. 2. 2. 3. 3. 3 (3, 10, 3; 3, 3, 10; 10, 3, 3, together 48).

2 Cp. III. 4. 1.

2. The forty-eight-versed (chant) is the end of all (the chants). Just as one, having climbed up to the top of a big tree, steps on from nearer stair, so he thereby by the (viṣṭuti) 'of nearer stair' steps on from the nearer stair[1].

1 Cp. III. 4. 2.

3. Fixed[1] by ten (verses) is (this viṣṭuti); the circulating (verses) are three in number, the virāj (metre) is tensyllabic; man comprises his self, his children, his wife; in that he fixes (this viṣṭuti) by ten (verses) and in that the circulating (verses) are three in number, he thereby gives to the Sacrificer finally a firm support in the virāj: the food. An eater of food becomes he who in chanting practises this (viṣṭuti).

1 Cp. note 1 on III. 1. 3.

FOURTH AND FIFTH CHAPTER.

(The gavām ayana.)

Introductory remark. The two next following chapters describe the gavām ayana, *i.e.*, the Soma-feast lasting a year of 360 days. The Jaim. br. describes it II. 372-442. For the precise schema cp. below XXIV. 20; see also the survey in the Introduction to the Ārṣeyakalpa, pages XXIV, XXV.

On the precise meaning of *ayana* we may remark that the translation of *gavām ayana*: 'the course' or 'the walk of the cows' suggests an idea that is not inherent in this word *ayana*; *yanti* with instr. and accusative of time denotes a continuous occupation with any sacrifice: *etābhir iṣṭibhiḥ saptāhāni yanti, ta etaṃ ṣaḍbhir māsair yanti, gavām ayanena yanti*, etc.

IV. 1.

1. The cows (once upon a time) held[1] that sacrificial session. In the course of ten months they obtained horns. They said: 'We have been successful, let us arise[2], horns have come to us'. They arose.

[1] Properly the root *sad* with *sattram* as object, is the regular expression to denote the participation in a Soma-feast of longer duration than twelve days.

[2] *utthāna* 'araising' is the term which designates the breaking off, the finishing of such a 'session.'

2. Some of them[1] said: 'Let us continue the session during these two (remaining: the eleventh and the) twelfth months, let us complete the year'. Their horns in the course of the twelve months got curved ('crumpled')[2], they obtained, however, all food[3]. These are the hornless ones, these start forth all the twelve months[4], for they had obtained all food[5].

[1] On *tāsaṃ tvevābruvan* see Introduction, Chapter III § 8 (under Sandhi).

[2] *prāvartanta* is usually taken in the sense of: 'they fell off'. It is not clear to me how *pravartate* can have this meaning and I am inclined to take it in the sense of: 'to get curved' (at the top), or 'round', 'circular', cp. *pravarta* 'a circular ornament,' *pravṛtta* 'round'. The cows all obtained horns during the ten months, but those who continued the sacrifice, of them these horns got curved at the top: a *tūpara* animal, therefore, is, if I am right, not only a hornless animal, but also one with small, inward bent horns.

[3] Either because they had undertaken the sattra in order to obtain food (as the Jaim. br. has it) or because they had continued their session also during the two months, the vedic names of one of these being *ūrj* (cp. Ait. br. IV. 17: *ūrjaṃ*

tv asanvan). These two months seem to form the rainy season (*tasmāt tūparā vārṣikau māsau prartvā* [so my conjecture, cp. Acta Orientalia, Vol. V, page 252]. *caranti*, TS. VII. 5. 1. 2) and seem here to be taken as the last two months of the year

[4] Probably the meaning is, that the hornless cows remain during the whole year in the meadows, which the other kind, the horned ones, are not equal to (*tasmād dvādaśa māsāṁs tuparāḥ prertvariś caranti daśa śṛṅgiṇīḥ*, Kaṭh. XXXIII. 1; *tasmād u tāḥ* (*sc. tūparāḥ*) *sārvān ṛtūn prāptvottaram uttiṣṭhanti*, Ait. br. IV. 17).

[5] For this legend cp. TS. VII. 5. 2 and VII. 5. 1. 1-2, Kāṭh. XXXIII. 1, Ait br. IV. 17. 2-3, Jaim. br. II. 374.

3. All food obtains he who knows this.

4. Prajāpati (at the beginning) was here alone, he desired; "May I multiply, may I beget progeny.' He saw this overnight-rite[1], he practised it, by means of it he begat day and night.

[1] The first day of the year's sattra.

5. In that this (day) in an overnight-rite, they[1] procreate day and night, they get a firm support in day and night. The year comprises the day and the night only; by the day and the night they thereby reach the year.

[1] The performers of a sattra, who all are Yajamānas.

6. In that it is a jyotiṣṭoma[1], they thereby complete the beginning of the sacrifice; that it is an ukthya[2], is for preventing discontinuity of the Soma-feast; that it is a night (-rite)[3], is for obtaining the whole.

[1] A sacrifice of 12 stotra-śastras.

[2] A sacrifice of 15 stotra-śastras.

[3] An ukthya followed by the *rātriparyāyas* and the *sandhistotra*.

7. He saw these stomas[1]: the light, cow- and life-stomas; these stomas are the worlds, the "light" (*jyotis*) is this world, the "cow" (*go*) is the middle one, the "life" (*āyus*) is the highest.

[1] Here the word stoma denotes the days called jyotiṣṭoma, goṣṭoma, āyuṣṭoma; cp. Introd. remarks on chapters II, III.

8. In that there are (in the year's sattra) these stomas, they generate these worlds, they get firm support in these worlds.

9. He (Prajāpati) applied again this three-day-period; by this six-day-period (*ṣaḍaha*) he procreated the seasons.

10. In that there is this six-day-period, they generate the seasons, they get firm support in the seasons.

11. He applied again this six-day-period; by means of these two six-day-periods he procreated the twelve months.

12. In that there are these two six-day-periods, they generate the months, they get firm support in the months.

13. He applied again these two six-day-periods; by means of these four six-day-periods he procreated the twenty-four half-months.

14. In that there are these four six-day-periods, they generate the half-months, they get firm support in the half months.

15. Having procreated this world, he brought strength into himself by means of the six-day-period with the pṛṣṭhasāmans.

16. In that there is this six-day-period with the pṛṣṭhasāmans, they finally establish themselves firmly in strength.

17. By means of this (month) he procreated the (other) months, the year. In that there is this month, they generate the year, they get firm support in the year.

IV. 2.

(The 'proceeding' day: prāyaṇīya-atirātra.)

1. There is this proceeding day (the opening day of the year's sacrifice, the second of the whole sattra).

2. By means of the proceeding day the gods proceeded to the world of heaven: because they proceeded, therefore it is called the proceeding day.

3. Therefore one[1] must become an officiating priest of (*i.e.* at) the proceeding day; for this (day) is nearest to the world of heaven; he who is not an officiating priest of this (day), is left out of the world of heaven (*i.e.* does not reach it).

[1] All the priests at a sattra are at the same time Yajamāna.

4. It is (a) twenty-four-versed (day)[1].

[1] A day of which all the lauds are twenty-four-versed, cp. II. 14–17.

5. The gāyatrī consists of twenty-four syllables; the gāyatrī is gleaming splendour and spiritual lustre. Having laid hands on gleaming splendour and spiritual lustre, they proceed.

6. It is (a) twenty-four-versed (day); twenty-four-fold is the year[1]: manifestly they lay hold on the year.

[1] As consisting of 24 half-months (J.Br. II. 377).

7. As many stotriya-verses as are contained in the twenty-four-versed day with uktha lauds[1], so many days there are in the year: by means of the stotriya-verses they thus reach the year.

[1] Again as so often *uktha* is equal to (or faulty instead of) *ukthya*.—The ukthya has 15 lauds each of 24 verses=360 in all.

8. There are fifteen lauds, the half-month has fifteen days, half-month by half-month they thus reach the year.

9. There are fifteen lauds and fifteen recitations (*śastras*); that makes a month, month by month they reach the year.

10. Regarding this they say: 'A wound as it were, is the hotrā[1] of the Achāvāka; if it (the sacrifice, the Soma-feast) closes after the (laud of the Chanters and the corresponding recitation of the) Achāvāka they are likely to become wounds[2]. If it is to be an ukthya, the traikakubha[3] and the udvaṁśīya[3] are to be fixed at the end; these two sāmans are strength: in strength they finally are firmly supported.

[1] The office of a hotraka (Hotṛ, Maitrāvaruṇa, Brāhmaṇācchaṁsin, Acchāvāka).

[2] On *īśvarermā* see Introduction, Chapter § 8, end.—Possibly the function of the Acchāvāka is called a wound, because he enters the service some time after the sacrifice has begun, leaving, so to say, an open space (as a wound may be a gaping in the flesh).

[3] See note on XV. 6. 4 and 6.—The traikakubha should in this case be taken as the Brahman's, the udvaṁśiya as the Acchāvāka's sāman.

11. Now, however, they say: 'it must be made an agniṣṭoma; the agniṣṭoma, indeed, is a sacrifice conducting to the world of heaven; for it rises upward after the (laud of the Chanters and the corresponding recitation of the)Hotṛ.

12. The agniṣṭoma is (contains) twelve lauds and the year is (contains) twelve months, thereby it (the sacrifice) is of equal measure with the year. There are twelve lauds and twelve recitations, that makes twenty-four: the year is (contains) twenty-four half-months, thereby it (the sacrifice) is of equal measure with the year.

13. Now, however, they say: it must be made an ukthya: for the obtainment of the day.

14. All the characteristics[1] are brought about, for all is reached by this day[2].

[1] *Viz.* of the ten day period, the daśarātra, as it seems, cp. the long passage Nid. sūtra IV. 13: *sarvānt stomān sarvāṇi pṛṣṭhāni sarvā vibhaktīr daśarātrarūpāṇīti vibhaktimātreṇaiva kalpayante*—This § as it seems must be connected with the following, where the *rūpāṇi* are described.

[2] It is remarkable that the praxis of the Ārseyakalpa (I. 1. s. f.): *agniṃ vo vṛdhantām iti satrāsāhīyaṁ saubharam udvaṁśīyam* does not agree with the Brāhmana. cp Nidānasūtra IV. 13: *uddharanty ācāryās traikakubhaṁ samānodarkayony aparūpaṃ prāyaṇārthe, tatraitat saubharaṃ pṛṣṭhānvitaṃ vikalpo vāsmād brāhmaṇacoditatvāt.* The meaning of this passage is not wholly clear to me.

15. (The verse beginning): 'The Soma (draughts) possessing a thousandfold vigour are being strained for the obtainment of booty'[1] in which occurs the word 'a thousand', is to be taken as opening (verse for the out-of-doors-laud).

[1] S.V. II. 539=RS. IX. 13. 3.

16. It (this verse) is the characteristic of the year[1]; he (*viz.* the Chanter) purifies them all[2] (*i.e.* all the partakers of the sattra) by means of this (opening-verse), he addresses them all.

[1] The year having so many days and the verse containing the word, 'thousand' (Comm.).

[2] Note the plural *pavante* of the verse.

17. Now, however, they say: '(the verse beginning) 'be strained as the first of speech'[1] should rather be taken (as opening verse of the out-of-doors-laud). The beginning of speech verily is the opening of the year: at the opening they thereby lay hold on the year'.

[1] This tristich (SV. II. 125-127=ṚS. IX. 62. 25-27) is prescribed in accordance with this Brāhmana by Maśaka in his Ārṣeyakalpa I. 1.b.

18. A copulation, as it were, is this utterance: the words: 'be strained' represent the male, and 'of speech', the female; 'of Soma' the male and 'with bright' the female. A copulation he produces on their behalf at the opening of the sacrifice for the purpose of progeneration.

19. The jarābodhīya-melody (sung on the tristich beginning:)

O Agni, harness those steeds of thine '[1] is to be taken as agniṣṭoma-chant. With the harnessed year they proceed (or begin). It is (composed) on (verses) of twenty-four syllables: the characteristic of the twenty-four-versed (chant).

[1] SV. I. 25=II. 733–735=ṚS VI. 16. 43-45 (with variants). On SV. II. 733–735 the Ūhagāna gives no jarābodhīya, neither does the Ārṣeyakalpa record this sāman. The tristich SV. II. 733–735 has no *viniyoga* in our ritual, only in the Brāhmaṇa (in this passage). We seem to be right in supposing that the uttarārcika (SV. II) was compiled later than the time of the Brāhmaṇa and that the author of the Brāhmana refers in this passage to the Ṛgvedic texts. The tristich *agne yuṅkṣva* is not found in the ārcika of the Jaiminīyas.

20. Now, however, they say: 'the yajñāyajñīya-chant only is to be taken' (as agniṣṭomasāman)[1].

[1] And so does Maśaka.

21. The yajñāyajñīya is the way: in this manner they do not leave the way.

IV. 3.

(The Brahman's chant during the year.)

1 The chant (sāman) of the Brahman (*i.e.* the pṛṣṭha-laud corresponding with the śastra of the Brahman or the Brāhmaṇācchaṃsin, the third laud (stotra) at the mid-day service, of all the abhiplava-six-day-periods and the three svarasāman days during the first half of the year) is the abhīvarta (sāman)[1].

[1] See note on § 3.

2. By means of the abhīvarta the Gods turned themselves to (*abhyavartanta*) the world of heaven. (The reason) why the Brahman's chant is the abhīvarta, is, that they may turn themselves to the world of heaven[1].

[1] Cp. Jaim. br. II. 378, Journ. of the Amer. Or. Soc., Vol. XVIII page 45.

3. It has a finale (*nidhana*) of one syllable[1]; of one syllable consists (the word) 'speech'; by means of speech thereby having taken hold of the world of heaven they reach it.

[1] The abhīvarta (Grāmegeyagāna VI. 1. 34 on SV. I. 236, finishing words: *indraṃ gīrbhir navāmahe*) closes: *iṃdrām gā' 1 ir bhī'2 ḥ* | *navā'3 mā' 2345* | *hā. 2345i*|| (with superscript accent marks: 1 over drā, 2 over gā, ∧ over 2, 3 2 over vā, 1 over mā, 3 over hā; 1 1 1 1 over 2345)

4. By means of a sāman (or 'with a sāman') they go hence, by means of a ṛc (or 'with a verse') they return[1].

[1] The sāman is the abhīvarta-sāman used in the first half of the year; in the abhiplava-six-day periods of the second half of the year the pragātha SV. II. 806-807 is used to chant on it each day a different melody (paurumīḍha, mānava, janitra, bhāradvāja, śyaita and naudhasa), cp. Ārṣeyakalpa II. 7 (and II. 5. 6). In this manner during the first half of the year the sāman is the same, the ṛc different, in the second half the ṛc is the same, but the sāman different.

5. Yonder world (the sky) is the sāman, this world (the earth) is the verse[1]; in that they go hence with a sāman, they go, after taking hold of the world of heaven; in that they return with a verse, they get a firm support on this world.

[1] We are reminded of the well-known formula: *amo 'ham asmi sā tvam sāmāham asmy ṛk tvaṃ dyaur ahaṃ pṛthivī tvam*, etc.

6. If they were to abandon the sāman (*i.e.* if during the first half of the year they did not use continually the sāman, the abhīvarta), they would fall from the world of heaven; if they were to quit their hold of the verse (during the second half of the year), they would vanish from this world (*i.e.* they would not reach again the earth).

7. The sāman is the same, the pragātha (on which it is chanted) is varied: to various bright (things) surely comes he who undertakes a journey.

8. The abhīvarta, forsooth, is a male, a seed-placer; he places the seed continually into the pragāthas; in that from here (*i.e.* in the first half of the year) the sāman is the same, but the pragātha different, they thereby place the seed. In that afterwards (*i.e.* in the second half of the year) the pragātha is the same, but the sāman different, they thereby cause the placed seed to spring.

9. By means of the sāman he milks from here (in the first half of the year) the pragāthas[1] (*i.e.* he gets the good out of them), by means of the pragātha he afterwards (in the second half) milks the sāmans: for the sake of congruency.

[1] Read *pragāthān* instead of *pragāthām*.

10. They who undertake a journey, each time returning, these do not perform their journey; they who undertake a journey without returning, these arrive[1].

[1] And in this manner the performers of a sattra, who during the first half of the year use other sāmans than during the second half, reach the world of heaven —Read: *punar nivartaṃ yanti.*

11. If they repeat a chant[1], it would be as if one would seat himself near a cow (in order to milk it), that has (already) been milked.

[1] See note on next §.

12. If they (do) not (repeat) a chant[1], they reach the fulfilment of all the desires they wish to see fulfilled.

[1] The precise meaning of *āstutam* is not clear to me. The meaning of these two sentences seems to be a recommendation not to repeat the brahmasāmans; these must be different in each half year.

13. The theologues argue: 'is the year used up[1], or is it not used up'? 'In this way it is not used up'[2], it should be answered: the other lauds return again, but the Brahman's sāman (alone) goes upward[3].

[1] Read: *yātayāmā* (nomin. from *yātayāman*) instead of *yātayāmāḥ*

[2] Read: *tenāyātayāmeti.*

[3] A repetition causes 'using-up'; as the other pṛṣṭhasāmans in the ṣaḍahas are day after day the bṛhat, rathantara, vāmadevya and kāleya, there is a fear of *yātayāmatva*: but the brahmasāmans, which are during the first half of the year chanted on different verses and in the second half of the year are chanted on different melodies, take away the fear of 'using-up'

IV. 4.

(The Brahman's chant; continued.)

1. In the (first) five months (of the year) the bārhata pragāthas[1] are used up[2] (for the brahmasāmans).

[1] A pragātha is a combination of two verses: either a bṛhatī (of 8+8+12+8 syllables) and a satobṛhatī (of 12+8+12+8 syllables), or a kakubh (of 8+12+8 syllables) and a satobṛhatī. By repetition, out of these two verses are made three When the bṛhatī precedes, the pragātha is called a bārhata pragātha, when the kakubh precedes, it is called a kākubha pragātha, cp. Vaitānasūtra XXII. 8. 9, XXV. 4. 5.

[2] For this translation of *āpyante* cp. XIV. 1, 1. Perhaps we might equally well translate here: 'are obtained' (*viz.* out of the Ṛksaṃhitā). According to Lāṭy. X. 6. 5, Nidānasūtra V. 3, and Kalpānupadasūtra I. 7, the Ṛksaṃhitā contains 104 bārhata pragāthas addressed to Indra (I count 106 of them, but am not sure about this). Four of these are destined for the bṛhat, the rathantara, the kāleya and that sāman on which during the second half of the year the

brahmasāman is chanted (*viz. indra kratuṃ na ābhara* ṚS. VII. 32. 16. 17=SV. II. 806, 807); moreover one is destined for the brahmasāman of the caturviṃśa opening day. The remaining 99 are to be used at the abhiplava-ṣaḍahas of the first five months for the brahmasāmans. These five months contain each four abhiplavas: together 120 days; as there are only 99 pragāthas left over for these 120 days (cp. Jaim. br. II. 381: 'before the fifth month the bārhata pragāthas are used up') the remainder are taken from the 29 sātobārhata tṛcas contained in the Ṛksaṃhitā (I am unable to point out which Ṛk-verses are meant). These satobārhata pragāthas are used on the third day of each abhiplava ṣaḍaha. The exact reckoning is not clear to me

2. These having been used up, they should proceed (during the remaining days) uniting two metres[1].

[1] For the brahmasāman during the sixth month, cp. Lāṭy. X. 6. 9 and Jaim. br. II. 381: 'having united two metres: the uṣṇih and the triṣṭubh, they should finish (with these) the five months; having united two metres: the anuṣṭubh and the paṅkti, they should finish the six months'.

3. They should be three uṣṇihs (and) one gāyatrī: these make three bṛhatīs[1].

[1] Uṣṇih: 8+8+12 syllables, gāyatrī: 8+8+8. Three uṣṇihs ad 28=84+one gāyatrī ad 24=108=3 bṛhatīs ad 36 syllables. In this manner the want of bārhata pragāthas in the Ṛksaṃhitā is supplied.

4. Regarding this they say (however): 'this uniting of the two metres, forsooth, is, as it were, a splitting up of the metres'.

5. They should (rather) apply the metres, which increase by four (syllables)[1].

[1] These metres are: the gāyatrī, uṣṇih, anuṣṭubh, bṛhatī, paṅkti, triṣṭubh, jagatī.—In order to make up the want of bārhata pragāthas, verses in gāyatrī metre are, according to Lāṭy. X. 6. 12, to be taken for the brahmasāman on the caturviṃśa day, in uṣṇih on the first abhiplava-day, in anuṣṭubh on the second day, in bṛhatī on all the other days; cp. below, § 7.

6. The metres, which increase by four (syllables), are the (f o u r-footed) cattle; thus by means of the cattle they afford a (means of) approaching the world of heaven[1].

[1] The accusative *svargaṃ lokam* seems to be governed by *ākramam*

7. They should apply one gāyatrī during one day (*viz.* the caturviṃśa-prāyaṇīya-day), one uṣṇih during one day[1], one anuṣṭubh during one day[2]; with the bṛhatī they should proceed during five months[3]; the paṅkti they should apply during one day[4]; with the triṣṭubh they

should proceed during the sixth month, and on the day immediately before the viṣuvat-day (*i.e.* on the third svarasāman-day) they should apply the jagatī.

[1] The first day of the first abhiplava of the first month.

[2] The second day of the first abhiplava of the first month.

[3] The third day of the first abhiplava of the first month and during the rest of the first month and the following five months.

[4] The sixth day of the second abhiplava of the sixth month.

8. Regarding this they say (however): 'unsuitable for the midday-service are these metres[1]; they should apply the bṛhatī and the triṣṭubh (only)'.

[1] As at the midday-service only gāyatrī, bṛhatī and triṣṭubh are regularly used.

9. These two metres[1], forsooth, are powerful[2], they are plainly the characteristic mark of the midday-service.

[1] The bṛhatī and triṣṭubh.

[2] Cp. Śat. br. V. 3. 1. 2: *vīryam triṣṭup* and Pañc. br. XV. 10. 11: *tasmād bṛhatī chandasāṃ vīryavattamā.*

10. On a rathantara-day[1] the bṛhatī is to be taken (for the brahmasāman); the bṛhatī, forsooth, is the special place of the rathantara (sāman)[2]; he thereby gives firm support to the rathantara in its own place. On a bṛhat-day[3] the triṣṭubh is to be taken: the triṣṭubh, forsooth, is the special place of the bṛhat (saman)[4]; thereby the rathantara and the bṛhat find continually firm support in their own place.

[1] *Viz.* on a day, on which the rathantara sāman is taken for the first (or Hotṛ's) pṛṣṭhalaud.

[2] They both are the typical Hotṛ-chants for the first pṛṣṭhalaud.

[3] *Viz.* on a day, on which the bṛhatsāman is taken for the first pṛṣṭhalaud.

[4] I do not see the reason for this assertion.

11. They should apply (for the brahmasāman at the pṛṣṭhalauds) thirty-three pragāthas; thirty-three in number are the deities; in the deities even they have (in this manner) continually a firm support. They should apply twenty-four: the year consists of twenty-four half-months; in the year even they have continually a firm support. They should apply twelve: the year consists of twelve months; in the year

even they have continually a firm support. They should apply six: six in number are the seasons; in the seasons they have continually a firm support. They should apply four: four-footed is cattle; in the cattle they have continually a firm support. They should apply three: three are these worlds; in these worlds they have continually a firm support. They should apply two: two-footed is the Sacrificer, for treading on the world of heaven; for, in walking, man stands firmly now on this, now on that foot[1].

[1] The exact of purport of what is said in this § is not clear to me. Probably the author permits for the brahmasāman in the first half of the year 33, or 24 or 12 etc. pragāthas; when these are used up they apply them again as long as need be. It seems that the Ārṣeyakalpa takes no notice of all the possibilities treated in IV. 4. On the whole cp. Lāṭy. X. 6-8, Nidānasūtra V. 3-4; the Jaiminīya brāhmaṇa (II. 382) agrees closely with PBr.

IV. 5.

(The svarasāman-days.)

1 There are the svarasāman (days)[1].

[1] The six days (three in the first half of the year preceding the middle or viṣuvat-day, three in the second half, following immediately on the viṣuvat-day), on which the sāmans called *svara* are chanted at the ārbhava-laud. The svarasāmans are four in number, composed on the verse *yaj jāyathā apūrvya* (Ār. ārcika II. 17, they are registered in the araṇyegeyagāna III. 2. 9-12, cp. Ārṣeyakalpa, page 18, note 1, page 20, note 1, page 21, note 2). On these days these sāmans are chanted: on the first day on SV. II. 736-738, on the second day on II. 168-170, on the third day on II. 222-224. Besides *svara* these sāmans are called also *spara* (§2) and *para* (§ 3).

2. The demoniac Svarbhānu struck the sun with darkness: by means of the svara (sāmans)[1] the Gods delivered (*asprṇvan*) it; that there are the svarasāman (days), is for delivering the sun (from darkness).

[1] According to the tradition of Kāṭh. XXXIII. 6: 32. 3 and TBr. I. 2. 4. 4 we expect *spara* (in harmony with *asprṇvan* and *sprti*), but cp. Kaus. br. XXIV. 3: *tad yad asprṇvata tasmāt svarasāmānaḥ* and Jaim. br. II. 16: *yad asprṇvaṃs tat svarāṇām svaratvam.*

3. By means of the para (sāmans) (thereupon) the Gods conveyed the sun to the world of heaven; because they conveyed (*apārayan*), therefore are they called the para (sāmans)[1].

[1] Cp. TBr. l. c. Kāṭh. l. c. line 5.

4. Him who knows this, him convey the para (sāmans).

5. They are seventeen-versed[1].

[1] Each laud of these days is made to consist of seventeen stotriya-verses.

6. Prajāpati is seventeenfold[1]; it is Prajāpati they reach (thereby).

[1] Cp. note 1 on II. 10. 5.

7 They[1] have the anuṣṭubh for their metre, Prajāpati is of anuṣṭubh-nature[2]; they (thereby) actually take hold of Prajāpati.

[1] *Viz.* the verses on which the svara's are chanted; these are in anuṣṭubh metre.

[2] Cp. below, IV. 8. 9 and Ait. br. III. 13. 2: as Prajāpati divided the metres among the gods, he retained the anuṣṭubh for himself, *athāsya yat svaṃ chanda āsid anuṣṭup*, etc.

8. Three are before (the viṣuvat-day), three after.

9. The Gods were afraid lest the sun should fall down from the world of heaven; they fastened it (there) by means of these seventeen-versed stomas; that there are these stomas, is for the sake of propping up the sun[1].

[1] Cp. Kath. XXXIII. 6: 31. 8, TBr. I. 2. 4. 2.

10 They are thirty-four-fold (stomas)[1]. The thirty-four-versed (stoma) is the highest goal; by means of the highest goal even do they fix it (*viz.* the sun, the viṣuvat-day)

[1] Taken together two and two.

11, 12. They feared lest it (*viz.* the sun) might fall across, to the farther side; they propped[1] it all round (*i.e.* above and below) by means of all the stomas: the two Abhijit and Viśvajit (days)[2]; these two stomas are strength, by strength even they thus prop[1] the sun all round: for the sake of holding (it), in order that it may not fall down nor fall across.

[1] Read *paryārṣan* and *paryṛṣanti*.

[2] The Abhijit and Viśvajit days are sarvastoma (cp. notes on Ārṣeyakalpa II. 1 and II. 6, pages 17 and 25) and below, note 2 on XX. 2. 1.—On the whole cp. Kāth. XXXIII. 6: 31. 9, TBr. I 2. 4. 2.

13. Regarding this they say (however): 'it is similar to falling into a pit, when after a thirty-three-versed (stoma) they undertake a

seventeen-versed (one)'[1] A pṛṣṭhya (six-day period) is to be put between.

[1] *Viz.* when after an Abhijit, the last stotra of which is thirty-three-versed (cp. Ārṣeyakalpa, page 17, note 1), follow the svarasāman-days, which are seventeen-versed (IV. 5. 5). This transition is similar to falling into a pit, because the transition of the stomas is abrupt.—Instead of *trayastriṁśat* read *trayastriṁśāt*.

14. (In this case) the seventeen-versed-day of it (of the pṛṣṭhya-ṣaḍaha) is to be put at the end, for the sake of congruency[1].

[1] If the third day of the pṛṣṭhya ṣaḍaha (which ṣaḍaha, on the whole, agrees with the first six days of the daśarātra), being seventeen-versed, precedes the svarasāman days, which also are seventeen-versed, there is no such abruptness The purport of § 13 and 14 is expressed more clearly in the Jaim. br. II. 386 (see Sāyaṇa's citation of the Śāṭyāyanaka *a. h. l.*): 'having performed the Abhijit before the pṛṣṭhya-ṣaḍaha, they should bring round the middle day of the pṛṣṭhya ṣaḍaha, that of seventeen-versed stoma, after (the last day of this ṣaḍaha) · the thirty-three-versed one: in this way they undertake after a seventeen-versed day (*viz.* the one of the ṣaḍaha) a seventeen-versed day (*i.e.* the first svarasāman day)

15. Regarding this they say (however): 'the seventeen-versed (stoma) is the belly of the stomas[1]. If they removed the seventeen-versed (stoma) from the middle, the offspring would suffer from hunger, the participants of the sattra would suffer from hunger.

[1] Probably because (cp. VI. 1. 10) it came forth from the middle of the body of Prajāpati.

16. The seventeen-versed (stoma) m u s t be undertaken after the thirty-three-versed one; the thirty-three-versed stoma is the highest goal and the seventeen-versed one (also) is the highest goal: from the highest goal thereby they step over unto the highest goal[1].

[1] They get as high as possible.

17. Regarding them (these svarasāman-days) they say: 'are they to be made ukthyas or agniṣṭomas'? If they are ukthyas—

18. the uktha-lauds are the cattle[1], cattle is a means of quenching[2], by means of a q u e n c h e d (ceremony) they undertake the viṣuvat (day)[3].

[1] Simply because of the plurality ?

[2] *As the cattle yields milk, butter, etc.*

[3] So that the viṣuvat, which is equal to the sun, be not overheated, *śānti* signifying also: 'the extinguishing of fire, the removal of heat'.

19. Regarding this they say (however): 'there would be no equilibrium [1], as it were, if the viṣuvat day as well as the Abhijit and Viśvajit days were to be agniṣṭomas, but the others (*viz.* the svarasāman-days) ukthyas'.

[1] *vivīvadham* 'not being *vivadha*', a *vivadha* being the shoulder yoke from each side of which depend two heavy objects (buckets, *e.g.*). If the viṣuvat and the Abhijit before it, and the Viśvajit after it, were made agniṣṭomas, but the svarasāman-days ukthyas, the weight on each side would be unequal, on each side would be a heavier and lighter load (?). Instead of *vivīvadham* the Jaim br. (II. 387) has *vilomā yajñaḥ*, which is more logical.

20. All (the svarasāman days) are (therefore) to be made agniṣṭomas.

21. The agniṣṭoma is strength; in strength they obtain even in the middle (of the year) firm support. Nine (days) are of equal number of stomas [1]: nine in number are the breaths [2]; in the breaths they (in this manner) obtain firm support.

[1] When all the svarasāmans are also agniṣṭomas, we obtain together with Abhijit and Viśvajit and viśuvat, nine of them. Sāyana seems to comprehend these words in a different way.

[2] Cp. note on II. 7. 8.

IV. 6.

(The viṣuvat or middle day.)

1. There is that viṣuvat(-day).

2. The viṣuvat(-day) is the world of the Gods; they thereby climb unto the world of the Gods.

3. It is (a) twenty-one-versed (day); the sun, forsooth is the twenty-first of this universe [1]; unto the world of the sun they thereby climb.

[1] See next §.

4. Twelve in number are the months, five the seasons, three the worlds, yonder sun is the twenty-first [1].

[1] The same statement is often met with, for instance Śat. br. XI. 2. 6. 11.

5. In the middle of the sacrifice even they get firm support.

6. (The tristich beginning:) 'O Vāyu, the bright (Soma) hath been offerded unto thee' [1] is the opening (tristich) (of the out-of-doors laud) containing the word 'bright': the characteristic of the sun [2].

1 SV. II. 978-980=RS. IV. 47. 1-3 (anuṣṭubh).

2 It is striking that the Ārṣeyakalpa prescribes a different tṛca as *pratipad*: perhaps this rests on the contents of § 8.

7. Of the Gods it is Vāyu, forsooth, that reaches him (*i.e.* the sun), of the metres it is the anuṣṭubh; if the opening (tristich) were a different one, he (the sun) would burn down (the Sacrificers)[1].

1 Cp. Jaim. br. II 339: 'an anuṣṭubh-verse addressed to Vāyu (the Wind) is the opening tristich: the Voice ('Word'), forsooth, and the Wind of the Gods reach him'.

8. 'They are severed from breath', they say, 'who depart from the opening tristich in gāyatrī-metre'[1]. In that, however, this tristich is addressed[2] to Vāyu, thereby they are not severed from breath, for Vāyu is breath.

1 *Viz.* who take as opening tristich for the pavamāna-lauds any other than a *pratipad* in gāyatrī-metre.

2 Read *bhavati* instead of *bhavanti*.

9. And they also appease[1] him by means of this (opening tristich), for Vāyu (Wind) is a (means of) appeasing[1].

1 On *śamayati* and *śānti* cp. note 1 on IV. 5. 18. The viṣuvat-day is again identified with the sun, whose too excessive heat thus is removed by the wind. Jaim br III. 389: 'if the wind did not blow, yonder (sun) would burn this (world) by its heat and Agni vaiśvānara would destroy the creatures'.

10. (This verse, containing the words:) 'Come along for the drinking of Soma' is addressed to Soma who is being clarified (to Soma pavamāna)[1].

1 And thus especially adapted for a pavamāna-laud: the bahiṣpavamāna-stotra.—The words are SV. II. 978. c.

11. It is a (verse) containing the word 'team'[1]; for the teams are cattle, the cattle is a (means of) quenching[2], by means of a quenched (ceremony) even they thereby go unto the sun (*i.e.* undertake the viṣuvat-rite).

1 *sparho deva niyutvatā*: 'desirable, O God, by (Vāyu), who drives with a team of horses', SV. II. 978. d.

2 Cp. note 2 on IV. 5. 18.

12. It (*viz.* the viṣuvat-day) has the divākīrtya (sāmans)[1] for its chants.

[1] Under the name divākīrtya are comprised the five ādityasya vrata śukriyāni: bhrāja, ābhrāja, vikarṇa, bhāsa, mahādivākīrtya (the divākīrtya par excellence). Of these the bhrājasaman (araṇyegeyagāna VI. 1. 5.) is composed on *agna āyūṁṣi pavase* (ār. ārc. V. 1); the ābhrāja (ar. gāna VI. 1. 6.) on *agnir mūrdhā* (ār. ārc. I. 27); the vikarṇa (ar. gāna VI. 1. 7) on *vibhrāḍ bṛhat* (ār. ārc. V. 2); the bhāsa (ar. gāna VI. 1. 8.) on *prakṣasya vṛṣṇaḥ* (ār. ārc. III. 8); the mahādivākīrtya (ar. gāna VI. 1. 9–18) on different stobhas and ār. ārc. V. 2 (*vibhrāḍ bṛhat*).

13. The demoniac Svarbhānu struck the sun with darkness: from it (from the sun) the Gods drove away the darkness by means of the divākīrtyas; in that there are the divākīrtyas, they drive away even the darkness from it. The divākīrtyas are the rays of the sun, by means of the rays even they thereby plainly take hold of the sun [1].

[1] Cp. TBr. I. 2. 4. 2, Kāth. XXXIII. 6: 31. 21.

14. The bhrāja ('shine'-sāman) [1] and the ābhrāja ('flame'-sāman) [1] are chanted at the beginning ('mouth', 'upper part') of the two pavamāna-lauds; from its (the sun's) very mouth ('upper-part') they by means of these two remove the darkness.

[1] The bhrāja is the second sāman (the gāyatra not being taken into account) of the midday-pavamāna-laud, the ābhrāja of the ārbhava-pavamāna-laud, see Ārseyakalpa II. 5.

15. The mahādivākīrtya [1] and the vikarṇa [2] are in the middle; from its (the sun's) middle part they by means of these two (sāmans) remove the darkness. The bhāsa is at the end [3]; from its (the sun's) feet (lower part) they by means of this (sāman) remove the darkness.

[1] As hotuḥ pṛṣṭha, Jaim. br. II. 390.

[2] As brahmasāman (Jaim. br. l. c.) *i.e.* as third pṛṣtha.

[3] As agniṣṭomasāman.

16. It (*viz.* the bhāsasāman) has ten stobhas [1], ten syllables contains the virāj; in the virāj [2] they get firm support.

[1] *ṛtaṃ me, bhadram, śreyaḥ, vāmam* etc., see Sāmaveda saṃhitā ed. Calc., Vol II, page 508 and cp. the Stobha-book II. 9 (ib. page 540).

[2] *Viz.* 'in food': *virāḍ vā annam.*

17. Now, regarding the saying of the theologians: 'by means of six months they go hence on their way, by means of six they return —where, then, is the world of heaven, for reaching which they hold the sattra'?

18. (It should be answered:) 'by (the tristich beginning:) 'the crest of heaven'[1] they take hold of the world of heaven.

[1] SV. II. 490-492=ṚS. VI. 7. 1, 4, 2; note that the Black Yajurveda (*e.g.* TS. I. 4. 13) has equally the verses ṚS. VI. 7. 1, 4.—On these verses the bhāsa is chanted.

19. By (the words): 'the disposer of the earth' they gain firm support on this world (the earth).

20. By (the words): 'Agni vaiśvānara, born in the sacred rite' the characteristic mark of the viṣuvat (day, *i.e.* the sun) is brought about.

21. By (the words): 'the wise universal-sovereign, the guest of men' they reach food.

22. By (the words): 'him the Gods have begotten as a vessel for their mouth'[1] they are born (in their offspring).

[1] Reading with the ṚS. *āsannā* instead of the Sāmavedic tradition *āsannah*.

23. It[1] is (performed) on jagatī- and triṣṭubh (metres)[2]; jagatī- and triṣṭubh-like, forsooth, is the sun[3]; if it were (performed) on (metres) different from these, they would fall from the world of heaven (they would not reach the world of heaven)

[1] *Viz.* the viṣuvat-day as to its first pṛṣṭha-stotra and its agniṣṭoma-stotra.

[2] The verse *vibhrāḍ bṛhat* is jagatī, *mūrdhānaṃ divaḥ* is triṣṭubh.—Cp. Nidāna-sutra V. 9: *atha khalvāha: triṣṭubjagatīṣu bhavatīti; kasyedaṃ brāhmanaṃ syād iti? pṛṣṭhāgniṣṭomasāmnor ity āhuḥ* etc. According to Sāyana the assertion that the viṣuvat-day is performed *triṣṭubjagatīṣu* refers only to the bhāsasāman (chanted on *mūrdhānaṃ divaḥ*), which being by itself *traiṣṭubha*, is by the words *yā devyā* also *jāgata*. This statement is to me incomprehensible.

[3] Because the earth is gāyatrī-like, the intermediate region triṣṭubh-like, the sky jagatī-like and the sun moves between intermediate region and sky, cp. Kauṣ. br. XXV. 3. 6: *triṣṭubjagatyor ha vā eṣa āhita ādityaḥ pratiṣṭhitas tapati*.

24. It (*viz.* the bhāsasāman) is (chanted) on (verses) containing the words: 'universal sovereign'[1]; the world of heaven is universal sovereignty. In the world of heaven even they get firm support.

[1] Cp. IV. 6. 21.

IV. 7.

(The Brahman's chant.)

1. The viṣuvat (day) is the body (the trunk) of the year; on both sides of it (*i.e.* before and after) are the two halves (of the year);

the abhīvarta [1], by means of which they depart hence, and the pragātha [2], which comes afterwards (*i.e.* in the second half), these both are brought into practice on the viṣuvat-day [3]. They thereby bring the halves into the body of the sacrifice: in order to reach the world of heaven.

[1] The brahmasāman, on which different verses are chanted during the first half of the year.

[2] The pragātha *indra kratuṃ na ābhara*, which is chanted on different melodies, see § 2.

[3] The abhīvarta falls (at the viṣuvat-day) on the midday-pavamāna-laud and the vikarnasāman is chanted on *indra kratuṃ na ābhara*.

2. It is the pragātha (beginning): 'O Indra, bring us ability' [1]

[1] SV. II. 806-807=ṚS. VII. 32. 26-27.

3. This (pragātha) has been 'seen' by Vasiṣṭha, after his son had been slain [1]; he then became rich in progeny and cattle. That it is this pragātha, is for the sake of obtaining progeny.

[1] *putrahata* as Kāṭh. XII. 10: 172. 12 against the regular *hatáputra* of TS. II. 5. 2. 1 and Jaim. br. I. 150, III. 26. According to the Anukramanika on ṚS. VII. 32. 26 (which is the pragātha here mentioned): *saudāsair agnau prakṣipyamāṇaḥ śaktir* (the son of Vasiṣṭha) *antyaṃ pragātham ālebhe* (began to recite the first half), *so 'rdharca ukte 'dahyata ; taṃ putroktaṃ vasiṣṭhaḥ samāpayateti śāṭyāyanakam ; vasiṣṭhasyaivārṣam iti tāṇḍakam*. On this legend cp. below VIII. 2. 3, XIX. 3. 8 and Jaim. br. II. 390, 392 in Journal of the Amer. Or. Soc., Vol. XVIII, page 47; cp. also Sāyaṇa on TS. VII. 4. 7. 1: *viśvāmitraśāpena hateṣu putreṣu... vasiṣṭhaḥ... saudāsān abhyabhavat*, and Kauṣ. br. IV. 8.

4. (The quoted pragātha contains the words): 'may we, living, attain to light'. They, forsooth, who happily traverse the year, attain, living, to the light.

5. 'Let no unknown, evil-minded tribes, let no unfriendly ones tread us down'. The evil-minded ones are the thiefs, the impostors. These they thereby overcome.

6. 'By thine help, o Hero, we will traverse the streams, the ever-flowing waters'. The streams, the ever-flowing waters, forsooth, are the year. This they thereby traverse.

7. (The pragāthas beginning:) 'to-day and to-morrow continually' [1], 'thee to-day and to-morrow the men' [2], 'h i m to-day and to-morrow' [3] are the linking pragāthas; one of these is to be taken (as

the Brahman's chant during the second half of the year), for the sake of congruency. They link (the religious performances) of each following day (with those of the preceding one).

[1] SV. II. 808-809=ṚS. VIII. 61. 17-18.

[2] SV. II. 163-164=ṚS. VIII. 99. 1-2.

[3] SV. II. 1041-1042=ṚS. VII. 66. 7-8.

8. Now they say, however: (the pragātha beginning:) 'O Indra, bring us ability' is to be taken[1], for the sake of prospering.

[1] And so does the author of the Ārṣeyakalpa II. 7, page 26.

9. Descending are the months[1].

[1] In the second half of the year the course followed in the first half is reversed, cp. Ārṣeyakalpa, Einleitung p. XXV.

10. In the manner as they climb from here (*i.e.* from the ground) on a tree, in the same manner they descend from it: having ascended unto the world of heaven, they thereby regain firm support in this world.

IV. 8.

(The go- and āyus-days.)

1. There are the go- and the āyus-stoma (days)[1].

[1] In the last month, after the three abhiplava six-day periods, follows an āyus and a go-day. Why runs the text: *gauś cāyuś ca* (as XXIV 14.1) instead of *āyuś ca gauś ca*? Jaim. br. has the same.

2. Two-footed is the Sacrificer: (these two must be performed) for obtaining firm support.

3. They have a plus and a minus[1]: after the plus and the minus, forsooth, the children are born[2].

[1] The goṣtoma contains 15 stotriya verses in the bahiṣpavamāna, 36 in the four ājyastotras, 85 in the mādhyandinasavana, and 105 in the tṛtiyasavana: together 241; here is a plus of one stotriya verse above the decimal number (the virāj); the āyuṣṭoma, on the other side, has 9 stotriya verses in the bahiṣpavamāna, 60 in the four ājyastotras, 85 in the mādhyandinasavana, and 105 in the tṛtīyasavana: together 259; here is a minus of one (cp. Ārṣeyakalpa page 7, note 2 and page 8, note 2.)

[2] The male has a plus: the member, the female has a minus: the vulva; in accordance with this plus and minus, *i.e.* out of it are born the young ones.—Cp. Kāṭh. XXXIII. 2: 27. 16: *ekayā gaur atirikta ekayāyur ūnaḥ* and TS. VII. 4. 11. 1-2.

4. They are virāj-like[1]; the virāj is food: in food even they obtain firm support.

[1] The number of stotriya verses of the two stomas, together being 500. is dividable by ten, cp. Kāṭh. l. c. *te saṁstutā virājam abhi sampadyante* and TS. l. c.

(The ten-day rite.)

5. There are the ten days of the twelve day-period[1].

[1] The dvādaśāha without the opening- and the closing day (prāyaṇīya and udayanīya).

6. The ten days are an accomplished virāj; in accomplished virāj (in perfect food) they obtain firm support.

7. There are (in this ten day period) the (six) pṛṣṭhas[1]; the pṛṣṭhas, foorsooth, are strength; in strength even they get firm support. There are the Chandomas[2]; the Chandomas are cattle; in cattle even they gain a firm support. Then there is that tenth day of used up stomas)[3], of used up metres[3], of used up cases[4], which is unexpressed[5] and Prajāpati-like[5].

[1] The six pṛṣṭhya days, on which successively the pṛṣṭhasāmans (rathantara, bṛhat, etc.) are the hotṛsamāns, *i.e.* serve for the first pṛṣṭhalaud.

[2] The 7th, 8th and 9th day of the daśarātra.

[3] *āptastoma āptacchandas*, in so far this day is the final clause (of the nine days), on which all the stomas, all the metres are again used in due order.

[4] *āptavibhaktika.* The rule is that the ājyastotras, at least one of them, contain a certain definite *vibhakti* (one of the seven case-forms of declension, the vocative being reckoned as eighth) of the name of the God invoked (*agni* or *indra*) see below X. 7–9 and Nidānasūtra III 9: *athaitāḥ sapta nāma vibhaktayaḥ : sa taṃ tena tasmai tasmāt tasya tasminn ity āmantritāṣṭamī ; sa khalu vibhaktim āmantritāṃ* ('the vocative') *prāthame 'hani karoti* (cp. the first ājyastotra: *agna ā yāhi*) :..*tam iti dvitīyā, tāṃ dvitīye* (*agniṃ dūtam..*); *teneti tṛtīyā, tāṃ tṛtīye* (*agnināgniḥ samidhyate*); *sa iti prathamā, tāṃ caturthe 'hani karoti* (*janasya gopā ....agniḥ*) etc.

[5] *aniruktaṃ prājāpatyam*; in the words of the pṛṣṭhastotra *kayā naś citra ābhuvad...kayā śaciṣṭhayā .. kas tvā* (SV. II. 32–34) instead of the name of the deity invoked, the pronoun *kaḥ* is used, which, as is well-known, represents Prājapati.

(The tenth day.)

8. What they reveal, that they overdo; therefore no revealing should be made[1].

[1] Read with the Leyden MS. *yad vyāhur* (instead of *yad adhyāhur*), cp. below XV. 7. 3 and Kauṣ. br. XXVIII. 1: *sa yo vyāha so 'tirecayati; vyāhur* is explained by Sāyaṇa as *vibruvanti* (so to be read instead of *vikravanti*). The meaning is: 'what is recited too much (or too less).' The tenth day is *avivākyam i.e.* if any mantra or any act has been forgotten during the service, or if any mantra or any act has been practised, that does not belong to it, no one should draw the attention to this fact, no one should express his opinion about it. Usually, if such be the case, a prāyaścitta should take place.

9. Cryptically they bring into practice the anuṣṭubh[1]; the anuṣṭubh, forsooth, is Prajāpati[2]; if they perceptibly brought into practice the anuṣṭubh, they would go unto Prajāpati[3].

[1] For the chants of the ārbhava-pavamāna-laud at a certain moment (cp. Einl. on Ārṣeyakalpa page XXIV) anuṣṭubh verses are to be taken, usually for the śyāvāśva and āndhīgava, which in the prakṛti are chanted on anuṣṭubh's (SV. I. 545, 546). At this occasion, on this tenth day, however, they are chanted on a peculiar kind of anuṣṭubh, *viz.* the *pipīlikamadhyā*, of 12+8+12 syllables, *viz.* SV. II. 714-716, cp. below XV. 11. 8, and especially XV. 7. 2, 5. According to Baudhāyana XVI. 6: 252. 10-253.7 this tenth day is *ananuṣṭubham*, cp. Āśvalāyana VIII. 12. 2-7, Kauṣ. br. XXVIII. 1: *utsṛjyate daśame' hany anuṣṭup.*

[2] See note 2 on IV 5. 7.

[3] They would attain the *prajāpateḥ sāyujyaṃ*, in other words they would die in the middle (before the end) of the sattra, and, as Sāyana remarks, the participants of a sattra, it is true, wish to attain this union with Prajapāti, but only after they have lived long and die at the normal end of life.

10. He, verily, who knows the pith of the sacrificial session, becomes (himself) the pith; of the chants (the sāmans) the vāmadevya is the pith, of the deities it is Agni, of the metres it is the virāj, of the stomas it is the thirty-three-versed one[1]. Having united all of this into one whole, they rise[2].

[1] Cp. below XV. 12. 2.

[2] This refers to the last laud of the last day but two of the gavām ayana, the tenth day of the daśarātra, after which they 'rise from the session' (*sattrād uttiṣṭhanti*) *i.e.* they finish the sacrificial 'session.'

11. The theologians say: 'have ye risen from a going-on, or from a still-standing session?'[1]

[1] *udasthātā3* can only be the pluti-form of *udasthāta*, 2nd p. plural aor. act. The tense and person in the question are remarkable. Cp. with this and the next §§ XV. 12. 3-5.

12. They who rise after chanting the rathantara (sāman), these rise from a going-on (session). Regarding these he should say: 'they will be devoid of a firm support.' They who rise after chanting the bṛhat (sāman), these rise from a still-standing (session). Regarding these he should say: 'still-standing (not increasing) will be their prosperity: they will not be better off'[1].

[1] And for this reason neither the rathantara nor the bṛhat are to be chosen as the last sāman.

13. They (on the contrary), who rise after chanting the vāmadevya, these rise from pith[1] to pith, from fullness to fullness, from support to support, for the young ones have the intermediate region as their support[2].

[1] Cp. IV. 8. 10.

[2] Sāyaṇa: *avakāśam antareṇa saṃcaraṇānupapattes tāsāṃ tadāyatanatvam*, cp. Śat. br. IV. 5. 2. 13: *antarikṣāyatanā vai garbhāḥ*. For the rest, the vāmadevya being identified with the intermediate region, they reach the antarikṣa and thereby *prajā*, which is *antarikṣāyatanā*; cp. also VII. 9. 6.

14. It is on (verses) of thirty-three syllables[1]: after gaining firm support among the thirty-three deities[2], they rise.

[1] The vāmadevya is chanted on the thirty-three-syllabic virāj: *agniṃ naro dīdhi°*, SV. I. 72=ṚS. VII. 1. 1-3.=SV. II. 723-725.

[2] Cp. IV. 4. 11.

15 The vāmadevya is Prajāpati-like[1]: after gaining firm support in Prajāpati they rise. The vāmadevya is cattle: after gaining firm support in cattle they rise.

[1] This sāman being composed on SV. I. 69: *kayā naś citra ābhuvad*; *ka* is the quasi-mystic name of Prajapāti.

IV. 9.

(The tenth day, continued; the mental laud, etc.)

1. Having performed the patnīsaṃyājas[1], they (*viz.* the Chanters) go up (out of the *prācīnavaṃśā śālā*, where these oblations have taken place) in easterly direction and address the (verse) of redundant metre (beginning): 'this one of thousand men'[2] to the āhavanīya-fire (standing before it, directed to the east)[3].

[1] Cp. C. H. § 252; the day closes with the patnīsaṃyājas, cp. Āpastamba XXI. 9. 14, 15. The Chanters also have to perform those oblations with a special mantra, Drāhy. IX. 3. 23.

[2] S. V. I. 458.

[3] According to Drāhy. IX. 4. 1-2 the Udgātṛ only chants the sāman (thrice), all three join in the nidhana.

2. The (verse) of redundant metre is (equal to) these worlds[1]; in these worlds they obtain firm support.

[1] This equation is not known from any other source.

3. The finale (nidhana) is *goḥ*[1]; the cow (*go*), verily, is the characteristic mark of the virāj[2]: in the virāj even they obtain firm support.

[1] The sāman (the first one of the two attributed to Gaur āṅgirasa), grāmegeyagāna XII. 1. 28, begins *ayaṁ*^{5} *saho*^{4} *hā*^{5} *i*, and closes: *go*^{3}*'2345ḥ*^{111}. Cp Drāhy. IX. 4. 1

[2] Probably because virāj is equal to food (milk).

4. Having entered with their face westward (into the sadas), they hold the (mental) laud with the verses[1] of Sārparājñī

[1] Ār. ārcika V. 4–6=SV. II. 726–728=ṚS. IX. 189. 1–3. They are chanted on the gāyatra-sāman. Cp. Kauṣ. br. XXXVII. 6: *te saṃprasṛpya sārparājñyā ṛkṣu stuvate* and TS. VII. 3 1. 3.

5. By means of these (verses) the Serpent Arbuda removed his dead skin; their dead skin even they remove by means of these (verses).

6. Sārparājñī is the earth; on the earth even they obtain firm support.

7. They chant three (verses); three in number are these worlds; on these worlds they obtain firm support.

8. Mentally he causes them to return[1].

[1] For all lauds with the exception of the three pavamāna-lauds the Adhvaryu holds the *upākaraṇa* saying: *upavartadhvam*: 'return ye', indicating thereby that the tristichs of these lauds are to be repeated, cp. Āp. XII. 17. 9, C. H. § 155, page 236. For the mental laud these words are not pronounced loudly, but only said *mente*. The conclusion of the stotra is indicated to the Hotṛ not by the word 'this (is the last verse)', but by looking at him.

9. Mentally he (the Udgātṛ) makes *him*; mentally he (the Prastotṛ) sings the prastāva, mentally he (the Udgātṛ) sings the ud-

gītha, mentally he (the Pratihartṛ) sings the pratihāra, mentally they (the three Chanters together) sing the finale[1]: for the sake of reaching the unreached.

[1] Cp. Baudh. XVI. 7: 254. 7 sqq., Āp. XXI. 10. 4.

10. What they (the participants of the sattra) do not reach by means of the voice, that they (the Chanters) make them reach by means of the mind.

11. On an enclosed space[1] they hold the laud: in order that they may encompass the brahman[2].

[1] Probably the two doors of the sadas are covered up.

[2] In this way will not go forth from them the mantras, the sacred texts.

12. They hold a colloquy on (the nature of) brahman[1]: in spiritual lustre even they gain firm support.

[1] *brahmodya*, *brahmavādya* or *brahmavadya*. According to Drāhy. IX. 4. 12-15 the Theologians of the Sāmaveda give different explications regarding the nature of this *brahmodya*. According to Śāṅkhāyana XVI. 4. 8 sqq. it is a dialogue in question and answer between Hotṛ and Adhvaryu, Brahman and Udgātṛ, Brahman and Sacrificer, according to Āp. XXI. 10. 13-11. 10 between, on the one side, Adhvaryu, Brahman, Hotṛ, Hotrakas, and Udgātṛ, and on the other side the Yajamāna, who answers the questions. These three texts give the questions which are addressed and the answers which are given, cp. also Āśv. X. 9. 2 and Ait. br. V. 25. 22.

13. The Hotṛ recites loudly the Four-hotṛ-formulas; he thereby holds the recitation following on the laud[1]; for that is no laud which is not followed by a recitation.

[1] When the Hotṛ mentally has repeated the verses of the laud, he recites by way of śastra (each stotra must be followed by a corresponding śastra) the Caturhotṛ-formulas. In the manuals of the Hotṛ these are given Śāṅkh. X. 14. 4 and Ait. br. V. 25. 3-13, Āśv VII. 13. 9-10.

14. They abuse[1] Prajāpati; now that they have got hold of him, this (fact) is now[2] proclaimed by them (as they think:) 'we have got hold of him.'

[1] The abusing of Prajāpati consists according to Drāhyāyaṇa (IX. 4. 17-18) either in mentioning the evil deeds of Prajāpati or in repeating the evil facts done by Prajāpati as recorded by the Adhvaryus and the Ṛgvedins. Of the Ṛgvedins is known the tale of the incest of Prajāpati (Ait. br. III. 33, cp. below VIII. 2. 10 and Śat. br. I. 7. 4). Āpastamba (XXI. 12. 3) cites several *prajāpatiparivāda*-

mantras, e.g. yat stenān yad vṛkān daṃśān maśakān yad aghāyavaḥ | tad u te vṛjinaṃ tv etad vratam etan na me matam.

2 Probably (note the place occupied in the sentence by *enam*) *tāvad* belongs to the preceding, not to *āpāmainam.*

15. The householder (Gṛhapati) holds the pillar of udumbara-wood; the householder, forsooth, is the reacher of food [1], food even he reaches to them.

1 Cp. *ūrg vā udumbaraḥ*, passim in all the Brāhmaṇas.—The Gṛhapati and all the Chanters after the completion of the mental laud must take hold of the pillar until the stars become visible, cp. Drāhy. IX. 4. 21, 23.

16. They restrain their speech [1].

1 Until the stars become visible, Drāhy. l.c., Āp. XXI. 12. 7.

17. Milked out, as it were, are now the metres, used up, and gone to end; these they thereby invigorate with juice,

18. and they also link the (religious performances) of the next (day) with (those of this day).

19. At a sattra the sacrificial fee is the (person) self [1].

1 At a sattra no cows are given as dakṣiṇā; a sacrifice devoid of dakṣiṇā is inauspicious; by the conception here given, the inauspiciousness is removed. The Brāhmaṇa is identical with TS. VII. 4. 9. 1.

20. When one cuts off [1] from himself, he reaches the fulfilment of whatever wish he has.

1 *avadyati* is the technical term for the cutting off from the havis, the sacrificial substance, such as a puroḍāśa.—The TS. l. c. has: *ātmānam eva dakṣiṇāṃ nītvā suvargaṃ lokaṃ yanti*, the Jaim. br. (II. 374) uses the expression *spṛṇvate* 'they free themselves' (?).

21 During two (months [1]: the first two) he cuts of his hair, during two (the two following months) his skin, during two his flesh, during two his bones, during two his mark, during two his fat and blood [2].

1 Thus Sāyaṇa, but it seems preferable to understand with the Jaim. br. (II. 374) *upasadbhyām*; if we accept this interpretation, the participants of the sattra begin their Soma-feast in a spiritual state, as it were. The gavām ayana is preceded by 12 dīkṣā- and 12 upasad-days, see *e.g.* Baudh. XVI. 13: 261. 1. If the Jaim. br. (II. 373) states that there are t h r e e upasads, this must be an error.

[2] Cp. TS. l. c. and Āp. X. 14. 10: *pīvā dīkṣate kṛśo yajati; yad asyāṅgānām mīyate juhoty eva tad iti vijñāyate.*

22. Their top-knots they one after another cause to be shaved; mishap even they thereby remove from themselves (as they think): 'let us go lighter to the world of heaven'[1].

[1] Cp. TS. VII. 4. 9. 1 s. f. *śikhām anu pravapanta ṛddhyā, atho raghīyāṁsaḥ suvargaṃ lokam ayāmeti*; Āp. XXI. 13. 4: *sattraṃ ced, vapanakāle saśikhāni (pra) vapante.* Ordinarily this shaving takes place after the offering of the *vaśā maitrāvaruṇī*, cp. C. H. § 256a, page 407, according to Lāṭy. IV. 4. 18, Drāhy. XI. 4. 19 the shaving takes place at the e n d of the gavām ayana and with this statement the Jaim. br. (II. 374) agrees: 'therefore (*i.e.* because the cows got curved horns or lost their horns, cp. above IV. 1.2) the participants of a sattra shave even their top-knots: they then become equal to the cows (who got all the food)'.

23. And they also become similar to the cows: in order to get all food[1].

[1] This refers to IV. 1. 2; cp. the quotation from Jaim. br. in the preceding note (on IV. 9. 22).

IV. 10.

(The mahāvrata.)

1. Prajāpati created (lit. let loose out of himself) the creatures; he was emptied out and fell down. To him the Gods altogether came up; they said: 'let us bring together a mighty (fast-)food (*mahad vratam*) that will restore him.'[1] For him they brought together what food ripens during a year; that they reached him, that he partook of[2]; that restored him. 'Mighty (*mahad*), forsooth[3], is that food (*vrata*) that has braced him.' Thence the name 'mahāvrata'.

[1] Cp TBr. I 2. 6. 1: *prajāpatiḥ prajāḥ sṛṣṭvā vṛtto 'śayat; taṃ devā bhūtānāṁ rasaṃ tejaḥ saṃbhṛtya tenainam abhiṣajyan*, etc. According to the Jaiminīyas the mahāvrata has its name from the words of the deities, who having brought to Prajāpati the pith of the regions, of the waters and of the food, exclaimed: 'We bring food (*vratam*) to the great one' (*mahate*), Jaim br. II. 409.

[2] Read *avratayat* instead of *avrajayat.*

[3] On *maryā (ḥ)* as an interjection or particle cp. Pischel, Vedische Studien I, page 61.

2. Prajāpati, forsooth, is great (*mahān*), his food even is this *vrata* (-rite)[1].

[1] According to the explanation of § 1 the word mahāvrata is a karmadhāraya compound, according to the second explanation it is a bahuvrīhi.

3. Regarding this (mahāvrata-rite) they say: 'in the middle of the year it is to be undertaken: in the middle (of the body: in the stomach) the food which has been eaten, restores.

4. . Regarding this (however), they (other theologians) say: 'if they undertake (it) in the middle of the year, they reach the (one) half of the food, but lose[1] the other.' At the end of the year even it is to be undertaken; for in the (course of the) year all food ripens.

[1] Read here and V. 9. 13 *chambaṭkurvanti* instead of *saṃvaṭkurvanti*.

5. This (a) twenty-four-versed (day); the year is twenty-four fold, food is the twenty-fifth[1].

[1] In this manner the mahāvrata is a pañcaviṃśa-day, cp. TBr. 1. 2. 6. 1-2: *pañcaviṁśastomo bhavati, caturviṁśatyardhamāsaḥ saṃvatsaro, yad vā etasminī saṃvatsare 'dhiprājāyata tad annaṃ pañcaviṁśam abhavat.*

6. The twenty-four-versed opening day (the first but one of the year's sattra) is (the same as) this finishing day[1].

[1] By this fact the beginning and the end of the year are the same. The purport of this sentence in this context (in the midst of the description of the mahāvrata) is not very clear. Perhaps this fact, which ought to be mentioned at the end of the description of the gavām ayana, is mentioned here by anticipation. before the lengthy treatment of the mahāvrata.

7. Because they bring[1] together the food after a year, this twenty-fifth (stotriya-verse) comes into existence.

[1] We expect the imperf., 'because they (the Gods) had brought together', cp. § 1. Perhaps the imperfect is intended; a few times also in the Śat. br. the present is used instead of the imperfect, see Introduction to the edition of the Kāṇvīya Śat. br. chapter III, § 29.—The author of our Brāhmaṇa implies in § 7, that properly the mahāvrata is a caturviṃśa day; § 7 seems to continue § 5.

FIFTH CHAPTER.

(The gavām ayana, continued.)

(The mahāvrata, continued.)

V. 1.

1. The vāmadevya is to be taken for the mahāvrata (laud)[1].

[1] *i.e.* that part of the first pṛṣṭha-laud, which is designated as the *ātman*, 'the trunk,' cp. V. 2. 1. Jaim. br. II. 411: *vāmadevyam evaitasyāhnaḥ pṛṣṭhaṃ kāryam iti.*

2. The 'head' is nine-versed [1].

[1] Literally 'thrice three fold.' The so-called 'head' of the mahāvrata laud (*i.e.* always of the first pṛṣṭha-laud of the midday service) is chanted in gāyatra melody on three tristrichs, *viz.* SV. II. 146–148=ṚS. I. 7. 1. 2. 4; SV. II. 263–265=ṚS I. 84. 13–15; SV. II. 800–802=ṚS. VIII. 93. 1-3.

3. For threefold is the head: hair, skin, bone [1].

[1] Cp. TBr. I. 2. 6. 2-3: *tridhāvihitaṁ hi śiro loma chavir asthi.*

4. Fivefold (or five-versed) is the other [1] trunk: hair, skin, flesh, bone and mark.

[1] *itara* used as ἄλλος, cp. § 7.

5. Having made once the *him*-sound they chant 'the head' (*i.e.* the stotriya-tristichs composing this part of the vratasāman) right off [1] (without repeating any of the nine verses, in their order as given above).

[1] Cp. TBr. l. c.

6. Therefore when the limbs grow fat, the head does not also grow fat, (and) when they grow lean, it does not also grow lean [1].

[1] *medyanti* and *kṛśyanti* accus. plur. neutr. Cp. TBr. I. 2. 6. 3: *tasmāt tat sadṛg eva na medyato 'numedyati, na kṛśyato 'nukṛśyati* and Jaim. br. II. 408: *tasmād idaṃ śiro na medyato 'numedyati, na kṛśyato 'nukṛśyati.*

7. Again and again returning [1] they chant the (tristichs constituting the) other trunk; therefore the other trunk (*i.e.* the parts except the head) grows fat and lean (but not so the head).

[1] *i.e.* repeating (cp. note 1 on IV. 9. 8.): for the other parts of the vratasāman are the pañcadaśa, saptadaśa, etc. stomas, the required number of verses for which is got by repetition after the rules laid down in Chapter 2 and 3. Cp. Jaim. br. II. 407: 'he makes (by repetition) fifteen verses out of the three; therefore the arm grows fat and lean w i t h the trunk.

8. The 'head' is (chanted) on gāyatrī-verses containing the word *arka* [1].

[1] SV. II. 146 (cp. § 2 note 1): *indram id gāthino bṛhad indram arkebhir arkiṇaḥ;* according to the Jaim. br. (II. 9) on Jaim. Saṃh. IV. 5. 2-4=ṚS. VIII. 16. 9-11: *tam arkebhis taṃ sāmabhiḥ.*

9. Arka, forsooth, is food, the gāyatrī is spiritual lustre: food even and spiritual lustre he puts at the beginning (ready for them)[1].

[1] Or: 'he brings in (their) mouth.'

10. The 'wings' are fifteen-versed and seventeen-versed; by means of the wings the Sacrificer, having become a bird, goes to the world of heaven.

11. Regarding these two they say: 'they are to be made equal: either both fifteen-versed or both seventeen-versed: for the sake of equilibrium.'

12. Regarding this, however, they (other theologians) say: 'if they are equal, then they are of equal strength.' They are to be made fifteen-versed (the one) and seventeen-versed (the other): the bird, forsooth, when holding his wings aslant [1], so to say, flies swifter.

[1] *sāciva.. kṛtvā*, probably tmesis for *sācīkṛtvā* (cp. *pradakṣiṇī... kurvate*, Baudh. X. 2: 2. 10), otherwise 'instead of *sācī* a dual. masc. would be required: but cp. ṚS. X. 142. 2.

13. On the right side (*i.e.* as right wing) the bṛhat (sāman) is to be taken: the right side of the trunk is the more powerful.

14. But they (*i.e.* others) say: 'it is to be taken on the left side: at the side of the Brāhmaṇācchaṃsin[1]; triṣṭubh-like is the bṛhat[2], triṣṭubh-like is the Brāhmaṇācchaṃsin[3], triṣṭubh-like is the fifteen-versed (chant)[4].

[1] Who has his seat in the sadas to the left side of the Hotṛ.

[2] Being chanted on triṣṭubh-verses: SV. II. 159 160=ṚS. VI. 46. 1-2.

[3] The Brāhmaṇācchaṃsin is the second of the Hotrakas, just as the triṣṭubh is the second metre of the *caturuttarāṇi* (Ind. Studien, Vol. VIII, page 16).

[4] Cp. VI. 1. 8.

15. At the right side the rathantara (sāman) is to be taken (*viz.* for the right wing); at the side of the Maitrāvaruṇa[1]; gāyatrī-like is the rathantara[2], gāyatrī-like is the Maitrāvaruṇa[3], gāyatrī-like is the seventeen-versed (chant)[4].

[1] Who has his seat to the right side of the Hotṛ.

[2] Because the rathantara sprang from the mouth of Prajāpati along with the gāyatrī.

[3] Because the Maitrāvaruṇa is the first of the Hotrakas, just as the gāyatrī is the first metre of the *caturuttarāṇi*.

[4] The rathantara (chanted on SV. II. 30-31=ṚS. VII. 32. 22-23) is on jagatī, and the jagatī contains twice the number of syllables of the gāyatrī, thus Sāyaṇa.

16. The 'tail' is (a) twenty-one-versed (chant).

17. The twenty-one-versed (stoma) is the support of the stomas, therefore a bird, having supported itself on its tail, flies up, and, having supported itself on its tail, sits down [1].

[1] Cp. Ait. br. I. 4. 3: *atho ekaviṃśo vai stomānāṃ pratiṣṭhā*, and: *tasmāt sarvāṇi vayāṃsi pucchena pratitiṣṭhanti pucchenaiva pratiṣṭhāyotpatanti.*

18. The yajñāyajñīya (sāman) is to be taken for the tail, for the yajñāyajñīyā (sāman) is the tail of the mahāvrata [1].

[1] Probably because the last laud, the agniṣṭomastotra, of the mahāvrata-day is chanted on the yajñāyajñīya.

19. But they (*i.e* other theologians) say: 'excessive for two-footed (creatures) is the yajñāyajñīya [1]; the bhadra (sāman) [2] is to be taken, for the sake of prosperity [3].

[1] Because the yajñāyajñīya on SV. II. 53, 54=ṚS. VI. 48. 1, 2 is on verses with f o u r padas, but the bhadra ('good' 'auspicious') is on d v i p a d ā triṣṭubhs (SV. II. 460-462=ṚS. X. 157. 1-3.)

[2] Araṇyegeyagāna III. 1. 21, composed on SV. I. 452.

[3] And so the Ārṣeyakalpa prescribes the bhadra for the 'tail.'

V. 2.

(T h e m a h ā v r a t a , c o n t i n u e d .)

1. The vāmadevya is to be taken for the mahāvrata (laud) [1]; its head is the gāyatra, its wings are the rathantara and the bṛhat, its tail is the yajñāyajñīya.

[1] Probably here also (cp. V. 1. 1) the *ātman*-part is intended; to this assertion the prescript of V. 2. 6 is a *vikalpa.*

2. Who knows the thousand [1] that are hitched in the mahāvrata, he obtains a thousand head of cattle.

[1] According to Ait. ār. II. 3. 4 the stotra has thousand verses, see the translation of Keith, page 219.

3. Its head is the eastern region, this is thousandfold through the metres; the one of its wings is yonder (world: the sky), this is thousandfold through the stars; its other wing is this (world: the earth), this is thousandfold through the plants and trees; its trunk is the intermediate region (the air), this is thousandfold through the birds; its tail is the western region, this is thousandfold through the

fires[1] and the rays (of the sun)[2]. He who knows thus, obtains a thousand head of cattle.

[1] Because, according to the Commentary, the gārhapatya and other fires, as the śālāmukhīya are in the western part of the sacrifical ground.

[2] Because the rays of the rising sun go all to the west (Comm.).

4. Regarding this they say (however): 'the vāmadevya is unfitting for the pṛṣṭha (laud)[1], for it is devoid of finale[2].

[1] *i.e.* for the pṛṣṭha stotra of the hotṛ; the usual pṛṣṭhasāmans for the hotuh pṛṣṭha are rathantara and bṛhat, which are *nidhanavat*, provided with a nidhana.

[2] *ṛco bahirbhūtaṃ nidhanaṃ yato 'sya nāsti*, cp. C. H. § 204, page 315.—For the anidhana sāmans cp. below, VII. 3. 5.

5. Without support is the chant that is devoid of finale.

6. The rājana (chant)[1] should be taken for the mahāvrata (laud).

[1] The melody of SV. I. 318 (araṇyagāna IV. 2. 19) chanted on S.V. II. 833-335 =ṚS. X. 120. 1-3.

7. The rājana (sāman) is plainly (equal to) food: it is fivefold[1], for food is fivefold[2].

[1] The rājana is fivefold either by the fact that all the five parts of it are to be repeated five times (Ait. ār. II. 3. 4.), or on account of the five times repeated stobha: *huṃ huṃ huṃ huṃ huṃ*, or on account of the five finales *vāg, iḍā, suvo, bṛhad, bhā*.

[2] Eating (*aśyam*), chewing (*khādyam*), sucking (*coṣyam*), licking (*lehyam*), drinking (*peyam*).

8. It is provided with the *him*-sound: thereby there is (that) characteristic of the vāmadevya[1].

[1] The vāmadevya has also (as the rājana, cp. note 1 to § 7) *hummā* in its pratihāra.

9. It is provided with a finale: thereby there is (that) characteristic of the pṛṣṭha (laud)[1].

[1] Which should have a finale, cp. V. 2. 5.

10. The vāmadevya[1] of five finales[2], (chanted) on (verses) of redundant metre[3], is to be taken as the (pṛṣṭha) sāman of the Brahman

[1] The melody of *kayā naś citra ābhuvad*: araṇyagāna II. 1. 30.

[2] *iha prajām iha rayiṁ rarāṇo; rāyaspoṣāya sukṛtāya bhūyase; aganma vāmam idaṃ bṛhat; idaṃ vāmam idaṃ bṛhat; carācarāya bṛhata idaṃ vāmam idaṃ bṛhat.*

[3] SV. II 836-838=ṚS. II. 22. 1. 3. 2.

11. The (verse) of redundant metre exceeds the other metres: the mahāvrata (day) thereby exceeds the other days.

12. By means of the Brahman's sāman thereby it (*viz.* the mahāvrata-day) makes the other days exceedingly thriving [1].

[1] Differently the commentary: *atimedayati ātmānaṃ vardhayati svatovṛddham api punaḥ rājanena sāmnā vardhata ity arthaḥ.*

13. It has five finales [1], for food is fivefold [2].

[1] Cp. note 1 on § 10.

[2] Cp. note 2 on § 7.

V. 3.

(The mahāvrata, continued.)

1. The ilānda [1] is to be taken as agniṣṭomasāman.

[1] The melody of ār. ārcika III. 12 (*agnir asmi janmanā*), registered in the araṇyagāna V. 1. 2 (Sāmav. ed. Calc. Vol. II, page 307), chanted on SV. II. 1166-1171 (cp. Lāṭy. X. 9. 6)=ṚS. X. 140. 1-6; ūhyagāna II. 2. 14 (SV. ed. Calc. Vol. V, page 452). Cp. Śāṅkh. XVIII. 23. 6, 7: *yady u sarvasmin salṛce stuvīran* etc.

2. The ilānda in a visible way is (equal to) food: it (the ilānda) is refreshing drink (*irā*) and food (*anna*); in refreshing drink even and food they finally [1] are supported.

[1] *Viz.* at the end of the gavām ayana.

3. Its (*viz.* the ilānda's) metre is the sea [1], waving and bristling [2]; a sea, as it were [3], waving, as it were, bristling, as it were. becomes he who is successful [4].

[1] The verses are compared with the ocean on account of their great number of syllables; two of them form a stotriyā of 80 syllables.

[2] Properly 'hairy', on account of the numberless hairs of man (?). On this passage cp. Weber in Indische Studien Vol. VIII, page 108 sqq.

[3] Cp. Ait. br. II. 3. 3: *sa eṣa puruṣaḥ samudraḥ sarvaṃ lokam ati*: the sea is typical of the endless.

[4] *yo bhavati*, cp. XXV. 4. 3. The Jaim. br. II. 413 has: *samudra ivākṣitās tuṣṭuvānā asāmeti.*

4. Therefore it is to be applied on these (verses), for the sake of prosperity.

5. The finale is *vratam* [1]; thereby the characteristic mark of the mahāvrata is brought about; it is *svar* [1], for reaching the world of

heaven; it is *śakuna* ('bird')[1]; as a *śakuna* the Sacrificer, having become a bird, goes to the world of heaven.

[1] Stobha II. 4, see SV. ed. Calc. Vol. II, page 536 and cp. ūhagāna II. 2. 14, ed. Calc. Vol. V, page 453.

6. The yajñāyajñīya is to be taken as agniṣṭomasāman[1].

[1] And so does the Ārṣeyakalpa II. 10. a (end). Both cases are known to the Bahvṛcas: *cyaveta ced yajñāyajñīyam, agne tava śrayo vaya iti ṣaṭ stotriyānurūpau yad ilāndam*, Ait. ār. V. 3. 2, and Śāṅkh. as cited under note 1 to § 1.

7. That (sāman) is to be taken as agniṣṭomasāman, which is not overreached ('overtuned') by another voice; the voice (of one person), surely, cannot overreach ('overtune') the voice (itself); the yajñāyajñīya is the voice[1], in the voice they finally find a firm support.

[1] This sāman has *vā(g)* for its finale.

8. The varavantīya[1] is to be taken as agniṣṭomasāman.

[1] Vāravantīyasāmans are grāmegeyagāna I. 1. 30; VIII. 2. 17; XV. 2. 12, 13. Probably the first of these is meant, cp. notes on XVII. 5. 7 and XVIII. 6. 16.

9. Agni vaiśvānara, forsooth, went burning this (world)[1]; of him the Gods were afraid; they warded him off by means of a varaṇa branch; because they warded him off (*avārayanta*), therefore it is called vāravantīya

[1] Cp. the well-known legend of Agni vaiśvānara burning the land, Śat. br. I. 4. 1. 10 sqq.

10. Therefore the varaṇa is endowed with healing power[1], for by it the gods defended themselves.

[1] See *e.g.* Ath. S. VI. 86. 1. *varaṇo varayātā ayaṃ devo vanaspatiḥ | yakṣmo yo asminn āviṣṭas tam u devā avīvaran* || and cp the remark of Bloomfield in his commentary on this sūkta, Sacred Books of the East, Vol. XLII, page 505.

11. Therefore a Brāhmin should not use for drinking a vessel of varaṇa (wood), lest he may extinguish Vaiśvānara[1].

[1] If he drank from such a vessel, he would suffer from indigestion. Vaiśvānara is the inner fire, whereby food is digested: *ayam agnir vaiśvānaro yo 'yam antaḥ puruṣe yenedam annaṃ pacyate yad idam adyate*, Śat. br. XIV. 8. 10.

12. The vāravantīya is cattle; cattle is a means of quenching[1]; from the year that has been quieted[2] they thereby rise.

[1] Cp. note 3 on IV. 5. 11.

[2] Or: 'come to rest' (*śāntād.*)

V. 4.

(The mahāvrata, continued.)

1. With the prāṇa (sāman)[1] they[2] address[2] the āhavanīya[3] (standing) to the east (of it, directed to the west); the prana (or out-breathing) they thereby gain.

1 The melody of araṇyagāna II. 2. 1, composed on SV. I. 318.

2 The Udgātṛ chants the sāman, the two other Chanters join in the finale.

3 Of a *cityāgni*, a high-altar built of bricks, because a gavām ayana sattra is always connected with the 'piling of agni.' The *parigāna* mentioned Jaim. śrs. 4, Āp. XVII. 12. 10, 11, Baudh. X. 49: 15. 15, Lāṭy. I. 5. 11 sqq., Drāhy. II. 1. 8. sqq., seems to be different from the practice here described, but cp. Lāṭy. III. 9. 4 sqq., Drāhy. X. I. 4 sqq.

2. With the apāna (sāman)[1] they address the tail (of the bird-shaped high-altar), (standing) to the west (of it, with their face directed to the east); the apāna (or in-breathing) they thereby gain.

1 The sāman (composed on the same verses as the prāṇa) recorded araṇyagāna II. 2. 2.

3. With the two vratapakṣas[1] (' wings of the [mahā] vrata) they address the two wings[2] (of the bird-shaped high-altar); the regions they thereby gain.

1 The two sāmans ār. gāna II. 2. 5, 6 (cp. Ed. Calc. Vol. II. page 438), composed on the same verse.

2 With the first the right wing, with the second the left one.

4. With the 'heart of Prajāpati'[1] they address the armpit[2]: excellence[3] they thereby gain.

1 The sāman araṇyagāna V. 2. 15 (cp. Ed. Calc. Vol. II, page 499) composed on stobhas.

2 The left one according to Drāhy. X. 1. 10: the seat of the heart.

3 Because Prajāpati is *jyeṣṭha*

5. With 'the invoking of Vasiṣṭha' (vasiṣṭhasya nihava)[1] they address the cātvāla; heaving reached thereby the world of heaven, they announce their welfare.[2]

1 Grāmegeya VIII. 1. 36 composed on SV. I. 313, cp. also § 6.

2 *śriyaṃ vadante*; they do this probably by the words of the verse (see next §), on which the sāman is chanted, *sumneṣv id vo antamā madema*.

6. It is (chanted) on a verse addressed to the All-gods[1]; to possess all forms is the peculiar mark of cattle; cattle they thereby gain.

1 This melody (of grāmegeyagāna VIII. 1. 36) is adapted to the verse of ār. ārcika III. 9, see Introduction, Chapter II (page XII.).

7. With 'the success of the session'[1] (sattrasyarddhi) they address the āgnīdhra; in success even they are supported.

1 The sāman ar. gāna IV. 1. 4 (SV. ed. Calc. Vol. II, page 465) on stobha: *aganma jyotir | amṛtā abhūma | antarikṣaṃ pṛthivyā adhyaruhāma | divam antarikṣād adhyaruhāma | avidāma devān | sam u devair aganmahi*, cp. ṚS. VIII. 48. 3.

8. It has a four-syllabic finale[1]: four-footed is cattle; in cattle even they are firmly supported.

1 *suvar jyotiḥ.*

9. They repeat the finale until the breath fails them: the whole (normal time of) life they (by doing thus) reach.

10. With the śloka[1] and anuśloka[2] they address the two havirdhāna (carts)[3]; glory[4] they thereby gain.

1 The sāman grāmegeya XII. 11. 1 (SV. ed. Calc. Vol. I, page 887) composed on SV. I. 439.

2 Grāmeg. XII. 11. 3 (ed. Calc. l. c. p. 889) composed on SV. I. 440.

3 The first they chant over the havirdhāna carts standing in front of them, directed to the west, the second standing behind them, directed to the east.

4 Because they are ś l o k a and anu ś l o k a.

11. With the yāma(sāman)[1] they address the mārjālīya; the world of the Fathers[2] even they thereby gain.

1 Ar. gāna III. 2. 3 composed on SV. I. 320 (cp. ed. Calc. Vol. II, page 461).

2 Both, mārjālīya and pitṛloka are in the south.

12. With the āyus- and the navastobhasāman[1] they address the sadas[2]; priesthood and nobility they thereby gain.

1 Ar. gāna III. 1. 13 and 14, composed on SV. I. 437.

2 The first they chant over the sadas, standing in front of it, directed towards the west, the second standing behind it, directed towards the east. Drāhy. X. 1. 17.

13. With the chant of Ṛśya[1] they address the gārhapatya[2].

1 Ar. gāna V. 1. 22, composed on ār. ārcika IV. 9 (ed. Calc. Vol. II, page 324).

2 This sāman they chant over the old āhavanīya: the śālāmukhīya-fire, according to Dhānaṃjayya standing on the inside of the mahāvedi with the face turned to the west; according to Śāṇḍilya behind it, outside the mahāvedi with the face turned to the east, Drāhy. X. 1. 18, 19.

14. All beings (once upon a time) praised Indra with a chant; Ṛśya noted that one[1] of his (*viz.* Indra's) members[1] had been omitted in (these) chants; that member of him he praised with this (chant), thereby he reached the place dear to Indra. Through this (chant) they reach the place dear to Indra.

1 *aṅga, guhyarūpa*, Comm., probably 'secret part.' According to Sāyaṇa this *bhogasādanaṃ guhyarūpam* is indicated by the words of the stobha: *ṛśyāsa indra bhuṅ, maghavann indra bhuṅ, prabhuṅ* and *indras tasarapūtaḥ* (Stobhagrantha II. 6, SV. ed. Calc. Vol. II, page 538); the word *bhuṅ* reminding us of the verb *bhuj* 'to enjoy.' Probably the membrum virile is meant.

15. If they undertook (*i.e.* chanted) the finale behind his back[1], they would fasten timidity upon themselves; they undertake (*i.e.* chant) the finale to his face[1]: timidity even they (thereby) put aside.

1 *parokṣam*: cryptically, here rather: behind the back (of the God), who is addressed in the verse: Indra; *pratyakṣam*: overtly, here rather: to the face of the God addressed. The meaning is that nought is to be spoken about Indra but that the God himself is to be addressed. This is partly the case in the finale, which contains the vocative *indra*. Perhaps these vocatives only are intended by the author of the Brāhmaṇa If one does not address a God (in vocative), he speaks about him, and this can be a sign of timidity, of a want of confidence in the power of the God. According to Lāṭy. III. 9. 22, Drāhy. X. 1. 20 the *pratyakṣavāda* is to commence after the word *indra* (because this is already a vocative), in this case only *indra tasarapūtaḥ* is to be changed into *indra tasarapūta* (voc.). The commentary of Dhanvin on sūtra 10 is to be emended: *tena indras tasarapūta iti prathamāntam* ('the case sign of the nominative') *apohya indra tasarapūteti saṃbuddhyantaṃ* ('in the vocative') *prayojyaṃ yathā ṛśyāsa, indra, maghavan indreti trīṇi saṃbuddhyantāni tadvad iti.* And somewhat later, instead of Reuter's conjecture *pragalbho hi bhrāntaṃ saṃbodhayituṃ kṣamaḥ*, we ought to read *pragalbho hrīmantaṃ s. k.* In the following words, which give an example for *pratyakṣavāda*: 'thou art able, o King, to rule the world', *paripālana* is to be substituted for Reuter's *paripālanaṃ*. As an example of *parokṣavāda* Dhanvin says: 'but the non-confident says in his own home: 'this king is able (to rule the world).'—Finally I subjoin the passage of the Nidānasūtra (VI. 7), which refers to our Brāhmaṇa, although I am not able to translate it: *ṛśyasya sāmni kiṃ pratyakṣaṃ kiṃ parokṣam iti. hrasvaṃ pratyakṣaṃ, drāghitaṃ parokṣam; api vendreti pratyakṣam indra iti parokṣam; api vā yathā grāma etad aṅgam ācaṣṭe, tat pratyakṣaṃ, tasyaiṣā stutiḥ syāt: tatsaram*

(sic !) iva te pāyur ṛjur anāskandha iti ; yathāsamāmnāyam evopeyur, evam hi brāhmaṇaṃ bhavati. yad vai manuṣyāṇāṃ pratyakṣaṃ tad devānāṃ parokṣam, atha yan manuṣyāṇaṃ parokṣaṃ tad devānāṃ pratyakṣam iti. tat kuśalaṃ yad asminn ahani devapratyakṣaṃ kuryuḥ.

Excursus on Pañc. br. V. 4.

The preceding khaṇḍa treats of the *parimād's*, *i.e.* the thirteen sāmans to be chanted over the different ports of the birdshaped high-altar and of the devayajana. According to the Sūtrakāras (see Drāhy. X. 1. 1, sqq.) these sāmans are chanted (by the Udgātṛ alone, the two assistant Chanters joining in the finale) immediately before the mahāvrata laud *i.e.* the first pṛṣṭhastotra at the midday-service of the mahāvrataday. These chants, although being *parisāmans* (Drāhy. I. 5. 1), are to be considered as forming part of the mahāvratastotra ; this is apparent from the fact that Maśaka in his Ārṣeyakalpa mentions them as belonging to the vrata (*vratam pṛṣṭhaṃ: trayodaśa parimādo brāhmaṇaklptā indram id gāthino bṛhad* etc. II 10. a) ; the Upagranthasūtra (I. 2) confirms this surmise : *vrate dviṣaṣṭiḥ śiraḥpakṣapucchānāṃ parimādbhis trayaḥ pañcaviṃśāḥ*, *i.e.*: 'the vrata (=mahāvratastotra) contains sixty-two verses from the head (9), the two wings (15+17) and the tail (21); together with the *parimād*'s (13) this makes three twenty-five-fold (stomas)' (62+13=75=3+25), cp. Varadarāja on Maśaka l c. : *eteṣāṃ pṛṣṭhāṅgatvaṃ pṛṣṭhasya pañcaviṃśasampatsiddhyartham uktam*, the whole mahāvrataday being a pañcaviṃśastoma, in which each laud consists of twenty-five stotriya verses.—As to the *parimāds*, it is only in the texts of the Jaiminīyas and the ritual of Śāṅkhāyana that they are also (as in PBr.) indicated by their name (TBr. I. 2. 6. 5 mentions the word only), *viz.* Śāṅkh. ār. I. 4[1], śrs. XVII. 12. 4, where it is prescribed that the Hotṛ should mutter (as he usually does before holding his śastra ; equally do the chanters) the verses on which the sāmans (*parimāds*) are built up. In Śāṅkhāyana as well as in the Taittirīyasaṃhitā the chants differ from those given by the Pañcaviṃśabrāhmaṇa ; according to Śāṅkh. (ār. l. c.) they are **1.** nidhanam āṅgirasam. **2.** bhūtecchadāṃ or bhūtechandasāṃ sāma[2]. The Jaimi-

[1] The word *parimāda* given in the Dictionary of St. Petersburgh does not exist; in stead of *athaitān parimādāñ japāñ japati* Śāṅkh. ār. l. c., śrs. l. c.) read *parimādāṃ j. j.*: 'he mutters the texts of the *parimāds*.'

[2] I here observe that the words following in the Śāṅkh. ār. are to be read, not *pratiṣṭhāyaitad rūpam*, but *pratiṣṭhāyai tad rūpam*.

nīyas give this name (in the last form) as another name for the ṛśyasya vratam (or ṛśyasya sāma), cp. Jaim Saṃh., Einl. page 25. The *arthavāda* following in Śāṅkh. immediately after this sāman: *priyam indrasya dhāmopajagāmeti* must refer to t h i s sāman, not, as Keith in his translation of the text (the Śāṅkhāyana āraṇyaka with an appendix on the mahāvrata, London 1908, page 4 note 2) deems more natural, to the next following one [1]. A comparison of PBr. V. 4. 14 makes this clear. **3, 4.** krośānukrośe (these sāmans occur in the grāmegeya). **5.** payaḥ (occurs in the araṇyegeya). **6, 7.** arka and arkapuṣpa (both occur ib.). The Taitt. Saṃh. (VII. 5. 8. 1—2) enumerates 1. krośa, 2. sattrasyarddhi (cp. PBr. V. 4. 7), 3 prajāpater hṛdaya (l. c. 4), 4, 5. śloka and anuśloka (PBr. V. 4. 7). Both traditions differ considerably from the Pañc. br.; the Taittirīyas stand nearer to the Kauthumas, whilst the tradition of Śāṅkhāyana stands nearer to that of the Jaiminīyas than to that of the Kauthumas. The Jaiminiyas (JBr. II. 398–403) enumerate: 1. viśveṣāṃ devānāṃ vrataṃ, 2. 3. krośānukrośau, 4. sattrasyarddhi, 5. 6. vratapakṣau, 7. 8. prāṇāpānau, 9. 10. ślokānuślokau, 11. 12. nihnavābhinihnavau, 13. aṅgirasāṃ ṣaḍviṃśatyakṣaranidhanam, 14. bhūtecchandasāṃ vratam; here we have one too many, as also appears from II. 404, where thirteen *parimāds* are mentioned.

[1] *jagāma* is probably 3rd ps., not 1st.

V. 5.

1. Having mounted a throne-seat the Udgātṛ chants (the rājana chant [1] of the vratalaud); under the eyes even of the Gods [2] he thereby gains a seat above (others) [3].

[1] That only this part of the stotra is meant, appears from V. 6. 7.

[2] *devasākṣya eva tad upariṣadyaṃ jayati*, cp. Śat. br. V. 2. 1. 22: *athāsmā āsandīm āharanty, upariṣadyaṃ vā eṣa jayati yo jayaty antarikṣasadyaṃ, tad enam upary āsīnam adhastād imāḥ prajā upāsate*; TBr. I. 2. 6. 5: *yasya talpasadyam anabhijitaṃ syāt sa devānāṃ sāṃyakṣe* (cp. note 2 on XII. 13. 26) *talpasadyam abhijayānīti talpam* (=*āsandīm*) *āruhyodgāyet, talpasadyam evābhijayati*, and Kāṭh. XXXIV. 5: 38. 23 (almost verbally agreeing with PBr.) *atho devasākṣya evopariṣadyaṃ jayanti*.

[3] Because he has been placed higher, nearer to the Gods.

2. It is (made) of udumbara (wood); the udumbara is food; food he thereby retains for himself.

3. Its measure[1] is a span: that he may not leave this world[2].

[1] The heighth of its feet, Drāhy. X. 3. 4.

[2] Therefore the feet are no more than a span high.

4. With the metres[1] he mounts: to the world of heaven even he mounts.

[1] With the formulas *vasavas tvā gāyatreṇa* *c h a n d a s ā rohantu tān anv adhirohāmi* etc., Drāhy. X. 4. 9.

5. With the metres[1] he descends: on this world (the earth) he gains a firm support.

[1] With the same formulas (changing *ārohantu* and *adhirohāmi* in *avarohantu* and *avarohāmi*) but in reversed order, Drāhy. X. 4. 9 (where *aparuhya* is to be corrected into *avaruhya*).

6. The whole 'trunk'[1] is to be chanted by the Udgātṛ after he has taken up (certain verses) from all (the other parts of the vratalaud)[2], in order that he may not be disjoined in these worlds[3].

[1] Here *ātman* again designates the rājanasāman.

[2] The explanation of the words is given below, V. 6. 2-5.

[3] In order that the *ātman* (*i.e.* his rājanasāman) may not be severed from its head, wings and tail; see V. 6. 5.

7. When one stotriya (verse) (*viz.* the last) is not (wholly) chanted[1], he brings down his feet (from the seat)[2].

[1] *Viz.* whilst the prastāva is being chanted.

[2] And at the moment when the finale is chanted, he places them on the ground (Drāhy. XI. 4. 7-8), as is implied in the next following §.

8. Simultaneously with the finale[1] they[2] reach a firm support[3]: on these worlds even they firmly stand.

[1] Of the last verse.

[2] All the Chanters; the Prastotṛ and Pratihartṛ have been sitting on kūrcas, see § 12.

[3] They put their feet on the ground.

9. The Hotṛ holds his recitation having mounted a swing[1]; thereby a characteristic mark of merriment[2] is brought about.

[1] Cp. Ait. ār. I. 2. 4, Śāṅkh. ār. I. 7, śrs. XVII. 15. 10. sqq.

[2] *mahas* according to Sāyaṇa means here *tejas*, which does not suit the context. Cp. TBr. I. 2. 6. 6: *maho vai plenkho mahasa evānnādyasyāvaruddhyai.*

10. When merriness seizes children, then they mount swings.

11. The Adhvaryu holds his responsorium having mounted a plank (of udumbara-wood)[1].

[1] Cp. *e.g.* Āp. XXI. 17. 14.

12. The others[1] take their seat on bundles (of kuśa-grass); they thereby keep ascending upwards[2].

[1] The Hotrakas, the two other Chanters, the Brahman and the Gṛhapati.

[2] Cp. Kāth. XXXIV. 5: 38. 23: *svargam u lokam ākramamāṇā yanti.*

13. There are the Abhigara ('praiser')[1] and the Apagara ('reviler')[1]; the one finds fault with them, the other eulogizes them. He who finds fault with them, drives away their evil lot, he who eulogizes them, praises what by them has been well-chanted and well-recited.

[1] From *abhigṛṇāti* and *apagṛṇāti*: 'to praise,' 'to revile'. Outside the Sāmaveda literature these two performers are given by Kāty. (XIII. 3. 4-5), who has taken them over from the Sāmavedic literature and in Kāṭh. XXXIV. 5; 39. 1 (almost verbally agreeing with PBr.): *abhigarāpagarau bhavataḥ; pra vā anyaḥ sattrinaḥ śaṁsati, nindaty anyo; yaḥ praśaṁsati yad evaiṣāṁ suṣṭutaṁ suśastaṃ tat sa praśaṁsaty, atha yo nindati yad evaiṣāṁ suṣṭutaṁ suśastaṃ tat so 'pahanti.* The name of at least one of these officials occurs in Baudh. II. 3: 37. 1-2: *abhigaro dhruvagopaḥ saṁśrāva iti sadasyasya (sc. puruṣāḥ)* In the texts of the Taittirīyakas (TBr. I. 2. 6. 7) the praising and reviling are combined with the ritual recorded in Pañc. br. V. 5. 14-17. According to the Taittirīyakas namely the Brāhmin says: 'these have succeeded, they have brought about welfare,' the Śūdra says: 'these are taking away (? *udvāsakāriṇaḥ*), these have brought about mishap'.

14. An Ārya[1] and a Śūdra fight for the hide[2]; of these two they cause to win the (member of the) Ārya-caste.

[1] According to the Commentators on the sūtras: a Vaiśya.—It is impossible to decide whether the author of the Brāhmaṇa means *arya* or *ārya*; the Kāṭh. points to *ārya*. According to the well-known rule of Pāṇini (II. 2. 34) the compound *śūdrāryau* means: 'an Āriya and a Śūdra.'

[2] The Ārya stands inside the mahāvedi with his face directed to the south, south of the Mārjālīya (how is this possible?), the Śūdra stands outside the mahāvedi with his face to the north; they tug at a round, white hide, striving to obtain it; first the Śūdra pulls; the Ārya must win, Drāhy. XI. 3. 4-7; cp. Kāṭh. l. c. (39. 3): *śūdrāryau carma vyāyacchete...āryaṃ varṇam ujjāpayati...antarvedy āryaḥ syād bahirvedi śūdraḥ; śvetaṃ carma parimaṇḍalaṁ syād ādityasya rūpam,* cp. also TBr. l. c., Āp. XXI. 18. 4, 19. 9-12.

15. The Gods and the Asuras fought about the sun[1]; the Gods got possession of it. Thereupon the Gods throve, the Asuras came to nought. He thrives himself, his rival comes to naught who knows this.

1 By tugging at it. Read *vyāyacchanta* instead of °*cchantas*. Oertel defends the reading with participle ('The disjunct use of cases,' page 39), but cp. Kaṭh. l. c. *devāś ca vā asurāś cāditye vyāyacchanta, taṃ devā abhyajayan* and TBr. I. 2. 6. 6.

16. In that they cause the (member of the) Ārya-caste to win, they thereby cause themselves[1] even to win.

1 On the singular *ātmānam* cp. Oertel, The disjunct use of cases, page 184.

17. It is a circular hide; thereby the characteristic mark of the sun is brought about[1].

1 Cp. Kāṭh. as cited under § 14 (note 1).

18. At all the corners (of the mahāvedi) the drums sound (*i.e.* are beaten)[1]; they thereby gain the voice that is in the trees[2].

1 Drāhy. XI. 3. 20, TS. VII. 5. 9. 2-3, Kāṭh. XXXIV. 5: 39. 6: *sarvāsu sraktiṣu dundubhayo vadanti yā dikṣu vāk tāṃ tenāvarundhate*; Āp. XXI. 18. 1, 19. 8.

2 Cp. below, VI. 5. 12, 13. The drums are made of w o o d.

19. There is the earth-drum[1]; they thereby gain the voice that is in the earth[2].

1 Behind the āgnīdhra-shed a hole is made in the ground, half inside, half outside the mahāvedi; over this hole an ox-hide with the hairy side above, is stretched, Drāhy. X. 3. 1—3, cp TS. VII 5. 9. 3. Kāṭh. l. c. (39. 7), Āp. XXI. 18. 2-3.

2 I am unable to trace a passage in the PBr. where it is said that *vāc* entered the earth. Maitr. Saṃh. II. 5. 9: 60. 2: *yāsurī vāg avadat semāṃ prāviśat*.

20. All (manner of) voices (*i.e.* music) resound[1]; they thereby gain that voice that is in these worlds.

1 TS. VII. 5. 9. 3: *sarvā vāco vadanti: sarvāsāṃ vācām avaruddhyai*, Drāhy. XI. 3. 21, 22, Śāṅkh. śrs. XVII. 14. 12: *kurvanti ghoṣaṃ ghoṣakṛtaḥ*.

21. Accoutred, clad in armour they[1] go around[2]; thereby the characteristic mark of courage is brought about, and they also pay honour to the mahāvrata.

1 The companions of the king, who, according to the Śūtrakāras, also fulfil a rôle at the feast (Drāhy. X. 2. 1. sqq).

[2] Having accoutred themselves with shields etc. to the east of the sacrificial ground, they go around to the south of it; Kāṭh. XXXIV. 5: 39. 15: *saṃnaddhakavacāḥ pariyanti, mahāvratam eva mahayanty atho sendratāyā eva.*

V. 6.

(The mahāvrata, continued.)

1. All the officiating priests together should chant the mahāvrata (laud)[1].

[1] The head, wings, tail and trunk, cp. TBr. I. 2. 6. 4: *sarveṇa saha stuvanti.*

2. The Adhvaryu should chant 'the head'[1], the Maitrāvaruṇa 'the right wing'[2], the Brāhmaṇācchaṃsin 'the left wing'[3], the Gṛhapati 'the tail'[4], the Udgātṛ 'the trunk'[5].

[1] The nine verses, see V. 1. 2 and Āp. XXI. 17. 3.

[2] The rathantara.

[3] The bṛhat.

[4] The bhadra.

[5] The rājana.

3. When they act in this way, they should each of them leave for the Udgātṛ[1] one of the stotriya verses (of the chant which he has to perform), after this (verse) has not (yet wholly) been chanted[2].

[1] Literally: 'they should, all of them, go near the Udgātṛ with' etc., cp. TBr. I. 2. 6. 4: *ekaikām ucchiṁṣanti.*

[2] Cp. note 1 on V. 5. 7.

4. Having chanted three (verses) of 'the trunk', the Udgātṛ should put in the (last) stotriya (verse) of 'the head' (left over by the Adhvaryu); having chanted the next three (verses of 'the trunk'), he should put in the (last) stotriya (verse) of 'the right wing' (left over by the Maitrāvaruṇa); having chanted the next three (verses of 'the trunk'), he should put in the (last) stotriya (verse) of 'the left wing' (left over by the Brāhmaṇācchaṃsin); when the last but three or the last but one stotriya (verse) (of 'the trunk') has been chanted, he should put in the (last) stotriya (verse) of 'the tail' (left over by the Gṛhapati)[1].

[1] In the same way the Jaiminīyas (Jaim. br. II. 408): *ta ekaikayāstutayodgātāram upasamāyanti; tābhir udgātodgāyaty; ātmann eva tad aṅgāni pratidadhāti; tasmād ātmann aṅgāni pratihitāny; ātmanottamayodgāyati* ('he himself [=*ātmanā*] chants this last verse left over by each of the others'): *tasmād idam ātmana ud iva śete.*

5. They thereby put the limbs on 'the trunk'[1], for the obtainment of the world of heaven[2].

[1] Cp. JBr. (in note on § 4) and TBr. I. 2. 6. 4: *ātman hy aṅgāni baddhāni.*

[2] The method here (in V. 6. 1. 5) set forth is one of the two (for the other see below, § 7) that may be practised in chanting the vrata laud. It has already been alluded to above (V. 5. 6). It is remarkable that of all the other vedic texts (besides the Jaim. br.) it is only the Taittirīya-saṃhitā that accepts this order of things. The passage of TS. can only be understood in the light of our Brāhmaṇa; Sāyaṇa appears to have no notion of its purport. We read then (TS. VII 5. 8. 2): *navabhir adhvaryur udgāyati...sarvā aindriyo bhavanti...apratihṛtābhir udgāyati,* whereupon follows the mention of the rathantara, bṛhat, bhadra and rājana; these nine verses have nothing to do with the anuśloka sāman (mentioned before), as Sāyaṇa believes, but they are the trivṛt śiras gāyatram, all the verses of which are indeed addressed to Indra. That they should chant them without pratihāra is new in the Taitt. Saṃh. Even Āpastamba (XXI. 17. 3) seems to have misunderstood his own Saṃhitā, as he joins the words *navabhir aindrībhir apratihṛtābhir adhvaryur udgāyati na vā* immediately after *anuślokaṃ stuvate.* Besides, in TS. l. c. 4, the two sentences *ekaikayāstutayā samāyanti* and *tābhir udgātodgāyati* agree, one of them nearly verbatim, with Jaim. br. II. 408 (see note 1 on § 4) and, as to the matter, wholly with Pañc. br. VI. 6. 3, but these words seem here (in TS.) to be out of the context, as they follow after *pañcadhā viniṣadya stuvanti,* on which see below, note 1 on VI 6. 7.

6. Now they say, however: 'how could an Adhvaryu or a Bahvṛca[1] (*i.e.* a Ṛgvedin) chant a sāman'? No other than the Udgātṛ should chant the whole (mahāvrata laud); that is (something) complete; in completeness they gain a firm support.

[1] As the Maitrāvaruṇa and, properly speaking, also the Brāhmaṇācchaṃsin.—This sentence alludes to V. 6. 2.

7. Having chanted in the havirdhānashed 'the head,' they should, taking hold of each other, go in a westerly direction; then, having gone round the dhiṣṇyas, to the south of them, and having taken their seat behind the dhiṣṇya of the Maitrāvaruṇa, they should chant the rathantara (sāman) of fifteenfold stoma; then they should go together in a northerly direction behind the dhiṣṇya of the Hotṛ and, having seated themselves behind the dhiṣṇya of the Brāhmaṇācchaṃsin, they should chant the bṛhat of seventeenfold stoma; then, having again gone out (of the sadas) along the same way by which they had entered (it), they should go round the āgnīdhra, to the north of it, and, having taken their seat behind the

gārhapatya (*i.e.* the śālāmukhīya), they should chant 'the tail' of twenty-one-fold stoma; then, having again entered (the sadas) along the same way, by which they had left it, they should seat themselves each on his own place, and the Udgātṛ, having mounted the throne-seat, should chant 'the trunk'[1].

[1] This, then, is the ritual recommended in contrast to the one formerly (V. 6. 1-5) described, by the author of the Brāhmaṇa. In this way there is still a connection between the sāman and those of the ṛtvij's, by whom, according to the formerly described, but now rejected ritual, it should be chanted. The ritual of § 7 enjoins the chanting of the whole mahāvrata to the Udgātr alone. The plural is due to the fact, that the Prastotr and Pratihartṛ also take part in the chanting. The words at the end: *te... upaviśya. ...udgātātmanodgāyati* contain an anacoluthon caused by the desire to indicate here the seat of the Udgātr. Strictly speaking, the text ought to run: *te..upaviśya ... ātmanā stuvīran, āsandīm āruhyodgātā stuvīta.*—To the ritual here described refers the author of Taitt. Saṃh VII. 5. 8. 4: *pañcadhā viniṣadya stuvanti*: 'having taken their seat on five different places.' Which are these places, is now apparent from Pañc. br. V. 6. 7. The commentary of Sāyaṇa here is utterly insufficient. Unknown to the Sāmagas is the prescription of TS. VII. 5. 8. 4 that the Chanters should perform the first five stotriyas standing, the following five sitting. Practically this seems impossible, since the *viṣṭuti* is to be marked on the garment by means of the little wooden pegs. The expression of TS. l. c. 4 *ekaikayāstutayā samāyanti* (cp. note on V. 6. 5 s. f.) seems to be in contradiction to the preceding words. Here we have a mixing-up of the two possibilities proposed by the Pañc. br.—We see from this § 7. that the essential part of the mahāvrata laud is the *ātman*, 'the trunk'; it is only for the chant of this piece that the Udgātṛ takes his seat on the *āsandī*.

8. The wives (of the Sacrificers, *i.e.* of the partakers of the session) accompany the (chant of the rājana) by (playing on) 'apaghāṭilās'[1]; the wives thereby fulfil the office of priests (whilst they think): 'let us go simultaneously to the world of heaven'.

[1] Behind the Choristers (on them cp. C. H. § 134. d, page 173) the wives of the Yajamānas take their seat; each of them has two instruments, a *kāṇḍavīṇā* and a *picchorā*; on these they play all together alternately, first on the *kāṇḍavīṇā*, then on the *picchorā*. The *kāṇḍavīṇā* is a flute of bamboo, the *picchorā* a guitar, which is beaten by means of a plectrum, Lāṭy. IV. 2. 5-7, Drāhy. XI. 2. 6-8. The Jaim. br. (cp. 'Das Jaiminīyabrāhmaṇa in Auswahl' No. 166) enumerates the following instruments; *karkarī, alābu, vakrā, kapiśīrṣṇī aiṣiki, apāghāṭalikā* (cp. Āp., below), *vīṇā kaśyapī* (cp. Ath. S. IV. 37. 4: *āghāṭāḥ karkaryaḥ* 'cymbels and lutes,' Whitney). Āp. XXI. 17. 6, 19 names three instruments: *apāghāṭalikā, tambalavīṇā* and *piccholā*: the second is according to R. Garbe (see his Introduction to Āp. vol. III, page VIII) a tamil guitar. Baudh. XVI. 20: 266. 9-10; 267. 9-10 names also three instruments: *āghāṭi, piccholā* and *karkarikā*, on whch cp. the Karmāntasūtra (Baudh. XXVI.

17, s.f.); Śāṅkh. XVII. 3. 12 has: *ghāṭakarkarīr avaghaṭarikāḥ kāṇḍavīṇāḥ picchorā iti*, read perhaps *āghāṭarīr avaghaṭa*', etc.; but the following passage (sūtra 15-17) is rather uncertain.

9. In every house (of all the Sacrificers) food is being prepared[1]. Now, if they should ask: 'wherefore do they prepare this?'[2] they should answer: 'these Sacrificers will eat food.'[3]

[1] During the other days of the year Brāhmins are to be fed in the house of the Gṛhapati (?), but on this day this should take place in the house of all the partakers of the session.

[2] Or: 'What are they doing there?'

[3] *Viz.* in yonder world.

10. Who speaks evil of those that have been initiated[1], takes a third part of their evil (on himself), who eats their food, a third part, the ants a third part[2].

[1] *Viz* of those who have undergone the *dīkṣā*-rite = the partakers of the sattra.

[2] The stress is to be laid evidently on the second third, as this § must be connected with the preceding one.

11. They perform with the *parimāds*; the *parimāds* are the skin and the hair of the mahāvrata; having thereby gained the skin and the hair of the mahāvrata, they retain it (*viz.* skin and hair)[1].

[1] The śruti quoted by Sāyana: *yad etān ha* (read: *yādṛg aha*) *vai puruṣo devebhyaḥ karoti tādṛg asmai devāḥ kurvanti* is Jaim. br. II. 386. On our passage cp. Jaim. br. II. 403: 'as man's hairs, nails, hairs on the body, beard, thus are they (*viz.* the *parimāds*) of it' (*viz.* of the mahāvrata) and TBr I. 2. 6. 4-5: *sarveṇa saha stuvanti, sarveṇa hy ātmanātmanvī, sahotpatanty; ekaikām ucchiṁṣanty ātman hy aṅgāni baddhāni; na vā etena sarvaḥ puruṣo; yad ita ito lomāni dato nakhān parimādaḥ kriyante, tāny eva tena pratyupyante*, i.e. 'they chant together the whole (mahāvrata laud), for through the whole 'trunk' he becomes possessed of a trunk: together they fly (as birds) upward: they each leave over one (of his stotriya-verses, cp. supra V. 6. 4), for on the trunk the limbs are fastened. Man, however, is not complete thereby (*i.e.* by the possession of solely limbs and trunk); that he gets here and here (*i.e.* on his limbs and trunk) hairs, teeth, nails thereby he now becomes complete); the *parimāds* are practised, thereby these hairs, teeth, nails) are fixed on (his body)'. I suppose the text has not been handed down correctly, as the accusatives *lomāni dato nakhān* hang in the air. Perhaps we should read *kurvanti* instead of *kriyante*: 'in that the *parimāds* bring about here and here hair, teeth, nails,' etc. For the rest, the Jaiminīyabrāhmaṇa raises the surmise, that in this context the word *parimādaḥ* may have a meaning different from the usual one (cp. excursus on V. 4) and that it indicates the music accompanying the chant: after the description of the lute the Jaim. br. II 46. has:

athaitā anyāḥ parimādaḥ kriyante, and II. 404: *athaitā vācaḥ pravadanti kṣudrāḥ parimādaḥ,* whereupon follows the description of the musical instruments.

12. They string the lute; the lute is the end[1] and the mahāvrata is the end[2]; thereby they salute by its music[3] the end by means of the end.

[1] As it is the last or most perfect of all the instruments.

[2] The end of the year, the last day (but one).

[3] *abhivādayanti* 'they salute:' and also: 'they play, make resound.'

13. It is provided with a hundred strings, man, forsooth, has a life of a hundred years, has a hundred powers[1].

[1] Cp. Jaim. br. II. 45, 418, Kāth. XXXIV. 5: 39. 10, TS. VII. 5. 9. 2.—The *vāṇa* is an instrument of wood, according to Śānkh. consisting of a kind of crate and a handle (cross-bar?); it is covered with the skin of a red ox, hairs on the outside, it has ten holes at its back side, over each of which ten strings are fastened; these strings are manufactured of *muñjā* or *darbha* grass. The strings are touched by the Udgātṛ by means of a reed or a piece of bamboo (with its leaves), that is bent of itself (not by the hand of man): *indreṇataya* (var. *indrana*) *iṣīkayā,* Jaim. br., and from this text the word is taken over by Lāṭy.-Drāhy. (On this word cp. note 3 on XV. 5. 21). The Udgātṛ does not properly play on this instrument, having touched the strings (see § 14) with the plectrum he orders a Brāhmin to play on it, Drāhy XI. 1. 1-10, cp. Āp. XXI. 18. 9, Śānkh. XVII. 3. 1-11.

14. He should grate on it[1] in upward direction muttering the formulas: 'for out-breathing (I grate on thee); for in-breathing (I grate on) thee; for through-breathing (I grate on) thee.' Having obtained thereby the out-breathing, the in-breathing and the through-breathing they retain these.

[1] He should touch the strings with the plectrum; probably this must be done thrice, each time with one of the formulas. The Jaim. br. prescribes the formulas: *mā no jyotiḥ, vāk satyam, mā no bhadraḥ.*

15. Females[1], bearing water-jars go[2] around the mārjālīya[3], (calling out:) 'here is honey, here is honey.'[4] Accompanied by loud noise they thereby, having become birds, go simultaneously to the world of heaven.

[1] Female slaves, at least five, at highest fifty or twenty five.

[2] 'Dance,' according to Baudh. Āp.

[3] Sunwise they go round according to Drāhy.-Lāṭy.; first thrice withershins (*apradakṣiṇam*), afterwards silently sunwise, according to Śānkh.

[4] According to Baudh. and Āp. this call: *haimahā, idaṃ madhu* is the refrain of a longer chant, the text of which is given by the Sūtrakāras of the Yajurveda.

V. 7.

(The gavām ayana, continued: the gaurīvita and other sāmans during the year.)

1. The Gods divided (distributed) the Voice, what pith of it was left over, that became the gaurīvita (sāman)[1]. This (pith, *i.e.* this sāman) revolves along with the anuṣṭubh[2]; the anuṣṭubh is Voice, the gaurīvita is the pith of Voice.

[1] Grāmegeya V. 1. 22, composed on SV. I. 168=RS. VII. 69. 4.

[2] The gaurīvita occurs on each day of the whole year's session *viz.* in the anuṣṭubh part of the ārbhavapavamāna laud, cp. Ārṣeyakalpa, Einl. page XXIV.

2. In that they chant day after day the gaurīvita, they thereby bring into the Voice the pith of the Voice.

3. He who knows thus, speaks with a pith-full voice[1].

[1] With a voice that is rich in pith, not 'dry' or harsh.

4. It has two 'raisings'[1]; these are the two that look out for a stopping-place in the (journey to the) world of heaven; by means of the first (former) they finish the first (former) day, by means of the following (the second), they pass, in chanting, across[2] to the following day.

[1] *dvyudāsam, udāsa=utkṣepa: utkṣepo nāma dīrghaviśeṣaḥ:* probably the notation *satyā*'3123 is meant, which occurs twice in the gaurīvita. Instead of *avasānadeśau* read *avasānadarśau* cp. XI. 5. 19 (which is identical with our §) and Jaim. br. II. 424: 'the gaurivīta forsooth is (that part of the sacrifice) which has relation to the to-morrow; what has relation to the to-morrow, is: progeny, cattle and the world of heaven. Just as one who has good knowledge of fields comes up to a village, thinking: 'here is a good path, along it we will go; here is a good ford, by it we will set across; here is a good dwelling, here we will dwell,' in this same way these two raisings of the gaurivīta wander (before the journeying troop) (as) the two (persons) that look out for a stopping-place;' the restored text runs: *etad dha vai yajñasya śvastanaṃ yad gaurivītaṃ, prajā śvastanaṃ, paśavaḥ śvastanam, svargo lokaḥ śvastanam sa yathā kṣetrajño grāmaṁ dhāvayed: adaḥ sugaṃ, tena yāsyāmo, 'daḥ sutīrthaṃ, tena tariṣyāmo, 'daḥ suvasaṃ, tad vatsyāma ity, evam etau gaurivītasyodāsāv avasānadarśau carataḥ*; that here also *avasānadarśau* (the ms. has *'daśau*) is the correct reading, is proved by Jaim. br. III. 17: 'just as in ordinary life two (persons) looking out for a stopping-place find a stopping-place (*avasāna*), so find these two raisings of the gaurivīta the to-morrow for the Gods;.. one of these raisings is the person looking out for a stopping-place, *avasāya itānyaḥ*.

It is herewith just as if one were to settle down after reaching grass and water that been looked for.'

2 The translation of *abhyativadati* (which occurs again VIII. 3. 6) would be in German: 'sie reden hinüber zum nächsten Tage.'

5. The gaurīvita is (that part) of the sacrifice which has relation to the to-morrow; if they were to let loose (*i.e.* not to practise during the whole year) the gaurīvita, there would be for them neither to-morrow nor progeny.

6. 'The other[1] (part of the) sacrifice,' they say, 'comes to an end, but the Voice has no finish.' In that there is day by day the gaurīvita, they thereby again bring into action the Voice for themselves[2].

1 Is 'other' used here as ἄλλος, or, with Śāyaṇa to be taken in the sense of *vāgrahitayajña*?

2 The gaurīvita being the pith of the Voice, see § 1.

7. Day by day there is the (sāman) that has the word *svar* ('heaven') for its finale[1].

1 The sujñānasāman, Grāmegeya XVII. 1. 26, composed on SV. I. 572=RS. IX. 106.10, chanted on different verses: the finale (*e*) *upā* of the Grāmegeya is to be changed into (*e*) *suvar*, cp. Lāty. VII. 10. 1 and 7.

8. To the region of the Gods ascend they who undertake (*i.e.* practise) the sāman with the word *svar* as finale. 'He verily, causes the participants of a sattra to undertake a sacrificial s e s s i o n,' they say, 'who makes them ascend to the region of the Gods.' No one s i t t i n g[1] in the region of the Gods comes to distress. In that there is day by day the sāman with the word *svar* as finale, they suffer no distress whatever.

1 *āsīnāḥ* is used because of the idea implied in *sattra* 'session.'

9. 'They verily swerve from this world,' they say, 'who practise the sāman with the word *svar* as finale. (But this objection is of no value, for) in that they by means of a v e r s e[1] undertake (*i.e.* chant) (the word) *svar*[2], they get a firm support in t h i s world, in that (there is) the *e*-sound, they get a firm support in the i n t e r m e d i a t e region, in that they by means of a s ā m a n (chant the word *svar*), they get a firm support in y o n d e r world. In all the worlds they get a firm support in chanting the svarṇidhana (sāman).

1 *ṛc* is equal to earth, *sāman* to heaven or sky; cp. the well-known mantra: *amo 'ham asmi sā tvam* etc.

2 I propose to read: *svar upayanti* instead of *svarūpaṁ yanti*. The expression *svar upayanti* used à double entente, meaning also 'they get to heaven.'

3 The nidhana being *e ṣuvar*, cp. note 1 on § 7.

10. It is the sujñāna (saman)[1].

1 Cp. note 1 (on § 8).

11. The Gods, in going to the world of heaven, were afraid of ignorance[1]; they saw this sujñāna (sāman) ('knowledge giving sāman'), and thereby attained knowledge. In that there is day by day the sujñāna (sāman), they attain knowledge.

1 Probably: 'were afraid lest they should not find their way heavenward.'

V. 8.

(The sāmans that must be chanted during the year, continued.)

1. They who feed the Voice with food, become eaters of food, they who let it (the Voice) be parched, get parched up.

2. The gaurīvita, the śyāvāśva (and) the nihava, these sāmans are the food of the Voice, of these the Voice is the food; in that these sāmans do not fall off[1] (*i.e.* are used day by day during the whole year), they thereby feed the Voice with food and so they all become eaters of food.

1 According to this Brāhmaṇa the three sāmans here designated, should day by day be chanted in the anuṣṭubh-part (=*vāc*, cp. V. 7. 1). For the gaurīvita (and the sujñāna) this rule holds in the ritual of the Ārṣeyakalpa, not for the śyāvāśva and the nihava. How is this incongruency to be explained?

3. Stepping on and stepping off they are: stepping on and stepping off verily is a characteristic feature of the Voice[1].

1 The meaning of this sentence is obscure to me.

4. There is day by day the plava (sāman)[1].

1 According to Sāyaṇa day by day in the bṛhatī part of the midday service. I do not find it in the Ārṣeyakalpa.

5. A sea they cross, who enter upon the (sacrifice of a) year; he, verily, who without a boat (*plava*) crosses the sea, does not come out of it; that there is the plava (sāman), is for reaching the world of heaven[1].

1 Cp. XIV. 5. 17.

6. By (the words of the finale of the sāman): 'may we overcome all difficulties'[1] they overcome what by them is wrongly chanted or recited (in stotra or śastra).

[1] These words are the nidhana of the plava, Grāmegeyagāna XIV. 1. 34, see the edition of Calcutta Vol. II, page 75.—The § is identical with XIV. 5. 18.

7. There is the (sāman) with the finale *okaḥ* ('house'), at the head (*i e.* beginning) of the six-day-period[1].

[1] See Ārṣeyakalpa I 2 end: *pra sunvānāyāndhasa* (SV. II. 736-738) *iti..auṣṇiham okonidhanam ekasyām* (on II 737). The okonidhana, Grāmegeya X. 1. 29, is composed on SV. I. 382; it has the word *okaḥ* as finale.

8. To the farthest distance get they who go to the end of the six-day-period; that there is the sāman with the word 'house' (*okaḥ*) as finale, is for knowing (the way)[1].

[1] *okonidhana* meaning also, 'having a house for (*i.e.* at) the end.'

9. When one arrives at his own house, he then knows the way in every direction, all is (as clear as) day[1] for him.

[1] *divā* cp. VIII. 1. 13. and Chand. up. III. 11. 3.

V. 9.

(The time for the consecration: *dīkṣā*.)

1. On the aṣṭakā par excellence[1] they should undergo the consecration.

[1] *ekāṣṭakā*. After each full-moon the eighth day is an *aṣṭakā*; the *aṣṭakā* par excellence is that *aṣṭakā* which falls after the Māghī paurṇamāsī, *i.e.* one week before the beginning of the new year, as it seems, cp. Āp. gṛhs. XXI. 10 etc.—This whole ninth khaṇḍa (on which see Weber, 'die vedischen Nachrichten über die Nakṣatra' page 341 sqq.) agrees almost verbatim with TS. VII. 4. 8.

2. The aṣṭakā par excellence is the spouse of the year[1], during this[2] night (=day), verily, it (the year) dwells with her (with its spouse the Ekāṣṭakā); having thereby obviously taken hold of the year, they undergo the consecration.

[1] Ath. S. III. 10. 2: *saṃvatsarasya yā patnī*, ib. 8: *saṃvatsaraḥ patir ekāṣṭake tava*.

[2] Read *etāṁ* instead of *gatāṁ*.

3. Of this (term) this is a defective feature that they descend into the water[1] without delight[2].

[1] *Viz.* at the avabhṛtha, the lustral bath which would then fall after a year, in winter-time.

[2] Cp. Jaim. br. II. 373: *seva tu paricakṣā yad apo 'nabhinandantaḥ śiśire vabhṛtham adhyavayanti* and Kauṣ. br. XIX 3: *saṃvepamānā avabhṛthād udāyanti.*

4. In regard to (a part) of the year that has been torn asunder they undergo the consecration, who undergo the consecration at the aṣṭakā par excellence[1].

[1] Because the *dīkṣā* would fall partly in the old, partly in the new year, the *dīkṣā*-days being twelve in number.

5. They are the two seasons that are called the last (of the year)[1]; in regard to (a part) of the year that is unhappy[2] they undergo the consecration, who undergo the consecration with regard to the two seasons that are called the last of the year.

[1] I combine the last words of § 4: *antanāmānāv ṛtū bhavataḥ* (so is to be read instead of *bhavate*) with § 5. The *dīkṣā*, undertaken on the ekāṣṭakā, falls in the last two seasons of the year, which are to be regarded as one whole.

[2] Being the last: *anta.*

6. Therefore the consecration is not to be undertaken on the aṣṭakā par excellence.

7. In Phālguna (month)[1] they should undergo the consecration.

[1] On Phālguna full-moon-day.

8. The Phālguna (full-moon-day) is the head (*i.e.* the beginning) of the year; at the head (the beginning of the year) having thereby taken hold of the year they are consecrated.

9. Of this (term) this is a defective feature, that the viṣuvat (day) then falls in with the cloudy (season)[1].

[1] Which would be of bad augurium, because the viṣuvat is the sun. The middle day of the year would thus fall on the śarad month āśvayuja, cp. Weber, op. cit page 343.

10. On Citra-full-moon they should undergo the consecration.

11. The Citrā-full-moon, verily, is the eye of the year; in the head (=at the beginning) is the eye; at the head (=in the beginning of the year) having thereby taken hold of the year they are consecrated. This term has no defective feature.

12. Four days before the day of full-moon they should undergo the consecration.

13. Their buying of the soma (then) falls together with the aṣṭakā par excellence; thereby they do not lose the aṣṭakā par excellence[1].

[1] The *dīkṣā* lasting twelve days and the *somakrayaṇa* following immediately after the *dīkṣā*, this last ceremony would, if the *dīkṣā* were to begin four days before Citrā-full-moon, fall not on the ekāṣṭakā, but on the aṣṭakā after Citrafull-moon, the ekāṣṭakā being the eighth day after Māgha-full-moon (see on V. 9. 1). I guess that §§ 12 and 13 had to follow originally immediately after § 2. Of the ritualistic Sūtras Āpastamba is somewhat uncertain about the question which *paurṇamāsī* is meant in TS.; his text (XXI. 15. 5, 6) runs: *caturahe purastāt paurṇamāsyai dīkṣeran | māghya ity āśmarathyaḥ | caitrya ity ālekhanaḥ*. More explicit is Baudh. XVI. 13: 260. 5. sqq.: *te caturahe purastān māghyai paurṇamāsyai dīkṣante, teṣām ekāṣṭakāyaṃ krayaḥ saṃpadyata, iti nu yadi samām avijñāya dīkṣante; yady u vā etasyām evaikāṣṭakāyāṃ samāṃ vijijñāsante* (according to the ritual of XIV. 13: 176. 6–16), *caturaha eva purastāt phālgunyai vā cāitryai vā paurṇamāsyai dīkṣante, teṣām aparapakṣasyāṣṭamyāṃ krayaḥ saṃpadyate, tenaikāṣṭakāṃ na chambaṭkurvanti*. Baudhāyana, then, speaks strongly in favour of my surmise. For the rest the Jaim. br. (II. 373), disapproving of the ekāṣṭakā for the same reason as the Pañc. br. (see note 2 on § 3), recommends for the *dīkṣā* the term of five or six days after new-moon in the month Phālguna.

14. For them[1] the sutyā (*i.e.* the Soma pressing, the beginning of the Soma feast days) falls on the first half (of the month, *i.e.* in the half of the waxing moon). The months are one after another finished in the first half (of the month), they rise in the first half; after them, having risen, cattle and herbs rise and lucky words are spoken (spread) about them: 'these partakers of the session have succeeded'[1]. They do succeed.

[1] *Viz.* if they undertake the *dīkṣā* four days before full-moon (either phālgunī or caitrī).

V. 10.

(The years-rite with dismissed day-rites: *utsargiṇām ayanam*.[1])

[1] Compare TS. VII. 5, 6 and 7, Kāṭh. XIII. 7, Lāṭy. IV. 8. 8—23, Drāhy. VIII. 4. 4. 8—28, Baudh. XVII. 22, Āp. XXI. 24, Śāṅkh. XIII. 20.

1. They who practise 'dismission'[1], make swell (or 'strengthen') the year.

[1] They who dismiss (remove, abandon) the ritual of certain days out of the year-rite, cp. note on V. 10. 4 and the text of V. 10. 5.

2. If no dismission out of it is made, the year is like an inflated leathern bag (*i.e.* like a leathern bag filled with air); if they did not practise dismission, they would die of strangurine.

[1] Cp. TS. VII. 5. 6. 2: *yad ahar notsṛjeyur yathā dṛtir upanaddho vipataty evaṁ saṃvatsaro vipatet* and Jaim. br. II. 393: *yo vai pūrṇa* (*i.e. pūrṇe*) *āvapati vi vā vai tat patati pra vā śiryate.*

3. The year is out-breathing[1], the months are in-breathing[1]; in that they practise dismission they put their in-breathing into their out-breathing[2]. The consecrated one who dies before the normal time of life, is afflicted by the distress of the year out of which no dismission has been made.

[1] *prāṇa* as the counterpart of *udāna* (usually this is *apāna*), as for instance Śat. br. XI. 2. 4. 5. The months are compared with in-breathing, because they make, as it were, holes in the year for the mouth.

[2] Elsewhere it seems to be considered as a b a d occurrence when the *udāna* passes into the *prāṇa* (Śat. br. XI. 5. 3. 9: when the gārhapatya-fire is extinguished...*udānaḥ prāṇam apyagāt*). The thought of § 3 is more clearly expressed in the Jaim. br. II. 393: 'from a vacuum (the lungs) the out-breathing starts forth. Prajāpati is the year, his out-breathings are the full-moon-days; by dismissing the full-moon days, they make for Prajāpati's out-breathing a way to pass out' (*prajapāter eva tāt prāṇān utsṛjante*).

4. Regarding this they say: 'must dismission[1] take place or not?'

[1] According to Baudh. and Āpastamba five days are to be dismissed in the first half of the year (before the viṣuvat-day), and five days in the second half (after the viṣuvat-day), *viz.* five jyotis-days: the f i r s t day of each first abhiplava-ṣaḍaha in the 2nd, 3rd, 4th, 5th and 6th month, and after the viṣuvat the l a s t day of each first pṛṣṭhya-ṣaḍaha in the 8th, 9th, 10th, 11th, and, in the 12th month, the last day of the last (3rd) abhiplava-ṣaḍaha (a jyotis-day). In the first and seventh month there is no *utsarga*. The ritual thus falling out is replaced by the offering of a he-goat to Prajāpati and different puroḍāśas, Baudh. XVII. 22: 301. 7—302. 7, Āp. XXI. 24. 1—25. 4.

5. In case they should prefer to practise dismission, they should dismiss the ukthas[1]; thereby dismission takes place and (at the same time) does not take place[2].

[1] Cp. Āp. XXI. 25. 6: *ukthāni vā* (*viz. utsṛjeyuḥ*). The uktha-stotras and corresponding śastras and grahas of the uktha-days should be dismissed. The statement given here finds, as it seems, its explanation in the Sūtra of Drāhy.-Lāṭy. l. c., and cp. Varadarāja on Ārṣeyakalpa I. 7. s.f. (page 12, note 3 of the edition), where it is set forth that the dismission should take place in this way, that in each

month the 6th day of the three opening abhiplava-ṣaḍahas should be ukthyas, but the 6th day of the last ṣaḍaha an agniṣṭoma. Now, as the ukthastotras at the end of the 6th day are optional (cp. Ārṣeyakalpa l.c.), it can be said that by doing so, on the one hand, *utsarga* is made, and, on the other hand, is n o t made.

[2] Cp. Āp. l. c. 7.

6. But they say also: 'it is to be made a 'one-and-three' stoma[1]. Thereby (on the one side) dismission has been obviously brought about, but on the other side, they press out the soma' (*i.e.* they perform sacrifices of soma).[2]

[1] The day, on which they agree to practise dismission, should be made an *ekatrika* stoma (cp. below, XVI. 16), consisting of stomas alternately of one stotriya and of three stotriyas. This is another way to obtain *utsṛṣṭam* and at the same time *anutsṛṣṭam*, cp. Drāhy. VIII. 4. 11—14. (Dhanvin is to be read: *so 'yaṃ stotriyālopo nāmotsarga iti*), and Āp. XXI. 21. 5, Śāṅkh. XIII. 20. 4.

[2] The printed text has *abhyutṣuṇvanti*; although this reading is repeated in the Commentary, it cannot be right, the *ṣ* and *ṇ* are not accounted for, and, moreover, a compound *abhyutsunoti* does not exist. Now, the Commentary on Lāṭy. IV. 8. 13 cites this passage with *abhyuruṣuṇvanti*; that an *u* must be read is proved by the Leyden MS., which rightly, as it seems to me, presents: *abhy u tu ṣuṇvanti* (*u* 'but', *tu* 'nevertheless'). The *ekatrika* soma i s a pressing, i s a sacrifice of soma.

7. 'There are, forsooth, holes in the year of those,' they say, 'who dismiss a stoma'[1].

[1] *Viz.* who shorten a stoma in the manner described above, §§ 5. 6.

8. They take hold of (*i.e.* they immolate) a victim; of the stoma even they thereby take hold, for the victim is a stoma[1].

[1] Because both are destined to offer homage to the Gods; probably the he-goat destined for Prajāpati is meant, cp. note 1 (end) on V. 10. 2, and TS. VII. 5. 7. 4, Śāṅkh. XIII. 20. 8.

9. On the day immediately before that day on which they intend to practise dismission, they drive away the calves from (the mother-cows)[1]. On the (following) morning they immolate the victim; they proceed with its omentum[2], then witht he savana-puroḍāśa, prepared on eight kapālas[3], for Agni, then with the coagulated sour milk destined for Indra, then with a mess of boiled rice (a *caru*) destined for the All-gods. Thereby the morning service comes about[4].

[1] To obtain the milk for the sāṃnāyya offering to Indra, cp. C. H. § 110.— Instead of *śva utsṛṣṭāḥ sma iti* read *śva utsraṣṭāsma iti*.

[2] Cp. C. H. § 141. c.

[3] Cp. C. H. § 143 and cp. § 121.

[4] Cp. TS. VII. 5. 7. 2-3, Baudh. XVII. 22 : 301. 3-12, Āp. XXI. 24. 3-7.

10. They then proceed with the paśupuroḍāśa prepared on eleven kapalas[1], then with the savana-puroḍāśa on eleven kapālas[2], then with a puroḍāśa prepared on eleven kapālas destined for (Indra) accompanied by the Maruts, then with a mess of boiled rice destined for Indra. Thereby the midday-service comes about[3].

[1] Cp. C. H. § 185.

[2] Cp. C. H. § 186.

[3] Cp. TS. l. c. 3, Baudh. l. c. 301. 12-15, Āp. l. c. 8.

11. They (then) proceed with the offering of the victim, then with the savana-puroḍāśa prepared on twelve kapālas, then with a puroḍāśa prepared on twelve kapālas destined for the All-gods, then with a mess of boiled rice destined for Agni and the Maruts. Thereby the third service comes about[1].

[1] Cp. TS. l. c. 3, Baudh. l. c. 301. 15—302. 1, Āp. l. c. 9.

12. Having proceeded with the pṛṣadājya they perform the patnīsaṃyājas[1].

[1] Cp. C. H. §§ 246, 252, Baudh. l. c. 302. 1-2, Āp. l. c. 12.

Sixth Chapter.

(In the Chapters VI—IX. 2 the jyotiṣṭoma, ukthya, atirātra, *i.e.* the *prakṛti* of all the ekāhas and ahīnas is described.)

(The jyotiṣṭoma-agniṣṭoma.)

(VI. 1, 2: Origin of the sacrifice, its stomas.)

VI. 1.

1. 'Prajāpati desired: 'may I be more (than one), may I be reproduced.' He saw that agniṣṭoma and practised it; by it he created the creatures.

2. It was by means of the eleventh laud (stotra) of the agniṣṭoma that he created them and by means of the eleventh month of the year;

then he laid hold of (seized)[1] them by means of the twelfth laud and the twelfth month of the year.

[1] *paryagṛhṇāt*, meaning as VI. 5. 14.

3. Therefore the creatures (the women), having borne their young ones during ten months, bring them forth in the eleventh month and do not bear them beyond the twelfth (month); for by means of the twelfth (stotra and month) they were seized. He, then, who knows this, gets the (born) children and brings forth the unborn ones[1].

[1] *pra jātā janayati* probably with the Leyden ms. is to be corrected, read: *prājātā janayati*, cp. TS. VII. 1. 1. 3.

4. From these (creatures) being seized (by Prajāpati) the mule went forth[1]; he went after it and took away its seed[2]; this he wiped off on (transferred to) the mare[3]; therefore the mare has double seed[4], therefore the mule is barren, for its seed had been taken away.

[1] Litt: 'passed beyond' *atyakrāmat*, cp. *atyapravata* of TS. VII. 1. 1. 2. which passage is nearly identical with PBr.

[2] Read *ādatta* instead of *ādattā*.

[3] Read *tad vaḍabāyām nyamārṭ tasmād*, etc.

[4] As it brings forth a horse and a mule, cp Śat. br. VI. 3. 1. 23.

5. Therefore it is not fit to be given as a sacrificial fee, for it exceeded (*i.e.* went beyond) the sacrifice[1], it could (however,) be the sacrificial fee for an excessive (or redundant) (sacrifice)[2], for congruence's sake: it must be given at the laud of a ṣoḍaśin: the ṣoḍaśin, forsooth, is an excessive (or 'redundant') sacrifice; he (then) gives at an excessive (sacrifice) an excessive (sacrificial fee).

[1] 'Prajāpati is the sacrifice' (see *e.g.* Maitr. S. III. 6. 5: 65. 3).

[2] One that exceeds the measure of a normal sacrifice, as does the ṣoḍaśin with its sixteenth laud.

[3] Cp. on VI. 1. 1-5 Oertel in Transactions of the Connecticut Acad. of Arts Vol. XV, page 176 sqq., where the corresponding passage of J. Br. is given.

6. He (Prajāpati) wished: 'may I create the sacrifice.' Out of his mouth he created (let forth) the ninefold (nineversed) stoma; along with it of the metres the gāyatrī came into existence, of the deities Agni, of the men the Brahmin, of the seasons the spring[1]. Therefore, of the stomas the ninefold one is the mouth (or the beginning or 'the chief one'), of the metres the gāyatrī, of the deities Agni, of the men

the Brāhmin, of the seasons the spring[1] Therefore, of the stomas the ninefold one is the mouth (or 'the beginning', or 'the chief one'), of the metres the gāyatrī, of the deities Agni, of the men the Brāhmin, of the seasons the spring. Therefore the Brāhmin by his mouth (his word) is strongest, for he is created from the mouth (of Prajāpati)[2].

1 A Brāhmin must perform the upanayana and establish his sacred fires in the spring.

2 With this and the following §§ cp. TS. VII. 1. 1. 4—6.

7. Strong with his mouth (his word) is he who knows this.

8. Out of his breast, his arms, he created the fifteenfold (or fifteen-versed) (stoma); along with it of the metres the triṣṭubh came into existence, of the deities Indra, of the men the Noble, of the seasons the summer[1]. Therefore the stoma for a noble is the fifteenfold one, his metre is the triṣṭubh, his season the summer Therefore his strength lies in his arms, for he is created from the arms (of Prajāpati).

1 A Kṣatriya must perform the upanayana and establish his sacred fires in the summer.

9. Strong with his arms is he who knows this.

10. Out of his middle, his membrum virile[1], he created the seventeen-fold (stoma), along with it of the metres the jagatī came into existence, of the deities the All-gods, of the men the Peasants, of the seasons the raining season[2]. Therefore the Peasant, although he is lived upon[3], does not decrease, for he is created from the membrum virile. Therefore he is rich in cattle, for the All gods are his deity[4] and the jagatī is his metre and the rainy season is his season[5]. Therefore the Brāhmin and the Noble must live upon him, for he is created (from the part) below (them).

1 'From the middle, the belly,' TS.

2 A Vaiśya must perform the upanayana and establish his sacred fires in the rainy season.

3 By Brāhmana and Kṣatriya.

4 Who are a plurality.

5 In which season cattle accrues.

11. Out of his feet, his firm support, he created the twenty-one-fold (stoma); along with it of the metres the anuṣṭubh came into existence, of the deities none, of the men the Śūdra. Therefore the Śūdra

is, it is true, rich in cattle, but excluded from the sacrifice, for he has no deity, as no deity had come into existence after him. Therefore he does not bring it farther than to the washing of the feet [1], for he is created out of the feet (of Prajāpati). Therefore the twenty-one-fold of the stomas is the firm support [2]; for it is created out of his firm footing (the feet of Prajāpati). Therefore they [3] do not transpose [4] the anuṣṭubh along with the metres [5].

[1] Of the three higher castes, see *e.g.* Hir. gṛhs. I. 12. 19.

[2] It is the last stoma of the agniṣṭoma (the yajñāyajñīya), on which the whole Soma-feast is resting (*pratitiṣṭhati*).

[3] The Chanters.

[4] In the vyūḍha-dvādaśāha, cp. Ait. br. IV. 27, Śat. br. IV. 5. 9, TS. VII. 2. 8.

[5] *I.e.* the anuṣṭubh metre is not transposed along with (*anu*) the gāyatrī, triṣṭubh and jagatī, but it retains its own place in the vyūḍha dvādaśāha.

12. For the sake of separating good and bad (prosperity and adversity)[1].

[1] In order that the good, the better (*viz.* the gāyatrī and the other two metres) may not be mixed up with the bad, the inferior (*viz.* the anuṣṭubh, sprung out of the feet).

13. Separation of good and bad comes (unto him) who knows this.

VI. 2.

(The stomas of the normal sacrifice.)

1. He, forsooth, who knows the stomas to be provided with an explanation[1], comes into the possession of the explanation[1].

[1] *I.e.* of the objects, indicated by the explanation in the next following §. Perhaps, though *upadeśanavat* has a different meaning, the one 'being in the possession of a explanation' does not seem to fit in with Kāṭh. IX. 16 : 119. 15 : *ya evaṃ devān upadeśanād vedopadeśanavān bhavati.*

2. The ninefold (stoma) is the breath[1]; the fifteenfold one is the half month [2]; the seventeenfold one is the year [3]; the twenty-onefold one is the sun [4]. These are the stomas provided with an explanation; in the possession of the explanation is he who knows this [5].

[1] The breath being threefold as *prāṇa, apāna, vyāna*, or, if we take *trivṛt* in the sense of 'containing nine', the seven prāṇas in the head: mouth, nose (2), ears (2), eyes (2) and the two in the body, thus Sāyaṇa

[2] The half-month consisting of fifteen days.

[3] The year consisting of seventeen parts, 12 months and 5 seasons.

4 The sun is the twenty-first, as there are 12 months, 5 seasons, 3 worlds, the sun being the 21st, see the passage of TS. in note 5.

5 C.p. TS. VII. 1. 1. 6: 'the trivṛt is the breath, the pañcadaśa is (equal to) the half months, the saptadaśa is Prajāpati, three are the worlds and the sun is the twenty-first (=ekaviṃśa stoma); on h i m (the ekaviṃśa) they repose, in h i m they have firm support; he who knows this, reposes on h i m, has firm support in h i m.'

3. The thrice nine-fold (*i.e.* twenty-seven-versed) (stoma) is (equal to) these worlds; through the Brāhmaṇa of the thrice-nine-fold (stoma) these worlds are thrice renewed [1].

1 Meaning doubtful, the words *triṇavasya vai brāhmanena* are passed over in silence by Sāyaṇa. On the whole cp. Śat. br. VIII. 7. 2. 17 *sarve hy ete lokās rivṛtaḥ.*

4. He who knows this, gets firm support in these worlds.

5. The thirty-threefold (stoma), forsooth, is (equal to) the deities: the eight Vasus, the eleven Rudras, the twelve Ādityas, Prajāpati and the Vaṣaṭkāra are the thirty-second and thirty-third [1].

1 *trayastriṁśau*, a similar kind of elliptic dual is *dvādaśau* IV. 1. 2.

6. A sacrifice at which the Gods are present [1] is performed by him who knows this.

1 Read *sadevena* as one word.

7. He who knows the ruler, becomes a ruler; the thirty-three-fold is the ruler of the stomas, man is the ruler of animals.

8. Therefore the other animals eat (with their head) bent down, but man (eats in) erect (position), for he is the lord.

9. Ruler over his equals becomes he who knows this.

VI. 3.

(T h e n a m e j y o t i ṣ ṭ o m a; i t s s t o m a s.)

1. The agniṣṭoma, forsooth, is t h e sacrifice.

2. The other sacrifices are performed for (the obtainment of) one (special) desire, (but) the agniṣṭoma for (the obtainment of) all [1].

1 Cp. a quotation in the Comm. of Sāyaṇa: *ukthyena paśukāmo yajeta ṣoḍaśinā vīryakāmo yajeta vājapeyenādhipatyakāmo yajeta*, and Āp. XIV. 1. 2.

3. The agniṣṭoma (comprises) twelve lauds, the year twelve months; in the course of the year the domestic animals bring forth, thereby it is conducive to cattle (and) successful.

4. There are twelve lauds (and) twelve recitations, that makes twenty-four; the year has twenty-four half-months: in the course of the year the animals bring forth, thereby it is conducive to cattle (and) successful.

5. On Agni the laud as well as the recitation reposes [1]; thereby it provides spiritual lustre.

[1] The last laud, the yajñāyajñīyastotra, is *āgneya* and thus also the last recitation: the āgnimāruta śastra.

6. 'Why is the jyotiṣṭoma called thus' they (the theologians) ask. When it is chanted through to the end, it becomes (equal to) the virāj [1] (and) the virāj is the light (*jyotis*) of the metres.

[1] The virâj is a metre of ten syllables (*daśākṣarā vai virāṭ*, Śat. br. I. 1. 1. 22) and all the stotriya verses of the whole jyotiṣṭoma are 190 in number (9 + 60 of the morning service, 15 + 68 of the midday service, 17 + 21 of the afternoon service), which number being dividable by 10, contains the number of syllables of the virāj, cp. Kauṣ. br. XV. 5: *virāḍ vā agniṣṭomo, navatiśatam stotriyāḥ saṃpadyante* and Jaim. br. 1. 235: *etad dha vai paramaṃ vācaḥ krāntaṃ yad daśety, etāvad dha paramaṃ vāk cakrame: tad yat paramaṃ vācaḥ krāntaṃ tat sarvam āpnavānīti*; .. *sā vā eṣaitāsām eva navatiśatasya stotriyāṇāṃ praśaṃsā, navatiśataṃ hy evaiṣo 'gniṣṭomaḥ saṃstutaḥ stotriyā bhavanti*; cp. also TS. VII. 1. 1: 'Light is generative; the light of the Gods is Agni; the light of the metres is the virāj, (the light) of the Word (is) the virāj; in Agni it (*i.e* the stotra destined for Agni) ends; it becomes the virāj; therefore (this Soma-rite) is called the agniṣṭoma, 'the Light-chant.' With this § cp. X. 2. 2.

7. A light among his equals becomes he who knows this [1].

[1] A light, as φάος = σωτηρία.

8. The agniṣṭoma, indeed, is the chief sacrifice [1].

[1] Or 'the sacrifice of the chief (God)' *viz.* Prajāpati, cp. TS. VII. 1. 1. 3-4: 'therefore they say: 'it is the chief sacrifice'. Prajāpati is the chief, for he sacrificed with it at the beginning.'

9. Prajāpati created the beings; these did not yield him the supremacy; he saw that agniṣṭoma and practised it. Thereupon the beings yielded him the supremacy.

10. Him his equals yield the supremacy, who knows this.

11. Now, as regards the saying: 'to the gāyatrī belongs the morning-service, to the triṣṭubh the midday-service, to the jagatī the afternoon-service,[1] where, then, (does) the fourth metre, the anuṣṭubh, (come in)?'

[1] This statement is found often e.g. TS. II. 2. 9. 5-6. Śat. br. IV. 2. 5. 20.—Strictly spoken, only the prātaḥsavana is chanted on verses in gāyatrī metre; the mādhyandina savana e n d s with a triṣṭubh and the tṛtīya savana with a jagatī, cp. Introduction to the edition of Ārṣeyakalpa, page XXIV. By a highly artificial reasoning the Jaim. br. (I. 242) reduces all the verses of the midday service to triṣṭubhs and all those of the afternoon service to jagatīs: 'of this agniṣṭoma, forsooth, the morning service results in gāyatrī, the midday service in triṣṭubh, the afternoon service in jagatī. The morning service results by itself wholly in the gāyatrī.—Four metres (convey) the midday service: the gāyatrī, the bṛhatī, the kakubh and the triṣṭubh. Of this kakubh of 28 syllables he puts 20 syllables on the gāyatrī and so this (gāyatrī) becomes a triṣṭubh (of 44 syllables); the remaining 8 (syllables of the gāyatrī) he puts on the bṛhatī (of 36 syllables) and so this (bṛhatī) becomes a triṣṭubh: the triṣṭubh (of the midday service) is (already) triṣṭubh.—Six metres (convey) the evening service: the gāyatrī, the uṣṇih and kakubh, the anuṣṭubh, the jagatī and the bṛhatī Of this gāyatrī of 24 syllables he puts 20 syllables on the kakubh (of 28 syllables), so this becomes a jagatī; the four remaining syllables he puts on the uṣṇih (of 28 syllables); this becomes an anuṣṭubh of 32 syllables; the anuṣṭubh is anuṣṭubh; this (anuṣṭubh) he divides in two equal parts and the 16 syllables (obtained in this manner) he puts on the anuṣṭubh (of 32 syllables), so this becomes a jagatī (32+16=48); the following one is of itself (already) a jagatī; the 16 remaining syllables he puts on the bṛhatī of the yajñāyajñīya; thence results a jagatī of 52 syllables (36+16): four too many for a jagatī; (these) are the four-footed animals, or the teats: the milking of the virāj, or the firm footing (the four feet of the domestic animals).' According to others, however, there are no four syllables left over; three of them are to be reckoned to the verses of the vāmadevya (SV. II. 32-34) and one to those of the yajñāyajñīya, the vāmadevya verses namely are short of three syllables in the padas *kas tvā satyo madānām, abhī ṣu ṇaḥ sakhīnām* and *avitā jaritṝṇām*; the yajñāyajñīya verses are short of one syllable in the pada *uta trātā tanūnām.*

12. Along with the suppression of the metres the Sacrificer is suppressed [1].

[1] And therefore the anuṣṭubh also ought to come in.

13. The gāyatrī has eight syllables, the *him*-sound is the ninth; the triṣṭubh has eleven syllables, and the jagatī twelve: by means of the metres he reaches the anuṣṭubh [1], in order that the Sacrificer may not be suppressed.

[1] Of 32 syllables: 8+1+11+12=32.

14. He forsooth, who knows the anuṣṭubh, coming along with the services, to reach everywhere[1] (to share in all), reaches everywhere (shares in all); the anuṣṭubh, indeed, coming along with the services, reaches everywhere; so he who knows this reaches everywhere (shares in all)[2].

[1] The Petersburgh Dict. takes *sarvatrāpi* as one word, an adjective, meaning 'reaching everywhere,' but from *sarvatrāsyāpi* it appears, that *sarvatrāpi* are two words.

[2] The precise meaning of this § is far from clear to me. The parallel passage of the Jaim. br. (I. 284) runs: 'he who knows the anustubh to reach everywhere, shares in all that is good: the gāyatrī is of 8, the triṣṭubh of 11, the jagatī of 12 syllables, the word 'voice' (*vāk*) is the nidhana of the yajñāyajñīya; that makes 32; the anuṣṭubh is of 32 syllables. She (the anuṣṭubh) shares in the morning service, in the midday service, in the afternoon service; she shares in the priesthood, in the nobility, in the peasantry; she shares in this world, in the intermediate region, in yonder world. He who knows the anuṣṭubh to share in all, shares in all that is good'. Probably we have here the compound *apibhavati*: from this *api* a quasi substantive is derived.

15. When the nobles undertake a journey, they yoke the strongest of their horses. The ninefold, fifteen-fold, seventeen-fold and twenty-one-fold, these are the strongest of the stomas, these he (the Chanter) yokes (*i.e.* applies), in order to reach the world of heaven.

16. It (*viz.* the agniṣṭoma-jyotiṣṭoma) is a catuṣṭoma[1]; the catuṣṭoma, forsooth, is a support[2]: in order to gain a support (it is practised).

[1] Comprising the (first) four stomas: trivṛt, pañcadaśa, saptadaśa and ekaviṃśa.

[2] Because of the number four (four feet of the animals).

VI. 4.

(The special functions of the Udgātṛ: the erection of the pillar.)

1. Prajāpati distributed the strength (life-sap, or food) to the Gods[1]; therefrom the udumbara came into existence. Related to Prajāpati, forsooth, is the udumbara, related to Prajāpati is the Udgātṛ. In that through his first[2] act the Udgātṛ takes hold of the pillar of udumbara (wood), he chooses by means of his own deity himself for the function of officiating priest[3].

[1] 'Udumbara (ficus glomerata) is *ūrj*', a common equation in the Brāhmaṇas, see VI. 4. 11 and Śat. br. III. 2. 1. 33, VI. 6. 3. 3: *tasmāt sa sarvārdraḥ sarvadā kṣirī,* further cp. TBr. I. 1. 3. 10: *'devā vā ūrjaṃ vyabhajanta; tata udumbara udatiṣṭhat.*

[2] The erection of the pillar is first act for which the Udgātṛ is required, see note 2 on the next §.

[3] The Udgātṛ not being 'chosen for the office, as are the other priests (cp. C. H. § 141. b); *vṛṇate 'nyān ṛtvijo nodgātā (ram)*, Jaim. br. I. 70.

2. He raises it (with the formula): 'Let Dyutāna[1], the son of the Maruts, raise thee; prop the sky! fill the air! make the earth firm'[2].

[1] Nitāna, Maitr. S., Kāṭh.

[2] See Lāty. I. 7. 1-3, Drāhy. II. 3. 1-3: 'When he (the Udgātṛ) is going to set up the pillar of udumbara wood, he should betake himself to the east of the sacrificial ground, if his dwelling be on the south of it, to the north of the sacrificial ground, if his dwelling be elsewhere (these restrictions are made to prevent the Udgātṛ from nearing the devayajana from the west side); (he should thereupon enter the sacrificial ground at the north side between utkara and cātvāla). Having entered (the sadas) *between the two holes destined for the doorposts of the sadas,* he should betake himself before (*i.e.* to the east of) the pillar of udumbara-wood (which is lying with its point to the east) and, standing with his face towards the north (and his back to the south), he should raise it, together with the Adhvaryu, with (the formula): 'Let Dyutāna thee.'—See the references in C. H. § 93. b.

3. He takes hold of it[1] with (the formula): 'I set thee in the seat of Āyu, in the shadow of the Favouring one[2], in the heart of the ocean'[2].

[1] Cp. Lāty. l. c. 4, Drāhy. l. c. 4.

[2] *i.e.*, according to Sāyaṇa, 'the protector of the sacrifice.'

4. Āyu, forsooth, is the sacrifice; for it this seat is prepared.

5. The sacrifice, forsooth, is the one that favours; for it this shadow is prepared.

6. In the middle of the trunk is the heart, therefore in the middle of the sadas the pillar of udumbara-wood is erected.

7. 'Salutation to the ocean! Salutation to the eye[1] of the ocean!' he says[2]; the ocean, forsooth, is the Voice, the eye[1] of the ocean is the Mind; to these two he thereby brings salutation.

[1] *cakṣuse, cakṣus,* although Lāty., Drāhy. and Jaim. śrs. have *caksase.*

2 'He', the Udgātṛ mutters this yajus after he has put down the pillar into the hole, Lāṭy. l. c. 5, Drāhy. l. c. 5.

8. 'May not Yūnarvan[1] leave me' he says; Yūnarvan, forsooth, is the sāman; being about to exercise his priestly function, he thereby brings salutation to the sāman.

1 The meaning of the word is unknown, Jaim. br. I. 70 has *yonorvāṃ*, Jaim. śrs. *yonorvā*. Sāyaṇa: *yūnardharcaḥ puruṣaḥ yūnarti prāpnotīti yūnarvā.*—The *viniyoga* of this yajus is the same as given under the preceding §.

9. He, who, having saluted the sāman in this manner, exercises with the sāman his priestlv function, is not deprived of the sāman, nor does the sāman repel him.

10. And he who curses him, comes to distress.

11. 'Strength art thou, the giver of strength; give me strength, put into me strength, give me food, put into me food'[1] (he says); the sadas, forsooth, is the belly of Prajāpati, the udumbara is strength; in that the (pillar) of udumbara-wood is created in the middle of the sadas, he brings to his children (and young ones) strength: food in the middle.

1 An *ity āha* or simple *iti* seems to be missing in the text. The *viniyoga* as under § 7.

12. Therefore, where this (pillar) becomes worn out[1], then the progeny becomes hungry.

1 According to Sāyaṇa this refers to the preceding formulas which accompany the setting up of the pillar: if it is set up w i t h these mantras, the pillar will n o t be worn out and the Sacrificer and his children and cattle will n o t suffer from hunger: *poṣukā ha tvai bhavanti*, Jaim. br. I. 71.

13. The food of the Gods is the sāman[1]; in the sāman (*i.e.*), in the food he thereby puts strength for the Gods and he himself. resting on strength[2], thereby distributes strength to his progeny.

1 Cp. Sāmavidh. br. I. 1. 2: *sa (prajāpatiḥ) vā idaṃ viśvaṃ bhūtam asṛjata, tasya sāmopajīvanaṃ prāyacchat.*

2 *ūrji śritaḥ*; in the Jaim br. I. 71 and in the Sūtras of Lāṭy. and Drāhy. the question is moved, whether the Udgātṛ must lean against the pillar, or not: *upaspṛśyā3ṃ nopaspṛśyā3m iti mīmāṁsante.* The conclusion of the Jaim. br. is: *upaspṛśya na svāspṛṣṭenaivodgeyaṃ*; perhaps we must restore *upaspṛśya svāspṛ°*: 'leaning lightly against it' because if he did not lean against the pillar, the Udgātṛ would exclude himself from food (=udumbara).

14. Sitting with his face directed to the north[1] chants the Udgātṛ; he thereby endows the northern quarter with strength. Sitting with his face directed to west[1] chants the Prastotṛ; he thereby endows the western quarter with strength. Sitting with his face directed to the south chants the Pratihartṛ; he thereby endows the southern quarter with strength. Directed to the east the other priests exercise their priestly functions[2]; therefore this one is the strongest of the quarters, for this (quarter) is favoured by the most (*i.e.* the plurality of the priests).

[1] The Sūtrakāras agree, with one slight exception: the Prastotṛ seats himself directed to the west, to the north the Udgātṛ; having gone behind (*i.e.* to the west of) the Udgātṛ, the Pratihartṛ seats himself, regarding the intermediate quarter: the south east, Lāṭy. I. 11. 9—21, Drāhy. III. 3. 28, cp. C.H. § 134. d.

[2] See *e.g.* Śāṅkh. I. 1. 13, Baudh. II. 2: 35. 18: *prāṅmukhaḥ..daivāni karmāṇi karoti.*

15. The theologians say: 'for which cause do the other officiating priests exercise their functions directed to the east but the chanters after they have turned round (to the) different[1] (quarters)?' 'For the seeking of the quarters, for the pleasing of the quarters' he should answer. Therefore food is found in all the quarters, for all the quarters are sought and pleased.

[1] Instead of *viparikramya* the Jaim. br. I. 72 has *viparyāvṛtya diśaḥ.*

VI. 5.

(Continuation: the placing of the droṇakalaśa, of the pressing stones, of the strainer; the pravṛta-oblations.)

1. Prajāpati desired: 'may I be more (than one), may I be reproduced'. He languished and out of the head of him who languished the sun was created (or 'came forth', 'came into existence'). This (sun) slew off his head[1]; that became the droṇakalaśa[2], therein the Gods took their soma-draughts. This woe, forsooth, he overlived by his life-time[3].

[1] In the Jaim. br. it is Agni, who, not wishing to be created out of the head of Prajāpati, throws up his brains (*mastiṣkaḥ*, but read perhaps *mastakaḥ* 'skull').

[2] Cp. Śat. br. IV. 4. 3. 4: *vṛtro vai soma āsīt. tam yatra devā aghnaṁs tasya mūrdhodvavarta, sa droṇakalaśo 'bhavat.*

[3] ? *āyuṣārtim atyajīvat.*

2. The woe he overlives by his life-time, who knows thus.

3. This (droṇakalaśa) he (the Udgātṛ) should push forward (muttering the formula): 'of the Lord of the forest (*i.e.* of wood) art thou; of Bṛhaspati art thou; of Prajāpati art thou; the head of Prajāpati art thou, the overliving vessel art thou, here I push myself forward in order to obtain glory and spiritual lustre'[1].

[1] See I. 2. 4, and C. H. § 130 and the references given there.

4. As to why he says: 'of the Lord of the forest art thou', he thereby pushes it forward in accordance with truth[1].

[1] The droṇakalaśa is actually made of wood: *vanaspatibhyo hy enam adhi kurvanti*, Jaim. br. I. 73

5. As to why he says: 'of Bṛhaspati art thou', he thereby appoints Bṛhaspati (as Udgātṛ), this God being the Udgātṛ of the Gods.

6. As to why he says: 'of Prajāpati art thou', the droṇakalaśa belongs indeed to Prajāpati by its deity.—As to why he says: 'the head of Prajāpati art thou', it is indeed the head of Prajāpati that was slain off.

7. As to why he says: 'the overliving vessel art thou', the droṇakalaśa surpasses indeed the other vessels[1], the droṇakalaśa that is the vessel of the Gods[2].

[1] Because, according to Jaim. br. I. 73, it is first of all the vessels taken in use and last of all 'loosened.'

[2] Cp. § 1.

8. Provided with the vessel of the Gods is he who knows this.

9. Regarding a Brāhmin whom he holds truly to be a Brāhmin, he should not make any consideration about the vessel[1]: he obtains the vessel of the Gods and is not deprived of that of men.

[1] *Viz.* 'he should not have doubts as to admitting him to the vessel.' Sāyaṇa takes *pātra* in the later sense of 'a fit or worthy person', but cp. Maitr. S. IV. 5. 5: 70. 11 (and Kāṭh. XXVII. 2, 139. 15, where *pātre na* instead of *pātreṇa* is to be read): *iyaṃ vai devapātraṃ, tad ya evaṁ veda pra vasīyasaḥ pātram āpnoti, brāhmaṇaṃ tu pātre na mimāṁseta yaḥ pātriya eva syāt.*—Weber, Indische Studien, Vol. X, page 47, takes *pātra* as '(common) meal.'

10. The Voice passed away from the Gods, it entered the Waters; the Gods claimed her back. They (the Waters) said: 'if we restore her, what would then be our share?' 'What you wish', they answered.

They said: 'what unclean substance man may throw into us, therewith may we not be mixed up.'

11. Pure (and) clean is water for him who knows this.

12. She, being restored (by the Waters to the Gods), passed beyond and entered into the trees; the Gods claimed her back, but they did not restore her; they cursed them: 'by means of your own handle[1] (as) a thunderbolt they will hew you.' Therefore they hew the trees by means of their own handle (as) a thunderbolt. For they had been cursed by the Gods.

[1] *i.e* of the axe to which a handle of w o o d is fixed.

13. The trees distributed her, (*i.e.*) the Voice, over four different objects: the drum, the lute, the axle, the reed-pipe[1]. Therefore this Voice of the trees (in the wooden instruments) is the loudest and most lovely; for it was the Voice of the Gods[2].

1 Thus according to Rudradatta on Āp. V. 8. 2: *tūnavo vaṃśaḥ*; according to Sāyana, on the contrary, it means: *dhanuṣi gune* 'in the bow-string'.

2 Cp. TS. VI 1. 4. 1: 'The Voice, not submitting to (be used at) the sacrifice, passed away from the Gods; she entered into the trees; this is the voice that is heard in the drum, the reed-pipe, the lute.' Maitr. S. III. 6. 8: 70. 16: 'The Voice, having been created, was split up four-fold, that part of her which prevailed entered into the trees; this is the voice in the axle, the drum, the reed-pipe, the lute'; cp. Kāṭh. XXIII. 4: 79. 9-11.

14. B e n e a t h the axle (of the Soma-cart) they push the droṇakalaśa forward: for the obtainment of this Voice (that is in the axle); a b o v e the axle they hand over the filtering cloth: from both sides they (thus) lay hold of the Voice[1].

1 'The Soma having been pressed, they (the Chanters) should lay hold of the droṇakalasa (which stands beneath the Soma-cart behind the axle) with (the formula): 'the vessel of righteousness art thou' (Pañc. br. I. 2. 4) and push it forward (underneath the axle, so that it comes to stand on the pressing stones which lay before the axle). In his left hand the Udgātṛ should take the fringed filtering cloth. If they should touch the axle (with the dronakalaśa, whilst pushing it forward), they should push it forward anew. Between the axle and the *viṣkambha, i.e.,* the pole (above the axle), on which the two shafts are fastened, they should push the fringed filtering cloth forward and lay it on the droṇakalaśa, taking care not to touch (the axle with their arms). Should they (the axle and the *viṣkambha*) be united (so that there is no room left), then (they should push it forward) above (the axle and the *viṣkambha*)', Lāṭy. I 9. 20-24 Drāhy. III, 1. 18-23.

15. (At the sacrifice of one) of whom he wishes 'may I make his sacrifice demoniac (*i.e.*, destined for the Asuras), may I possess myself of his (power of) speech' he should, whilst pushing the droṇakalaśa forward, touch the axle with his arms. Thus he make his sacrifice demoniac and possesses himself of his (power of) speech. (At a sacrifice of one) who is dear to him, he should push it forward without touching the axle. The droṇakalaśa is the breath; thus he brings his breathings in good order.

16. As to what they (the theologians) say: 'the other officiating priests being elected [1] by the Voice (by the Word), for which reason are the Chanters n o t elected before they exercise their priestly function?'

[1] The *pravara* here alluded to is described C. H. § 141 b.

17. In that they seat themselves near [1] the droṇakalaśa, thereby the Chanters are elected.

[1] *upasīdanti: prohanti*, Sāyaṇa but cp. the next §§. The verb *upasīdanti* is probably used here to denote all the acts with the droṇakalaśa which begin with their seating themselves turned to the east, cp. C. H. § 120 beg. and cp. § 125. 0.

18. To Prajāpati belong the Chanters, to Prajāpati belongs the droṇakalaśa; it is the droṇakalaśa that elects them for their priestly function.

19. Turned to the east they seat themselves near it, (thinking): 'we will, at the beginning of the sacrifice, undertake our function turned toward the east [1]'.

[1] During the chanting they are orientated differently (VI. 4 14), but by pushing the droṇakalaśa to the east, they also come, so to say, in the possession of this much desired region.

20. The easterly region, forsooth, is the unconquerable one of the Chanters; that they push the droṇakalaśa in easterly direction, is for conquering (this) region.

21. As to what they (the theologians) say: 'between the traces the horse is yoked, between the hames [1] the bullock; what is the yoking of the Chanters?' The fact that thy seat themselves near the droṇakalaśa is their yoking Therefore they (who are about to undertake a journey) should have (their draught-animals) yoked near them, for an unyoked (chariot) cannot convey.

[1] Read *śamye* instead of *śamya*.

VI. 6.

(Continuation.)

1. Having laid together the pressing stones, they shove on them the droṇakalaśa. The pressing stones are the peasantry[1], soma is the food, the droṇakalaśa is the nobility[2]. By shoving the droṇakalaśa on the pressing stones, they raise the nobility over the peasantry (*i.e.* they make the peasantry, the people, the Vaiśyas, subject to the Baron, the Kṣatriya).

[1] Simply because they also are a plurality.

[2] *rāṣṭram* is equivalent to *kṣatram*, cp. Ait. br. VII. 22. 6 : *kṣatram hi rāṣṭram* and cp. the often occurring phrase (*e.g.* T. S. III. 4. 8. 1) *rāṣṭraṃ bhavati* 'he obtains the reign over his subjects.' With our passage cp. Śat. br. III. 9. 3. 3.

2. For whom he hates he should put down the pressing stones with their faces[1] averted and then shove (the droṇakalaśa) away with (the formula): 'Here[2] I shove away (*i.e.* I separate), from the clan so and so, from the food thus and thus, so and so, the member of the Gotra so and so, the son of the mother so and so.' He thereby shoves him asunder (separates him) from the clan, from food.

[1] *mukha* 'face,' 'the thick end', cp. note 3 on § 5.

[2] Read here and § 3 *idam aham amum āmuṣyāyaṇam,* see Lāṭy. I. 10. 11, and *annādyān nirūhāmi* instead of *annādyāṃ ni°*.

3. For him who is dear to him, he should put down the pressing stones with their 'faces' towards each other and then shove (the droṇakalaśa) on (them) with (the formula): 'Here I put on the clan so and so, on food thus and thus, so and so, the member of the Gotra so and so, the son of (the mother) so and so.' He thereby puts him over the clan and in food.

4. But he may also disregard both (these practices) and shove (the droṇakalaśa) on (the pressing stones, whose 'faces' are turned to each other) with (the formula): 'Here I put myself in glory and spiritual lustre.' He thereby puts himself in glory and spiritual lustre.

5. For a noble whom he wishes to be slain by his clan, he should shove asunder the pressing stones, put the droṇakalaśa below[1] and lay on it the *upāṃśusavana*[2] with (the formula): 'Here I slay by the clan so and so the noble so and so.' He thereby slays the noble by the clan[3].

1 *i.e.* not on the stones but directly on the leather on which usually the stones are deposited.

2 The peculiar stone used for pressing the 'silent draught' of Soma, cp. C.H. §127c.

3 For the different practices mentioned VI. 6. 1—5 cp. Lāty. I. 10. 1-6, Drāhy. III. 2. 1-21: 'Having returned (to the place, where in the havirdhāna-shed the pressing is going to be performed) he should join together the pressing stones from right to left in the intermediate quarters, putting their thickest parts at the inner side; these thickest parts are 'the faces' (mentioned in the Brāhmaṇa VII. 2, 3: *vimukhān, saṃmukhān*), the first in the south-east; having touched them they should mutter (the formula) 'ye children of Marut' (Pañc. br. I. 2. 5). (So they should first lay down on the leather the first pressing stone with its thickest part turned to the middle, in the south-east; the second in the south-west, the third in the north-west, the fourth in the north-east). According to Dhānaṃjayya they should mutter this (formula) on the 'seat of righteousness' (*i.e.* on the same place where they have muttered t h i s formula, see note on I. 2. 2) and then (touch the stones) with (the last part of this formula, I. 2. 5): 'put to are ye, draw!' Thereupon they should shove the droṇakalaśa (on the stones) either from the west (to the east) or from the south (to the north), with (the formula: 'here I (push) this (Sacrificer)' (Pañc. br. I. 2. 6). The word '(this) Sacrificer' they should everywhere bring in in accordance with the facts (*i.e.* if the Soma-feast is a sattra, the word should be put in the plural). Should this act (of putting the droṇakalaśa on the stones) be performed by another, then they should mutter the two mantras (Pañc br. I. 2. 5 and 6) after (the act has been performed).' In no other of the ritual texts known to us, the putting of the droṇakalaśa on the stones is executed by any other than the Chanters; the *grāvṇāṃ saṃmukhakaraṇam*, on the contrary, is, according to the Adhvaryusūtras, done by the Adhvaryus (see *e.g.* Āp. XII. 12. 11, Baudh. VII. 6: 208. 11). This ritual regards the observances which are undertaken in view of certain wishes (Pañc. br. VI. 6. 2. 5), except the precepts given in the Brāhmaṇa (*i.e.* all that is said in the Sūtra of Drāhy. III. 2. 1-9, prevails also for the *kāmya* observances, but in these the special rules laid down in the Brāhmaṇa, *e.g.* the way of putting down the pressing stones, etc., are to be practised), except the ritual for one whom he hates (Pañc. br. VI. 6. 2). Here the order is to be reversed (*i.e* the laying down of the pressing stones is *prasavyam*: the first is laid down in the north-east, the second in the north-west, the third in the south-west, the fourth in the south-east, and the stones have their thick ends at the outer side) and without formulas (take place) the joining (of the stones) and the putting (of the dronakalaśa) on (them); moreover, he should with (the formula): 'here I (shove away) so and so' (P. Br. l. c.) shove away the droṇakalaśa to the south-west (*i.e.* the region of Nirṛti, 'Destruction'). The formulas for the enemy and friend (P.Br. VI. 6. 2 and 3) he should apply only for a king (in case the Yajamāna is a king) and he should indicate (instead of 'so and so') the name of his clan and this clan with the food (so the formula of the Brāhmaṇa (VI. 6. 3.): *idam aham amum āmuṣyāyaṇam amuṣyāḥ putram amuṣyāṃ viśy amuṣminn annādye 'dhyūhāmi,*

should run, *e.g.*, thus: *idam ahaṃ yudhiṣṭhiraṃ bhāratam kuntyāḥ putraṃ bhīmārjunādirūpāyāṃ viśi kurukṣetrarājyarūpe 'nnādye 'dhyūhāmi*). There is a fifth pressing stone, called *upāṃśusavana*; this he should put upon the droṇakalaśa, if he wishes to kill a noble, and he should indicate (by name) the neighbouring clan that is mighty (which should overcome the noble in accordance with the words of the formula; this last sūtra refers to P. br. VI. 6. 5). After he has practised one of these (*kāmya*'s, recorded in the Brāhmaṇa VI. 6. 2-5, exc. 4) he should, according to Gautama, perform the normal one; this one only (*i.e.* only the *kāmya*), according to Dhānaṃjayya; according to Śāṇḍilya he should perform the *kāmya* at the end of the pṛṣṭhas (*i.e.* at the end of the pṛṣṭha lauds, at the close of the midday service), having left (the sadas) by the eastern door.'

6. He, forsooth, who knows the divine purifiers, becomes purified (and) able to sacrifice. The divine purifiers, now, are the metres, by means of them they purify the droṇakalaśa.

7. 'Let the Vasus purify thee[1] with the gāyatrī-metre, let the Rudras purify thee with the triṣṭubh-metre, let the Ādityas purify thee with the jagatī-metre.' These (formulas) are the divine purifiers; purified (and) able to sacrifice is he who knows this.

[1] At I. 2. 7 these formulas are given with *sammṛjantu* instead of *punantu*; the formulas of the Jaim. br. are more in accord with P.Br. I. 2. 7: *vasavas tvā sammṛjantu gāyatreṇa chandasā*, etc. (Jaim. br. I. 8: and śrs. 9: 11. 3). Sāyana proposes to take *punantu* in our passage as a *vyākhyāna* of I. 2. 7, or to admit it as a *vikalpa*.—Lāṭy. I. 10. 17-19, Drāhy. III. 2. 22-26: 'With the strainer (*pavitra*) he should wipe the droṇakalaśa off, the bottom with (the formula): 'Let the Vasus,' the middle part with: 'Let the Rudras', the mouth (or upper part) with 'Let the Ādityas' According to Dhānaṃjayya he should with each of these three (formulas) wipe it off thrice at each service (with the first at the morning, with the second at the midday, with the third at the afternoon-service), according to Śāṇḍilya with all (the three) at each service, according to some with all (the three) the bottom, the middle and the upper part or (in reversed order) the upper part, the middle and the bottom.

8. The daemoniac Svarbhānu struck the sun with darkness; the Gods did not discern it (the sun, hidden as it was by darkness): they resorted to Atri; Atri repelled its darkness by the bhāsa[1]. The part of the darkness he first repelled became a black sheep, what (he repelled) the second time (became) a silvery (sheep), what (he repelled) the third time (became) a reddish one, and with what (arrow)[2] he set free its original appearance (colour), that was a white sheep[3].

[1] *bhāsena*; probably here also (as below, XIV. 11. 14) the sāman grāmegeyagāna XIII. 1. 5 is meant, although Sāyana does not say it. After all,

Hopkins (Transactions Conn. Acad. of Arts and Sciences, vol. XV, page 35) may be right in assuring that *bhāsa* originally meant 'lightening' and that the sheep may originate in an old error, *kṛṣṇāvir* having been taken as *kṛṣṇā avir* instead of *kṛṣṇā āvir*. The three kinds of sheep in the Jaim. br. are *kṛṣṇā, dhūmrā* and *phalgunā*.

2 The fem. *yayā* is somewhat doubtful; I suppose that *iṣuṇā* is to be supplied. Sāyaṇa interprets: *yena prayogeṇa*. If my interpretation is right, we have to imagine Atri as shooting with arrows towards the sun to drive away the daemon of darkness.

3 There are many parallels to this myth, which are collected by Oertel in J.A.O.S., Vol. XXVI, page 191. The chief are (besides Jaim. br. I. 80, 81) TS. II. 1. 2. 2, Maitr. S. II. 5. 2: 48. 11, Kāṭh. XII. 13: 175. 1. In these texts the fourth time an *avir vaśā* springs from that which the Gods had cut forth from the sun's *adhyasthāt* ('upper bone', 'cranium'?).

9. Therefore the strainer is white (*śukla*)[1], the soma is clear (*śukra*): for clear (soma's) congruity's sake.

1 On the strainer, made partly of white wool. cp. C. H. § 124, note 8, § 130, note 4.

10. (At a sacrifice) of one whom he (the Chanter) hates, he should make the two strainers (*pavitra*)[1] (partly) of those[2] colours; with a bad lot, with darkness he smites him, for darkness is black. (At a sacrifice) of one who is dear to him, he should make it purely white[3]; gold, forsooth, is light, he (thereby) brings light unto him.

1 On the two *pavitras* (one strainer, one purifier) cp. C. H. § 122, note 8.

2 Of those colours, *viz*. the colours other than white, mentioned in the preceding §.

3 *āsaktiśukla* cp. *āsaktipūnam* Śat. br. (Kāṇviya) I. 3. 1. 9, *āsaktisatyam āsaktyánṛtam*, Śat. br. IX. 5. 1. 17, which words perhaps are also compounds. In the Kāṇvīya recension of Śat. br. (IV. 6. 1. 7) *āsaktayaḥ* answers to *kevalyaḥ* of the Mādhy. recension.—On the whole cp. Jaim. br. I. 81: *sa yaṃ kāmayeta pāpīyan syād iti kṛṣṇam asya pavitre 'pyasyet*.

11. Therefore they seek the Ātreya by means of gold[1]; for Atri had set free its (the sun's) light[2].

1 Cp. C. H. § 191. c, Jaim. br. I. 80: *tad etad atrihiraṇyaṃ hriyate, śatamānaṃ ha sma purā hriyate, 'thaitarhi yāvad eva kiyac ca dadati*, Maitr. S. IV. 8. 3: 11. 1. (Kāṭh. XXVIII. 4: 158. 10): 'The daemoniac Svarbhānu struck the sun with darkness; Atri detected it; by giving gold to an Ātreya he repels darkness from himself.'

2 The first word of § 12 *abhyatṛṇat* belongs to § 11.

12. They spread out the strainer [1]; hereby a manual performance of the sacrifice is brought about; the spreading of the strainer, now, is the manual performance (that falls to the share) of the Chanters [2].

1 They spread the strainer over the droṇakalaśa, cp. C. H. § 130 and Lāṭy. I. 10. 20, Drāhy. III. 2. 27-28: 'having shaken the strainer they should spread it out with its fringed part to the north (*udīcīnadaśam* also Jaim. br. I. 81) and its central part (where the white wool is fixed) below, with (the verse, cp. Pañc. br. I. 2. 8): 'thy strainer'; with the three verses (beginning with the words 'thy strainer') according to some.' These *eke* do not refer to Pañc. br. I. 2. 8 but to SV. II. 225-227=ṚS. IX. 83. 1-3. The Jaiminīyas use either the tristich (Jaim. br. I. 81 and Jaim. śrs. 9: 11. 7) or one of the three verses, each for the obtainment of a different wish.

2 Otherwise it are the Adhvaryus only, to whose share fall the manual performances.

13. Not deprived of handicraft is he who knows this.

14. Him who does not spread out (the strainer) [1], they cut off from breath.

1 *i.e.* probably 'who does not stretch firmly his part of the strainer in holding it over the droṇakalaśa, but holds it loosely, unstably.'

15. He should say to him: 'shivering (by fever) will thou die'; he will die shivering.

16. With (the formula): 'Let the clear Goddess Prayer go forward from us, as a chariot well carpentered and swift' [1] the Udgātṛ addresses the stream (of Soma running through the strainer into the droṇakalaśa).

1 Pañc br. I. 2. 9. a.

17. 'For my long life become thou strained, for my glory become thou strained; of earth and sky the origin [1] they know; let hear the Waters that flow down. 'Sing thou, o Soma, here as Chanter,' he says, 'on my behalf, for glory and spiritual lustre' [2].

1 See note 1 on Pañc br. I. 2. 9.

2 These last words differ from I. 2. 9, but they may be intended as a kind of explanation of *āyuṣe* and *varcase*, and originally the yajus may have ended after *udgāya*.—For the act described in these two §§ cp. C. H. § 131 (page 161, middle) and Lāṭy. I. 10. 21-24, Drāhy. III. 2. 29-34: 'When the stream (of soma) flows continuously (through the strainer), the Udgātṛ should mutter (the formula): 'Let the clear' (I. 2. 9); with (the words): 'for the reign of so and so (i. e., end), he should (instead of 'so and so') indicate the name of the king who is dear to him, or (mutter) 'for the reign of the king' or 'for the reign of the Sacrificer, the king,' or

'for the reign of King Soma.' He should (rather) say only 'of Soma,' for the brāhmins have Soma (only) as their king.'

18. This, forsooth, is the Udgātṛ's chanting of the Soma, that he (Soma) is cleared (*i.e.* flows being cleared through the strainer); he (thus) chants a sāman at which Soma officiates as Udgātṛ.

19. They clear (it whilst it flows) continuously; they (thus) make the sacrifice as well as the breaths continuous. Uninterruptedly they clear it, for the continuity of the sacrifice.

VI. 7.

(Continuation.)

1. Bṛhaspati exercised the function of Udgātṛ (at the sacrifices) of the Gods; him the ogres sought to slay, but he had recourse, with a share (*i.e* offering a share), to the rulers of these worlds.

2. He sacrifices with (the formula): 'Let the sun protect me from the side of heaven, the Wind from those from the intermediate region, the Fire from those from the side of the earth, *svāhā!*'

3. These are the rulers of these worlds, to them he had recourse with a share.

4. Strong by his voice is he, no injury in the assembly[1] suffers he, who knows thus.

[1] *sadasyām ārtim ārchati*, an expression not occurring elsewhere, as far as I see, and unexplained by Sāyana.

5. The Voice went away from the Gods; the Gods addressed her; she answered: 'I am shareless; let me have a share.' 'Who could make a share for thee?' 'The Chanters' she said. It are the Chanters who make a share for the Voice.

6. He should sacrifice to her (muttering): 'Bekurā by name art thou; acceptable to the Gods; homage to the Voice! Homage to the Lord of the Voice! O Goddess Voice, what from thine (voice) is most sweet, therein place me. To Sarasvatī *svāhā!*'

[1] On this and the preceding §§ (Pañc. br. I. 3. 2 and 1) cp. C. H. 134. c. page 170 and Lāty. I. 11. 9, Drāhy. III. 3. 17: 'After the Adhvaryu has sacrificed, they should offer the two *pravṛta* offerings in the order of their entrance (firstly the Prastotṛ, then the Udgātṛ, then the Pratihartṛ) with (the formula): 'Bekurā by name art thou,' 'Let the Sun protect me.'—Note that in the Brāhmaṇa the

second mantra is given first, the first second; the Sūtrakāras adopt, as it seems, the sequence of the Jaim. br. (I. 82, 83).

7. Sarasvatī, forsooth, is the Voice, of her even he thereby lays hold by means of a share.

8. (At the sacrifice) of one whom he hates. he should, whilst offering this[1] oblation, think in his mind of the Voice; he thereby possesses himself of his (*viz.* the enemy's) Voice (power of speech).

[1] The last, *viz.* the one mentioned in § 6.—It is not certain whether our author intends to say, that in this case the mantra is to be muttered, or thought only.

(The out-of-doors-laud.)

9. They move[1] towards (the place where) the out-of-doors-laud (is going to be performed). They thereby move towards the world of heaven.

[1] See the note of Eggeling in Sacred Books of the East, Vol. XVI, page 299 and cp. C. H. § 134. c., Lāṭy. I. 11. 16-17, Drāhy. III. 3. 25, 26.

10. Somewhat stooping they move, for up-stream from here (from the earth), as it were, is the world of heaven[1], stealing along[2], as it were, they move; the sacrifice, indeed, is of the same nature as the deer—in order to soothe, to not terrify the sacrifice.

[1] Cp. Āp. XII. 17. 3-4. 'stealing along, as it were, licking (their mouths), as it were, bending their heads, as it were, they move; for the sacrifice is as a deer.' The sentence *pratikūlam iva hītaḥ svargo lokaḥ* occurs exactly so also T.S. VII. 5. 7. 4, Kāṭh. XXXIII. 7 : 33. 9; Jaim. br. I. 35: *pratikūla* (n. b. not '*kūlam*) *iva vā itaḥ svargo lokaḥ.—pratikūla* litt 'up-stream,' the journey to heaven being an ascension: when one goes up-stream he ascends along the bank.

[2] *i.e.* 'not making any noise with their feet.'

11. They restrain their speech[1]; the sacrifice they thereby restrain; did they break the silence, they would reveal the sacrifice; therefore the silence is not to be broken.

[1] They speak no profane words; the muttering of mantras is not forbidden.

12. Five officiating priests[1] move (towards the out-of-doors-laud), holding on to each other[1]; five-fold is the sacrifice[2]; as much as is the sacrifice, that they (thereby) connect together[3].

[1] The three Chanters preceded by the Adhvaryu and followed by the Brahman, cp. C. H. § 134. c, Lāṭy. I. 11. 2-6, Drāhy. III. 3. 11-13.

[2] Cp. Śat br. IV. 2. 5. 4.—The fivefoldness of sacrifice is proved, according to Sāyaṇa, by the following passage of the Taitt. saṃh. (VI. 5. 11. 4): 'The number five is reached neither by the verse, nor by the formula; what, then, is the fivefoldness of sacrifice? the *dhānās*, the *karambha*, the *parivāpa*, the *puroḍāśa* and the *payasyā* (cp. C. H. § 121), thereby the number five is reached, this is the fivefoldness of sacrifice.' Sāyaṇa on IX. 5. 11. explains: 'the three services, the avabhṛtha and the anūbandhya-cow', or 'the five: '*dhānāḥ*, *karambha*, *payasyā*, *parivāpa*, *puroḍāśa*'.

[3] Note the word *saṃtanvanti*, which also is the typical expression to denote the continuity of the priests in their procession to the bahiṣpavamāna (Lāṭy. I. 11. 2).

13. If the Prastotṛ is severed (if he lets go his hold of his foreman), the head of the sacrifice is severed. Having granted to the Brahman a boon[1], he himself[2] is to be chosen again. He thereby restores the severed head

[1] 'A cow' Sāyaṇa.

[2] *sa eva*, the Prastotṛ. I do not comprehend Sāyaṇa who says: *sa eva brahmā vartavyaḥ*.

14. If the Udgatṛ is severed, the Sacrificer is deprived of the sacrifice. This sacrificial rite is to be finished without sacrificial fees, and then it is to be performed anew; at this (new sacrifice) is to be given what he intended to give (at the original one).

15. If the Pratihartṛ is severed, the Sacrificer is deprived of his cattle; the Pratihartṛ, forsooth, is the cattle; (in this case) his (*viz.* the Sacrificer's) entire property is to be given; if he does not give his entire property, he is deprived of his all[1].

[1] With the last three §§ cp. the rules of Āp. XIV. 26. 3-6, Kāty. XXV. 11. 7-9, which these two authors have apparently taken from our Brāhmaṇa. Cp. also Upagranthasūtra I. 6 and Atharvaprāyaścittasūtra IV. 5: *bahiṣpavamānaṃ cet sarpatāṃ prastotā vicchidyeta, brahmaṇe varaṃ dattvā tatas tam eva punar vṛṇīyād; yad udgātā vicchidyeta, sarvavedasadakṣiṇena yajñena yajetaivam sarveṣām vicchinnānām sarpatām ekaikasmin kuryāt.*

16. The Adhvaryu bears the prastara (bunch of grass)[1].

[1] Cp. C. H. § 134.c (note 13).

17. The bunch of grass is the Sacrificer[1]; he thereby bears the Sacrificer to the world of heaven[2].

[1] A common equation, see *e.g.* Śat. br. I. 8. 3. 11.

[2] The moving to the bahiṣpavamāna is equal to an ascension to heaven, cp. VI. 7. 10.

18. The sacrifice, having taken the form of a horse, went away from the Gods; the Gods brought it to a standstill by a bunch of grass; therefore a horse being wiped with a bunch of grass, is pleased. That the Adhvaryu bears the bunch of grass, is for soothing, for not terrifying the sacrifice.

19. Prajāpati created the domestic animals; these, after being created, being hungry, went away from him. He presented them a bunch of grass as food; they turned toward him. Therefore the Adhvaryu must wave slightly the bunch of grass[1], for the animals turn to a (stalk of) grass that is being waved (before them).

[1] Cp. *e.g.* Baudh. VIII. 8: 212. 16, Āp. XII. 17. 4, Mān. śrs. II. 3. 6. 4.

20. Cattle will turn to him who knows this[1].

[1] The Sacrificer being equal to the prastara (§ 17).

21. He should chant after putting down the bunch of grass (on the ground), to prevent the sacrificial substance from being spilt[1].

[1] The prastara bunch usually is laid down on the vedi (Śat. br. I. 3. 3. 3) and on it afterwards the havis (the ājya or puroḍāśa) is deposited (see *e.g.* Śat. br. I. 3. 4. 14).

22. But (in doing so) he holds the Sacrificer away from the world of heaven[1].

[1] The prastara bunch, being the Sacrificer, is, by this act, l o w e r e d and put down on the ground, the earth.

23. He (the Udgātṛ) should chant whilst touching (it) with his knee; thereby the sacrificial substance is not spilt by him nor the Sacrificer held away from the world of heaven[1].

[1] The prastara rests with one of its ends on the ground (and the havis is not spilt), with its other end the Udgātṛ touches his knee, so that it points to the sky. Is this the meaning? As to the acts described in § 16 sqq. cp. Lāṭy. I. 12. 1-2, Drāhy. III. 4. 16-17 (C. H. § 134.c): '(When the Chanters are seated on the āstāva), the Prastotṛ, who has received (from the Adhvaryu) the prastara bunch, says: "Brahman, shall we chant, Praśāstr?" and hands it over to the Udgātṛ; with it he should touch the calf of his right leg and 'yoke' the laud with (the formula): 'with Agni's brilliancy' (Pañc. br. I. 3. 5).

24. They chant the out-of-doors-laud having looked towards the cātvāla. Here, forsooth, yonder sun was (once) (placed); by means

of the out-of-doors-laud the Gods bore it to the world of heaven In that they chant, having looked towards the cātvāla, they bear the Sacrificer to the world of heaven.

[1] Cp. Lāṭy. I. 11. 18, Drāhy. III. 3. 27; by the Jaiminīyas the looking towards the cātvāla is enjoined to the Sacrificer only. The corresponding passage of the Brāhmana (I. 87) runs: 'The sun (originally) was here on earth on the place of the cātvāla and yon (in the sky) was the fire. The Gods, being afraid lest it (the fire) burn down all, said: 'This (fire) will burn down all, let us make these two change their places.' By means of the (first) three verses of the out-of-doors-laud they raised it (the sun) from here, by means of the three (following verses) from the intermediate region and by means of the (last) three they made it ascend heaven... The Sacrificer whom they wish to reach the world of heaven, they should, before beginning the chant, cause to look towards the cātvāla'.—Śat. br. IV. 2. 5. 9: *atra ha vā asāv agra āditya āsa.*

VI. 8.

(The out-of-doors-laud, continued.)

1. 'He, in truth, can only be said to offer the sacrifice,' it is said, at the beginning of whose sacrifice they put the virāj[1] in.'

[1] The metre of ten syllables, cp. § 3.

2. They chant nine (verses), the *him*-sound is the tenth, of ten syllables is the virāj; they (thereby) put in the virāj at the beginning of his sacrifice.

3. They chant nine (verses); nine are the vital airs[1]; they make thrive his vital airs; the *him*-sound is the tenth; therefore the navel, being unpierced, is the tenth of the vital airs[2].

[1] Thus also Śat. br. I. 5. 2. 5; cp. note 1 on VI. 2. 2.

[2] This seems to be the only passage, where the navel is reckoned as a *prāṇa*; elsewhere (*e.g.* in the well-known mantra: *prāṇānām granthir asi*) it is called the knot of the vital airs.

4. They chant nine (verses): the Adhvaryu at the morning service draws nine (soma) draughts[1]; these they thereby strain, the vital airs of these they let loose[2].

[1] *Viz.*, the grahas which precede the out-of-doors-laud.

[2] What is the exact purport of these last words?

5. The *him*-sound is Prajāpati[1], the (verses) of the out-of-doors-laud are women[1]. By holding, after the sound *him* has been made, the

prastāva, he effectuates a copulation even at the beginning of his (the Sacrificer's) sacrifice, in order that he (the Sacrificer) may procreate.

[1] The word *hiṃkāra* being of masculine, the word *ṛcaḥ* of feminine gender.

6. The *him*-sound is the 'yoking' of the stoma; by holding, after the sound *him* has been made, the prastāva, he begins the chant with a 'y o k e d' stoma

7. The *him*-sound is the sap of the sāmans; by holding, after the sound *him* has been made, the prastāva, he begins the chant after moistening[1] these (*viz*, the verses of the out-of-doors-laud) with s a p.

[1] *abhyudya,* Sāyaṇa: *abhivandanam kṛtvā*! It is certainly the gerund of *abhyunatti.*

8. With regard to the wild animals they chant this out-of-doors-laud; they chant verses of one form[1]; therefore the wild animals are of one colour.

[1] They are all addressed to one deity: Soma.

[2] Of grey colour? Or has the word *rūpa* a wider sense?

9. They chant them thitherward (right off, *i.e.* without any returning, without any repetition) Therefore (the cattle) begets thitherward[1] and disperses thitherward.

[1] This alludes to the position in which the copulation of the animals comes to pass, in opposition of that of men: *samyañco bhūtvā dvipadā retaḥ siñcanti,* Ait. br. II. 38. 5.

[2] *Viz.* to the meadow, cp. TS.V. 2. 5. 4: *tasmāt parāñcaḥ paśavo vitiṣṭhante pratyañca āvartante.*

10. On the open[1] they chant; therefore the wild animals[2] live on the open[3].

[1] On a not enclosed spot, in contrast to the other lauds, which are all held in the (enclosed) sadas.

[2] With regard to which (see § 8) the bahiṣpavamāna is held.

[3] Litt.: 'are not enclosed.'

11. Out of doors they perform the laud. in-doors[1] they perform the subsequent recitation[2]; therefore they consume the (wild animals. the game) that have been brought to the village[3].

[1] Within the sadas.

[2] The Hotṛ and his assistants recite their śastras within the sadas.

[3] After the śastra the rests of the Soma-cups are consumed within the sadas.

12. In view of the domestic animals, forsooth, they chant the ājyas[1]; they chant verses of various forms[2]; therefore the domestic animals are of various forms (colours).

1 The ājyalauds, cp. VII 2. 6.

2 As they are addressed to different deities (Agni, Mitra-varuṇa, Indra, Indrāgni).

13. They chant (them, *viz.* the ājyalauds) constantly returning[1]; therefore the cows, having gone forth to freely roam about (on the meadows)[2], do return.

1 *i.e.* repeating: the ājya-and pṛṣṭhalauds are chanted on three verses, which are repeated in various ways, see chapters 2 and 3 and for our passage VII. 2. 6 end.

2 For *pretvan* cp. Acta Orientalia Vol. V, page 252.

14. On an enclosed (space) they chant (them *i.e.* the ājyas); therefore the domestic animals live on an enclosed space.

1 Within the sadas: *ājyāny antaḥsadasaṃ stuvanti*, Jaim. br. I. 106.

15. In view of yonder world they chant the (verses of the) out-of-doors laud; o n c e only for these is made the *him*-sound and they are thitherward directed (not repeated), for yonder world is once and for all away from here[1].

1 There is no return from yonder world: once and for all they depart from hence thither (*unde nefas redire quemquam !*) cp. the well-known phrase: *sakṛt parāñcaḥ pitaraḥ*.

16. In view of this world (the earth, earthly existence) they chant the ājya(laud)s; they chant them constantly returning; therefore this world is again and again returning[1].

1 The creatures procreate themselves constantly.

17 'Thitherward directed are the vital airs of those'[1], it is said, 'who chant the (verses) of the out-of-doors-laud thither directed' (*i e.* without repetition, straight off). He should (therefore) chant as last (verse) one containing (the word) 'hither'[2], for the retainment of his vital airs.

1 If the vital airs do not return into the body, death needs must follow.

2 SV. II. 9, finishing: *agmann ṛtasya yonim ā*.

18. 'They, forsooth, vanish from this world,' it is said, 'who chant the (verses) of the out-of-doors-laud thither directed'; he should chant the last (verse) with the sounds (*i.e.* after the manner) of the rathantara [1]: the rathantara is the earth [2]; he thereby retains a firm support on the earth.

[1] Cp. Lāṭy. I. 12. 10-11, Drāhy. III 4. 24-25: 'the last verse, which has the peculiarities of the rathantara, dismisses not its *him*-sound (*i.e.* instead of *hum ā*, the pratihāra of the bahiṣpavamānastotra, cp. C.H. § 14, note 36, only *hum* is chanted); the four syllables after the prastāva of this verse he should replace by a stobha' *viz.* (cp. Lāṭy. VII. 11. 6) by the stobha *bhā*. The prayogas consulted by me (see C. H. § 134 g, page 179) take no notice of this peculiarity. The peculiarities to be observed at the chanting of the rathantara are treated below, VII. 7. 9, sqq.

[2] That the rathantara is equated to the earth and the bṛhat to the sky, is common in the Brāhmaṇa literature, see *e.g.* Śat. br. I. 7. 2. 17.

VI. 9.

(The verses of the out-of-doors-laud.)

1. (The tristich beginning) 'Sing ye, o men, unto (*upa*) him' [1] he should take as opening one for one who is desirous of a village [2].

[1] SV. II. 1-3=ṚS. IX. 11. 1-3.

[2] *i.e.* of the supremacy over the inhabitants of his village.

2. The 'men' [1] are the village belonging to the Gods, he (thereby) drives unto (*upa*) him a village [2].

[1] Mentioned in the verse.

[2] *i.e.* he subjugates to him the inhabitants of the village.

3. The food is 'unto' (*upa*): food he drives unto him.

4. (The tristich beginning:) 'Unto (*upa*) the born active' [1] he should take as opening one for one who is desirous of offspring.

[1] SV. II. 685-687=ṚS. IX. 61. 13-15.

5. The offspring is 'unto' (*upa*); this by the word 'born' he produces [1].

[1] On §§ 4-5 cp. the Kṣudrasūtra (I. 1, n° 2): 'for one who is desirous of offspring the stotriya (tristich) is the one (beginning): 'unto the born active'; the Brahman's chant (the third pṛṣṭhalaud) is the first janitra melody composed on 'not you in the least even' (SV. I. 241=ṚS. VII. 59. 3) (the melody of grāmegeya VI. 2. 18) chanted on the verses of the naudhasa (SV. II. 35-36); the viṣṭuti, from

the Hotṛ pṛṣtha (stotra) onward, is the middleless seventeenfold stoma (Pañc. br. II. 10 and cp. especially II. 10. 3); the rest is similar to the Jyotiṣṭoma.

6, 7*a*. (The tristich beginning) 'Be thou clarified for the weal of our cow'[1] he should take as opening one in a year in which the Great God[2] slays his cattle.

1 SV. II. 3, 2, 1=ṚS. IX. 11. 3, 2, 1 see note on § 9.

2 Rudra.

7*b*. By (the words): 'be thou clarified for the weal of our cow' he heals his quadruped(s).

8. By (the words). 'for the weal of our people' (he heals) his biped(s), 'for the weal of our runner' (he heals) his one-hoofed animal(s).

9. Smeared with poison, forsooth are the herbs in that year, in which the Great God slays the cattle. By saying: 'for the weal, o King, of our herbs' he makes the herbs palatable for him; both kind of herbs ripen and become palatable for him: the kind that ripens uncultivated as well as the kind that ripens cultivated[1].

1 On §§ 6-9 cp. Kṣudrasūtra (I. 1, no. 3): 'in which year the Great God slays his cattle, the opening tristich (are the verses): 'be thou clarified for the weal of our cow' in reversed order (cp. Lāṭy. VI. 3. 2); the Brahman's chant is the ātharvana melody (araṇyegeya I. 1. 23) chanted on the naudhasa verses; the *viṣṭutis* are the ascending ones (optionally, Pañc. br. II. 12, or II. 15, or III. 2); the rest is similar to the Jyotiṣṭoma.'

10. (The tristich beginning) 'Be clarified as the foremost of speech'[1] he should take as opening one for one whom he wishes to become excellent among his equals

1 SV. II. 125-127=ṚS. IX. 62. 25-27.

11. By (the words): 'be clarified as the foremost of speech' he brings him round to the foremost point.

12. The foremost point is excellency; he brings him[1] to excellency[2].

1 Read: *śriyam evāsmin dadhāti.*

2 On §§ 10-12 cp. Kṣudrasūtra (I. 1, No. 4): 'for one who desires excellency the opening (tristich) is the one containing (the word), 'foremost'; the ājyalauds are connected with the bṛhat (cp. Ārṣeyakalpa page 33, note 3); the Hotṛ's pṛṣṭha (laud) is the bṛhat; the Brahman's pṛṣṭha (laud) is the śyaita; on the uṣṇih-part (in the ārbhavapavamāna laud) is chanted the śrudhya; the rest is similar to the jyotiṣṭoma.'

13. (The tristich beginning), 'these Soma-drops have effused'[1] he should take as opening one for a plurality (of Sacrificers)[2].

[1] SV. II. 180-182=ṚS. IX. 62. 1-3.

[2] Cp. note 3 on § 23 and Jaim. br. I. 94: *bahūnāṃ saṃyajamānānām.*

14. By (the word) 'these' he addresses them all; for (their) welfare[1], (their) prosperity.

[1] Read *ṛddhyai* instead of *ṛddhai.*

15. By (the word) 'these' Prajāpati created the Gods; by (the words) 'have effused' (*asṛgram*) he created (*asṛjata*) men, by (the word) 'Soma-drops', the Fathers; by (the words) 'through the strainer'[1], the Soma-draughts; by (the word) 'swift', the laud; by (the word) 'all', the recitation; by (the words) 'unto riches', the other creatures[2].

[1] Read *pavitram iti* instead of *pavitra iti.*

[2] Sāyaṇa explains this exposition of creation by all kinds of fanciful etymologies and combinations.

16. In that (he said): 'these', therefore all the Gods that (were) in the beginning, (exist) even now.

17. And they enjoyed all possible prosperity[1]; for stationary is this word[2].

[1] Read *sarvām v ṛddhim ārdhnuvant sthi*.

[2] The purport of these two §§ is not clear to me.

18. In that (he said): 'have effused', therefore men are created[1] day by day.

[1] *sṛjati* meaning as well 'to effuse, to emit' as 'to create'.

19. In that (he said): 'Soma-drops', the Fathers namely are, as it were, the Soma-drops[1].

[1] Perhaps the author had in mind the well-known attribute of the Pitaras: *somyāsaḥ.*

20. (For they are) 'mind' (only), as it were[1].

[1] Being only perceptible by the mind, not by the eye. The equation *mana iva pitaraḥ* being comprehensible, it is not intelligible how the *indavaḥ* can be compared to *manas.* Sāyaṇa quotes from Chānd. up. (VI. 5. 4): *annamayaṃ hi saumya manaḥ,* but here *saumya* is a vocative and has no relation to *manaḥ.*

21. The prosperity enjoyed by those creatures after they were created, falls to the share of those for whom he (the Udgātṛ), thus knowing, takes this (tristich) as opening one.

22. The metres, forsooth, fetched the Soma; the Gandharva Viśvāvasu stole it (from them) and with it entered the water; the Gods sought after it, Viṣṇu spied it in the water; he doubted: 'Is it he (the Soma) or not?' 'He poked it with his foot and from it (from the Soma thus poked) drops effused; he announced to the Deities who stood near: 'These Soma-drops have effused.' Through the out-of-doors-laud, verily, the Sacrificer comes into existence; in that he chants (as prastāva) the words: 'These Soma-drops have effused', he announces to the Deities the sacrifice that has come into existence[1].

[1] Just as Viṣṇu announced to the Deities that he had found out the Soma in the water. On the myth of the stolen Soma cp. Lévi, la doctrine du sacrifice dans les Brāhmaṇas, page 32, and below, VIII. 4. 1.

23. Deprived of prosperity and not conducive to cattle, verily, is the morning service, for it is devoid of *iḍā*[1]; by saying: 'the *iḍā* for us uninterruptedly'[2] he makes the morning service provided with *iḍā* and with cattle[3].

[1] In the chants of the morning service the finale is not, as mostly otherwise, *iḍā* (but *ā*). Note the well-known equation *iḍā vai paśavaḥ*.

[2] Third pada of the last verse in the same stotriyatṛca (cp. VI. 9. 13).

[3] To §§ 13-23 refers the Kṣudrasūtra (I. 1, n°. 5): 'for a plurality of Sacrificers (i.e. in a sattra) who are not friendly disposed to each other, the stotriya (tristich of the out-of-doors-laud) is: 'these Soma drops are effused'; the *viṣṭuti* for the pṛṣthastotra is the *saptāsthuā* belonging to the seventeenfold one (Pañc. br. II. 9, especially § 3); the rest is similar to the jyotiṣṭoma.'

---

24. (The tristich beginning): 'By fiercely brilliant lustre'[1] he should take as opening one for a joined group (of Sacrificers)[2].

[1] SV. II. 4-6=RS. IX. 64. 28-30.

[2] See note 1 on § 26.

25. (The words): 'by fiercely brilliant lustre' represent the gāyatrī[1]; (the words): 'by loudly sounding' (represent) the triṣṭubh[2]; (the word) 'voice'[3] (represents) the anuṣṭubh[3]; (the words) 'the Soma-(draughts) (are) bright, mixed with the milk' (represent) the jagatī[4]. This (verse) represents all the metres; the metres, forsooth, are a

joined group as it were; by taking this (tristich) as opening one, he makes them prosper by their own feature [5].

[1] For the gāyatrī is splendour and spiritual lustre, it is said in the holy script (Ait. br. I. 5. 2).

[2] A pun on the root *stubh* in *pari ṣ ṭ o b h ayantyā* and *tri ṣ ṭ u b h*.

[3] I have rendered *kṛpā* by 'voice' in accordance with Sāyaṇa *kṛpeti vāṅnāma*, and *vāg ghy anuṣṭup* (Śat. br. III. 1. 4. 2.).

[4] The point of agreement between the jagatī and the pada *scmāḥ śukrā gavāśiraḥ* is, according to Sāyaṇa, that both: the word *jagatī* and the word *gavāśiraḥ* have in common the syllable *ga*; for another explanation see note 1 on XII. 1. 2.

[5] 'Feature' or 'nature.'

26. A joined group, verily, is devoid of courage and strength; the metres are courage and strength; he makes them possessed of courage and strength [1].

[1] To § 24-26 refers the Kṣudrasūtra (I. 1, no. 6): 'for a plurality of Sacrificers, who are friendly disposed to each other, the stotriya (tristich) is 'by fiercely brilliant lustre'; 'sing ye unto him' (SV. II. 1-3) is the corresponding (tristich); the *viṣṭuti* for the pṛṣtha-laud is the *saptāsthitā* belonging to the seventeenfold stoma; the rest is similar to the jyotiṣṭoma.'

VI. 10.

(The verses of the out-of-doors-laud, continued.)

1. (The tristich beginning) 'Agni, thou purifyest the lives' [1] he should take as opening one for those dīkṣitas amongst whom one dies.

[1] SV. II. 868-870=ṚS. IX. 66. 19-21.

2. Unclean, as it were, are the dīkṣitas amongst whom one dies; in that the opening (tristich) is addressed to Agni pavamāna, Agni drives away from them the heat (the defilement) and the wind (or Soma pavamāna) purifies them [1].

[1] Cp XVI. 5. 9, 10.

3. In saying 'the lives' he puts life [1] into them who are living [2].

[1] *Viz.* the normal lease of life, so that they do not die of any other cause than old age.

[2] The same matter is treated more fully IX. 8.—To § 1-2 refers the Kṣudrasūtra (I. 1, No. 7): 'when a dīkṣita has died, the opening (tristich) is: 'O Agni, thou purifyest the lives' except on the days at which a transposition (of metres:

stotras and śastras) takes place; if he dies on (one of) the days at which a transposition takes place, the tristich of t h a t day, on which the tristich in gāyatrī-metre is the opening one, is to be taken as opening one, with the exception of the udayanīya atirātra; the rest is similar to that (day)

---

4. (The tristich beginning): 'For us, o Mitra and Varuṇa'[1] he should take as opening one for one suffering from a lingering disease.

[1] SV. II. 13-15=ṚS. III. 62. 16-18.

5. Gone away are the out- and inbreathing of him, who suffers from a lingering disease; Mitra and Varuṇa are the out- and inbreathing[1]; out- and inbreathing he (thereby) puts into him[2].

[1] Cp. Śat. br. VIII. 4. 2. 6: *prāṇo vai mitro 'pāno varuṇaḥ*.

[2] To §§ 4, 5 refers Kṣudrasūtra (I. 2, No. 7, 8): 'for one who suffers from a lingering disease the out-of-doors-laud consists of the tristichs: 'for us, o Mitra and Varuṇa' (II. 13–15), 'by fiercely brilliant lustre' (II. 4–6), 'from thee, that art being clarified, o Sage' (II. 7-9=ṚS. IX. 66. 10-12): or the opening (tristich of the out-of-doors-laud) is to be composed of different parts of the Veda (*saṃbhārya* cp. Introduction, Chapter II) (and to comprise the following verses): 'for us, o Mitra and Varuṇa' (II. 13), 'be clarified as the foremost of speech' (II. 125), and 'sing ye unto him, o men' (II. 1); 'o Agni, come hither to the feast' (II. 10–12) is (the Hotṛ's ājya-laud): the rathantara one (see note 4 on page 33 of Ārṣeyakalpa); the three other ājya-lauds are the bṛhat ones (see ib.); or the first two are the bṛhat ones (the first being II. 140–142) and the last two the rathantara ones. (In the midday-service) on 'being clarified by the stream' (II. 25–26) are chanted the raurava, the yaudhājaya and the dairghaśravasa (or instead of this last the udvat prājāpatya); these are ekarcas; the rathantara on three (verses) (II. 25–26); the bṛhat is the Hotṛ's pṛṣṭhalaud, the traiśoka the pṛṣṭha-laud of the Brāhmaṇācchaṃsin, and the kāleya is chanted on 'they all have magnified Indra' (II. 177-179). On 'entice the withdrawing' (II. 111=ṚS. IX. 19. 6) the sapha (is chanted), the śrudhya on the uṣṇih-part. He puts the two kakubhs at the end of the rathantara (the exact meaning of these words, which recur No. 39, is not clear to me; probably they refer to the chanting of the rathantara on *punānaḥ soma dhārayā*). The *viṣṭuti* is the *brahmāyataniya* of the seventeenfold stoma (Pañc. br. II. 8. 2) for the Hotṛ's pṛṣṭhalaud, and the ascending one belonging to the twenty-one-fold (Pañc. II. 1) for the agniṣṭoma chant. The rest is similar to the jyotiṣṭoma.'

---

6. (The tristich beginning): 'Driving away the enemies thou art strained, away, o Soma, the envious'[1] he should take as opening one for one who is calumniated falsely.

[1] SV. II. 563–565=ṚS. IX. 61. 25–27. The verse is quoted here by a longer pratīka than is usual and strictly necessary, because of its tendency.

7. Envious verily are they, who calumniate falsely; these he drives away from him.

8. By (the words): 'going to Indra's agreed place' he causes him to go, cleaned [1] (of the false imputation) and fit for (taking part at) the sacrifice, to Indra's agreed place [2].

[1] Note the pun '*pūtam*' with reference to *pavase* of the verse.

[2] To §§ 6–8 refers the Kṣudrasūtra (I. 2, No. 9): 'for one who is calumniated falsely the stotriya-tristich is 'driving away the enemies thou art strained'; on the verses of the naudhasa is chanted as pṛṣṭha-laud for the Brāhmaṇācchaṃsin the śuddhāśuddhīya which has a pada for nidhana; the *viṣṭuti* for the agniṣṭoma-chant is the 'lamp' belonging to the twenty-one-fold stoma (Pañc. br. II. 17, see especially § 4). The rest is similar to the jyotiṣṭoma.'

---

9 (The tristich beginning): 'Be thou, a bull, strained by the stream' [1] he should take as opening one for a noble. The noble, forsooth, is a bull; he (thereby) makes him a bull.

[1] SV. II. 153–155=ṚS. IX. 65. 10–12.

10. By (the words): 'and jovial to (Indra) accompanied by the Maruts', the Maruts being the peasantry [1] of the Gods, he attaches the peasantry to him; the peasantry does not desert him.

[1] Or 'the clans, the subjects, the people.'

11. By (the words) 'possessing thyself of all thine might' he by might, by courage afterwards [1] encompasses for him the peasantry; the peasantry does not desert him [2].

[1] *parastāt* the text, *purastāt* Sāyaṇa.

[2] To §§ 9–11 refers the Kṣudrasūtra (I. 2, No. 10): 'for a Sacrificer who is a king, the opening stotriya (tristich) is 'be thou, a bull, strained by the stream'; the pṛṣṭha-laud of the Brāhmaṇācchaṃsin is the vṛṣan-sāman chanted on the verses of the śyaita, the e k a vṛṣa-sāman, if he is a s o l e king. The rest is similar to the ritual of one who is desirous of excellency' see Kṣudrasūtra I. 1, No. 4 as quoted in note 2 on VI. 9. 12.

---

12. (The tristich beginning): 'Be thou, a bull, o Soma, strained after being pressed' [1] he should take as opening one for one who desires: 'may I fare well in the foreign country' [2].

[1] SV. II. 128–130=ṚS. IX. 61. 28–30.

[2] Or, perhaps: 'may I fare well amongst men' *i.e.* in the assembly; cp. the author's paper 'Altindische Zauberei' (Wunschopfer) note 36 on page 6.

9

13. By (the words), 'make us honoured among men' he will fare well in the foreign country[1].

[1] To §§ 12, 13 refers the Kṣudrasūtra (I. 2, No. 11): 'for one who desires to fare well in a foreign country, the (opening) stotriya (tristich) is 'be thou, a bull, o Soma, strained after being pressed'. The rest is similar to (the ritual of) one who is desirous of excellency', cp. note 2 on § 11.

14. (The tristich beginning): 'You both are Lords of light'[1] he should take as opening one for two (Sacrificers); he (thereby) causes them to participate equally in the sacrifice: he bestows[2] upon both of them the glory of the sacrifice[3].

[1] SV. II. 351, 350, 349=ṚS. IX. 19. 2, 3, 1. (*svaḥpatī* SV., *svarpatī* ṚS). Originally the author of the Brāhmaṇa may have meant the Ṛgveda-verses IX.19. 2-4 and the reading *svaḥpatī* may have been introduced afterwards, in accordance with the gāna.

[2] *arpayati*.

[3] To §§ 13, 14 refers the Kṣudrasūtra (I. 3, No. 12): 'for two Sacrificers the opening stotriya (tristich) is, in reversed order 'you both are Lord of light'; on 'being clarified by the stream' (II. 25–26) are chanted the raurava, yaudhājaya and dairghaśravasa (or udvat prājāpatya) as ekarcas; on these (verses) the first aśvinor vrata; on 'by fore conquest, from your (Soma) plant' (II. 47-49), the śyāvāśva, the āndhigava, the audala, as ekarcas; on three (verses) the last aśvinor vrata. The rest is similar to the jyotiṣṭoma.'

15. (The tristich beginning): 'The streams have flowed forward'[1] he should take as opening one for one who is desirous of rain.

[1] SV. II. 1115–1117=RS. IX. 29. 1–3.

16. By (the words): 'the streams have flowed forward' he causes the rain to fall from heaven; by (the words): 'of the bull that with vigour has been pressed' (he causes it to fall) from the intermediate region.

17. By (the words): 'that presents itself to the Gods' he brings it down on the earth.

18. By means of vigour, of strength, is given forth what (after being promised or due) is held back; by (saying): 'of the bull that with vigour has been pressed' he procures to him by means of vigour, of strength, the rain from heaven[1].

[1] To §§ 15–18 refers the Kṣudrasūtra (I. 3, No. 13): 'for one who wishes to obtain rain the (opening) (stotriya tristich) is: 'the streams have flowed forth';

on 'being clarified by the stream, o Soma' (are chanted) the raurava, yaudhājaya and dairghaśravasa (or udvat prājāpatya) as ekarcas; on (all the) three (verses), the first apām vrata; on the verses of the naudhasa as pṛṣṭha-laud of the Brāhmaṇācchaṃsin, the saubhara with hīṣ as nidhana (cp. below, VIII. 8. 19); on 'by fore-conquest, from your (Soma) plant', the śyāvāśva, the āndhigava and the audala as ekarcas; on all three, the last apām vrata. The rest is similar to the jyotiṣṭoma.'

---

19. (The tristich beginning): 'Become thou strained by this stream, by which the cows may come hither, the alien ones, to our dwelling'[1] he should take as opening one for one who desires that alien cows may fall to his lot, that his dominion may obtain alien cows; by the fact that this (tristich) is the opening one, the alien cows fall to his lot, his dominion obtains alien cows[2].

1 SV. II. 786-788=ṚS. IX. 49. 2-4.

2 To this § refers the Kṣudrasūtra (I. 3, No. 14): 'for one who desires alien cows, the (opening) stotriya (tristich) is: 'become thou strained by this stream, by which alien cows may come hither'; on 'being strained, o Soma, by the stream' (are chanted) the raurava, the yaudhājaya and the dairghaśravasa (or udvat prājāpatya) as ekarcas; on (all) three, the first gavām vrata; on the verses: 'verily thou shalt extol' (SV. I. 247=II. 1073-1074=ṚS. I. 84. 19-20), the traikakubha is chanted as pṛṣṭha-laud for the Brāhmaṇācchaṃsin; on 'by the most sweet, most intoxicating' (SV. II. 39-41=ṚS. IX. 1. 1-3), the gāyatra, the saṃhita and the satrāsahīya as ekarcas; on (all) three the last gavām vrata. The rest is similar to the jyotiṣṭoma.'

Seventh Chapter.

VII. 1.

(The gāyatra-sāman on which the out-of-doors-laud is chanted.)

1. The gāyatra is (equal to) these (three) worlds (earth, intermediate region, sky)[1]; the chant belonging to it is to be performed in three sections[2]; for three in number are these worlds; by chanting (the gāyatra) in three sections, he makes him[3] equal to these three worlds.

1 Usually the gāyatrī is identified with the earth, the triṣṭubh with the intermediate region and the jagatī with the sky.

2 *āvṛt* is a part of the udgītha; to this Brāhmaṇa refers Lāṭy. VII 10. 21, according to which passage the udgītha, *e.g.* of S.V. II. 1, which runs in the ārcika *pavamānāyendave* | *abhi devām̐ iyakṣate*, is to be divided into three āvṛts in

the following manner: 1. *pā2va2 mānāyendāvā 2*; 2. *abhi devāṁ iyā 1212*; 3. *kṣāto*. Cp. also Jaim. br. I. 111 and Jaim. up. brāhm. III. 11. 5, III. 39. 2 (*tad etat tryāvṛt tryudānaṃ gāyati*.

[3] The Sacrificer.

2. Twice he should stretch the tone, the third (time) he should make *him*[1].

[1] *avanardati* according to Sāyaṇa is equivalent to *avasvarati* and consists in a lowering of the musical tone by one interval; probably *avanardana* has the same value as the later term *karṣaṇa*, and especially the first kind of *karṣaṇa* designated *e.g.* by $\overset{1}{\text{ā}}$2, see R. Simon in his Introduction to the Puṣpasūtra, page 519 (cp. also C. H page 466). Now, as the *him* sound is always chanted thus: $\overset{1}{\text{hūm}}$ *ā 2*, it appears that in the gāyatra-chant this *avanardana* takes place three times. The ritualistic authorities have always been at variance about the question as to how the *avanardana* is to be practised the first two times: "the first two sections (*āvarga*=*āvṛt*) are to be 'stretched', according to Dhānaṃjayya; in the middle section he should put in two stobhas, and these are to be 'stretched' according to Gautama, *e.g. abhi devāṁ* $\overset{2}{\text{iyā}}$ *1212*" (see Sāyaṇa on Pañc. br. VII. 1. 2), Lāṭy. VII. 10. 22–24. It seems that the usual way of chanting the gāyatra is the one recommended by Gautama, it is found in all the prayogas. The expression: 'he should put in two stobhas' may be understood, if we consider that all the words of the udgītha are replaced by the syllable *o*, which can be considered as a stobha.

3. In that he stretches thrice[1], he thereby makes the gāyatra redundant.

[1] Cp. note 1 on the preceding §. The purport of this § is far from clear to me.

4. He who chants an unresponded gāyatra[1], has no firm support; the response of the gāyatra is the *him*-sound.

[1] *i.e.* a gāyatra without response, without pratihāra.

5. It is to be thought mentally; he thus chants a responded gāyatra and gains a firm support[1].

[1] To this § refers Lāṭy. VII. 11. 3–5: 'after the *retāsyā* (verse, *i.e.* the first verse of the out-of-doors-laud) he should, leaving over two syllables (*i.e.* before the last two syllables) utter the *him*-sound: $\overset{1}{\text{hūm}}$ *ā 2*; this *him*-sound the Pratihartṛ should think mentally in the *retasyā*, not in the other (verses), according to Gautama; in the other verses (only), not in the *retasyā*, according to Dhānaṃjayya and Śāṇḍilya,' cp. also Lāṭy. I. 12. 8, 9: 'the first verse, the *retasyā* is devoid of *him*, the other verses are provided with it'. Lāṭyāyana, then, accepts the view of Gautama, the words of the Brāhmaṇa leaving it open to doubt; Ṣaḍv. br. II. 1. 4:

na hiṃkuryād seems to refer equally to the *retasyā* only, cp. also Jaim. br. I. 100: *na hiṃkuryād, yad dhiṃkuryād vajreṇa hiṃkāreṇa reto vicchindyāt*, and Jaim. śrs. 11: 13. 9.

6. He who chants the gāyatra in view of these worlds, is not severed from these worlds; for his sake these worlds clothe themselves with strength (or 'food')[1].

[1] *enam..abhi saṃvasate*, Sāyana: *enam ūrjānnena samācchādayanti*. I take *enam* as governed by *abhi*; *saṃvasate* 3rd pl. to *saṃvaste*.

7. He should begin softly, then (chant) louder, and then still more loudly[1]; thereby he chants in view of these worlds.

[1] *mandram, tārataram, tāratamam* could equally well mean 'deep, higher, highest' (pitch of the voice), as relating to the three octaves (*grāmas, sthānas*), which are equally designated as *mandra, madhyama, tāra* (Taitt. prātiś. XXII.11), and said to reside successively in the chest, the throat and the head (ib. 10 and cp. Nāradīya Śikṣā I. 7: *uraḥ kaṇṭhah śiraś caiva sthānāni triṇi vāṅmaye*), each of these *sthānas* comprising seven tones.—The first third part (the first *āvṛt*, the *ādi*, cp. *ādadīta* in this §) he should chant *mandreṇa*; the second *āvṛt, tārataram*; the third *āvṛt, tāratamam*. Sometimes four *sthānas* are given: *upāṃśu, mandra, madhyama, uttama* (thus Sāyaṇa), with which compare Jaim. up. br. I. 51. 6 sqq.: *mandram, ugram, valgu, krauñcam*, cp. TS. II. 5. 11. 1: *krauñcam, mandram*.

8. The chant (of the gāyatra) must be performed 'unexpressedly'[1]. That which is expressed of the gāyatra is terrible; by chanting 'unexpressedly' he avoids what is terrible in it.

[1] Each syllable of the verse is replaced by *o*, cp. C. H. §§ 178, 180.

9. The gāyatra is breath[1]; he should not take breath (whilst chanting the udgītha), to prevent the breath from being cut off. If he takes breath, he will die before (his time), if he does not take breath, he lives his whole life.

[1] According to Sāyaṇa because there are nine stotriya-verses in the out-of-doors-laud and there are nine 'breaths' (*sapta śirṣaṇyā dvāv avāñcau*), but elsewhere the gāyatrī is identified directly with *prāṇa*: below, XVI. 14. 5 and Śat. br. VI. 2. 1. 24, VI. 4. 2. 5 etc.

10. If (however) he should take breath, he should take breath in the middle of the verse: the gāyatra, verily, is breath, the tone[1] is breath; he thereby puts breath in the midst, into his body: he lives his whole life[2].

[1] Possibly *svara* here also means circumflex, cp. XVII. 12. 2. Compare the passage, which to me is not clear, of the Jaim. br. I. 112: *sāmno 'ntararaṇyaṃ*

nāvetyaṃ,...etad dha vai sāmno 'ntararaṇyaṃ yat prastutam abhisvaritam (ms. *ābhi°*) *ādīyate ; svarenolpādyodgāyet.*

[2] Cp. Jaim. up. br. I. 37. 7 : *tad anavānaṃ geyaṃ ; tat sāmna evā pratihārād anavānaṃ geyaṃ, tat prāṇo vai gāyatraṃ ; tad vai prāṇam ṛdhnoti, tathā ha sarvam āyur eti,* and Jaim. br. I. 112 : *yadi sāmi tāmyen, madhya ṛco 'vānyāt.*

11. As nidhana [1] he should take (the word) *iḍā* [2] for one who desires cattle; *svaḥ*,[3] for one who desires (to reach) heaven; *yaśaḥ*[4], for one who desires spiritual lustre; *āyuḥ*[5], for one who suffers from disease; *haṁsi*[6], for one who exercises magic (spell for malevolent purpose)[7].

[1] Instead of the regular *ā*.

[2] *iḍā* is equal to cattle.

[3] 'Heaven.'

[4] 'Glory.'

[5] 'Long life.'

[6] 'Thou slayest'.

[7] To this § refers Lāṭy. VII. 11. 15. sqq.: 'if he desires to use any of the finales, that are recommended for (the fulfilment of special) wishes, he should, according to Gautama, put them (*i.e.* the words, that express them) in the place of the last two syllables, or after finishing the whole verse, *e.g. abhi devāṁ iyakṣata* 1212 (instead of the syllable *u*); according to Dhānaṃjayya he should, without changing, chant the whole gāyatra and put them in at the place of *ā*, for they (the words *iḍā*, *svaḥ*, etc) are intended as finales.'

12. These, forsooth, are the milkings [1] of the gāyatra.

[1] The instruments, as it were, to obtain from the gāyatra, as a milch-cow, all one wishes.

13. Into the possession of spiritual lustre, of cattle [1] comes he, who knows this.

[1] And of heaven, long life, etc. cp. § 11.

VII. 2.

(The ājya-lauds.)

1. Prajāpati, having changed himself into the sacrifice, gave himself over to the Gods. These did not agree together as to the precedence. He said to them: 'Run ye a race for it'. They ran a race (*ājim āyan*). Because they ran a race, therefore the ājya (-lauds) are called ājyas (*āj-yā*).

2. Indra understood: 'Agni, forsooth, will win in the first place.' He said (to Agni): 'Whichever of us both shall win in the first place, shall share with the other'. Agni was the first to win, thereon Mitra and Varuṇa, thereon Indra. Now, there was this o n e Hotṛ-function (still) to be won. Indra said to Agni: 'According to our agreement this one must be shared by us two'. This is the Hotṛ-function consecrated to Indra-agni: one and a half (of the) laud belongs to Agni, one and a half to Indra[1].

[1] The four ājya-lauds are 1. *āgneyam* (hotur ājyam), C. H. § 55; 2. *maitrāvaruṇam* (maitrāvaruṇasyājyam) C. H. § 160; 3. *aindram* (brāhmaṇācchaṃsina ājyam) C. H. 164; 4. *aindrāgnam* (acchāvākasyājyam) C. H. § 169. In the Jaim. br. this quasi-myth is more logically represented; here (I. 105) Agni, Mitra and Varuṇa, and Indra win first, and then Indra and Agni make the agreement about the fourth ājya that is left over: *athaikam anujjitam āsit, tad indro 'ved: agnir vāvedam ujjeṣyatīti. so 'bravid: agne, yatara āvayor idam ujjayāt tan nau sahāsad iti*, etc.

3. Four in number are they (the ājya-lauds) with six deities[1].

[1] Agni, Mitra, Varuṇa, Indra and for the last stotra again Indra and Agni together.

4. In six ways disposed[1] is the sacrifice; the whole of the sacrifice he thereby lays hold off.

[1] *ṣaḍḍhāvihitaḥ*, cp. *tridhāvihitaḥ* ('*tripartitus*'). Probably we are to understand: the agniṣṭoma-catuṣṭoma (comprising t h r e e services), the ukthya, the ṣoḍaśin and the atirātra.

5. All the ājya-(lauds) are *svāra*[1]; this is a sameness[2]; they chant (verses) addressed to different deities[3]: for the sake of taking away the sameness.

[1] *i.e.* provided with *svarita*: having at the end, as all gāyatra-chants have, a final ending on $\overset{111}{345}$, cp. R. Simon, Puṣpasūtra page 525, in voce *svāra*.

[2] Why the sameness, the *jāmitvam*, is unfruitful, is made clear by the following passage of the Jaim. br. (I. 300): 'Devoid of pairing and offspring is the sameness, just as when two men or two women were lying together, neither the two men would bring forth any child, nor the two women, if they did not get a copulating partner. That, on the other side, which is devoid of sameness, is a copulation, a generation'. Moreover, the consequence of sameness is *yātayāmatvam*!

[3] Cp. Jaim. br. I. 106: *tad āhur: yad ājyāni sarvāṇi samānanidhanāni, kenājāmi kriyata iti.*

6. In view of the domestic animals they chant the ājya (-lauds)[1]. They chant (them) constantly returning[2]; therefore they (the animals, the cattle) beget thitherward[3] and are born hitherward[4]; therefore also they (the cows), having started to the (meadows), return[5].

1 Cp. VI. 8. 12.

2 Cp. VI. 8. 9.

3 Cp. VI. 8. 9.

4 The young ones, being born, come 'hitherward' out of the womb.

5 Cp. VI. 8. 13.

VII. 3.

(The midday-pavamāna-laud.)

1. The midday-service is purified[1] by the following:

1 This must mean: 'the midday-service is brought about' or 'the midday-pavamāna-laud is held.'

2. by three metres[1] and five sāmans[2].

1 Gāyatrī, bṛhatī, triṣṭubh, cp. Introduction to Ārṣeyakalpa, page XXIV and Ait. br. III. 17. 4: *ṣaṭsu vā atra gāyatrīṣu stuvate ṣaṭsu bṛhatīṣu tisṛṣu triṣṭupsu.*

2 Gāyatra, āmahīyava, raurava, yaudhājaya and auśana.

3. By chanting the midday-pavamāna (-laud)[1] they strain the midday-pressing.

1 *i.e.* the first laud (stotra) in the midday-service.

4. The (sāmans used) at the midday-pavamāna (-laud) are (equal to) a l l the sāmans (of the whole midday-service).

5. (They are) the gāyatra (sāman), the sāman w i t h finale, the one d e v o i d of finale, the one with *iḍā* as finale[1].

1 With finale (*stauṣe*) is chanted the āmahīyava (grāmegeya XII, 2. 13); without finale proper the yaudhājaya (grām. XIV. 1. 36) and the auśana (grām. XV. 1. 32); with *iḍā* as finale the raurava (grām. XIV. 1. 35). In the same way the rathantara or hotuḥ pṛṣṭhastotra (araṇyegeya II. 1. 21) is chanted with finale (*as*); the vāmadevya or maitrāvaruṇasya pṛṣṭhastotra (grām. V. 1. 25) is chanted without finale (cp. V. 2. 4), likewise the naudhasa (grām. VI. 1. 37) or brahmaṇaḥ pṛṣṭhastotra is chanted without finale; the kāleya or acchāvākasya pṛṣṭhastotra (grām. VI. 2. 7) is chanted with *iḍā* as finale.

6. In chanting the midday-pavamāna-(laud) they chant a l l the sāmans (of the midday-service)[1].

1 See note 1 on the preceding paragraph.

7. The pavamāna (-laud) is the trunk of the service, the gāyatrī (metre) is its mouth; the gāyatra (sāman) is the breath; in chanting the gāyatra on the gāyatrī (metre) they put the breath into the mouth (of the sacrifice).

8. These metres[1] are the out- and in-breathing[2]: the gāyatrī is the out-breathing, the bṛhatī is the through-breathing, the triṣṭubh is the in-breathing; that they chant with these metres is for the continuity of the out- and in-breathing.

[1] Cp. § 2.

[2] Elliptic for out-, through- and in-breathing, as appears from what follows.

9. These metres are (equal to) these worlds: the gāyatrī is this world (the earth), the bṛhatī is this middle (world), the triṣṭubh is yonder highest (world). That they chant with these united metres is for the continuity of these worlds.

10. If another metre were to come in between them, he would disjoin these worlds[1].

[1] Read *vyaveyād imāṃllokān*.

11. Having chanted a gāyatra, they chant a sāman with finale[1]. The gāyatra is the earth; thereby an abode is made on the earth (for the Sacrificer)[1].

[1] The āmahīyava of the ordinary agniṣṭoma, see note 1 on § 5.—Besides 'finale', *nidhana* means also 'residence, abode'.

12. Were they to chant at the beginning a (sāman) without finale[1], the Sacrificer would be deprived of abode.

[1] 'without finale'='without abode'.

13. They chant a (sāman) with finale; the gāyatrī is strength, the finale is strength; by strength he (thereby) augments his strength.

14 With a (sāman) having (the word) *iḍā* (as finale)[1] they commence the bṛhatī (part) (of the laud).

[1] The raurava of the ordinary agniṣṭoma, cp. note 1 on § 5.

15. *Iḍā* is cattle[1], the bṛhatī is cattle[2]; in the cattle he thereby puts cattle.

[1] *iḍā* is one of the names for cow, Pañc. br. XX. 15. 5; Śat. br. IV. 5. 8. 10.

[2] *bārhatāḥ paśavaḥ*, Śat. br. XII. 7.2. 15.

16. (Moreover,) on the bṛhatī most of the sāmans are (chanted).

17. On it[1] (is) also (chanted) a (sāman) with three finales[2].

[1] On the bṛhatī part.

[2] The yaudhājaya in the ordinary agniṣṭoma; it has no finale in the proper sense, *viz.* no finale which is added to the words of the verse (such as *iḍā*, *as*, *hiṣ*, etc.), but three parts of the verse itself are taken as nidhana ($\overset{3}{\text{sā}}\text{234s}\overset{5}{\text{ī}}$; $\overset{3}{\text{dā}}\text{234s}\overset{5}{\text{ī}}$; $\overset{3}{\text{ṇyā}}\text{345y}\overset{5}{\text{āḥ}}$, etc.) see C. H. § 178h, page 281.

18. The middle world, forsooth, is the least strong[1] (of the three), as it were; to it thereby an abode is procured.

[1] The antarikṣa (being identified with the triṣṭubh, see § 9) cannot stand of itself, but is supported on both sides by heaven and earth, and thereby the least strong of the three! It now gets three *nidhanas*, three resting-places.

19. There is a (sāman) with three finales; three rents there are in the services[1], these are covered by it.

[1] In the morning-, midday- and afternoon-service of the Soma-feast. The purport of these words (cp. Jaim. br. I. 304: *atho trīṇi yajñasya chidrāṇi dve apidhattasya (?) āyatana ekaṃ bhavati*) was not certain to the ancients; they are discussed in the Nidānasūtra (II. 11): *atha khalv āha trīṇi savanānāṃ chidrāṇi tāni tenāpidhīyanta iti; katamāni chidrāṇīti? pavamānā ādevatā stutayas, tāni chidrāṇīty; athāpy antareṇa pavamānāṃś cāvartini ca havirbhiḥ pracaranti, tāni chidrāṇīti.* The text of the first explanation is doubtful (Sāyaṇa differs, as he reads: *pavamāna-devatāstutayas*) and to me unintelligible; probably the stotras beside the pavamānas are intended; the second explanation is clear: the author refers to the savanīyapuroḍāśas which follow after each pavamānastotra (cp. C. H. §§ 143, 186, 344).

20. There is a (sāman) with three finales; three are these worlds; in these he (thereby) obtains a firm support.

21. There is a (sāman) with three finales; by means of the (sāman) with three finales the midday-service becomes firmly established; if there were no (sāman) with three finales, the midday-service would not be firmly established.

22. The finales are of two syllables[1], the Sacrificer is a biped; he (thereby) instals the Sacrificer in the sacrifice, in cattle.

[1] Cp. note 2 on § 17.

23. A (sāman) devoid of finale is at the end (*i.e.* is the last of the

midday-pavamāna-laud)[1], to prevent (him) from falling across the world of heaven.

[1] The auśana in the ordinary agniṣṭoma, cp. note 1 on § 5.

24. If it were one with finale, he would expel the Sacrificer from the world of heaven[1].

[1] A highly casuistical reasoning! We would expect that the last chant was one provided with nidhana, the nidhana being an abode, in order that the Sacrificer might abide in heaven! But the author of these Brāhmaṇas had to reckon with the facts, and one of these was that the last sāman is *anidhana*. He now apparently seeks to explain this difficulty by assuming an etymological (and therefore, for one of h i s time and views, real) connection of *nidhana* with *nirhanti!* Sāyaṇa's attempt to explain this passage is unacceptable; he thinks that, the nidhana being a firm footing (*i.e.* the earth, containing food and cattle), the Sacrificer having gone up to heaven, would be tempted to return to earth (read in the commentary *svargād imam eva lokam* instead of *svargādikam eva lokam*). But note *ati* in *anatipāda* of the preceding §.

25. It is 'circumflected'[1].

[1] *svāra, i.e.* at the end, provided with the *padānusvāra*, ending: *nt*$\overset{5}{\text{ā}}$*656yi*, cp. R. Simon, Puṣpasūtra page 521 *in voce.* Sāyaṇa: 'a sāman which ends with a *svarita* tone on the last vowel, is called *svāra*; nowhere more than four endings of a sāman are met with: the *svāra*, the finale, (the word) *iḍā*, (the word) *vāg*'.

26. By means of the tone (*svara*)[1] food is offered to the Gods towards the end; he thereby offers, by means of the tone. food to the Gods towards the end.

[1] *svareṇa* a double entente: meaning here besides 'tone' also the (loud) voice, *viz.* such a word as *svāhā* or *vau3ṣaṭ* at the end of the offering verse, the *yājyā* in which an oblation is consecrated to a deity.

27. The gāyatra (sāman) is at the beginning, the circumflected one at the end.

28. The gāyatra is breath, the tone is breath; he thereby puts breath in at both sides; therefore animals have breath at both sides[1].

[1] The *prāṇa* is exhalation, the *apāna* inhalation, but also the wind in the belly. Or are we to think of the two ears, which equally are reckoned among the *prāṇas?*

29. Because the gāyatra is at the beginning, the circumflected (sāman) at the end, therefore he starts[1] by means of out-breathing and gains firm support through[2] in-breathing[3].

[1] *praiti* *i.e.* he begins, cp. XVIII. 8. 16 and Śat. br. XII. 2. 4. 16: *udānena hy udyanti.*

[2] Read *apānena* instead sf *apāne* (?).

[3] The rules laid down in this khanda, especially in §§ 11 sqq., are of great importance for the identification of the sāmans in general. They seem to agree with the ample prescripts of Jaim. br. I. 299 sqq. Here four kinds of sāmans are distinguished regarding their ending, *svārāṇi, nidhanavanti, aiḍāni* and *ṛksamāni*, cp. Sāyana on Pañc. br. VII. 3. 25, where, instead of the last group (the meaning of *ṛksama* is unknown to me; elsewhere, I. 307, the *ṛksamam* is declared identical with *svāra*; cp. the St. Petersb. Dict. s.v. *ṛksaman*), are given the sāmans ending on the word *vāk*. These rules intend, apparently, to prevent *jāmitva*, 'sameness' (cp. note 3 on VII. 2. 5). Further, we learn from the Jaim. br. (I. 311) the following important rule, which, as it seems, is also observed by the other Sāmavedists, that the places for inserting in, or taking out from, the *prakṛti* (*i.e.* the schema of the normal jyotiṣṭoma) those sāmans which must be added or taken out in order to obtain the required number of stotriya-verses, are: the gāyatrī, the bṛhatī, and the anuṣṭubh-part. In each sacrifice, therefore, only one sāman i chanted on the triṣṭubh, the kakubh, the uṣṇih and the jagatī. Jaim. br. I. 311 runs: 'three bellies, forsooth, has the sacrifice: the gāyatrī, the triṣṭubh and the anuṣṭubh, here they insert, hence they take out, just as man is filled in the middle (the stomach) or hungers (in the middle), but the other stotras are not liable to alteration, just as the other members of man are not altered (by hunger)'. The Jaim. br. in the same book gives some more rules, the exact understanding of which would without doubt provide us with much more data to identify the sāmans that are to be applied; one of these rules (I. 307) is that, where three sāmans are applied, they should be taken in this order: first the *aiḍam*, secondly the *svāram* and thirdly the *nidhanavat*.

VII. 4.

(The metres used in the midday-pavamāna-laud.)

1 The midday-service is that part of the sacrifice, which is conducive to heaven, the pavamāna (-laud) (is that part) of the midday-(service), (which is conducive to heaven), the bṛhatī (part) is that part of the pavamāna (-laud) (which is conducive to heaven); the sacrificial fees, being given at the chant of the bṛhatī (-part)[1], are thereby given on the place of the world of heaven.

[1] This statement (cp. Ait. br. III. 25.3: *tasmān madhyandine dakṣiṇā nīyante triṣṭubho loke*, and cp. Kāṭh. XXIII. 10: 86. 11, Maitr. Saṃh. III. 7. 3: 77-12, TS. VI 1. 6. 3) must not be taken too literally, for the dakṣiṇās are never given during the mādhyandina pavamānastotra, but after its completion, cp. C. H. § 178 (pav.), § 191 (dakṣ.).

2. The Gods said to the metres: 'Through you, let us reach the world of heaven'. They employed the gāyatrī, through it they did not reach it. They employed the triṣṭubh, through it they did not reach it. They employed the jagatī, through it they did not reach it. They employed the anuṣṭubh, through it they nearly[1] reached it. They now squeezed[2] out the essences of the quarters and added (these essences as) four syllables to the anuṣṭubh; that became the bṛhatī, by means of it they reached these worlds[3].

1 Read *tayālpakād iva* and cp. Delbrück, Altind. Syntax, page 113.

2 *prabṛhya*, pun on *bṛhatī*.

3 We expect rather 'the world of heaven' cp. XVI. 12. 7. –Cp. Śat br. III. 5. 1. 9: *bṛhatyā vai devāḥ svargaṃ lokaṁ samāśnuvata.*

3. 'Verily[1], it is the bṛhatī through which we have reached these worlds' (they said) and so the bṛhatī ('great one') has its name.

1 *maryā(h)* cp. note 3 on IV. 10. 1.

4. What they had added[1] to it (*i.e.* to the anuṣṭubh, from which resulted the bṛhatī) was the cattle; the bṛhatī, forsooth, is cattle; in that the sacrificial fees (the cows) are given at the chant of the bṛhatī (part), they are thereby given on their own place[2].

1 When the Gods squeezed out the quarters, § 2.

2 Cp. Śat. br. XII. 7. 2.15: *bārhatāḥ paśavo, bṛhatyaivāsmai paśūn avarunddhe.*—For §§ 2–4 cp. Jaim br. I. 120: 'Three metres convey the sacrifice: gāyatrī, triṣṭubh and jagatī; after these the anuṣṭubh is joined in; by means of it the Gods wished to reach the world of heaven; by it they did not reach it; they added to it (to the anuṣṭubh of 32 syllables) the four (kinds of) domestic animals: cow, horse, goat, sheep, and in this manner got to heaven. Having got there, they said: 'a great one (*bṛhatī*), forsooth, has this one been, through which we have reached this'. Hence its name 'bṛhatī'.

5. As to what they (the theologians) say: 'There are other metres which are larger, why is it called bṛhatī ('the great one')'? (one could answer): 'This one, indeed, and none of the other metres, reached these worlds. The seven metres, which increase by four (syllables), each[1] pass over into the bṛhatī[2]; therefore it is called bṛhatī'.

1 The gāyatrī of 24, the uṣṇih of 28, the anuṣṭubh of 32, the bṛhatī of 36, the pankti of 40, the triṣṭubh of 44 and the jagatī of 48 syllables.

[2] Taking together the gāyatrī and the jagatī we obtain 72 syllables, the double of the bṛhatī; the same is the fall with uṣṇih and triṣṭubh, with anuṣṭubh and paṅkti. To this passage Kātyāyana refers in his Upagranthasūtra (I. 1): *sapta caturuttarāṇīti, gāyatrījagatyau dve bṛhatyāv, uṣṇiktriṣṭubhau ca dve, paṅktyanuṣṭubhau* (*ca dve*), *saiva* (the bṛhatī itself) *saptamī*.

6. As to what they say: 'The morning-service is gāyatrī-like, the midday-service is triṣṭubh-like, the afternoon-service is jagatī-like, for what cause do they chant at midday the bṛhatī (part)'?

7. By means of the out-of-doors-laud, forsooth, the Gods carried the sun to the world of heaven; but it (the sun) could not hold itself (there); they then fixed it at midday by means of the bṛhatī; therefore they chant at the midday (-service) the bṛhatī (part), for it is this (metre) that props up the sun at midday[1].

[1] Cp. Śat. br. XII. 8. 3. 24: *bṛhatyāṃ vā asāv ādityaḥ śriyāṃ pratiṣṭhāyāṃ pratiṣṭhitas tapati.*

8. With whichever of the metres they chant at the midday-service, these all amount to the triṣṭubh (or: 'pass into the triṣṭubh', 'become equal to the triṣṭubh')[1]; therefore they do not depart from the triṣṭubh: the midday-service.

[1] This passage is treated by Kātyāyana in the Upagranthasūtra (I. 1): *yair u kaiś ca chandobhir iti; ṣaṣṭis triṣṭubhas; tāsāṁ siddhis: trayoviṁśatir gāyatryah, pañcacatvāriṁśataṃ bṛhatyo, dvādaśa kakubhaś catasṛbhir gāyatrībhis, tā bṛhatyas; tāḥ saptapañcāśataṃ; tāvanty akṣarāṇi gāyatryas; tais tās triṣṭubhas; tisraś cauśane*, which means: 'as to (the words of the Brāhmaṇa): 'with whichever of the metres (they chant)': there are sixty bṛhatīs in the whole midday-service; these are attained (by the following reckoning): there are 23 gāyatrīs (the gāyatra and āmahīyava yield 6, and the second pṛṣṭhastotra 17 gāyatrīs, together 23); 45 bṛhatīs (the raurava and yaudhājaya of the mādhyandina pavamāna, consisting each of 3 bṛhatīs, yield together 6 bṛhatīs; the first pṛṣṭhastotra (contained in the first *viṣṭāvas* of each *paryāya*) yield 5 bṛhatīs; the third pṛṣṭha and the fourth pṛṣṭha comprise each 17 bṛhatīs: 6+5+17+17=45); the twelve kakubhs (left over from the first pṛṣṭha in the two last *paryāyas*, see C. H., page 308) together with 4 (of the) gāyatrīs (mentioned first) yield $(12\times 28=336+[4\times 24=]\,96=432;\ \frac{432}{36}=12)$ (12) bṛhatīs; (45+12=)57 bṛhatīs (on the whole); by the fact that the (remaining 19) gāyatrīs contain the same number (*viz.* 57) of pādas (3×19), they are also equal to triṣṭubhs, and lastly, the auśana (in the mādhy. pavamāna) has 3 triṣṭubhs; that makes 60 triṣṭubhs (for the whole midday-service)'.

VII. 5.

(The sāmans of the midday-pavamāna-laud.)

1. Prajāpati desired: 'May I be more (than one), may I be reproduced'. He was in a languishing and unhappy (*amahīyamānaḥ*) state; he saw this āmahīyava[1] (melody); by means of it he created these creatures; these, being created, were happy (*amahīyanta*); because they were happy, therefore it is the āmahīyava[2].

[1] The first chant after the gāyatra in the midday-pavamāna-laud, *viz.* grāmegeya XII. 2. 13 composed on SV. I. 467, *i.e.* S.V. II. 22, 23, 24=ṚS. IX. 61. 10, 12, 11; the Vāj. Saṃh. XXVI. 16-18 has the same sequence of the verses as SV.

[2] A fanciful etymology, made 'pour le besoin de la cause'; the meaning of *āmahīyavaṃ sāma* is: 'the chant of (the seer) Amahīyu'.

2. These (creatures), being created (by him, or 'emanating from him') went away from him; (through the words): 'the earth took (it) that was[1] in heaven' he took their vital airs and, their vital airs having been taken (by him), they returned to him; (through the words): 'a formidable protection, a great glory' he rendered them their vital airs. They struggled against him[2], but he broke their anger (through the words): 'I will laud'[3]; thereupon they yielded him the supremacy.

[1] *divi sad* SV. and Vāj. S. against *divi ṣad* of ṚS.

[2] Reading (see Sāyana) *asmā ud evāyo°* instead of *asmād ud evāyo°*.

[3] The final of this sāman is *stauṣe*, an expanded form of *stuṣé*.

3. The equals yield the supremacy to him who knows this.

4. The āmahīyava is not only a creation of creatures[1] but also a separation of good and bad (prosperity and adversity).

[1] *i.e.* a means to get children and young cattle, as Prajāpati had practised it with this aim.

5. Separation of good and bad[1] comes unto him who knows this.

[1] Cp. note 1 on VI. 1. 12.

6. The Gods Agni, Indra, Vāyu and Makha, desirous of glory, performed a sacrificial session. They said: 'The glory that will come to (one of) us, must be in common to (all of) us'. Of them it was Makha to whom the glory came. He took it and stepped forth. They

tried to take it from him by force and hemmed him in[1]. He stood there, leaning on his bow[2], but the end of the bow, springing upwards[3], cut off his head. This (head) became the pravargya; Makha, forsooth, is the sacrifice; by holding the pravargya (ceremony), they put the head on the sacrifice[4].

[1] *paryayatanta*, Śat. br. *samantaṃ pariṇyaviśanta.*

[2] *sa dhanuḥ pratiṣṭabhyātiṣṭhat*, Śat. br. *sa dhanurārtnyā śira upaṣṭabhya taṣṭhau*; *dhanuḥ pratiṣkabhya*, TĀ.

[3] Because the ants had gnawed the bów-string.

[4] This myth is known to us from several other Brāhmaṇas: Śat. br. XIV. 1. 1, Maitr. Saṃh. IV. 5. 9, TĀ. V. 1. 1–5, and for the Kaṭhas, Sitz. Ber. der. Kais. Akad. der. W. in Wien, phil.-hist. cl., Band CXXXVII. (No. IV.) page 114, line 3 from bottom.

7. The Gods divided that glory among themselves; of it Agni seized upon the raurava (sāman).

8. By doing so he seized upon the strength of the cattle[1].

[1] Because its finale is *iḍā* and *iḍā* is cattle.

9. Rich in cattle becomes he who knows this.

10. Agni, forsooth, is burning (*rūra*), to him belongs this rauravai (sāman)[1].

[1] This § is identical with XII. 4. 24 —The raurava, according to Jaim. br. I. 122, has its name either from *agni ruru* or from a certain sage *rura vṛddhra.*

11. The Asuras hemmed the Gods in; thereupon Agni saw these two burning[1], all-divergent stobhas[2]; through these he scorched them and, being scorched, they howled (*aravanta*), therefore (there is) the raurava

1 The text has *rūro*, the comm. *rurau.*

[2] The stobhas of the raurava sāman (grāmegeya XIV. 1. 35 on SV. I. 5 11, *i.e.* ṚS. IX. 107. 4, 5=SV. II. 25, 26) are in the grāmegeya *óhā*^{2} *'32vā*^{2} and *au*^{2} *'3ho*^{4}*vā*^{5} Why are they called 'divergent' or 'dispersing'?

12. Then Indra seized upon the yaudhājaya[1]; by doing so he seized upon the thunderbolt; the yaudhājaya, forsooth, is the thunderbolt.

[1] Grāmegeya XIV. 1. 36 composed on the same verses as the raurava.

13. A thunderbolt at his rival he hurls who knows this.

14. Indra, forsooth, is the winner of battle [1]; to him belongs that yaudhājaya.

[1] *yudhājit*; in Jaim. br. I. 122 he is called *indro yudhājivan* (or °*jīvan*).

15. 'In battle (*yudhā*) verily [1], we have won (*ajaiṣma*)' (thus Indra thought); therefore (there is) the yaudhājaya.

[1] *maryā(ḥ)* cp. IV. 10. 1, VII. 4. 3.

16. But Vāyu seized upon the auśana [1].

[1] Grāmegeya XV. 1. 32 on SV. I. 523=ṚS. IX. 87. 1–2= SV. 27–28. There are on this triṣṭubh (a triṣṭubh is required, see above, VII. 3. 2) chanted f i v e auśanas, three of which are *svāra* (cp. VII. 3. 25 and 27), *viz.* grāmegeya XV. 1. 28, 31 and 32. A comparison with the ūhagāna proves that the last of the three is to be taken.

17. By doing so he seized upon the vital airs; the auśana, forsooth, is (equal to) the vital airs.

18. He who knows this, lives his whole (normal lease of) life.

19. Vāyu is the willing one (*uśan*), to him belongs that auśana.

20. Uśanas Kāvya, forsooth, was the chaplain of the Asuras; him by means of the wish-cows the Gods invited to come over to their side [1]; they gave over to him those auśana(sāman)s [2]; the auśana(sāman)s, forsooth, are the wish-cows.

[1] Cp. Baudh. śrs. XVIII. 46: 403. 2 sqq.: 'he (Indra) went to Uśanas and cajoled him by (offering him) his daughter Jayantī and four wish-cows; he, (thus) directed, came over from the Asuras to the Gods'. In the Jaim. br. (I. 126, see Journal of the American Or. Society, Vol. XXVIII, page 83) Uśanas is won over by the wish-cows of Virocana, the son of Prahlada. Oertel is wrong in not accepting the word *kāmadugha* as a substantive.

[2] Probably the five: grāmegeya XV. 1. 28–32.

VII 6.

(The pṛṣṭha-lauds: rathantara and bṛhat.)

1. Prajāpati desired: 'May I be more (than one), may I be reproduced': He meditated silently [1] in his mind; what was in his mind that became the bṛhat (sāman).

[1] *tūṣṇīm* is equal to *vācaṃyamaḥ*, cp. § 3.

2. He bethought himself: 'This embryo of me is hidden; through the Voice I will bring it forth'.

3. He released his voice ('speech')[1] and this voice (*i.e.* this speech, the words uttered by him) became the rathantara[2].

[1] *i.e.* he now became *visṛṣṭavāc*, as he spoke the words mentioned in the next § (?).

[2] *sā vāg rathantaram anvapadyata*: litt. 'this voice fell to the share of the rathantara'. The author of our text seems to have chosen this expression in order to come to the etymology of the next §. The rathantara existed in reality before the bṛhat, cp. below, § 10 and TS. VII. 1. 1. 4, where it is said that firstly Prajāpati created the trivṛtstoma, Agni, the gāyatrī and the rathantara, and then the pañcadaśa stoma, Indra, the triṣṭubh and the bṛhat. That vāc is identical with rathantara appears also from § 17, and cp. Jaim. br. I. 128: 'when Prajāpati created the rathantara and the bṛhat, he first saw the mind: the bṛhat, he spoke over it the voice: the rathantara'.

4. 'The chariot[1] (*ratham*), verily, it has swiftly[2] reached' (*atārīt*) (said Prajāpati[3]) and for this cause it is called '*rathaṃ-tara*'[4].

[1] With the chariot here perhaps is meant the vehicle of Prajāpati's thought: his voice; the voice often is called a vehicle, *e.g.* Śat. br. I. 4. 4. 2.

[2] Read *kṣepṇā* (instead of *kṣeplā*) with the Leyden ms. and the Petersb. Dict. in kürzerer Fassung.

[3] Indra, according to Sāyaṇa.

[4] A different but equally fanciful etymon of the name is given in the Jaim. br. (I. 135): by means of the rathantara the Gods went upwards to the world of heaven. 'These Asuras and ogres, nine nineties (in number), covered these worlds; they were Rathas by name; the Gods, having chanted the rathantara and ascended the rathantara (as vehicle), went to the world of heaven and said: 'We have crossed (' overcome', *atāriṣma*) these Rathas'. Thence the name rathantara'.

5. Then, after it (after the rathantara) the bṛhat came into existence. 'This, verily, is the great (*bṛhat*) (thing): long time has it been concealed'[1] (said Prajāpati)[2] and for this cause it is called bṛhat.

[1] Cp. § 1.

[2] Indra, according to Sāyaṇa.

6. As an eldest son (to a human father) thus is the bṛhat to Prajāpati.

7. Indeed, it has a prior brāhmaṇa[1].

[1] The brāhmaṇa-sentence in which the origin of the bṛhat is expounded (VII. 6. 1) is prior to that of the rathantara! Simply a pun, to come to following statement.

8. To priority (amongst his equals) comes he who knows this.

9. As to what they say: 'The bṛhat arose first in Prajāpati, why is it, that the rathantara has come to be yoked ('applied') first'[1]?

[1] Everywhere, when these two sāmans are used simultaneously, it is the rathantara that takes the first place; for instance, in the dvādaśāha, where the first day has the rathantara as it pṛṣṭhastotra, the second the bṛhat; in the abhiplava six-day-period (cp. Ārṣeyakalpa I. 2, compared with I. 3). Perhaps this whole quasi-myth of the birth of the two chants is to be explained by the fact that a grammatical (*dvandva*) compound of the two words *rathantara* and *bṛhat* could not be otherwise than *bṛhadrathantare* (cp. note 1 on V. 5. 14); the precedence of the bṛhat is then only a precedence in appearance.

10. It is true that the bṛhat arose first, but the rathantara had been created actually prior to it[1]; therefore it comes to be yoked ('applied') first.

[1] At the time when the bṛhat existed only in the mind of Prajāpati as an embryo (§ 1), the rathantara had already come into existence (§ 3), cp. note 2 on § 3.

11. These two (bṛhat and rathantara) (originally) had the same finale; they did not agree to this[1] and ran a race (to decide the question as to which of them it should belong)[2]. Of them the bṛhat by its finale *has* won the out-breathing, the rathantara by its finale *as* envelopped the in-breathing[3].

[1] *tasmin nātiṣṭhetām, tiṣṭhate* here with locative instead of the usual dative.

[2] Differently the Jaim. br. (I. 298): *te abrūtām ājim anayor nidhanayor ayāveti.*

[3] The rathantara (araṇyegeya II. 1. 21) on SV. I. 233=ṚS. VII. 32. 22, 23=S.V. II. 30, 31; nidhana: *as*; the bṛhat (araṇyegeya I. 1. 27) on SV. I. 234=ṚS. VI. 46. 1, 2=SV. II. 159, 160; nidhana: *has*. Note (see note 1 end on § 9) that of the verses on which *bṛhadrathantare* are chanted, the pūrvārcika gives in the first place the verse for the rathantara, in the second place the verse for the bṛhat.—In the Nidānasūtra (II. 9, beg.) the speculations of different authorities are recorded, as to what this original nidhana, in common to both sāmans, had been: *has*, or *a*, or *sa* (*sakāram evāham anayoḥ samānaṃ nidhanaṃ manya iti dhānaṃjayyaḥ, sa hy ubhayatra dṛśyata iti*).

12. The bṛhat and rathantara, forsooth, are out- and in-breathing; for one who is suffering from a lingering disease, both should be applied[1]; gone forth, verily, are the out- and in-breathing of him, who suffers from a lingering disease; he (thereby) puts into him out- and in-breathing.

[1] *Viz.* the rathantara in the midday-pavamāna-laud in the bṛhatī-part (probably instead of the yaudhājaya) and the bṛhat as hotuh pṛṣṭhastotra.

13. As to what they say: 'Both the bṛhat and the rathantara have their finale outside the (verse), how is it that the bṛhat partakes of (chants) that have their finale o u t s i d e [1], (but) the rathantara of (chants) that have their finale i n s i d e [2] (the verse)'?

[1] As in the śyaita (see second day of the daśāha, Ārṣeyakalpa page 206).

[2] As in the naudhasa (see first day of the daśāha, Ārṣ. k. page 205).

14. The bṛhat is the o u t-breathing, therefore it partakes of the (chants) that have their finale o u t s i d e, for outside is the out-breathing. The rathantara is the i n-breathing, therefore it partakes of the (chants) that have their finale i n s i d e, for inside is the in-breathing.

15. Two big trees, forsooth, are the bṛhat and the rathantara; (their) nidhanas must not be put together [1].

[1] *nidhane na samarpye*, means probably: 'their n. should be kept asunder, must not be the same'.

16. If two big trees come into collision, then there lies (on the ground) a great shattering, a great breaking down (of branches) [1].

[1] And therefore the finales should be kept asunder. Similarly the Jaim. br. (I. 133): 'He should part ('differentiate') the bṛhat and the rathantara; if he did not part them, just as two big trees having come into collision, would break down their branches, so would these two break down the (young) children and cattle; *ho vā u hā* is the (finale of the) bṛhat, *o vā hā* (of) the rathantara; thus he differentiates the bṛhat from the rathantara; parted from bad lot is he who knows this.' According to the gāna of the Jaiminīyas the rathantara ends: *o v ā h ā u vā ās*, the bṛhat *h o v ā h ā u vā hās*.

17. The bṛhat is *irā*-like, the rathantara *iḍā*-like; the bṛhat is mind, the rathantara voice; the bṛhat is the melody, the rathantara the verse; the bṛhat is the out-breathing, the rathantara the in-breathing; the bṛhat is yonder world ('heaven, sky'), the rathantara this world ('earth'). Having meditated on these (equations) he should chant (either the bṛhat or the rathantara); then he chants them well equipped [1].

[1] To this brāhmana refer Lāṭy. II. 9. 7–10 and Drāhy. VI. 1. 11–14: 'when he is about to chant either the bṛhat or the rathantara, he should, b e f o r e the 'yoking' of the stoma meditate upon the ten 'great words': 'the bṛhat is *irā*-like' etc.; at the rathantara (he should recite) only the verse (Pañc. br. VII. 7. 19.): 'with the greatness that is in the cows'; a f t e r the 'yoking' of the stoma he should perform this recitation of the 'great words' and the verse, according to

Śāṇḍilya and the verse before the 'great words'; the other view is that of Dhānamjayya

VII. 7.

(Rathantara and bṛhat, continued.)

1. The bṛhat and rathantara are cattle[1]; the (first) eight syllables of the first verse he (the Prastotṛ) takes as prastāva[2]; he thereby gains the eight-hoofed cattle.

[1] More especially are designated by the Jaiminīyas (Jaim. br. I. 128) the *anyatodantaḥ* as belonging to the rathantara, the *ubhayādantaḥ* as belonging to the bṛhat; from ib. I. 297 we learn that the rāthantara animals, who go on bone (horn, hoof!), are *ādyās*, but the bārhata animals, who walk on flesh, are the eaters (*attāraḥ*).—I here remark that, although *bṛhadrathantare* should be translated: 'rathantara and bṛhat,' I am not sure that for the author of our Brāhmaṇa this was the meaning; he rather takes it as: 'bṛhat and rathantara.

[2] Cp. the chant of the rathantara in C. H., page 308.

2. The (first) two syllables of the last two verses he takes as prastāva[1]; the Sacrificer is a biped, he (thereby) firmly establishes the Sacrificer in the sacrifice[2], in the (possession of) cattle.

[1] Cp. C. H., pages 308, 309.

[2] More clear is the Jaim. br. I. 135: 'he takes eight syllables of the first verse, two of each of the last two verses; that makes twelve syllables; of twelve months consists the year; Prajāpati, sacrifice is the year, he thus reaches Prajāpati: the sacrifice.'

3. Five syllables of the rathantara he (the Pratihartṛ) takes for his respond (pratihāra); he thereby gains the fivefold cattle[1].

[1] Cp. note 2 on II. 4. 2.

4. Four syllables of the bṛhat he takes for his respond; he thereby gains the quadruped cattle.

5. Neither the bṛhat nor the rathantara was sustained by one single metre; so they put two kakubhs after it; therefore the first (verse) is a bṛhatī and the last two are kakubhs[1]; therefore they perform the bṛhat and the rathantara on one verse[2], for they were not sustained by one metre.

[1] For this see C. H. pages 307 and 308.

[2] What is the exact meaning? Both the sāmans being actually chanted not on one but on two verses.

6. He makes nine risings in the bṛhat[1]; nine in number are the vital airs[2]; he thereby retains the vital airs.

2r 1r r 2 1
[1] Cp. the commentary on Puṣpasūtra VIII. 96, note 1 (*sātau vājā ; vṛtrā iṣuv*
1
ā·i ; sū 2 ārvā 234) and cp. araṇyegeya I. 1. 27 in SV. ed. Calcutta, Vol. II, page 492. For the risings of the bṛhat the Nidānasūtra II. 9 gives some particulars, which, without commentary, are unintelligible to me.

[2] Cp. note 1 on VI. 2. 2, and on VI. 8. 3.

7. Three risings he makes in the first (verse); the past, the present, and the future he retains by these; three in the middle (verse); (the life of) himself, his progeny and cattle he retains by these; three in the last (verse); three are these worlds; in these worlds he gains a firm support.

8. All wishes are fulfilled for him, who, knowing this, makes the risings in the bṛhat.

9. In chanting the prastāva of the rathantara the Prastotṛ hurls a thunderbolt against the Udgātṛ; he (the Udgātṛ) should chant his part of the chant (the udgītha), after putting an ocean between; (the word) 'voice' (*vāk*) is to be made the beginning of the part chanted by him[1]; an ocean, forsooth, is the voice[2]; he puts an ocean between, for security's sake.

[1] *ādeyam* (wrongly Sāyaṇa : *manasy ādhānam kartavyam dhyātavyam ity arthaḥ*) is the gerundive to *ādatte*, cp. *ādi* 'the first part of the udgītha' (Jaim. śrs. 17 : 21. 12 : *rathantare prastute ho ity uktvādim ādadīta, bṛhati prastute ā iti*). Further cp. C H. pages 308, 309, where the Prayogas insert this word in the place as indicated by the Brāhmaṇa.

[2] *samudravat sarvapadārthānām svāntarnidhānād vāk samudra ity ucyate*, Sāyaṇa.

10. The chant must be performed (by the Udgatṛ) strongly; he (thereby) throws back the hurled thunderbolt.

11. The chant must be performed stammeringly[1] (and) confoundedly[2], as it were; he (thereby) confounds the thunderbolt.

[1] He must speak unintelligibly, cp. note on § 13.

[2] *abhilobhayatā* ; for *abhilobhayati* the Petersburgh Dictionary gives the meaning unlocken', which is unsatisfactory here.

12. The chanting should be performed swiftly, for the attainment f the world of heaven[1].

[1] The Jaim. br. (I. 329) gives another reason for the s w i f t chanting: Mind ('thought') comes first, then Voice; the bṛhat is the mind, the rathantara is the voice. When bṛhat and rathantara ran their race, the bṛhat won the race and the rathantara was left behind. By chanting the rathantara swiftly, he makes thought and voice (or 'word') equal (*i.e.* coming together). Then the rathantara thinks: 'he who has made me equal (to the bṛhat), come, let the bad lot leave him swiftly'

13. The rathantara is the God-chariot; its chanting should be performed whilst he (the Udgātṛ) causes it to stand firmly on each syllable, for a chariot stands firmly on each wheelspoke (successively)[1].

[1] Cp. Jaim. br. I. 135: *akṣareṣṭhaṃ rathantaraṃ karoti, tasmād ārenārena rathaḥ pratitiṣṭhann eti.*—On § 11 and 13 cp. C. H. page 307 and Lāṭy. II. 9. 12, Drāhy. VI. 1. 16: 'He should mentally join to each syllable loudly the stobhas' (*i.e.* whilst t h i n k i n g each syllable of the chant in its verse-form, according to the the text as handed down in the ārcika, he should u t t e r it audibly with stobhas), which are to begin with *bh* and to end on *a* (in so doing the Udgātr chants in accordance with the prescript given in the Brāhmaṇa, VII. 7. 11), in which no duplication of consonants is to take place (where, for instance, the ārcika has *maghavann wa*, the chant should not be: *bhabhabha b h b h a bha* but *bhabhabha b h a-bha*, and hereby the Udgatṛ, according to Dhanvin, at least, executes the prescript of the Brāhmaṇa in § 13), of which stobhas the last has the *dvitīyā* ('the third') musical tone, the others the second (*prathamā*)'. These prescripts of the Sūtrakāras do not agree entirely with the praxis, see the gāna as figured in C. H. page 308, 309 according to the Prayoga's.

14. He, forsooth, who mounts the God-chariot without taking hold (of it), falls down from it: the God-chariot (*viz.* the rathantara) is the earth; he should perform the udgītha whilst taking hold of the earth, then he does not fall down from it[1].

[1] See note 1 on § 15.

15. The rathantara, forsooth, is liable to destroy the eye-sight of the Udgātṛ; whilst its prastāva is being chanted, he should shut his eyes and open them at (the words): 'seeing the light'; (in this manner) he is not deprived of his eye-sight.

[1] On § 14 and 15 cp. C. H. page 307 and Lāṭy. II. 9. 11, 14, Drāhy. VI. 1. 15-16 (last words) and 17: 'Whilst the prastāva of the rathantara is being performed, he (the Udgātṛ) should everywhere (*i.e.* at each stotriya-verse) shut his eyes and open them everywhere at the beginning of the last four syllables (of the udgītha) before the respond (the pratihāra)'. The Sūtrakāras add the word 'everywhere', because strictly speaking the Brāhmaṇa refers only to the first stotriya-verse.—The fact that the Prayogas, used in constituting the chanting of

the rathantara in C. H. l.c., allow the chanting of the syllables *svar dṛśam* etc. not with stobha (and cp. C. H. page XIV, note 4) rests on Drāhyāyaṇa (VI. 1. 16), who takes the words *prāk pratihārāc caturakṣaraṃ śiṣṭva* to the prescript for the chanting on stobha, whereas Lāṭyāyana takes them to the following sentence, *tat sarvatra pratīvīkṣeta.* Drāhy. here agrees with the Jaiminīyas (br. I. 330, 331): 'sixteen syllables (of the udgītha) he chants with the stobha (chanting instead of *adugdhā iva dhenavaḥ ; abhubhā bhibhabhebhava*, cp. Jaim. br. I. 330), (the words) *svar dṛśam* he chants distinctly (as they are handed down, not replacing the consonants by *bh*).

16. The rathantara, forsooth, is the procreative force; if he says: of the still-standing '[1], the voice of the Udgātṛ becomes standing still ('restrained')[2], and it (the rathantara) destroys his procreative force; (instead of it) 'of the not standing still'[3] is to be said, or, 'of the well-standing'[3]; (then) the voice of the Udgātṛ becomes not still-standing (*i.e.* will not be restrained during the chanting) and it (the rathantara) does not destroy his procreative force.

1 The last word of the first verse: *īśānam indra t a s t h u ṣ a ḥ .*

2 The rathantara is also the voice (of Prajāpati, VII. 6. 3).

3 *asthuṣaḥ, susthuṣaḥ* (!).

17. The pṛṣṭhas were created; by means of them the Gods went to the world of heaven; of these (pṛṣṭhas) the rathantara on account of its greatness could not fly upwards[1].

1 *nāśaknod utpatat, śaknoti* with participle, an unknown construction. Sāyaṇa interprets: *utpatad api svargaṃ gantuṃ nāśaknot.*

18. Vasiṣṭha having distributed its 'greatnesses'[1], chanted it and went to the world of heaven. He (the Udgātṛ) should chant (the rathantara) after putting together these ('greatnesses')[2]

1 As indicated in the mantra in § 19. By doing so the greatness (heaviness) of the rathantara had got such a nature that it could go up and convey Vasiṣṭha to the world of heaven (?).

2 He should, before chanting, recite the mantra of § 19, see C. H. page 307 and the Sūtrakāras as cited under VII. 6. 17 (note 1).

19. 'With thy greatness that is in the cows, that is in the water, or that is in the chariot, in the thunder, with thy greatness that is in the fire, therewith be thou united, o Rathantara; be full of riches for us'[1]!

1 Cp. Jaim. śrs 17 : 21. 3 sqq.

VII. 8.

(The second pṛṣṭha-laud, the vāmadevya.)

1. Unto the Waters came the seasonal period (the period favourable for conception). Vāyu (the Wind) moved over their back ('surface'). Therefrom came into existence a beautiful (thing). This was espied by Mitra and Varuṇa[1]; they said: 'A beautiful (*vāmam*) (thing), verily, has here been born in the Gods' (*deveṣu*)[2]. Therefore there is the vāmadevya (chant).

[1] Litt.: 'in this (part of the water) Mitra and Varuṇa saw themselves reflected'. The second pṛṣthastotra runs parallel with the śastra of the Maitrāvaruna-priest.

[2] *i.e.* 'in the Waters', instead of *devīṣu*, etymologiae causa!

2. Laying hold of it they said: 'We two have found this; do ye not dispute us it'[1]. About it Prajāpati said: 'Out of me, forsooth, it has been born[2], to me it belongs'. About it Agni said: 'After me, forsooth, it has been born[3], to me it belongs'. About it Indra said: 'Belonging to the most excellent is this, I am the most excellent of you all, to me it belongs'. About it the All-gods said: 'Us for deity has that which has come into existence out of the Waters, to us it belongs'. Then Prajāpati said about it: 'Let it belong to all of us, let us all live upon it'. They deposited it in the pṛṣṭhas. Pertaining to all the deities, forsooth, in the vāmadevya.

[1] *mābhyartiḍhvam*, according to Böhtlingk (in the Dict. of Petersburgh in kürzerer Fasung), is incorrect for *mābhyarthidhvam* (from *abhyarthayati*). But it may be the injunctive of the iṣ-aorist to *abhyrtīyate*, Dutch: 'b e - twisten'.

[2] Śat. br. VI. 1. 3. 1: *tasmāt (prajāpateḥ)... āpo 'sṛjyanta.*

[3] Sāyaṇa quotes a śruti: *agner āpaḥ.*

3. In that it is (chanted) on verses containing (the word) *ka*[1], thereby it belongs to Prajāpati, for Prajāpati is Ka; in that it is (chanted) on 'unexpressed' verses[2], thereby it belongs to Prajāpati, for Prajāpati is 'unexpressed'[3].

[1] The vāmadevya (grámegeya V. 1. 25) is composed on SV. I. 169 (beginning: *kayā naś citra ā bhuvat*)=ṚS. IV. 31. 1–3=SV. II. 32–34.

[2] Cp. VII. 1. 8. Prajāpāti is unexpressed or *anirukta*, because he is called not by his name, but designated as *ka*.

[3] §§ 3—7 give the quasi-facts, on which the quasi-myth of § 1 and 2 is based.

4. In that it is (chanted) on verses in gāyatrī metre, thereby it belongs to Agni; for Agni has the gāyatrī as his metre.[1]

[1] Cp. Śat. br. V. 2. 1. 5: *gāyatram agneś chandaḥ*.

5. In that they deposited it in the pṛṣṭhas[1], thereby it belongs to Indra, for all the pṛṣṭhas belong exclusively to Indra[2].

[1] Cp. § 2, end.

[2] The four niṣkevalyaśastras run parallel to the pṛṣṭhastotras, cp. Sacred Books of the East, Vol XXVI, page 325, note 2.

6. In that the Maitrāvaruṇa recites his śastra after (the vāmadevya-stotra)[1], thereby it belongs to Mitra-Varuṇa.

[1] Cp. C. H. § 204 with § 203.

7. In that the last quarter (of the last verse) has a plurality of deities[1], thereby it belongs to the All-gods. In all forms[2] he (thereby) gains a firm support.

[1] Because of the word *śatam* in the untranslatable *śataṃ bhavāsy ūtaye*.

[2] 'In all forms' (*rūpeṣu*), kinds of domestic animals (?).

8. Prajāpati forsooth, saw this womb, the gāyatrī (metre)[1]. He thought: 'Out of this womb I will create the pṛṣṭhas'.

[1] The vāmadevya is chanted on gāyatrī-verses.

9. He created the r a t h a n t a r a; after it the chariot's noise was created[1].

[1] And for this cause (Lāṭy. III. 5. 1, Drāhy. IX. 1. 1) at the pṛṣṭhya-ṣaḍaha (*i.e.* the first six days of the daśarātra, see Ārṣeyakalpa, Anhang (page 205) 4. a—4.f) during the chanting of the rathantara a chariot should ride along. Jaim. br. I. 143: *tasmād rathantarasya stotre rathaghoṣaṃ kurvanti*.

10*a*. He created the b ṛ h a t; after it the noise of the thunder was created[1].

[1] And for this cause at the pṛṣṭhyaṣaḍaha during the chanting of the bṛhat a drum should be beaten, Lāṭy. l.c. 2, Drahy. l.c. 2, Jaim. br. I. 143 and III. 118: *tasmād bṛhata stotre dundubhīm udvādayanti*.

10*b*. He created the v a i r ū p a; after it the noise of the wind was created[1].

[1] And for this cause at the pṛṣṭhyaṣaḍaha, during the chanting of the vairūpa, wind should be made by the Chanters by shaking their garments, Lāṭy. l.c. 3, Drāhy. l.c. 3. Jaim. br. I. 143 and 118: *tasmād vairūpasya stotre grāmaghoṣaṃ kurvanti*.

11. He created the vairāja; after it the noise of fire was created[1].

[1] And for this cause at the pṛṣṭhyaṣaḍaha, during the chanting of the vairāja, fire should be churned with the churning sticks, Lāṭy. l.c. 5, Drāhy. l.c. 5; cp. XII. 10. 12–19. Jaim. br. l.c. *tasmād vairājasya stotre 'gnim manthanti.*

12. He created the śakvarī-verses[1]; after it the noise of the waters was created[2].

[1] Or 'mahānāmnī-verses.

[2] And for this cause at the pṛṣṭhyaṣaḍaha, during this chant, water is put near and has to be shaken, Lāṭy. l.c. 13 sqq., Drahy. l.c. 14 sqq.; cp. XIII. 4. 8. Jaim. br. l.c.: *tasmāc chākvarasya stotre 'pa upanidhāya stuvanti.*

13. He created the revatī-verses; after it the noise of the cows was created[1].

[1] And for this cause at the pṛṣṭhyaṣaḍaha, during the chant of the vāravantīya-sāman, some cows and calves, having been separated from each other, should be caused to bellow, Lāṭy. III. 6. 1 sqq., Drāhy. IX. 2. 1 sqq. Jaim. br. l.c. *tasmād raivatasya stotre paśughoṣaṃ kurvanti: vatsān mātṛbhiḥ saṃvāśayanti*; cp. note 1 on XIII. 10. 9.

14. Together with these noises, forsooth, these (the pṛṣṭhas) were created.

15. In him[1] forsooth, who knows this, all noises, all auspicious voices sound.

[1] This means 'in his neighbourhood'.

VII. 9.

(The vāmadevya, continued.)

1. The vāmadevya, forsooth, is the father, the pṛṣṭhas are the sons.

2. Out of this womb, verily, they were created[1].

[1] Cp. VII. 8.8.

3. Therefore, they chant the vāmadevya after the laud of the pṛṣṭhas[1], for appeasement[2].

[1] When the vāmadevya is not used for the pṛṣṭhastotra, then it must be applied later; for instance, on the tenth day, cp. Ārṣeyakalpa, page 217.

[2] Probably an appeasement is required, because of the pṛṣṭhasāmans five, at east, belong to the araṇyegeyagāna: the collection of chants that, because of

their greater sacredness or tabu-quality, are studied in the forest, outside the community.

4. For the unauspicious (or 'unappeased') (deeds) achieved by the sons are appeased by the father[1].

[1] Cp. § 1.

5. The vāmadevya, forsooth, is this middle world (the antarikṣa), out of it these two worlds, *viz.* the bṛhat and the rathantara, were created apart[1].

[1] The bṛhat is heaven or sky, the vāmadevya is the intermediate region, the atmosphere, the rathantara is the earth: a very common equation *e.g.* in the invocation of the *iḍā* (see for instance Śat. br. I. 8. 1. 19). Here, heaven and earth are said to have been created out of the intermediate region, whilst elsewhere it is set forth that at one time heaven and earth were together.

6. By the chanting of the rathantara those domestic animals, which belong to the rathantara[1], lean on the intermediate region[2]; by the chanting of the bṛhat those animals, which belong to the bṛhat, lean on the intermediate region. These animals are gained by the chanting of the vāmadevya[3].

[1] Read *rāthantarāḥ* instead of *rathantarāḥ*.—On *rāthantara* and *bārhata* animals cp. note 1 on VII. 7. 1, and below, X. 2. 5 (goat, horse) and 6 (cow, sheep); see also IV. 8. 13 and Lāṭy. II. 10. 1, Drāhy. VI. 2. 1, where it is ordained that before the chanting of the vāmadevya the Udgātṛ should think on 'cows and horses, goat and sheep, rice and barley', cp. Jaim. śrs. 17 : 22. 1.

[2] *upaśrayanti* 'lean on', 'dwell in'. *antarikṣāyatanā hi prajāḥ*, IV. 8. 13.

[3] Which is equal to *antarikṣa*.

7. He should sit without moving whilst chanting the vāmadevya, in order that the domestic animals may turn to him[1].

[1] Read *upāvṛttyai*.—Cp. Jaim. br. I. 138 : 'he should chant it without moving (*anejan*), in order that the cattle may not get lost'. In the Jaim. br. the *vāmam vasu* is directly the cattle.

8. To him turn the domestic animals, who knows this.

9. The vāmadevya is the intermediate region, he must chant (is) without shaking (his limbs), for unshaken is the intermediate region. The vāmadevya is cattle; he must chant (it) without hurting[1], in order not to hurt the cattle.

[1] See § 11 first half.

10. 'How (then) is the vāmadevya to be chanted' they ask.

11. In the same manner as a she-cat[1] takes her young ones between her teeth without hurting them by biting, (or) in the same manner as the wind blows gently over the water.

[1] *aṅkulī* according to Sāyaṇa is *mārjārī*. It could equally well be some other animal belonging to the feles.

12. Independently[1] the vāmadevya must be chanted.

[1] Properly, 'having a yoke of its own'; cp. § 15.

13. He who chants the vāmadevya independently, becomes independent.

14. Another goes h i s way[1], but he does not go another's way.

[1] 'follows him, is dependent on him'.—For § 12 and 14 cp Jaim. br. 144: *tat svadhūr geyam, noccair iva na nīcair iva; yad uccair gāyec, chreyaso bhrātṛvyasya niyānena yāyād; yan nīcair gāyet, pāpīyaso bhrātṛvyasya niyānena yāyāt*; and ib. I. 333: *no hānyasyānuvartma geyam; īśvaro hopajīvī bhavitor yo 'nyasyānuvartmā gāyati: svadhūr eva geyam.*

15. It must not be chanted conformably to the bṛhat and the rathantara[1]; on its own support it must be chanted; he (thereby) comes into the possession of a support.

[1] This means probably that the special prescripts for the chant of the bṛhat and rathantara (such as are given VII. 7. 1) must not be applied at the chanting of the vāmadevya.

16. The Gods divided the domestic animals among themselves; they excluded Rudra[1]; he fixed his looks on them during the laud of the vāmadevya[2].

[1] Whilst in the Śat. br. (*e.g.* XII. 7. 3. 20: *rudraḥ paśūnām īṣṭe*) Rudra is ruler of the cattle, he gains, according to other texts (*e.g.* Kāṭh. XXV. 1: 102. 16) this reign only for a few days in the year.

[2] The vāmadevya is cattle (IV. 8. 15); at the moment of its chanting Rudra hopes to obtain it, as he was excluded by the Gods from obtaining a share in them.

17. It must be chanted 'unexpressedly'[1].

[1] Or 'unuttered,' cp. VII. 1. 8, note 1. But the praxis takes no heed of this.

18. By 'uttering' he delivers the cattle to Rudra. Rudra during this year is apt to slay the cattle[1].

[1] But if one does not utter the words of the chant, Rudra will be prevented from hearing it and he will not know that here was an occasion to obtain the cattle!

19. One who is desirous of (obtaining) cattle should chant the vāmadevya on the verses[1] containing (the words) 'ye prosperous ones'.

[1] SV. I. 163 (*revatir na sadhamāde*)=ṚS. I. 30. 13-15=SV. II. 434-436.

20. The prosperous ones are the Waters; the vāmadevya is cattle; out of the Waters he (thereby) produces cattle for him.

21. The contrary of ruin in cattle (it is true, thereby) falls to his share, but his young ones shrink, as it were[1].

[1] *mīliteva* (also XVIII. 4. 4), cp. Śat. br. VII. 1. 2. 7: *yac cakṣur adhyaśeta sa candramās, tasmāt sa mīlitataro, 'nnaṁ hi tasmād asravat.* According to Sāyaṇa, because in a country where abundance of water is found, the young ones cannot thrive (!). The Jaim. br. I. 140 has simply: *paśumān bhavatīśvaro ha tv aprajātir bhavitoḥ, kavatibhyo hy eti prājāpatyābhyaḥ*, but Bharadvāja saw a way out of this dilemma: he chanted the sāman on three verses, the first and the last *kavatī*, the middle *revatī*: SV. II. 32, 434, 34.

22. For he deviates from the verses containing (the word) *ka*[1] (*i.e.*) from Prajāpati[2].

[1] Cp. VII. 8. 3.

[2] And this is another reason why he should not chant the sāman on the revatī-verses. Sāyaṇa seems to misunderstand this passage.

VII. 10.

(The third pṛṣṭha-laud, the naudhasa and śyaita.)

1. These two words (sky and earth) (once upon a time) were together (*i.e.* not separated by the intermediate region); when they went asunder they said: 'Let us contract a marriage on equal terms'[1].

[1] Cp. Ait. br. IV. 27. 5: *imau vai lokau sahāstām.. tau saṃyantāv etaṃ devavivāhaṃ vyavahetām.*

2. Of these (worlds) this (world) (*i.e.* the earth) gave the śyaita[1] to yonder (world) (*i.e.* to heaven), yonder (world) to this (world) the naudhasa[2].

[1] Grāmegeyagāna VI. 1. 62 on SV. I. 235=ṚS. VIII. 49. 1–2=SV. II. 161–162.

[2] Grāmegeya VI 1. 37 on SV. I. 236=ṚS. VIII. 88. 1–2=SV. II. 35–36.

3. Thereupon the finales of both of them changed places[1]; the naudhasa and śyaita, forsooth, are a God-marriage.

[1] *viparikrāmati* means, according to the Dict. of Petersburgh, 'rings herum schreiten'. That the meaning is 'to change places', is apparent from Āp. śrs. VIII. 15. 1 (see Rudradatta *a. h. l.*) and Baudh. śrs. V. 13 : 147. 3.

[2] On § 1–3 cp. Jaim. br. I. 145 : 'These worlds, being together, went asunder (in discordance ?); nothing whatever reached them (*i.e.* nothing from earth reached heaven and *vice versa*): Gods and men suffered hunger, for the Gods live upon what is given from here (*i.e.* the offerings) and men upon what is given from there (rain, and in consequence : food). Then rathantara and bṛhat (*i.e.* earth and heaven) said : 'Let us interchange those of our manifestations' (lit. 'let us contract a marriage with those of our m.) that are dear to us.' Now, originally, the śyaita was the manifestation dear to the rathantara, the naudhasa to the bṛhat. These they interchanged (lit. : 'with these they contracted a marriage'). Yonder world from thence gave the *ūṣas* to this world as marriage gift, and this world from here, the fog to yonder world; yonder world from thence gave the rain to this world as marriage gift, and this world from here, the divine service to yonder world....These manifestations (śyaita and naudhasa) said : 'Let us then interchange our nidhanas' (litt. : 'let us contract a marriage with our n.'). Now, originally, the śyaita had a verse-quarter as nidhana, the naudhasa (the word) "*vasu*". These they interchanged. Since then they dwell in each other's house, formerly they had dwelled each in his own house.' So far the Jaim. br. We note that the nidhana of the śyaita consists of the word *vasu* and of the naudhasa *mahe* (of the last pada of SV. I. 236 ?). Cp. also C. H. § 207.

4. He who knows this, lights on a better marriage.

5. These worlds keep arranging themselves from hence upwards and (on the other side) from above downwards[1].

[1] The regular succession is e i t h e r earth or rathantara, intermediate region or vāmadevya, sky or naudhasa, or: sky or bṛhat, intermediate region or vāmadevya, earth or śyaita.

6. In that they chant the rathantara (earth), he yokes by means of it this world (the earth); by means of the vāmadevya, the intermediate region; by means of the naudhasa[1], yonder world (heaven). In that they chant the bṛhat, he yokes by means of it yonder world; by means of the vāmadevya, the intermediate region; by means of the śyaita[2], this (world).

[1] Which, according to § 2 belongs to the earth.

[2] Which (*l.c.*) belongs to the heaven.

7. He sits by (well-) arranged worlds, who knows this [1].

[1] For one who knows this, the worlds are well arranged.

8. The naudhasa and the śyaita are (the same as) the rathantara and the bṛhat. In that they use the naudhasa correspondingly to the rathantara, they thereby use the bṛhat correspondingly to it, for the bṛhat cryptically is the naudhasa. In that they use the śyaita correspondingly to the bṛhat, they thereby use the rathantara correspondingly to it, for the śyaita cryptically is the rathnatara [1].

[1] The naudhasa originally belonged to the heaven (bṛhat), the śyaita to the earth (rathantara), cp. § 2.

9. He who knows this, chants both: the rathantara and the bṛhat [1].

[1] Although chanting the rathantara alone, he chants, in applying at the third pṛṣṭhalaud the naudhasa, the bṛhat also, and although chanting the bṛhat only at the first pṛṣṭhalaud, he chants, in applying at the third pṛṣṭhalaud the śyaita, the rathantara also.

10. The Gods divided amongst themselves the sacred lore (the bráhman); unto them came Nodhas, the son of Kakṣīvat; they said: 'A seer has come unto us; let us give him the sacred lore.' They granted him this sāman; in that they granted (it) to Nodhas, therefore it is called the naudhasa ('the sāman of Nodhas').

11. The naudhasa is sacred lore. One who is desirous of spiritual lustre should in chanting use t h i s (sāman): he comes in the possession of spiritual lustre [1].

[1] On § 10 and 11 cp. Jaim. br. I. 147: 'Now the naudhasa. Nodhas, the son of Kakṣīvat, went about a long time finding no firm support. He desired: 'May I find a firm support'. He came unto the Gods, who were dividing the sacred lore, and said: 'I am a seer, a maker of mantras: a long time I have gone about finding no firm support. Give ye to me that by which I may get a firm support'. To him they gave the essence of sacred lore: that became the naudhasa. He used it in chanting and then he got a firm support'.

12. Now (as to) the śyaita.

13. Prajāpati created the domestic animals; these, being created, went forth from him; he uttered over them this sāman, they gave way to him and submitted (*śyetyā abharan*) [1]; because they submitted, therefore it is the śyaita.

[1] It appears from TS. V. 5. 8. 1-2 and TBr. I. 1. 8. 3 (*śyeti kurute, śyetī akurvata*) that instead of *śyetyā abhavan* must be restored either *śyetyabhavan* or *śyeti abhavan*. The Jaim. br. (I. 148) has correctly: *so 'bravic chyetī vā imān paśūn akṛṣīti* and *śyetīkṛtā enaṃ paśava upatiṣṭhante*. Sāyaṇa on our passage is worthless.

14. The śyaita is cattle; one who is desirous of (obtaining) cattle should in chanting use t h i s (sāman); he comes into the possession of cattle.

15. Prajāpati created the creatures; these, being created, languished; he sniffed at them by means of the śyaita with *hummā* [1]; thereupon they throve. The young ones thrive during that year, in which he chants, knowing this, the śyaita.

[1] The last words of the udgītha of this sāman.

16. The Udgātṛ, forsooth, is the Sacrificer's creator (Prajāpati). In that he makes *him* (*i.e. hum*) by means of the śyaita, he becomes Prajāpati and sniffs at the young ones (thus causing them to thrive).

17. It has (the word) 'good' (*vasu*) for its finale [1]; cattle is a good (thing); he finds a firm support amongst cattle.

[1] *vā '234sū* (3, 5 above), cp. Calcutta ed. of SV., Vol. I, page 484.

EIGHTH CHAPTER.

VIII 1.

(V a r i a t i o n s o f t h e t h i r d p ṛ ṣ ṭ h a l a u d.)

1. At (a sacrifice) fit for charming (or 'bewitching') he should apply as the Brahman's chant [1] the (sāman) with (the word) *vaṣaṭ* as finale and at the midday-pavamāna (-laud) the (sāman) with (the word) *abhi* ('on to') as finale [2].

[1] As third pṛṣṭhalaud, corresponding with the śastra of the Brahman, *i.e.* the Brāhmaṇācchaṃsin.

[2] The printed text cannot be right; so as it stands it implies that the āṣkāra-ṇidhana kāṇva (grām. VII. 1. 28 on SV. I. 261=ṚS. VIII. 33. 1-3.=SV. II. 214-216) is chanted as the Brahman's sāman, changing its finale *āṣ* into *vaṣaṭ*, and the same sāman with *abhi* instead of *āṣ* at the bṛhatī part of the midday pavamāna laud. But in the first place, for the brahmasāman a bārhata pragātha is required, whilst SV. II. 214-216 are triṣṭubhs, and, secondly, neither Sāyaṇa nor the

Kṣudrasūtra agree with the literal sense of the printed text of our Brāhmaṇa. Sāyaṇa is silent about the words *āṣkaraṇidhanaṃ kāṇvam*, and the Kṣudrasūtra (I. 4, No. 16) runs: 'for one who bewitches, the opening (tristich of the out-of-doors-laud) and the ājyalauds are those of the śyena (see Ārṣeyakalpa III. 7); on 'being clarified by the stream' are chanted the raurava, the abhinidhana kāṇva (grām. VII. 1. 30), and the dairghaśravasa (or instead of the last the udvat prājāpatya), each on one verse, (and these three together replace here the raurava on all three of the normal agniṣṭoma); then, on the three (same verses), the yaudhājaya; the vaṣaṭkāranidhana (grām. VII. 1. 19, on SV. I. 256=ṚS. VIII. 3. 7-8=SV. II. 923-424) is the Brahman's chant; the kāleya (fourth pṛṣṭhalaud) on: 'this Brahman, the regular one' (SV. I. 438=SV. II. 1118-1120; this tristich is not found in the Ṛksaṃhitā, but must once have belonged to it, as not only the Ait. br. but also the Ait. ār. quote it by its pratīka, see Bloomfield's Concordance, in voce). The *viṣṭutis* are the ones pertaining to abhicāra (cp. Ṣaḍv. br. III. 2-6). The rest is similar (to the normal) jyotiṣṭoma).' For all these reasons it seems almost certain that the first two words *āṣkāraṇidhanaṃ kāṇvam* are interpolated, and the cause of the interpolation is apparent: the second khaṇḍa of Chapter VIII begins with precisely these same two words.—On the vaṣaṭkāraṇidhana cp. note 1 on IX. 6. 1.

2. The word *vaṣaṭ*, forsooth, is the God-arrow, and with (the word) 'on' (*i.e.* 'on to him': *abhi*) Indra hurled his thunderbolt towards Vṛtra; having hurled with (the word) 'on' a thunderbolt (*i.e.* a deadly weapon) towards him (towards his enemy whom he wishes to damage by charm), he shoots him with the God-arrow: the word *vaṣaṭ*.

3. For one who is desirous of (obtaining) cattle he should perform on the verses: 'Verily thou shalt extol'[1] the traikakubha[2] as Brahman's chant.

[1] SV. I. 247=ṚS. I. 84. 19-20=SV. II. 1073-1074.

[2] Grāmegeya X. 2. 12-14 are recorded three traikakubha sāmans, of which the last two have $\overset{2}{i}$'234 $\overset{5}{\text{mdrāḥ}}$ for nidhana (cp. § 7). From the ūhagāna it appears that the last of the two is meant.

4. Indra gave the Yatis over to the hyaenas. Three of them were left over: Rāyovāja, Bṛhadgiri and Pṛthuraśmi. These said: 'Who will support (or 'bear') us (as his) sons?' 'I' answered Indra and he, the three-humped[1], having put (them) on (his back), went along. He saw this chant. Because the three-humped (*trikakubh*), had seen it, therefore it is the traikakubha[2].

[1] Is Indra thought of here as a three-humped b u l l?

[2] For this myth cp. below XIII. 4. 17 and Jaim. br. I. 18. 5 in Journal of the

Amer. Or. Soc. Vol. XIX, page 125, where other references are given; add to these Maitr. Saṃh. III. 9. 3: 116. 15.

5. He again resorted to himself[1] with (the verse): 'Verily thou, a God, shalt extol the mortal, o most mighty! Than thee there is no other giver of joy, o Lord! Unto three, o Indra, do I speak this word.' By this pragātha and[2] this sāman he created a thousand head of cattle and gave them over to them. They got a firm support.

[1] *i.e.* 'he addressed himself' (?).

[2] The word *ca*, in the text erroneously given in the words of the verse, should be put before *sāmnā*.

6. He who is desirous of (obtaining) cattle, and he who is desirous of (finding) a firm support, should chant this sāman on this pragātha; he gains a thousand head of cattle and gets a firm support

7. Of triple strength and triple courage, verily, is this chant: to Indra are addressed the verses, to Indra is addressed the sāman, and (the word) '*indra*' is its finale; he gets a firm support in strength and courage[1].

[1] To § 3–7 refers the Kṣudrasūtra (I. 4, No. 17) saying: 'The (ritual) for one who is desirous of (obtaining) cattle has been arranged'; the author refers to his own text: I. 2, No. 14, see above, note 2 on VI. 10. 19.

8. He should take the traiśoka[1] as the Brahman's sāman for one who is suffering from a lingering disease.

[1] Gramegeya IX. 2. 35 composed on SV. I. 370=ṚS. VIII. 97. 10, 1 1, 1 2 =SV. II. 2 8 0, 2 8 2, 2 8 1 (with various readings).

9. These worlds (earth, intermediate region, sky) were (once) joined[1]; they languished. Indra by means of this chant removed their languor; in that he removed (it) from the three (*tri*) languishing (*śocatām*) (worlds), therefore it is the traiśoka.

[1] This is clearer in the Jaim. br., cp. note 1 on § 10.

10. The (languor) he removed from t h i s world (from the earth), entered the harlot; that which (he removed) from the intermediate region, (entered) the impotent (the eunuch); that which (he removed) from yonder (world), (entered) the wicked (or 'sinful') man[1].

[1] From the Jaim. br. (III. 72) I cite, correcting the obvious blunders, the following passage: *ime vai lokāḥ saha santas tredhā vyāyaṃs; te 'śocan yathaikas tredhāvicchinnaḥ śoced evaṃ; te devā abruvann: eteṣāṃ trayāṇāṃ lokānāṃ tisraḥ*

śuco 'pahanāmeti; ta etat sāmāpaśyaṃs, tenāstuvata, tenāiṣāṃ trayāṇāṃ lokānāṃ tisraḥ śuco 'pāghnan... tāḥ klībe kitava puṃścalyāṃ nyaveśayaṃs; tasmād ete śucā viddhāḥ śocante; na hāsyaita (read: *aitā, sc. śucaḥ*) *ājāyante ya evaṃ veda; tasmād u haiteṣāṃ nopabruvīta, nec chuco 'pabhajā iti.*

11. Therefore no thought of these ought to be cherished; to him who cherishes a thought of these he[1] assigns a part of the languor.

[1] Either the guilty or the harlot or the eunuch, cp. the last words of the passage cited from Jaim. br. under note 1 on § 10.

12. Hurt by languor, verily, is he, who suffers from a lingering disease; in that the Brahman's chant is the traiśoka, he removes from him the languor.

13. They undertake ('they chant') as finale (the word) *divā*; *divā* ('by day'), forsooth, is the dawning; he makes it dawn upon him[1].

[1] So that he will see the following dawnings or days —To § 8–13 refers the Kṣudrasūtra (I. 4, No. 18): 'The (ritual) for one who suffers from a lingering disease has been arranged', *viz.* under No. 8 of this same text, see note 2 on VI. 10. 5.

VIII. 2.

(Variations of the third pṛṣṭha-laud, continued.)

1. The kāṇva (sāman) of which (the syllable) *āṣ* is the finale[1], he should take as the Brahman's chant for one who desires firm support.

[1] Grāmegeya VII. 1. 28 on SV. I. 261=ṚS. VIII. 33. 1–3=SV. II. 214–216.

2. Kaṇva[1] saw this sāman (as it was) without (any) finale; he did not get (by its chanting) a firm support; he heard a cat[2] sneezing (and making the noise) *āṣ*; he saw this as finale and thereupon (by chanting the chant with this finale) he got a firm support; (the reason) why this is the sāman, is for getting a firm support[3].

[1] In Jaim. br. III. 46 it is Kaṇva the son of Nṛṣad (*nārṣada*).

[2] Jaim. br. has *pṛṣadaṃśa* (as against *vṛṣadaṃśa* of Pañc. br.), which may be the better reading (gaṇa *utsādi*).

[3] To § 1–2 refers the Kṣudrasūtra (I. 4, No. 19). 'For one who is anxious to obtain a firm support, the Brahman's chant is the kāṇva (sāman) with *āṣ* as finale, (chanted) on the verses of the naudhasa (the sāman grām. VII. 1. 28 chanted on the words of grām. VI. 1. 37, *i.e.* SV. I. 236=ṚS. VIII. 88. 1–2=SV. II. 35–36). The rest is similar to the (normal) jyotiṣṭoma'.

3. The janitra of Vasiṣṭha[1] he should take as the Brahman's chant for one who desires to obtain offspring.

[1] Cp. note 1 on VI. 9. 5; the vague statement of the Brāhmaṇa (there are more than one sāmans of this name) is specified by the sūtra.

4. Vasiṣṭha, whose son had been slain[1], saw this sāman; he got (by chanting it) children and his cattle was multiplied; (the reason) why it is this sāman, is for procreation[2]

[1] Cp. note 1 on IV. 7. 3.

[2] To § 3-4 refers the Kṣudrasūtra (I. 4, No. 20): 'The (ritual) for one who is desirous of offspring has been arranged', *viz.* in No. 2 of this text, cp. note 1 on VI. 9. 5.

5. The ātharvaṇa (sāman)[1] he should take as the Brahman's chant for one who desires (to reach) the world[2].

[1] Araṇyegeya I. 1. 23 (on SV. I. 33) chanted on the naudhasa-verses.

[2] From § 6 appears that the world of immortality is meant.

6. The Atharvans, forsooth, desiring to reach the world, saw this sāman; they by means of it saw the world of immortality. (The reason) why it is this sāman, is for getting to know (the way to) the world of heaven[1].

[1] To § 5 and 6 refers the Kṣudrasūtra (I. 4, No. 21): 'For one who is desirous of (reaching) the world, the Brahman's chant is the ātharvaṇa (-sāman), chanted on the verses of the naudhasa; the *viṣṭutis* are the ascending ones (see the Brāhmaṇa II. 1. 1); the rest is similar to the (normal) jyotiṣṭoma.—In this manner, if its pṛṣṭha (*i.e.* the hotuḥ pṛṣṭha, the first pṛṣṭhalaud) is chanted on the rathantara, but if it is chanted on the bṛhat, the introductory (tristich) must contain (the word) 'foremost' (cp. note 1 on VI. 9. 10), the ājya-(laud)s are *bārhata* (cp. note 4 on page 33 of the edition of Ārṣeyakalpa), the pṛṣṭha is the bṛhat (sāman); the ātharvaṇa (sāman), (chanted) on the verses of the śyaita, is the Brahman's chant, and on the uṣṇih (part) the śrudhya is chanted (instead of the pauṣkala, see Anhang on Ārṣeyakalpa, page 203). The *viṣṭutis* are the ascending ones. The rest is similar to the jyotiṣṭoma'.

7. The abhīvarta[1] he should take as the Brahman's chant for one who has a rival.

[1] Cp IV. 3. 1 and XV. 10. 3 and 11.

8. By means of the abhīvarta the Gods turned themselves against (*abhyavartanta*) the Asuras. (The reason) why the Brahman's chant is the abhīvarta, is for turning against the rival[1].

[1] Cp. IV. 3. 2.—To § 7 and 8 refers the Kṣudrasūtra (I. 4, No. 22): 'For one who has a rival, the Brahman's chant is the abhīvarta, the *viṣṭutis* are those that are used for *abhicāra* (cp. Ṣaḍv. br. III. 2–6) The rest is similar to the (normal) jyotiṣṭoma'.

9. The śrāyantīya[1] he should take as the Brahman's chant for one who goes amiss[2] in a sacrifice.

[1] Gramegeya VIII. 2. 5 on SV. I. 267=ṚS. VIII. 99. 3-4 (with varr.)=SV. II. 669-670.

[2] Cp. XVII. 8. 2 as compared with ib. 4.

10. Prajāpati longed to possess his own daughter Uṣas[1]. He lost his seed; this was poured down on the earth; he strengthened[2] it, (thinking): 'may this of me not be spoiled'[3]; he set it right and made the cattle out of it.

[1] For parallels cp. Lévi, Le sacrifice dans les Brāhmanas page 20, 21.

[2] *śrīṇāti* is the counterpart of *vibhraṃśate* (see XVI. 12. 4).

[3] Cp. Ait. br. III. 33. 6: *te devā abruvan medaṃ prajāpate reto duṣad iti*; because they had said *mā duṣat*, the *māduṣa* came into existence which cryptically is equal to *mānuṣa*'. The recension of the myth in our Brāhmaṇa is apparently abbreviated and by consequence only partly comprehensible. The fuller recension has been handed down in the Jaim. br. III. 261, 262, but the text is rather corrupt. I give the translation so far as I understand the passage 'The Gods, undertaking a sacrificial session, said: 'what of us is horrid, that we will produce, in order not to undertake the sacrifice w i t h (that) horrid (part).' What was horrid of them that they produced, and cleansing it, put it down on (between) two earthen plates, thereupon they undertook the sacrificial session. Therefrom (from the two plates, the *śarāvas*) that *akhala* ('not-wicked', euphemistic as *śiva*) God was born. Because he was born out of the plates, that is his name (probably the author has in mind the name Śarva=Rudra). It was Agni that here was born (Agni sometimes is identified with Rudra). He who knows this, is not hurt by this (God). He (Agni-Rudra) said to the Gods: 'For what have ye caused me to come into existence'? 'For carefully watching', they replied, 'thou shalt kill him who may transgress'. Now, Prajāpati had set his mind on his own daughter, the Dawn. He (Rudra) put an arrow on his bow and shot at him. Thereupon, he (Prajāpati) put on the form of an antelope and went upward. This (arrow shot by Rudra) is (the constellation called) 'the three-knotted arrow'.... After he (Prajāpati) was shot, his seed fell down and came down on the Himavat. It became *mānuṣa* (probably a lake, the forerunner of the classical *mānasaṃ saras*). About this the Gods and the Seers, coming together, said: 'Let not this be spoiled'. Because they had said 'let it not be spoiled' (*mā idaṃ duṣat*), hence it was *māduṣam*, and *māduṣaṃ* is called *mānuṣam* ('man'). They set it to flames on all sides by Agni, the Maruts blew on it, by means of

the *śrāyantīya* they strengthened it (*aśriṇan*): hence the name *śrāyantīya*. Thereupon cattle was created (out of the strengthened seed of Prajāpati); those (animals) that first came into existence are the red ones; those that came into existence out of the (seed) when it was being heated, are the reddish brown ones; those that came into existence out of the (seed) when it was heated, are the brown ones; those that came into existence out of the (seed), when it was being burned, are the mules and the black (animals), and therefore, this same fire burns the white as well as the black (animal); out of the sparks were created the goats and the antelopes; out of the coals (*añjāra*) the Angirases, out of the ashes mixed with coals were created the three *vaśās*: the one dedicated to Mitra and Varuṇa, the one dedicated to Bṛhaspati and the one dedicated to the All-Gods; out of the ashes the donkey was created; therefore he is (in colour) the counterpart of the ashes; therefore he lives being ridden'. The Sanskrit text may be consulted in: 'Das Jaiminīya brāhmaṇa in Auswahl' No. 207.

11. (The reason) why the Brahman's chant is the śrāyantīya, is that it (this sāman) strengthens him and sets him right [1].

[1] To § 9–11 refers the Kṣudrasūtra (I. 4, No. 23): 'For one who is deprived of a sacrifice, the Brahman's chant is the śrāyantīya; the kāleya (grāmegeya VI. 2. 7) is (chanted) on the verses (SV. I. 408=ṚS. VIII. 21. 1. 2=SV. II. 58–59): 'We (call) thee, o incomparable one!' The rest is similar to the (normal) jyotiṣṭoma'.

VIII. 3.

(The fourth pṛṣṭha-laud, the kāleya.)

1. The Gods and the Asuras contended for (the possession of) these worlds. The Gods resorted to Prajāpati; he gave them this sāman, (saying): 'By means of this sāman ye will be able to drive them away' [1]. By it they drove them away from these worlds. Because they drove them away (*akālayanta*), therefore it is (called) the kāleya [2].

[1] Read (*kālayiṣyadhva iti* instead of *kālayiṣpaddham iti*.

[2] See note 1 on VIII. 2. 11.—Besides other myths to explain the name kāleya, the Jaim. br. (I. 154, 155) has the following interesting quasi-myth: 'Gods, Fathers and Men were on one side, Asuras, Ogres and Piśācas on the other side. These contended about (the possession of) these worlds. Now, the Kali-Gandharvas moved in the middle, not heeding either party. The Gods, the Fathers and the Men overcame the Asuras, Ogres and Piśācas, and they divided these worlds among themselves. The Gods took as their share the world of the Gods, the Fathers the world of the Fathers, the Men the world of the Men. Then arrived the Kali-Gandharvas and said, 'Grant us also subsequently a share in these worlds'. 'No', they said, 'ye, forsooth, have kept yourselves neutral, not heeding either party'. They answered: 'But in our mind we have attended on

ye, so give us a share'. 'No' they said, 'the worlds are well-divided by us, we cannot mix them up again'. They said: 'Then let that be ours what we ourselves see'. They granted them these Kalindās (the land of Kalinda ?), saying: 'Among these practise ye austerities'. Because they granted the Kalindās to the Kalis, thence the Kalindās have this name.—This Kali, the son of Vitadanya, saw this sāman, he practised it in chanting and saw by means of it this *avāntaradeśaṃ duryantaṃ lokam*; this he conquered. This sāman is a world (or 'room') gaining one, he who has practised it in chanting finds room, but the status of a Gandharva he does not reach, he gains only the world of the Gandharvas. Because Kali, the son of Vitadanya, saw this sāman, therefore it is (called) kāleya.' See the Sanskrit text in Jaim. br. in Auswahl, No. 47.

2. He who knows this, drives away his rival from these worlds.

3. The stoma, 'strength' (*tara*) by name, was with the Gods; the sacrifice, 'finding treasure' by name, was with the Asuras. The Gods by means of this stoma: 'by strength your treasure finding one'[1] took away the sacrifice of the Asuras[2].

[1] The verses of the kāleya begin: *tarobhir vo vidadvasum*.

[2] Similarly the Jaim. br.

4. He who knows this takes, by means of the stoma, the sacrifice of his rival away.

5. There were (once) (certain) Gods called Sādhya. These, having cut off the afternoon-service, went together with the midday-service to the world of heaven. This (cut off afternoon-service) the Gods connected by means of the kāleya[1]. That there is the kāleya, is for connecting the afternoon-service (with the midday-service).

[1] The kāleya is the last laud of the midday-service.

6. The afternoon-service, forsooth, is 'finding treasure' (*vidadvasu*): by taking as prastāva (the verse quarter) 'by strength your treasure-finding one' he passes, in chanting, across[1] to the afternoon-service.

[1] *abhyativadati* (cp. V. 7. 4), *abhilakṣyātivadati, atīti dhātvarthānuvādaḥ*, Sāyaṇa.

7. The kāleya is (equal to) all the characteristics: in that it has a (whole) verse-quarter as prastāva, thereby it is rathantara-like[1]; in that it makes the same risings as the bṛhat[2], thereby it is bṛhat-like; in that its respond contains a stobha, thereby it is bṛhat-like[3]; in that it has a 'running' *iḍā*[4], thereby it is rathantara-like[5]. In all characteristics he is firmly established.

[1] Cp. VII. 7. 1.

[2] Cp. VII. 7. 6. I am uncertain about the *rohas* in the kāleya, perhaps:

1 2 1 2 1
drāṁ sa..(1); *bā* | *dhā* (2); *ntā 234ḥ* (3), cp. the musically figured chant in C. H. page 324.

[3] In the bṛhat: *auhovā*, in the kāleya: *vā ovā*.

4
[4] *dravaḍiḍa*: *ho 5i* | *ḍā* (close of the kāleya), cp. also X. 11. 1 and X. 12. 4.

[5] How in this respect the kāleya is rathantara-like, is not very clear. Sāyaṇa quotes a passage from the Nidānasūtra, which I cannot find exactly so in our text (II. 11 beg.) The meaning seems to be that the pṛṣṭhastotras on the uneven (3, 5) days of the ṣaḍaha (on which the rathantara is replaced by the vairūpa- and śākvarasāmans) are *dravaḍiḍa* (as the kāleya), whilst the pṛṣṭhastotras of the even (4, 6) days (on which the bṛhat is replaced by the vairāja and raivata-sāmans) are *ūrdhveḍa* (*au 2345* | *ḍā*). In this way we note at least a kind of correspondence between kāleya and rathantara.

VIII 4.

(The ārbhava-pavamāna-laud, its metres and chants.)

1. There were (once) (certain) Gods called Sādhya. Together with the whole sacrifice they went to the world of heaven. The Gods said to the metres: 'Bring ye the soma hither.' They sent off the Jagatī; she returned leaving behind three syllables and having become monosyllabic; they sent off the Triṣṭubh; she returned leaving behind one syllable and having become trisyllabic; they sent off the Gāyatrī—at that time, forsooth, the metres consisted of four syllables—she returned bringing with her not only those syllables (that had been left behind by the two others), becoming thus octosyllabic, but also the three pressings, two in her hands, the third (in her mouth), biting it with her teeth. Therefore two pressings are provided with shoots, but the third is sucked out[1], because she had fetched it beween her teeth, sucking it out[2]. The shoots of it (of the soma), that fell down as it was being fetched, became the pūtikas[3]; the blossoms that fell out, became the arjunas[4]; what she shook off[5] (*prāprothat*), that became the praprothas[5]. Therefore, at the afternoon-service (or 'the third pressing') they pour out the sour milk[6]: the soma which is eaten by the cows[7]; thereof they pour out the sap, in order that there may be soma in it.

[1] The Jaim. br. relates this *in extenso* (cp. Jaim. br. in Auswahl No. 102): further cp. Śat. br. IV. 3. 2. 7, Ait. br. III. 25-28, TS. VI. 1. 6. 1-5, Kaṭh. XXIII. 10, Maitr Saṃh. III. 7. 3.

[2] The first two pressings are obtained from the soma-shoots itself, the third, however, (cp. C. H. § 218) from the pressed-out soma-husks.

[3] A kind of herb used as surrogate for the soma, see below, IX. 5. 4, and cp. Eggeling in Sacred books of the East, Vol. XLIV. page 451, note 1.

[4] Equally a kind of grass used as substitute for soma, probably equivalent to *phālguna*, cp. Āp. XIV. 24. 12, Baudh. XIV. 29: 201. 25, TBr. I. 4. 7. 5.

[5] Thus Sāyaṇa (*adhunutāṅgāni*): elsewhere the meaning is 'to snort'. The meaning of *praprotha* is unknown. It must also denote a kind of herb palatable to cows.

[6] *Viz.* in the pūtabhṛt to the pressed soma, cp. C. H. § 220 and Ait. br. III. 27. 2.

[7] When they eat the herbs, mentioned above, which originated from the soma.

2. Triṣṭubh and Jagatī said to Gāyatrī: 'Let us join thee'[1]. She answered: 'What will result therefrom for me'? 'What thou wishest' they said. She replied: 'To me must belong the whole morning-service, and I must have the lead of the last two services'. Therefore, the whole morning-service belongs to the Gāyatrī and the last two services are introduced by it[2].

[1] *upa tvāyāva*, usually this is the expression of one who wishes to become pupil to another.

[2] The prātaḥsavana is chanted on verses in gāyatrī-metre only, whilst the first chant of the midday- and afternoon-lauds are likewise on verses in gāyatrī.

3. Triṣṭubh joined her with (her) three syllables[1], so that she (Gāyatrī) became of eleven syllables; Jagatī joined her with (her) one syllable[1], so that she (Gāyatrī) became of twelve syllables.

[1] Triṣṭubh had become trisyllabic and jagatī monosyllabic after their endeavour to fetch the soma; in this manner they were absorbed into the gāyatrī.

4. Therefore, it is said that the gāyatrī is (equal to) all the metres, for the gāyatrī went making those increases[1].

[1] *i.e.* increased so as to encompass the two other metres.

5. Indra, loathing the afternoon-service[1], got away. The Gods by means of (the words): 'by the most sweet'[2] made it sweet; by means of (the words): 'by the most intoxicating' they made it intoxicating ('strong'); by means of (the words): 'by the stream become thou, o

Soma, clarified' they clarified it, and on (the words): 'pressed out for Indra to drink' Indra returned to it. (The reason) why he makes the prastāva with 'by the most sweet, most intoxicating' is that Indra may take a share in the afternoon service.

[1] Because its soma was pressed only out of the husks and therefore not sufficiently strong and intoxicating.

[2] The gāyatra and the first sāman (the saṃhita) are chanted on the gāyatrī-verses SV. I. 468=ṚS. IX. 1. 1-3=SV. II. 39-41: *svādiṣṭhayā madiṣṭhayā pavasva soma dhārayā | indrāya pātave sutaḥ.*

6. 'The most sweet' were the domestic animals among the Gods, 'the most intoxicating' amongst the Asuras; by (the words): 'by the most sweet, most intoxicating' the Gods took away the animals of the Asuras.

7. He who knows this takes away the cattle of his rival.

8. On these (verses is chanted) the saṃhita [1].

[1] Grāmegeyagāna XII. 2. 19 on the verses quoted in note 2 on § 5.

9. There were (once) (certain) Gods called Sādhya. These, having cut off the afternoon-service, went, together with the midday-service, to the world of heaven. The Gods (however) united it (*samadadhuḥ*) by means of the saṃhita (sāman); because they united it, therefore it is the saṃhita ('united').

10. The kāleya goes before, the saṃhita comes afterwards; for by means of these two (sāmans) is the afternoon-service linked (with the midday-service) [1].

[1] Cp. VIII. 3. 5.

11. The saṃhita is (equal to) all the characteristics: in that it has a (whole) verse-quarter as prastāva, thereby it is rathantara-like; in that it makes the same risings as the bṛhat [1], thereby it is bṛhat-like; in that is has after each verse-quarter a finale [2], thereby it is rathantara-like. In all characteristics he is firmly established.

[1] I am not able to point out these *rohas* in the saṃhita-sāman. On the whole, the chant as figured in the ūhagāna and the Prayogas differs considerably from the grāmegeya; this is probably due to certain special rules for chanting on gāyatrī-metre.

[2] *padanidhana*, cp. X. 10. 1; perhaps in the saṃhita-sāman the syllables *pavā*, *yāpā* and *sūtāḥ* (cp. C.H. page 340) are to be taken as finales.

VIII. 5.

(The ārbhava pavamāna-laud, its metres and chants, continued.)

1. There are the kakubh and the uṣṇih[1].

[1] After the saṃhita sāman two chants follow in the jyotiṣṭoma, the first on kakubh-metre (of 8+12+8 syllables): the sapha, the second on uṣṇih-metre (of 8+8+12 syllables): the pauṣkala. The sapha is grāmegeya XVII. 2. 5 on SV. I. 578=ṚS. IX. 108. 1(-2)=SV. II. 42(-43) (kakubh satobrhatī). The pauṣkala is grāmegeya XVII. 1. 5, on SV. I. 566=ṚS. IX. 106. 1(-3)=SV. II. 44(-46).—Although here only two verses are applied (*viz.* II. 42 and 44), the uttarārcika gives, after 42, one verse more and after 44 two more, because these come in later on, at the 10th day.

2. By means of the kakubh and the uṣṇih, Indra hurled his thunderbolt on Vṛtra; at the kakubh he made a stride onward, by means of the uṣṇih he hurled it. Therefore, the middle verse-quarter of the kakubh has the highest number of syllables, for it is a striding-on. Thereupon, he drew together[1]; therefore, the last verse-quarter of the uṣṇih has the highest number of syllables, for in front the thunderbolt is, as it were, heavy[2].

[1] *tad abhi samauhat;* for *abhisamūhati* the Dict. of Petersburgh in kurzerer Fassung gives the meaning 'zusammenhäufen'. I propose to take *tad abhi* together, and suggest that *padau* is to be understood as object to *samauhat*; being about to hurl the thunderbolt, Indra strides out; at the moment of hurling, he draws his feet together (he draws the left foot, which was behind the right one, forward). Sāyaṇa comments: *abhitaḥ ubhe pārśve samauhat, aṣṭākṣarau pādau samyag avahat*; he takes as subject *kakubh.* The Jaim. br. (III. 294) has: 'striding out he drew together its syllables (*parākramamāṇo hy asyākṣarāṇi* (read *asyā a* °?) *samauhat*).

[2] The parallel passage in the Jaim. br. (I. 158, 159) runs as follows: 'By means of the kakubh and the uṣṇih Indra, standing on two gāyatrīs (the metre of 24 syllables) (as his feet), hurled his thunderbolt on Vrtra. These two (gāyatrīs) were not able to support him; he added to them the fourfooted animals: cow, horse, goat and sheep, and those (*i e.* the metres which arose in this way, the metres of 24+4=28 syllables, the kakubh and uṣṇih) supported him. Standing on the kakubh and uṣṇih, making the sabha and pauskala his two arms, he hurled (the thunderbolt) and slew him (*viz.* Vṛtra). He who knows this slays his spiteful enemy. He (Indra) stepped with one foot forward, the other one coming after; the foot that was directed forward, became the kakubh; therefore of the kakubh the greatest number of syllables is in the fore part (8+12+8); the foot that came after, became the uṣṇih; therefore of the uṣṇih the greatest number of syllables is in the hind part (8+8+12). See Jaim. br. in Auswahl, No. 50.

3. A thunderbolt (*i.e.* a deadly weapon) he who knows this, hurls on his rival.

4. The kakubh and the uṣṇih are the nostrils (the nose) of the sacrifice. Therefore, although being the same metre, they both convey in different ways the sacrifice; therefore from each of the nostrils, although they are similar, the two breaths issue in a different way[1].

[1] As out- and inbreathing.

5. The kakubh and the uṣṇih are the breaths (the vital airs); therefore they (the priests) do not make *vaṣaṭ* with them[1]. If they made *vaṣaṭ* with them, they would put the vital airs into the fire.

[1] They must not be used as yājyās, to accompany a burnt-offering; at the end of a yājyā the word *vaṣaṭ* is pronounced.

6. On these (verses)[1] the sapha (sāman) is (chanted). Devoid of *pha*[2], forsooth, is the afternoon-service; (this sāman is chanted) to make the afternoon-service provided with *pha*[2]. As for the pauṣkala, by means of this (sāman) Prajāpati created the domestic animals in abundance (*puṣkala*); to them he brought form (or 'beauty'); (the reason) why it is this sāman, is that he (thereby) brings beauty to his beasts[3].

[1] Properly the sapha only on the first.

[2] What the meaning of *pha* is, according to our author, is unknown. Nor is the meaning of the name *sabha*, as this sāman is called by the Jaiminīyas (Jaim. br. I. 160), very clear. "On these the sabha (is chanted), in order that the sacrifice may be *sabha* (possessed of *bhā*, 'light' ?). All that is wrongly chanted or recited, or incomplete in the sacrifice, for clearing up (*sabhatāyai*) (all) that (it is adhibited). They chant this sāman, hoping that it may be shining, illuminated (?)—By means of the sabha, the Gods (possessed themselves) of the splendour, the power, the valour, the strength, the cattle and the food of the Asuras, by means of the sabha, they made themselves lighting (*sabham atmānam adhyakurvata*).'—By means of the sabha, Prajāpati makes the cattle remain with him; therefore, he said: 'I have become 'shining out' through cattle (*sabho vai paśubhir abhūvam*)' etc. See. Jaim. br. in Auswahl No. 51.

[3] Cp. Jaim. br. I. 160: 'He (Prajāpati) did not know the domestic animals (the cows) from one another, as they were of one colour (*ekarūpa*). He saw the pauṣkala and, thereby, distinguished their colours: they became of different colour: white, reddish, and black; formerly, forsooth, they had been of one colour, r e d even they were' (Auswahl No. 52).

7. (The three verses, beginning): 'By fore-conquest from your plant' are a verse-quarter-virāj[1] and syllabic-virāj.[1] By means of the

verse-quarter-virāj, the Gods went to the world of heaven, by means of the syllabic virāj, the seers after (them) came to know the way to it That there are those verse-quarter-virāj and syllabic virāj (verses), is for knowing the way to the world of heaven.

[1] After the sapha and pauṣkala follow in the ārbhavapavamāna-laud the śyāvāśva and the āndhīgava sāmans on three verses, the first of which is an anuṣṭubh, the second and third gāyatrīs. These three verses together comprehend 10 verse-quarters (the anuṣṭubh: 4, each gāyatrī: 3) and, the virāj being of 10 syllables, they form together a *padyā virāj*. They contain together 80 syllables (the anuṣṭubh: 32, each gāyatrī: 24), together, they form an *akṣaryā virāj*; 80 being a plurality of 10.—The three verses are SV. I. 545=ṚS. IX. 101. 1-3=SV. II. 47-49. The śyāvāśva (on SV. I. 545) is grāmegeya XVI. 1. 11, the āndhīgava (on the same verse) is grām. XVI. 1. 12.

8. On these (verses) the śyāvāśva (is chanted).

9. Śyāvāśva, the son of Arcanānas, who was taking part in a sacrificial session, was brought (by his fellow-sattrins who wished to kill him) to a desert ('dry soil'). He saw this sāman and by means of it created rain. Thereupon, he became all right and found salvation This sāman, forsooth, is a means to get salvation [1].

[1] In the Jaim. br. (I. 163, 164) this legend is somewhat differently told Śyāvāśva, the son of Arcanānas, had absented himself to collect fuel for the sacrifice, the sattra. He was left behind by his fellow-sattrins, who by themselves went to the world of heaven. He desired: 'May I reach after them the world of heaven, may I be united with my fellow-sattrins'. He saw this sāman and practised it in chanting. By the verse: 'By fore-conquest of your plant' the Maruts called him to the world of heaven, the thrice repeated stobha of the sāman being *ehyā* ('come'). Thereupon, he was united with his fellow-sattrins. And so Śyāvāśva is united with the Maruts (*sa haisa marudbhir eva saha śyāvāśvaḥ*). See the text in Jaim. br. in Auswahl, No. 54.

10. He who has chanted this (sāman) finds salvation and becomes all right.

11. Indra, loathing the afternoon-service, got away [1]. The Gods by means of the śyāvāśva (and especially by its stobha): 'come, come' [2] called him back. (Thereupon) he returned. The reason why there is this sāman, is that Indra may have a share in the after-noon-service [3].

[1] Cp. note 1 on VIII. 4. 5.

[2] The stobha is *aihayi*, *ehiyā* which are the chanting forms of *ehi*: 'come hither'.

3 Similarly the Jaim. br. I. 164. In the text of Pañc. br. read *ehiyety anvahvayant, sa* etc.

12. Then the āndhīgava. Andhīgu, desiring (to obtain) cattle, saw this sāman; by means of it he created a thousand head of cattle[1]. (The reason) why it is this sāman, is that the cattle may flourish. It has a finale in the middle[2] (and) has (the word) *iḍā* (as closing finale)[2]. Thereby the afternoon-service becomes all right[3]. If it were not provided with a finale in the middle and if it had not *iḍā* (as closing finale), the afternoon-service would not be all right.

1 Cp. Jaim. br. I. 165: 'The descendants of Śakti (the Śāktyas), being desirous of obtaining food, were consecrated (*i.e.* they undertook a sacrifice of soma). Then Andhīgu, the Śāktya, saw this sāman and practised it in chanting; he applied the decasyllabic virāj in the middle; the virāj is decasyllabic, the virāj is food; thereupon they obtained the virāj, *viz.* the food', cp. Auswahl No. 56.

2 Cp. C.H. page 342.

3 This is more clearly expressed in the Jaim. br. (I. 165, Auswahl No. 55): 'It has a nidhana in the middle: for obtaining a firm support. They who undertake the ārbhava-laud, go crossing a sea without hold (?); that it (the sāman) has a nidhana in the middle, is for obtaining a firm support. Just as in daily life one, who has descended with his ship into a sea, comes across an island, and having gone on land, takes a rest, in the same manner they, having undertaken (litt. 'come unto') the nidhana, might take a rest'.

13. They make ('chant') in the middle a finale of ten syllables; the virāj is of ten syllables; he (the Sacrificer) gets a firm support in the virāj[1].

1 Cp. the Jaim. br. as cited in note 1 under § 12.

14. (On the verses beginning:) 'Unto the dear ones he is clarified'[1] is chanted the kāva(sāman)[1]; it is the chant of Prajāpati.

1 Grāmegeyagāna XVI. 2. 6 on SV. I. 554=ṚS. IX. 75. 1-3=SV. II. 50–52 (jagatī-metre).—According to the Jaim. br. (I. 166) this sāman was seen by Kavi Bhārgava who desired amidst the Gods the immortal world of the Gandharvas. This Kavi Bhārgava is, according to the Sarvānukramaṇa, the Seer of ṚS IX. 75.

15. The 'dear ones' are the children, the 'dear ones' are the domestic animals; he gets a firm support in children and domestic animals.

16. The auśana and the kāva are the strings of the sacrifice[1]; this God-case[2], forsooth, is closed up with regard to the sacrifice.

(The reason) why these two (sāmans) are the last, is, that the sacrifice may be uninjured (or 'well kept').

[1] The sacrifice is, so to say, kept in a case which is closed up or pressed together by means of two strings: the auśana, the last of the midday laud (cp. VII. 5. 16) and the kāva, the last of the ārbhava-laud.

[2] Cp. Ath. S. X. 2. 27. *tad vā atharvaṇaḥ śiro* d e v a k o ś a ḥ s a m u b - i t a ḥ.

VIII. 6.

(The agniṣṭoma-laud.)

1. The Gods divided among themselves the sacred lore; what pith of it was left over, that became the yajñāyajñīya (sāman)[1].

[1] Grāmegeyagāna I. 2. 25 on SV. I. 35=ṚS. VI. 48. 1–2=SV. II. 53-54.

2. The yajñāyajñīya, forsooth, is the pith of the sacred lore. By chanting the yajñāyajñīya they establish the sacrifice in the pith of the sacred lore.

3. The yijñāyajñīya is a womb: out of this womb Prajāpati created (emitted, brought forth) the sacrifice; in that he created sacrifice after sacrifice (*yajñaṃ yajñam*), therefore it is (called) yajñā-yajñīya[1].

[1] The word yajñāyajñīya, containing twice the word *yajña*, induces our author to speak of 'sacrifice after sacrifice', 'sacrifice' alone being sufficient.

4. Therefore, formerly the Brāhmins used to hold[1] the out-of doors-laud with t h i s (sāman)[2], (thinking): 'Beginning at its womb let us go on to extend the sacrifice'. But, by chanting it at the end[3], they establish the sacrifice in its womb.

[1] On the aorist with *purā* (also VIII. 9.7) cp. Delbrück, Altind. Syntax, page 286.

[2] Similarly the Jaim. br. (I. 173): 'Formerly they used to hold all the lauds with this (sāman)': *etena ha sma vai purā sarvāṇi stotrāṇi stuvanti.*

[3] Read *yad v antataḥ* instead of *yajñantataḥ*.

5. With the Asuras (once) was the whole sacrifice. The Gods saw the yajñāyajñīya. By means of (the words): 'by sacrifice on sacrifice in honour of Agni' they took from them the agnihotra; (by the words) 'and by hymn on hymn in honour of the skilful', the full- and new-moon sacrifices; by (the words): 'continually we (will extol) the

immortal Jātavedas', the seasonal sacrifices, and by (the words) 'as a dear friend I will extol', the sacrifice of soma.

6. At that time the metres (the verse-quarters of it) were: 'By sacrifice in honour of Agni; by hymn in honour of the skilful; we (will extol) the immortal Jātavedas; as a dear friend I will extol'. Now, the Gods by means of the verses, repeating each time the beginning, (the first word of each verse quarter), took the sacrifice away from the Asuras[1].

[1] Because the verses of the Gods in this manner had grown bigger and stronger than those of the Asuras! The verse runs: *yajñāya a j ñ ā vo agnaye girāg i r ā ca dakṣase* | *prap r a vayam amṛtaṃ jātavedasaṃ priyaṃ mitraṃ na śaṁsiṣam.*

7. He who knows this takes, through the verses, the sacrifice of his rival away.

8. A brahman, Kūśāmba, the son of Svāyu, a Lātavya (by gotra), used to say about this (chant): 'Who, forsooth, will to day be swallowed by the dolphin[1] that has been thrown on sacrifice's path?'[2]

[1] A female dolphin or porpoise; perhaps a crocodile is meant.

[2] 'Sacrifice's path' is the way prescribed for going hither and thither on the sacrificial ground.—The text should run at the end: *gariṣyatīti.*

9. Now, the dolphin thrown on sacrifice's path is the yajñāyajñīya (sāman). By saying: 'by hymn on hymn' (*girāgirā*)[1], thereby the Udgātṛ swallows himself.

[1] A pun on the word *girā*, which is in appearance inauspicious, because it can be connected, as 2nd pers. imperative, with *girati* ('to swallow'), (instead of *gṛṇāti* 'to extol').

10. He should (therefore) perform his part of the chant, making (the) *irā* (-sound)[1]; the Udgātṛ (thereby) establishes the sacrifice in food (*irā*) and will not die prematurely.

[1] Instead of by *girāgirā* he introduces the Udgītha by *irā irā*, see C.H. page 370. Read in the text *yad yajñāyajñīyaṃ.*

[2] On these §§ cp Jaim. br. I. 174, 175: (He should chant the Udgītha in the following manner:) "*o(y)irā (y)irā cā dākṣāsā*' (instead of *o gā irā girā cā dākṣāsā* of the gāna). If he were to say: *girā girā ca*, Agni vaiśvānara would swallow up (*gired*) the Sacrificer, but by saying: *o(y)-irā (y) irā cā dakṣāsā, irā* being food, he puts food into the mouth of Agni vaiśvānara (=as he brings the word *irā* at the beginning [*mukha* meaning 'mouth' as well as 'beginning'] of the yajñāyajnīya, which is identified with Agni vaiśvānara). However, he is apt to become parched

up by saying *o(y)irā o(y)irā cā dākṣāsā* ; he should (rather) say *o(y)irā ihā cā dākṣāsā*, and so he does not become parched up. About this (chant) the Brāhmins of former times used to speculate: 'Who, forsooth, will to day come safely across the opened mouth of the crocodile (*śiṃśumārī*) ?' The yajñāyajñīya, forsooth, is the crocodile that stands with opened mouth waiting at the small path; it is in h i s mouth that he puts food, whereupon he passes safely by him'. See the text in Jaim. br. Auswahl No. 62.

11. Unto (Agni) vaiśvānara the Udgatṛ surrenders himself[1] by saying: *prapra* ('forth! forth') *vayam*; he should say *praprīṃ*[2] *vayam*. In this manner he will pass over Vaiśvānara.

[1] Is Agni vaiśvānara here a reminiscence of the Jaim. br.? cp. note 2 on § 10. According to the Jaim. br. (I. 169, 170) it is also Agni vaiśvānara out of whose *haras* the yajñāyajñīya is sprung forth.

[2] Suggesting the idea of *prīṇāti* (?).

12. He, forsooth, who recites a declining verse, will, after the performing of the chant, fare worse. Now, the (part of the yajñāyajñīya which contains the words) *na śaṁsiṣam* ('I will n o t extol')[1] is a declining verse; he should (rather) say *nu śaṁsiṣam* or *suśaṁsiṣam* ('I will extol'; 'I will extol allright'). He then recites no declining verse, and after the chanting will fare better.

[1] As if *na* were the negation, whilst it is equal to *iva*. Similarly the Jaim. br. (I. 176) prescribes the change *nu śaṃsiṣam*.

13. The sacrifices that have (the word) *vāc* ('voice') at the end, leak through the cleft of the voice. Now, the sacrifices that end with the yajñāyajñīya[1], have (the word) *vāc* at the end. Untruth is the cleft of the voice; a f t e r the untruth that is spoken by one who performs the agniṣṭoma, the sacrifice leaks; on a syllable[2] it must finally be established; by the syllable forsooth, he covers up the cleft of the sacrifice[3].

[1] As does the normal agniṣṭoma, of which the yajñāyajñīyastotra is the last.

[2] Cp. note 3 on § 14.

[3] With §§ 12, 13 cp. Jaim. br. I. 178: 'They (the theologians) remark: 'The verses of the yajñāyajñīya are one syllable too short (this refers to the last pāda: *uta trātā tanūnām*). This is a gap in the yajñāyajñīya; after the gap in the yajñāyajñīya the sacrifice leaks; after the sacrifice, the Sacrificer; after the Sacrificer, his children. In this (gap) he should put tho (the word) 'voice'; the voice, forsooth, is the sacred lore', etc.

14. The syllable[1], forsooth, is Virāj's form[1]: in Virāj[2] he is finally established[3].

[1] *akṣara* 'syllable' means also 'imperishable'.

[2] And virāj is food: *annaṃ virāṭ* (*e.g.* Śat. br. VIII. 3. 2. 13).

[3] The ritualistic authorities are at variance regarding the meaning of the Brāhmaṇa. Nidānasūtra (II. 10) cites our passage and adds the remark: 'What is the untruth, which the syllable?' *vā* is the syllable, *i e.*, a syllable beginning with '*vā*' and ending on 'ā'. (This remark is added because from the words *vety etad akṣaram* one might otherwise infer that *va*, and not *vā*, was meant). 'Ending on *g*', say some. Considering that the Brāhmaṇa condemns the dropping of the *g*, they should recite w i t h it; in this way he covers by means of a whole syllable the cleft of the sacrifice'. Another meaning is that the last syllable of the verse (and not the stobha) is intended by the author of the Brāhmaṇa, and this is the meaning of the Sūtrakāra (Lāṭy. II. 10. 18), who expressly states that the syllable *nām* (not *vā*=*vāg*) must be the nidhana of the last stotriya, cp. note 1 on VIII. 7. 2.

VIII. 7.

(The agniṣṭoma-laud, continued.)

1. At the morning, verily, the metres are applied from hence upwards[1], from thence downwards[2] they are applied at the laud of the yajñāyajñīya; *yajñā vo agnaye girā ca dakṣase* is (the metre) of twelve syllables; *pra vayam amṛtaṃ jātavedasam* is (the one) of eleven syllables, *priyaṃ mitraṃ na śaṁsiṣam* is (the one) of eight syllables[3].

[1] *i.e.* increasing in number of syllables: the gāyatrī (3×8) at the morning-service, the triṣṭubh at midday (4×11), the jagatī at the evening-service (4×12 syllables).

[2] In reversed order.

[3] By this reasoning we understand, that the Sacrificer, after he has reached temporarily and spiritually the world of heaven, will again descend on earth (cp the next following §), to live his whole life.

2. He transforms the last (verse of the yajñāyajñīya-stotra) into an anuṣṭubh[1]. The anuṣṭubh in the earth: on the earth he (the Sacrificer) (thereby) gains a firm support.

[1] How this is brought about, is explained by the Sūtrakāras (Lāṭy. II. 10. 18–19, Drāhy. VI. 2. 18–19). 'At the last stotra-verse he should repeat (the syllables *bhuvadvāje* in this manner:) *bhuvadvājāyi, bhuvadvājeṣu*; and its nidhana is (the syllable) *nām*; for he (the author of the Brāhmaṇa) says: 'the last (he transforms) into an anuṣṭubh' and 'on a syllable it must finally be established' (VIII. 6. 13).

(It is known that out of the pragâtha, on which the yajñâyajñîya is chanted, are made three verses: a bṛhatî of 36, and two kakubhs each of 28 syllables; by adding the four syllables *bhuvadvāje* [for *bhuvadvājāyi* is only the sâman form of these four syllables], the last kakubh becomes an anuṣṭubh, of 32 syllables) —'But the teachers (are of opinion) that no repetition is to be made (according to Dhanvin, because we have already an anuṣṭubh, if the last time the first verse is read, as is done in the Brâhmaṇa in VIII. 7. 1, omitting the syllables *yajñā, girā*, and *pra*; in this manner the triṣṭubh of 36 becomes an anuṣṭubh of 31 syllables; reasoning with Ait. br. I. 6. 2: *na vā ekenākṣareṇa chandāṃsi viyanti na dvābhyam*, this can be taken as an anuṣṭubh of 32 syllables, or we are to take the finale of one syllable *vā*, to the 31 syllables) and the finale should be as handed down in the sacred text, according to Śâṇḍilya'.

3. (Moreover) the anuṣṭubh is the voice[1]; in the voice he is firmly established; the anuṣṭubh is pre-eminence; in pre-eminence he is firmly established.

[1] Cp. v. 7. 1.

4. How, now, must the yajñâyajñîya be chanted?' they ask. 'Like an ox discharging urine, t h u s indeed and t h u s indeed'[1].

[1] With 'thus' the person who recites the Brâhmaṇa must have made a gesture, indicating the precise manner.

5. 'The Udgâtṛ is continually nearing himself unto (Agni) vaiśvânara'[1] they say, 'if he speaks the verse of the yajñâyajñîya manifestly'[2]. It should be chanted by him while he passes over[3], as it were; he (thereby) passes over (Agni) vaiśvânara.

[1] To whom this chant is attributed in the anukramaṇikâ of the grâmegeya; cp. VIII. 6. 11.

[2] Or 'rightly' *ṛjunā*, *i.e.* without changing anything in the words of the chant.

[3] *i.e.* deviates from the text in the manner as indicated VIII. 6. 10–12.

6. Unto (Agni) vaiśvânara the Adhvaryu gives over (*abhisṛjati*)[1] the persons seated in the sadas, by causing them to return to[2] the laud of the yajñâyajñîya. It should be chanted whilst he covers himself completely up (with his garment)[3], in order to prevent their being burned by (Agni) vaiśvânara.

[1] The Adhvaryu summons the priests before the chant of those stotras that are formed by repetition out of three verses, by the words; *asarjy asarji vāg asarji...upāvartadhvam*, Âp. XII. 17. 9; Śat. br. IV. 2. 5. 8, *upāvartadhvam ity anyāni stotrāṇi (sc. upākaroti)*.—The persons seated inside the sadas are the Hotrakas and the Chanters, the Brahman and the Yajamâna.

[2] *i.e.* 'to repeat', cp. note 1.

[3] Cp. C. H. § 241 c.

7. The Fathers, however, do not know[1] one who has completely covered himself (by his garment) and at the laud of the yajñāyajñīya the Fathers want to know (him) properly: up to the ears (only) the covering must be made. Thereby he is covered and (at the same time) n o t covered; so the Fathers know (him) and (Agni) vaiśvānara does not hurt (him).

[1] The reason why at this particular moment the Fathers must be able to know their descendants is perhaps to be sought in the fact, that at the afternoon-service, immediately before the yajñāyajñīya-stotra two chips from a *saumya caru* are offered to Soma accompanied by the Fathers, cp. C. H. § 237a. II. The Jaiminīyas disapprove of this practice; we read in their Brāhmaṇa (I. 174): 'Now' they say: 'He should chant (the yajñāyajñīya-stotra) having covered himself completely up. The yajñāyajñīya, forsooth, is Agni vaiśvānara: for appeasing it and for not being burned by it.' He is, however, apt to get the Fathers for his deity, if he should chant (it), being completely covered (probably because at a sacrifice destined for the souls of the Dead the performer covers himself). They say also: 'As far as his ears are (*i.e.* up to his ears), so far having covered himself, he should chant.' They (others), however, say: 'By means of the ears he hears, by means of the eyes he sees; of this (eyesight and hearing) he would deprive himself, if he should chant (it), being covered.... Being uncovered he should (therefore) chant it.'

8. Behind (the gārhapatya)[1] the wives[2] pour down water; they thereby extinguish (or 'appease') (Agni) vaiśvānara; for water is a means of extinguishing (or 'appeasing').

[1] Or: 'afterwards'. According to the Adhvaryusūtras (see C. H. § 241. d) this action takes place inside the sadas.

[2] The plural, in case it is a sattra.

9. Besides, they (the partakers of the sattra) thereby emit semen[1], for the semen is a fluid.

[1] And thus are sure to obtain progeny.

10. They (the wives) pour it (the water) along their right thighs; for from the right side the semen is emitted[1].

[1] Cp. Śat. br. II. 5. 2. 17: *dakṣiṇato vai vṛṣā yoṣām upaśete* and the other passages collected by Oertel in Journal of the Amer. Or. Soc., vol. XXVI, page 188.

11. Rather a great (part of the garment) must be pushed back[1] (by the wives); they thereby engender spirit for him[2].

[1] Cp. TS. VI. 5. 8. 6: 'she pours down water; thereby semen is poured out; along the thigh she pours it down; for along the thigh the semen is poured out; having bared her thigh she pours it out; for after the thigh is bared, cohabitation takes place, semen is emitted, children are born.

[2] For the son, as appears from Kāṭh. XXVI. 1: 122. 7: *dūram upary udūhetāhṛitamukhy asyā jāyate* 'he will get an *ahṛitamukhin* (son).'—For §§ 8-11 cp. Jaim. br. I. 173: 'They hold the laud, having put (a vessel filled with) water near. The yajñāyajñīya, forsooth, is Agni vaiśvānara: for extinguishing it and for not being burned (by it); along the thigh the wife (of the Sacrificer) pours it out; it is Agni vaiśvānara she thereby extinguishes; having bared her thigh she pours it out, for, after the thigh is bared, the wife *vīryaṃ karoti*' ('takes the seed of the male up'?).

12. They[1] cause her to be looked at by the Udgātṛ, for impregnation's sake.

[1] The Adhvaryus, cp. TS. l.c.: 'he causes her to be looked at by the Udgātṛ; the Udgātṛ, forsooth, is Prajāpati: in order that she may bring forth progeny'.

13. At the *him*-making[1] they cause her to be looked at; for after the *him*-making the seed is implanted (the pregnancy follows)[2].

[1] At the beginning of each turn of the chant the Chanters make *him* (*hum*).

[2] Sāyaṇa here quotes Āp. V. 25. 11, see also the references given in the German translation of Āpastamba.

14. Unto the third verse of the laud[1] they cause her to be looked at, for threefold[2] is the semen[3].

[1] This implies that the Udgātṛ should look at the wife (or the wives) only during the first three stotra-verses, beginning with the first *hum*.

[2] I compare TS. V. 6. 8. 4: *trīṇi vāva retāṁsi pitā putraḥ pautraḥ*.

[3] To § 8 sqq. refer Lāṭy. II. 10. 15-17 and Drāhy. VI. 2. 15-17: 'At the *him*-making of the yajñāyajñīya the Udgātṛ should look at the wife (of the Sacrificer); at the finale (of the first three verses of the laud) the wife should pour down water upon her right thigh; when the prastāva of the third verse of the laud has been chanted, she should pour down all this water'.

VIII. 8.

(The three uktha-lauds.)

1. The Gods, forsooth, having acquired by conquest the agniṣṭoma, could not conquer the ukthas. They said to Agni: 'Let us

gain the conquest by thee as leader'. He answered: 'What will therefrom result for me?' 'What thou wishest' they said. He replied: 'On verses addressed to me may they introduce the ukthas'.

2. Therefore, they introduce the ukthas on verses addressed to Agni[1].

[1] Cp. Kauṣ. br. XVI. 11: *āgneyīṣu maitrāvaruṇāya praṇayanty, aindrīṣv itarayoḥ.*

3. And therefore, on gāyatrī-verses, for Agni has the gāyatrī as his metre.

4. Having made Agni their leader, they strode on, together with the horse[1]; because together with the horse (*sākam aśvena*) they strode on, therefore there is the sākamaśva (sāman)[2].

[1] With Agni who had taken the form of a horse, cp. Ait. br. III. 49. 7: *tān agnir aśvo bhūtvābhyatyadravat.*

[2] An ukthya-sacrifice consists of 15 stotras and śastras; to the ordinary twelve lauds of the normal agniṣṭoma three more are added, thereby the afternoon service comes to comprise, as each of the other services, five lauds. The three new ones are 1. the uktha-stotra (running parallel to the śastra) of the M a i t r ā v a r u ṇ a, addressed to Indra and Varuṇa; 2. the uktha-stotra (running parallel to the śastra) of the B r ā h m a ṇ ā c c h a ṃ s i n, addressed to Indra and Bṛhaspati; 3. the uktha-stotra (running parallel to the śastra) of the A c c h ā v ā k a, addressed to Indra and Viṣṇu (see *e.g.* Āp. XIV. 1. 9).

I. The m a i t r ā v a r u ṇ a s y o k t h a s t o t r a is the sākamaśva: grāmegeya I. 1. 14 on SV. I. 7=ṚS. V I. 1 6. 1 6 – 1 8=SV. II. 55–57 (gāyatrīverses); the śastra of the Maitrāvaruṇa consists (cp. Āśv. VI. 1. 2, Śāṅkh. IX. 5. 2) of ṚS. V I. 1 6. 1 6 – 1 8 (stotriya tṛca); VI. 16. 19–21 (anurūpa tṛca); III. 51. 1–3 (Indra) and VIII. 42. 1–3 (Varuṇa) (the ukthamukha); VI. 82 (sāṃśaṃsika); VII. 84 (paryāsa) both addressed to Indra and Varuṇa together; VI. 68. 11. (yājyā).

II. The u k t h a s t o t r a o f t h e B r ā h m a ṇ ā c c h a ṃ s i n is the saubhara: grāmegeya XI. 1. 14 (but cp. note 1 on VIII. 8. 13) on SV. 1. 408=ṚS. V I I I. 2 1. 1 – 2=SV. II. 58-59 (kakubh and satobṛhatī); the śastra of the Brāhmaṇācchaṃsin (Āśv. l.c., cp. Śāṅkh. IX. 3, Vaitānasūtra XXV. 3. 11) consists of ṚS. V I I I. 2 1. 1 – 2 (stotriya); VIII. 21. 9-10 (anurūpa); I. 57 (ukthamukha, addressed to Indra); X. 68 (sāṃśaṃsika, addressed to Bṛhaspati); X. 43. 1–11 (paryāsa addressed to Indra); VII. 97. 10 (yājyā).

III. The u k t h a s t o t r a o f t h e A c c h ā v ā k a is the nārmedha: grāmegeya I. 2. 27 (but cp. note 2 on VIII. 8. 22) on SV. I. 406=ṚS. V I I I. 9 8. 7 – 9=SV. II. 60–62 (bṛhatī and satobṛhatī); the śastra of the Acchāvāka consists

of ṚS. VIII. 98. 7–9 (stotriya); VIII. 13. 4–6 (anurūpa); II. 13 (ukthamukha, addressed to Indra), VII. 100 (Viṣṇu), I. 156 (Viṣṇu); VI. 69 sāṃśaṃsika (Indra and Viṣṇu); VI 69. 3 (yājyā).

5. Therefore, they lead on (introduce) the uktha (-laud)s with the sākamaśva; for by it at the beginning they conquered them.

6. Now, Indra said: 'Who is going to follow together with me?' 'I' said Varuṇa. Varuṇa stood behind him and Indra fetched (the uktha). Therefore a (hymn) addressed to Indra and Varuṇa is recited (by the Hotraka) after (the laud)[1].

1 See note 2 on § 4 (I).

7(*a*). The same (God) said: 'Who is going to follow together with me?' 'I' said Bṛhaspati. Bṛhaspati stood behind him and Indra fetched (the uktha). Therefore a (hymn) addressed to Indra and Bṛhaspati is recited after (the laud)[1].

1 Cp. note 2 on § 4 (II).

7(*b*). The same (God) said: 'Who is going to follow together with me?' 'I' said Viṣṇu. Viṣṇu stood behind him and Indra fetched (the uktha). Therefore a (hymn) addressed to Indra and Viṣṇu is recited after (the laud)[1].

1 Cp. note 2 on § 4 (III).—With § 6 and 7 cp. Ait. br. III. 50.

8. What he had fetched for them was the cattle[1]; the ukthas forsooth, are the cattle. He who desires (to obtain) cattle should perform an ukthya (sacrifice)[2].

1 According to Jaim. br. I. 181 they were the six wish-cows: cow, horse, goat, sheep, rice and barley.

2 A jyotiṣṭoma followed by the three ukthastotras and corresponding śastras. Here, as so often in the printed text, the words *uktha* and *ukthya* are interchanged (misprint!)

9. By means of the bṛhat, forsooth, Indra hurled his thunderbolt on Vṛtra; the sharpness (or 'lustre', 'splendour') of it fell down and became the saubhara (-sāman).

10. 'A sameness is brought about in the sacrifice' they say, 'if the pṛṣṭha(-laud)[1] and the twilight(-laud)[2] are both the rathantara (-sāman) and no chant of the bṛhat comes between (these two)'. By

chanting (however) the saubhara, the chant of the bṛhat is brought about between (these two), for the saubhara is the sharpness of the bṛhat[3].

[1] The hotuḥ pṛṣṭhastotra.

[2] The sandhistotra, which also is chanted on the rathantara-melody (Ārṣeya-kalpa, page 204 s.f.)

[3] Cp. § 9.

11. If the over-night-rite (the atirātra) is chanted on the bṛhat (sāman)[1], then the saubhara must be taken as the Brahman's chant in the uktha (laud)s[2]. He thereby furnishes the bṛhat fully with (its own) splendour.

[1] If the hotuḥ pṛṣṭhastotra is the bṛhat.

[2] Then equally the uktha-laud of the Brāhmaṇācchaṃsin (the second uktha) must be the saubhara: for in this case there is no 'sameness of performance'.

12. (But) if it (the over-night rite) is (chanted) on the rathantara, he should take the saubhara (as the Brahman's chant)[1], for avoiding sameness.

[1] The text runs *yadi rathantarasāmnā saubharaṃ kuryāt.* This gives no good sense. I guess: *yadi rathantarasāmā (sc. atirātraḥ syāt).* But even so the purport is not wholly clear.

13. When the Gods went to the world of heaven, the quarters collapsed. By means of the saubhara (and more especially by its finale) *ū*[1], they propped them u p (*u d astabhnuvan*). Thereupon, they (*i.e.* the quarters) became fixed (or 'fastened') and got a firm support. Then the Gods knew the (way to the) world of heaven. He who desires (to reach) the world of heaven and to get a firm support, should chant the saubhara; he gets knowledge of the way to the world of heaven and gets a firm support.

[1] The saubharasāman in the grāmageya (on Sv. I. 408, cp. note 2 on § 4 [II]). has no *ū* for nidhana; the saubhara as given ūhagāna I. 1. 16 points to the saubhara of grāmageya III. 1. 31 (on SV. I. 109), where the nidhana *ū* is given. To this sāman also the Jaim. br. points. However, the nidhana *ū* may be facultative, cp. the next following §§, especially § 19.

14. Prajāpati created the creatures; these, having come into existence, suffered from hunger; by means of the saubhara (and more

especially by the finale) *ūrj* ('food') he gave them food. Thereupon they throve.

15. The creatures (*i.e.* children and young domestic animals) thrive in that year when he, knowing this, chants the saubhara.

16. They (*i.e.* the creatures nourished by Prajāpati) said: 'Well reared hast thou us'[1]; hence (the name) saubhara.

[1] *subhṛtaṃ no 'bhārṣiḥ*. On § 4–16 cp. Jaim. br. I. 187 (Auswahl No. 71): 'Prajāpati created the creatures: these being created by him, perished; they became the reptiles other than the snakes. He created a second kind; these perished also; they became the fishes. He created a third kind; these also perished: they became the birds. He thought: 'How might these creatures not perish?' He saw this sāman; by means of it (and especially of its nidhāna) *ūrj*, he touched them and they throve, being anointed by him with *ūrj* ('food'). He said: 'Well-reared have I these creatures' (*subhṛtaṃ*...*abhārṣam*). Thence the name saubhara'. N.B. the first saubhara, on SV. I. 109, has *ūrk* as nidhana.

17. The food, verily, that he gave them, was the rain.

18. He who wishes for rain, for food, and for the world of heaven, should chant the saubhara.

19. As finale for one who wishes for rain, he should take (the sound) *hīs*; for one who wishes to obtain food, (the word) *ūrj*; for one who wishes to reach the world of heaven, (the syllable) *ū*.

20. The saubhara (represents the fulfilment of) all wishes; in all that he wishes he comes to be established.

21. Now, as to the nārmedha(-sāman).

22. As Nṛmedhas of the Angiras-clan was taking part in a sacrificial session, they (*i.e.* his fellow-Sacrificers) set dogs on him[1]. He resorted to Agni with (the verse): 'Protect us, o Agni, by one'[2]. (Agni) vaiśvānara came and encircled him. Thereupon he got a firm support and found a refuge[3].

[1] Delbrück, Altind. Syntax, page 261, suggests *abhyādravan* for *abhyāhvayan*.

[2] The nārmedha-melody grāmegeyagāna I. 1. 27 (see SV. ed. of Calcutta, Vol. I, page 152) composed on SV. I. 36=ṚS. VIII. 60. 9–10=SV. II. 894–895, is chanted on SV. I. 406=ṚS. VIII. 98. 7–9=SV. II. 60–62 (see ed. Calc. vol. III, page 192), cp. below, §§ 24–26 and Puṣpasūtra X. 70 with Simon's remark. This manner of indicating a sāman seems to be irregular.

[3] The very interesting recension of the legend of Nṛmedha in the Jaim. br. (I. 171, see the text in Jaim. br. in Auswahl, No. 61) is only partly intelligible to me. What I can make of it is the following: 'Nṛmedha and Suvrata (were) brothers: these...; now, Nṛmedha acted as Udgātṛ for Suvrata. When the laud of the yajñāyajñīya was not (yet wholly) finished, they came running to him (to Suvrata), saying: 'The son of thee, who art the yajamāna (for whom Nṛmedha is the Udgātṛ) has been murdered by the two sons of thine Udgātṛ: Antakadhṛti, the son of Suvrata by Nakira and Śakapūta'. Seizing him (*viz.* Nṛmedha) by the arms, he (Suvrata) said: 'Ye brāhmins, this is your sacrifice, perform it for whom ye wish; I, forsooth, by means of this one will punish this'. Having bound him (Nṛmedha) to the pillar of fig-wood he (Suvrata) set fire on him by means of hempen-chips. He (Nṛmedha) desired: 'May I get out of this; may I find a way out, a deliverer; may not this fire burn me'. He saw this sāman and lauded with it. Thereupon, he found a way out, a deliverer, and the fire did not burn him; it even burned down the bond with which he was fastened (to the pillar)'. Note that in the Sarvānukramaṇī Śakapūta is called the son of Nṛmedha; Nakira may find his explanation in the words *nakir asya* of ṚS. X. 132. 3; for Antakadhṛti cp. ṚS. l.c. 4: *antakadhruk*.

23. This sāman is a refuge procuring one; he who has used it in chanting finds a refuge and gets a firm support.

24. The verses (of the nārmedha) are of different metres: the characteristic of day and night.

25. For the characteristic of the ukthas is neither that of day nor that of night[1].

[1] They are something between, as they fall on the afternoon. By a different reasoning the Jaim. br. (I. 188) arrives at the same result: 'This sāman has the features of day and night: to Indra belong the verses, to Agni belongs the sāman (the nārmedha forms part of the āgneya-section in the gāna), to Indra belongs the day, to Agni the night. He who at an atirātra deviates from this sāman (does not apply it), would be removed from the features of day and night. If one were to say about him: 'he (*viz.* the Udgātṛ) has removed him from the features of day and night', it would be in truth thus. Therefore, at an atirātra this sāman must not be deviated from'.

26. The first (verse)[1] is a kakubh; then (comes) an uṣṇih[2], then a pura uṣṇih anuṣṭubh[3]. They thereby do not deviate from the anuṣṭubh: (the metre of) the Acchāvāka's chant.[4]

[1] ṚS. VIII. 98. 7=SV. II. 60.

[2] ṚS. VIII. 98. 8=SV. II. 61.

[3] ṚS. VIII. 98. 9 (pura-uṣṇih), whilst SV. II. 62 at the end has four syllables more.

[4] This refers, according to Sāyaṇa, to the fact that the Acchāvāka, before partaking of the soma, has to recite certain anuṣṭubh-verses (ṚS. V. 25. 1—3, VI. 42, cp. C.H. § 148), cp. Ait. br. III. 13. 2: *athāsya yat svaṃ chanda āsīd anuṣṭup tām udantam abhyauhad acchāvākīyam abhi.*—To our Brāhmaṇa refers a remarkable passage in the Nidānasūtra (II. 11): *atha nārmedhastotriye vadati: kakup prathamāthoṣṇig atha pura-uṣṇig-anuṣṭub iti; kakub eva prathamoṣṇig dvitīyā pura-uṣṇik tṛtīyā, dāśatayenādhyāyena tāṃ bahvṛcā adhīyate* (namely in ṚS. VIII. 98. 9): *yuñjanti harī iṣirasya gāthayorau ratha uruyuge | indravāhā vacoyujeti. tatra vayaṃ catvāry akṣarāṇy upāharāmaḥ: svarvideti* (*i.e. suvarvidā iti*), *sānuṣṭub bhavaty upariṣṭājjyotiḥ*'. The uttarārcika, indeed reads: *yuñjanti harī iṣirasya gathayorau ratha uruyuge vacoyujā | indravāhā svarvidā* (12+12+8 syllables). This addition of the four syllables must be very old, as the Jaiminīyas also have it already in their uttarārcika. Must we infer from this fact, that the author of our Brāhmaṇa was acquainted with the uttarārcika? See on this question the Introduction, Chapter II, page XVI. I subjoin the parallel passage of the Jaim. br. (I. 188): 'They argue: from the anuṣṭubh, forsooth, they, who perform the acchāvāka's chant on uṣṇih-verses, deviate'. One of these (uṣṇih-verses, which are the same as uttarāoika II. 60-62 of the Kauthuma-Rāṇāyanīyas=ṚS. VIII. 98. 7–9) is an arvāg-uṣṇih, one a madhya-uṣṇih, one a pura-uṣṇih, *anavadhṛtaṃ chando 'navadhṛtaṃ vāg vadati,* and the anuṣṭubh is the voice. Thereby, they do not deviate from the anuṣṭubh. (Moreover) the last of these (verses) is a visible anuṣṭubh. Thereby, also, they do not deviate from the anuṣṭubh'. The Jaim. br., then, seems to recognise also the Sāmavedic recension of SV. II. 62 (as an anuṣṭubh).

VIII. 9.

(The variations of the uktha-lauds.)

1. There is the hārivarṇa (-chant) [1].

[1] Grāmegeyagāna X. 1. 34 (that the last of the four hārivarṇas is meant, appears from XII. 6. 9) on SV. I. 383=ṚS. VIII. 15. 4-6=SV. II 230-232. How it is to be applied, is explained in § 5.

2. The Asuras were in these worlds. The Gods expelled them, by means of (the words): 'of golden splendour' [1], from this world; by 'thou shinest' [1] from the intermediate region; by 'for day and day' (*dive dive*) [1] from yonder world (the sky, *div*).

[1] The last word of each of the three verses, being used as their finale, cp. XII. 6. 9.

3. So, he who knows this, expels his rival from these worlds and ascends (himself) these worlds.

4. Harivarṇa[1], who desired to possess cattle, saw this sāman: by it he created a thousand head of cattle; that it is this sāman, is for the thriving of the cattle.

[1] An āngirasa, according to the Jaim. br. (I. 183), see § 5.

5. When the Angirases went to the world of heaven, they were pursued by the ogres; by means of this (sāman) Harivarṇa repelled them. That it is this sāman, is for repelling the ogres[1].

[1] To §§ 1-5 refers the Kṣudrasūtra (I. 5, No. 25): 'Now (the arrangement) of the (jyotiṣṭoma) which ends with the uktha(-laud)s, and in which the āṣṭādaṃṣṭra is the Acchāvāka's sāman (cp. below § 20). On 'thou hast made merry, the fullness has been drunk' (SV. II. 782-784=ṚS. I. 175. 1-3; the verses do not occur in the pūrvārcika) the kāleya (grām. 2. 7. VI, in stead of the normal one on SV. II. 37-38); on 'on all sides run forth' (SV I. 427=ṚS. IX. 109. 1=SV. II. 717) the sapha; the sākamaśva, the hārivarṇa and the āṣṭādaṃṣṭra are the ukthas (resp. of Maitrāvaruṇa, Brāhmaṇācchaṃsin, and Acchāvāka). The rest is similar to the (normal) jyotiṣṭoma'.

6. The pṛṣṭhas[1] were created; their redundant lustre, their pith was collected (brought together, united) by the Gods, and that became the udvaṁśīya(-chant)[2].

[1] The pṛṣṭhasāmans.

[2] Grāmegeyagāna IX. 1. 16 on SV. I. 342=ṚS. I. 10. 1-3=SV. II. 694-696.

7. The udvaṁśīya is the lustre of all the pṛṣṭhas; therefore they formerly did not apply it for a tribesman[1], in order to hold apart the good and the bad[2].

[1] A tribesman, *sajāta*, who seeks equal or greater influence than the Sacrificer; *sajāta* with hostile meaning is common, cp. *e.g.* TS. II. 2. 1. 2, where it is equal to *bhrātṛvya* 'rival'.—On the aorist with *purā* cp. note 1 on VIII. 6. 4.

[2] If he were to apply for a rival the udvaṃśīya, which means lustre, the good (prosperity) would fall to the share of the rival.

8. For he who chants the udvaṁśīya, has chanted[1] the pṛṣṭhas.

[1] Note the participle used as verbum finitum.

9. The udvaṁśīya is (equal to) all the characteristic features[1].

[1] This sāman contains all the features of the pṛṣṭhas.

10. The (syllable) *ā* (after the first verse-quarter of the udvaṃśīya): 'thee celebrate the seers'[1] is the characteristic of the rathantara; for *ā* is the rathantara[2].

4r 5 r r 4 5 4
[1] The sāman begins: *gāyanti tvā gāyatriṇa ā.*

2 r
[2] Which begins: *ā bhi tvā* (araṇyegeyagāna II. 1. 21).

11. The beginning[1] is (that) of the bṛhat, for the bṛhat is, as it were, upwards[2].

[1] The sound *u* of the name *udvaṁśiya.*

[2] Being the sky, the heaven.

12. The presence of manifold stobhas[1] is (that) of the vairūpa[2]; for provided with manifold stobhas[3] is the vairūpa.

[1] The exact meaning of *pariṣṭubh* is not certain. The expression seems to mean: 'to include the *iḍā* before and behind by a stobha' (cp. X. 11. 1).

[2] Araṇyegeyagāna I. 1. 3. The udvaṁśīya has the following stobhas only: *ho,1i,*
2 2
up, hā i.

[3] Read *pariṣṭubdhaṁ.*

13. The repeated push is (that) of the vairāja[1]; for the vairāja is (chanted) with repeated push.

[1] The expression 'repeated push' is an effort to translate the Dutch 'naslag'. The vairāja (grāmegeya X. 2. 32, on SV. I. 398, or ar. gā. II. 1. 31 (?) on the same
1 2 1 2
verse, XII. 10.6–11) has: *mā-datu tvā '3-datu tvā* (original text: *mandatu tvā*);
1 2 2 2 3 5 1 3
the udvaṁśīya has: *udvaṁśam iva yā' 1 imī'3re | udvaṁśā '234 mī | vā yā '32 u vā*
'2 2 2 2 3 5 3 2 1 2
'3-up-mā' 1i-mī '3 re | udvaṁśā '234 mī | vā yā '32 uvā '3-up-mā '2 iro '35 | hā i
(original text: *ud vaṁśam iva yemire*).—On *anutud* cp. X. 6. 4, XII. 9. 17, XII. 10. 11.

14. The *ardheḍā* ('half-*iḍā*) is (that) of the śākvarī(-verses)[1], the *atisvāra* (that) of the revatī(-verses)[2].

[1] The ardheḍā, as *up*, is found in the udvaṁśīya, as *iṭ* in the mahānāmnīs (cp. the Calcutta edition of the SV. Vol. II, pages 372, 377, 380). On the term cp. also Simon, Puṣpasūtra page 517, bottom.

[2] On *atisvāra* cp. note 1 on XIII. 12. 11. The raivatasāman (araṇyegeya I.
2
2. 19) has twice *hā31,* the udvaṁśiya *iro '35.*

15. The Gods, by means of the half-*iḍā* having repelled the Asuras, ascended, by means of the 'overtuning' (*atisvāra*) the world of heaven.

16. He who knows this, having by the half-*iḍā* repelled his rival, ascends the world of heaven by the 'overtuning

17. By the half-*iḍā*, forsooth, they finish the preceding sacrifice[1], by the 'overtuning' they begin the subsequent one[2].

1 The ukthya, according to Sāyaṇa.

2 The ṣoḍaśin, according to Sāyaṇa. I must confess that the purport of this § is not clear to me.

18. A subsequent sacrifice falls to the share of him, who knows this.

19. Fivefold, verily, is this sāman[1]; the sacrifice is fivefold[2] and cattle is fivefold[3]; in sacrifice and cattle he becomes firmly established[4].

1 The sāman is chanted on an anuṣṭubh of four verse-quarters, but by the repetition (cp. VIII. 9. 13) comes to have five.

2 Cp. VI. 7. 12, note 2.

3 Consisting of hair, skin, flesh, bone, mark (Sāyaṇa).

4 He is sure to be asked as an ṛtvij for a sacrifice and will possess cattle.

20. (One of) the two āṣṭādaṁṣṭra(sāman)s he should take (for the uktha-laud of the Acchāvāka) for one who desires prosperity.

1 Grāmegeya IX. 1. 20 and 21 on SV. I. 343=ṚS. I. 11. 1-3=SV. II. 177-179 (anuṣṭubhs).

21. Aṣṭādaṃṣṭra, the son of Virūpa, grew old without sons, without progeny. He thought he had torn asunder these worlds[1]. In his old age he saw these two sāmans[2], but feared lest they should not be taken into practice. He said: 'He shall thrive, who will chant these two sāmans of mine'[3].

1 Because he had no progeny, no continuity of race (*santatyabhāva*) and consequently the continuity of the three worlds would be destroyed (!).

2 'And got children by them' must according to Sāyaṇa be supplied, which to me does not seem certain.

3 Because he was too aged to teach them to others (?). The Jaim. br. (I. 191) gives no light.

22. This[1] is the product of the seer's fervent wish. (The reason) why they are the āṣṭādaṁṣṭra (sāmans, that are to be applied), is for thriving.

1 This pair of sāmans.

2 To VIII. 9. 6–22 refers the Kṣudrasūtra (I. 5, No. 26): 'Now (the arrangement) of the (jyotiṣṭoma) which ends equally with the uktha (laud)s, and in which the udvaṃśīya is the Acchāvāka's chant; of the naudhasa (grām. VI. 1. 37) the six kakubhs (the meaning is not quite clear to me); on (the verses): 'thee like a car

to aid us' (SV. I. 354=ṚS. VIII. 68. 1-3=SV. II. 1121-1123), the kāleya; on (the verse): 'he is pressed, who of goods' (SV. I. 582=ṚS. IX. 108. 13=SV. II. 446), the sapha and on (the verse): 'run about for Indra' (SV. I. 427=ṚS. IX. 109. 1=SV. II. 717), the pauṣkala. The sākamaśva, hārivarṇa and udvaṁśīya are the uktha(laud)s. The rest is similar to the (normal) jyotiṣṭoma'.

VIII. 10.

(The variations of the uktha-lauds, continued.)

1. On gāyatrī (verses) they should lead on the uktha(laud)s for one who desires spiritual lustre; on gāyatrī (metre), the Brahman's sāman; on anuṣṭubh (metre), the Acchāvāka's sāman; this (last thereby) becomes gāyatrī[1].

[1] As the ukthastotras are twenty-one-versed, there are in the Acchāvāka's laud (which is based on anuṣṭubh-verses of 32 syllables) 32 × 21 = 672 syllables; this number is divisable by 24 (the number of syllables contained in the gāyatrī); by this reckoning the 21 anuṣṭubhs are equal to 28 gāyatrīs. The sākamedha of itself being already chanted on gāyatrī, all the ukthas are (cryptically) chanted on gāyatrī.

2. Spiritual lustre is splendour; splendour also is the gāyatrī[1]; he obtains (by chanting gāyatrīs) spiritual lustre[2].

[1] So also Śat. br. XIII. 2. 6. 4 (as the gāyatrī is āgneyī, cp. VI. 1. 6).

[2] To § 1-2 refers the Kṣudrasūtra (I. 5, No. 27): 'For one who desires spiritual lustre, on (the verses): 'by thy most sweet, most intoxicating' (SV. II. 39-41) is chanted the gāyatra, the saṁhita and the satrāsāhīya, each on one verse consecutively; the aiḍa kautsa (grām. V. 1. 4, probably) on all three; on (the verses): 'by foe-conquest from your plant' (SV. II. 47-49), the śyāvāśva on the first (on SV. II. 47); on the second (verse, 48) the second krauñca (of those three krauñcas which are composed) on 'this Pūṣan' (SV. 1. 546; grām XVI. 1. 14), the audala on the third (verse, SV. II. 49), and the āndhīgava on all three (SV. II. 47-49); (the ukthastotras are:) the sākamaśva, the saubhara chanted on (the verses): 'for thus art thou a hero' (grām. XI. 1. 14 or III. 1. 31? on SV. I. 232=ṚS. VIII. 92. 28-30=SV. II. 174-176); on (the verses): 'all (songs) have caused Indra to grow' (SV. I. 343=ṚS. I. 11. 1-3=SV. II. 177-179) the nārmedha. There are ten not-chanted gāyatrīs, seventy chanted ones. The rest is similar to the (normal) jyotiṣṭoma'. Here the seventy chanted gāyatrīs are 21 (Maitr. uktha), 28 (Brahman's uktha, out of the 21 anuṣṭubhs, cp. note 1 on § 1) and 21 (of the Acchāvāka's uktha). I do not see what is meant by the ten gāyatrīs that are *not* chanted.

3. On gāyatrīs they should lead on the uktha (laud)s for one who desires (to obtain) cattle; on uṣṇih (metre) the Brahman's sāman, on

anuṣṭubh (metre) the Acchāvāka's sāman; this (last thereby) becomes uṣṇih[1].

[1] Seven gāyatrīs are in number of syllables equal to six uṣṇihs; in the ukthastotra, which comprises 21 verses, the 21 gāyatrīs of the first one thus amount to 18 uṣṇihs; in the third ukthastotra, which consists of 21 anuṣṭubhs, each seven anuṣṭubhs being equal to eight uṣṇihs, are comprised 24 uṣṇihs.

4. The uṣṇih is cattle; he (thereby) obtains cattle[1].

[1] To this passage refers the Kṣudrasūtra (I. 6, No. 28), 'for one who desires (to obtain) cattle, the kāleya is (chanted) on (the verses) 'he has made merry; the strong (draught) has been drunk by thee'; on 'run about for Indra' the sapha; (the ukthas are:) the sākamaśva, the saubhara (chanted) on 'this intoxicating draught we announce to thee', (and) the nārmedha (chanted) on 'all (songs) have caused Indra to grow'. There are nine not-chanted uṣṇihs, 63 chanted ones (*viz.* 18 out of the 21 gāyatras, 21 *ipso facto* of the second uktha and 24 out of the 21 anuṣṭubhs). The rest is similar to the (normal) jyotiṣṭoma'.

5. On gāyatrīs they should lead on the uktha (-laud)s for one who desires men[1]; on kakubh(-metre) the Brahman's sāman; on anuṣṭubh (-metre) the Acchāvāka's sāman; this (last thereby) becomes kakubh[2].

[1] Probably slaves.

[2] As the number of syllables of the kakubh is the same as that of the uṣṇih the reckoning is similar to note 1 on § 3.

6. The kakubh is man[1]; he (thereby) obtains men[2].

[1] The middle part of man is broader and bigger than the upper and lower parts and the kakubh likewise is bigger in the middle : 8+12+8 syllables.

[2] Kṣudrasūtra (I. 6, No. 29): 'for one who desires men the kāleya (must be chanted) on: 'he made merry, the strong (draught) has been drunk by thee'; the sapha on: 'run about for Indra'; (the ukthalauds are) the sākamaśva, the saubhara, and the nārmedha (chanted) on: 'all (songs) have caused Indra to grow'. There are 9 not-chanted kakubhs, 63 chanted ones. The rest is similar to the (normal) jyotiṣṭoma'.

7. On virāj[1] they should lead on the uktha (laud)s for one who is desirous of obtaining food; on uṣṇih (metre) the Brāhman's sāman; on anuṣṭubh (-metre) the Acchāvāka's sāman; this (last thereby) becomes virāj[2].

[1] On verses of 30 syllables, although, in fact, here is applied a virāj of 3×11 syllables, (Ait. br. I. 6. 2) cp. note 1 on § 8.

[2] The 21 virājs of the first uktha comprise 630, the 21 uṣṇihs of the second comprise 588, the 21 anuṣṭubhs of the third comprise 672 syllables, together 1890 syllables, which number, being divided by 30 (the number of syllables of the virāj) yields 63 virājs.

8. The virāj is food; he (thereby) obtains food[1].

[1] Kṣudrasūtra (I. 6, No. 30): 'for one who desires food, the kāleya (must be chanted) on the tristich (ṚS. I. 3. 4-6: SV. II. 496-498) of which the middle (verse): 'Indra, impelled by prayer, come hither' is to be taken as the first (*i.e.* on SV. II. 497, 496, 498); the sākamaśva (is chanted) on: 'he who illuminates the strong fortress' (ṚS. I. 149. 3-5=SV. II. 1124-1126, n o t i n t h e p ū r v ā r c i k a; virāj); on (the uṣṇih verses): 'this intoxicating (draught) we announce to Indra', the saubhara; on 'all (songs) have caused Indra to grow', the nārmedha. There are 9 not chanted virājs; 63 chanted ones (cp. note 2 on § 7). The rest is similar to the (normal) jyotiṣṭoma'.

9. On akṣarapanktis they should lead on the uktha (laud)s for one who desires precedence; on uṣṇih(-metre) the Brahman's sāman; on anuṣṭubh (-metre) the Acchāvāka's sāman; this (last thereby) becomes anuṣṭubh[1].

[1] The reckoning is too intricate to be undertaken here; from the Kṣudrasūtra we gather that the three ukthas together must be equal to 56 akṣarapanktis.

10. The anuṣṭubh is precedence; he (thereby) obtains precedence[1].

[1] To §§ 9 and 10 refers the Kṣudrasūtra (I. 6, No. 31): 'for one who desires precedence, the kāleya (must be chanted) on: 'the singers chant unto thee'; on: 'he is pressed out who of goods' the sapha; (the ukthas are) the sākamaśva on: 'O Agni, this (sacrifice) to day with hymns as a steed' (akṣarapaṅkti); the saubhara on: 'this intoxicating (draught) we announce to thee'; the nārmedha on: 'all (songs) have caused Indra to grow'. There are 8 not-chanted anuṣṭubhs, 56 chanted ones. The rest is similar to the (normal) jyotiṣṭoma'.

NINTH CHAPTER.

IX. 1.

(The night-rite: rātriparyāyas and twilight laud.)

1. The Gods, having conquered (from the Asuras) the uktha(laud)s, could not conquer the night[1], (for) they could not discern the Asuras, who had entered the night: the darkness. They saw that pragātha, which has an anuṣṭubh at the beginning[2]: the virāj[3] ('the shining one') (*i.e.*) the light. By means of the shining one (the virāj): (*i.e.*) the light, they discerned them and by the anuṣṭubh, (*i.e.*) the thunderbolt[4], they drove them away out of the night.

1 The night-rounds, the *rātriparyāyas*.

2 *Viz.* 'him who drinks of the soma': SV. I. 155=ṚS. VIII. 92. 1-3=SV. II. 63-65. Properly speaking, this is not a pragātha, but the Nidānasūtra (I. 3) remarks: *ānuṣṭubhā api pragāthā bhavantīty eke; 'nuṣṭup prathamā gāyatryā uttare, yathā purojitī vo andhasa* (SV. II. 47-49), *ā tvā ratham yathotaye* (SV. II. 1121-1123), *viśo viśo vo atithiṃ* (SV. II. 914-916), *pāntam ā vo andhasa* (SV. II. 63-65) *iti*.

3 As the anuṣṭubh contains 32 syllables and the two gāyatrīs each contain 24 syllables, the whole pragātha has 80 syllables, which number, being divisible by 10, can be qualified as a virāj.

4 Vāc is equal to anuṣṭubh (V. 7. 1) and *vāc* is a *vajra* (Ait. br. II. 21. 1).

2. In that it is that pragātha with an anuṣṭubh at the beginning, he first discerns his rival by means of the virāj (*i.e.*) the light, and then drives him away out of the night by means of the anuṣṭubh (*i.e.*) the thunderbolt.

3. Encircling them on all sides, they drove them away; because they drove them away, encircling (*paryāyam*) them, therefrom the 'rounds' (the *paryāyas*) derive their name[1].

1 Cp. Ait. br. IV. 5. 3; *tān vai paryāyair eva paryāyam anudanta; yat paryāyaiḥ paryāyam anudanta, tat paryāyāṇāṃ paryāyatvam*.

4. The first verse-quarters[1] are repeated of the first round[2].

1 The first verse-quarters of each second and third verse; in this manner the chant is given in the ūhagāna I. 1. 18, cp. the Calcutta ed. Vol. III, page 197. Ait. br. IV. 6. 4: *prathamena paryāyeṇa stuvate, prathamāny eva padāni punar ādadate.*—See further §§ 16 and 19.

5. For, by repeating the first verse-quarters, they (the Gods) drove them (the Asuras) out of the first (part of the) night[1].

1 Cp. Ait. br. IV. 5. 4 (*pūrvarātrād*).

6. He begins the chants[1] on (the verses beginning): 'him who drinks of the soma'[2].

1 *prastauti* seems here to be used in a general sense, not in that of 'he chants the prastāva'.

2 Cp. note 2 on § 1.

7. The day, forsooth, is 'him who drinks'[1], the night is the soma[2]; by means of the day even they thus lay hold[3] of the night.

1 *pāntam*, derived by our author from *pāti* 'he who protects'.

2 The word *andhas* is taken by our author in the sense: 'darkness'.

[3] Or 'they begin', which also is the meaning of *ārabhate.*—*pāntam* (day) goes before *andhas* (night).

8. On these (verses they chant) the vaitahavya (sāman)[1].

[1] Grāmegeyagāna IV. 2. 18.

9. Vītahavya, the son of Śreyas[1], being a long time held off (from his dominions or his possessions, by his enemies), saw this sāman. He (thereupon) returned (was restored to his dominions) and was firmly established. He who has applied this (chant) returns and is firmly established.

[1] In the Jaim. br. I. 214 it is Vītahavya āśrāyasaḥ.

10. Into darkness do they enter who undertake the night (-rite). That (the word) 'house' is the finale[1] at the commencement of the night (-rite), is for finding the way.

[1] The chant ends: *o3kā2345ḫ* (see the Calcutta edition of the SV. Vol. I, page 357).

11. When a man comes to his own house, then he recognises all, all is for him (as clear as) by day.

12. They (the Asuras after they were driven out of the first part of the night) retired into the middle (the second)-round; by means of the aurdhvasadmana (sāman)[1], they (the Gods) appropriated their voice.

[1] Cp. note 1 on § 14 and IX. 2. 10.

13. The voice of his rival he appropriates who knows this.

14. It has a triple finale[1].

[1] The aurdhvasadmana, grāmegeya XVI. 1. 10, on *purojitī* SV. I. 545 (ed. Calcutta, Vol. II, page 152) has the triple nidhana:
2 1 2 1r 2
suvṛktibhir | *nṛmādanam* |
1 r , 3 2
bhare 2 ṣuvā 1 |

15. Just as of the day (rite) the midday-service has a triple finale as resting-place[1], so of the night (-rite) has the middle round a triple finale as resting place, for the sake of congruity.

The yaudhājaya also is *triṇidhana*, cp. C. H. § 281.

16 The middle verse-quarters are repeated of the middle round; for by repeating the middle verse-quarters they (the Gods) drove them (the Asuras) out of midnight[1].

[1] Cp. Ait. br. IV. 6. 5: *madhyamena paryāyeṇa stuvate, madhyamāny eva padāni punar ādadate*, and cp. §§ 4 and 19.

17. They (the Asuras) retired into the last round; by means of the (sāman), which has (the word) 'fat-dripping' for finale[1], they took away their cattle; fat-dripping, forsooth, is the cattle[2].

1 Grāmegeyagāna V. 1. 12 on SV. I. 165=ṚS. III. 51. 10—12=SV. II. 87-89, ending ghṛtaścutā' 2345ḥ. (superscript 2 1 3 1 1 1 over ghṛtaścutā')

2 i.e. giving milk from which the ghṛta is produced. In Burnell's edition of the Ārṣeyabrāhmaṇa page 24 under 165, read: *ghṛtaścunnidhanaṃ prājāpatyaṃ mādhucchandaṃ vaiva*, cp. IX. 2. 17.

18. He who knows this appropriates the cattle of his rival.

19. The last verse-quarters are repeated of the last round; for by repeating the last verse-quarters they (the Gods) drove them (the Asuras) forth out of the last (part of the) night[1].

1 Cp. Ait. br. IV. 16. 6: *uttamena paryāyena stuvata, uttamāny eva padāni punar ādadate*; cp. §§ 4 and 16.

20. By means of the junction[1], they then put them to flight[2].

1 The junction, *sandhi*, of day and night, at which moment the *sandhistotra* or twilight-laud is chanted.

2 *palāyanta* with causative force; so also the Jaim. br. I. 205.

21. By means of the āśvina (śastra)[1] they dispersed them[2].

1 The recitation of the Hotr, following on the sandhistotra.

2 *asaṃhāyyam agamayan* ('finished them finally?), cp. Oertel, in Transactions of the Conn. Acad. of Arts and Sciences, Vol. XV, page 172.

22. He who knows this, finishes his rival finally.

23, 24. The night rite, forsooth, is the match of the agniṣṭoma: the agniṣṭoma comprises twelve lauds[1] and the night (-rite) comprises twelve lauds[2].

1 Out-of-doors laud, four ājyalauds, midday pavamāna-laud, four pṛṣṭha-lauds, ārbhava-pavamāna-laud and agniṣṭoma (or yajñāyajñiya-laud).

2 Each of the three rounds comprises four stotras (of the Hotṛ, the Maitrāvaruṇa, the Brāhmaṇācchaṃsin and the Acchāvāka). A similar reasoning Ait. br. IV. 6. 10.

25, 26. The night(-rite)[1] is the match of the ukthya: there are uktha (-laud)s[2] and the twilight (-laud) has three deities[3].

1 *i.e.* the sandhistotra.

2 Of Maitrāvaruṇa, Brāhmaṇācchaṃsin and Acchāvāka.

3 Agni, Uṣas and the Aśvins.

27. Just as of the day (-rite) the uktha (-laud)s are, so of the night (-rite) is the twilight (-laud): of different features are the ukthas[1], of different features are the tristichs[2].

[1] By their metres.

[2] By their deities, note 3 on § 25, 26.

28. The rathantara (sāman) he should take as twilight (-laud) for one who wishes firm support[1].

[1] The sandhi-stotra is chanted on: *snā vo agniṃ namasā* SV. I. 45=ṚS. VII. 16. 1-2=SV II. 99-100 (*agneḥ sāma*); *praty u adarśy āyatī* SV. I. 303=ṚS. VII. 81. 11-12=SV. II. 101-102 (*uṣassāma*) *imā u vaṃ diviṣṭayaḥ* SV. I. 304=ṚS. VII. 74. 1-2=SV. II. 103-104 (*aśvinoḥ sāma*). Their melody is that of the rathantara: ar. gāna II. 1. 21.

29. The rathantara is the earth; on the earth he gets a firm support.

30. The bṛhat (-sāman) he should take as twilight-laud for one who wishes (to reach) the world of heaven.

31. The bṛhat is the world of heaven; in the world of heaven he gets a firm support[1].

[1] In this case, the same pragāthas are chanted on the bṛhat-melody of ar-gāna I. 1. 27; see Kṣudrasūtra I. 7, No. 33.

32. The vāravantīya[1] or the vāmadevya[2] or the śrudhya[3], one of these he should take as twilight (-laud) for one who desires cattle.

[1] Grāmegeya I. 1. 30.

[2] Grām. V. 1. 25.

[3] Grām. III. 1. 15.—These sāmans are to be chanted on the same verses, cp. § 28.

33. These sāmans are the cattle[1]; in the (possession of) cattle he is firmly established.

[1] Cp. V. 3. 12, IV. 8. 15, XV. 5. 34.

[2] To §§ 32 and 33 refers the Kṣudrasūtra (I. 7, No. 34): 'The vāravantīya or the vāmadevya or the śrudhya, one of these he should take for the sandhi(-stotra) for one who desires cattle, on the same pragāthas (as usual). If the sandhi sāman is *aiḍa* (*i.e.* has the word *iḍā* as finale), he should replace the kautsa by the udvaṃśīya on the verses: 'Let the Soma enter thee'.—The udvaṃśīya is grām. IX. 1. 16, chanted on SV. I. 197=RS. VII. 92. 22-24=SV. II. 1010-1012, cp. uhagāna XIX. 1. 1. The kautsa (on SV. I. 381=II. 96-98), grām. X. 1. 26 is *aiḍam*, but this is not the case with the udvaṃśīya, grām. IX. 1. 16. This change is made in order to avoid sameness of performance (*jāmitva*).

34. After (the laud) the Hotṛ recites the āśvina(-śastra)[1].

[1] Cp. *e.g.* Eggeling in 'Sacred Books of the East', Vol. XLI, page XVIII.

35. Prajāpati, forsooth, created that thousand (head of cattle)[1]; this he gave to the Gods. They could not come to terms about it (about its possession). Then they made the sun the goal, and ran a race (about it).

[1] According to Sāyaṇa, the *sahasrasaṃvatsara* sacrifice is meant, but cp. Ait. br. IV. 7. 1, and, especially, Kauṣ. br. XVIII. 1. When Savitṛ gave away his daughter Sūryā in marriage to king Soma, or when Prajāpati (read *prajāpatis* instead of *prajāpates?*) gave away the thousand (cows) to his daughter when she was married, these thousand cows belonged to these deities (*i.e.* were given over to them), etc. But it is clear that the thousand cows are made equal to the thousand verses of the āśvina śastra by the author of our Brāhmaṇa. For the version of the Jaiminīyas cp. Jaim. br. I. 213 (Transactions of the Conn. Acad of Arts and Sciences, Vol. XV, page 165).

36. Of them the two Aśvins were foremost in the race. They (the other Gods) called after them: 'Let it be in common to us'. They answered: 'What would therefrom result for us both?' 'What ye wish' they (the Gods) said. They said: 'Let this recitation be called after us'. Therefore it is called 'the aśvin's (recitation)'.

37. All the deities, forsooth, are mentioned in the recitation[1].

[1] Because, in accordance with the compact made with the Aśvins, all must have a share in the thousand.

38. It is to be recited swiftly; for they run a race, as it were. Before sunrise he should recite (it), for they had made the sun the goal.

IX. 2.

(The chants of the 'rounds'.)

1. 'On (the verses beginning): 'him who drinks of the soma'[1] the vaitahavya (is chanted). Into the field of another they enter, who enter upon the night (-rite). That at the beginning of the night(-rite) there is the (chant) with (the word) 'house' as finale[2], is for the purpose of not going astray from his house.

[1] Cp, note 2 on IX. 1. 1 and IX. 1. 8.

[2] Cp. IX. 1. 10.

2. On (the verses beginning): 'Unto Indra an intoxicating '[1], the gaurīvita[2].

[1] SV. I. 156=ṚS. VII. 31. 1-3=SV. II. 66-68.

[2] The gaurīvita or śāktya is registered grāmegeya IV. 2. 19.

3. When the Gods divided the sacred lore, that which was left over from it (or 'that which surpassed it') became the gaurīvita.

4. Left over (or 'surpassing, excessive') is the gaurīvita and excessive is the night (-laud)[1]; he brings the 'left-over' into the excessive.

[1] The night laud is excessive or surpassing, as it exceeds or surpasses, the three savanas, which close with the yajñāyajñīya-stotra. Cp. XI. 1. 15.

5. On (the verses beginning): 'We herein intend thee[1]', the kāṇva[2].

[1] SV. I. 157=ṚS. VIII. 2. 16-18=SV. II. 69-71.

[2] Grāmegeya IV. 2. 26 (IV. 2. 25 is equally kāṇva, but from Jaim. br. I. 216 it appears that the second one of the two is meant. Is the Pañc. br. inaccurate?)

6. By means of this (sāman), Kaṇva[1] came into harmony (friendship) with Indra. By means of it he comes into harmony with Indra.

[1] According to the Jaim. br. I. 216 is was Kaṇva nārṣada.

7. On (the verses beginning): 'To Indra, who is given to joy, the pressed out (soma)'[1] the śrautakakṣa[2]. It is a might-chant, through it he becomes mighty[3].

[1] SV. I. 158=ṚS. VIII. 92. 19-21=SV. II. 72-74.

[2] Grām. IV. 2. 19.

[3] According to Jaim. br. I. 217, this chant was seen by Śrutakakṣa, the son of Kakṣivat, who desired to obtain cattle.

8. On (the verses beginning): 'This soma, o Indra, for thee'[1], the daivodāsa[2].

[1] SV. I. 159=ṚS. VIII. 17. 11-13=SV. II. 75-77.

[2] Grām. IV. 2. 32.

9. By means of the agniṣṭoma the Gods conquered this world; by means of the ukthya, the intermediate region; by means of the overnight (rite), yonder world. They longed again for this world (the earth); by the (word) 'here'[1] they got a firm support on this

world. (The reason) why it is this sāman, is for getting a firm support (on earth).

[1] The nidhana of the daivodāsa is *ī'234 hā* (*iha*, 'here').

10. On the (verses) which accompany the night (-rite) they use, by way of modification, the aurdhvasadmana.

[1] Grām. XVI. 1. 10 (cp. IX. 1. 12) chanted on the same verses as the daivodāsa.—In the text read *apiśarvariṣu.*

11. The Asuras, forsooth, were in these worlds; by means of the aurdhvasadmana the Gods drove them out of these worlds.

12. Therefore he, who knows this, performs, after driving his rival out of these worlds, a sacrificial session on his own abode[1].

[1] To §§ 10–12 refers the Nidānasūtra (VIII. 1): *madhyamasya rātriparyāyasya hotṛsāmani vicārayanti daivodāsaṃ vā syād aurdhvasadmanaṃ veti; vikalpo vā syād api vā daivodāsam ahīne kuryāt purvādhyāyaṃ pūrve yajñasthāna, aurdhvasadmanaṃ sattreṣūttarādhyāyam uttare yajñasthāne; 'thāpy asmint sattravādarūpo bhavaty: aurdhvasadmanam apiśarvariṣu prohantīti.* From these words so much is clear that, of old, the ritualistic authorities regarded the aurdhvasadmana as optional instead of the daivodāsa, or the daivodāsa as applicable on ahīnas, the aurdhvasadmana on sattras. The Jaiminīyas (br. I. 218, 219) allow only the aurdhvasadmana.

13. On (the verses beginning): 'For us, o Indra, rich in food'[1], the ākūpāra[2].

[1] SV. I. 167=ṚS. VIII. 81. 1–3=SV. II. 78–80.

[2] Grāmeg. V. 1. 18.

14. There was (once upon a time) a female Angiras, named Akūpāra. As the skin of a lizard, so was her skin. Indra, having thrice cleansed her by means of this chant, made her sun-skinned; that, forsooth, she had wished. Whatever they desire as they chant this sāman, that desire is fulfilled for them[1].

[1] On this well-known legend see the parallels in Journal of the American Oriental Soc., Vol. XVIII, page 26 sqq.

15. On (the verses beginning): 'Unto the soma thee, o Bull'[1], the bull-chant (ārṣabha)[2]. It is a might-chant; by it he becomes mighty[3].

[1] SV. I. 161=ṚS. VIII. 45. 22–24=SV. II. 81–83.

[2] Grāmeg. V. 1. 3.

[3] This is illustrated by the Jaim. br. I. 222: 'It (*i.e.* the ārṣabhasāman) is also called daivodāsa (cp. Jaim. ārṣeyabr. page 8). Divodāsa, the son of Vadhryaśva, wished: 'May I obtain both: priesthood and nobility, may I, who am a king, become a seer (*rājā sann ṛṣiḥ syām iti*). He saw this sāman' etc.

16. On (the verses beginning): 'Here, o Good one, is the pressed plant'[1], the gāra[2]. By means of this (sāman) Gara pleased Indra. Pleased by him (by the Udgātṛ) is Indra through this (sāman).

[1] SV. I. 124=ṚS. VIII. 2. 1-3=SV. II. 84-86.

[2] Grām. III. 2. 23 (21 and 22 are likewise gāra, but alone 23 is *aiḍam*, and this, according to Jaim. br. is required).

[3] Differently, the Jaim. br. (I. 223): 'From the Gods the Asuras (read perhaps: from the Asuras the Gods) had swallowed poison (*gara*); they had swallowed this unknowingly, holding it for food. They believed that they had swallowed poison and wished: 'May we drive out from ourselves the poison that has been swallowed by us'. They saw this sāman and by it drove out from themselves the poison they had swallowed. That became the mountains (*giri*)...He who believes himself to have swallowed poison, having eaten food from one, from whom no gift may be accepted, from one whose food may not be eaten, he should apply this sāman' etc.

17. On (the verses beginning): 'For through this with might'[1] the mādhucchandasa[2]; hereby, forsooth, the not-worn-out form of Prajāpati is applied.

[1] SV. I. 165=ṚS. 51. 10-12=SV. II. 87-89.

[2] Or ghṛtaścunnidhanam, cp. IX. 1. 17. It is registered grām. V. 1. 12; its other name is *prājāpatyaṃ mādhucchandasam* and it is attributed to Prajāpati. How Sāyaṇa can assert *asya tṛce ādye dve anirukte*, I fail to comprehend.—According to the Jaim. br. (I. 224) Ghṛtaścut and Madhuścut were two Angirases, who, when the other Angirases went to the world of heaven, were left behind; by these sāmans they joined their clansmen.

18. On (the verses beginning): 'Come ye hither and take place'[1], the daivātitha[2].

[1] SV. I. 164=ṚS. I. 5. 1-3=SV. II. 90-92.

[2] Grām. V. 1. 9.

19. Devātithi, who went about hungering together with his sons, found gourds in the wilderness; he approached them with this sāman; they appeared unto him, having become spotted cows. (The reason) why it is this sāman, is for the thriving of the cattle[1].

[1] This sāman is called maidhātitha by the Jaiminīyas, and its origin is told in the following passage (I. 226; the text is too corrupt for translation): *kāṇvāyanāḥ*

sattrād utthāyāyanta āyuñjānās; te hodgīthā (var. *hodgtāhā, hodgathā*) *iti kimudvatyaitaddhanām* (var. *aitardhanvām*) *urvārubahupravṛttaṃ śayānam upeyus. te 'kāmayantemān eva paśūn bhūtān utsṛjemahīti. sa etan medhātithiḥ kāṇvaḥ sāmāpaśyat; tenopanyaṣīdann ā tvetā niṣīdatendraṃ..*(SV. II. 90-92)*..purandhyām iti. paśavo vai rayis, tato vai te tān paśūn bhūtān udasṛjanta, hiṃkāreṇa haivainān utsasṛjire. te haite 'tra paścād urvārupṛśnaya iva paśavaḥ.*

20. On (the verses beginning): 'At every conjunction the very mighty'[1], the saumedha[2]. It is a night-chant, for the flourishing of the night(-rite)[3].

[1] SV. I. 163=ṚS. I. 30, 7, 8, 9,=SV. II. 93, 95. 94.

[2] Grāmegeya V. 1. 8.

[2] Besides saumedha, this sāman is called paurvatitha, because it was seen by Pūrvatithi (otherwise he is called Pūrvātithi), the son of Arcanānas, the younger brother of Śyāvāśva, who desired and obtained by it abundance of cattle (Jaim. br. I. 227).

21. On (the verses beginning): 'O Indra, at the pressed soma'[1], the kautsa[2].

[1] SV. I. 381 (with various readings)=ṚS. VIII. 3. 1-3=SV. II. 96-98.

[2] Grām. X. 1. 26.

22. Kutsa and Luśa called in rivalry each upon Indra. Indra turned towards Kutsa. He bound him (Indra) with a hundred straps by the scrotum. Luśa said to him (to Indra):

> 'Free thyself, leave Kutsa and come hither.
> Why, pray, should one like thee remain bound by the scrotum?'[1]

Then, Indra broke these (straps) and ran forth. Thereupon, Kutsa saw this sāman; with it he called after him and he (Indra) turned back[2].

[1] The half-verse is ṚS. X. 38. 5. c.d: but with two variants, PBr. *āṇḍayor*, ṚS. *muṣkayoḥ*; PBr. *āsātai*, ṚS. *āsate*.

[2] See for parallels Oertel in Journ. of the American Or. Soc., Vol. XVIII, page 31.

23. That it is this sāman, is for securing Indra's attendance.

(The rest of Chapter IX describes the prāyaścittas, the expiations.)

IX. 3.

1. If they have undergone the consecration for a sacrificial session and (one of them) rises in the middle[1], he should take a part his part of the soma and (therewith) perform a Viśvajit-overnight-rite, at which he gives all his possessions as sacrificial fee. In view of the whole[2] they undergo the consecration; the whole he (thereby) reaches[3].

[1] *i.e.* leaves off the sattra before its end, for cause of illness or a similar reason.

[2] Sc. 'sacrifice.'

[3] And in this manner he obtains the same result as he would have obtained, if he had finished the sattra. The viśvajit-atirātra contains all the 6 pṛṣṭha-stotras, and he gives all his possessions.

2. By the sacrificial fees he gives, he even exceeds (the session)[1].

[1] At a sattra, where all participants are dīkṣitas, no sacrificial fees are given, but at an ahīna, as is the Viśvajit, they are given. This whole matter is treated at length in the Upagranthasūtra I. 8–9 and briefly in the Kṣudrasūtra (I. 7, No. 35): 'For one who rises from a sattra before its end, the arrangement has been given, *viz.*, a Viśvajit-overnight-rite (cp. Ārṣeyakalpa III. 1. e.); all his possessions are the sacrificial fee'. Cp. TBr. I. 4 7. 7: 'To all the deities, to all the pṛṣṭhas he addicts himself, who addicts himself to a sattra; man, forsooth, is as great as his possession; he should perform a sacrifice at which he gives his whole possession, and his soma (feast) should contain all the pṛṣṭha(stotra)s. From all the deities and all the pṛṣṭhas (to which he had addicted himself) he (thereby) redeems himself.' See further Jaim. br. I. 348: *viśvajitātirātreṇa sarvapṛṣṭhena sarvavedasena yajeran*, Baudh. XIV. 29: 202. 12–203. 2, Āp. XIV. 13. 3–11 (the first sūtra agrees closely with PBr. IX. 3. 1) and Śāṅkh. XIII. 13, Āśv. VI. 6. 1.

3. If day-break falls in before the chant of the rounds has been completed, they should chant, on fifteen verses for the Hotṛ, on five for each of the others[1].

[1] They should chant the stotra, which corresponds with the śastra of the Hotṛ, on fifteen verses, the stotras of the Maitrāvaruṇa, the Brāhmaṇācchaṃsin and the Acchāvāka each on five verses; the last three, which, normally, are also on fifteen stotra-verses, are thus shortened each by ten.—Āpastamba (XIV. 23 12–14, following apparently the Jaiminīya śākhā, Jaim. br. I. 348) gives the following specification: 'If day-break falls in before the chant of all the rounds has been completed, they should chant the stotra for the Hotṛ (*i.e.* the

stotra corresponding with the Hotṛ's śastra) on six verses addressed to Indra and Viṣṇu, on three for the others. If day-break falls in before the chant of t w o of the rounds has been completed, (*i.e.*, if only the first has been chanted) they should chant for the Hotṛ and the Maitrāvaruṇa (at the second round only) on the first round, and for the Brāmaṇācchaṃsin and the Acchāvāka on the last, (*i.e.*, they should take for Hotṛ and Maitrāvaruṇa their own *paryāya*-chant of the second round; of the last, for the two others; in this manner the last two of the second, and the first two of the third round fall out). If day-break falls in before the chant of one (the last round) is completed, they should chant for the Hotṛ on fifteen and for each of the others on five verses'. Somewhat different are the prescripts of Āśv. VI. 6. 1–7, Śāṅkh. XIII. 10. 4-10 and Mān. śrs. III. 7. 2.

4. On (the verses beginning): 'O Agni, Uṣas' forth-shining[1]', they should perform the twilight (-laud). Among the stomas, the threefold (or 'nine-versed') one is (equal to) the (three) vital airs, of the sāmans the rathantara is the support. They (thereby) come into the possession[2] of vital airs and of support[3].

1 SV. I. 40=ṚS. I. 44. 1–2=SV. II. 1130–1131.

2 Literally: 'they undertake', the usual expression as relating to a sacrifice of soma.

3 The sandhi-sāman, in order to shorten the service, is now chanted not, as is usual, on nine, but on three verses, as *trika stoma.* The melody is, as in the normal ritual, the rathantara. With § 4 cp. Āśv. VI. 6. 8–9, Āp. XIV. 23. 15.

5. Three hundred and sixty (verses) are recited by the Hotṛ[1].

1 Cp. Āśv. VI. 6. 10 and Śāṅkh. XIII. 10. 11 (instead of the usual thousand).

6. So many days there are in the year; by a number of verses equal to that of the (days in the) year they thus reach the āśvina (recitation)[1].

1 To §§ 3–6 refers the Kṣudrasūtra (I. 7, No. 36): 'If they fear for the falling in of day-break (during the chant of the rounds), they should chant on fifteen (verses) for the Hotṛ, on five for each of the others; on the (verses): 'O Agni, Uṣas' forth-shining', they should chant the twilight (-laud), on the threeversed stoma. Having intentionally * left over (of) the soma, they should on (the verses): 'The buffalo in the bowls, the barley-mixed' chant (instead of the rathantara) the bṛhat on the forty-eight versed (stoma); in the two last but one (stotra-verses) he leaves out the additions *pracetaya* †. The rest is similar to the (normal) jyotiṣṭoma.'

(* I now prefer to read *nikāmāt* instead of *anikāmat*, as the Comm. remarks: *tadarthaṃ buddhipūrvaṃ somam atiricya.*)

(† This means apparently the two additions (taken from the mahānāmnī-verses) *pracetana pracetaya*; they are not found in the Ṛgveda text. It is rather strange that the ūhagāna V. 1. 5 (ed. Calcutta, Vol. V, page 535) takes no notice of this prescript. The verses are SV. I. 457=ṚS. II. 22. 1, 2, 3=SV. II. 836, 838, 837. Are they *aindrāvaiṣṇavyaḥ*? cp. Āp. XIV. 23. 12; Śāṅkh. XIII. 7. 3, 8. 3, 9. 3, prescribes such verses for the *somātireka*. On the whole cp. Śāṅkh. XIII. 10, 3 sqq.)

7. What is chanted too short, that is not-chanted; what is chanted exactly, that is chanted; what is chanted over (*i.e.* too much), that is well chanted[1].

[1] More logically the Jaim. br. I. 356: 'What is chanted too short, that is not-chanted; what is chanted over, that is badly chanted; what is chanted exactly, t h a t is chanted'.

8. If they chant too short, (*i.e.*, if the number of stotra-verses or the required amount of syllables is too little) they should chant (in the next stotra, extra) as many stotra-verses as have been omitted, or they should increase (the next stotra) by as many syllables (as have been omitted).

9. If they chant too many, they should (in the next stotra) leave out as many (stotra-verses) as have been chanted too many, or they should shorten (the next stotra) by as many syllables (as have been chanted over).

10. If they chant too short, a sāman with triple *iḍā*[1] must be taken as agniṣṭoma-sāman; one *iḍā* is the finale, by means of the two others the equilibrium is brought about.

[1] *i.e.* the mahāvaiśvāmitra-sāman, grām. XII. 2.2. (which ends: $\overset{3}{\textit{ho}}$' 4 $\overset{5}{\textit{iḍā}}$, $\overset{3}{\textit{ho}}$ '4 $\overset{5}{\textit{iḍā}}$, $\overset{3}{\textit{ho}}$ '2345 *i-ḍā*.)

11. If they chant too much, a circumflected sāman must be taken as agniṣṭoma-sāman; the circumflex, forsooth, is, as it were, the minus of the sāman[1]; by means of it the equilibrium is brought about[2].

[1] Because such a sāman is shorter than the usual one which has *iḍā* as finale.

[2] To §§ 8 and 10 refers the Kṣudrasūtra (I. 7, No. 37): 'If they chant too short, they should chant extra as many (stotra-verses) as have been omitted or as many syllables more (as have been omitted), or they should take a sāman with triple *iḍā* for agniṣṭomasāman. The ritual in this case is: on (the verses beginning): 'by fore conquest of the soma' the śyāvāśva, the āndhīgava and the audala (are chanted), each on one of the (three) stotra-verses; the yajñāyajñīya on all three; on the verses of the yajñāyajñīya, the mahāvaiśvāmitra (see note 1 on § 10) is chanted by way of agniṣṭomasāman. The rest is similar to the (normal)

jyotiṣṭoma'.—To §§ 9 and 11 refers the same text (No. 38): 'If they chant too much, they should leave out as many (verses) as have been chanted too many or as many syllables (as have been chanted over), or they should take a circum flected (sāman) as agniṣṭomasāman. The ritual in this case is: on the verses of the kāva, the yajñāyajñīya (is chanted) as last sāman (of the midday-pavamāna-laud); on the verses of the yajñāyajñīya, the dairghaśravasa (which sāman, grām. II. 1. 6, ends thus: (*gnā*[4]) *'5yo '6 hā*[5] *i*) is (chanted) as agniṣṭomasāman. If after the agniṣṭomasāman they chant either too short or too much, they should bring about the equilibrium of the stotra-verses or of the syllables (and in this case no other modifications are to be applied in the chant).'

IX. 4.

(The saṃsava.)[1]

1. If two sacrifices of soma are held simultaneously[1], he (the Adhvaryu) should, in the dead of night, make the summons for the morning-litany[2].

[1] *Viz.*, by two rivals in the neighbourhood of each other.

[2] Cp. C. H. § 108 and Eggeling in Sacred Books of the East, Vol. XXVI, page 229; further TS. VII. 5. 5. 1 and Kāṭh. XXXIV. 4.

2. He (then) is the first to appropriate the Voice, the metres and the deities[1].

[1] TS. l.c., Kāth. l.c.

3. He should take as opening (tristich of the out-of-doors-laud) one that contains (the word) 'bull'[1]. Indra, forsooth, is a bull, he (thus) from their morning-service takes away Indra.

[1] See note 2 on § 18, and cp. TS. l.c. Kāṭh. l.c., Āp. XIV. 19. 5: *marutvatīr vṛṣaṇvatīr vā pratipadaḥ*.

4. But they (the theologians) say (also): 'At the beginning of each service it (such a verse) is to be taken'[1]; he (thereby) takes Indra away from the beginning of each service of theirs[2].

[1] Each pavamānalaud (also the midday- and the ārbhava) should begin with a verse as indicated in § 3.—After *kāryā* an *iti* fails, see Kāṭh.

[2] This § agrees with TS. and Kāṭh.

---

[1] Cp. Jaim br. I. 342-344; Maitr. Saṃh. III. 7. 5; Kāṭh. XXXIV. 4; TS. VII. 5. 5, III. 1. 7; TBr. I. 4. 6. 1-3; Śāṅkh. XIII. 5. 4-6; Baudh. XIV. 4: 157. 1-11; Āp. XIV. 19 and 20. 1-4; Kāty. XXV. 14, 16; Lāṭy. I. 11. 10-14; Drāhy. III. 3. 18-23.

5. On well flaming fire is to be offered[1]. All the deities, forsooth, are (equal to) Agni[2]; (thus) he offers whilst seeing (by the flames of the fire) all the deities.

[1] This § is nearly equal to Jaim. br.—The offering here mentioned is described in § 6.

[2] Sāyaṇa quotes a *śrutyantara*: 'the Gods and the Asuras contended together; the Gods, fearing, entered Agni; therefore they say: all the deities are (equal to) Agni'.

6. He sacrifices with (the formulas): 'For lying down, for sitting down[1]! For the conquest of the gāyatrī-metre, *svāhā*!—For lying down, for sitting down! For the conquest of the triṣṭubh-metre, *svāhā*! —For lying down, for sitting down! For the conquest of the jagatī-metre, *svāhā*![2]'

[1] TBr. I. 4. 6. 4 and TS. III. 1. 7 have *saṃveśāya tvā, upaveśāya tvā*. The original intention may have been 'I offer thee that my rival may lie down and sit down (may not be active)'. Sāyaṇa interprets differently.

[2] According to the Sūtrakāras (Lāṭy. 1. 11. 10, Drāhy. III. 3. 18) the Udgātṛ, after his *pravṛta* offerings of each savana (cp. C. H. § 134. b, page 170; § 178. a, page 277; § 221, page 337) makes (in the āgnīdhra-fire, according to Jaim. br. I. 342) an offering with each of the three formulas; with the first at the morning-service, with the second at the midday-service, with the third at the afternoon-service.

7. The conquests, forsooth, are the metres; by means of these he conquers them (his rivals).—Both sāmans, the rathantara and the bṛhat must be applied[1].

[1] See note 2 on § 18.—Jaim. br. I. 343, TS. III. 1. 7. 2, TBr. I. 4. 6. 2 agree.

8. Where are, forsooth, the two bay (steeds) of Indra, there is Indra. Now the rathantara and the bṛhat are Indra's bay (steeds). In that both, the rathantara and the bṛhat, are applied, he is the first to lay hold of Indra's bay (steeds)[1].

[1] Cp. Jaim. br. I. 343: *ubhe bṛhadrathantare bhavata; indrasya vā etau harī yad ubhe bṛhadrathantare; yajño devaratha; indrasyaiva haribhyāṃ yajñena devarathenājim ujjayati.*

9. The two tauraśravasa (-samans) must be applied.

[1] See note 2 on § 18.

10. Turaśravas and the Pārāvatas (once upon a time) performed simultaneously sacrifices of soma. Thereupon, Turaśravas saw these

two sāmans. For these, (*i.e.*, in recompense of these) Indra carried off, unto him, by means of[1] a cotton tree from the side of the Yamunā[2] their (the rival's) offering substances. In that there are the two tauraśravasa (sāmans), he appropriates their (his rivals') offering substances.

[1] Sāyaṇa gives the periphrase with an instrumental, I presume that *śalmalinā* is to be read with the Leyden MS. instead of *śalmalināṃ*. But Sāyaṇa's interpretation: *svakīyenāyudhaviśeṣeṇa* is not clear to me.

[2] *yamunāyāḥ*, Sāyaṇa joins it as a genitive with *havyam*. Read perhaps *yamunayā*: along the Yamunā.

11. They should be the first to press out the soma.

12. Those (ships)[1], forsooth, that are the first to enter the water, are the first to reach the stairs of the landing place (on the opposite shore or bank); (in this way) they are the first to lay hold of Indra.

[1] To the feminine *yāḥ* and *tāḥ* I supply *nāvaḥ* (Sāyaṇa: *prajāḥ*); *prasnānti*, then, is here used with the meaning of *praplavanti*, just a Kaṭh. XXXIII. 5 : 30. 18 *prasnānti* as against TS. VII. 5. 3. 2 *praplavanti*.

13. The vihavya (hymn) must be recited (by the Hotṛ)[1].

[1] TS. and Kāṭh.: *sajanīyaṁ śasyaṃ, vihavyaṁ śasyam, agastyasya kayāśubhīyaṁ śasyam*; Jaim. br. (I. 344): *vihavīyaṃ sajanīyam agastyasya kayāśubhīyam ity etāni śastrāṇi bhavanti* (cp. § 17). See Āśv. VI. 6. 14-16, Śāṅkh. XIII. 5. 15-17.

14. Jamadagni and the seers[1] performed (once upon a time) simultaneously sacrifices of soma. Thereupon, Jamadagni saw this vihavya (-hymn). To him Indra turned himself. In that the Hotṛ recites the vihavya, he takes away Indra from them (from the rivals).

[1] In TS. III. 1. 7. 3 Viśvāmitra and Jamadagni contend against Vasiṣṭha.

15. If the other (sacrifice of soma) be an agniṣṭoma, then an ukthya must be performed; if an ukthya, then an atirātra[1]. That sacrifice which is larger is welcome to Indra; by the larger sacrifice he takes away Indra from them.

[1] Cp. TS. III. 1. 7. 3, TBr. I. 4. 6. 3-4.

16. But they say also: 'Difficult to reach, so to say, is the further path[1]; from the sacrifice which he undertakes in the beginning he should not depart' (he should hold on to that sacrifice and not strive to perform a larger one than his rival)[2].

[1] *paraḥ panthāḥ*, the path followed by the other, the rival.

[2] And in this case the measure exposed in § 17 will secure him the priority.

17. The sajanīya (hymn) must be recited, the kayāśubhīya (-hymn) of Agastya must be recited [1].

[1] Cp. note 1 on § 13.

18. From this (world) and from yonder (world), from the to-day and the to-morrow, from the pair [1], from the day and the night he excludes them [2].

[1] Probably from sons and daughters, or from cows and horses.

[2] This § has no intimate connection with § 17 but has a general purport, cp. TS. III. 1. 7. 3: 'both, rathantara and bṛhat are to be applied; the rathantara is the earth, the bṛhat is the heaven; from these he excludes him. The rathantara is the to-day, the bṛhat is the to-morrow; from the to-day and the to-morrow he excludes him. The rathantara is the past, the bṛhat is the future; from past and future he excludes him. The rathantara is the limited, the bṛhat is the unlimited; from the limited and the unlimited he excludes him'. Jaim. br. I. 343: *idaṃ vai rathantaram ado bṛhad, asmād amuṣmād adyaśvāt sumithunād evainān antaryanti.*— The saṃsava is treated in the Kṣudrasūtra (I. 8, No. 39) in the following manner: 'If two sacrifices of soma take place simultaneously, the out-of-doors-laud consists of the tristich:

(Morning Service.)

1–3. *pavasvendo v ṛ ṣ ā suta* (II. 128–130)

4–6. *davidyutatyā rucā* (II. 4–6)

7–9. *pavamānasya te kave* (II. 7–9);

or (its opening tristich) is to be composed (of the following verses):

pavasvendo vṛṣā sutaḥ (II. 128)

upāsmai gāyatā naraḥ (II. 1)

pavasva vāco agriyaḥ (II. 125).—

agna ā yāhi vītaye (II. 10–12) is the hotṛ's ājya (stotra), the rathantara-one (cp. Ārṣ. k. page 33, note 4), the (other) three ājya(stotra)s are the bārhata-ones; or the ājya(stotra)s are of the two kinds, on *agniṃ dūtaṃ vṛṇimahe* (II. 140–142, and the following, cp. Ārṣ. k. page 34, note 3).

(Midday Service.)

On: *vṛṣā pavasva dhārayā* (II. 153–155) (are chanted)

1–3. the gāyatra,

4–6. the āmahīyava; on:

punānaḥ soma dhārayā (II. 25-26)

7. the raurava, on one (verse),

8. the yaudhājaya, on one (verse),

9. the circumflected t a u r a ś r a v a s a, on (one verse): aranyegeya III. 1. 6, see ed. of Calcutta Vol. II, 448, composed on SV. I. 298: *yad indra śāsaḥ*; not in the ṚS. and not being the first verse of a tristich, as it is chanted *ekasyām*; ending *hā* 5 *yo* 6 *hāi*.

10–12. the rathantara, on all three; on:

vṛṣā śoṇaḥ (II. 156–158)

13–15. the pārtha as the last (of the midday-pavamāna-laud).

The bṛhat, vamadevya, śyaita and kāleya (are the prstha-lauds)

(Afternoon-service.)

On: *acikradad v ṛ ṣ ā hariḥ* (II. 392–394) (are chanted)

1–3. the gāyatra,

4–6. the saṃhita; on:

pavasva, indram acchā (II. 42-46)

7–9. the sapha and

10–12. the śrudhya; on:

purojitī vo andhasaḥ (II. 44–49)

13. the śyāvāśva, on one (verse),

14. the tauraśravasa, with nidhana, on one (ar. gāna III. 1. 5, S.V. ed. Calc. l.c.),

15. the audala, on one,

16–18. the āndhīgava, on all three;

19–21. the kāva, as the last (of the ārbhavapavamāna-laud).

The yajñāyajñīya is the agniṣṭomasāman. For a (samsava-rite,) at which the rathantara is taken (as first pṛṣṭha)[1], two kakubhs are the last (of the midday- and the arbhavāpavamāna)[2]. The *viṣṭuti* is the *brahmāyataniya* of the seventeen-versed stoma (Pañc. br. II. 8. 2) for the Hotṛ's pṛṣṭha. The offerings, at which the metres are the deities (see Pañc. br. IX. 4. 6), are in each service the third of the two *pravṛta*-offerings (see note 2 on IX. 4. 6). In the kayāśubhīya(-hymn) (ṚS. I. 165) the nivid(-formulas) of the marutvatīya(śastra) (which runs parallel to the midday-pavamāna, C. H. § 196, pages 300, 302) should be put in; in the

1 If it is allowed to read *rāthantarasya* instead of *rathantarasya*.

2 This is not certain!

sajanīya (-hymn) (ṚS. II. 12), those of the niṣkevalya (śastra) (which runs parallel to the Hotṛ's pṛṣṭha, cp. C. H. § 200, page 310, 312); in the vihavya(-hymn) (ṚS. X. 128), those of the vaiśvadeva (śastra) (which runs parallel to the ārbhava-pavamāna, cp. C. H. § 235, pages 354, 358); or he may, after reciting these hymns, recite, before the hymns, in which the nivids are put in, the nivids in their proper place' (and this is the practice of Āśv. VI. 6. 14–16). The saṃsava is also treated at length in Upagranthasūtra I. 13.

IX. 5.

(Expiation in case the soma has been taken away.)

1. If they (*i.e.*, some rivals) take away the soma before it has been bought[1], other soma must be bought[2].

[1] Cp. C. H. § 33.

[2] Cp. Kāṭh. XXXIV. 3: 37. 12, TBr. I. 4. 7. 5, Baudh. XIV. 29: 201. 17, Āp. XIV. 24. 9, Mān. śrs. III. 6. 3.

2. If they take it away after it has been bought, other soma, which is to be found in the vicinity, must be obtained[1]; but he should give something (some fee) to the soma-buyer[2].

[1] A renewed buying does not take place: Jaim. br. I. 354: *yenaivāsyāyaṃ pūrvakrayeṇa krīto bhavati, tenaivāsyāyaṃ krīto bhavati.*

[2] Cp. Kāṭh., Āp., Mān. śrs. ll. cc.; Jaim. br. l.c. *somavikrayiṇe tu kiñcit kaṃ deyaṃ, nen no 'bhiṣavo hato 'sad iti.*

3. If they cannot obtain any soma, they should press (instead of the soma) pūtīkaplants; if he cannot obtain *these*, then arjuna-plants[1].

[1] Cp. Kāṭh. l.c. (*ārjunāni*), TBr. l.c. Āp. l.c. 12 (both *phālgunāni*); according to Mān. śrs. l c., the arjunas (or ārjunas) must be red-tufted, if they replace the soma originating from the Hemavat-mounts, but brown-tufted, if they replace the soma originating from the Mūjavat-mounts; cp. also below, § 7. The pūtīkas seem to be the same as ādāras.

4. The Gāyatrī fetched the soma; a soma-guard discharged an arrow after her and cut off a feather of her (off Gāyatrī); that shoot of it (of the soma) which fell down, became the pūtīka (-plant); in it

the Gods found help (*ūti*); it verily is the pūtīka; in that they press out the pūtīkas, they find help for him[1].

[1] Cp. VIII. 4. 1.—Kāṭh. XXXIV. 3: 37. 15 sqq. agrees closely with Pañc. br. (read *tasyāḥ* instead of *tasya*, line 15) and cp. also Ait. br. III. 26. 3, 4. I suspect that the original reading of Pañc. br. was: *ūtīko vā eṣa yat pūtīko yat pūtīkān abhiṣuṇvanti*, etc., cp. Kāṭh. *ūtīkā vai nāmeti yat pūtīkā yat pūtīkān abhiṣuṇvanti*, etc. The Jaim. br. (I. 354) knows only the ūtīka, not the pūtīka: 'Indra, having hurled his thunderbolt on Vṛtra, believed that he had not destroyed him; he entered the ūtīkas; these found a refuge (or 'help') for him: *yadi tan na vindeyur ūtīkān abhiṣuṇuyur; indro vṛtraṃ vajreṇādhyasya nāstṛṣīti manyamānaḥ sa ūtīkān eva prāviśat; tasmai ta evotim avindan.*

5. Fresh milk and pūtīkas (are to be pressed instead of the soma) at (the) morning (-service); boiled milk and pūtīkas at (the) midday (-service); sour milk and pūtīkas at (the) afternoon (-service)[1].

[1] This nearly agrees with Kāṭh. XXXIV. 3: 37. 20; cp. also TBr. I. 4. 7. 6-7, Āp. XIV. 24. 14, Āśv. VI. 8. 9-11; Śāṅkh. XIII. 6. 3.

6. 'The soma-draught, forsooth, goes away from him', they say, 'whose soma they take away'. It enters the plants and the cattle: (in substituting the pūtīkas and the different kinds of milk) he retains him (the soma) out of the plants and the cattle[1].

[1] Cp. Kāṭh. l.c. page 37. 21. sqq.

7. Indra slew Vṛtra. The soma which flowed out of his (Vṛtra's) nose, that became the brown-tufted arjunas; that which flowed out of his omentum, as it was cut out, became the red-tufted ones. The brown-tufted arjunas he should press (if no pūtīkas are obtainable); this, forsooth, (*viz.*, the brown colour) is the feature of the brāhmin; (in doing so) he actually presses the soma[1].

[1] Almost identical with Jaim. br. I. 354. The Kāṭhaka (l.c. 37. 17) runs: 'Indra slew Vṛtra; his blood became the red-tufted arjunas; the fluid that streamed together out of his neck, when it was pulled off, became the brown-tufted arjunas; this (however) is an Asuric soma, as it were; therefore it is not to be taken for pressing'.

8. The śrāyantīya (-sāman) must be taken as the Brāhman's chant[1]; thereby he puts him (the soma) all right[2].

[1] For this and the sāman of § 9, cp. Āśv. VI. 8. 12-13.

[2] *satkaroti*, by strengthening (*śrāyantīya-śrīṇāti*) him.

9. The yajñāyajñīya (-sāman) he should shift on to the anuṣṭubh (-part)[1]; he (thereby) makes him thrive by the voice[2]. The vāravantīya must be taken as agniṣṭomasāman, in order to encompass valour (and) strength[3].

[1] In the ārbhavapavamāna, before the last (the kāva) sāman.

[2] Because the yajñāyajñīya has the word *vāc* as finale.

[3] Because the vāravantīya, so called because of the word *vārayantam* (SV. I.17), reminds of 'restraining, opposing' (the rival).

10. Five sacrificial fees (cows) must be given[1].

[1] Mān śrs. III. 6. 6; differently TBr. I. 4. 7. 7 and Āp. XIV. 24. 18, Śat. br. IV. 5. 10. 6 ('one cow he should give to these same priests as sacrificial fee'), cp. Āśv. VI. 8. 14, Śānkh. XIII. 6. 4 (who allows five cows in case the soma has been lost by burning cp. below IX. 9. 15).

11. Fivefold is the sacrifice[1]; as much as is the sacrifice, that he (thereby) lays hold on.

[1] Cp. note 2 on VI. 7. 12.

12. Having come up (returned) from the lustral bath, he should undergo anew the consecration[1].

[1] After the close of this soma-sacrifice, he should, by way of indemnification, of atonement, recommence a sacrifice of the same order as the one he has now performed. The same thought is expressed in TBr. l.c., Āp. l.c. 19 by the words: 'he should again buy soma', cp. also Mān. śrs. l.c. 17, Āśv. VI. 8. 14.

13. On the occasion of this (sacrifice) he should give the sacrificial fees that he intended to give[1].

[1] That he intended to give at the sacrifice, which he had been unable to perform in the ordinary manner, because his soma had been taken away; with this § cp. Āp. l.c. 21, Mān. śrs. l.c. 8, Baudh. XIV. 29: 202. 10, Āśv. VI. 8. 15.— To Pañc. br. IX. 5 refers the Kṣudrasūtra (I. 8, No. 40): 'If the soma has been taken away, the Brahman's chant is the śrāyantīya; on 'we there, o uncomparable one' the kāleya (is chanted); on 'by fore-conquest of the plant' the śyāvāśva, the āndhīgava and the audala each on one verse, the yajñāyajñīya on all three; on the verses of the yajñāyajñīya, the vāravantīya as agniṣṭomasāman; five sacrificial fees (are to be given). The rest is similar to the (normal) jyotiṣṭoma. For the sāmans see the Index. The Upagranthasūtra II. 1, 2 treats also at length of this prāyaścitta.

IX. 6.

(Expiation in case the soma-trough bursts.)

1. If the soma-trough bursts, he should take as the Brahman's chant the sāman which has the word *vaṣaṭ* as finale.[1]

[1] The so-called vaṣaṭkāraṇidhana (grāmegeyagāna VII. 1. 19, on SV. I. 256=ṚS. VIII. 3. 7-8=SV. II. 923-924) has, as nidhana, *ū234pā* (with 3 and 5 printed above) (thus also has the ūhagāna). Sāyana on VIII. 1. 1 remarks: *tatra upā nidhanam asti, tatsthāne vāṣāḍ iti nidhanaṃ kuryāt*; cp. Lāṭy. VII. 10. 1 *upāsthāneṣv anyāni nidhanāni*, see also XI. 10. 14, XIII. 3. 13, XIV. 5. 22.

2. The soma of him, whose trough bursts, is spilled, as it has not been consecrated by the word *vaṣaṭ*[1]; in that the Brahman's chant is the one that has *vaṣaṭ* as finale, his soma becomes consecrated by the *vaṣaṭ*.

[1] After each libation of soma, the word *vaṣaṭ* is uttered by the Hotṛ (or by the Hotraka), see, *e.g.*, C. H. page 200.

3. It is to be applied on the verses (beginning): 'Wandering (*dadrāṇa*) alone in the midst of many'[1].

[1] The vaṣaṭkāraṇidhana must be chanted on SV. I. 325=ṚS. X. 55. 5-7=SV. II. 1132-1134.

4. For this trough bursts 'in the midst of many'.

5. Here (however) they say: 'A mishap should not be bespoken by a (word of) mishap: he, who, after the trough has burst, applies (the chant) on verses containing (the word) *dadrāṇa*[1], now bespeaks a mishap by a (word of) mishap.

[1] This word is by the author of the Brāhmana derived as part. perf. med. from the root *dṛ*, 'to burst'.

6. The śrāyantīya only is to be taken (as the Brahman's chant, and not the vaṣaṭkāraṇidhana).

7. Prajāpati created the creatures; he thought himself milked out, emptied out. He saw this śrāyantīya (sāman); by means of it he braced himself fully[1] by progeny, cattle (and) strength.

[1] Cp. note 2 on IX. 5. 8.

8. Milked out, as it were, emptied out is he, whose trough bursts; in that the śrāyantīya is the Brahman's chant, he braces himself again fully with progeny, cattle (and) strength.

9. If the śrāyantīya is the Brahman's chant, he should apply the sāman, which has the word *vaṣaṭ* as finale, on anuṣṭubh (-verses) addressed to Viṣṇu[1].

[1] *i.e.*, (see note 1 on § 11) on SV. II. 366, 367, 368=ṚS. (with variants) IX. 100 6, 7, 9. According to the Taittirīyas (TS. VII. 5. 5. 2) and the Kaṭhas (Kāṭh. XXXIV. 4: 38. 13), on verses addressed to Viṣṇu śipiviṣṭa, *i.e.*, probably on SV. II. 975, 976, 977=ṚS. VII. 100, 6, 5, 7; but these verses cannot be meant by the Pañc. br. as they are triṣṭubhs.

10. What (part) of the sacrifice trickles away (by the fissure in the trough), that part trickles away towards the Voice; the anuṣṭubh is the Voice, and Viṣṇu is the sacrifice. By means of the Voice, (*i.e.*, the anuṣṭubh) he covers the fissure in the sacrifice.

11. What (part) of the sacrifice trickles away, that part trickles away at the end. The vāravantīya must be taken as agniṣṭomasāman. He (thereby) covers up (*vārayati*) the fissure in the sacrifice[1].

[1] Cp. on the whole Jaim. br. I. 352, TS. VII. 5.5.2, Kāṭh. XXXIV. 4 (second half), Āp. XIV. 26.10—27.2, Baudh. XIV.7, Śāṅkh. XIII. 12. 1-2, Mān. śrs. III. 6.11.— To the sixth khaṇḍa refers the Kṣudrasūtra (I.8, No. 41): 'If the trough bursts, the first two savanas (are) similar to (those of) the preceeding, (*i.e.*, of No. 40, see note 1 on IX. 5.13); on 'he is pressed out who of the riches' and 'invite them who hold themselves aloof' (are chanted) the sapha and the pauṣkala; on 'thou sustainest sky and earth' (SV. II. 368), reverting (the sequence of the verses of) the tristich (II. 366-368), the śyāvāśva on one (on II. 368), the āndhīgava on one (on II. 367), the vaṣaṭkāraṇidhana on one (on II. 366); on 'by fore-conquest of the plant,' the yajñāyajñīya on all three (on II. 47-49), the first (II. 47) is anuṣṭubh, the last two (II. 48, 47) are gāyatrīs; on the verses of the yajñāyajñīya, the vāravantīya (is chanted) as agniṣṭomasāman. The rest is similar to the (normal) jyotiṣṭoma' (This is the arrangement, the *kḷpti*, with reference to Pañc. br. IX. 6.5-11). 'Now the (jyotiṣṭoma), which has the vaṣaṭkāraṇidhana as the Brahman's chant, and the śrāyantīya on the anuṣṭubh (part) (cp. Pañc. br. IX. 6. 1-4): on 'wandering alone in the midst of many,' the Brahman's chant (or third pṛṣṭhastotra): on 'this Brahman, the regular one,' the kāleya; on 'run about for Indra,' the sapha; on 'thou sustainest sky and earth,' reverting the tristich, the śyāvāśva on one, the āndhīgava on one, the śrāyantīya on one; on 'by fore-conquest of the plant' the yajñāyajñīya: on three verses, all anuṣṭubhs (the two gāyatrīs, II 48, 49, are transformed into anuṣṭubhs by adding a verse-quarter from the preceding verse, cp. ūhagāna VIII. 2.16 in the edition of Calcutta Vol. III, page 141); on the verses of the yajñāyajñīya the vāravantīya as agniṣṭomasāman. The rest is similar to the (normal) jyotiṣṭoma.'

IX. 7.

(Expiation in case some of the soma is left over.)

1. If there is left over (of the) soma from the morning service [1], they should chant the gāyatra (melody) on the verses in which the Maruts are invoked (which begin): 'This soma is pressed out' [2].

[1] At the end of each savana all the soma must be poured out, offered and drunk, cp., *e.g.*, C.H. § 167, 239 (the sampraiṣa in this case is: *mātirīricaḥ*; but if a residue must be left during the savana for a subsequent libation, the sampraiṣa runs: *somaṃ prabhāvaya*). If it happens that some quantity of soma is left over in the trough, this residue must be offered subsequently at the end of each savana, with an extra stotra, śastra and bhakṣaṇa.

[2] SV. I. 174=RS. VIII. 94. 4-6=SV. II. 1135-1137. This tristich is also prescribed by the hautrasūtrakāras as *stotriya tṛca* for the śastra of the Hotṛ (Āśv. VII. 7.2, Śāṅkh. XIII. 7.2). The texts of the Jaiminīyas (Jaim. br. I. 350) and the Taittirīyas (TBr. I. 4.5, Baudh. XIV. 25: 196.9, Āp. XIV. 18.5) prescribe in the first place the tristich 'the cow of the Maruts sucks' (RS. VIII. 94.1-3), which according to Āśvalāyana is to be taken as *anurūpa tṛca*.

2. The soma which is left over from the morning-service, is left over coveting the midday-service. Therefore, they chant on verses, in which the Maruts are invoked, for at the midday-service the Maruts are invoked [1], and therefore also (they chant) gāyatrī-verses, for gāyatrī-like is the morning-service.

[1] The first śastra of the midday-service is the marutvatīya-śastra. In doing thus, 'they depart neither from the morning-, nor from the midday-service' TBr. I. 4.5. 1-2.

3. The same (kind of) stoma is to be taken as that after which it (the soma) is left over [1], for the sake of congruence.

[1] So *e.g.*, the stoma which follows after the morning-service, must be trivṛt, that after the midday-service, seventeen-versed.

4. The Hotṛ addresses, after (the laud), a (hymn) addressed to Indra and Viṣṇu [1].

[1] Cp. Āśv. VI. 7. 2-5, Śāṅkh. XIII. 10. 3.

5. Indra, forsooth, is valour, Viṣṇu is the sacrifice, in valour even and in the sacrifice he is firmly established [1].

[1] To § 1-5 refers the Kṣudrasūtra (I. 10, No. 42): 'If any soma is left over from the morning-service, they should chant, as fifth ājya (laud), the Marut-verses:

'This soma is pressed out' on the gāyatra-melody; the Brahman's and the Acchāvāka's chants, (*i.e.*, the third and the fourth pṛṣṭhastotra) should be successively nine- and fifteen-versed (instead of seventeen-versed). The rest is similar to the (normal) jyotiṣṭoma.'

6. If there is left over from the midday-service, they should chant the gaurīvita (melody) [1] on the verses, in which the Sun is invoked, (beginning): 'Verily, thou art great, o Sun' [2].

1 Grāmegeya V. 1. 22 composed on SV. 1. 168; Cp. TBr. I. 4. 5. 2-3, Āp. XIV. 18. 9-11.

2 SV. I. 276=ṚS. VIII. 101. 11-12 (var.)=SV. II. 1138-1139.

7. The soma which is left over from the midday-service, is left over coveting the afternoon-service. Therefore, they chant verses in which the Sun is invoked, for at the afternoon-service the Sun is invoked [1], and therefore also (they chant) bṛhatī (verses)[2], for bṛhatī-like is the midday-service.

1 The afternoon-service begins with the ādityagraha (C.H. § 217), which, however, is properly not a graha destined for Āditya, the Sun, but for the Ādityas.

2 The verses SV. II. 1138-1139 are bṛhatī and Satobṛhatī.

8. The same (kind of) stoma is to be taken as that after which it (the soma) is left over [1], for the sake of congruence. The Hotṛ recites, after the (laud), a (hymn) addressed to Indra and Viṣṇu [2]. Indra is strength, Viṣṇu is the sacrifice, in strength even and in the sacrifice he is firmly established [3].

1 Cp. note 1 on § 3.

2 Cp. Āśv. VI. 7. 6, Śāṅkh. XIII. 8. 3.

3 To § 6-8 refers the Kṣudrasūtra (I. 10, No. 43): 'If any soma is left over from the midday-service they should chant, as f i f t h pṛṣṭha (laud), the āditya (-verses): 'verily, thou art great, o Sun' on the gaurīvita (melody); the afternoon-service they should make nine-versed. Its arrangement is: on 'run about for Indra' the sapha (should be chanted); on: 'round about do thou run,' the śyāvāśva; on: 'be clarified, o Soma, (as) a great sea,' the āndhīgava. The rest is similar to the (normal) jyotiṣṭoma.'

9. If there is left over from the afternoon-service, they should chant the gaurīvita (melody) on verses addressed to Viṣṇu śipiviṣṭa [1].

1 Cp. Baudh. XIV. 25: 197. 8, Āp. XIV. 18. 14, Āśv. VI. 7. 8, Śāṅkh. XIII. 9. 2.

10. Viṣṇu śipiviṣṭa is the sacrifice; in the sacrifice, in Viṣṇu he (thereby) is firmly established.—Redundant (or 'excessive') is the

gaurīvita: he (thus) puts the redundant (soma) into the redundant (gaurīvita)[1].

1 The gaurīvita is a surplus, is redundant or excessive because (see V. 7. 1) it is sprung from the pith that was l e f t o v e r at the division of the Voice.

11. They should, further, do the following: the uktha (laud)s should lead on further[1]. This (soma), which is left over from the agniṣṭoma, is left over coveting the uktha (laud)s. If there is left over from the uktha (laud)s, an overnight-rite should be performed. This (soma) which is left over from the uktha(laud)s is left over coveting the night (-rite). If there is left over from the night (-rite), they should chant the verses addressed to Viṣṇu śipiviṣṭa on the bṛhat (melody). 'That soma, however', they say, 'is left over, which is left over from the night (-rite)'.

1 Not wholly certain; read perhaps (cp. the Kṣudrasūtra) *etad anyat kuryur ukthāny anyat praṇayeyur.*

12. That (soma) verily which is left over from the night (-rite), is left over coveting yonder world. They should chant the bṛhat (melody); the bṛhat is able to reach yonder world[1]: that same (world) he reaches (by means of the bṛhat)[2].

1 Usually the bṛhat is declared to be yonder world, the sky, the heaven (VII. 6. 17).

2 To 9–12 refers the Kṣudrasūtra (I. 10, No. 44): 'If there is left over from the afternoon-service, they should chant the verses addressed to Viṣṇu śipiviṣṭa (see note 2 on IX. 7. 9) on the gaurīvita (melody,) as s e c o n d agniṣṭoma-sāman. They should, further, do the following: the ukthas should lead on further. If there is left over from the ukthas, a night (-rite) is to be performed (and on this occasion an extra-laud must be performed and the soma, which has been left over, must be offered). If there is left over from the night (-rite), they should chant the bṛhat (melody) on the verses addressed so Viṣṇu śipiviṣṭa as nine-versed stoma, following on the twilight-laud'.

IX. 8.

(Expiation in case one of the dīkṣitas dies.)[1]

1 Cp Jaim. br. II. 345–347; Kāṭh. XXXIV. 2: 36. 23–37. 11; TBr. I. 4. 6. 5–7; Baudh. XIV. 27: 198. 14–200. 2; Āp. XIV. 21. 8–22. 15; Mān. śrs. III. 8. 4–7; Kāty. XXV. 13. 28–46; Āśv. VI. 10. 1–31; Śāṅkh. XIII. 11.

1. If one of those who have undergone the consecration for a sacrifice of soma, comes to die, they should, having cremated him, tie

up his bones[1]; then they should consecrate (in his place) him who stands in relation nearest to him[2] and perform the sacrifice with him.

[1] In his black deer-hide, cp. Āp. XIV. 22. 11.

[2] His son or his brother, Śāṅkh.

2. They should, further, do the following: having pressed out further the soma[1], they (the Chanters) should, before taking the soma-draughts[2], perform a laud either at the southern corner[3] or at the mārjālīya[4].

[1] A similar expression above IX. 7. 11 and cp. Jaim. br. I. 345: *etad anyat kuryur: abhiṣutya somam anyad agṛhītvā grahān*, etc.

[2] The aindravāyava and following ones, C. H. § 132.

[3] The south-eastern corner of the mahāvedi.

[4] The dhiṣṇya situated to the south of the mahāvedi. The south is the quarter of the dead.—read: *mārjālīye vā*.

3. He forsooth, who dies, being consecrated, has a right to a share in the sacrifice[1]; him they thereby appease.

[1] *api vā etasya yajne* (*sc. bhavati*), the same construction as Jaim. br. I. 284: *sarvatra haivāsyāpi puṇye bhavati*. Sāyaṇa (*saptamyarthe ṣaṣṭhī!*) would have us believe that *etasya yajñe* is equivalent to *etasmin yajñe*, or he proposes to take *asya* in the sense 'of the Gṛhapati'. For the thought cp. Jaim. br. I. 345: *samānāya vā ete yajñāya samānāya sukṛtāya samārabhya dīkṣante, tenaivainaṃ niravadayante.*

4. They chant the yāma (melody)[1]; they (thereby) lead him to the world of Yama.

[1] Cp. note 1 on § 7.

5. Three verses they chant; for in the third world (reckoned from here) are the Fathers[1].

[1] The Manes, the departed Ancestors.

6. They chant them right off (or 'thitherward', *i.e.*, without repeating)[1], for yonder world is (situated) thitherward from this (world).

[1] As a *trika stoma*.

7. They chant the verses of the Sārparājñī[1].

[1] Read: *sārparājñyā* instead of *sārparājñā*; cp. IV. 9. 4.—Cp. note 1 on IV. 9. 4; the verses are chanted on the yāma-sāman: araṇyegeyagāna IV. 1. 13, composed on ār. saṃh. III. 4: *agnim īḍe.*

8. By means of these (verses) the Serpent Arbuda removed his dead skin; their dead skin even they remove by these (verses)[1].

1 =IV. 9. 5.

9. Reciting these verses after (the laud), they[1] walk around the mārjālīya, beating their left thighs[2].

1 Not only the Chanters but all the participants.

2 The circumambulation is performed thrice from right to left (withershins), *i.e.*, while turning their left side to the mārjālīya, where, according to some authorities, the urn with the bones of the deceased has been deposited. They wear their over-garments over the right shoulder (they are *prācīnāvītinaḥ*) and beat their left thigh with their left hand. The recitation of the verses that have been chanted, takes the place of the śastra, for, as the Black Yajurveda texts have it: 'deficient is a laud, which is not followed by a recitation.'

10. He[1] (in doing thus) recites the (verses of the) śastra after the laud. In yonder world they fan him[2].

1 The Hotṛ, who, according to other authorities, goes in front of them all.

2 Translation somewhat doubtful. Read with the MS. Leyden *nidhuvanti*, and cp. Jaim. br. I. 345 (immediately after the description of the circumambulation): *amuṣminn evainaṃ tal loke nidhuvate.* Probably the meaning is the same as expressed by Āpastamba in his words *sigbhir abhidhūnvantas* (*triḥ...pariyanti*), cp. *atho dhuvanty evainam, ny evāsmai hnuvate*, TBr., and cp. Kāṭh. *dhuvanty evainam etad, atho ny evāsmai hnuvate.* The words following in the Jaim. br. immediately: *abhy enam amuṣmiṃlloke vāyuḥ pavate,* seem to prove that our rendering of *nidhuvanti* is right. Then, there cannot be any logical connection between the two sentences of our § 10.

11. 'They swerve from the path', they say, 'who officiate for a deceased.' They take the soma-draughts in this order, that the one destined for Indra and Vāyu comes first[1]. In this way they return to the path.

1 Although this is the usual practice (cp. C. H. § 132) it is here (as by Śāṅkh. and Baudh.) expressly mentioned, as there are other possibilities.

12. (The tristich beginning): 'O Agni, thou purifyest the lives'[1], must be taken as the opening one. In those, who live, he (therby) puts life[2].

1 Cp. VI. 10. 1.

2 Cp. note 1 on VI. 10. 3.

13. After a year[1], they should perform a sacrifice for the bones (of the deceased)[2]. The year is the allayment of all[3]; were they

to perform the sacrifice before the (end of the) year, the speech (or 'voice') would become wounded (and) mangled[4].

[1] At the end of the year's sattra.

[2] *asthīni yājayeyuḥ*, the bones representing the deceased are treated exactly as if they were the man himself, as if they were the Sacrificer, the Yajamāna: 'at each laud he (the Adhvaryu) puts the bones in the vicinity (during the other acts the urn is deposited on the place usually occupied by the Yajamāna); the soma-draughts (which under normal circumstances are drunk by the Yajamāna) they pour down at the mārjālīya', Āp. and Śāṅkh. 'When the time appointed for the drinking of the soma-rests has come, they should make him, (*viz.*, the deceased) partake of the essence of them and pour them out at the mārjālīya', Āśv.

[3] Time allays all.

[4] *vāc* is the sacrifice. For this last passage cp. Śat. br. XIII. 3. 6. 6: *sarvā vai saṁsthite yajñe vāg āpyate, sūtrāptā yātayāmnī bhavati, krūrīkṛteva hi bhavaty aruṣkṛtā, vāg yajñaḥ*, etc.

14. The laud should be illimited[1], for illimited is yonder world; (or) the pāvamāna-(laud)s (the out-of-doors laud, the midday-pavamāna-laud and the ārbhava-pavamāna-laud) should be threefold, (*i.e.*, nine-versed) all the rest seventeen-versed[2].

[1] *asammitaṃ stotram*, Śāṅkh. The choice is open.

[2] Āśv.: 'it is a seventeen-versed day; threefold are the pavamāna (laud)s; it is an agniṣṭoma with the rathantara as pṛṣṭha (the Hotṛ's pṛṣṭhastotra, the first pṛṣṭha, is chanted on the rathantara)'.

15. As to why the pavamāna(-laud)s are threefold: threefold are the vital airs; (by undertaking the threefold stoma) they come unto the vital airs (they are left in possession of the vital airs). As to why all the rest is seventeenfold: Prajāpati, forsooth, is seventeenfold; (by undertaking the seventeenfold stoma) they come unto Prajāpati.

16. 'Of out-breathing and in-breathing are those deprived', they say, 'who officiate for a deceased'. They take the soma-draughts in this order, that the one destined for Mitra and Varuṇa comes first; Mitra and Varuṇa are the out- and in-breathing, (in this manner) they are fully provided with out- and in-breathing[1].

[1] To khaṇḍa 8 refers the Kṣudrasūtra (I. 11, No. 45): 'If one of those, who have undergone the consecration for a sacrifice of soma, comes to die, they should, having cremated him, tie up his bones; then they should consecrate him who stands nearest to him in relation and perform the sacrifice with h i m . Further, they should do the following: having pressed out further the soma, they should, after the offering of the upāṁśu and antaryāma (C. H. §§ 128, 131) and

before the other soma-draughts have been taken out, leave the (havirdhāna-shed) by the eastern door, take their seat to the north of the mārjālīya with the face turned southward and perform a laud of three verses, chanting the (verses) of Sārparājñī on the yāma (-melody), the *yoni* of which is: *agnim īḍe purohitam* (see note 1 on § 7). The yoking of the stoma and the words (subsequently) to be uttered by the Sacrificer (see the Brāhmaṇa: I. 3. 5 and I. 3. 8.) fall forth. After (the completion of the laud) they should, while muttering these verses, (*i.e.*, the same verses that have been chanted by the Udgātr) walk round the mārjālīya from right to left, beating their left thighs: they then should walk thrice round (the mārjālīya) sunwise and return, without touching each other and without looking backward, (into the havirdhāna-shed). Having touched water, they should take out the soma-draughts, beginning with the one destined for Indra and Vāyu. Of this day (the tristich beginning): 'O Agni, thou purifyest the lives' should be the opening tristich (for the out-of-doors-laud). The rest is similar to that (day), (*i.e.*, the sacrifice during this day, on which the dīkṣita has deceased, is performed in the usual manner).—After a year they perform a sacrifice (an agniṣṭoma) for the bones (of the deceased); its stotras are illimited, or its pavamāna-(lauds) are threefold (nine-versed) and its 'returning' (lauds) (the four ājya-lauds, the four pṛṣṭha-lauds and the agniṣṭoma-laud) are seventeen-versed. Of this (jyotiṣṭoma), at which the pavamāna-lauds are threefold, the arrangement is as follows:

(The bahiṣpavamāna is the usual one, cp. C. H. page 503, only the pratipat stotriya is SV. II. 868-870.

The ājyastotras are the usual ones, cp. C. H. l.c.; the only difference being that they are seventeen-versed).

On: *uccā te jātam andhasaḥ* (are chanted):

1. The gāyatra, on one (verse),
2. The āmahīyava, on one (verse),
3. The abhīka, on one verse;

   on: *punānaḥ soma dhārayā:*

4. The raurava, on one (verse),
5. The yaudhājaya, on one (verse),
6. The kāleya, on one (verse).

   (on: *pra tu drava pari kośam:*

7-9. The auśana). (this is the mid-day pavamāna).

The pṛṣṭhastotras are: rathantara, vāmadevya, the Brahman's chant (or third pṛṣṭhastotra) is the śrāyantīya, the Acchāvāka's chant (or fourth pṛṣṭha-stotra) is the vaikhānasa. (In the ārbhavapavamāna there is a difference only in the distribution of the numbers of the stotriya-verses: gāyatra, saṁhita, each on one verse (1. 2); sapha and pauṣkala, each on one verse (3,4); śyāvāśva and andhīgava, each on one verse (5, 6), kāva on three verses (7, 8, 9).—The yajñāyajñīya is on seventeen verses). The graha destined for Indra and Vāyu and the graha destined for Mitra and Varuṇa change their places. The rest is similar to the (normal) jyotiṣṭoma'.

IX, 9.

(Expiation in case the quantity of soma is deficient, etc.)[1]

[1] Cp. Kāṭh. XXXV. 16: 61. 11–16; TBr. I. 4. 7. 4; Baudh. XIV. 29: 201. 11–17; Āp. XIV. 24. 7–8; Mān. śrs. III. 6. 18–19.

1. Whose (soma in the) trough becomes exhausted[1], the breath of that one becomes exhausted along with the exhaustion of the (soma in the) trough, for soma is the breath.

[1] This is the counterpart of the case treated in IX. 7, when soma is left over.

2. About this (case) they say: 'He should pour milk into (the trough)'.

3. But they (other authorities) say: 'Concealed, as it were, is the milk[1]; he should (rather) pour water out on (a piece of) gold and (the soma) out on the gold'.

[1] As it is enclosed in the udders of the cows. Apparently the fact that it is concealed or has vanished makes it inappropriate to replace the exhausted soma.

[2] He should put a piece of gold into the droṇakalaśa and pour *vasatīvarī* water on it; afterwards, when the soma is poured in the camasas (C. H. § 228), he should put equally first a piece of gold into each camasa, cp. Upagrantha-sūtra II. 6: *droṇakalaśe hiraṇyam avadhāya tatrāpo 'bhyavanayeyur; hiraṇyam eva camaseṣv avadhāya teṣv apo 'bhyunnayeyuḥ*. The same, though in other words, is prescribed by the author of the TBr.

4. Water, forsooth, is (equal to) the vital airs; gold is (equal to) immortality[1]; he (thus) puts his vital airs into immortality[1]; he (the Sacrificer) lives his whole life.

[1] *amṛtam*: 'the not dying before the normal term of life.'—§§ 1–4 are almost identical with Kāṭh.

5. Whose nārāśaṃsa (cup) is dried up[1], the breath of that one becomes exhausted along with the drying up of the nārāśaṃsa cup, for soma is the breath.

[1] On the camasas called *nārāśaṃsa* cp. Lāṭy. II. 5. 13; they are the camasas on which the *āpyāyana* has taken place (C. H. § 147 note 25, page 220). With our passage (in which *upavīyantam* should be corrected into *upavāyantam*) the Kāṭh. XXXV. 16 : 61. 16 agrees almost to the letter.

6. Of the graha, which the Adhvaryu draws as the last, he should pour a small quantity [1] (in the nārāśaṃsa-cup) [2].

[1] *aptum* (read thus instead of °*āsum*); Sāyaṇa reads and explains *āptum* // It is a word wellknown from the Baudh. sūtra (see the Index to this work), cp. Upagranthasūtra II. 6: *tasyāptum avanayed ity*; *alpam avanayed ity artham manyante*; *'ptum iti hi śaśvad dakṣiṇājā alpam ācakṣate.*

[2] Cp. Āp. XIV. 28. 1, Kāṭh. l.c.; on *aptu* cp. also note 1 on XX. 3. 5.

7. For the sake of atonement the graha is drawn [1]; by means of an atonement he makes atonement for him [2].

[1] How is this to be explained?

[2] Read: *prāyaścityaivāsmai.*

8. If soma of which has been drunk and soma of which not (yet) has been drunk, come to be mixed up, he should, having shifted some coals inside the enclosing pegs (of the āhavanīya-fire), make an offering (of it on these coals) with (the formula): 'From the offered and the not-offered, from the not-offered and the offered, from the drunk and from the not-drunk soma partake ye both, o Indra and Agni, the pressed out, *svāhā*!' This is the atonement therefore [1].

[1] For the other sources see Bloomfield's concordance *in voce*: *hutasya cāhutasya ca.*

9. From the soma which is unfit for drinking [1], he should pour out an offering with (the words): 'To Prajāpati, *svāhā*!' in the north-eastern resounding-hole [2].

[1] Because an insect or a hair has fallen into it,

[2] Cp. Mān. śrs. III. 6. 14, Kāṭh. XXXV. 16: 62. 4.

10. With (the formula): 'The drop has gone down on the drop' he should partake of soma on which rain has fallen.

11. 'Of thee, o Drop, (*i.e.*, o Soma), that hast been drunk by Indra, of thee that containest vigour, that art accompanied by thy whole troop, that art invited, I partake, accompanied by my whole troop and being invited' [1].

[1] This formula is a continuation of § 10, see Āp. XIV. 29. 2, Mān. śrs. III. 6. 15, Śāṅkh. śrs. XIII. 12. 10.

12. For one over whose soma-cup the summons has been made [1], he should perform, having gone to the āgnīdhra, (*i.e.*, in the āgnīdhrīya-fire) an offering with clarified butter with (the verse): 'The golden

embryo was evolved at the beginning; it was, when born, the sole Lord of beings; it maintained earth and heaven; thee, o Soma, (who art) that (Lord), we honour with offering, *svāhā*!' This is the atonement therefore.

[1] *i.e.*, if the *stotropākaraṇa* is made by the Adhvaryu and the Udgātṛ before the camasa-group has been drunk, cp. Āp. XIV. 29. 5, Śāṅkh. XIII. 12. 11, Kāty. XXV. 11. 33, 34, Mān. śrs. III. 6. 19. The Upagranthasūtra II. 7 discusses the possibility, if the word *ājya* in the Brāhmaṇa can be taken to mean *ājyastotra* (and this would indeed seem possible, cp. Āp. l.c.: *stotreṇābhyupākaroti*; moreover, the instr. *ājyena* with *ājuhuyāt* is strange, we expect the accus.); the author, however, rejects this surmise, quoting a remarkable passage from a smṛtisūtra of the Kātyāyanīya Adhvaryus: *yasya camaso 'bhyupākṛtaḥ syāt sa enam uttarasicāvachādya pūrvayā dvārā sadas 'pani(r)hṛtya* (cp. Śāṅkh. XIII. 12. 12: *avacchādya ca nirharet*) *purastād āgnīdhrīyasya nidhāyājyam juhuyāt*. This passage is not found in any of our ādhvaryavasūtras. The Jaim. br. I. 351 has: *yadi camasam abhyupākuryāt tam uttaravargeṇābhiprāvṛtyāsīta*, etc.,; for *uttaravarga* cp. Baudh. (see the Index verborum) *uttaravargya*, where the reading *uttaravarga* is also found, meaning upper-garment or 'hem of the upper-garment.'

13. If (during the act of pressing the soma) one of the stones used for pressing breaks off, the Sacrificer is deprived of his cattle. The stones for pressing, forsooth, are the cattle.[1] They should chant the sāman of Dyutāna of the Maruts [2].

[1] Because both procure milk and soma-sap (Sāyaṇa).

[2] Cp. Kāṭh. XXXV. 16: 62. 1-4. On the sāman, see XVII. 1. 6, and note 2 on § 14, below.

14. Of the Maruts, forsooth, are the stones for pressing [1]; by their own feature they thereby make them thrive [2].

[1] I 2. 5 they are addressed as 'children of the Marut.'

[2] Cp. Śāṅkh. XIII. 12. 3: *grāvṇi dīrṇe vṛtrasya tvā śvasathād īṣamāṇā iti* (ṚS. VIII. 96. 7) *dyutānena mārutena brāhmaṇācchaṃsine stuvate, uttaro* (l.c. 8) *'nurūpaḥ*; Āp. XIV. 25. 7, 8; Kāty. XXV. 12. 15; Mān. śrs. III. 6. 10.—To § § 13-14, refers Kṣudrasūtra (I. 11, No. 46); 'If a stone used for pressing breaks off, on: 'being clarified, o Soma, by the stream' (is chanted) the raurava on one (verse), the dyautāna sāman', *viz.*, the first of the two (that are recorded in the gāna) on one verse, namely *vṛtrasya tvā śvasathād īṣamāṇāḥ* (SV. I. 324, grām. VIII. 2. 22); the dairghaśravasa (or the udvat prājāpatya) on one; the yaudhājaya on all three. The rest is similar to the (normal) jyotiṣṭoma'. The Kṣudrasūtra does not agree with most of the other authorities, who, in accordance with Jaim. br. I. 353: *dyutānasya mārutasya brahmasāmnā stuvīran*, prescribe the dyautāna as the sāman for the third pṛṣṭha stotra.

15. If the soma is burnt, the Adhvaryu should mark[1] the grahas, the Udgātṛ the stotras, the Hotṛ the śastras, and, then, they should (on another, newly chosen place for worship) proceed with the sacrifice in due order. Five (cows) must be given (as) sacrificial fee. Fivefold is the sacrifice, as much as is the sacrifice, that he (thereby) lays hold on. Having come up from the lustral bath, he should undergo the consecration anew and (at this new sacrifice of the same order as the former) should give what he intended to give (as sacrificial fee at the first sacrifice, at which the soma was burnt). He should undergo the consecration before the twelfth (day); if he were to extend it beyond the twelfth (day), it would vanish.

1 *spāśayeta*: in order that they may know exactly, at which point the sacrifice on the new devayajana is to be continued.

2 Cp. Kāṭh. XXXV. 6 (almost identical with our passage). Āp. XIV. 25. 1-4, Mān. śrs. III. 6. 22–26. The Upagranthasūtra (II. 8) quotes from an (unknown ?) ādhvaryavabrāhmana : 'if the soma is burnt, they should press over the ashes of the soma' (*some 'bhidagdhe somabhasmany abhiṣuṇuyuḥ*), and from the Śāṭyāyanibrāhmaṇa: 'it should be mixed with other herbs' (*anyābhir oṣadhibhir abhisaṃsṛjyeta*). With § 15 cp. IX. 5. 10-13.

IX. 10.

(Expiations for various occasions.)

1. If the mahāvīra (the pot used at the pravargya-ceremony) breaks, he should touch, when it is broken (muttering the three verses): 'He, who, even without a clamp, before the piercing of the neck-ropes, makes the combination, he, the bountiful, the one of much good, removes again what is spoiled.—Let us not fear as strangers, o Indra, as removed from thee ! O God with the thunderbolt, we thought ourselves ill-famed, as trees that are devoid (of leaves).—We thought ourselves slow and weak, o Slayer of Vṛtra ! May we once more, o Hero, through thy great liberality be gladdened after our praise', [1] (with these verses) he should touch the broken mahāvīra (pot). This is therefore the atonement.

1 ṚS. VIII. 1. 12-14 with some variants ; the first verse also SV. I. 244. Kāty. XXV. 5. 30 is the only other source, where the touching of the mahāvīra, at least with the first of these three verses, is ordained ; cp. Āp. XV. 17. 8.

2. Assuming[1] an asuric character, the lustre, valour, strength, food, children and cattle recede from him, whose sacrificial post takes leaves; he is liable to come to worse fortune[2].

[1] Read *kṛtvā* instead of *kṣatvā*.

[2] Almost identical with Kāṭh. XXXIV. 2: 36. 20 (where the grammatically correct *īśvaraḥ* is found). Cp. TBr. I. 4. 7. 1.

3. He should immolate to Tvaṣṭṛ a multi-colour animal (a he-goat). Tvaṣṭṛ, forsooth, is the fashioner of the colours (forms); to him he thereby resorts; he provides him with lustre, splendour, valour, strength, food, children and cattle. This is therefore the atonement[1].

[1] Cp. Kāṭh. and TBr. ll. cc., Āp. IX. 19. 15, Kāty. XXV. 9. 15; 10. 1, Mān. śrs. III. 6. 1.

TENTH CHAPTER.

(The twelve-day rite in general; its stomas.)

X. 1.

1. Through fire, earth and plants, thereby this world is threefold; through wind, intermediate region and birds, thereby that world is threefold, which stands between; through sun, sky and stars, thereby yonder world is threefold. This is the base of the threefold (stoma[1], which consists of thrice three verses), this is its connection.

[1] The stoma of the first day of the six-day period, belonging to the twelve (ten-)day rite.

2. Provided with a firm base and connections is he, who knows this.

3. They call this (stoma) also 'the firm foundation', for the trivṛt is firmly founded on these worlds.

4. The base of the fifteen-versed (stoma)[1] are the half-months, these are its connection.

[1] The stoma of the second day of the six-day period.

5. Provided with a firm base and with connections is he who knows this.

6. They call this (stoma) also 'vigour (and) strength'[1], for half-month-wise the children and (young) cattle foster vigour (and) strength[1].

[1] The meaning probably is, that each half month the growth of young ones is perceptible.—The text should run *tamvojo, i.e.,* : *tam u ojo.*

7. The base of the seventeen-versed (stoma)[1] is the year: (there are) twelve months (and) five seasons. This is the base of the seventeen-versed (stoma), this its connection.

[1] Of the third day of the six-day-period.

8. Provided with a firm base and with connections is he who knows this.

9. They call this (stoma) also 'the production', for after a year (of pregnancy) the children and (young) cattle are produced (born).

10. The base of the twenty-one-versed (stoma)[1] is the sun: (there are) twelve months, five seasons, the sun is (number) twenty-first. This is the base of the twenty-one-versed (stoma), this its connection.

[1] Of the fourth day of the six-day-period.

11. Provided with a firm base and with connections is he who knows this.

12. They call this (stoma) also 'the bed of the Gods'; he who knows this, reaches the bed of the Gods.

13. The base of the thrice-ninefold (or twenty-seven-versed) (stoma)[1] is the threefold (stoma), this is its connection.

[1] Of the fifth day of the six-day-period.

14. Provided with a firm base and with connections is he who knows this.

15. They call this (stoma) also 'the increase', for it is an increased three-fold one.

16. The base of the thirty-three-versed (stoma)[1] are the deities: (there are) thirty-three deities and Prajāpati is the thirty-fourth[2]. This is the base of the thirty-three versed (stoma), this its connection.

[1] Of the sixth day of the six-day-period.

[2] Thus also Śat. br. V. 1. 2. 13, V. 3. 4. 23.

17. Provided with a firm base and with connections is he who knows this.

18. They call this (stoma) also 'the firmament' (*nāka*), for Prajāpati is (causes) pain to nobody (*nākam, na akam*)[1].

[1] Cp. Śat. br. *na hi tatra gatāya kasmai canākam.*

19. The base of the chandoma (-days)[1] are the metres, this is their connection.

[1] The three days following on the six-day-period, successively of 24-, 44-and 48-fold stoma; *chandoma* or 'metre-measuring', 24=gāyatrī, 44=triṣṭubh, 48=jagatī.

20. Provided with a firm base and with connections is he who knows this.

21. They call these (stomas) also 'the thriving', for the chandomas are cattle[1].

[1] Cp. note 1 on III. 8. 2.

X. 2.

(General remarks on the twelve-day-period.)

1. Prajāpati had created the creatures; he was exhausted; for him the Voice raised up a light[1]; he said: 'who is it, that has raised up a light for me?' 'Thine own Voice', she answered. He spoke to her: 'Let them sacrifice, having applied thee, the light among the metres, the Virāj'.

[1] *jyotis*: *lucem*, φάος, a means of deliverance=σωτηρία.

2. Therefore, they call that stoma, which amounts to (or 'results in') the virāj, the jyotiṣṭoma-agniṣṭoma ('the Light-stoma')[1]; for the virāj is the light of the metres.

[1] Cp. VI. 3. 6.

3. A light among his equal[1] becomes he who knows this.

[1] *samānānām*.

4. The anuṣṭubh[1] and the seventeen-versed (stoma)[1] copulated; the anuṣṭubh brought forth the metres which increase by four syllables[2], the seventeen-versed (stoma) brought forth the stomas which increase by six (stotra-verses)[3]. These two generated her (the virāj) in the middle[4].

[1] *i.e.*, the voice and Prajāpati.

[2] Cp. IV. 4. 5.

[3] The stomas of 9, 15, 21, 27 and 33 verses, which, together with the seventeen-versed, are the stomas of the six-day-period.

[4] 'Her': *etām*, or, with the ms. of Leyden, *enām*. According to Sāyaṇa, they generated, between uṣṇih and anuṣṭubh, the virāj of 30 syllables. The exact meaning of these words eludes me.

5. The thrice-threefold (or nine-versed, stoma) and the thrice-ninefold (or twenty-seven-versed, stoma) are connected with the rathantara[1]; after these two, goat and horse were created; therefore, these two (goat and horse?) push the rathantara-day in front of them.[2]

[1] Cp. Āśv. VII. 5. 1–3: *abhiplavapṛṣṭhyāhāni rathantarapṛṣṭhāny ayujāni, bṛhatpṛṣṭhānītarāṇi.*

[2] Meaning? Cp. VII. 9. 6.

6. The fifteenfold and the twenty-one-fold stomas are connected with the bṛhat[1]; after these two, cow and sheep were created; therefore, these two (cow and sheep?) illuminate the bṛhat-day in front of them[2].

[1] Cp. note on preceding §.

[2] Equally not clear.

7. About him who knows this, they say: 'Even of the domestic animals he understands the language'.

X. 3.

(General remarks on the twelve-day-period, continued.)

1. Prajāpati desired: 'May I be more (than one), may I be reproduced'. He perceived in himself the seasonal period[1]. Therefrom, he created the officiating priests; because he created them from the seasonal period (*ṛtva*), therefore they are called *ṛtvij*. By means of them he approached (or 'undertook') the twelve-day-rite, and prospered.

[1] *ṛtva,* Jaim. br. III has the regular *ṛtviya.* Prajāpati as a mother-being we find also elsewhere, below XIII. 11. 18, MS. I. 6. 9: 101. 15, Śat. br. II. 5. 1. 3 (wrongly interpreted by Eggeling).

2. (Thinking) 'Our father[1] has prospered', the months undertook (the twelve-day-rite). They prospered by means of the consecration (*dīkṣā*); at the upasads they consecrated the thirteenth (month); this one came behind (or 'was dependent on the others')[2]. Therefore, one who has undergone the consecration on the upasad(-day)s, comes behind (or 'is dependent on the others')[3]; for they (some theologians) teach a thirteenth month and (others do) n o t (teach it)[4].

[1] Prajāpati being the year.

[2] The meaning of *anuvyam* is not altogether certain, cp. Kāṭh. XXXIV. 9: 43. 2: *tasmāt so 'nāyatana itarān upajīvati*; on this word cp. my remark in the Introduction to the Kāṇvīya Śat. br. page 51.

[3] Cp. Āp. XXI. 1. 11-13: 'A single person may perform the twelve-day-rite, or three persons, or six, or twelve, or thirteen; of these they consecrate the thirteenth on the upasad(day)s. Therefore, at a twelve-day-rite the Brahman must not be the thirteenth, according to some'. Similarly the Jaim. br. (III. 4): *yady u bhūyāṃso yajeran dvādaśa vā trayodaśa vā yajerann: ime catvāra (ime catvāra) ime catvāro 'yam eka iti nirmimīran, yaṃ kāmayerann imaṃ yajñasya vyṛddhir anviyād iti; taṃ haiva yajñasya vyṛddhir anveti; yady u bhūyāṃso yajeran ṣoḍaśa vā saptadaśa vā yajerann: ime catvāra ime catvāra ime catvāra ime catvaro 'yam eka iti nirmimīran, yaṃ kāmayerann imaṃ yajñasya vyṛddhir anviyād iti; taṃ haiva yajñasya vyṛddhir anveti; yady u bhūyāṃso yajeraṃś caturviṃśatir vā pañcaviṃśatir vā yajerann: ime pañceme pañceme pañceme pañceme pañceme catvāro 'yam eka iti nirmimīran, yaṃ kāmayerann imaṃ yajñasya vyṛddhir anviyād iti; taṃ haiva yajñasya vyṛddhir anveti, sarva itara ṛdhnuvanti*, cp. § 4 of this khaṇḍa.

[4] Cp. Śat. br. V. 4. 5. 23: *dvādaśa vā trayodaśa vā saṃvatsarasya māsāḥ* and Kāṭh. XXXIV. 13 (end): *uta vai trayodaśaṃ māsaṃ vidur uta na viduḥ.*

3. One (person) may undertake the consecration[1], for Prajāpati, (being) one, prospered; twelve (persons) may undertake the consecration, for the months, (being) twelve, prospered; twenty-four may undertake the consecration, for the half-months, (being) twenty-four, prospered.

[1] A dvādaśāha may be performed by one person as Yajamāna.

4. If a twenty-fifth undertakes the consecration, they should point (them) out in the following manner: 'These are five, these are five, these are five, these are five, these are four, so and so is one'. Whom they wish ill-luck, him ill-luck reaches, all the others prosper[1].

[1] From this it appears that, when a dvādaśāha is performed by twenty-five participants, one of these is liable not to reach the success he hopes to gain by it, cp. note 3 on § 2 and Āp. XXI. 1. 13.

5. He who knows the Gṛhapati of the Gods, arrives at the house-lord's position, reaches the house-lord's position[1].

[1] Of all the priestly participants one is called the Gṛhapati; it is he who performs the duties otherwise incumbent on the Yajamāna, cp. Hillebrandt, Ritual-literatur § 79 (page 154).

6. The house-lord of the Gods is the year; he is Prajāpati and the months are his fellow-dīkṣitas.

7. He who knows this finds fellow-dīkṣitas, arrives at the house-lord's position, reaches the house-lord's position[1].

[1] With §§ 5–7 cp. Jaim. br. II. 4: 'He who knows the house-lord and the house-mistress of the sattra, arrives at the house-lord's position, reaches the house-lord's position. The year, forsooth, is the house-lord, the earth is the house-mistress', etc.

8. He, forsooth, who knows the ruler of the metres, arrives at rulership. The bṛhatī, now, is the ruler of the metres; he who knows this arrives at rulership, reaches ruleship.

9. It is this one (the bṛhatī), forsooth, that, for the sake of food, they undertake ('practice') with this twelve-day sacrificial session, dividing it into several parts: the twelve days of consecration, the twelve upasads, the twelve pressing-days; these are (together) thirty-six-days and the bṛhatī has thirty-six syllables[1].

[1] Cp. Ait. br. IV. 24. 6 and, for this sentence, below, X. 5. 8.

10. He is born, forsooth, by the consecration, he is purified by the upasads, he reaches the worlds of the Gods by the sacrifice of soma.

11. These days, forsooth, are the force and strength in the year: the twelve full-moon-days, the twelve ekāṣṭakās[1], the twelve new-moon-days. The whole force and strength that is in the year he reaches and obtains by this twelve-day-rite[2].

[1] Each eighth day following on a full-moon-day.

[2] Solely because the t w e l v e-day-session is preceded by twelve dīkṣās and twelve upasads: together equally thirty-six.

12. The virāj is of thirty syllables; six in number are the seasons; through the virāj he finds a support in the seasons, through the seasons in the virāj[1].

[1] The dvādaśāha by its number of 36 (see note 2 on § 11) comprises not only the virāj (of 30 syllables) but also the seasons (six in number). Similarly the Jaim. br. III. 5.

13. The anuṣṭubh is of thirty-two syllables, the anuṣṭubh is the voice; fourfooted is cattle; by means of the Voice, (*i.e.*, the anuṣṭubh) he supports the cattle; therefore they (the cattle, the cows) approach when reached by the voice, when summoned by the voice; therefore also they know their name[1].

[1] Of the number 36 (see note 2 on § 11) the first 32 syllables are the anuṣṭubh: the voice; then follow four: the cows, which thus lean on the voice, are supported

by the voice, that precedes them, calling them as it were; cp. Jaim. br. III. 5, *anuṣṭubhaṃ vāvaitām āsate yad dvādaśāham; dvātriṃśadakṣarānuṣṭup, catuṣpadāḥ paśavo, vāg anuṣṭub: vācā paśūn dādhāra; tasmāt paśavo vācā siddhā vācā hūtā (ā)yanti.*

X. 4.

(General remarks on the twelve-day-rite, continued.)

1. The first overnight-rite [1] is the past, the last is the future; the first is earth, the last is sky; the first is the fire, the last is the sun; the first is the out-breathing, the last is the in-breathing [2].

[1] Each dvādaśāha is enclosed by an atirātra at the beginning and at the end.

[2] Here *udāna* is used as *apāna*.

2. The two overnight-rites [1] are the eyes, the two agniṣṭomas [2] are the pupils of the eye. Because the two agniṣṭomas are at the inside of the two overnight-rites, therefore, the pupils, being at the inside [3] ('in the middle'), are profitable [4].

[1] Mentioned in the preceding §.

[2] The first and the last day of the daśarātra are agniṣṭomas, all the others being ukthyas, see § 5.

[3] *antara* with ablative as Śat. br. III. 2. 1. 11. Note the unequal sandhi *antarā(v)agniṣṭomāv atirātrābhyām.*

[4] If they are not just in the middle, they are not profitable, because, then, one squints.

3. The two overnight-rites are the fangs of the year [1]; on these (days) one ought not to sleep, lest he may set himself on the fangs of the year.

[1] It is true that here the dvādaśāha is treated, but this rite is the image of the year: *saṃvatsarapratimā vai dvādaśa rātrayaḥ.*

4. Regarding this, they say: 'Who is able to remain awake? [1] Verily, when the breath is awake, t h e n (the condition of) being awake is (fulfilled)'.

[1] An infinitive with *a* priv.; Jaim. br. II. 8: *ko hāsvapnasyeśe.*

5. It is the gāyatrī with wings of light (*jyotiṣpakṣa*), forsooth, that they undertake (practise) with this twelve-day sacrificial session: there are eight ukthya(-days) in the middle and two agniṣṭoma (-days) on both sides [1]; by means of lustre, having reached the world of heaven, he eats resplendent until old age, food suitable for Brāhmins [2].

1 With the gāyatrī of 3×8 syllables are compared the eight ukthyadays in the middle; its wings of light (*jyotis*) are the two j y o t iṣṭoma-agniṣṭomas (cp. § 2) on both sides; cp. Ait. br. IV. 23. 5: *tasya yāv abhito 'tirātrau tau pakṣau.*

2 From the words: 'till old age' it appears that the author has not in mind a description of heavenly bliss, but of material welfare, after the Sacrificer has reached (mentally and ideally) the world of heaven through his sacrifice and returned to the world of the living; the same thought is expressed III. 6. 2, IV. 7. 10, etc. Sāyaṇa takes *dīpyamānaḥ* as meaning 'being heated by fever': *madhye madhye jvarādibhiḥ tapyamānaḥ san* (!).

6. Thrice they enter upon ('they apply') the rathantara at the beginning[1]; threefold is the voice[2]; having attained the whole voice, all food, they extend ('perform') the twelve-day (-rite).

1 They apply the rathantarasāman as first pṛṣṭhalaud on the first three days of the daśarātra.

2 Or 'the word', either as *sup* (verbal-suffix), *tiṅ* (case-suffix) and *kṛt* (derivative suffix) or as representing the three Vedas (Sāyaṇa).

7. 'A sameness of performance is brought about in the sacrifice' they say, 'in that at the beginning they enter thrice upon the rathantara'. The Brahman's chant for the 'uktha(laud)s is the saubhara (sāman); thereby the sameness is avoided[1].

1 How the *jāmitvam* is taken away by the saubhara is not clear to me, nor is it explained by Sāyaṇa, but cp. perhaps VIII. 8. 10. For the rest, the usual practice (see Ārṣeyakalpa, page 205 sqq.) follows neither this prescription nor that given in §§6 and 9.

8. The opening verses of the beginning day contain the word *pratna*[1]; thereby also this sameness is avoided[2].

1 The out-of-doors-laud of the beginning day begins: *asya pratnām anu dyutam,* SV. II. 105-107=ṚS. IX. 54.1-3.

2 *teno eva tad ajāmi* seems to refer to the same matter as treated in § 7. I do not see its purport. Sāyaṇa seems to refer the sameness to this beginning day: *teno tena u tenaiva..tat prāyaṇīyam ahar ajāmi* and then the *ajāmitvam* is found therein, that no other day of the daśarātra begins with these verses.

9. And[1] thrice they enter upon ('apply') the rathantara afterwards[2]; threefold, forsooth, is the Voice (or 'the Word'); having attained the whole Voice. all food, they rise from the twelve-day sacrificial session.

1 *trir u eva,* referring to § 6.

2 They apply the rathantarasāman on the last three days of the daśarātra (the 8th, 9th, 10th) as first pṛṣṭhalaud. The usual ritual (see Ārṣeyakalpa, page

212 sqq.) is not wholly conform to this prescription (8: rathantara; 9: bṛhat; 10: rathantara).

X. 5.

(General remarks on the twelve-day-period, continued.)

1. The twelve-day-rite is (equal to) three three-day-rites[1]: the first trirātra (three-day-rite) has the gāyatrī at the beginning, the second has the gāyatrī in the middle, the third at the end[2].

[1] If neither the tenth-day is taken into account nor the opening and closing atirātra.

[2] The morning service of the first three days is on gāyatrī metre; of the second trirātra (4th-6th days) the midday service is on gāyatrī metre (at least the beginning and the end of it); of the third trirātra (7th-9th days) the afternoon service is on gāyatrī metre (at least the beginning and the end); cp. also Sāyaṇa on Ait. br. IV. 25. 10.

2. Because the first (trirātra) has the gāyatrī at the beginning, therefore, the fire[1] flames upwards; because the second has the gāyatrī in the middle, therefore, the wind[1] blows horizontally; because the third has the gāyatrī at the end, therefore, the sun[1] sends its rays downwards[2].

[1] The three trirātras are compared with the three worlds (cp. X. 1. 1) of which Agni, Vāyu and Āditya are the deities.

[2] The Jaim. br. III. 6 has nearly the same. On the whole cp. Ait. br. IV. 25. 10.

3. By splendour the gāyatrī supports the first trirātra, by verse-quarters the second, by syllables the third[1].

[1] See § 4.

4. The threefold-(*i.e.*, nine-versed) (stoma) is the splendour of the gāyatrī[1] and the opening day (the first of the navarātra) is a threefold-stoma day; by it the first trirātra is supported. Of three verse-quarters is the gāyatrī, and a three-day rite is in the midst; by it the second trirātra is supported. Of twenty-four syllables is the gāyatrī and the seventh day is twenty-four-versed; by it the third trirātra is supported[2].

[1] Because, according to VI. 1. 6, the trivṛt stoma and Agni sprang from the mouth of Prajāpati.

[2] Jaim. br. l.c. closely agrees.

5. With splendour (*i.e.*, gāyatrī), forsooth, they depart[1] (*i.e.*, 'begin'), splendour they put in the middle, in splendour they finish[1]; with light, forsooth, they depart, light they put in the middle, in light they finish; with eye-sight they depart, eye-sight they put in the middle, in eye-sight they finish; with breath they depart, breath they put in the middle, in breath they finish—who depart with gāyatrī, put gāyatrī in the middle and finish in gāyatrī.

[1] *prayanti* and *udyanti*, cp. the term *prāyaṇīyam ahaḥ* 'beginning day' as opposed to *udayanīyam ahaḥ* 'finishing day.'

6. In (performing) the twelve-day rite, a web is stretched out ('a cloth is woven'); its pegs are the gāyatrīs[1]; in order that it may stand perfectly firm[2].

[1] Cp. Ath. Saṃh. X. 7. 42: 'a web with six pegs' *ṣaṇmayūkhaṃ tantram*. The comparison of the performance of a sacrifice with a web that is woven, is well known.

[2] Litt. the gāyatrī in its pegs (*tasyaite mayukhā yad gāyatry, asaṃvyāthāya*). Therefore, at the beginning, at the middle, and at the end a 'gāyatrī-peg' is fastened.

7. 'O Girikṣit, son of Uccāmanyu' said (*i.e.*, asked) Ābhipratārin, the son of Kakṣasena, 'how (is) the twelve-day rite?' As a felly encompasses the spokes, so the gāyatrī encompasses it (*viz.*, the twelve-day, rite), in order to prevent it from slipping down: as the spokes are upheld in the nave, so is the twelve-day rite upheld in it (*i.e.*, in the gāyatrī)[1].

[1] Cp. Jaim. br. III. 6: *kathaṃ gāyatrī dvādaśāham* (supply *dādhāra*) *ity āhur; yathārān nemiḥ sarvataḥ paryety, evaṃ gāyatrī dvādaśāhaṃ sarvataḥ paryety, avisraṃsāya; yathā rathanābhāv ārā dhṛtā evaṃ gāyatryā dvādaśāho dhṛto 'saṃplavāya; mayūkho vā eṣa dharuṇo yad gāyatrī; tasyāṃ dvādaśāho dhṛto, 'saṃvyāthāya.*

8. It is the anuṣṭubh, forsooth, that, for the sake of food, they undertake ('apply') with this twelve-day sacrificial session, dividing it in several parts[1].

[1] The same manner of expression X. 3. 9, X. 4. 5, Jaim. br. III. 6: *anuṣṭub vā eṣā pratāyate yad dvādaśāhaḥ.*

9. By means of eight (of its) syllables the anuṣṭubh lifts up the first day of the twelve-day rite; by means of eleven, the second day; by means of twelve, the third[1].

[1] The first day of the first trirātra being, theoretically, *gāyatra* (3 × 8 syllables), the second *traiṣṭubha* (4 × 11 syllables), the third *jāgata* (4 × 12 syllables).

10. A syllable of three sounds remains: that he distributes successively over the next trirātra (*i.e*, one over each)[1].

[1] The first trirātra has 31 syllables (8, gāy.; 11, triṣṭubh; 12, jagatī) of the anuṣṭubh (of 32 syllables); the remaining one, which is *vāc*, anuṣṭubh being 'Voice' (cp. Ait. br. V. 3. 1–3: *akṣaraṃ tryakṣaram* is *vāk*), is added to the second trirātra, to each of its days one and in this manner the full anuṣṭubh is found in the second trirātra.

11. The metres belonging to this (anuṣṭubh)[1] convey the third trirātra[2]

[1] Cp. X. 2. 4.

[2] The stomas of the last three (7th, 8th, 9th) days are resp. 24-versed, 44-versed, 48-versed, *i.e.*, they contain the numbers of the metres springing from the anuṣṭubh, and thus implicitly it is the anuṣṭubh that conveys them.

12. This (anuṣṭubh) is undertaken ('applied') coming on[1], crosswise[2], and retiring[3], for the sake of (obtaining) food; therefore the creatures (*i e.*, men) live upon the cattle (the cow) that is coming on (to the meadows), standing crosswise (when being milked) (and) retiring (from the meadows).

[1] During the first trirātra.

[2] During the second trirātra.

[3] During the third trirātra.—Cp. Jaim. br. III. 7: *tām etāṃ pratīcīṃ parācīṃ tiraścīm annādyāyāsate; tasmāt paśuṃ pratyañcam parāñcaṃ tiryañcam upajīvanti.* The exact meaning of *pratīcī, tiraścī* and *parācī*, as referring to the anuṣṭubh, is not clear to me.

13. Each of the metres (once upon a time) set their mind on the place occupied by the others: the gāyatrī on that occupied by the triṣṭubh; the triṣṭubh on that occupied by the jagatī, the jagatī on that occupied by the gāyatrī. They transposed them[1] according to their several places. Thereupon, they reached (the fulfilment of) all the wishes they, each of them, cherished.

[1] Probably the Gods transposed the metres. The commentary here is defective. So much is certain that here is mentioned the *vyūḍha-dvādaśāha*, cp. Ait. br. IV. 27.1, Śat. br. IV. 5. 9 with Eggelings note, Ṣaḍv. br. III. 7, and Jaim. br. III. 7: *prajāpatir jāyamāna eva saha pāpmanājāyata; so 'kāmayatāpa pāpmānaṃ hanīyeti; sa etaṃ vyūḍhacchandasaṃ dvādaśāham apaśyat; tam āharat, tenāyajata*, etc.

14. With whatever wish he performs the twelve-day rite with transposed metres, that wish is fulfilled for him.

15. The twelve-day rite, forsooth, is the home of the Gods. The deities that have entered upon the twelve-day rite are comparable to men that have entered this world (the earthly existence). He who, knowing this, performs the twelve-day rite, performs a (twelve-day rite) at which the deities are present.

16. The twelve-day rite is the house of the Gods; there is no fear of being house-less (for him who performs this rite).

17. He who knows the twelve-day rite as being fitted by the agniṣṭoma, for him it becomes fitted. By the morning-service even the first trirātra becomes fitted; by the midday-service, the second trirātra, by the afternoon-service, the third, and, by the agniṣṭomasāman, the tenth day becomes fitted [1].

[1] In this manner the dvādaśāha (*viz.*, its ten days, without the opening and concluding atirātras) is comparable to the agniṣṭoma-jyotiṣṭoma. Jaim. br. III. 8: *yo vā agniṣṭomena daśāhaṃ kalpamānaṃ veda kalpate 'smai*, etc.

18. For him who knows this, it becomes fitted.

X. 6.

(General remarks on the twelve-day-period, continued.)

1. 'Hither' (or 'with the word *ā*')[1], 'forth' (or 'with the word *pra*')[2], combined with 'swift' (or 'having the word *āśu*')[3], combined with a feast (or 'having the word *vīti*')[4], combined with lustre (or 'having the word *ruc*')[5], combined with splendour (or 'having the word *tejas*')[6], (and) 'being harnessed'[7] is the characteristic of the first day, of the thrice threefold (or 'nine-versed') stoma, of the gāyatrī metre, of the rathantara (or first pṛṣṭha-) sāman[8].

[1] *e.g.*, in SV. II. 10: *agna ā yāhi.*

[2] *e.g.*, in SV. II. 119: *pra somāso madacyutaḥ.*

[3] *e.g.*, in SV. II. 31: *aśvāyanto* (sic!), *aśva* being derived from *āśu.*

[4] *e.g.*, in SV. II. 10: *agna ā yahi vitaye.*

[5] This can only refer to *davidyutatyā rucā* (SV. II. 4), which verse, however, is not used at the first day, at least, according to the Comm. on Ārṣeyakalpa.

[6] According to Sāyaṇa, SV. II. 106 is meant, where *sūrya* is mentioned.

[7] Cp. SV. II. 17: *ā tvā brahma yujā harī.*

[8] The Jaim. br. has the same as here expressed in § 1; comp. on the whole also Ait. br. IV. 29. 3.

2. Combined with 'a bull' (or 'having the word *vṛṣan*')[1], fiend-slaying (or 'containing the words *vṛtra* and *han*')[2], combined with riches (or 'having the word *rayi*')[3], containing all (or 'having the word *viśva*')[4] and 'come near' (*upasthita*)[5], is the characteristic of the s e c o n d day, of the fifteen-versed stoma, of the triṣṭubh-metre, of the bṛhat-sāman[6].

[1] *e.g.*, in II. 127: *pavasvendo vṛṣā sutaḥ.*

[2] *e.g.*, in II. 162: *hanti vṛtrāṇi.*

[3] *e.g.*, SV. II. 139: *rayiṃ vīravatīm.*

[4] *e.g.*, SV. II. 125: *abhi viśvāni kāryā.*

[5] *e.g.*, SV. II. 127: *mahimne soma tasthire*, but this is not precisely what we would expect.

[6] With § 2 cp. Ait. br. IV. 31. 1, 3.

3. An ascent (or 'containing the word *ud*')[1], containing three (or 'having the word *tri*')[2], containing the quarters (or 'containing the word *diś*')[3], possessing cows (or 'containing the word *go*')[4], possessing bulls (or 'containing the word *ṛṣabha*')[5], is the characteristic of the t h i r d day, of the seventeen-versed stoma, of the Jagatī-metre, of the vairūpasāman (as first pṛṣṭhalaud).[6]

[1] *e.g.*, in SV. II. 22: *uccā te jātam andhasaḥ.*

[2] *e.g.*, in SV. II. 219: *tisro vāca udīrate.*

[3] Cp. XII. 3. 11.

[4] *e.g.*, SV. II. 221: *gāvo minanti dhenavaḥ.*

[5] *e.g.*, SV. II. 215: *indra svabdīva vaṁśagaḥ*, where the last word is equivalent to *ṛṣabha.*

[6] Cp. Ait. br. V. 1. 1, 3.

4. Combined with the king (or 'containing the word *rājan*')[1], containing the people (or 'containing a word derived from the root *jan*')[2]; combined with the sun (or 'containing the word *sūrya*')[3], combined with the virāj's 'repeated push'[4] is the characteristic of the f o u r t h day, of the twenty-one-versed stoma, of the anuṣṭubh-metre, of the vairājasāman (as first pṛṣṭhalaud)[5].

[1] *e.g.*, in SV. II. 261: *rājānāv anabhidruhā.*

[2] *e.g.*, SV. II. 239: *pavamāno ajījanat.*

[3] *e.g.*, SV. II. 246: *uṣāḥ sūryo na raśmibhiḥ.*

[4] Cp. VIII. 9. 13 note 1, and XII. 9. 17.

[5] Cp. Ait. br. V. 4. 1, 2.

5. Combined with wonderful (or 'containing the word *citra*')[1], combined with the young ones (or 'containing the word *śiśu*)[2], the

paṅkti (the verse of five verse-quarters)[3], the śākvarī less by two syllables[4], combined with cows (or 'containing the word *go-*')[5], combined with bulls (or 'containing the word *ṛṣabha*')[6], provided with a thunderbolt (or 'containing the word *vajra*')[7], and being 'towards' (or 'containing the word *abhi*')[8], is the characteristic of the f i f t h day, of the thrice-ninefold (or twenty-seven-versed) stoma, of the paṅkti metre, of the śākvara-sāman (as first pṛṣṭhalaud)[9].

[1] SV. II. 349: *yat soma citram ukthyam.*

[2] SV. II. 363: *prāṇā śiśur mahīnām.*

[3] SV. II. 352-353 are in paṅkti metre.

[4] The Jaim. br. III. 329 has the plural *śakvaryo dvyūnākṣarāḥ.* I do not see what is meant by the author; the treatment of the mahānāmnī-verses in XIII. 4 gives no light. Sāyana gives no explanation.

[5] SV. II. 305: *govit pavasva.*

[6] SV. II. 306: *pavamāna vṛṣabha tā vidhāvasi.* The Jaim. reads not *ṛṣabhavat* but *vṛṣabhavat.*

[7] SV. II. 356: *vajraṁ hinvanti sāyakam.*

[8] SV. II. 371: *abhi vratāni pavate.*

[9] On the whole cp. Ait. br. V. 6. 1 sqq.

6. Combined with 'around' (or 'containing the word *pari*')[1], combined with 'against' (or 'containing the word *prati*')[2], the (verse) of seven verse-quarters[3], the (verse) of two verse-quarters[4], the *nārāśaṃsa*-less (verse)[5], combined with cows (or 'containing the word *go*')[6], combined with bulls (or, 'containing the word *ṛṣabha*')[7], is the characteristic of the s i x t h day, of the thirty-three-versed stoma, of all the metres, of the raivata-sāman (as first pṛṣṭhalaud)[8].

[1] SV. II. 420: *bhinddhi viśvā apa dviṣaḥ pari bādhaḥ.*

[2] SV. II. 417: *prati vāṁ sūra udite.*

[3] Cp. XIII. 10. 18.

[4] SV. II. 457-459, cp. XIII 12. 1.

[5] It seems that the verses SV. II. 407-410 are meant; why they are called *vinārāśaṃsa* here and XIII. 7. 14, is not clear to me.

[6] SV. II. 430: *gobhir añjāno arṣasi.*

[7] I find in this day no verse containing the word *ṛṣabha* (or *vṛṣabha*, as the Jaim. br. has it).

[8] Cp. XIII. 10. 4.

7. Because this diversity of the six-day rite, being the same, is different in characteristics, therefore, the year is multiform.

8. Multiform (progeny and cattle) is born unto him, who knows this.

X. 7.

(General remarks on the twelve-day-period, continued.)

1. 'O Agni' (vocative) is for the first day the characteristic of Agni's variety (or 'grammatical case-form')[1]; '(thee)' Agni' (accusative) for the second (day)[2]; 'by Agni' (instrumental) for the third (day)[3]; '(thou), Agni' (nominative) for the fourth (day)[4].

[1] SV. II. 10 (in the âjyalauds) *agna āyāhi vītaye*; more clearly the Jaim. br. III. 330: *agna iti prathamasyāhno vibhaktiḥ*.

[2] SV. II. 140: *agniṃ dūtaṃ vṛṇīmahe*.

[3] SV. II. 194: *agnināgniḥ samidhyate*.

[4] SV. II. 257: *janasya gopā ajaniṣṭa jāgṛvir agniḥ* (all in the âjyalauds).

2. The Gods sought Fortune; they found her neither on the first nor on the second, nor on the third day (of the nine-day rite), but found her on the fourth day. He who knows this, finds Fortune. 'From Agni' (ablative) is (the variety) of the fifth (day)[1], and thereby, they say, that Fortune is rejected[2].

[1] The first âjyalaud of the fifth day is on SV. II. 332: *tava śriyo varṣyasyeva vidyuto 'g n e ś cikitra uṣasām ivetayaḥ*, and on the word *śriyaḥ* rests the quasi-myth.

[2] Probably: 'is repulsed from his adversary' (because of the ablative-meaning).

3. He who knows this is not contradicted by his rival.

4. 'O Agni' (vocative) is (the variety or case-form) of the sixth (day)[1]: with what characteristic they begin[2], with that they finish.

[1] SV. II. 414: *agne sakhye mā riṣāmā vayaṃ tava*.

[2] Cp. § 1.

5. Because this variety of Agni, being the same, is of different characteristic, therefore the sun shines (differently) according to the seasons.

X. 8.

(General remarks on the twelve-day-period, continued.)

1. 'O Indra' (vocative) is for the first day the characteristic of Indra's variety (or 'grammatical case-form')[1]; '(thee), Indra' (accusative), for the second (day)[2]; 'by Indra' (instrumental), for the third

(day)[3]; '(thou) Indra' (nominative), for the fourth (day)[4]; 'from Indra' (ablative), (for the fifth (day)[5]; 'O Indra' (vocative), for the sixth (day)[6]: with what characteristic they begin, with that they finish. Because this variety of Indra, being the same, is of different characteristic, therefore the fruits ripen (in different times) according to the seasons[7].

1 SV. II. 16: *āyāhi suṣumā hi ta indra somaṃ pibā imam.*

2 SV. II. 146: *indram id gāthino bṛhat.*

3 SV. II. 200: *indreṇa saṁ hi dṛkṣase.*

4 SV. II. 263: *indro dadhīca asthabhiḥ.*

5 SV. II. 340: *indrāt pari tanvaṃ mame.*

6 SV. II. 422: *yad vīḍāv indra yat sthire.*

7 Jaim. br. III. 332: *tasmād asāv āditye yathartu tapati śito hemantam uṣṇo grīṣmam.*—On khaṇḍa 7 and 8 cp. Nidānasūtra III. 9.

X. 9.

(General remarks on the twelve-day-period, continued.)

1. That he performs the prastāva with the (mere words of the) verse, is of the first day the characteristic of the tunes' variety[1]; that the (prastāva) is preceded by a stobha, of the second (day)[2]; that it is preceded and followed by a stobha, of the third (day)[3]; that it is pushed repeatedly, of the fourth (day)[4]; that it is begun again and again, of the fifth (day)[5]; that the word 'here' is repeated, is of the sixth day[6] the characteristic of the tunes[7].

1 The mere words of the verse, *i.e.*, the first verse-quarter, cp. X. 12. 2, serve as prastāva, *e.g.*, in the āśva-sāman (cp. note 1 on XI. 3. 4), see SV. ed. Calcutta, vol. III, page 269.

2 *e.g.*, in the yauktāśvasāman (grām. XII. 2. 30, composed on SV. I. 469: *vṛṣā pavasva dhārayā*), beginning: *āuho ho hā i-vṛṣā.* (5r 4 3 4 5)

3 *e.g.*, in the gautamasāman, grām. II. 1. 1, beginning: *hā u 'tvam it saprathā asi hā u* (SV. ed. Calcutta, Vol. I, page 162). (5r r)

4 See note 1 on VIII. 9. 13.

5 *yad abhyārabdham.* Sāyaṇa explains as follows: 'All the other sāmans are chanted each on one single verse, but the śākvara melody is chanted on three verses; therefore, it is said here that a renewed taking up should take place; in this manner each stotriya-verse consists of three ṛks in the (first) pṛṣtha laud of the fifth day. And so also it is said by Āśvalāyana (see his śrs. VII. 12. 10): 'the verses which by their natural form are nine in number, become three'. —The nine mahānāmnīs are given in the Appendix to the araṇyegeyagāna (SV. ed.

Calcutta, Vol. II, pages 371, 375, 379) and for the Ṛgvedins in the Khila, Adhyāya V. 4 (ed. Scheftelowitz, page 134) and Ait. ār. IV (ed. Keith, page 141).

[6] This refers to the ihavad vāmadevyam, grām. gā. I. 2. 6, where the stobha *iha* occurs thrice.—According to the Nidānasūtra (III. 10) the Brāhmana refers to auśanam for the first day; vāsiṣṭham for the second day; ubhayataḥ stobhaṃ gautamam for the third day; ābhīśavam for the fourth day: grām. gā. XIV. 2. 6,
5 r r 7
beginning: *parīto ṣiñcatā sutam* | *e* | *e* |, cp. XII. 9. 15-17; ānūpam for the fifth day: grām. gā. VII 2. 23, composed on SV. I. 277: *aśvi rathi surūpa it*, the
4 5 4 5
sāman begins, : *aśvī aśvi*; for the sixth day the ihavad vāmadevyam, grām. gā. I. 2. 6. Probably where the Nidānasūtra differs from Sāyaṇa, the sūtra is right, not Sāyana.

[7] I presume that the word *svarāṇām* of § 2 in the printed text, belongs to § 1.

2. Because this variety of tunes, being the same, is of different characteristic, therefore the wind blows (differently) according to the seasons [1].

[1] 'Cold during the winter, hot during the summer', Jaim. br. III. 332.

X. 10.

(General remarks on the twelve-day-period, continued.)

1. A (sāman) that has a finale at (each) verse-quarter [1] is of the first day the characteristic of the finales' variety; a (sāman) that has the finale outside (the verse) [2], of the second (day); a (sāman) with the word 'quarters' (*diś*) for finale [3], of the third (day); a (sāman) that has ī for finale [4], of the fourth (day); a (sāman) that has the word *atha* for finale [5], of the fifth (day); a (sāman) in which the word here (*iha*) is repeated (as finale) [6], is the characteristic of the sixth day for the finales. Because this variety of finales, being the same, is of different characteristic, therefore the worlds, being together, are apart.

[1] The yaudhājaya has the nidhana at each pada: grām. XIV. 1. 36.

[2] The yauktāśva, grām. XII. 2. 30, the finale of which, being outside the verse,
2 3 2
is *o i-jvarā ā*.

[3] The kṣullakavaiṣṭambha, grām. XIII. 1. 11; nidhana: 3 5 *dī'234 śāḥ*.

[4] The mahāvātsapra, grām. VIII. 2. 11; nidhana: 31111 *ī 2345*.

[5] The mahānāmnis (SV. ed. Calcutta, Vol. II, page 372) end: 1 2 2 1r indrā | dyumnāya
1 1
iṣā i | athā.

6 The bhadra, ar. gāna III. 1 2 (SV. ed. Calcutta, Vol. II, page 454) ends:

$\overset{1}{\textit{ihā}}$ | $\overset{1}{\textit{ihā}}$ | $\overset{1r}{\textit{au}}\overset{1r}{\textit{ho}}\,\overset{3}{\textit{i}}\overset{2}{\textit{hā}}$ *34* | $\overset{2r}{\textit{au}}\overset{r}{\textit{ho}}$ *vā* | $\overset{2}{\textit{e}}$ *3* | $\overset{2}{\textit{bha}}\overset{1}{\textit{dram}}$.

X. 11.

(General remarks on the twelve-day-period, continued.)

1. A (sāman) with a 'running' *iḍā*[1] is of the first day the characteristic of the *iḍās*' variety; a (sāman) with 'ascending' *iḍā*[2], of the second (day); a (sāman) with a stobha on both sides of the *iḍā*[3], of the third (day); an *iḍābhir aiḍam* (sāman)[4], of the fourth (day); a (sāman) with one and a half *iḍā*[5], for the fifth (day); a (sāman) with repeated *iha*[6], for the sixth day is the characteristic of the *iḍās*. Because this *iḍās*' variety, being the same, is of different characteristic, therefore cattle (cows), being the same, is of different characteristic (or 'colour' or 'form').

1 *dravadiḍa* (cp. VIII. 3. 7, XI. 4. 11), the kāleya: $\overset{4}{\textit{ho}}$ *5 i* | *ḍā*. Instead of *dravadiḍa* the Jaim. br. uses the term *prasṛtela*.

2 *ūrdhveḍa* (cp XI. 9. 7), the mādhucchandasa (grām. VIII. 1. 23): $\overset{1}{\textit{o}}$*'2345 i* | *ḍā*.

3 *pariṣṭubdheḍa* (cp. VIII. 9. 12 and Sāyana on X. 12. 4), the raurava (grām. XIV. 1. 35) which ends: $\overset{2}{\textit{au}}$ *'3* $\overset{4}{\textit{ho}}$ $\overset{5}{\textit{vā}}$ | $\overset{4}{\textit{ho}}$ *'5 i* | *ḍā* (cp. XII. 4. 27).

4 The pṛśni (grām. I. 2. 29): $\overset{1}{\textit{iḍā}}$ *'23* $\overset{2}{\textit{bhā}}$ *'343* | $\overset{1}{\textit{o}}$ *'2345 i* | *ḍā*.

5 *adhyardheḍa*, the rāyovājīya (ar. gāna III. 1. 15, SV. ed. Calcutta, Vol. II, page 452) ending: $\overset{1}{\textit{iṭ}}$ | *iḍā* $\overset{1}{2}\,\overset{1}{3}\,\overset{1}{4}\,\overset{1}{5}$; cp. also VIII. 9. 14.

6 Here is some uncertainty. According to the Nidānasūtra the goṣṭha (grām. XIV. 2. 14) is meant, ending: *ihā* | $\overset{3}{\textit{upā}}$ *'*$\overset{1}{2}\,\overset{1}{3}\,\overset{1}{4}\,\overset{1}{5}$, which, according to the ūhagāna (SV. ed. Calcutta, Vol. IV, page 43) is repeated four times in each stotriya verse. According to Sāyaṇa the vāravantīya (gram. I. 1. 30) is meant, which, however, has $\overset{1}{\textit{i}}\overset{3}{\textit{hā}}$ but once. As all the other chants, here mentioned, are the last pṛṣṭhastotra of each day, we might be tempted to emend *yad ihakārenābhyastam* into *yad iḍākāreṇābhyastam*. If this is right, the śyena (last pṛṣṭha of the sixth day) may be meant, which has (see SV. ed. Calcutta, Vol. II, page 453) five times *iḍā*, cp. however X. 12. 4 (end).

X. 12.

(General remarks on the twelve-day-period, continued.)

1. The descendants of Bharadvāja (once upon a time) performed a sacrificial session. Of them they (*i.e.*, the other seers) asked: 'What did ye accomplish by the first day?' They answered: 'We went forth (or 'we began the sacrifice')'. 'What by the second (day)?' 'We made our provisions' (they answered). 'What by the third day)?' 'We journeyed about'. 'What by the fourth (day)?' 'With the good we did cover up the good'. 'What by the fifth (day)?' 'We went destroying the lives'. 'What by the sixth (day)?' 'We returned hither' [1].

[1] The statements made in khaṇḍa 11 are here repeated in a mystical way and the six kinds of *iḍā* are here compared to so many acts of a raid to procure cattle (cows). The comparison of the *iḍās* with these acts rests mostly on puns: so the answer: 'We went forth' (*pra* in *praima*) reminds of the *prasṛteḷa* (so the Jaiminīyas instead of *dravaḍida*, cp note 1 on X. 11. 1) of the first day. 'We have covered up the good with the good' means: 'We have seized upon cows after cows' (*iḍābhir iḍām=paśubhiḥ paśūn*, *iḍā* being equal to cattle). 'We went away destroying the lives' ('the cows' Jaim.) is the mystical expression for the one and a half *iḍā*, because here the *iḍā* (the cattle!) in the first time is cut off, etc. All this now becomes clear by the Jaim. br. (III. 331, 332) where, however, the technical expressions differ somewhat from those of the Kauthumas. In the text of the Jaim. it is the Naimiśīyas who are asked by a seer Cahola Vāyaska (name uncertain).

2. By the (sāman), the prastāva of which is chanted on a (mere) verse-quarter and which then is circumflected, the Gods beheld the cattle. By that (sāman), which is preceded by a stobha and then circumflected, they let loose the cattle. By that (sāman), which is preceded and followed by a stobha and then circumflected, the Gods brought from these (three) worlds foods unto the cattle. By that (sāman), which has a repeated push and then is circumflected, they appropriated them (? *upāśikṣan*). By that (sāman), in which the finale is in the middle and which then is circumflected, they (the domestic animals) were impregnated. By that (sāman), which contains the word 'here' (or 'hither,' *iha*), and which is circumflected, they caused them to bring forth (*i.e.*, to give birth to the conceived fruit) [1].

[1] Cp. X. 9. 1, all the sāmans as given by the Nidānasūtra (see note 6 on l. c.), seem to be *svāra* (circumflected) at the end.

3. The Gods, forsooth, conquered this (earthly) world by means of the (sāman), which has its finale at (each) verse quarter; yonder (world) by means of the (sāman), which has its finale outside (the words of the verse); the intermediate region by means of the (sāman), which has 'the quarters' for finale; they reached immortality by means of the (sāman), which has ī as finale; they obtained priestly lustre by means of the (sāman), which has the word *atha* as finale; in this world they gained firm support by means of the (sāman), which has (the word) 'here' as finale[1].

[1] Cp. X. 10. 1.

4. The Gods, forsooth, conquered this world by means of the (sāman) with running *iḍā*; yonder (world) by means of the (sāman) with upward *iḍā*; the intermediate region by means of the (sāman), the *iḍā* of which is preceded and followed by a stobha; they retained a firm support by means of the (sāman), which has *iḍābhir iḍā* (as its finale); having got a firm support[1], they conquered finally by means of the (sāman), which has one and a half *iḍā*, and, by means of the (sāman), which has the word 'here' as its *iḍā*, they found a firm support on this world[2].

[1] Read: *pratiṣṭhāyārdheḍena.*

[2] Cp. X. 11. 1.

5. The Word[1] (or 'the Voice') does not sound beyond the year[2], (but) it is the *iḍā* that sounds beyond the year; by means of the embryo, having turned round, it (*i.e.*, the *iḍā*, *i.e.*, the cattle) is born in (or 'after') a year and thereby sounds beyond the year.

[1] The author has in mind the word *vā(k)* ('Word, Voice') as nidhana, and sets forth why this nidhana is inferior to the word *iḍā* as nidhana.

[2] Because young children begin to speak before their first year is finished, according to Sāyaṇa: the contrary is said in TS. VI. 6. 1. 7: *tasmād ekahāyanā manuṣyā vācaṃ vadanti.* I am inclined to compare this with TS. II. 2. 6. 2: *saṃvatsarāya vā etau samamāte yau samamāte.* Seen in the light of this quotation our passage could mean: 'an oral engagement is binding no longer than a year.'

6. These (*i.e*, the following) four *iḍās* go beyond the six-day period[1]: this *anunūtā* one[2], this *viṣūcī* one (the all-pervading one), this *pratīcī* (or backward turned one) and this (sāman) with double *iḍā*[3].

[1] *i.e.*, occur also in the days following on the six-days of the daśarātra.

[2] The meaning of *anunūta* is unknown. The Kāṭh. (XXXIV. 6), where all the ten kinds of *iḍā* are enumerated (1. *ihīḍaṃ sāma;* 2. *ūrdhveḍaṃ sāma;* 3. *iḍābhir*

aiḍaṃ s.; 4. *pariṣṭubdheḍaṃ s.*; 5. *adhyardheḍaṃ s.*; 6. *ho iḍaṃ sāma*; 7. *punar nitunnām iḍām*; 8. *viṣvagaiḍaṃ sāma*; 9. *ho iḍaṃ sāma*; 10. *dviḍaṃ sāma*) has *punar nitunna*. The Pañcavidhasūtra (ed. Simon, page 67) cites our passage, which certainly has not been rightly interpreted by Simon, who follows Sāyaṇa.

[3] Cp. Nidānasūtra III. 10: *athaiṣā chandomeṣv iḍāvibhaktir: jarābodhīyaṁ saptama, iḍānāṁ saṃkṣaro 'ṣṭamasya satī* (meaning ?) *navame 'hani kriyate, pratīcī-neḍaṃ kāśītaṃ navama, utsedho daśame.* The jarābodhīya (of the 7th day) has for
5 3r 2
iḍāvibhakti (cp. grām. 1. 12. 26) *dṛśīko '3 4 5 i | ḍā.* The iḍānāṃ saṃkṣāra (of the
4
9th day) (cp. grām. III. 2. 13), *ho '5 i | ḍā* (see the designation in the Kāṭh. under note 2). The pratīcīneḍa kāśīta (of the 9th day; on the meaning of the word
4 5 4 5
cp. XV. 5 16) (cp. grām. V. 2. 8): *au '2 3 ho vā | iḍā.* The utsedha (of the 10th day)
3 1 1 1 1 2 2
(cp. grām. XIV. 2. 23): *ū '2 3 4 5*, within the sāman it has twice *ū '34pā.* I am unable to point out, even by means of this passage in the Nidānasūtra, which kinds of *iḍā* are meant by the terms of the Brāhmana; only the term *pratīcī* is clear. Sāyaṇa's interpretation of our passage is wholly different from the one given above.

7. Agni is the year, the year is the Voice; in that Agni is distributed (*i.e.*, is mentioned in different varieties as explained in X. 7) they thereby distribute the Voice[1].

[1] Agni is the year, the year is the Voice, and consequently Agni is the Voice; in distributing Agni he distributes the Voice.

8. They distribute each time two syllables[1], for one season is (equal to) two months; and thus also the characteristic of the months is brought about.

[1] *agne, agnim, agneḥ, agniḥ*, cp. X. 7.

9. Six days are differentiated[1]; six in number are the seasons: for holding the seasons, for the firm standing of the seasons; and so also is the characteristic of the seasons brought about. Six in number also are the persons (the priests) on whose behalf the fire is taken out.

[1] As described in X. 6.

[2] On the dhiṣṇyas (in the sadas) of six ṛtvijs the fire is taken out from the āgnīdhrīya, cp. C. H. § 139.

10. Because at this particular moment the fire (Agni) is taken out diversely, (and) because the sun[1] is directed towards all beings on earth, therefore these two deities (only) attain the differentiation and no other whatever.

[1] Here Indra is the Sun; this refers to the case-forms of the name *indra*, X. 8.

Eleventh Chapter.

(Pṛṣṭhya six-day period of the twelve-day rite.)
(First day.)

(Out-of-doors-laud.)

1. For the days of a sacrificial session the laud is yoked ('begun') by means of verses containing the words 'old' (*pratna*) and 'upon' (*upa*)[1].

[1] The bahiṣpavamāna consists of the following verses:
asya pratnām SV. II. 105-107=Ṛs. IX. 54. 1-3.
eṣa pratnena SV. II. 108=Ṛs. IX. 3. 9.
eṣa pratnena SV. II. 109=Ṛs. IX. 42. 4 (var. reading).
duhānaḥ pratnam SV. II. 110=Ṛs. IX. 42. 4 (with var. reading).
upa śikṣa SV. II. 111=Ṛs. IX. 19. 6.
upo ṣu jātam SV. II. 112=Ṛs. IX. 61. 13.
upāsmai gāyatā SV. II. 113=Ṛs. IX. 11. 1.

2. In that the verses containing the word 'old' are yoked ('ranged') before those containing the word 'upon', therefore, the priesthood is yoked ('ranged') before the nobility[1], for the priesthood comes before the nobility.

[1] Probably because *pratna* recalls *pra* 'before', and *upa*, 'near to'.

3. Thereby, the mind is yoked ('ranged') before the voice; for the mind comes before the voice[1], for all that has been thought out (firstly) by the mind, is (afterwards) uttered by the voice.

[1] Cp. Śat. br. III. 2. 4. 11: *manasā vā iyaṃ vāg dhṛtā, mano vā idaṃ purastād vācaḥ.*

4. Thereby, the bṛhat is yoked ('ranged') before the rathantara[1]; for the bṛhat comes before the rathantara; through conquest, however, the rathantara has obtained a prior yoking[2].

[1] According to VIII. 6. 1 the bṛhat is sprung from the mind of Prajāpati, but voice is connected with rathantara. Jaim. br. II. 12: 'the bṛhat is the mind, the rathantara is the voice'.

[2] It is applied practically before the bṛhat: the Hotṛ's pṛṣṭhastotra at the first day of the daśarātra is not the bṛhat, but the rathantara. Cp. further VII. 6. 9 sqq.

5. The tristichs (of the out-of-doors-laud) are to be brought together ('composed')[1]. He composes them ('brings them together') just

as he would compose ('bring together', 'yoke together') the swiftest and best drawing (oxen): for starting.

[1] On *saṃbhārya* 'to be brought together (from different parts of the sacred texts)' cp. the Introduction, Chapter II, page XV; cp. XVI. 5. 11 and XVIII. 8. 8. Seen from a Sāmavedistic standpoint, the verses, which are mentioned in note 1 on § 1, can hardly be qualified as *saṃbhārya*, but from a Ṛgvedistic standpoint, they are truly *saṃbhārya*.

6. They are nine in number: in order to yoke ('begin') the nine-day rite: by means of each verse he yokes ('begins') a day. He, thereby, puts the yoke-pins of the nine-day rite in [1], just as he would put in the yoke-pins of a (cart) that is going to be put into motion [2]: for starting.

[1] He fastens them, just as the yoke-pins fasten the draught-oxen.

[2] I see only one way out of the difficulty presented by the word *prārthasya*, *viz.*, by reading, with a slight change of the devanāgarī characters, प्रार्प्यस्य instead of प्रार्थस्य, *prārpya* to be taken as a gerundive of *prārpayati* 'to bring into motion.' The word *prārtha* occurs, besides in our passage, twice: Ath. Saṃh. v. 22. 9: *ábhūd u prā́rthas takmā́ sá gamiṣyati bā́lhikān*; here the word *prārtha* has met with no acceptable explanation; but if we emend here also *prārpyas*, all becomes clear. Strongly in favour of this emendation speaks the metrum: *ábhūd u prā́rpiyas takmā́*. About the third place where the word occurs, *viz.*, T. Br. II. 1. 2. 12, I am not certain that this emendation is commendable. It is not impossible that Sāyaṇa in his Tāṇḍya-text has read also *prārpyasya*, as he comments. *prakarṣeṇa iyarti gacchatīti prārtho 'naḍvān*. The Jaim. br. II. 12, with its passage *yathā naddhayugasya śamyā avadadhyāt tādṛk tat*, seems to speak in favour of our emendation.

7. The stoma is the threefold (*i.e.*, nine-versed) one, for the sake of obtaining splendour and priestly lustre.[1]

[1] Because Agni is the deity connected with the trivṛt stoma, cp. VI. 1. 6.

XI. 2.

(The ājya-lauds of the first day.)

1. The verses of the out-of-doors-laud are yoked ('begun') by both characteristics [1]; what sāman the stoma has (as first pṛṣṭha-laud) that is (represented) in the ājya-lauds [2].

[1] By both, bṛhat and rathantara; the verses with *pratna* point to the bṛhat (XI. 1. 4), those with *upa* to the rathantara.

[2] The verses of the ājya-lauds vary according to the nature of the first pṛṣṭha-laud: is this the rathantara, then, the verses for the ājyas are SV. II. 10-21; if it is the bṛhat, then, they are SV. II. 140-152, see *e.g.*, Ārṣeyakalpa page 33, note 4.

2. Containing a 'calling-out[1]' are the (verses of the) ājya-lauds: after it (*sc.* the first day) has been yoked[2], he calls it by means of these (ājya-lauds).

[1] They contain an addressing of the Deities, *i.e.*, vocative cases; all the verses for the ājya-lauds of the first day contain indeed vocatives; *nirāhavat* stands, as Sāyaṇa remarks, for *nirāhavavat*, a fine specimen of haplology! cp. XI. 7. 2.

[2] See the preceding §.

3. (The verses for the ājya-lauds are:) 'O Agni, come hither to the feast'; 'Hither, o Mitra and Varuṇa, to our'; 'Come hither, for we have pressed for thee'; 'O Indra and Agni, come to our soma'[1]. He thereby brings to light ('displays') the characteristic of the rathantara[2]. The stoma (is given)[3].

[1] SV. II. 10–12=Ṛs. VI. 16. 10–12.
SV. II. 13–15=Ṛs. III. 62. 16–18.
SV. II. 16–18=Ṛs. VIII. 17. 1–3.
SV. II. 19–21=Ṛs. III. 12. 1–3.

[2] Because all the verses contain the word ā, cp. X. 6. 1.

[3] Cp. XI. 1. 7.

XI. 3.

(The midday-pavamāna-laud of the first day.)

1. (The verses on which this laud is chanted are:) 'Forth (*pra*) the wise somas,' a gāyatrī (verse), to promote the 'going forth' (*pra*) (or 'the beginning'); 'On to (*abhi*) the trough the brown ones,' to promote the stepping on (*abhikrānti*); 'Pressed for Indra (and) Vāyu,' to promote the equipment[1]; 'Forth (*pra*), o God Soma, to the feast,' to promote the going forth (*pra*); 'Run forth (*pra*), now'[2], to promote the going forth (*pra*); by means of this (first) day, indeed, they go forth (they start, they begin).

[1] *saṃskṛtyai* ('for the cooking, the dressing') here 'for the preparation of the soma,' because of the word 'pressed.'

[2] The verses are SV. II. 114–116=Ṛs. IX. 33. 1–3 (with var. reading); SV. II. 117-118=Ṛs. IX. 107. 12-13 (with var.); SV. II. 27-28=Ṛs. IX. 87. 1-2 (with var.).

2. There is the gāyatra (chant).

3. The brāhmaṇa of the gāyatra is the same (as the one already given).[1]

[1] See khaṇḍa 1 of Chapter VII.

4. There is the horse-chant (the āśva-sāman).[1]

[1] Grāmegeyagāna III. 2. 5 (on SV. I. 116) with the nidhana: *de'* $\overset{1111}{2345}$ *ḥ*.

5. Prajāpati. having become a horse[1], created the creatures; he was reproduced (and) became multiplied. He who has chanted the horse-chant is reproduced and becomes multiplied.

[1] A she-mule, according to Sāyaṇa. Besides this explanation of the name, the Jaim. br. (III. 14) has another, according to which the sāman has been seen by Aśva, the son of Samudra, who desired to get plurality of cattle.

6 They undertake ('chant') one syllable as finale[1]: so as not to exceed the rathantara in speaking.[2]

[1] See note 1 on § 4.

[2] Which (see VII. 6. 11) has also one syllable as finale. This day, namely, is a rathantara-day.

7. The rival of him who knows this, will not be able to out-talk him.

8. There is the soma-chant.[1]

[1] As it must be *aiḍam*, the somasāman grām. XIII. 1. 2 composed on SV. I. 470 must be understood, see SV. ed. Calcutta, Vol. II, page 15 and ūhagāna I. 2. 12 in the Calcutta edition, Vol. III, page 269.

9. Soma (formerly) was just as these other herbs[1]; he performed penance and saw this soma-chant; by means of it he came to royalty[2], to supremacy and became honoured. He who lauds with the soma-chant, comes to royalty, to supremacy and becomes honoured.

[1] He was equal in rank to them.

[2] He became their King: *soma rājā*.

10. There is the yaudhājaya[1]; the brāhmaṇa of the yaudhājaya is the same (as the one already given)[2].

[1] Grām. XIV. 1. 36, chanted on SV. II. 117-118=Ṛs. IX. 107. 12-13.

[2] See VII. 5. 6 and 12.

11. (*a*). (There is) the auśana[1]; the (brāhmaṇa) of the auśana (has been given).[2]

[1] Cp. note 1 on VII. 5. 16.

[2] See VII. 5. 16-20.

11. (*b*) The stoma (is given).[1]

[1] See XI. 1. 7.

XI. 4.

(The pṛṣṭha-lauds of the first day.)

1 (In the verses beginning:) 'Unto (*abhi*) thee we shout loudly'[1] (the word) 'unto' is characteristic for the rathantara[2]; for this is a rathantara-day[3].

1 *abhi tvā śūra nonumaḥ*: SV. I. 233=Ṛs. VII. 32. 22-23=SV. II. 30-31.

2 Because it is the first day, where the idea of 'going unto' is appropriate.

3 *i.e.*, a day on which the first pṛṣṭha-laud is the rathantara. This sāman is registered in the araṇyegeyagāna II. 1. 21, based on SV. I. 233, see SV. ed. Calcutta, Vol. II, page 425 and cp. Vol. V, page 381.

2. (The verses beginning:) 'By which assistance shall the bright one help us' contain (the word) 'which' (*ka*). Thereby, they are Prajāpati-like, for Prajāpati is 'who' (*kas*): in order that they may reach (*i e.*, become equal to) Prajāpati[1].

1 For the vāmadevya (the second pṛṣthastotra) cp. VII. 8. 3.

3. (The verses beginning:) 'Him who works wonders, enduring the onslaught, who drinks of the salutary plant, as milch-cows unto (*abhi*) their calf in the stables'[1] are by (the word) 'unto' characteristic for the rathantara; for this is a rathantara-day.

1 For the naudhasa (the third pṛṣṭha-laud) cp. note 2 on VII. 10. 2.

4. (By the words): 'We call Indra with our songs'[1] they call him.

1 Last words of the first verse on which the naudhasa is chanted: SV. I. 236 (II. 35). In reading *indraṃ girbhir havāmahe* as against *indraṃ girbhir navāmahe* of SV. and Ṛs., the Pañc. br. deviates from its Saṃhitā (the pada with *havāmahe* occurs Ṛs. VIII. 76. 5). About this difference of reading, the author of the Nidānasūtra remarks (III. 10); *atha naudhase vadatīndraṃ havāmaha iti; tat khalu havāmaha ity eva kartavyaṃ; vidhipramāṇāḥ katham anyathāvidhi kuryāmety; āmnāyadvaitena brāhmaṇam upavarṇayatīty aparaṃ; tan niyogāya na prabhavatīty; etenaitad vyākhyātam akrānt samudraḥ parame vidharmann iti yāni caivaṃjātīyāni*, i.e., 'About the naudhasa, it (the Brāhmaṇa) says: 'We call (*havāmahe* instead of *navāmahe*) Indra with our songs'; that (sāman) must be applied with *havāmahe* (not with *navāmahe*). How could we, conforming ourselves to the rules (laid down in the Brāhmaṇa), perform (the chant) against the rules? But there is another explanation of this, *viz.*, that the Brāhmaṇa describes a duality of sacred lore and that this has no value for the practice. This same remark prevails for (the words): *akrānt samudraḥ parame vidharman* (Pañc. br. XV. 1. 1; here the SV. and the Ṛs. have *prathame* instead of *parame*) and such-like cases'.

5. (In the verses beginning:) 'With strength him who finds treasures'[1] the strength is the stoma; 'he who finds treasures' is the sacrifice; by means of the stoma the sacrifice is yoked ('brought into action'); in that he says: 'With strength him who finds treasures' he yokes the sacrifice.

[1] On these verses (SV. I. 237=Ṛs. VIII. 66. 1-2=SV. II. 37-38) the kāleya (grām. VI. 2. 7) is chanted as fourth pṛṣṭha-laud, cp. note 1 on VIII. 2. 11.

6. There is the rathantara; the rathantara, forsooth, is sacred lore, the introductory day is sacred lore; thereby, they go forth (start, begin), stepping from sacred lore unto sacred lore[1].

[1] The same manner of expression in § 9 and in XI. 9. 4.

7. There is the vāmadevya; the vāmadevya is cattle[1]: for the retainment of cattle. The vāmadevya is Prajāpati-like[2]: having got a firm support in Prajāpati, they perform the sacrificial session.

[1] Cp. IV. 8. 15, VII. 9. 9.

[2] Cp. XI. 4. 2.

8. The rathantara is the earth; having got a firm support on the earth, they perform the sacrificial session.

9. There is the naudhasa; the naudhasa is sacred lore; the introductory day is sacred lore; thereby they step from sacred lore unto sacred lore.

10. There is the kāleya; the kāleya and the rathantara belong to the same world[1]; the rathantara is the earth, the kāleya is cattle; having got a firm support on the earth and in cattle, they perform, the sacrificial session.

[1] Because wherever the rathantara is the first pṛṣṭhastotra, the kāleya is the fourth.

11. It is of 'running' *iḍā*,[1] for thus is the characteristic of this day. The stoma (has been given).[3]

[1] Cp. VIII. 3. 7.

[2] Cp. X. 11. 1 (note 1).

[3] Cp. XI. 1. 7.

XI. 5.

(The ārbhava-pavamāna-laud and the agniṣṭoma-laud of the first day.)

1. (The verse beginning:) 'Forth (has) the intoxicating (*mada-cyut*) Soma'[1] is the gāyatrī; intoxicating (having *mada*) (and) rich in sap is the afternoon service; he, thereby, puts intoxication (and) sap (in it). (The verse beginning:) 'By this (stream) become thou clarified, devoted to the Gods'[2] is by (the word) 'hither'[3] the characteristic of the rathantara[4], for this is a rathantara-day. (The verse): 'The coveted fallow one is being clarified'[5] is the characteristic of the bṛhat[6]; the bṛhat he, thereby, yokes ('applies') on this day; this, being yoked, is undertaken ('chanted') on the next day. (The verses:) 'Forth (*pra*) for the one that is being pressed from the herb'[7] contain[8] (the word) 'forth,' for this day is rather apt to bring forward (*pra*). (The verse:) 'Unto the dear ones he is clarified willingly'[9] is by the (word) 'unto' (*abhi*) characteristic of the rathantara; for this is a rathantara-day.

1 SV. I. 447=Ṛs. IX. 32. 1, 3, 2=SV. II. 119–121.

2 SV. II. 122=Ṛs. IX. 106. 14 (but a, c, b). Ṛs. is an uṣṇih (8+8+12 syllables), SV. a kakubh (8+12+8); the verse-quarters of the Ṛs. are here transposed, because immediately after the gāyatra must come a kakubh (s. Einleitung on Ārṣeyakalpa, page XXIV). The short *u* in *devayu* before *re°* proves the transposition.

3 There is no preposition *ā*, but there is a long syllable *ā* in *ayā*.

4 Cp. X. 6. 1.

5 SV. I. 576=Ṛs. IX. 106. 13=SV. II. 123; Ṛs. IX. 65. 25 has the same *pratīka*, but as an uṣṇih is required here, this last verse, being gāyatrī, is excluded.

6 Why?

7 SV. I. 553=Ṛs. IX. 101. 13=SV. II. 124, see the next note.

8 Although it is o n e verse only, the author uses the plural; probably this is a mistake. Sāyana seeks to explain the plural by referring it to the two sāmans that are chanted on it. But it is striking that the Jaim. br. (III. 16) has equally the plural: *pra sunvānāyāndhasa iti pravatīr anuṣṭubho bhavanti*, although the saṃhitā (Jaim. s. III. 12. 8) gives one single verse.

9 SV. I. 554=Ṛs. IX. 75. 1=SV. II. 50.

2. (Then there are the verses beginning:) 'Through sacrifice on sacrifice, in honour of Agni'[1]. The sacrifice, forsooth, is Agni: he thereby establishes (finally) the sacrifice into the sacrifice.

1 Cp. note 1 on VIII. 6. 1.

3. There is the gāyatra (-chant); the brāhmaṇa of the gāyatra is the same (as already given)[1].

[1] Cp. VII. 1. 1 sqq.

4. There is the saṃhita with a finale of two syllables[1]: for obtaining a firm support[2]. Having become firmly supported, they perform the sacrificial session.

[1] Grām. XII. 2. 22 with the nidhana *sū'234 tāḥ* (5).

[2] Because man is supported on t w o feet.

5. There is the sapha[1].

[1] See note 1 on VII. 5. 1; here it is chanted on SV. II. 122.

6. By means of the sapha, the Gods reached (*sam-āp-nuvan*) these worlds; therefore, the sapha is called sapha[1]. Having by means of this (sāman) reached these worlds, they perform the sacrificial session.

[1] The etymological connection aimed at by the author is far from convincing; cp. VIII. 5. 6, note 2.

7. There is the ākṣāra[1].

[1] Grām. X. 2. 19, composed on SV. I. 391, here chanted on SV. II. 123.

8. There were (once) those[1] eight wish-cows; one of these broke down, it became the ploughing. He who knows this, has luck in ploughing.

[1] Those (*etāḥ*), according to Sāyaṇa 'the metres'. I should prefer to take the pronoun as pointing to what follows: those cows, the first of which was changed into agriculture, and the other seven were fought over by the Gods and the Asuras (§ 9). Perhaps there is some connection with the wish-cows of Uśanas (VII. 5. 20), see Baudh. XVIII. 47: 404. 9 sqq., where it is set forth that of the four wish-cows three were changed by Indra into the ukthas, but the fourth was given to Manu, who deposited the cow on the earth and she became the ploughing (probably *kṛṣi* is here the better reading). In the Jaim. br. I. 181 six wish-cows are mentioned in connection with the ukthas (they are: cow, horse, goat, sheep, rice, barley), and still more explicit is another rather corrupt passage in the second book (84), where there seem to be seven of them: the first one is deposited into the earth, this is the one that they ('the men') seek after with the curved (piece of) wood: the plough. Then are mentioned three others and finally it is said: 'the three that were left over, of these they made the ukthas'.

9. About these[1] the Gods and the Asuras contended; by means of the ākṣāra(sāman) the Gods repelled the Asuras from the wish-

cows. He who uses in chanting the ākṣāra (sāman) repels his rival from the wish-cows.

[1] The seven remaining ones. On this contention cp. Jaim. br. I. 127 in Journ. of the Amer. Or. Soc., vol. XXVIII, page 87.

10. From these worlds the sap ('pith') went forth; by means of the ākṣāra(sāman)[1] Prajāpati made it flow (again) forth (*ākṣārayat*). Hence this chant has its name.

[1] Meaning 'flowing toward'.

11. Therefore, he, who having been formerly successful, afterwards fares worse, should take the ākṣāra(sāman) as the Brahman's chant[1]. Unto him it (this sāman) causes to flow ('to return') valour, strength (and) pith.

[1] The Nidānasūtra III. 10 treats at length of this case: *athākṣāre vadati: yaḥ purā puṇyo bhūtvā paścāt pāpīyānt syād ākṣāraṃ brahmasāma kurvīteti; kiṃ tasya sthānaṃ syād ity; ete evānyo'nyasya sthāne vyatiharen: naudhasam uṣṇihi kuryād iti*, etc.

12. They are naturally consisting of one single verse[1]: for supporting the day. What (part) of this day is not supported, that he supports by means of these two (sāmans, chanted each on a single verse).

[1] The two verses (SV. II. 122, 123), on which sapha and ākṣāra are chanted, are by nature single verses, they are not parts of a tristich or a pragātha. Probably it is the number two of them, that brings about the firm support, on the two feet.

13. There is the gaurīvita[1].

[1] Grām. V. 1. 22 composed on SV. I. 168.

14. Gaurīviti, the son of Śakti, saw this (sāman) as it was left over from sacred lore[1]; that became the gaurīvita (sāman)[2].

[1] When the Gods divided the 'Voice', V. 7. 1, IX. 2. 3.

[2] The origin of the name is explained more fully in the Jaim. br. (III. 18, see the text in Das Jaim. br. in Auswahl, n.° 170): 'The Śāktyas, who used to offer meat-cakes, (once upon a time) performed a sacrificial session. Gaurivīti, one of these Śāktyas, had shot a deer (to obtain the meat for the sacrifice). Tārkṣya Suparṇa came flying to him from above. He (Gaurivīti) put (his arrow) on (his bow) and aimed at him. He (Tārkṣya) addressed him: 'Seer, do not shoot at me. That which has relation to the to-morrow I will declare to thee; the to-day only thou knowest, not the to-morrow'. He imparted to him this gaurivita (sāman), etc. For the beginning words of this tale cp. below, XXV. 7. 2.

15. In lauding the ahīnas with the gaurīvita (sāman)[1], they laud that which has been left over ('that which is excessive, what is surpassing') by means of that which is left over ('excessive, surpassing'): it includes the (ritual of the day) of to-morrow, and also is fit for (obtaining) progeny[2].

[1] The ahīnas (cp. note 2 on V. 7. 1) have, with the exception of the last day, the gaurīvita towards the end of the ārbhava-pavamāna, to connect each day with the following one.

[2] Cp. XII. 13. 10.

16. This sāman, forsooth, is a bull (and is) strong; the bull is the seed-placer; to-day they laud, to-morrow he brings forth[1] (obtains progeny).

[1] The sentence refers to the last words of § 15.

17. It is performed on the anuṣṭubh of the (different) metres, (which are applied in the ārbhava-laud). for the anuṣṭubh is the womb of the metres[1]; he thereby places the seed into his own womb[2]: for the sake of procreating.

[1] Cp. X. 2. 4.

[2] *i.e.*, into the womb of his own wife and his own female domestic animals.

18. He who knows this brings forth and is multiplied.

19. It has two 'raisings'; these raisings are the two that look out for a stopping place in the (journey to the) world of heaven. By means of the first ('the former') they finish the first ('former') day, by means of the following, they pass, in chanting, across to the following day[1].

[1] This § is nearly identical with V. 7. 4, see the notes on that passage.

20. Just as in daily life[1] people on a journey each time take their resting place after reaching water and grass that has been looked for on the preceding day,[2] thus they (the performers of an ahīna-rite) make their journey, taking by means of these two ('raisings', *i.e.*, stopping places) their resting place in view of the world of heaven.

[1] *adaḥ*.

[2] Each day the stopping place is chosen there, where they have made certain that food for the draught-animals may be obtained, cp. note 1 on V. 7. 4.

21. There is the gautama (the chant of Gotama).[1]

[1] Grām. IX. 1. 25 composed on SV. I. 344.

22. A sāman, being of Ṛṣi-descent[1], is fit for (reaching the world of) heaven. He who applies (it) in lauding falls not from the world of heaven.

1 As is this sāman that has been seen by the Ṛṣi Gotama, who reached by it the world of heaven; *ārṣeyavat* occurs in this sense XI. 9. 6, XII. 11. 14, XII. 16. 5, XIII. 3. 19, XIV. 10. 5. For the gautama-sāman the Jaim. br. (III. 44) has this remarkable, but to me not wholly comprehensible statement: 'Gotama, the son of Rahūgana, desired: 'may I be in the possession of booty' (*sātasaniḥ syām*, refers probably to the gifts that are collected by the participants of a soma-feast, cp. C. H. § 23). He saw this sāman and practised it in lauding. Thereupon, he came into the possession of booty. They perform a sacrificial session hoping to come into the possession of booty; they g e t booty. Both kinds of seers, as well those who are upward from Gotama as those who are downward, revere the seer Gotama (*tad ye ca ha vai gotamād ṛṣayaḥ parāñco ye cārvāñcas te gotamam evarṣim ubhaya upāsate*), for he saw this *samabhimānam* (meaning ?). Both kinds of Fathers, as well those who are upward from him as those who are downward, revere him who knows this (*i.e.*, even after his death and after the death of his sons and grandsons these all will revere him, cp. also below, XIII. 12. 3). And because Gotama, the son of Rahūgana, had seen this sāman, therefore, it is called the gautama-sāman.'

23. The brāhmaṇa given for the anuṣṭubh (verse) with a finale in the middle,[1] is the same for this (sāman) also[2].

1 Cp. VIII. 5. 12-13.

2 If this means that the gautama (sāman) ought to have a nidhana of 10 syllables in the middle (as the āndhīgava has), the chant registered grām. IX. 1. 25 seems to agree with this prescript; the nidhana in the middle is (cp. SV. ed.
3 2∧3r 5 3 2∧3r 5
Calcutta, vol. IV, page 439 sqq.): *hatā auho 234 vā makhā auho 234 vā.*

24. There is the kāva (chant)[1].

1 Grām. XVI. 2. 6, composed on SV. I. 554.

25. It is a room finding chant; he who lauds with this chant finds room.

26. It is circumflected as to its tone[1]; for by means of the tone[2] food, at the end, is given to the Gods; by means of the tone he gives at the end (of the laud) food to the gods.[3]

1 Ending on *656*, see note 1 on VII. 3. 25; cp. the sāman as it is figured in C.H., page 342.

2 *svareṇa* (but Jaim. br. I. 166: *svāreṇa vai devebhyo 'ntato 'nnādyaṃ pradiyate*) cp. however VII. 1. 10 note 1.

3 Cp. VII. 3. 26.

27. There is the yajñāyajñīya (sāman)[1].

[1] Cp. note 1 on VIII. 6. 1.

28. The yajñāyajñīya is the voice[1]; in the voice the sacrifice is established; they thereby (*i.e.*, in chanting this sāman at the end of the rite) finally establish the chant in the voice, and from the voice he begins it again on the next following day.

[1] Because its nidhana is *vā(k)*, cp. note 3 on VIII. 6. 13.

29. Threefold ('nineversed') is the stoma (of this whole first day), for the obtainment of splendour and priestly lustre.

XI. 6.

(The out-of-doors-laud of the second day.)

1. 'Be clarified as the first of speech'[1] is the opening (tristich) of the second day.

[1] SV. II. 125–127=Ṛs. IX. 62. 25–27 (with var. readings).

2. (The words): 'be clarified' are the characteristic of the rathantara, (the words) 'as the first,' of the bṛhat[1]. He lays hold on both characteristics, in order to prevent the two-day-rite from slipping asunder[2].

[1] *agriya* is the *rūpa* of the brhat, because, according to the Brāhmaṇa (VII. 6), the bṛhat existed before the rathantara.

[2] In order to put these two days, the rathantara-day and the bṛhat-day, fixedly together.

3. 'Be clarified, o Soma, as a bull, being pressed'[1] is the corresponding (tristich, the antistrophe): combined with the bull[2], Indra-like and of triṣṭubh nature[3] is this second day; this (day) he thereby addresses.

[1] SV. II. 128–130=Rs. IX. 61. 28–30 (var. reading in 30).

[2] Cp. X. 6. 2.

[3] Cp. note I on X. 5. 9 (*traiṣṭubhaṃ dvitīyam ahaḥ*).

4. And, moreover, after the former characteristic he thereby speaks the latter characteristic; that he speaks after (*anu*) the former characteristic (*rūpa*) the latter characteristic, is the reason why the corresponding (tristich) is called *anurūpa*.

5. A son resembling (in good qualities) to him[1] he gets, who knows this.

[1] Note the construction *anurūpa enam*, where the accusative depends on the compound adjective.

6. The stotriya and the anurūpa are tristichs, for retaining the breathings (or vital principles)[1].

[1] Probably the dual *prāṇāpānau* is elliptic for *prāṇavyānāpānāḥ* (cp. VII. 3. 8, note 2); hence the tristich.

7. The tristichs[1] contain the word 'bull,' for the attainment of valour and strength.

[1] SV. II. 128–136.

8. A tristich is the last[1].

[1] SV. II. 137–139.

9. With which breath they start, in that they finish (the laud)[1].

[1] According to Sāyaṇa because there is a semblance between the first (SV. II. 125–127) and the last (SV. II. 137–139) tristich, as both are addressed to Soma pavamāna. But so are the others! Rather: because they have begun with tristichs and these are (cp. § 6) the *prāṇas*.

10. Fifteenfold (or 'fifteen-versed') is the stoma.

11. In vigour and strength he thereby is established: the fifteenfold stoma is vigour and strength[1].

[1] The pañcadaśa stoma is sprung forth from the breast and the arms of Prajāpati, see VI. 1. 8.

XI. 7.

(The ājya-lauds of the second day.)

1. By both the characteristics the verses of the out-of-doors-laud are yoked[1]; what sāman the stoma has, that is (represented) in the ājya-(lauds)[2].

[1] Cp. XI. 6. 2.

[2] Cp. XI. 2. 1.

2. Come near in consequence of the calling-out[1] are the (verses of the) ājya(laud)s.

[1] This a conjectural translation of *nirāhopasthitāni*; on *nirāha* cp. XI. 2. 2, note 1. Exactly as on the first day the ājya verses contain vocatives, so in the second, they contain accusatives of the names of the deities. Strictly speaking, if my explanation of this passage is correct, it ought to run: 'containing a coming-near in consequence of a calling-out'. By the vocatives of the first day (X. 7. 1,

X. 8. 1) the Gods are called and now that they have approached, the verses are spoken about them with their names in the accusative (Cp. X. 7. 1, X. 8. 1). Sāyaṇa's interpretation is not clear to me.

3. (By the verses beginning): 'Agni we choose as our messenger'; 'Mitra do we call'; 'To Indra the singers call loudly' (*bṛhat*); 'On Indra, on Agni, a laud (*bṛhat*) praise',[1] he makes plain the characteristic of the bṛhat[2].—The stoma (has been given)[3].

[1] SV. II. 140–142=ṚS. I. 12. 1-3; SV. II. 143–145=ṚS. I. 23. 4–6 (with one var. reading); SV. (II. 146, 147, 148, 149=ṚS. I. 7. 1, 2, 4, 3; SV. II. 150–152=ṚS. VII. 94. 4-6. As to SV. II. 146–149, it is far from clear why here are given four verses in the ārcika, as in the praxis always the last must be omitted according to Lāṭy. VI. 4. 10 (see Introduction to the Ārṣeyakalpa, page XVII). If we start from the supposition that the uttarārcika was not known to the author of our Brāhmaṇa, but that he draws directly on the Ṛgveda, the matter is clear, for then he simply refers to ṚS. I. 7. 1-3.

[2] By the word, bṛhat, which occurs in two of the tristichs.

[3] Cp. XI. 6. 10 and XI. 11. 14.

XI. 8.

(The midday pavamāna-laud of the second day.)

1. 'Be thou, a bull, clarified by the stream' (*dhārā*)[1] is the gāyatrī, for supporting[2] the day.

[1] SV. I. 469=ṚS. IX. 65. 10–12=SV. II. 153-155.

[2] A pun on *dhārā*. *dhṛtyai*.

2. Containing the word 'bull'[1] they are, by their characteristic, triṣṭubhs[1], for this day is a triṣṭubh-day.

[1] Cp. X. 6. 2.

3. (The verses beginning): 'Being clarified, o Soma, by the stream' (*dhārā*)[1] are for propping[2].

[1] For the verses see note 2 on VII. 5. 11.

[2] See note 2 on § 1.

4, 5. (The verses beginning): 'The red bull, roaring unto the cows'[1] containing (the word) 'bull,' are triṣṭubhs by their characteristic (and) they are lucky ones; this second day, forsooth, is combined with the bull, it is indra-like and of triṣṭubh-nature; this (day) he thereby addresses[2].

[1] SV. II. 156-157=ṚS. IX. 97. 13-14 (a var. reading in 13).

[2] See notes 1 and 2 on XI. 6. 3.

6. There is the gāyatra (-chant); the brāhmaṇa of the gāyatra is the same[1].

[1] Cp. VII. 1. 1 sqq.

7. There is the yauktāśva[1].

[1] Grām. XII. 2. 30 on SV. I. 469, the first of the two given by the gāna, see note 1 on § 8 (end).

8. Yuktāśva of the Angiras-clan exchanged two young ones immediately after their birth; from him the veda went forth; (in order to recover it) he underwent austerities and saw this yauktāśva (-sāman) (and lauded with it) To him the veda returned. That, forsooth, he had desired then (when he underwent austerities). The yauktāśva is a wish-granting chant. He (who applies it) obtains (the fulfilment of) his wish[1].

[1] This tale is apparently shortened and by consequence incomprehensible. It is made clearer by the Jaim. br. (III. 23, see das Jaim. br. in Auswahl. no. 171): 'Vasiṣṭha was the house-chaplain (the *purohita*) of Sudās Paijavana, the king of the Ikṣvākus (cp. Śāṅkh. śrs. XVI. 11. 14 and Ait. br. VIII. 21. 11). This Sudās Paijavana entrusted his mares to Vasiṣṭha just as they use to entrust (their possessions) to a purohita. Now, Vasiṣṭha, going out after booty (*sani*, cp. note 1 on XI. 5. 22), said to his younger brother Yuktāśva: 'Mayest thou be the surveyor of these (mares) that are to be kept by us'. Yuktāśva exchanged the young ones that were born of the king's mares (with those that belonged to himself): the beautiful ones he drove away for himself, the bad ones he drove amongst the king's mares. Thereupon they perceived that he had exchanged the young animals that had been born, and they drove him away, saying: 'Thou art a thief, thou art a non-seer'. He wished: 'May I obtain faith, may they invite me (again to the participation in the sacrifices).' He saw this chant and practised it in chanting. He undertook (*i.e.*, chanted) as finale (the words): '*o i jvarā*.' Thereupon he found faith and was invited.' The nidhana of the f i r s t yauktāśva in the recension of the Kauthumas (see SV. ed. Calcutta, vol. II, page 13) is equally
2 3 2
o i | jvara ū.

9. There are the two āyāsya (chants)[1].

[1] The *aiḍam* and the *triṇidhanam*: grām. XIV. 1. 25 and 28, both chanted on SV. I. 511=SV. II. 25-26.

10. Ayāsya of the Angiras-clan had eaten food of the Ādityas, who had been initiated (by the dīkṣā); he was (consequently) afflicted by sickness[1]; he undertook austerities and saw these two sāmans; by means of these he drove away the sickness. He who applies in chanting the two āyāsya (sāmans) drives away sickness.

[1] Read *taṁ śug ārchat.*—Apparently Ayāsya himself was not initiated, not a dīkṣita, cp. Āp. śrs. X. 15. 15: 'one should not wear the garment of one initiated neither mention his faults nor eat his food.' In the Jaim. br. (III. 187, 188) a different cause is given for the origin of these sāmans. Here the well-known tale is related of the Ādityas and the Angirases, who wish to reach before each other the world of heaven. The Angirases prepare a *svaḥsutyā* and send one of them: Agni, as their messenger to the Ādityas. Upon receiving the invitation from the Angirases to act as their officiating priests, the Ādityas invent an *adyasutyā*, a sadyaskrī sacrifice, and the Angirases are won over by them: Agni as their Hotṛ, Gaus as their Adhvaryu, Bṛhaspati as their Udgātṛ, and Ayāsya as their Brahman (cp. Kauṣ. br. XXX. 6). Having given as sacrificial fee to Ayāsya, their Brahman, the sum in the form of a white horse purveyed with a horse-bridle, they went to heaven, the Angirases being left behind. But Ayāsya having accepted a gift that either was equal to himself or better than himself, decayed (*so 'yāsyaḥ sadṛśav ātmanaḥ* [read probably *sadṛśaṃ vātmanaḥ*] *śreyāṃsaṃ vā pratigṛhya vyabhraṃśata*). He wished: 'May I be restored' (*sam ātmānaṃ śrīṇiya*) and saw this sāman; by means of it he rehabilitated himself.' Cp. also below, XIV. 3. 22.

11. From these worlds (once upon a time) the rain retired; by means of the two āyāsya(sāman)s Ayāsya caused it to fall. He who in chanting applies the two āyāsya (sāman)s causes the rain to fall.

12. It was the food, forsooth, that thereby retired from these worlds: by means of the two āyāsya (sāman)s Ayāsya caused it to fall[1]. He who in lauding applies the two āyāsya (sāman)s, causes food to fall.

[1] By the absence of rain the herbs did not grow, the falling of the rain caused the food to reappear.

13. There is the vāsiṣṭha (sāman)[1] (the chant of Vasiṣṭha).

[1] The *ihavad vāsiṣṭham (svāram)* is probably grām. XV. 2. 6 (on SV. I. 526, see SV. ed. Calcutta, vol. II, page 116).

14. Vasiṣṭha, the son of Viḍu, having lauded with this (sāman), straightway beheld the world of heaven; (so it is) for beholding the world of heaven. He who applies it in lauding falls not from the world of heaven.—The stoma (has been given)[1].

[1] Cp. XI. 6. 10, and XI. 11. 14.

XI. 9.

(The pṛṣṭha-lauds of the second day.)

1. (The verses beginning): 'For thee we hail'[1] are through (the word) 'thee'[2] the characteristic of the bṛhat, for this day is a bṛhat-day.

[1] SV. I. 234=ṚS. VI. 46. 1-2=SV. II. 159 160.

[2] Being the accusative, which is the feature of the second day (X. 7. 1).

2. 'Towards him, of good gifts'[1]: by means of the former (the first) day they yoke (*i.e.*, begin the sacrifice or the ten-day rite), by means of this (day) they go forward.

[1] SV. I. 235=ṚS. VIII. 49. 1-2=SV. II. 161-162.

3. 'Thee the men but yesterday'[1]: the present (day) and the (day of) yesterday they (thereby) undertake together, for preventing the two-day-period from slipping asunder.

[1] SV. I. 302=ṚS. VIII. 99. 1-2 (var. r.)=SV. II. 163-164.

4. There is the bṛhat[1]; the bṛhat, forsooth, is the summit, the second day is the summit; from the summit unto the summit they step[2].

[1] See note 3 on VII. 6. 11.

[2] Cp. the expression II. 1. 3.

5. There is the śyaita[1] (and thereby) a wedding of the two sāmans[2]: for the continuity of the sacrifice.

[1] See note 1 on VII. 10. 2.

[2] The śyaita of this day and the naudhasa of the preceding day, cp. VII. 10. 1-3.

6. There is the mādhucchandasa[1]; a sāman, being of Ṛṣi-descent[2], is fit for reaching the world of heaven. He who applies it in lauding, does not fall from the world of heaven.

[1] Grām. VIII. 1. 23 composed on SV. I. 302=SV. II. 163—164.

[2] Cp. XI. 5. 22. From the Jaim. br. (III. 27) we learn that this sāman was seen by Madhucchandas, the son of Viśvāmitra, who by means of it became the first, the principal, and possessed of priestly lustre.

7. It is of ascending *iḍā*[1], for so is the characteristic of this day.—The stoma (has been given)[2].

[1] See note 2 on X. 11. 1.

[2] Cp. XI. 6. 10, and XI. 11. 14.

XI. 10.

(The ārbhava-pavamāna-laud of the second day.)

1. 'The intoxication (*mada*) desirable for thee'[1] is the gāyatrī (-verse).

[1] SV. I. 470=ṚS. IX. 61. 19-21=SV. II. 165-167.

2. Intoxicating (*madavat*), rich in sap is the afternoon-service (or the third pressing); he (thereby) puts (in it) intoxication and sap[1].

[1] This § is found also in XI. 5. 1, XIV. 11. 1, XV. 11. 1.

3. 'Be clarified as the most sweet'[1]: for they are clarified, as it were, by this day; 'as the most sweet,' honey (*madhu*), forsooth, is food; he thereby puts food into the Sacrificer.

[1] SV. I. 578=RS. IX. 108. 1-2=SV. II. 42-43.

4. 'Unto Indra this soma'[1]: for retaining valour and strength.

[1] SV. I. 566=ṚS. IX. 106. 1-3=SV. II. 44-46 (var. r.).

5. (The verses beginning): 'This Pūṣan, Rayi, Bhaga'[1], being anuṣṭubhs, are, by their characteristic, triṣṭubhs[2], for this day is a triṣṭubh-day.

[1] SV. I. 546=ṚS. IX. 101. 7-9=SV. II. 168-170.

[2] Because of the word *rayi*, cp. X. 6. 2.

6. (The verses beginning): 'The conspicuous bull of the prayers is clarified,'[1] being jagatīs, are, by their characteristic, triṣṭubhs[2]; for this day is a triṣṭubh-day.

[1] SV. I. 559=ṚS. IX. 86. 19-21=SV. II. 171-173 (with var. read.).

[2] By the word *vṛṣan*, cp. X. 6. 2.

7. There is the gāyatra (chant); the brāhmaṇa of the gāyatra is the same[1].

[1] Cp. VII. 1. 1 sqq.

8. There is the hāviṣmata (-sāman) (the chant of Haviṣmat)[1].

[1] Grām. IV. 1. 19 (the second of the two composed on SV. I. 138).

9. Haviṣmat and Haviṣkṛt belonged to the Angiras-clan: on the second day Haviṣmat prospered, on the ninth Haviṣkṛt[1].

[1] By means of the two sāmans seen and applied by them on these days, cp. XV. 5, 17, see also TS. VII. 1. 4. 1; according to the Jaim. br. (III. 28) Haviṣmat and Haviṣkṛt were two Angirases who were left behind when the Angirases ascended to heaven. By these sāmans they reached likewise the world of heaven.

10. (By the words): 'This one is possessed of oblations' (*haviṣmat*)[1] he announces to the Gods that the day has been produced ('is at hand'), that the soma has been produced, and for his (the Sacrificer's) benefit he by means of the sāman invokes a blessing; for the sāman is a true blessing.

1 This apparently is an allusion to the last word (stobha) annected to the sāman : *haviṣmate*' 2345 (2 1 3 1111) (see SV. ed. Calcutta, Vol. I, page 328). By adding to the words of SV. I. 138 : 'This great help do we then choose of the Gods, of the mighty ones, for our benefit' the word *haviṣmate* : 'for him who is rich in oblations', a blessing is invoked for the Sacrificer. On the whole cp. Jaim br. III. 29 : 'These two sāmans are (respectively) the announcement and the declaration (*proktiś ca* . . *niruktiś ca*) of the oblations. In that the hāviṣmata (-sāman) is (applied) on the second day, they (*i.e.*, the participants of the sattra) announce (*prāhuḥ*) to the Gods that they are possessed of oblations; in that the hāviṣkṛta(-sāman) is applied on the ninth day, they declare (*nirāhuḥ*) that they have prepared (and offered) the oblations, for at this moment they h a v e prepared (and offered) the oblations.

11. There is the śaṅku[1] (the 'pin-chant'), for propping the day; that (part of the sacrifice) which is not propped, he props by means of the śaṅku ('the pin').

1 Grām. XVII. 2. 18 composed on SV. I. 581.

12. They call it (this sāman) also the sīdantīya ; by means of it Prajāpati went upright to these worlds[1]; because he went (*asīdat*), therefore, it is called sīdantīya. He who applies this (chant) in lauding goes upright to these worlds.

1 ? *ūrdhva imāṃllokān asīdat.* More comprehensible is the Jaim. br. III. 30 : 'The Gods wished : 'may we gain a seat (*sīdema*) in the world of heaven', etc.

13. There is the sujñāna (-sāman)[1].

1 Grām. XVII. 1. 26, composed on SV. I. 572 (see SV. ed. Calcutta, Vol. II, page 214); grām. XVII. 1. 27 is likewise sujñāna, but it must be a *nidhanavat sāma*.

14. A (sāman) containing (the word) *svar*[1] ('heaven') is the characteristic of the rathantara[2], a (sāman) with (the word) *svar* as finale is the characteristic of the bṛhat[3].

1 The sāman as given in the grāmegeyagāna contains no *svar*, but the verses on which it is chanted, have it (SV. II. 44 : *śruṣṭe jātāsa indavaḥ svarvidaḥ*). Moreover, the Sūtrakāra (Lāṭy. VII. 10. 1 sqq.) teaches that for *upā* (thus ends the sujñāna in the gāna) may be substituted other nidhanas, and he says this expressly about the sujñāna (l.c. 7.). For an analogous case cp. IX. 6. 1, XII. 9. 19.

2 Which contains the word *svardṛśam* (SV. I. 233, II. 30).

3 Because the bṛhat is the sky, the heaven.

15. It has the word *svar* as finale, for so is the characteristic of this day [1].

[1] Which is *bahirnidhanam*, see X. 10, 1.

16. In (chanting) these two (sāmans) (śaṅku and sujñāna) they push near two boats, for reaching the world of heaven [1].

[1] The twelve-day rite is again compared to a voyage over the water.—About the origin of the sujñāna the Jaim. br. (III. 31, see Auswahl No. 172) has the following interesting tale: 'The Asuras sought to slay the Gods, ever changing themselves, by entering among the Gods in that appearance which belonged to the Gods (by disguising themselves as Gods). Those of the Gods, who kept studying in the forest, they sought to slay by assuming the form of the Gods who were in the village, and those (of the Gods) who were in the village, they sought to slay by assuming the form of those (of the Gods), who kept themselves studying the veda in the forest. In this manner continually changing themselves, they sought to slay them. The Gods perceived this. They said (among themselves): 'Let us think out a question to be answered' (a kind of password). They thought out a question to be answered: 'When anybody comes near and we ask him: 'Unto whom dost thou come?' he (the person asked) must answer; 'Unto Indra do I come' (cp. the opening words of the veda-verse, on which the sujñāna is chanted, XI. 10. 4). So, whenever anybody came near and they asked him: 'Unto whom dost thou come?' he (*viz.*, that of the Gods to whom the question was addressed) answered: 'Unto Indra do I come', and then they said: 'Thou art well recognised (*sujñāna*) .. but whosoever, being asked, did not respond, him they slew'.

17. There is the gaurīvita. The brāhmaṇa of the gaurīvita is the same [1].

[1] Cp. XI. 5. 13 sqq.

18. There is the krauñca (-sāman) [1].

[1] Grām. XVI. 1. 15 (13 and 14 also are krauñca, but the last of the three is required as it must be *aiḍam*) composed on SV. I. 546.

19. The krauñca is the voice, the twelve-day rite is the voice; so they chant the voice (the krauñca) in the voice (the twelve-day rite), for the prevalence of the sacrifice [1].

[1] About the krauñca, we read in the Jaim. br. (III. 32, Auswahl No. 173): 'Kruñc of the Angiras-clan obtained a day that was *iṣya*, as it were (the word must have the same meaning as *eṣya* of our Brāhmaṇa XIII. 9. 11, XIII. 11. 20); *iṣya*, as it were, is this second day; therefore, the krauñca is applied on the second day. There was (then) only one single day. This Kruñc of the Angiras-clan desired: 'May I form a (second) day out of the (now only existent) day. He saw this sāman and practised it in lauding. Thereupon, he formed a (second) day out of the (single) day...It is this day, forsooth, that the

Angiras Kruñc by drinking discriminates. As to the usual saying: 'the Kruñc (or curlew) discriminates the milk, in drinking', it is not the curlew that discriminates (the milk from the water), but it is the Angiras Kruñc who in drinking discriminates the (second) day from the (only existent) day'. Cp. Vāj. Saṃh. XIX. 73: *adbhyaḥ kṣīraṃ vyapibat kruṅṅ āṅgiraso dhiyā.*

20. There is the yāma (sāman) (the chant of Yama) [1].

[1] Grām. XVI. 2. 18 composed on SV. I. 557; there are many yāmasāmans, but this one is, as it must be, *svāra* (ed. Calc. Vol. II, page, 181).

21. By means of this (sāman), Yama obtained the unassailable sovereignty over yonder world. He who in lauding uses the chant of Yama, obtains the unassailable sovereignty over yonder world.

22. By means of this (sāman) Yamī brought Yama to the world of heaven [1]; (so it is) for beholding the world of heaven. He who in lauding applies (it), does not fall from the world of heaven.—The stoma (has been given) [2].

[1] The myth of Yama who died first and left his mourning sister and wife behind, is well known, see *e.g.*, Maitr. Saṃh. I. 5. 12: 81. 2.

[2] See note 3 on XI. 7. 8.

XI. 11.

(The uktha-lauds of the second day.)

1. (The verses beginning:) 'Come hither, I will gladly sing to thee' [1] contain (the words) 'come hither': for calling near the third day, and for the sake of connection.

[1] SV. I. 7=ṚS. VI. 16. 16–18=SV. II. 55–57.

2. That part of the sacrifice, which consists of the uktha(laud)s, is a cutting, as it were [1]; that it contains (the word) 'hither' [2], is for the sake of congruence.

[1] It is a separate piece in so far as it follows on the agniṣṭoma-sāman, which ends the normal jyotiṣṭoma.

[2] The preposition *ā* in *ehi*, first word of SV. I. 7.

3. (The verses beginning:) 'For thus art thou a hero' [1] are (verses) saying the same [2]: 'let it thus be here'.

[1] SV. I. 232=ṚS. VIII. 92. 28–30=SV. II. 174–176.

[2] By the word *evā* ('thus'), which occurs in several of the verse-quarters.

4. (The verses): 'All (songs) have caused Indra to grow[1]', for they[2] throve at that time; by means of this (verse) they make the Sacrificer thrive.

[1] SV. I. 343=ṚS. I. 11. 1-3=SV. II. 177-179.

[2] The Gods, according to Sāyaṇa; cp. XII. 12. 2. For this expression the Jaim. br. has only: *vṛddhaṃ hy etad ahar yad bārhatam.*

5. There is the sākamaśva (sāman)[1]: in order to conquer the ukthas, in order to stride on them.

[1] See note 2 on VIII. 8. 4 (chanted here on the same verses).

6. For by means of this (sāman) they, at the beginning, conquered the ukthas and strode on them[1].

[1] As set forth in VIII. 8. 1-5.

7. There is the āmahīyava(-sāman); a success (or 'arranging' ?) and food are brought about in (verses) which say the same[1]: 'let it thus be here'[2].

[1] Gram. VI. 1. 25 composed on SV. I. 232, chanted on SV. II. 174-176. This āmahīyava must be taken here because it must be *nidhanavat.*

[2] Cp. § 3. The purport is not quite clear.

8. This day verily expresses the nobility[1]; in that it is a fifteen-fold (stoma) and the Brahman's chant[2] is performed on gāyatrī (-verses)[3], he brings in union the priesthood and the nobility: he places the priesthood before the nobility and makes nobility and peasantry following after (and dependent on) the priesthood.

[1] As being pañcadaśa, cp. VI. 1. 8.

[2] The āmahīyava on the gāyatrīs SV. II. 174-176.

[3] The pañcadaśa stoma is connected with nobility, the gāyatrī with priesthood (VI. 1. 6), both are here taken together and thus a union of both is caused.

9. The former (the first) day is the priesthood [1], the second day is the nobility[2]; in that the Brahman's chant[3] is performed on gāyatrī (-verses)[3], he causes the priesthood to flourish by fame, for the gāyatrī is the priesthood.

[1] Because it is a gāyatrī-day and a trivṛt-day, cp. VI. 1. 6, 8.

[2] Because it is a triṣṭubh-day and a pañcadaśa-day, l.c.

[3] See note 2 on § 8.

10. Therefore it (*viz.*, the Brahman's chant) is performed on (verses) that say the same [1], for the cause of flourishing.

[1] Cp. note 2 on § 3.

11. There are the two āṣṭādaṃṣṭra (-sāmans) [1].

[1] Grām. IX. 1. 20 and 21 composed on SV. I. 343; both sāmans being *aiḍa*, it is not apparent from the Brāhmaṇa, which of the two is intended; according to the later sources it is the first; cp. below, XII. 9. 13.

12. By means of (the stobha): *aiyāhai* [1] Indra slew Vṛtra, by means of: *aiyādau hovā* [2] he brought him down; these two sāmans are victorious (and) powerful.

[1] The stobha of the first āṣṭādaṃṣṭra: *aiyāhā i.* (4 5)

[2] The stobha of the second: *aiyādau-ho' 6 vā.* (5r 4r 4r 5 5)

13. Vigour and strength he gains by means of these two (sāmans).

14. Fifteen fold (fifteen-versed) is the stoma; in vigour (and) strength he thereby is firmly established. The fifteen fold (stoma) is vigour (and) strength [1].

[1] Cp. XI. 6. 10. 11.

TWELFTH CHAPTER.

(Pṛṣṭhya six-day period of the twelve-day-rite.)

(Third day.)

XII. 1.

(Out-of-doors-laud of the third day.)

1. (The verses beginning:) 'By 'fiercely brilliant lustre' [1] are the opening (tristichs) of the third day.

[1] Cp. note 1 on VI. 9. 24.

2. The gāyatrī is 'fiercely brilliant', the triṣṭubh is 'loudly sounding', the jagatī is 'mixed with milk' [1]. (In taking this tristich as opening one), he lays hold of the three characteristics [2]: in order that the three-day period may not slip off.

[1] *davidyutatyā rucā pariṣṭobhantyā kṛpā / somāḥ śukrā gavāśiraḥ*, cp. notes 1–3 on VI. 9. 25. The jagatī is 'mixed with milk' because the tṛtīyasavana, which is jāgata, contains the offering of the *āśir*. A different explanation is given on VI. 9. 25.

[2] The first day is gāyatra, the second traiṣṭubha, the third jāgata.

3. (The tristich beginning:) 'These soma-drops have been effused'[1] is the corresponding one (the antistrophe).

[1] Cp. note 1 on VI. 9. 13.

4. By (the word) 'these' Prajāpati created the Gods; by 'have been effused', the men; by 'soma-drops' the Fathers[1]. To this he thereby refers[2].

[1] So far this § is identical with VI. 9. 15.

[2] ? *tad eva tad abhivadati.*

5. And, moreover, after the former characteristic he speaks the latter characteristic. That he speaks after the former characteristic the latter characteristic is the reason why the corresponding tristich is called *anurūpa*. A son resembling himself gets he who knows this[1].

[1] This § is identical with XI 6. 4–5.

6. The stotriya and the anurūpa are tristichs. for retaining the breathings.

[1] Cp. XI. 6. 6.

7, 8. The tristich (beginning:) 'The king with prayers is besought, being clarified, in man, to go through the intermediate region'[1] has the intermediate region as its deity; the third day has the intermediate region as its deity[2]; to this he thereby refers.

[1] SV. II. 183, 184, 185=ṚS. IX. 64. 16, 18, 17.

[2] This statement is a consequence of the fact that the first, or rathantara-day, is identified with earth, the second or bṛhat-day, with heaven.

9. There is a pentastich; the pankti(-verse) has five verse-quarters, the food is five fold[2]: for retaining food.

[1] SV. II. 186, 187, 188, 189, 190=ṚS. IX. 48. 1, 2, 3, 5, 4.

[2] *aśyam, peyam, khādyam, lehyam, coṣyam*, Sāyaṇa on XII. 4. 6.

10. A tristich is the last[1]; with which breath they start, in that they break up (finish the laud)[2].

[1] SV. II. 191–193=ṚS. IX. 64. 13–15.

[2] Identical with XI. 6.8, 9.

11. Seventeen fold (or 'seventeen-versed') is the stoma, for gaining a firm support, for procreating[1].

[1] Because Prajāpati is *saptadaśa*.

XII. 2.

(The ājya-lauds of the third day.)

1. (The tristich beginning:) 'Agni is kindled by Agni'[1], is the ājya-(laud) addressed to Agni[2].

[1] SV. II. 194, 195, 196=ṚS. 12. 6, 8, 9.

[2] The first or *hotur ājyam*.

2. In view of the two former days which are kindled, he thereby kindles the third day[1].

[1] Which, at least, has the instrumental *agninā* for its characteristic, cp. X. 7. 1.

3. (The tristich beginning:) 'Mitra of holy might I call for'[1] is the rathantara-like (ājya-laud)[2] addressed to Mitra and Varuṇa[3].

[1] SV. II. 197–199=ṚS. I. 2. 7–9.

[2] This is explained in the next §.

[3] The second ājya running parallel to the śastra of the Maitrāvaruna.

4. 'I call for thee' is the characteristic of the rathantara[1].

[1] Because the verses on which the rathantara is chanted (SV. II. 30, 31) contain the words: 'rich in cows we call for thee'.

5. The vairūpa is cryptically (equal to) the rathantara[1]. He thereby displays the characteristic of the rathantara.

[1] This remark is made, because, the ājyalauds being rathantara-like, we expect also the rathantarasāman as first pṛṣṭhastotra, whilst on this day the vairūpa is used, not the rathantara. The vairūpa can be identified in a sense with the rathantara, as it is its *garbha*, cp. Ait. br. IV. 28. 1.

6. (The tristich beginning:) 'For together with Indra thou art seen[1]' is (the ajya-laud) addressed to Indra.

[1] SV. II. 200, 201, 202=ṚS. I. 6. 7, 4, 5; with this agrees Āśv. VII 2. 3, but according to Śāṅkh. (XII. 1. 4) ṚS. I. 6, 7, 8, 9 are used. May we infer from this that the uttarārcika was known to Āśvalāyana, but not to Śāṅkhāyana?

7. Together, as it were, (once upon a time) these worlds were seen[1]; the third day has the intermediate region as its deity[2]; to this he thereby alludes.

[1] Cp. VII. 10. 1.

[2] Cp. note 2 on XII. 1. 8; in chanting on *saṃ..dṛkṣase* he (the chanter) makes implicit mention also of the antarikṣa.

8. (The tristichs beginning:) 'These two I call for, whose[1]', is the rathantara-like (ājya-laud) addressed to Indra and Agni.

[1] SV. II. 203-205=ṚS. VI. 60. 4-6.

9. 'I call for' is the characteristic of the rathantara[1]; the vairūpa is cryptically the rathantara; he thereby displays the characteristic of the rathantara[2].—The stoma (is given)[2].

[1] This is identical with §§ 4 and 5.

[2] Cp. XII. 1. 11.

XII. 3.

(The midday-pavamāna-laud of the third day.)

1. 'On high (*uccā*) born of thy plant'[1] (*andhas*) is the gāyatrī.

[1] SV. I. 467=ṚS. IX. 61. 10, 12, 11=SV. II. 22-24.

2. An ascent ('containing the word 'up', *ut*), forsooth, is the third day[1], this he thereby expresses.

[1] As it follows, higher up, after the first two days, and cp. X. 6. 3.

3. It (the verse) contains (the word) 'plant'. the plant, forsooth, is the day[1]: it is the laying hold of the day.

[1] Because this day is upward, and the plants grow upward ?

4. (The verses beginning:) 'The living somas, unto' (*abhi*)[1].

[1] SV. I. 518=ṚS. IX. 107, 14-16 (var. read.)=SV. II. 206-208.

5. 'Unto' is the characteristic of the rathantara[1], 'great'[2] of the bṛhat; he undertakes ('applies') the characteristic of both (rathantara and bṛhat) together, for this (third) day is (equal) to both these aspects (*varṇa*).

[1] Which begins *abhi tvā śūra*.

[2] In the words of SV. II. 207: *rājā deva ṛtaṃ bṛhat*.

6. 'Three words are uttered by the running one[1]' is the characteristic of the third day[2]; thereby he lays hold on the third day.

[1] SV. I. 525=ṚS. IX. 97. 34-36=SV. II. 209-211.

[2] Because of the word 'three', cp. X. 6. 3.

7. Being triṣṭubhs they (these verses) are jagatīs by their characteristic[1]; for this day is a jagatī-day.

[1] Solely by the word 'three', which belongs to the third day, which is *jāgata*.

8. There is the gāyatra (-chant); the brāhmaṇa of the gāyatra is the same[1].

[1] Cp. VII. 1. 1 sqq.

9. There is the vaiṣṭambha (-sāman)[1].

[1] Grām. XIII. 1. 11, composed on SV. I. 471, called also *kṣullakavaiṣṭambham*.

10. This day (once upon a time) collapsed; by means of the vaiṣṭambhas[1] the Gods fixed (its) different (parts) (*vi-stambh*); that is the cause, why they are called the vaiṣṭambhas.

[1] The plural is strange; there are either two or one vaiṣṭambha. The Jaim. br. speaks of them in the dual.

11. They undertake (apply) as finale the word 'quarters'[1], for propping the quarters.

[1] The nidhana of this sāman is: *di'234 śāḥ* (with 3 and 5 above); cp. X. 6. 3.

12. There is the paurumadga (-sāman)[1].

[1] Grām. I. 2. 32 composed on SV. I. 39.

13. When this day collapsed[1], it was pursued by the ogres; the Gods, by means of the paurumadga[2], repelled the ogres from it. He who in lauding uses the paurumadga, repels his evil lot.

[1] Cp. § 10.

[2] In the Jaim. br. (III 43) the sāman is seen by Purumudga an Angiras, who wished for cattle. The name of the sāman there is paurumudga.

14. The Gods and the Asuras were contending The Gods by means of the paurumadga destroyed their boroughs. Because they destroyed (or 'made sink') their boroughs (*puro' majjayan*)[1], therefore it is called paurumadga. His hurtful rival he destroys by (lauding with) this (sāman).

[1] In the Jaim. br. the derivation of the name rests on the pun: *tad yat (devā asurān) pūrve (samudre)'majjayaṃs, tad v eva paurumudgasya paurumudgatvam.*

15. There is the gautama (-sāman).

[1] Grām II. 1. 1; there are several gautamasāmans, but see § 17.

16. The brāhmaṇa of the gautama (-sāman) is the same[1].

[1] See XI. 5. 22, 23.

17. It is the one which has a stobha on both sides[1], for so is the characteristic of this day[2].

[1] The first verse-quarter is enclosed by the stobha *hā u*, see SV., ed. Calcutta, Vol. I, page 162.

[2] See X. 9. 1, note 3.

18. There is the antarikṣa (-sāman)[1].

[1] Araṇyegeyagāna I. 1. 9, composed on SV. I. 239.

19. The third day has the intermediate region for its deity[1]; in the intermediate region (=on the third day) they laud with the 'intermediate region' (the antarikṣasāman), in order to get a firm footing[2].

[1] Cp. note 2 on XII. 1. 7, 8.

[2] Because of the verses on which it is chanted (SV. II. 206–208), the last of which is a virāj of two verse-quarters. On the antarikṣa cp. Jaim. br. III. 45 : *tasyobhayataḥ padaṃ pariṣṭobhayanty antarikṣasya rūpam: ubhayata iva hīdam antarikṣaṃ pariṣṭubdham ābhyāṃ lokābhyām.*

20. There is the kāṇva (-sāman) with (the syllable) *āṣ* as finale[1].

[1] Grām. VII. 1. 28 composed on SV. I. 261; finale : $\overset{3}{\text{ā}},\overset{1}{2}\overset{1}{3}\overset{1}{4}5\text{s}$.

21. (The syllable) *as* is the characteristic of the rathantara[1], *has* of the bṛhat[1]; they thereby (*i.e.*, in chanting *āṣ* as nidhana) undertake ('apply') a third characteristic: for the sake of flourishing.

[1] Cp. VII. 6. 11.

[2] The syllable āṣ has three moras and the number three is the *rūpa* of the third day, see X. 6.3.

22. There is the (chant called) 'the united yell of the Angirases' (angirasām saṃkrośa)[1].

[1] Grām. XV. 2. 3; there are on SV. I. 525 three saṃkrośas, but only the third is *svāram*, see SV. ed. Calcutta, Vol. II, page 113 as compared with Vol. III, page 430.

23. By means of this (sāman), all yelling together[1], the Angirases went to the world of heaven: it is for beholding the world of heaven; he who in lauding uses it, falls not from the world of heaven.—The stoma (is given)[2].

[1] Some of them calling loudly the stobha of one of the saṃkrośasāmans, others answering them with the stobha of the other, according to the Jaim. br. III. 47: *hūtiś ca ha khalu vā ete sāmanī pratiśrutiś ca ho ye ho vā hā ho ity evānenāṅgiraso 'hvayan hā vā o vā ity etena pratyaśṛṇvan.*

[2] See XII. 1. 11.

XII. 4.

(The pṛṣṭha-lauds of the third day.)

1. (The verses beginning:) 'If thou hadst, o Indra, a hundred heavens[1]' contain (the word) 'hundred'.

[1] SV. I. 278=ṚS. VIII. 20. 5-6=SV. II. 212-213. The plural is used, although we have to do with a pragātha, because, in chanting, the two verses are made three.

2. Possessed of hundred and thousand is the characteristic of cattle[1]; the characteristic of cattle he retains through these (verses).

[1] *i.e.*, strongly multiplying themselves.

3. (The verses beginning:) 'We with the soma thee[1]' are satobṛhatī (verses)[2]; (in chanting on these) he steps on to a larger metre[3]: in order not to fall down[4].

[1] SV. I. 261=ṚS. VIII. 33. 1-3=SV. II. 214-216.

[2] How these bṛhatī-verses can be designated as satobṛhatīs is not clear to me: the same difficulty in XII. 4. 22, XIII. 10. 1, XVII. 1. 11. See Nidānasūtra I, 2 (end): *bārhatam api tṛcaṃ satobṛhatya ity evācakṣate yathā vayaṃ gha tvā sutāvanta iti* (this is precisely the verse of this passage). On the Nidāna-passage cp. Weber in Indische Studien, Vol. VIII, pages 45, 46.

[3] From the bṛhatī of 36 syllables unto the satobṛhatī of 40 syllables.

[4] By getting a larger base.

4. (There are the verses beginning:) 'The swift one wishes to gain victory with Purandhi as his joiner; by a song of praise I bring unto you (*ā vaḥ* .·. *name*) the much summoned Indra'[1]; the word 'helping' (is) contained (in them)[2]; raised up, as it were[3], is the third day; in that there is this word 'helping', he thereby firmly establishes this day.

[1] SV. I. 238=ṚS. VII. 32. 20-21=SV. II. 217-218.

[2] As if *ā* (the preposition) and *vaḥ* (the enclitic of *tvam*) were equivalent to *āvad*, a participle of *āvati*!

[3] The *rūpa* of the third day is 'up' (*ud*), cp. X. 6. 3.

5. The vairūpa (-sāman) of five finales[1] is the pṛṣṭha (laud)[2]: for propping the quarters[3].

[1] Araṇyegeyagāna I. 1. 3, composed on SV. I. 278, see SV. ed. Calcutta, Vol. II, page 388; the five finales are: *diśaṃ*, *viśaṃ*, *has*, *aśvā śiśumatī*, *iḍā*.

[2] The first or hotuḥ pṛṣṭhastotra.

[3] The four quarters and the zenith (five nidhanas!). Where these midhanas in chanting are to be produced, is taught by the sūtrakāra (Lāṭy. VII. 5. 15–17), and cp. Nidānasūtra III, 11 middle.

6. The paṅkti has five verse-quarters[1]; food is five fold: for retaining food.

[1] The connection with the preceding sentence is perhaps this, that the four-footed bṛhatī and satobṛhatī of SV. II. 212, 213 are transformed into paṅktis, by adding the nidhanas *aśvā śiśumatī*, etc.

[2] Cp. note 2 on XII. 1. 9.

7. The vairūpa is the quarters' chant, for by it he refers to the quarters[1].

[1] By the nidhana *diśam*, see note 1 on § 5.

8. Further, in that it is of five finales, thereby (it belongs) to the seasons, for five in number are the seasons.

9. By the seasons and the quarters, verily, these worlds are enveloped[1]; in both of them he firmly establishes the Sacrificer; after the firm establishment (in them) of the Sacrificer, the Udgātṛ, who, knowing this, uses in lauding the vairūpa, is firmly established (in them).

[1] Strictly speaking, only by the quarters.

10. It has (the word) 'quarter', for repelling the rival[1].

[1] Whom he thereby excludes from the quarters, so that he must die.

11. As finale they undertake ('apply'): 'the quarter, the peasantry[1]': for propping the quarters.

[1] The nidhana *disaṃ viśam*.

12. After the (finale indicating the) quarters they undertake ('apply') the finale *has*; thereby it (the chant) is bṛhat-like[1].

[1] For the nidhana of the bṛhat see VII. 6. 11.

13. This world (the earth) is rathantara-like, yonder world (the sky) is bṛhat-like; by means of the characteristic of rathantara and bṛhat[1]. he gains[2] both the worlds.

[1] In § 12 has been said only that the vairūpa by its finale *has* is bṛhat like but we must keep in mind that the nidhana of rathantara and bṛhat is reported to have once been the same (VII. 6. 11) and, moreover, the vairūpa is sprung from the rathantara.

[2] *aparādhnoti* is used here with a meaning opposed to the ordinary one.

14. Rathantara and bṛhat are the bullocks that convey the Sacrificer to the Gods; these he yokes now[1]: in order to reach the world of heaven

[1] Through the vairūpa, the nidhana of which is equal to that of rathantara and bṛhat.

15. There is the (finale) containing (the word) 'horse'[1]: for the sake of procreation.

[1] The nidhana *aśvā śiśumatī*: 'the mare w i t h i t s f o a l.

16. As a frog makes *āṭ* ('croakes')[1], so they undertake ('produce') the finale: for the sake of unimpaired vigour.

[1] Perhaps this means (cp. 'for the sake of unimpaired vigour') 'with equal strength, with unexhausted strength of tone'. About this passage the Nidānasūtra (III 11) remarks: *atha vairūpe vadati: yathā maṇḍūka āṭ karoty evaṃ nidhanam upayantīti; kasyedam brāhmanaṁ syād iti? kṛtā rāthantarīḍākṛtā bārhatīti kautsas, tad idam akṛtakāraṃ brāhmanam ardheḍābrāhmaṇaṁ syād iti; pañcameḍeyaṃ pratyāhṛtā bhavatīti gautamas, tāṃ parokṣīkṛtyābhivyūhareyur, evaṃ pañcame 'hany ayātayāmā bhavatīti; tad apy evaṃ brāhmaṇaṃ bhavaty: ayātayāmatāyā iti; tatra kaḥ parokṣībhāva ity: ākāraṭakārau vā kuryur ikāraṇakārau vaivam ekavarṇavikāra, ikāraṃ tv evāyikārīkuryur, etasmin parokṣībhāva upalabhyata iti.* The corresponding passage of the Jaim. br. (III 49) runs: *sa yathā maṇḍūka iṭ kuryād evam arteṭ kuryat, tena pañcamam ahar ayātayāma kriyate.*

17. There are twelve characteristics (in the vairūpa)[1]; the year consists of twelve months; in the year he (by these) is firmly established.

[1] I read: *dvādaśa vai rūpāṇi* but it is difficult to explain which parts of the sāman our author has in mind. If we read *dvādaśa vairūpāni bhavanti*, the sense is: 'there are twelve vairūpasāmans.' To this interpretation seems to point the Nidānasūtra (III. 11): *atha khalv āha: dvādaśa vairūpāṇi bhavantīti; kasyedaṃ brāhmaṇaṁ syād iti? saṃvatsarabrāhmaṇam ity āhuḥ: saṃvatsare dvādaśa kṛtvo hotṛsāma bhavati.* The Anupadasūtra, on the other side, seems to favour my explanation, but the text is too corrupt for citation.

18. Multiform is the year[1], multiform is food[2]; (so it serves) for retaining food.

1 By its twelve months, its twenty-four half-months, its five (or six) seasons.

2 As consisting of rice, barley, etc.

19. The great vaiṣṭambha (-sāman[1]) is the Brahman's chant[2]: for retaining food[3].

1 Grām. VII. 1. 31, composed on SV. I. 261.

2 Or third pṛṣṭha-laud.

3 See the next §.

20. When a person eats food, then he is internally supported (*viṣṭabdha*).

21. The (word) 'quarters' they undertake ('apply') as finale[1]: for propping the quarters.

1 The nidhana (see SV. ed. Calcutta, vol. I. page 542) is: *dā̆ 234 śāḥ*.

22. They chant (it) on satobṛhatī (-verses)[1], for counterpoising the two preceding days[2].

1 Cp. note 2 on XII. 4. 3.

2 On the first two days the Brahman's sāman is chanted on bṛhatī-verses, here on quasi-satobṛhatīs; here, then, it is chanted on (seemingly) larger verses.

23. The raurava (-sāman)[1] is the Acchāvāka's chant[2].

1 Grām. XIV. 1. 35 composed on SV. I. 511, chanted on SV. II. 217, 218 (*aiḍam*) (See SV. ed. Calcutta, Vol. II, page 76).

2 Or the fourth pṛṣṭha-laud.

24. Agni, forsooth, is burning (*rūra*)[1], Agni is Rudra.

1 Cp. VII. 5. 10.

2 Cp. TS. VI. 3. 5. 1: *rudro vā eṣa yad agniḥ* and ṚS. III. 2.5.

25. It is Agni who (as Rudra ?) causes the cattle to go forth from him, from whom it goes forth, it is Agni who causes the cattle to approach him, whom it approaches.

26. Constantly the cattle approaches him, who, knowing this, lauds with the raurava (-sāman)[1].

1 Because this chant is the cattle, VII. 5. 8.

27. It has an *iḍā* preceded and followed by a stobha[1]; for such is the characteristic of the third day[1].—The stoma (is given)[2].

1 See note 3 on X. 11. 1.

2 Cp. XII. 1. 11.

XII 5.

(The ārbhavapavamāna-laud of the third day.)

1. (The verses beginning:) 'Three voices go up[1]' (contain) the characteristic of the third day[2]; thereby they lay hold on the third day.

[1] SV. I. 471=ṚS. IX. 33. 4-6=SV. II. 219-221.

[2] See X. 6. 3 (by the words *ut* and *tri*).

2. Containing the words 'up' and 'three' is the third day; this (day) he thereby addresses.

3. (The verses beginning:) 'Press ye (the soma), sprinkle ye around'[1] contain the word 'around' (*pari*).

[1] SV. I, 580=ṚS. IX. 168. 7-8=SV. II. 744-745.

4. The third day is the end[1]; these (verses) (serve) to close (*paryāpti*) it.

[1] Of the three-day period, when in itself constitutes a whole.

5. (There are the verses beginning): 'Ye friends, be ye seated down'[1]; raised up, as it were, is the third day[2]: by saying: 'be ye seated down' he firmly establishes the day[3].

[1] SV. I. 568=ṚS. IX. 104. 1-3=SV. II. 507-509.

[2] Cp. note 3 on XII. 4. 4.

[3] It is remarkable that the uttarārcika gives these verses (507-509) later on and not in this context, whereas the Jaiminīyas have them, but only the first of each pragātha, in their right place, see Jaim. Saṃh. III. 20. 5-6, page 67 of the edition. This inaccuracy of the diascouast's is perhaps due to the fact, that here, on the third day, only the first verses of each pragātha are used for the sāmans (kakubh and uṣṇih).

6. (The verses beginning:) 'The pressed out, most sweet'[1], being anuṣṭubhs, are, by their characteristic, jagatīs[2], for this day is a jagatī-day.

[1] SV. I. 547=ṚS. IX. 101. 4-6=SV. II. 222-224.

[2] Because, according to Sāyaṇa, the words 'most sweet' point to the evening service, which also is *jāgata* and also 'most sweet' by the pouring out of the *āśir*.

7. (Then there are the verses beginning:) 'The strainer is stretched out for thee, o Lord of sacred lore'[1].

[1] SV. I. 565=ṚS. IX. 83. 1-3=SV. II. 225-227 (var. read.).

8. Stretched out, as it were, is this intermediate region, between these two[1]; the third day has the intermediate region as deity[2]; this he thereby addresses.

[1] Between heaven and earth.

[2] Cp. note 2 on XII. 1. 8.

9. There is the gāyatra (-sāman). The brāhmaṇa of the gāyatra is the same[1].

[1] VII. 1. 1 sqq.

10. There is the pāṣṭhauha (-sāman)[1].

[1] Grām. XIII. 1. 12, composed on SV. I. 471; for the identification cp. § 11.

11. Paṣṭhavāh of the clan of the Angirases heard the voice of the fourth day[1] speaking this (sāman)[2]. He undertook ('applied') the finale: 'hey, Voice'! and so this day had been expressed by him.

[1] The nidhana of this sāman (see SV. ed. Calcutta, Vol. II, page 18) is $\overset{2r}{\textit{hā}}$ $\overset{1}{\textit{o}}$ $\overset{2}{\textit{vā}}$ | $\overset{1}{\textit{o}}$ $\overset{3}{\textit{vā}}$ $\overset{1111}{\textit{2345}}$; as usual, the melodic interjection *vā* is identified with *vāk* ('Voice,' 'Word'). By this nidhana (*ho vāk!*) the fourth day (the second trirātra) comes to be mystically connected with the third day (cp. note 1 on X. 5. 10).

[2] The instrumental *etena* in the words *etena....caturthasyāhno vācaṃ vadantīm upāśṛṇot* belongs to *vadantīm*, the construction is analogous to that of *stu*.

12. There is 'the chant of the Voice' (*vācas sāma*)[1].

[1] Grām. XVII. 2. 15 composed on SV. I. 580; probably here a *svāraṃ sāma* is required.

13. The twelve-day rite is the voice[1]: in the voice (or 'during the twelve-day rite') they laud with the voice (the vācassāman): for the prevalence of the sacrifice.

[1] Cp. XI. 10. 19.

14. The Niṣkirīyas[1] (once upon a time) performed a sacrificial session; they did not know the (practice of the) third day; chanting this melody[2], the Voice came drifting near to them; through it (*i.e.*, this sāman) they learned the (practice of the) third day. They said: 'She forsooth, has caused us to behold the third day'. This (melody) is a (means of) beholding the third day.

[1] In the Jaim. br. (III. 52) they are called *niṣkaryadevāḥ*, read: *niṣkaryāḥ*; II. 357 occur the *niṣkaraṇiyāḥ*. As Sāyaṇa derives the name *niṣkiriya* from *niṣkara*, the name is probably *niṣkarīya*.

[2] *tān etat sāma gāyamānā vāg upāplavata*, Sāyaṇa interprets *gāyamānān*, but *gāyamānā* only is right, cp. also Jaim. br. III. 52: *tān vâk sāma gāyamānopāplavata.*

15. There is the śaukta (-sāman)[1].

[1] Grām. XVII. 1. 15, composed on SV. I. 568 (there are five śauktasāmans, but here, as it seems, a *nidhanavat sāma* is required).

16. Śukti of the Angiras clan by means of this (sāman) beheld straightway the world of heaven; (so it serves) for beholding the world of heaven. He who lauds (with it) falls not from the world of heaven.

17. There is the gaurīvita (-sāman)[1]; the brāhmaṇa of the gaurīvita is the same[2].

[1] Grām. V. 1. 22, composed on SV. I. 168 (*svāram*), chanted on SV. II. 222–224.

[2] Cp. XI. 5. 14–20.

18. There is the melody of Tvaṣṭṛ's daughters (tvāṣṭrīsāman)[1].

[1] Grām. XVI. 1. 16, composed on SV. I. 547, see SV. ed. Calcutta vol. II, page 155; there are two sāmans of this name, but the *madhyenidhanaṃ sāma* is required; according to the Ārṣeyakalpa the *triṇidhanam*.

19. When Indra was suffering from a disease of the eyes, the (other) beings could not cause him to sleep, (but) the daughters of Tvaṣṭṛ by means of this melody brought sleep to him, for such had been their wish at that moment.

20. Wish granting is the tvāṣṭrīsāman; he (who applies it) gets (the fulfilment of) his wish.

21. Indra, being afraid of Vṛtra, entered a cow[1]. About him the daughters of Tvaṣṭṛ said: 'Let us produce (him)'. By means of these melodies[2] they produced him[3]. They perform the sacrificial session (wishing): 'Let us be (re)produced.' They a r e (re)produced.

[1] It is a well-known trait of the Indra-myth that after the slaying of Vṛtra the God hides himself, *e.g.*, in the water, see, for instance, TS. II. 5. 3. 6, Śat. br. VII. 4. 1. 13. For the rest, Indra is known to delight in songs: Śat. br. III. 6. 1. 24.

[2] The plural because the chant of one of the many sāmans of this name is optional (?).

[3] The Jaim. br., not containing the legend of Tvaṣṭṛ's daughters, has at III 19 a legend similar to the one given above in § 21: 'Indra, having hurled his thunderbolt on Vṛtra, entered the cows, thinking: 'I have missed him'; these wished: 'may we give birth to Indra'; they saw these tvāṣṭrī-sāmans' (*etāni sāmāni*). Furtheron the tvāṣṭrīs are designated as the cattle: *paśavo vai tvāṣṭryaḥ.*

22. There is the ariṣṭa (-sāman)[1].

[1] Araṇyegeyagāna I. 1. 11, composed on SV. I. 565, chanted here on SV. II. 225–227.

23. The Gods and the Asuras were contending; whom they slew of the Gods, that one did not come to life again, whom (they slew) of the Asuras, that one came to life again. The Gods performed austerities; they saw that ariṣṭa(-sāman); thereupon whom they slew of the Gods, that one came to life again, whom of the Asuras, that one did not come to life again[1]. (Because they now thought:) 'We have through this (sāman) come out unharmed' (*nāriṣāma*), therefore it is called ariṣṭa ('free from harm'). The ariṣṭa is applied at the end (of the ārbhava-pavamāna-laud) in order to be free from harm.

[1] A similar legend of the reviving of the slain Gods is found in Śat. br. II. 6. 1. 1: *atha yān evaiṣāṃ tasmint saṃgrāme 'ghnaṃs tān pitṛyajñena samairayanta.*

24. It has a triple *iḍā*[1]: to support the three-day period.

[1] *ho iḍā* (3r 4 5r) | *ho iḍā* (3r 4r 5r) | *ho 2345 i* (3) | *ḍā*.

25. The last *iḍā* they undertake, (*i.e.*, 'chant') 'running[1]' for connecting the fourth day.—The stoma (is given)[2].

[1] 'Swiftly', not extended, not lengthened; the term *dravantīm iḍām* seems not to have the technical meaning of *dravadiḍā* (XII. 11. 1).

[2] See XII. 1. 11.

XII. 6.

(The uktha-lauds of the third day.)

1. (There are the verses beginning:) 'Sing ye unto the very great one'[1].

[1] SV. I. 107=ṚS. VII. 103. 8–9=SV. II. 228–229.

2. By (the words) 'sing ye' the characteristic of power is brought about[1].

[1] According to Sāyaṇa, because mighty princes have many singers at their court.

3. (There are the verses beginning:) 'This intoxicating draught we announce to thee'[1]; possessed of intoxicating draught, possessed of pith is the afternoon service; he thereby puts (into it) intoxicating draught (and) pith.

[1] SV. I. 383=ṚS. VIII. 15. 4–6=SV. II. 230–232.

4. (The verses beginning:) 'Hear thou the summons of Tiraścī[1]' is (are) for hearing only.

5. There is the pramaṃhiṣṭhīya (-sāman)[1].

[1] Grām. III. 1. 26, composed on SV. I. 107 (first of the three sāmans of this name, it must be *svāram.*)

6. By means of the pramaṃhiṣṭhīya, Indra hurled his thunderbolt on Vṛtra and cast him down. One who has a rival should introduce the uktha (-laud)s with the pramaṃhiṣṭhīya; he casts down his rival and himself fares better.

7. There is hārivarṇa(-sāman)[1].

[1] Grām. X. 1. 34, composed on SV. I. 383 (there are four sāmans of this name, but the last is required, because this only has the nidhana mentioned in § 9, see SV. ed. Calcutta, Vol. I, page 789).

8, 9. Indra and the Asuric Namuci made an agreement: 'of us two not (one) shall kill the other either by night or by day, either with (what is) wet or (what is) dry'. Indra cut off his head at dawn before sunrise with foam of water[1]; what is at dawn before sunrise, is neither by night nor by day, and foam of water is neither wet nor dry. This head, a greater evil[2], (than the unslain himself had been) rolled after him, (calling out): 'Man-slayer, thou hast cheated, thou hast cheated!' Neither by verse nor by chant could he repel it (this head)[3], (but) by means of the finale of the hārivarṇa-(sāman)[4] he repelled it.

[1] Perhaps the plates of the ray, the *nadīsisa* of Kauś. sūtra VIII. 18, which is equivalent to *nadīphena*; this material is, it seems, used also for washing the hands.

[2] *pāpīyaṃ*, remarkable form instead of *pāpīyas*. Sāyaṇa connects it with *vācam* (his bhāṣya is printed by error partly under § 6). The translation of Hopkins in his paper 'Gods and Saints of the great Brāhmaṇa' (Transactions of the Conn. Ac. of Arts and Sciences, Vol. XV, page 47) is partly wrong.

[3] On this legend cp. Maitr. Saṃh. IV. 3. 4: 43. 7–13, TBr. I. 7. 1. 6–7, Śat. br. XII. 7. 3. 1.

[4] The nidhana is: *hariśriyā 2345m* (accents: 2 1 111).

10. He who lauds with the hārivarṇa (-sāman) repels, by its finale, distress and comes to fortune (*śriyam*) and energy.

11. There is the tairaścya (-sāman)[1].

[1] Grām. IX. 2. 2, composed on SV. I. 346, see SV. ed. Calcutta, Vol. I, page 708.

12. When the Angirases went to the world of heaven, they were pursued by Ogres. Tiraścin of the Angiras clan[1] circumambulated them slantingly[2] with this (sāman); because he had circumambulated them slantingly (*tiryañ*), therefore it is called tairaścya. It was, forsooth, the bad lot that pursued them; this they repelled by means of the tairaścya (-saman). He who lauds with the tairaścya (-sāman) repels his bad lot.

[1] Read *yato* instead of *yanto* and *tiraścy āṅgirasas tiryañ paryavaid; yat tiryañ paryavait tat*, etc. Against the masc. *tiraścy āṅgirasaḥ*, the ṚS. (VIII 95. 4) points to a female *āṅgirasī*: *tiraścī*.

[2] It is not clear which is the exact kind of manœuvre executed by the Ṛṣi: the word *tiryañ* is taken into the text as it seems, simply to explain the origin of the name. This is differently explained in the Jaim. br. (III. 56, cp. Auswahl No. 175): 'The other Gods and Seers had gained the upward world, but Tiraści of the Angiras-clan (*tiraścir āṅgirasaḥ*) wished to gain the slanting worlds (*tiraśco lokān*), where the waters flow, where the wind blows, where sun, moon and stars move. He saw this sāman and by lauding with it he gained those worlds.' Further on we read that this same Tiraści gained men and cattle by applying this chant. A third tale is as follows: 'When the Gods went up to the world of heaven, they were pursued by the Ogres. They wished to repel these Ogres and saw this chant. They made of it a god-stronghold (*devapuram*) and drew it across (*tiryak paryauhan*). By it they repelled the Ogres.'

13 The stoma is seventeenfold (seventeen-versed), for getting firm support, for getting progeny.

(FOURTH DAY.)

XII. 7.

(Out-of-doors-laud of the fourth day.)

1. (The verses beginning:) 'Forth on thy behalf the mares, o Pavamāna'[1] are the opening (tristich) of the fourth day.

[1] SV. II. 236, 237, 238,=ṚS. VIII. 86. **4, 6, 5** (with var. read.)

2. Now that the three-day period has been reached ('finished, used up'), they start with the characteristic of the gāyatrī[1]: 'forth' is the characteristic of the gāyatrī[2].

[1] The morning service as a rule, begins with gāyatrī verses; here are jagatīs, because the second three-day period is: *jāgatam, gāyatram, traiṣṭubham.*

[2] Cp. X. 6. 1.

3. The opening (tristich) is (in) jagatī (-metre): the third day is a jagatī-day: from jagatī they step on to jagatī.

4 If the opening (tristich) were any other (than on jagatīs), there would be an adverseness or a conformity [1].

[1] The idea of conformity is difficult to grasp.

5. (The verses beginning:) 'The pavamāna (soma) has produced [1]' is the corresponding tristich (the antistrophe) [2].

[1] SV. II. 239-241=ṚS. IX. 61. 16-18 (var. read.)

[2] That the stotriya is on jagatī, the anurūpa on gāyatrī, is caused by the fact that the author here treats of the dvādaśāha with transposed metres (*vyūḍha-dvādaśāha*). In the *samūḍha-dvādaśāha* all the days ought to begin with gāyatrī; for the *samūḍha-ṣaḍaha* cp. Ārṣeyakalpa I. 9. a, page 14 of the printed text.

6 Containing (words derived from the root) *jan* is the fourth day [1]; he produces food, he produces the virāj [2], he produces the twenty-one-fold stoma.

[1] Cp. X. 6. 4.

[2] The virāj is food, and besides, the first pṛṣṭhastotra of this day is the vairāja-sāman.

7. And, moreover, after the former characteristic he thereby speaks the latter characteristic; that he speaks after the former characteristic the latter characteristic, is the reason why the corresponding (tristich) is called anurūpa. A son resembling to him he gets, who knows this [1].

[1] Identical with XI. 6. 4, 5.

8 The stotriya and the anurūpa are tristichs, for retaining the breathings [1].

[1] Cp. XI 6, 6.

9. There are two hexastichs [1], for propping the (six) seasons.

[1] SV. II. 242-247=ṚS. IX. 41. 1-6 (var.); SV. II. 248-253=ṚS. IX. 39. 1, 2, 4, 3, 5, 6, (with var. read.). Whilst the verses are not indicated in the Pañc br., the Jaim br. treats of them at length, as it does also of the verses mentioned in § 10

10. A tristich [1] is the last; with which breath they start, in that they break up ('finish the laud').—The stoma is the twenty-one-fold (or 'twenty-one versed'), for gaining a firm support. He (thereby) gets a firm support.

[1] SV. II. 254-256=ṚS. IX. 65. 1-3 (var.).

XII. 8.

(The ājya-lauds of the fourth day.)

1. (The verses beginning:) 'The protector of the people has been born, the wakeful one'[1], are the ājya (-laud) addressed to Agni.

[1] SV. II. 257, 258, 259=ṚS. IV. 11. 1, 6, 2.

2. Containing (words derived from the root) *jan* is the fourth day; he produces food, he produces the virāj, he produces the twenty one-fold stoma[1].

[1] Identical with XII. 7. 6.

3. (The verses beginning:) 'Here for both of you, o Mitra and Varuṇa,'[1] are the bṛhat-like[2] (ājya-laud) addressed to Mitra and Varuṇa.

[1] SV. II. 260–262=ṚS. II. 41. 4–6.

[2] This is explained in § 4.

4. The vairūpa is cryptically (equal to) the bṛhat[1]; he thereby brings to light ('displays') the characteristic of the bṛhat.

[1] Because, according to Ait. br. IV. 28. 3, the vairūpa is the *garbha* of the bṛhat.

5. (The verses beginning:) 'Indra from the bones of Dadhyañc,'[1] are the tristich related to Dadhyañc.

[1] SV. II. 263–265=ṚS. I. 84. 13–15.

6. Dadhyañc of the Angiras clan was the chaplain of the Gods[1]; the office of chaplain is the food of the brahman (the priest); (so these verses serve) for retaining food.

[1] For the version of the Jaiminīyas cp. Journ. of the Amer. Or. Soc., Vol. XVIII, page 17.

7. (The verses beginning:) 'For both of you, from this prayer,'[1] are the (ājya-laud) addressed to Indra and Agni.

[1] SV. II. 266–268=ṚS. VIII. 94. 1–3.

8. 'O Indra and Agni, the excellent praise, as rain from a cloud, has come forth'[1]—anuṣṭubh-like, forsooth, is the rain[2], anuṣṭubh-like is the fourth day[3]: two united virājs he puts in[4], for the sake of food[5].— The stoma (is given)[6].

1 The second and third verse-quarters of SV. II. 266.

2 Because of a certain connection of the anuṣṭubh with *vāc*, cp. X. 5. 10.

3 Because the anuṣṭubh is the metre which, after the three (gāyatrī, triṣṭubh, jagatī), came into existence as the fourth, Ait. br. IV. 28. 6.

4 So there are at this day two anuṣṭubhs (from the rain and the *rūpa* of this day); if from the anuṣṭubh the two syllables, which are day and night, are not taken into account, there are left over two virājs (each of 30 syllables).

5 *annaṃ virāṭ*, *e.g.*, T Br. I. 6.3.4.

6 See XII. 7. 10.

XII. 9.

(The midday-pavamāna-laud of the fourth day.)

1. (The verse beginning:) 'Be clarified, thou who accomplishest energy' [1], is the gāyatrī: for the sake of accomplishment.

1 SV. I. 434=Rs. IX. 25. 1, 3, 2=SV. II. 269, 270, 271.

2. (The words) 'be clarified' are the characteristic of the bṛhat [1], for this day is a bṛhat-day.

1 The second day of the whole period, a bṛhat-day, begins equally with *pavasva*, XI. 6, 1 cp, however, ib. § 2.

2 Cp. note 1 on XII. 8. 4.

3. (There is the tristich:) 'In thy friendship, o Soma, day by day I take the greatest joy, o Drop! Many difficulties, o brown one, assault me; do thou pass beyond these hedges' [1].

1 SV. I. 516=ṚS. IX. 107. 19-20=SV. II. 272-273.

4. For they are passed beyond [1]– 'as birds, have we flown beyond', for they have flown beyond [2].

1 They are now passed over the first three-day period.

2 Last verse-quarter of SV. II. 273.

5. (There is the tristich beginning:) 'Being clarified he has stepped upon' [1].

1 SV. I. 488=ṚS. IX. 40. 1-3=SV. II. 274-276.

6. Being gāyatrī (-verses) they (these) are triṣṭubhs by their characteristic [1]; therefore, they are applied on the (proper) place of the triṣṭubh [2].

1 As containing the words *viśvā* (SV. II. 274. b), *vṛṣā* (275.b), *rayim* (276.a) Cp. X. 6. 2.

2 The last sāman of the midday-pavamāna is on triṣṭubh-verses.

7. There is the gāyatra (-sāman). The brāhmaṇa of the gāyatra is the same [1].

[1] Cp. VII, 1. 1, sqq.

8. There is the ātharvaṇa- (sāman) with four finales [1], for propping the four-day period [2].

[1] Aranyegeyagāna I. 1. 23, composed on SV. I. 33, here chanted on SV. II. 269–271; its four finales are: *āvat, sūvah, jyotiḥ,* ī 2 3 4 5, see SV ed. Calcutta, Vol. II, page 400.

[2] According to the Jaim. br. (III. 66), the Atharvans had gone to the world of heaven, situated 'above the falcon', but here they found no firm support: they saw this sāman and by applying it they found a firm support in the world of heaven.

9. Of four verse-quarters is the anuṣṭubh, and the fourth day is an anuṣṭubh- day [1].

[1] And, therefore, this sāman with its four finales is commendable.

10. The sāmans seen by the Atharvans, forsooth, are medicine [1]; he thus applies medicine.

[1] We have apparently to think of the *śānta*-part (the 'white magic') of the Atharvaveda, cp. Bloomfield, the Atharvaveda (in the 'Grundriss der Ar. phil.') page 8. Jaim. br (l. c.): *tad u bheṣajam eva prāyaścittir; atharvabhir vai bheṣajam kurvanti.*

11. There is the finale-wishing (sāman) (nidhanakāma)[1].

[1] Grām. IV. 2. 13, composed on SV. I. 152, called in Jaim. br. III. 67 *nidhanakāmaṃ vairājam.*

12. One wish (only) he acquires by any other announced finale, but this nidhanakāma (-sāman) (serves) for obtaining (the fulfilment of) all wishes.

13. There is the āṣṭādaṃṣṭra (-sāman).[1]

[1] Grām. IX. 1. 20, 21 are both thus designated, cp. XI. 11. 11; here, according to Sāyana, the last of the two is required. According to Jaim. br. III. 67 it is *ūrdhveḷam.*

14. The brāhmaṇa of the āṣṭādaṃṣṭra is the same [1].

[1] See XI. 11. 12, 13.

15. There is the ābhīśava (-sāman) ('bridle- chant') [1], for supporting the day.

[1] Grām. XIV. 2. 6, composed on SV. II. 512, here chanted on II. 272-273.

16. What is not sustained, that he sustains by means of a bridle.[1]

1 Besides the explanation of the name as 'bridle', the Jaim. br. has also this, that the sāman was seen by Abhīśū, the son of Śyāvāśva, who wished that the Gods might drink of his soma.-Sāyana periphrases the word *abhīśú* by *śaṅku* 'a peg'.

17. He chants it with 'repeated push'[1], for such is the characteristic of this day[2].

1 On *anutunna* and its translation see VIII. 9. 13, X. 6. 4, XII. 10. 11. The *anutoda* in this sāman is the twice occurring syllable *e* at the end of the prastāva: *parīto ṣiñcatā sutam* | *e* | *e*, see SV. ed. Calcutta, Vol. II, page 79.

2 See X. 6. 4.

18. There is the āṅgirasa (-sāman) (chant of the Angirases) with four finales[1], for sustaining the four-day period.

1 Grām. XV. I. 18, composed on SV. I. 518. The four nidhanas are probably *auho vā*; *ū* 234 *pā*; *ū* 234 *pā*, and *cyū*-234 *tāḥ*, see SV. ed. Calcutta, Vol. II, page 98.

19. It has (the word) *svaḥ* ('light, heaven') at its back (*i.e.* in its middle)[1], for such in the characteristic of this day[2].

1 Instead of one of the nidhanas in the middle of the sāman, the word *svaḥ* must be chanted. The ritualistic authorities are at variance as to where exactly this *svaḥ* should be put in: instead of the first or instead of the second *ū 234 pā*; according to Gautama and Dhānañjayya, the second must be replaced by *sū 234-vāḥ* (Lāṭy. V. 10. 8-9), cp. Nidānasūtra III. 12: *atha svaḥpṛṣṭhasyāṅgirasasya nidhanayor ānupūrvye vivadante: svaḥ pūrvam iḍottarety eke* (as Lāṭy. and Drāhy.; for *upā* may to replaced by *iḍā*); *evam etayoḥ sāmāntayor ānupūrvyam bhavati; iḍāṃ vayam pūrvāṃ kurma* (as do Gautama and Dhānañjayya), *evam anayoḥ samānopāyād abhivyāhāraṃ paśyāmo yathā rājane mādhucchandasa iti.* It is remarkable that the ūhagāna (see SV. ed. Calcutta, Vol. III, page 520) seems not to notice this prescript; for a similar case cp. XI. 10. 14. But a prayoga consulted by me has: *ā 234 vā* | *ī 234 ḍā* | *a* | *sū 234 vāḥ* | *a* | *paridhīm rā 23* |; the *a* denotes *antarnidhanam.* So this prayoga is in accord with the *vayam* of Nidāna and with Gautama and Dhānañjayya. With this disposition agrees also the Jaim. br. (III. 69): *ta etāṃ madhya-iḍām upetya svar ity upariṣṭād upāyan.*

2 The connection is sought by Sāyana in the fact that this day is a vairāja, has the vairāja as *hotuḥ pṛṣṭhastotram.*

20. There is the satrāsāhīya (-sāman)[1].

1 Grām. V. I. 27, composed on SV. I. 170; the second of the two sāmans of this name is required, because it must be *svāram* (SV. ed. Calcutta, Vol. I, page 387).

21. What had been (left) unconquered of (the possessions of) the Asuras, that was conquered by the Gods by means of the satrāsāhīya (-sāman). (Because they thereupon said or thought:) 'We have conquered (*sah*) them finally (*satrā*), therefore, the satrāsāhīya is called thus[1].

[1] Cp. Jaim. br. I. 182, see the text in 'Auswahl' No. 67.

22. He who lauds with the satrāsāhīya, conquers finally his rival.

23. They chant (it) on gāyatrī (verses), for the sake of getting a firm support[1], for (the obtainment of) priestly lustre; with which breath they start, in that they go up ('finish the stotra')[2].

[1] Because the gāyatrī has three versequarters, three feet! So Sāyana.

[2] The stotra begins and ends with gāyatrī-verses.

24. They are gāyatrī (-verses) containing (the word) 'bull'[1]; thereby, they do not depart from the characteristic of the triṣṭubh.[2]—The stoma (is given)[3].

[1] *gamad indro vṛṣā sutam*, SV. II. 275. b.

[2] The last sāman of the midday-pavamāna-stotra ought to be chanted on triṣṭubh metre (Ārṣeyakalpa, Einleitung, page XXIV). As the gāyatrī-verses contain the characteristic of the triṣṭubh, the word *vṛṣan* (see X. 6. 2), this condition is fulfilled and in a cryptic way they chant triṣṭubhs. The reasoning of Sāyana here seems false.

[3] Cp. XII. 7. 10.

XII. 10.

(The pṛṣṭha-lauds of the fourth day.)

1. (There are the verses the first of which is:) 'Drink, o Indra, the soma, let it gladden thee; the soma that has been pressed for thee, o (God) with the bay horses, by the stone, (that is) as a steed well controlled (*suyata*) by the arms of the presser'[1]; long-drawn (*āyata*), as it were, is the fourth day: in order to control it (*yatyai*).

[1] SV. I. 398=ṚS. VII. 22. 1-3=SV. II. 277-279.

2. (The verse beginning:) 'The men him who prevails in all battles'[1] is an excessive jagatī[2]; he, thereby, steps on to a larger metre: in order not to slip down.

[1] SV. I. 370=ṚS. VIII. 97. 10, 12, 11=SV. II. 280, 281, 282 (with var.).

[2] An atijagatī with one or more verse-quarters of 13 instead of 12 syllables.

3. A slipping down it is, as it were, if after a larger metre he applies a smaller one. That on the fourth day an excessive jagatī is applied, (serves) for not slipping down.

4. (There are the verses beginning:) 'He, who the king of men

1 SV. I. 273=ṚS. VIII. 70. 1-2=SV. II. 283-284.

5. For, at this moment they have arrived at the reign of the voice[1]; he causes through this (verse) the Sacrificer to come to reign.

1 This rests on the word 'king'; for the rest, the purport is not clear; a similar expression XII. 11. 4; the Jaim. br. III. 75 uses the same expression but with the singular of the verb.

6. By means of the metres the Gods brought the sun to the world of heaven; it did not hold (there); by means of the finale of the vairāja(-sāman)[1] they fastened it; therefore, the sun shines thitherward and hitherward[2], for thitherward and hitherward is the sound ī[3].

1 The finale of the vairāja, araṇyegeyagāna II. 1. 31, composed on SV. I 398 (SV. ed. Calcutta, Vol. II, page 433) is ī *2345*; cp. above, X. 10. 1: *īnidhanam caturthasya (ahnah)*.

2 Thitherward at night, for then the stars are visible; hitherward, at day, for then the earth is illuminated by the rays of the sun. Here we meet with the view of the sun, found in the Brāhmanas, cp. E. Sieg, 'Der Nachtweg der Sonne,' S. 7.

3 As being articulated in the mouth between *a* and *u*.

7. Having chanted the prastāva, he applies the 'props'[1]; he, thereby, puts food into his (own) mouth, for the prelude (prastāva) is the mouth[2] of the chant.

1 The stobhas: *matsva, ojaḥ, sahaḥ, balaṃ, indraḥ, vayaḥ, bṛhat, ṛtaṃ, svah jyotiḥ, dadhe*, each followed by *hā u*, see SV. ed. Calcutta l.c.

2 *mukha* meaning 'mouth' and 'beginning'.

8. Ten times[1] he 'props'; of ten syllables is the virāj, virāj-like is food: for the obtainment of food.

1 Probably the last stobha: *dadhe*, is not counted as viṣṭambha.

9. Thirty times[1] he 'props', for retaining more food.

1 The viṣṭambhas are applied in each of the three verse-quarters. For the rest, it is remarkable that the ūha (see SV. ed. Calcutta, Vol. V, page 391) does not insert these viṣṭambhas, but the Prayogas, consulted by me, do. On these the author of the Nidānasūtra (III. 12) remarks: *atha katame viṣṭambhā iti? devatā ity āhur, devatābhiḥ padāni viṣṭambhānīti. tad āhur: ekādaśemā devatā, daśa kṛtvo viṣṭabhnātīti, daśaitāḥ satyamprāyā bhavanty apivā ya ete devatāntareṣu daśa stobhās tān viṣṭambhān avocat, tair devatā viṣṭabdhā iti.*

10. There is the vairājasāman; they chant (it) on virāj-verses[1]; the 'props' are virāj-like[2]; united virājs he puts in, for the sake of food.

[1] SV. II. 277-279 are in virāj-metre.

[2] Because they are ten in number.

11. He chants (it) with repeated push[1], for impregnation's sake; for from the repeated push[2] seed is implanted (pregnancy follows).

[1] See note 1 on VIII. 9. 13. The chant of ar. geya II. 1. 31 begins with thrice repeated *ho iyâ* (2r, 1).

[2] *viz.* of the penis in the vagina.—For the anutoda cp. also Nidānasūtra III. 12: *atha vairājaṃ tryanutodam eke kurvanty* (see J. Br. III 70: *trir anutudati*): *evam chāndaso 'dhyāya iti; caturanutodam vayam: evam ācāryavaca iti: tena vātsapraṁ samādadhyād* ('he should make to agree): *yadi vairājaṃ tryanutodam, vātsapram api tryanutodam; yadi caturanutodam, vātsapram api caturanutodam, evam eva brāhmaṇaṃ bhavaty: etasmin vai vairājam pratiṣṭhitam iti* (XII. 11 24)

12. On the right thigh of the Udgātṛ they churn fire[1]; for from the right side the seed is discharged[2].

[1] Cp. VII. 8. 11.

[2] Because *dakṣinato vṛṣā yoṣām upaśete*, Śat. br. VI. 3. 1. 30 and cp. the other passages collected by Oertel in Journ. of the Amer. Or. Society, Vol. XXVI, page 188.

13. When it (the stotra, the laud) is brought near (*i.e* announced by the Adhvaryu), but before the *him*-sound has been made, they churn; when it (the fire) has been produced, he makes the *him*-sound over it.

14. Therefore, when a young (a calf) has been born, the cattle makes the *him*-sound over it (sniffs at it)[1].

[1] Cp. Kāth. XXVII. 9: 150 4: *tasmād gaur vatsam jātam abhihiṃkaroti.*

15. About this (fire), after it has been produced, they (the theologians) are in doubt: 'shall we throw it into the gārhapatya or into the āgnīdhra or into the āhavanīya?'[1]

[1] On the dative *tasmai* and the impf. *amīmāṁsanta* cp. Introduction, Chapter III § 8 (page XXVIII).

16. They throw it into the āhavanīya; for the āhavanīya is the resting place of the Sacrificer[1]. He, thereby, makes his own resting place provided with light.

[1] During the sacrifice he is seated south of the āhavanīya.

17. Possessed of light and priestly lustre is he who knows this.

18. On it he pours out a libation, for (the sake of) appeasing (it) He pours on it a libation of clarified liquid butter (*ājya*). Ājya, forsooth, is brilliance. brilliance he thus puts into himself.

19. He pours it out with the virāj (-verse): 'Kindled, blaze forth, o Agni, before us'[1]; the virāj is food: for the obtainment of food[2].

[1] ṚS. VII. 1. 3=SV. II. 725.

[2] To §§ 12-19 refers the Sūtrakāra (Lāṭy. III. 5. 5-12, Drāhy. IX. 1. 5-13): 'When the stotra of the vairāja-chant has been announced, he (the Udgātṛ) should put on his thigh, lengthwise, a chip of wood and two blades of grass; on it he should put crosswise the churning-apparatus, turning the (fire-) generating part towards himself. Then (whilst, according to Jaim. br. III. 71, the Prastotṛ and the Pratihartṛ keep hold of the apparatus) he should churn thrice from right to left on (his thigh), (with the formula): 'Be produced along with the gāyatrī-metre; along with the triṣṭubh-metre; along with the jagatī-metre; along with the anuṣṭubh-metre; along with the virāj-metre,' so, according to Gautama; with four of these formulas, according to Dhānañjayya; with three, according to Śāṇḍilya. Having touched the point of contact of the two churning sticks, he should smell at his hands with the formula: 'Thou art brilliancy, put brilliancy into me'. Whilst the fire is being churned (the act accomplished by the Udgātṛ is no churning proper, but only an imitation of the act), he should 'yoke' the stoma. When the fire is produced, they should chant the laud. Having caused the Sacrificer to say his say (cp. I. 6. 3), he should mutter over the fire: 'Return again with sap! again, o Agni, with strength and life! Protect us again from trouble.—Return again with wealth, o Agni; pour forth the all-enjoying stream from all sides!' (SV. II. 1182, 1183), and then offer into it; this has been set forth in the Brāhmana (*viz.* XII 10. 18, 19); with (the simple word) *svāhā*, he should make the second offering' —It is probable that this *anumantraṇa* with SV. II. 1182, 1183 is taken from the Jaim. br. (III. 71), otherwise, the verses, as they occur in the uttarārcika, would have been indicated by their pratīka. Another, equally possible, conclusion would be that at the time of the Sūtrakāras the Uttarārcika did not yet exist

20. The traiśoka(-sāman)[1] is the Brahman's chant[2].

[1] Grām. IX. 2. 35, composed on SV. I. 370.

[2] The third pṛṣṭha-laud.

21. They chant it on excessive jagatīs[1], for the stepping up of this day; for, indeed, they step up by this day.

[1] Cp. notes on § 2.

22. (The words) 'by day' they undertake ('apply') as finale[1], for repelling evil[2]. He who applies in lauding the traiśoka(-sāman), repels evil[3].

1 The nidhana is (cp. SV. ed. Calcutta, Vol. I, page 734) di234vā. (3 5 above)

2 Because day repels darkness: evil.

3 About the origin of the traiśoka the Jaim. br. (III. 72, see the text in 'Auswahl' No. 176) preserves the following interesting tale: 'Kaṇva Nārṣada had married the daughter of Akhaga, an Asura. By her he begot two sons: Triśoka and Nabhāka. She, being angry, returned to her relations. He went after her. The Asuras, smearing him (his eyes) with a sticking substance, addressed him: 'Now discern the day-break, (and announce it to us), if thou art a (true) brāhmaṇa.' The two Aśvins perceived this, the Aśvins, who amongst the Gods are those that untie the fastened. These two approached unseen (by the others) and said to him: 'The moment we will, touching the lute, pass thee, flying above thee (in the air), thou shalt discern day-break.' During this night they (the Asuras) leaped up again and again, (calling out): 'Arise ye, the day has come! Yoke your ploughs!' But each time he said: 'It dawns not yet, for sure.' Then these two (the Aśvins), touching the lute, passed flying above (him), and (now) he said: 'Take ye away this (sticking substance from my eyes), the day has come now, yoke your ploughs.' They said: 'Verily, this one was a brāhmaṇa, a seer. Here with his wife! Let us give her to him.' They gave her to him. She said to him: 'They seek again to slay thee in a hidden way. I have heard them conversing. They will put down for thee in the shadow (?) a golden seat: do not sit down upon it!' They went away; they had put down for him in the shadow a golden seat. He, not taking heed, sat down on it. But, turning into stone, it entangled him. Then his sons, Triśoka and Nabhāka, perceived that the Asuras had entangled their father in stone. They approached. Nabhāka uttered the wish: 'May I cause it (the stone-seat) to fall down.' He saw this hymn attributed to Nabhāka* and sang it over him. He (Kaṇva) became visible in it (in the seat), just as in a jewel the jewel-string is visible. Thereupon Triśoka uttered the wish: 'May I throw it asunder'. He saw this sāman (the traiśoka) and by means of it he caused it to fall asunder in two parts. He (Kaṇva), being (still) senseless, returned to life. He (Triśoka) wished: 'May he live' and touched him, (whilst uttering the nidhāna): 'Hey, live'†. So he lived, but it was as darkness for him. He (Triśoka) wished: 'May it be day to him'. He touched him (whilst muttering the nidhana): 'Hey, day*'. He wished: 'May I make him reach the world of heaven', and (by muttering the nidhana): 'Hey, to heaven' he made him reach the world of heaven'‡.

(* To Nabhāka Kāṇva are attributed three sūktas in the Ṛksaṃhitā: VIII. 39-41.)

(† The nidhana of the traiśoka in the Jaim. gāna is: o i jivā.)

(‡ This tale of Kaṇva must have been known to the poets of the Ṛksaṃhitā, as appears from I. 117.8, 118.7. c, d, VIII. 5. 23.)

23. Bharadvāja's 'various chant' (*pṛśni*)[1] is the Acchāvāka's chant[2].

[1] Grām. I. 2. 29, composed SV. I. 37.

[2] The fourth pṛṣṭhastotra.

24. The Gods call food 'various,' (so it serves) for obtainment of food.

25. It (the pṛśnisāman) is *iḍābhir aiḍam* [1], for thus is the characteristic of the fourth day [2].—The stoma (is given) [3].

[1] See note 4 on X. 11. 1.

[2] See X. 11. 1.

[3] See XII. 7. 10.

XII. 11.

(The ārbhava-pavamāna-laud of the fourth day.)

1. (The verses beginning:) 'Round (*pari*) the dear, the wise of heaven' [1] contain (the word) 'round'; the fourth day is the end [2]; these (verses) (serve) to close it (*p a r y āptyai*) [3].

[1] SV. I. 476=ṚS IX. 9. 1. 3, 2 (the Jaim. agree with the sequence of the ṚS)=SV. II. 285, 286, 287.

[2] The fourth day is the last of a catūrātra (!).

[3] Read *anto vai caturtham ahas, tasyaitāḥ paryāptyai*, cp. XII. 5. 4.

2. (In the verses beginning:) 'Yes, thou, the divine' [1], (the word) 'thou' is the characteristic of the bṛhat, for this day is a bṛhat-day.[2]

[1] SV. I. 583=ṚS. IX. 108. 3-4=SV. II. 288, 289.

[2] Cp. the verses, on which the bṛhat is chanted, which begin *tvām id dhi havāmahe*, and XI. 9. 1.

3. (There are the verses, the first of which is:) 'Soma being clarified by the wave, flows through the wool of the sheep, the Pavamāna, roaring at the front of speech' [1].

[1] SV. I. 572=ṚS. IX. 106. 10-12=SV. II. 290-292.

4 For at this moment they have arrived at the front of speech; by means of this (verse) they cause the Sacrificer to come to the tront [1]

[1] Cp XII. 10. 5, XII. 11. 3 and 4.

5. (The verses beginning:) 'By fore-conquest, from your plant' [1], are the two virāj (verse)s [2], for this day is a virāj-day [3].

1 SV. I. 545=ṚS. IX. 101. 1-3=SV. II. 47-49

2 Cp. note 1 on VIII. 5. 7.

3 Because of its first pṛṣṭhastotra: the vairāja-sāman.

6. (There are the verses beginning:) 'Soma is clarified, the engenderer of thoughts' [1]: the ṣoḍaśin-cup, which is drawn during the morning service [2], this they engender during the afternoon-service [3].

1 SV. I. 527=ṚS. IX. 96. 5-7=SV. II. 293-295.

2 See *e.g.* Āp. śrs. XIV. 2. 3-4.

3 This cup is offered during the afternoon-service, see *e.g.* Āp. XIV. 3. 1, sqq. This fourth day namely has a ṣoḍaśin at the end.

7. Being triṣṭubhs they are, by their characteristic, jagatī (verse)s [1]; therefore, they are applied at the place of the jagatī (verse)s [2].

1 Because they contain in the last verse-quarter: *ūtiṣṭhati vṛṣabho goṣu jānan*, features of the third day (cp. X. 6. 3), which is *jāgatam*.

2 At the end of the ārbhava-laud, cp. Ārṣeyakalpa, Einleitung, page XXIV.

8. There is the gāyatra (-sāman). The brāhmaṇa of the gāyatra is the same [1].

1 See VII. 1. 1 sqq.

9. There is the aurṇāyava (sāman) (Ūrṇāyu's chant) [1].

1 Grām. XIII. 1. 38, composed on SV. I. 176, the second of the two, cp. the next following §.

10. The Aṅgirases (once upon a time) performed a sacrificial session, and (in consequence of it) they reached and won the world of heaven, but the path leading to the Gods they did not know [1]. One of them, Kalyāṇa of the Aṅgiras-clan, went out (away from his fellow-Sacrificers) to study [2]. He came upon the Gandharva Ūrṇāyu, who was swinging amidst the Apsarases. Whenever he (Ūrṇāyu) indicated one of these by (the words): 'this one' [3], she desired him. He (Ūrṇāyu) addressed him: 'Kalyāṇa, reached verily and won by you (*i.e.* by thee and thy fellow-Sacrificers) is the world of heaven, but the path leading to the Gods ye do not know. This chant is conducive to the attainment of heaven. By using it in lauding ye will get to the world of heaven. But do not say: 'It is I who have seen it'.

1 It is a well-known theme in the Brāhmaṇas, that the Gods got to heaven and after them the seers knew the way to heaven, see *e.g.* VIII. 5. 7.

[2] Cp. note 1 on XV. 5. 20.—Sāyaṇa reads *āṅgiraso dhyāyam udavrajat*, and takes *dhyāyam* as gerund. The text has *āṅgiraso 'dhyāyam udavrajat*, and this reading seems to be supported by XV. 5. 20: *ṛṣim adhyāyam udvrajitam* In the Jaim. br. (III. 77) it is the Angiras Śvitra who goes out to collect fuel: *samiddhārah parait.*

[3] *iyām* is apparently the nidhana of the second aurṇāyava: *1 '3yā2345m*, the chant-form for *iyam*, designating at the same time the sāman which it concludes.

11. Kalyāṇa returned and said (to the other Angirases): 'Reached, forsooth, and won by us is the world of heaven, but the path leading to the Gods we do not know. This chant is conducive to the attainment of heaven; by using it in lauding we will get to the world of heaven'. (They said:) 'Who is it that has told it to thee?' 'Even I myself have seen it' (he said). Having applied it in lauding they got to the world of heaven, (but) Kalyāṇa was left behind, for he had told a lie[1] He is the leper here on earth[2].

[1] In the same way it is told of Cyavana that, when either the Bhṛgus or the Angirases reached heaven, he was left behind old and decrepit. Śat. br. IV. 1. 5. 1

[2] Differently the Jaim. br. (III. 77): 'He (Śvitra the Angiras) became a *śvitra* (probably a kind of viper): the *śvitras* are the vipers (*ahi*); because he was left behind (*ahīyata*), thence they derive their name (of *ahi*): the others are the serpents'.

12. Conducive to the attainment of heaven is this sāman; he who applies in lauding the aurṇāyava(-sāman) shares the world of heaven, the world of bliss.

13. There is the bṛhatka (-sāman)[1].

[1] Grām XI. 1. 1, composed on SV. I. 401 (it is *svāram*).

14. It is a sāman commendable by its Ṛsi-descent[1]. (The verses beginning:) 'Yes, thou'[2], (serve) to obtain food; by means of (the word) 'Yes', indeed, food is given[3], and, besides, he lifts up with this (sāman) the ṣoḍaśin (-cup)[4].

[1] It is not wholly certain that this is the meaning of *sāmārṣeyeṇa praśastam*. Perhaps: 'by the words of the verses themselves'. The same expression XIII. 3. 19, XIV. 10. 5.

[2] See § 2, above.

[3] An affirmative answer is indicated by the particle *hi*; see examples in Delbruck, Altindische Syntax, page 524.

[4] See note 3 on § 6.

15. There is the ātiṣādīya (-sāman)[1].

[1] Grām. XVII. 1. 31, composed on SV. I. 572 (the last of the two, being *nidhanavat*).

16. The ātiṣādīya (-sāman), forsooth, is life[1]; (it serves) for attaining (long) life.

[1] *āyuḥ* is the normal length of human life. Perhaps this sāman is identified with *āyus*, because its name reminds of *atiṣādayati* 'to (set) bring across'.

17. They undertake ('chant') the finale until their breath fails[1]; (by doing so) they reach the full space of life[2].

[1] They keep on chanting the nidhana as long as their breath permits.

[2] This statement seems to yield a good sense only, when seen by the light of the Jaim. br. (III. 79): 'The creatures, created by Prajāpati, fainted away. Prajāpati touched them with this sāman and they again recovered their breath,' etc.

18. There is the nānada (-sāman)[1].

[1] Grām. IX. 2. 13, composed on SV. I. 352.

19. (It is) of larger repetitions; passing over the fifth day (it is thereby) a laying hold of the sixth day; thereby, they lay hold of the sixth day: for the sake of continuity[1].

[1] I am not at all sure about the interpretation and the meaning of this sentence. Sāyana is not very explicit. Perhaps the 'larger repetitions' are explained by § 20. Perhaps XIII. 10. 2 may be compared.

20. Sixteen syllables[1] he takes for the prelude (prastāva). Moreover, the ṣoḍaśin (-cup) he thereby lifts up (for its libation)[2].

[1] The first sixteen syllables.

[2] Cp. note 3 on XII. 11. 6.

21. There is the āndhīgava (-sāman)[1].

[1] Grām. XVI. 1. 12, composed on SV. I. 545.

22. One (kind of) virāj is the verse-quarter virāj, another is the syllabic virāj[1]. By means of the verse-quarter virāj he (in chanting on the verses SV. II. 47–49) obtains the food from this world, from yonder world by means of the syllabic virāj. He who in lauding applies the āndhīgava (-sāman), obtains the food of both these worlds.

[1] See note 1 on VIII. 5. 7.

23. There is the vātsapra (-sāman)[1].

[1] Grām. VIII. 2. 11, composed on SV. I. 317, SV. ed. Calcutta, Vol. I, page 639; grām. VIII. 2. 9 and 10 are equally ī-*nidhana*, and *anutunna*.

24. On this chant the vairāja (-sāman) is established[1]; he who in lauding applies the vātsapra, gets firmly established.

[1] Because the vātsapra as well as the vairāja (cp. XII. 10. 6) has the 'repeated push', the *anutoda*, both are *anutunna*, cp. Lāṭy. VII. 7. 28–30: 'The last words of its (the vairaja's) verse-quarters they should repeat four times or thrice; thus also of the vatsapra of the fourth day; but there should be agreement (*i.e.*, if the vairāja is made with four, the vātsapra also should have four *anutodas*)', and cp. the passage cited from the Nidānasūtra in note 2 on XII. 10. 11. The Jaim. br III. 81 remarks: *vairājasya ha khalu vā etad anurūpam sāma*.

25. Vatsaprī, the son of Bhalandana[1], could not find faith (*śraddhā*); he performed austerities and saw this vātsapra(-chant). Thereupon, he found faith. (Thinking) 'we will find faith', verily, they perform the sacrificial session; faith he finds.

[1] Vatsaprī is known also from the pravarasūtras (Āp. XXIV. 10. 16, Baudh. pravarasūtra 53: page 465 of the Calcutta ed. of Baudh. śrs.). According to the sūtra of Baudhāyana, his father is also Bhalandana, his son Mankila. A vaiśya should in his pravara proclaim these as his ṛṣi-ancestors; cp. also TS. V. 2. 1. 6, Maitr. Saṃh. III. 2 2: 16. 9.

26. It has (the syllable) ī as finale, for such is the characteristic of the fourth day[1].—The pavamāna-lauds finish[2] on a finale[3], to support the day.—The stoma (is given)[4].

[1] Cp. X. 10. 1.

[2] The same is found XIII. 5. 28.—Cp. Ṣaḍviṃśa br. III. 7. 1. 3, 5.—The prescripts that the pavamanas finish at the first trirātra on a chant with *svara*, at the second on a chant with *nidhana*, at the third on a chant with *iḍā*, seem to prevail for the samūḍha-dvādaśāha.

[3] Cp. note 1 on XIII 5. 28.

[4] Cp. XII. 7. 10.

XII. 12.

(The uktha-lauds of the fourth day.)

1. (There are the verses beginning): 'The thriving Agni'[1].

[1] SV. I. 21=ṚS. VIII. 102. 6–8=SV. II. 296–298

2. For they throve[1] at that time[1]; by means of this (verse) they make the Sacrificer thrive.

1 The Gods, at the afternoon service, when they performed the sattra, cp. XI. 11. 4.

3. (There are the verses beginning): 'Thee, o incomparable one, we'[1]; for at that time they got to the incomparable form ('manifestation') of Prajāpati. To an incomparable (state) he by this (verse) brings the Sacrificer.

1 SV. I. 408=ṚS. VIII. 21. 1-2=SV. II. 58-59.

4 (There are the verses beginning): 'Drink thou, o Indra, this excellent immortal gladdening soma'[1]; for at that time they got to the excellency of Voice; by this (verse) he brings the Sacrificer to excellency.

1 SV. I. 344=ṚS. I. 84. 4, 6, 5=SV. II. 299-301.

5. There is the saindhukṣita (-sāman)[1].

1 Grām. I. 2. 1, composed on SV. I. 21; the first of the three saindhukṣitas is required: *svāram.*

6. Sindhukṣit, a king-seer[1], being held off[2] a long time (from his realm), saw this saindhukṣita (-sāman). He returned (by means of it) (to his realm) (and) was firmly established. He who in lauding applies the saindhukṣita, returns (to his estate) (and) is firmly established.

1 The Jaim. br. (III. 82) calls him a king of the Bharatas (*bhārato rājā*), dwelling at the Sindhu and, therefore, called Sindhukṣit.

2 On the construction cp. Oertel, Disjunct use of cases, page 20.

7. There is the saubhara (-sāman)[1]; it is the sharpness (splendour) of the bṛhat[2].

1 Grām. III. 1. 31, composed on SV. I. 109; the first of the three sāmans of this name is required: *nidhanavat.*

2 Cp. VIII. 8. 9.

8. Gone down, as it were, is the fourth day[1]; by means of this splendour of the bṛhat, (which is) the saubhara, he props it.

1 The preceding days have their first pṛṣṭhalaud on larger verses (on bṛhatī-verses) than the fourth day (on virāj-verses).

9. There is the chant dear to Vasiṣṭha[1] (*vasiṣṭhasya priyam*).

1 Grām. IX. 1. 27, composed on SV. I. 344.

10. By means of this (sāman) Vasiṣṭha won Indra's favour[1]; he who in lauding applies the (sāman) of Vasiṣṭha wins the favour of the deities.—The stoma (is given)[2].

1 Vasiṣṭha is the Seer who alone saw Indra before his mental eye; Indra revealed to him the stomabhāga-formulæ, TS. III. 5. 2, Kāṭh XXXVII. 17.

2 Cp. XII. 7. 10.

XII. 13.

(The sixteenth laud of the fourth day.)

1. Indra and the bṛhat (once upon a time) came together[1]. The bṛhat surpassed Indra through one of its manifestations. Indra was afraid of this (manifestation), lest it (*viz.* the bṛhat) should overcome him by means of it. He (Indra) said: 'Let this be for thee the ṣoḍaśin-soma-feast.' It became the ṣoḍaśin; this (is) its origin.

1 With hostile intentions or to vie with each other (?). Sāyana's explanation of *samubhavatām*, based on VI. 1. 8, seems to be unacceptable.

2. In prosperity his rival is surpassed by him, who chants on two-footed gāyatrī (-verses) the bṛhat as ṣoḍaśin.

3. The two-footed gāyatrī (-verses)[1] are: 'Unto our soma, with the bay (steeds)'[2]; on these the chant is to be held[3].

1 The verses (see note 2) are properly gāyatrīs with three verse-quarters, but the last verse-quarter of each verse is a repetition of the first verse-quarter of the first verse and so is not taken into account.

2 SV. II. 1140-1142=ṚS. VIII. 93. 31-33.

3 In the ūhagāna no bṛhat-sāman on these verses is recorded, probably because it is optional, see the following § §.

4. Indra, saying; 'I will slay Vṛtra', resorted to Prajāpati. To him (Indra) he gave this anuṣṭubh[1] devoid of energy; by means of this (verse) he (Indra) did not vanquish (Vṛtra); because, being unvanquished, he roared (*vyanadat*), therefrom the nānada (-sāman) has its name.

1 The nānada-sāman (grām. IX. 2. 13) is composed on the anuṣṭubh SV. I. 352; it is worked out ūhagāna X. 1. 1, in agreement with Ārṣeyakalpa III. 1. d (SV. ed. Calcutta, Vol. IV, page 517).—Cp. Ait. br. IV. 2. 2: *nānadaṃ ṣolaśisāma kartavyam ity āhuḥ*.

5. He (Indra) again resorted to him (to Prajāpati). He (Prajāpati) formed the energy of the seven Hotrā(-function)s and gave it to him[1].

1 The seven *hotrās* are the functions of the Hotṛ, the Maitrāvaruṇa, the Brāhmanācchaṃsin, the Acchāvāka, the Potṛ, the Neṣṭṛ and the Āgnīdhra.

6. He (Indra) vanquished him (Vṛtra). He who knows this, vanquishes him whom he wishes to vanquish.

7. Therefore, they (the Chanters) chant on (verses) containing (the word) *hari* [1], they (the Hotṛs) recite (verses) containing (the word) *hari* [2], the cup (the graha) is drawn (by the Adhvaryu) with (verses) containing (the word) *hari* [3]; for, having formed the energy (*haras*), he had given it to him (Prajāpati to Indra).

[1] SV. I. 347=ṚS. I. 84. 1, 3, 2=SV. II. 378–380; cp. below, § 17.

[2] Āśv. VI. 2. 2 prescribes ṚS. I. 84. 1-3; Śāṅkh. differs, he prescribes no *harivat*-verses.

[3] The Adhvaryus (cp. Āp. XIV. 2. 12, Baudh. XVII. 1: 283. 10, Kāty. XII. 5. 2) use ṚS. I. 84. 3 or (cp. TS. I. 4. 38-42) other verses, among which are ṚS. I. 84. 1,2.—Cp. Śat. br. IV. 5. 3. 4: *taṃ vai harivatyarcā gṛhṇāti, harivatīṣu stuvate, harivatīr anuśaṁsati: vīryaṃ vai h a r a indro surāṇāṃ sapatnānāṁ samavṛṅkta, etc.*

8. The ṣoḍaśin has twenty one resting places, for seven priests make *vaṣaṭ* at the morning-service, seven at the midday-service, seven at the afternoon-service [1].

[1] The remark is made with respect to § 5. For the rest, all the stotras of this day are twenty-one-versed.

9. It is the gaurīvita (-sāman) [1].

[1] Grām. V. 1. 22, composed on SV. I. 168, chanted on SV. II. 302–304, cp. § 22. Ait. br IV. 2. 1: *gaurivītaṃ ṣolaśisāma kurvīta.*

10. Gaurīviti, the son of Śakti, saw this (sāman), as it was left over from sacred lore; that became the gaurīvita (-sāman). In lauding the ṣoḍaśin with the gaurīvita, they laud that which has been left over by means of that which has been left over: it (the ṣoḍaśin) includes the day of to-morrow and is also fit for (obtaining) progeny [1].

[1] Cp. XI. 5. 14-15; with a few variants § 1–10 occur also in Jaim. br. I. 203, 204.

11. 'He (*i.e.* my Udgātṛ?) has by means of a creeper happily encircled the big one,' thus (once upon a time) spoke Upoditi, the descendant of Gopāla, 'he has applied on the anuṣṭubh(-part) [1] the nānada, and has chanted the ṣoḍaśin on the gaurīvita(-melody); thereby, he has got straightway to prosperity, from prosperity [2] I am not deprived' [3].

1 That part of the ārbhava-pavamāna laud which precedes the last part (in this case, the nānada is chanted on SV. II. 47–49, cp. Appendix 4. d on the Ārṣeyakalpa, page 208 of the edition).

2 *śriyā* for *śriyāḥ*, ablative.

3 We are tempted to change all the third persons of the words uttered by Upoditi into first person singular, but, as the Jaim. br. presents equally the third person, we must take as subject 'the Udgātṛ.' The parallel passage occurs twice in the Jaim. br. (I. 204, III. 80) in these words: *aupoditir ha smāha gaupālayo: viśālaṃ libujayābhyadhād, anuṣṭubhi nānadam akran* (or *akṛt*), *gaurivītena ṣoḍaśinam atuṣṭuvan, na śriyā (a)vapadya iti; na ha vai sriyā (a)vapadyate ya evaṃ veda.*—For the rest, we have here an attempt to reconcile the different views: the nānada, mentioned in § 4 and the gaurīvita of § 9.

12. He, forsooth, happily encircles, by means of a creeper, the big one, who, having applied the nānada on the anuṣṭubh(-part), chants the ṣoḍaśin on the gaurīvita; straightway he comes to prosperity, from prosperity he is not deprived.

13. On the śakvarī(-verses)[1] the ṣoḍaśin should be chanted by him, who wishes: 'May I be possessed of a thunderbolt' ('a destructive weapon)'.

1 Probably SV. II. 1151–1153=ṚS. X. 133. 1–3 (cp. TS. II. 2. 8. 5 with ib. I. 7. 3. 0); to the author of the Kāthaka (X. 10; 136. 8 sqq.) the mahānāmnī-verses are the same as the śakvarī-verses, as it seems, cp. my note 272 on 'Altindische Zauberei, die Wunschopfer,' page 100, and cp. Nidānasūtra II. 13: *atha khalv āha · śakvarīṣu ṣoḍaśinā stuvīteti; tatraike mahānāmnīḥ pratiyanty, etāḥ śakvaryo bhavantīty; etāsv eva śakvarīpravādo bhavatīty aparam, etāś cādhikṛtā bhavantīti.* Laty. X. 2. 1 sqq.: *śakvarīṣu soḍaśinā stuvīteti; gaurīvitaṃ mahānāmnīṣu syād ṛkcodanā hi tatprakaraṇe; mahānāmnyas tv eva ṣoḍaśisāma syur, na hy etāsv anyat sāmāpadyate.* The Sūtrakāra, then, prefers to take the mahānāmnī-verses as the chant of the ṣoḍaśin. As there exists in the ūhagāna no gaurīvita on SV. II. 1151–1153, the author of this text seems to accept the view of the Sūtrakāra.

14. The ṣoḍaśin, forsooth, is a thunderbolt, the śakvarī(-verses) are a thunderbolt; by means of a thunderbolt he grants him a thunderbolt: he becomes possessed of a thunderbolt (a deadly weapon)[1].

1 Cp. Ait. br. IV. 1. 2.

15. On anuṣṭubh(-verses)[1] should he hold the ṣoḍaśin(-laud), who wishes, 'May not the word (of my rival) outtalk me'[2].

1 Cp. § 17.

2 Jaim. br. I. 205: *na mānyā vāg ativaded iti.*

16. The ṣoḍaśin is a thunderbolt, the anuṣṭubh is the word; by means of a thunderbolt he grants him the word; the word does not out-talk him.

17. 'The soma has been pressed out for thee, o Indra'[1], on these (verses) the laud must be held (in this case).

[1] The verses are recorded in note 1 on § 7.

18. On virāj (-verses)[1] should he hold the ṣoḍaśin-laud who wishes food; the ṣoḍaśin is a thunderbolt, food is virāj-like[2]; by means of a thunderbolt he grants him food: he becomes an eater of food.

[1] Cp. § 19.

[2] Cp. IV. 8. 4.

19. 'Bring ye unto the great of great prosperity'[1], on these (verses) the (ṣoḍaśin-) laud should be held (in this case).

[1] SV. I. 328=RS. VII. 31. 10-12=SV. II. 1143-1145.

20. These virāj(-verse)s are of thirty-three syllables: by the twenty-one[1] of their syllables they are a support[2], by the twelve[1] they are a (means of) procreation[3].

[1] 33 may be divided in to 21+12.

[2] Cp. II. 14. 3.

[3] Because, according to Sayana, the young ones are born a year of 12 months after the conception.—The Jaim. br. I. 204 expresses the same thought more logically: *tato yāny ekaviṃśatiḥ pratiṣṭhā sātha yāni dvādaśa prajananaṃ tat.*

21. He who knows this gets a firm support and gets offspring, and, moreover, he is not deprived of the (progeny) being in the womb[1].

[1] This is only a conjecture for rendering *nāntasthāyāṃ jīyate.* The Jaim. br. I. 204 has precisely the same words, but elsewhere (II. 105) we find the following passage: *tasya* (*i.e.* of the ekāha called abhibhū) *trivṛtau madhye bhavatas trayastriṃśāv abhito; brahma vai trivṛt, kṣatraṃ trayastriṃśaḥ; kṣatreṇa tad ubhayato brahma parigṛhṇāti, yado vai kṣatreṇa brahma parigṛhṇāty, atha sa tasyāntasthāṃ tiṣṭhaty; atitiṣṭhaty antasthāṃ, nāntasthāyā jīyate.* My translation rests on a reading *antasthāyā* (*ḥ*).

22. Now (there are) those one-footed, three-syllabic bhurij-śakvarīs: Viṣṇu's metre[1].

[1] This is the designation of the liturgical interpolations (*upasargas*) in SV. I. 302-304 (cp. above, § 9, note 1); *pra vaha, hariha, matir na; navyaṃ na, divo na s(u)var na; mitro na, yatir na, bhṛgur na.* Nidānasūtra II. 12: *tasyaitā* (*tasya*

viz. ṣoḍaśinaḥ) ṛcaḥ pañcaviṁśatyakṣarāḥ pañcapadāḥ pañcākṣarapādā navopasargākṣarāś cāditas, trayāṇām padānām trīṇi triṇy upasargākṣarāṇi pādānteṣu bhavanti, te 'ṣṭākṣarāḥ sampadyante, pañcākṣarāv uttarau daśākṣarāv ekas; tāś catustriṁśadakṣarāḥ sampadyante. na sthā upasṛṣṭāḥ kano vidyāmetīttham hy eva vayam adhīmahe, tathā bahvṛcā iti (see Kauṣ. br. XVII. 1. and Śāṅkh. śrs. V. 5. 2); *brāhmaṇenety āhuś* (XII. 13. 24): *catustriṁśadakṣarāḥ saṁstuto bhavatīty anupasṛṣṭaḥ kanīyān iti vai tad bhavaty; athāpy uddhriyamāṇeṣūpasargākṣareṣu naivārtho hīyate, na vṛttir duṣyaty, athāpi śaśvad enā anupasṛṣṭā ātharvaṇikā adhīyate; 'thāpi nidhāritānām upasargākṣarāṇām vadaty* (XII. 13. 22): *atha vā etā ekāpadās tryakṣarā viṣṇoṣ chando bhurijaḥ śakvarya iti, tryakṣarā hy api bhurijo bhavantīti.* The meaning of these words is, on the whole, clear, only the passage *na sthā upasṛṣṭāḥ kano vidyāmeti* is, to me at least, incomprehensible. The author's remark that the Atharvavedins read this hymn without the *upasargas,* refers to the Paippalāda-śākhā (II. 7, in the Journal of the Amer. Oriental Society, Vol. XXX, page 196). The verses do n o t occur in the pūrvārcika, but are found in the Ṛgveda texts, cp. Weber, Ind. Studien, Vol. XIII. page 144, Whitney's remark on AV. II. 5 and Scheftelowitz, 'Die Apokrypha des Ṛgveda', page 18.—The *upasargas* are called *viṣṇoś chandaḥ* (so also the Jaim. br. I. 205) because of Viṣṇu's three renowned steps: *tripadasāmānyāt tredhā nidadhe padam iti,* says the Anupada-sūtra III. 12. It is noteworthy that the Aitareyins use as *upasargas* certain parts of the mahānāmnī-verses, which elsewhere are called also *śakvaryaḥ*, cp. note 1 on XII. 13. 13.

23. By means of these (verses) Indra slew Vṛtra; swiftly, forsooth, he (the Sacrificer, or the Chanter) slays by means of these (verses) his bad lot, swiftly he fares better.

24. There are thirty-four syllables, when they (the interpolations) are taken up in the laud[1]. Thirty-three in number, are the deities[2], Prajāpati is the thirty-fourth of the deities; (so) they come unto Prajāpati: so as not to be hurt.

1 SV. II 302-304 comprise: the *upasargas* which consist of 3×3=9 syllables, not taken into account, five verse-quarters: of five syllables each: 25+9=34.

2 Eight Vasus, eleven Rudras, twelve Ādityas, Indra and the *vaṣaṭ*-call. The same statement Śat. br. IV. 5. 7 2, V. 1. 2. 13, V. 3. 4. 23.

25. They perform the ṣoḍaśin-laud, whilst passing on from hand to hand (a piece of) gold[1]. His ṣoḍaśin(-feast) (thereby) is provided with light.

1 Cp. Lāṭy. III. 1. 9.-11, Drāhy. VII. 1. 9-11: the gold must be held in the hand by those of the three Chanters, who actually chant: during the prastāva in the hand of the Prastotṛ, during the udgītha in the hand of the Udgātṛ, during the pratihāra in the hand of the Pratihartṛ, during the nidhana either the Udgātṛ should hold it, or all three should touch the gold. Baudh. XVII. 3: 235. 15: *hiraṇyaṁ sampradāya stuvate,* Jaim. br. I. 205: *hiraṇyam sampradāyam stuvanti.*

26. A black horse stands near[1] (during the ṣoḍaśin-laud); for presence's sake[2]. It stands (near), blowing away ('scattering') the dwelling place of (his) rival.

[1] Cp. Lāty. III. 1. 4-8, Drāhy. VII. 1. 4-8: 'A black horse should stand with its head directed to the west, at the eastern door of the sadas, according to Śāṇḍilya with its head directed to the east, at the western door, according to Dhānañjayya. If no black horse is to be got, it should be a brown one; if such a one is not to be got, it should be of any colour available. If no horse is to be got, it should be a cow or a goat'. Cp. Baudh. XVII. 3: 285 14, Āp. XIV. 3. 3.

[2] On *sāmyekṣya* see note 5 on Jaim. br. in Auswahl § 77.

27. The monosyllabic metre was the lowest one in possession of the Gods, the heptasyllabic their highest; the enneasyllabic one was the lowest of the Asuras, the metre of fifteen syllables was their highest. The Gods, now, and the Asuras were contending with each-other. Prajāpati, having become of anuṣṭubh-nature, took place between them. The Gods and the Asuras called him to join them and he joined the Gods. Thereupon the Gods throve, the Asuras perished[1].

[1] As the Gods had now obtained a higher metre than the Asuras possessed. This passage refers to the Anuṣṭubh-verses mentioned in XII. 13. 7, which may be used for the ṣoḍaśin-stotra.

28. He himself thrives, his rival perishes, who knows this.

29. By means of the monosyllablic metre the Gods took away the metre of fifteen-syllables belonging to the Asuras; by means of the disyllabic metre, the metre of fourteen syllables (belonging to the Asuras); by means of the trisyllabic metre, the metre of thirteen syllables (of the Asuras); by means of the four-syllabic metre, the metre of twelve syllables (of the Asuras); by means of the five-syllabic metre, the metre of eleven-syllables; by means of the six-syllabic metre, the metre of ten syllables; by means of the seven-syllabic metre, the metre of nine-syllables (of the Asuras); by means of the eight syllables (of the anuṣṭubh-metre representing Prajapati), they took away the eight syllables (of the Asuras).

30. In this same manner he who knows thus takes away the welfare of his rival.

31. The ṣoḍaśin (soma-feast) is, as it were, a sacrifice (to be performed) for one who is held away (from his realm, his dominion): weaker, as it were, were the Gods at that time, stronger the

Asuras; he who knows this, though he be weaker, takes away his rival, though he be stronger.

32. (Muttering the verse): 'Higher than whom no other is born, he who encompasses all beings: Prajāpati, being united with creatures, is associated with the three lights[1], he, the ṣoḍaśin': the Udgātṛ looks down on the soma that has been drawn (by the Adhvaryus)[2].

1 The three lights are probably the three services or savanas of an ukthya-ekāha: 1. out-of-doors-laud and four ājya-lauds; 2. midday-pavamāna-laud and four pṛṣṭha-lauds; 3. ārbhava-pavamāna-laud, the agniṣṭoma-laud and three uktha-lauds; on these follows as sixteenth laud the ṣoḍaśin.

2 Cp. Lāṭy. III. 1. 1-3, Drāhy. VII. 1. 1-3: 'At a ṣoḍaśin soma-feast they should take their seat (in the sadas) in the prescribed manner, and then enter the havirdhāna-shed, where the Udgātṛ should look down on the graha destined for Indra ṣoḍaśin, (muttering the verse): 'Higher than whom'. The same should take place at the morning-service and also at the midday- and the afternoon-service, when they (the Adhvaryus) draw (at those services) the soma'. Cp. Jaim br. 1. 205, Jaim. śrs. 15: 18. 14-19. 3, Baudh. XVII. 1: 283. 10, Āp. XIV. 2. 4-7, Kāty. XII. 5. 2-5.

33. Provided with light is the ṣoḍaśin of him who knows this.

34 The stoma is the twenty-one-fold (twenty-one-versed): for obtaining a firm support; he gets a firm support[1].

1 Cp. II. 14. 3.

Thirteenth Chapter.

(Pṛṣṭhya six-day period of the twelve-day rite.)

(Fifth day.)

XIII. 1

(Out-of doors-laud of the fifth day.)

1. (The verses beginning:) 'Be clarified, procuring cows, procuring wealth, procuring gold'[1] are the opening (tristich) of the fifth day.

1 SV. II. 305-307=ṚS. IX. 86. 39, 38, 37 (with various readings: the Jaim. agrees with the words of ṚS., but has equally the reversed order).

2. Procuring cows, procuring wealth, procuring gold are the śakvarī (-verse)s[1].

1 Which form the hotuḥ pṛṣṭhastotra.

3. The śakvarī(-verse)s are cattle[1]; by means of cattle he gets all.

[1] See note 1 on XIII. 4. 13.

4. (There are the words:) 'Thou, o Soma, procuring all, possessest good men'[1]; he, forsooth, possesses good men, who has cattle; to this he thereby refers

[1] SV. II. 305. c.

5. 'Let these pour out on thy behalf butter and milk full of sweetness'[1]: the cattle, forsooth, pours out butter and milk full of sweetness; to this he thereby refers.

[1] SV. II. 307. c.

6. (The verses beginning:) 'Of thee who art being clarified'[1] are the corresponding (tristich, the antistrophe).

[1] SV. II. 308–310=ṚS. IX. 64. 7–9. (var. r. in 310)

7. To all (kinds of) wealth he thereby refers, for through cattle he obtains all.

8. 'Thy streams have been produced'[1]: for produced, as it were, are now the days[2].

[1] SV. II. 308. b.

[2] *Viz.* in the preceding four.

9. And, moreover, after the former characteristic he thereby speaks the latter characteristic; that he speaks after the former characteristic the latter characteristic, is the reason why the corresponding tristich is called anurūpa. A son resembling to him he gets, who knows this. The stotriya and the anurūpa are tristichs, for retaining the vital airs[1].

[1] This is identical with XI. 6. 4–6.

10. There are two heptastichs[1]: for propping the metres[2].

[1] SV. II. 311–317=ṚS. IX. 24. 1, 2, 3, 5, 4, 6, 7 (a sūkta, with various readings); SV. II. 318–324=ṚS. IX. 20. 1–7 (a sūkta).

[2] Because there are *sapta caturuttarāṇi chandāṃsi*, Jaim. br. III. 86

11. There is a tetrastich[1]: for gaining firm footing.

[1] SV. II. 325–328=ṚS. IX. 55. 1–4 (a sūkta; with var. r.).

12. A tristich is the last[1]: with which breath they start, in that breath they break up[2] ('finish the laud').—Thrice ninefold is the chant: for obtaining firm support, for increasing; for this chant is the increased ninefold one[3].

[1] SV. II. 329–331=ṚS. IX. 62 7–9 (var. readings).

[2] Cp. note 1 on XI 6.9.

[3] In having thrice the size of the trivṛt.

XIII. 2.

(The ājya-lauds of the fifth day.)

1. (The tristich beginning:) 'Thy beautiful manifestations as from the lightning of the rainy (cloud)'[1] is the ājya-laud addressed to Agni[2].

[1] SV. II. 332–334=RS X. 91. 5, 7, 8 (with var. readings).

[2] The first, or hotur ajya.

2. Cattle is a beautiful manifestation, the śakvarī (-verse)s are a beautiful manifestation; to this he thereby refers.

3*a*.—'of Agni, have shone forth as the coming forth of the downs',[1] for come forth, as it were, are now the days.

[1] SV. II. 332. c.

3*b*. 'Thy chariot (-horses) abide, as separately'[1]: for now these days abide, as it were.

[1] SV. II. 333. c.

4. (The tristich beginning:) 'For wide-extending is now, o Varuṇa (and Mitra), your help'[1] is the ājya-laud addressed to Mitra and Varuṇa[2]. That (part) of the sacrifice, which is performed badly, is seized by Varuṇa; this he thereby removes in sacrificing.

[1] SV. II. 335–337=RS. V. 70. 1–3 (with var. readings).

[2] The second ājya-laud.

5. (The tristich beginning:) 'Arising with power'[1] is the (ājya-laud) addressed to Indra.

[1] SV. II. 338–340=ṚS. VIII. 76. 10–12.

6. The five seasons are a characteristic of the arising[1].—(He says the words) 'with power': with power even (and) strength they arise[2]

[1] *pañca vā ṛtava utthānasya rūpam.*

[2] They will arise at the end of the sattra, they will finish the sacrificial session with strength.

7. (The tristich beginning:) 'You both, o Indra and Agni, these',[1] is the rathantara-like [2] (ājya-laud) addressed to Indra and Agni [3].

[1] SV. II. 341–343=ṚS. 60. 7–9.

[2] The ājya, which is required at a rathantara-day, a day on which the first pṛṣṭha-laud is the rathantara, cp. the next §.

[3] The fourth ājya-laud.

8. The śakvarī (-verse)s are in a cryptic way the (same as the) rathantara [1]; he thereby displays the characteristic of the rathantara.—The stoma (is given) [2].

[1] Cp. Ait. br. IV. 28. 3 and above, XII. 2. 5.

[2] Cp. XIII. 1. 12.

XIII. 3.

(The midday-pavamāna-laud of the fifth day.)

1. The verses (beginning): 'Flow, o Soma, bright'[1] are gāyatrīs containing (the word) 'Viṣṇu.'

[1] SV. II. 503=ṚS. IX. 65. 19–21=SV. II. 344–346.

2. The gāyatrī is the priesthood [1], Viṣṇu is the sacrifice: in the priesthood he thereby establishes firmly the sacrifice.

[1] Cp. VI. 1. 6.

3 (The verses beginning): 'Soma, being pressed by the pressers'[1] are the characteristic of the simās [2]; by means of their own characteristic he makes them flourishing.

[1] SV. I. 515=ṚS. IX. 107. 8–9=SV. II. 347–348.

[2] This is another name for the mahānāmnī- or śakvarī-verses; the verses are characteristic of the śakvarīs, as they contain the word 'cow' (in SV. II. 348. a, b), the śakvarīs being identified with cattle.

4. (The verses beginning:) 'What bright, praiseworthy, o Soma'[1], being gāyatrīs, are triṣṭubhs by their characteristic [2]; therefore they are applied in the place of the triṣṭubhs [3].

[1] SV. II. 349–351=ṚS. IX 19. 1, 3, 2 (with var. r.)

[2] Because they contain the word *vṛṣan* (in SV. II. 350. a), cp. X 6. 2.

[3] The triṣṭubh is used at the end of the midday-pavamāna.

5. There is the gāyatra (-sāman) The brāhmaṇa of the gāyatra is the same[1].

[1] Cp. VIII. 1 14 sqq.

6. There is the yaṇva (-sāman)[1]. The yaṇva is cattle[2]: for retaining cattle.

[1] Araṇyegeyagāna III. 1. 11, composed on SV. I. 198 and araṇyaka-saṃhitā II. 3, 4, see SV. ed. Calcutta, Vol. II, page 267; in the ūhyagāna (SV. ed. Calcutta. Vol. V, page 394) it is I. 1. III.

[2] It is not clear why the yaṇva is identified with cattle The Jaim. br. (III. 91) records that by this sāman Prajāpati withheld the cattle that had run away.

7. He chants (it) connectedly,[1] for the sake of the continuity of the sacrifice[2].

[1] By leaving out the prastāvas of the second and third verses, on which the yaṇva is chanted (but there are different views!), Lāṭy. VI. 1. 14; Drāhy. XVI. 1. 15. A prayoga (India office, No. 1671) has: *yaṇve prathamāyāṃ pratihāro nāsti, uttarayoḥ prastāvo nāsti, prastāvābhāvād oṃkārenodgīthādānam api na.* Differently the Jaiminīyas (br. III. 92), who chant thrice (once in each verse) the prastāva. make once the pratihāra and chant thrice the nidhana.

[2] In order not to break the sacrifice in the midst.

8. It is of one and a half *iḍā*[1], for such is the characteristic of this day[2].

[1] The *iḍā* is: *iṭ* | *iḍā 2345.* (1 1 1 1 1)

[2] See X. 11. 1, note 5.

9. There is the śākala (-sāman)[1].

[1] Grām. III. 2. 27, composed on SV. I. 126, chanted on SV. II. 344-346 (see § 1).

10. By means of this (sāman) Śakala on the fifth day gained a firm support.

11. There is vārśa (-sāman)[1].

[1] Grām. XIV. 1. 2, composed on SV. I. 498, chanted on the same verses (SV ed. Calcutta, Vol. II, page 56, first of the three vārśas).

12. Vṛśa, the son of Jana, was the house-chaplain of Tryaruṇa. Tridhātu's son, of the Ikṣvāku family. This (Tryaruṇa) of the Ikṣvāku-family, (once) riding out[1] on his chariot, destroyed (ran over) the child (boy) of a Brāhmin. He said to his chaplain: 'Under thy chaplainship has such a thing happened unto me.' He (Vṛśa) by means of this melody

restored him to life : such had been his wish at that moment. Wish-granting is the vārśa-sāman ; he (who applies it in lauding) gets (the fulfilment of) his wish [2].

[1] Read with the Leyden ms. : *aikṣvāko dhūvayan.*

[2] For the parallel version of the Jaiminīyas cp. Jaim. br. III. 94 in Journal of the Amer. Or. Society, vol. XVIII, page 21, and 'das Jaim. br. in Auswahl' No. 180 ; also Bṛhaddevatā V. 14 sqq.

13. It is of one and a half *iḍā* [1], for such is the characteristic of this day [2].

[1] The nidhana is $\overset{2}{\bar{a}}$'$\overset{5}{3234}$*pā* (according to the Jaiminīyas *ā ūpā*) but cp. note on IX. 6. 1.

[2] See X. 11. 1.

14. There is the mānava (-sāman) [1].

[1] Grām. II. 1. 23, composed on SV. I. 54, chanted on SV. II. 347–348 (see above, § 3), the second of the two.

15. By means of this (sāman) Manu got offspring and multiplication; he who applies in lauding the mānava (-sāman), becomes procreative and is multiplied.

16. There is the ānūpa (-sāman) [1].

[1] Grām. VII. 2. 23, composed on SV. I. 277, chanted on II. 347–348. The first of the two sāmans of this name is required: *svāram*, and, according to the Jaim. br. *anutodavat*, beginning : $\overset{4}{a}\overset{5}{\acute{s}}\overset{4}{v\bar{\imath}}$ $\overset{5}{a\acute{s}v\bar{\imath}}$.

17. By this sāman Vadhryaśva, the son of Anūpa, reached abundance of cattle. Having applied in lauding the ānūpa (-sāman), he reaches abundance of cattle [1].

[1] In the Jaim. br. (III. 97) it is Anūpa Dhitāni (name uncertain !), who, being a king, wished to become also a Seer : to obtain priesthood and nobility.

18. There is the vāmra (-sāman) [1].

[1] Grām. VII. 2. 6, composed on SV. I. 268, chanted (see § 3) on SV. II. 347–348. There are many sāmans of this name, but cp. § 20.

19. It is a sāman commendable by its ṛṣi-descent [1]. The bull, the horse or the man, whom they (people) commend (wish to praise), they commend, saying; 'a good one (it is)' [2]. By this sāman they commend the day.

1 Cp. XII. 11 14. According to the Jaim. br. (III. 99) this melody was seen by Vamra, the son of Vikhanas.

2 *vāma*, a feeble pun on *vāmra*!

20 It is of one and a half *iḍā*[1], for such is the characteristic of this day[2]

1 The sāman ends: *ā 3234 pā*, cp. note 1 on § 13.

2 See X. 11. 1.

21. There is the (sāman) of Agni with triple finale[1], for obtaining firm footing[2].

1 Grām. XIV 2. 20, composed on SV. I. 514, chanted on SV. II. 347-348 I am not able to point out, which parts are the three nidhanas. According to the Prayoga, the nidhanas are certain parts of words of the verses, perhaps *nā 234 sā*, *gr 234 vih*, *ścu 234 tām*, see SV. ed. Calcutta. Vol. II. page 86.

2 According to Sāyana this refers to tripods (*tripadāḥ phalakādayaḥ*).

22. Fire (Agni), having been created[1], did not flame. With this sāman, Prajāpati blew on it (or: fanned it) and thereupon it did flame. This sāman, forsooth, is brilliancy and spiritual lustre. By means of this (sāman) he obtains brilliancy and spiritual lustre[2].

1 Being emitted from Prajāpati's mouth, cp VI. 1. 6

2 According to the tradition of the Jaiminīyas (br III. 101, see the text in 'Auswahl', No. 181) this sāman, besides *āgneyam trinidhanam*, is also called sākamaśva (as such it is not designated in the Jaim. ārṣeyabrāhmana). About the origin of this name we read the following interesting record: 'Kakṣīvat asked Priyamedha: 'Who is it, who being kindled, does not flame, Priyamedha?' This he did not comprehend, and he answered: 'Let my progeny answer this (question)'. Now Kakṣīvat possessed a basket (made) of *nākuli*, filled with grains of priyangu or adhikata; of these (grains) he threw away one each year: so long was life granted to him (*i.e.* as long as the grains would last). Now Sākamaśva was born out of Priyamedha as ninth (descendant). (Read *navamaḥ* in stead of *nāvamaḥ*). He (Sākamaśva) wished: 'May I overcome this (difficulty), may I find a way out: an answer (to the question addressed to my ancestor)'. He saw this sāman and chanted it over (Kakṣīvat). Thereupon he saw the answer He ran up to Kakṣīvat. When he (Kakṣīvat) saw him running up to him, he said: 'Throw ye this basket of mine into the water: here I see him, who having answered, shall overcome the difficulty of the question put by me'. Then he (Sākamaśva) approached him (*viz.* Kakṣīvat) and said: 'He who practises a verse but not a chant, does not shine, being kindled, but he who practises not only a verse but also a chant, (*i.e.* who knows the chant to be sung on a verse), he is kindled, he shines. This is the answer I give thee, this (is the answer that gives thee) my father, my grand-

father, my great-grandfather' he said, and cited his ancestors up to Priyamedha, etc.

23. There is 'the (sāman) of the young one' (the śaiśava-sāman)[1].

[1] Grām XII. 2 8, composed on SV. I. 467, chanted on SV. II. 349-351. There are two sāmans of this name (see SV. ed Calcutta, Vol. V, page 4), but the first, being *svāram*, is required.

24. Śiśu of the Angiras clan was a mantra-maker amongst the mantra-makers; he used to address his Fathers as ('my) sons'. To him said his Fathers: 'Thou doest wrong in addressing us, who are thy Fathers, as (thy) sons'. He answered: 'I am, forsooth, the Father, I who am a mantra-maker'. They resorted to the Gods (for a decision). The Gods said: 'He indeed, is the Father, who is a mantra-maker'. So he triumphed then. He who in lauding applies the śaiśava (-sāman), triumphs[1].

[1] To this story allude Baudhāyana (dhś. I. 3. 47) and Manu (II 151-153), and cp. Harivaṃśa I, 17th adhy., M.Bh. IX 51. 46 sqq

25. They chant (it) on gāyatrī (-verses)[1], for obtaining firm support and priestly lustre. With what breath they start[2], in that they finish.

[1] Cp. § 4.

[2] The laud begins (§ 1), and ends on gāyatrī-verses.—cp. XII 9. 23.

26. They are gāyatrī (-verses) containing the word 'bull'[1]; thereby they do not depart from the characteristic of the triṣṭubh[2].—The stoma (is given)[3].

[1] Cp. XII. 9. 24; SV. II. 350. a: *vṛṣā punāna āyūṃṣi*

[2] See note 2 on XII. 9. 24. Sāyaṇa's explication here seems to be false also.

[3] See XIII. 1. 12.

XIII. 4.

(The pṛṣṭha-lauds of the fifth day.)

1. Indra wishing to slay Vṛtra, resorted to Prajāpati. He formed out of the metres valour and strength and delivered it to him, saying: 'Be able (to slay him) by means of this' (*śaknuhi*); hence the *śakvarī* (-verse)s have their name. (By means of it) he (Indra) split (Vṛtra's) skull, (*sīmānam*, properly 'the suture of the skull'); therefore (these verses are called also) the *simās*. He (Indra) made *mahnyā*[1]; therefore (these verses are called also) the *mahnyās*. There was a great noise

(*mahān ghoṣaḥ*); therefore (these verses are called) also the *mahānāmnīs.*

[1] This seems to be a kind of interjection, designating a certain noise. The corresponding name in the Jaim. br. is *maṭviḥ* (from *maṭu* ?).

2. The five-footed (śakvarī-verse) supports the (five) quarters; the six-footed one, the (six) seasons; the seven-footed one, the (seven) metres, the two-footed one (supports) man [1].

[1] The śakvarī- or mahānāmnī-verses in the sāmavedic recension are given in the SV. ed. Calcutta, Vol. II, pages 371–386. Each of the three (the *puruṣapadāni* not taken into account) is said to contain two elements: the śakvarī-parts proper (*śākvaram*) and the not-śakvarī-parts (*aśākvaram*), which are regarded as stobhas. Each of the three is subdivided into eight parts.

1. the *dvipadā* (1. *vidā...diśo*; 2. *vidā...anu*; 3. *indram...aparājitam*); this part is *aśākvaram.*

2. three padas (1. *śikṣā....abhiṣṭibhiḥ*; 2. *maṁhiṣṭham...maghonām*; 3. *sa naḥ...adrivo*); these three padas are *śākvarāḥ.*

3. the *dhātu* (1. *svaɜr nāṁśuḥ*; 2. *aṁśur na śociḥ*; 3. *aṁśur madāya*); this part is *aśākvaram.*

4. the *vatsa* (1. *pracetana pracetayo*; 2. *cikitvo abhi no naya*; 3. *sumnā ādhehi no vaso*), equally *aśākvaram.*

5. the *ūdhar* (1. *indra dyumnāya na iṣe*; 2. *indro vide tam u stuhi*; 3. *pūrtiḥ śaviṣṭha śasyate*); this pada is *śākvaraḥ.*

6. the *puruṣa* (1. *evā hi śakro*; 2. *īśe hi śakraḥ*; 3. *vaśī hi śakraḥ*); this part is *aśākvaram.*

7. three padas (1. *rāye...ṛñjase*; 2. *tam ūtaye...dviṣaḥ*; 3. *nūnaṃ...bravāvahai*) these padas are *śākvarāḥ.*

8. the *adhyāsa* (1. *āyāhi piba matsva*; 2. *kratuś...bṛhat*; 3. *sakhā advayuḥ*); is *aśākvaraḥ.*

In this way the first śakvarī-verse proper is seven-footed (parts 2, 5, 7); the first verse, for instance, runs:

śikṣā śacīnāṃ pate | pūrvīṇāṃ purūvaso | ābhiṣ ṭvam abhiṣṭibhiḥ | indro dyumnāya na iṣe | rāye vājāya vajrivaḥ | śaviṣṭha vajrinn ṛñjase | maṁhiṣṭha vajrinn ṛñjase ||

The second śakvarī-verse proper is said to be of six padas, one of its padas (*maṁhiṣṭha vajrinn ṛñjase*) having occurred already in the first. The third śakvarī-verse proper is said to be of five padas, two of its padas (the twice repeated *sa naḥ parṣad ati dviṣaḥ*) having occurred already in the second. Cp. Lāṭy. VII. 5. 9–10: *tāsāṃ* (viz. *mahānāmnīnām*) *prathamadvitīye pade dvipadās*; *trīṇi śākvarāṇi*; *dhātur, vatsa, ūdhas, tac chākvaram*; *puruṣas*; *trīṇi śākvarāṇy, adhyāsyeti padāny*; *uttamā tu dvyadhyāsā* (viz. *śūro...gacchati* and *sakhā..advayuḥ*). See also Nidānasūtra III. 13: *athaitāsu mahānāmnīṣu vipratipādayantīdaṁ śākvaram idam aśākvaram ity*; *aśākvarī prathamā dvipadā, śākvarāṇi trīṇi parāṇi padāni dhātur aśākvaraḥ pañcākṣaraḥ, sa eṣa kṛtākṛto bhavati* (this *dhātu* is indeed missing in the Ṛgvedic and the Jaiminīya recensions of the mahānāmnīs, but in the āraṇyagāna of the last mentioned *śākhā* it is inserted as a stobha); *vatso 'śākvaro 'ṣṭākṣara ; ūdhaḥ śākvaram aṣṭākṣaram ;...puruṣo 'śākvaraḥ pañcākṣaraḥ ; śākvarāṇy eva trīṇi parāṇi padāny ; adhyāso 'śākvaro 'ṣṭākṣaraḥ ;... etenaivottarayoḥ śākvarāṇi cāśākvaraṃ ca vyākhyātāni ; dvyadhyāsottamā śakvarī bhavati*, and a little farther: *atha khalv āha diśaḥ pañcapadā*..(Pañc br. XIII. 4. 2)..*dvipadeti pratilomaṃ vadati* (or *vadanti*), *padataś ced roho bhaviṣyatīti ; saptapadā prathamā śakvarī, ṣaṭpadā dvitīyā : yad dhi prathamāyā uttamaṃ padaṃ* (viz. *maṁhiṣṭha vajrinn ṛñjase*) *tad dvitīyāyāḥ prathamaṃ, pragāthasādhu pṛṣṭham* (?) *iti ; pañcapadottamā, yad dvitīyāyā uttamaṃ* (viz. *sa naḥ parṣad ati dviṣaḥ*) *tat tṛtīyāyāṃ prathamaṃ ca dvitīyaṃ ca.*

3. Taken as a whole laud (stotra) they (the mahānāmnīs) are of double point (*dvyopaśa*)[1], therefore cattle is double-horned (*dvyopaśa*).

[1] According to Sāyana the stotra being twenty-seven-versed and the *puruṣapadāni* being five in number (XIII. 1. 12), the whole stotra contains 32 stotriya-verses: two more than a virāj; these two he declares to be the two *opaśas* or redundant stotriyas. This explanation seems to be forced and unacceptable. The two points are rather the double *adhyāsa* of the last mahānāmnī, cp. Nidānasūtra III. 13: *atha khalv āha dvyopaśāḥ saṁstutā bhavantīti ; kasyedaṃ brahmaṇaṁ syād ity ? uttamāyā dvyadhyāsyā ity āhur. ekādhyāse pūrve dvyadhyāsottamā, tasyā idam abhinandaṃ brāhmaṇaṃ vaded iti* and cp. also Jaim. br. III. 112: *atha yad uttamaṃ padaṃ upaśa eva sa ; paśceva dvitīya āgacchat, tasmād uttamā dvyupaśā.* For the rest, we must bear in mind that the mahānāmnīs are identified with cattle.

4. Two *iḍās* (are) on either side of the word *atha*[1]; therefore the horns (are) sharper than the upper part of the head between the horns.

[1] The *ūdhar*-part of each mahānāmnī-verse (see note 1 on § 2) is repeated twice, preceded and followed by *iḍā*, and between them *áthā* ; the word *iḍā* with its long last syllable is longer and therefore sharper than the middle *atha.*

5. He chants them with the small (parts)[1]; therefore, cattle are mixed up with smaller ones[2].

[1] *upakṣudra* refers apparently to the *aśākvara*-parts, which are smaller than the *śākvara*-parts (the *dvipadās*, the *dhātu* or *aṁśu*, the *vatsa* and the *puruṣa*), cp. Anupadasūtra IV. 1: *upakṣudrā gāyatīti dvipadāṁśuvatsapurīṣityadādhyasyopagānāt* (*sic !*); *vikṣudra* of Ait. br. V. 6. 5 (*vikṣudrā iva paśavaḥ*) seems to have the same meaning as *upakṣudra.*

[2] *Viz.* the calves.

6. He chants them unconnectedly[1]; therefore domestic animals (cattle) are unconnected[2].

[1] The exact meaning is not clear; according to Sāyaṇa the *śākvara*- and *aśākvara*-parts are meant.

[2] As they go about according to their inclination, according to their different nature (Sāyana).

7. He chants them being of various characteristics [1]; therefore cattle is of different forms.

[1] Cp. note 1 on § 6: *kṣudraśākvarāṇāṃ vairūpyāt*, Anupadasūtra IV. 1.

8 The waters had milk as their fluid. The Gods were afraid of a confusion of things (of a mixture of good and bad) [1]. That he puts water near, whilst chanting (the śākvara-stotra) [2], is for keeping apart good and bad.

[1] Lest their milky nature might be changed (?).

[2] Cp. VIII. 8. 2; Lāṭy. III. 5. 13-23, Drāhy. IX. 1. 14-22: 'Having put near (a vessel filled with) water with avakās (Blyxa octandra, a water-plant) they should chant the mahānāmnīs. On whomsoever rests the (chanting of a) part of the sāman, he should (by shuttling the vessel) cause the water to produce noise. Having made the Sacrificer say his formula (*viz.* Pañc. br. I. 3. 8), he should pour it out on the āstāva (the place, outside the sadas, where the out-of-doors-laud has been held) with (the formula): 'Unassailable art thou (fem.). Let King Soma favour thee. Whom (fem.) the Waters, not tasted, approach, the śakvarī-bulls that are self-willing, let these flow, let these rain, let these produce strength, refreshment and welfare. May I obtain this' (the unintelligible mantra is in part a variant on Ath. S. IX. 1. 9), or with the verse: 'Some assemble' (SV. ār. saṃh. III. 6), or with the verse: 'To the ocean I send you forth' (given in full before, Lāṭy. II. 1. 8, Drāhy. IV. 1. 8), or with all (those mantras). The avakās they should insert between their knees; he who desires rain, should have them thrown on the roof (of his dwelling), according to Śāṇḍilya; in a cow-stall, one who desires cattle; in a hall, one who desires glory; on a place for cremation, one who wishes to exercise magic charm'.

9. Separation of good and bad comes (to him) who knows this [1].

[1] This § is identical with VI. 1. 13.

10. It is the gāyatrī-track [1] with (the word) *svar* [2] as nidhana for one who desires priestly lustre; with honey it [3] approaches (him) in yonder world. It is the triṣṭubh-track [1] with (the word) *atha* [2] as nidhana for one who desires strength; with clarified butter it [3] approaches (him) in yonder world. It is the jagatī-track [1] with (the word) *iḍā* [2] as nidhana for one who desires cattle; with milk it [3] approaches (him) in yonder world

[1] *ayana* in the sense which it has in *gavām ayana*, denoting a longer course of sacrificial days: here the *dvādaśāham ayanam*. The designation *gāyatra, traiṣṭubha, jāgata* rests, as it seems, solely on the fact that *brahmavarcasa, ojas, paśu* are

connected with these metres, being destined resp. for a brāhmaṇa, a kṣatriya, a vaiśya, cp. VI. 1. 6. 8, 10.

[2] As to where these words should be applied as nidhana, the ritualistic authorities maintain different views; Lāṭy. X. 2. 6-9: 'The nidhanas of the śakvarī(-verse)s, on which rests (the fulfilment of) different desires, should be inserted at the place of each *iḍā*, according to (our) Teachers, for this is the most frequently occurring (syllable in this chant). In the *ūdhar*-part only (cp. note 1 on XIII. 4. 2) according to Gautama and Dhānañjayya, for to this place it (*viz.* the brāhmana, XIII. 4. 4.) designs the nidhana. On the place of *atha* (these nidhanas should be applied, cp. the brāhmaṇa, l.c.), according to Śaucivṛkṣi, for in this way the modification is the slightest (in this case only one change finds place as the word *atha* occurs only once in each śakvarī-chant). Without any restriction (these *kāmyāni nidhanāni* must be applied) at the places of all the nidhanas, according to Kautsa.'—The Nidānasūtra (IV. 1) discusses at length this same topic.

[3] I take as subject *ayanam*, differing from Sāyaṇa, who takes as subject 'he' ('he meets with' etc.).

11. Rajana, the son of Kuṇi, said (once upon a time) to Alamma, the son of Parijānat: 'Ārya, of the Mālya family, has stopped[1] the śakvarī(verse)s by means of a straight (chanting), when he will be able to establish them firmly'. This is their straight (chanting), thereby are they firmly established, if he (the Chanter) performs quickly their prastāva and their udgītha.

[1] The meaning of the whole sentence, especially of the word *prārautsīt* is far from clear to me.

12. Having chanted the śakvarīs. they chant the *purīṣa* (-part)[1].

[1] The five *purīṣapadāni* are given SV. ed. Calcutta, Vol. II, page 384. Here also the authorities differ regarding the manner of applying the *purīṣas*. Lāṭy. X. 2. 10-12: 'According to Dhānañjayya, the *purīṣa*(-part) is connected with the last stotriya-verse, because (in the gāna) it immediately follows (after the śakvarī-chants). As by the words: 'having chanted the śakvarīs' it (*viz.* the brāhmaṇa) designs a separation, and then says '(they chant) the *purīṣa* (-part)', it should be unconnected (and only applied once). It should fall at the end of a round or at the end of the stotra'. The question is discussed at length also in the Nidānasutra IV. 1, 2.

13. The śakvarī (-verse)s, forsooth, are cattle[1], the *purīṣa* (-part) is the cow-pen; they thus (in chanting the *purīṣa*-part at the end) erect a cow-pen for the cattle and drive (the cows) within: in order that they may not slip away.

[1] We are to think of those parts called *ūdhar* and *vatsa*.

14. (There are the verses beginning:) 'Indra has thriven for the carouse'[1], for at that time they throve[2].

[1] SV. I. 411=ṚS. I. 81. 1-3=SV. II. 352-354; these are the verses on which the third or Brahman's pṛṣthastotra is chanted.

[2] Cp. XII. 12. 2, XI. 11. 3. Read, perhaps, *avardhata* ('Indra throve at that time'). Sāyaṇa takes h e r e *yajamānāḥ* as subject.

15. On these the bārhadgira (-saman)[1] (the chant of Bṛhadgiri) (is chanted).

[1] Aranyegeyagāna III. 1. 16, composed on SV. I. 411.

16*a*. (There is the tristich beginning:) 'Of the sweet, thus being in the midst[1]'. The fifth day, forsooth, is in the midst[2].

[1] SV. I. 409=ṚS. I. 84. 10-12=SV. II. 385-357 (with var. r.). These are the verses for the fourth, or Acchāvāka's pṛṣthastotra.

[2] This reckoning is inexact. It is neither the middle of the twelve-day period, nor of the ten-day period.

16*b*. On these the rāyovājīya (-sāman)[1] (the chant of Rāyovāja) (is chanted).

[1] Araṇyegāna III. 1. 15, composed on SV. I. 409.

17. Indra gave the Yatis over to the hyaenas. Three of them were left over: Pṛthuraśmi, Bṛhadgiri and Rāyovāja. These said: 'Who will bear ('support') us (as his) sons?' 'I', answered Indra and he, having put them on (his back), roamed about tending them. Having tended them he said: 'Boys, choose ye a boon'. 'Might for me', said Pṛthuraśmi. To him he gave, by means of this pārthuraśma (-sāman), might. One who desires might, should apply this (sāman) in lauding. To his share falls the lustre of might. 'Priestly lustre for me', said Bṛhadgiri. To him he gave, by means of this bārhadgira (-sāman), priestly lustre. One who desires priestly lustre, should apply this (sāman) in lauding. He becomes possessed of priestly lustre. 'Cattle to me', said Rāyovāja. To him he gave, by means of this rāyovājīya (-sāman), cattle. One who desires cattle, should, in lauding, apply this (sāman). He becomes rich in cattle[2].

[1] Read, probably, with the two Leyden MSS.: *paricaryācarad* instead of °*caran*, but cp. Oertel, Disjunct use of cases, page 21.

[2] For references see note 1 on VIII. 1. 4.

18. He should take the pārthuraśma (-sāman)[1] as Brahman's chant for a noble, the bārhadgira (-sāman) for a priest, the rāyovājīya (-sāman) for a peasant. By means of their own characteristic (by means of what naturally belongs to them, see § 17) he thereby makes them prosper[1].—The stoma (is given)[2].

[1] Araṇyegeya III. 1. 18, composed on SV. I. 409 (SV. ed. Calcutta, Vol. II, page 453), cp. note 1 on page 209 of my edition of the Ārṣeyakalpa. To the references there given may be added Lāṭy. X. 2. 13-15: 'When applying on the fifth day the rāyovājīya as the Brahman's chant, he may apply in its place what is in accordance with his wish and manner of living (in accordance with his wish, whether *kṣatram*, *brahmavarcasam* or *paśu*; in accordance with his manner of living, whether he be a priest, a noble, or a peasant). He should apply the bārhadgira, for this (chant) is contained in the araṇyegeya (gāna), being of the same metre and intended for the same day. When applying the pārthuraśma (composed on SV. I. 409=II. 355-357), he may apply it on the verses of the bārhadgira (composed on SV. I. 411=II. 352-354), in order to avoid the meeting of the (same) verses.' Because, otherwise, there would be *jāmitvam*.

[2] Cp. XII. 1. 12.

XIII. 5.

(Ārbhava-pavamāna-laud of the fifth day.)

1. (The verse beginning:) 'The soma-shoot has been pressed for intoxication'[1], is the gāyatrī; intoxicating (having *mada*) (and) rich in sap is the afternoon-service; he thus puts intoxication (and) sap (in it)[2].

[1] SV. I. 473=ṚS. IX. 62. 3-5=SV. II 358-360.

[2] See XI. 5. 1.

2. (In the verses beginning:) 'Unto (*abhi*) us lustre and great (*bṛhat*) glory'[1], the word 'unto' is characteristic of the rathantara[2], the word 'great', of the bṛhat. He undertakes ('applies') the characteristics of both (rathantara and bṛhat) together, for this day (has) both these features[3].

[1] SV. I. 579=ṚS. IX. 108. 9-10 (var. r.)=SV. II. 361-362.

[2] See note 2 on XI. 4. 1.

[3] Because it follows immediately after a bṛhat-day and is itself a rathantara-day (Sāyaṇa).

3. (The verses beginning:) '*Prāṇā*[1], the young of the great ones'[2] are the characteristic of the simā (or śakvarī-verse)s, for the simās are

the great ones Through their own characteristic he thereby makes them prosper.

1 *prāṇā*, untranslatable: *krāṇā* the ṚS.

2 SV. I. 570=ṚS. IX. 102. 1-3 (var. r.)=SV. II. 363-365.

4. (The verses beginning:) 'Be clarified for the obtaining of booty'[1] are anuṣṭubhs addressed to Viṣṇu[2].

1 Not in the pūrvārcikā! ṚS. IX. 100. 6, 7, 9=SV. II. 366-368.

2 Because of the words (II. 366. c): *indrāya soma viṣṇave*.

5. Viṣṇu is the sacrifice; what here (on this day) is not brought about, that he brings about through Viṣṇu (who is) the sacrifice.

6. (The verses beginning:) 'The swift soma is clarified *gonyoghās*'[1], are characteristic of the simās[2]. By means of their own characteristic he thereby makes them prosper.

1 SV. I. 540=ṚS. IX 97. 16-12 (var. r.)=SV. II. 369-371.

2 Probably because of the word *go* in *gonyoghās*, the śakvarīs or simās being the cows.

7. Being triṣṭubhs they are jagatīs by their characteristic[1]; therefore they are applied at the (proper) place of the jagatīs[2].

1 As they contain the word 'cow' and cow is connected with jagatī (VI. 1. 10).

2 The last sāman in the midday-laud is regularly on jagatī-metre.

8. There is the gāyatra (-sāman). The brāhmaṇa of the gāyatra is the same[1].

1 See VII. 1. 1. sqq.

9. Their is the santani (-sāman)[1], for connecting (*santati*) the fifth day.

1 Grām. XVII. 2. 32, composed on SV. I. 584 and 585, chanted on SV. II. 358-360. This sāman is given in SV. ed. Calcutta, Vol. II, page 238 as chanted on one single verse, but the Grantha edition of the Grāmegeya gives it on three stotriyas (on SV. I. 584 the first: on I. 585 *a, b* the second, on I. 585 *c, d*, the third). Only the Grantha edition is right here, cp. the Sūtrakāras (Lāṭy. VI. 1. 1, Drāhy. XVI. 1. 1.), who enjoin that the santani sāman is to be chanted wholly: each stotriya of the gāna on each verse of the tṛca in the pūrvārcikā. It seems that the prastāva of each second and third stotriya falls out and that this fact brings about the santānagāna, cp. note 1 on XIII. 3. 7.

10. The twelve-day period is the stretched (or 'prolonged') voice. Of this voice the fifth day is the midst[1] This (voice) he connects by means of this (sāman).

[1] Cp. note 2 on XIII. 4. 16*a*.

11. There is the cyāvana (-sāman)[1] (the chant of Cyavana).

[1] Grām. XIII. 1. 28, composed on SV. I. 473, chanted on SV. II. 361-362: there are four cyāvanas on this verse, but the last only is (and must be) *svāram*, cp. SV. ed. Calcutta, Vol. II. page 24.

12. The cyāvana (-sāman) is a (means of) procreation[1]: he procreates and is multiplied who, in lauding, has applied the cyāvana.

[1] Because of the connection of the word *cyāvana* with *cyavate* 'to fall forth from (the womb).'

13. The rain (once upon a time) receded from these worlds; by means of the cyāvana (-sāman) Prajāpati caused it to fall; because he caused it to fall (*acyāvayat*), therefore, it is the cyāvana. He who in lauding has applied the cyāvana (-sāman) causes the rain to fall[1].

[1] For the parallel of the Jaim. br. cp. Journal of the American Oriental Society, Vol. XXVI, page 58. sqq. and Jaim. br. in Auswahl No. 186.

14. There is the krośa (-sāman)[1] (the yell-chant).

[1] Grām. XI.1. 24, composed on SV. I. 381, chanted or SV. II. 363-365.

15. By this (sāman), forsooth, Indra (once upon a time) at Indrakrośa yelled (*akrośat*): 'Viśvāmitra and Jamadagni, here are cows!'[2] The krośa (-sāman) is applied for gaining cattle.

[1] The two ṛsis occur combined also ṚS. X. 167. 4.

[2] This passage of the Kauthuma-brāhmaṇa is only a fragmentary piece of information. It is comprehensible only by the tradition as preserved in the Jaim. br. à propos of the vaiśvāmitrasāman, which is identical with the maidhātitha (Pañc br. XIV. 12. 8). We read, then, in the Jaim. br. (III. 237, cp. Jaim. br. in Auswahl, No. 204): 'The Bharatas (once upon a time) were on one bank of the Sindhu hard pressed (?) by the Ikṣvākus. With them (with the Bharatas) stayed Viśvāmitra and Jamadagni. Now, Indra asked of Bhayada, the son of Asamāti, the two bay (steeds) (*viz.* the two bay steeds of the Gods that, through the help of Pratīdarśa, had come into his possession, cp. Jaim. up. brāhm. IV. 8. 7; from J. Br. III. 167 we may infer, that Asamāti, the father of Bhayada, was an Ikṣvāku). He did not give them to him. These not having been given, he (Indra) called at Indrakrośa (cp. Pañc. br.): '*ammakas tasmi(ṃ)s tiṣṭhantu*', he said, 'Viśvāmitra and Jamadagni, acquire ye these cows of the Ikṣvākus.' These two, being on the

opposite bank (of the Sindhu) heard this. They said to the **Bharatas**: 'Indra calls unto us: acquire ye these cows of the Ikṣvākus; come along, let us acquire them.' (They answered:) 'Then make you two this (Sindhu) fordable for us.' 'Then yoke ye (your horses)' (the two answered). They (the Bharatas) yoked (their horses to their chariots) and descended unto (the river). Then these two said: 'Throw away all your *palpūlanīs*'. They threw them away. Now a rājanya-bandhu, who possessed a *palpūlanī*, bound this (*palpūlanī*) beneath the axle (of his chariot). They (Viśvāmitra and Jamadagni) wished: 'May this (Sindhu) be fordable for us.' Viśvāmitra saw this sāman, he lauded with it. They (V. and J.) came unto (the river), addressing (to Indra) these (verses): 'The destroyer of the strongholds, the young, wise Indra of immeasurable strength, was born as the supporter of every deed, armed with his thunderbolt, praised by many.—Thou, o yielder of the stone, hast opened the hole of the cow-retaining Vala; thee have the fearless angry Gods helped; by thy favours, o Hero, am I come, addressing thee, unto the Sindhu' (Jaim. Saṃh. III. 58. 16–18*b*=ṚS. I. 11. 4-6*b*). With (the remaining part of the last verse) 'Come near are the wise ones (or 'the chanters') o (God) who lovest the praise, they attend to thee as (being) such' they approached respectfully the water. For them the (stream) became fordable and they crossed by the ford. On (the track of the chariot on) which that *palpūlanī* was (fastened) there even the waters receded (split up)....These two having passed behind (the cows of the Ikṣvākus) hemmed them in in front...Thereupon they acquired the cattle.'—This remarkable legend may be considered as a kind of illustration of ṚS. III. 33.

16. There is the gaurīvita(-sāman)[1]. The brāhmaṇa of the gaurīvita is the same[2].

[1] Grām. V. 1. 22, composed on SV. I. 168, here chanted on SV. II. 366–368.

[2] See XI. 5. 13. sqq.

17. There is the ṛṣabha-śākvara (-sāman)[1] (the śakvarī-bull).

[1] Aranyegeyagāna I. 2. 21, composed on SV. I. 409, chanted on SV. II. 366–368.

18. The śakvarī (-verse)s are the cattle; in his cattle he thereby produces a copulation[1], in order that it may procreate, for not without a bull does cattle (cow) procreate.

[1] On this fifth day, which has the śakvarīs ('the cow') as its first pṛṣṭha-stotra, is now applied the 'bull' (chant).

19. There is the pārtha (-sāman)[1] (the chant of Pṛthī).

[1] Grām. VIII. 2. 6, composed on SV. I. 316, chanted on SV. II. 366–368. There are two pārthasāmans, but the second of the two is required, being, according to Jaim. br. III. 131, *dvyabhyāsam*, see SV. ed. Calcutta, Vol. I, page 637.

20. Through this (sāman) Pṛthī, the son of Vena, got the supremacy over both (kinds of) animals[1]. He who in lauding has applied the pārtha (-sāman) gets the supremacy over both kinds of animals.

[1] Wild and domesticated. Wrongly Keith in Vedic Index *s.v.* pṛthī.

21. There is the padastobha (-sāman) with eight *iḍās* [2].

[1] The sāman which has a stobha in each (?) verse-quarter.

[2] Aranyegeyagāna I. 2. 25, composed on SV I. 558; it has eight times the word *iḍā*, see SV. ed. Calcutta, Vol. II, page 414

22. Indra raised his thunderbolt against Vṛtra, but he (Vṛtra) encircled him with sixteen coils. He (Indra) saw this padastobha (-sāman) and by means of it winded (them) off. He should chant the udgītha (-part), winding off, as it were[1], in order to repel the evil.

[1] Probably the Udgātṛ must, in chanting, make the gesture of one who winds himself loose from an encircling evil The Anupadasūtra (IV. 4) treats of this expression, which also occurs in the Jaim. br. (III. 129), but the text is too corrupt even to be cited.

23. The evil, forsooth, had seized him (Indra); through the padastobha (-sāman) he had repelled it. He who in lauding applies the padastobha (-sāman) repels the evil.

24. At his feet (*padoḥ*) he saw the last (*stobha*)[1], therefore, it is called the *padastobha*.

[1] The coils of Vṛtra fell off gradually while Indra was chanting the sāman; the last four of the sixteen fell off from his feet, when he chanted the last stobha.

25. It has twelve nidhanas[1], for gaining a firm support[2].

[1] According to Lāṭy. VII. 7. 1, the four verse-quarters are also to be regarded as nidhanas (*i.e.* must be chanted by a l l the Chanters); these, together with the eight *iḍās*, make twelve.

[2] According to Sāyaṇa, this refers to the year and its twelve months.

26. There is the dāśaspatya (-sāman).

[1] Grām. XV. 2. 29, composed on SV. I. 540, chanted (see § 6) on SV. II. 369–371. It is the third of the four sāmans of this name, being *nidhanavat*, see SV. ed. Calcutta, Vol. II, page 140.

27. The cow they wish to praise, they praise saying: 'she is a *dāśaspatya*,'[1]. They, in applying this sāman, praise this (fifth) day.

[1] 'A cow of Dāśaspati' (?), 'a cow of the bountiful lord' (?). According to Sāyana, the meaning is 'a cow that gives much milk.'

28. The pavamāna-lauds (of this day) finish on a nidhana[1]: for propping the day.—The stoma is (given)[2].

[1] There are four different endings of a sāman: a svara, a nidhana, the word *iḍā* and the word *vā(k)*. A sāman is *svarānta*, when it ends either on a syllable with *svarita* (the musical notation *656*, cp. note 1 on VII. 3. 25) or on the word *hā-i* (Lāṭy. VI. 9. 6); it is *nidhanānta*, when it ends neither on a svara or on the words *iḍā* or *vā(k)* (Lāṭy. l.c. 7). The last sāman of the three lauds (bahiṣpavamāna, mādhyandinapavamāna, ārbhavapavamāna) end on a nidhana in this sense of the word, cp. XII. 11. 26, XIII. 11. 24 (as compared with § 23).

[2] Cp. XIII. 1. 12.

XIII. 6.

(The uktha-lauds of the fifth day.)

1. (There are the verses beginning:) 'Hither, for thee, Agni, may we light.'[1]

[1] SV. I. 419=ṚS. V. 6. 4, 5, 9 (with var. r.)=II. 372-374 These verses are destined for the first uktha-laud.

2. That part of the sacrifice, which consists of the uktha (-lauds), is a cutting, as it were: that it contains the word 'hither,' is for the sake of congruence[1].

[1] See XI. 11. 2, notes.

3. (The verses beginning): 'For Indra chant ye a melody'[1] are full kakubhs[3]. Thereby, he comes to be not hungring.[2]

[1] SV. I. 388=ṚS. VIII. 98. 1-3 (var.)=SV. II. 375-377.

[2] He will have his fill, just as the kakubhs are full.

[3] But they are uṣṇih-verses! How must we explain this? Cp. XIV. 6. 2.

4. The kakubh is man[1] (*puruṣa*); he thereby (by taking the kakubh-verses for the middle uktha-laud) gladdens man in the middle.

[1] Cp. note 1 on VIII. 10. 6.

5. (The verses beginning:) 'The soma has been pressed, o Indra, for thee'[1], are the characteristic of the simās[2] (or śakvarī-verses); by means of their own characteristic he makes them thrive.

[1] SV. I. 347=ṚS. I 84, 1, 3, 2=SV. II. 378-380.

[2] The connection between these verses and the śakvarīs is difficult to see. Sāyaṇa's explanation is too forced to be true.

6. There is the saṃjaya (-sāman)[1] (the chant of victory).

1 Grām. XI. 2. 2, composed on SV. I. 419, chanted (see § 1) on SV. II. 372–374. There are two saṃjaya sāmans on this verse and both are svāra; from Jaim. br. III. 132: *tad v evācakṣate dvihiṃkāraṃ vāmadevyam*, it appears that the second saṃjaya is intended which (see SV. ed. Calcutta, Vol. I, page 855) in the middle has
2 2∧
huȝm hum.

7. The Gods and the Asuras made a compact that cattle should fall to the share of that of the two (contending) parties, which should vanquish (the other). By means of the saṃjaya (-sāman) the Gods vanquished the Asuras. Because they had vanquished (the other) (*samajayan*), therefore, it is the saṃjaya. The saṃjaya (-sāman) is applied for gaining cattle.

8. There is the saumitra (-sāman)[1] (the chant of Sumitra).

1 Grām. X. 2. 11, composed on SV. I. 388, chanted (see § 3) on SV. II. 375–377. There are three sāmans of this name on SV. I. 388; according to Jaim. br. III. 132, it is *pañcākṣaranidhanam*, the nidhana (see SV. ed. Calcutta, Vol. I, page 797) is
2 1 1111
e | *panasya ve 2345.*

9. A (certain) female, sacrifice-destroying, Ogre, Dīrghajihvī, kept here licking at the (butter of the) sacrifices. Indra despaired of slaying her by any stratagem whatever. Now, Sumitra, the Kutsa[1], was a handsome (young man). To him he (Indra) said: 'Call her to thee.' He called her to him. She said to him: 'This truly is unheard by me[2], but it is rather pleasant to my heart'. He (Sumitra) came to an understanding with her. At the trysting-place they both (Indra and Sumitra) slew her. That forsooth, had been at that moment their wish. The saumitra (-sāman) is a wish-granting chant. Through this (sāman) he obtains (the fulfilment of) his wish.

1 *kutsa*, probably, is identical with *kautsa*: 'the Son of Kutsa'.

2 *i.e.* 'never before have I been invited', reading *śuśruve* as passive perfect, although the two MSS. of Leyden read as the printed text: *śuśruva*.

10. (But) an (inauspicious) voice addressed him (Sumitra) thus: 'Being Sumitra ('good-friend') thou hast done a bloody deed'. Grief tormented him[1]; he performed austerities, he saw this saumitra (-sāman). Through it he drove away his grief. He who, in lauding, has applied the saumitra (-sāman), drives away his grief[2].

1 Read *ārchat* instead of *ārthat.*

2 The legend of Dīrghajihvī has been treated by H. Oertel in: Actes du onzième Congrès International des Orientalistes, Paris, 1897, section arienne,

page 225 sqq.; here all the parallels are given. As these 'Actes' are difficult to obtain and, moreover, the text and the translation can in some places be emended I here subjoin the version of this legend according to the Jaiminīyabrāhmaṇa (I. 161–163): 'Dīrghajihvī was a female Asura. She used to lick at all the soma. She was (installed) at the (bank of the) northern sea. The soma that was being pressed at the southern sea, that at the eastern (sea), that at the western (sea), at that soma she used to lick even from that (place, where she was at the northern sea because so long was her tongue!). Indra, wishing to seize her (read *jighṛkṣan*) could not seize her. He said: 'Let nobody sacrifice, for this Dīrghajihvī licks at all the soma.' Now Sumitra, the son of Kutsa, was a handsome (young man). To him said Indra: 'Sumitra, thou art handsome: with a handsome (young man) women like to chat; make this Dīrghajihvī chat with thee'. He (Sumitra) went and said to her (the reading of the MSS: *tāṃ hetyovāca* is correct and ought n o t to changed to *tāṃ haityovāca*) 'Dīrghajihvī, love me'. She said: 'Thou hast one single penis, but I have on each member a cunnus. This does not agree'. He returned (to Indra) and said: 'She says to me that I have only one penis, whilst she has on each member a cunnus, and that this does not agree. He (Indra) said: 'On each member of thine I will make a penis'. Having covered these (penes) with his uppergarment he came to her (read: *tāni hābhiprāvṛtyeyāya i.e. abhiprāvṛtya eyāya*). He said to her: 'Dīrghajihvī, love me'. She said: 'Thou hast one single penis, but I have on each member a cunnus, This does not agree'. He said; 'On each member of mine, forsooth, I have a penis'. She said: 'Well, let (them) see me'. He showed them to her. They pleased her. 'So come then,' she said, 'what is thy name?' 'I am Sumitra by name'. 'Thou hast a beautiful name', she answered. They now lay down together. As soon as he had obtained his wish with her, he laid hold of her. She said: 'Sirrah, hast thou not called thyself Sumitra?' He answered: 'I am Sumitra ('Good-friend') to a good friend (read, *sumitra evāha sumitrāya*), and Bad-friend to a bad friend'. He saw those saumitra (-sāmans) and lauded with them. By means of these he called Indra near. He, Indra, raising up that anuṣṭubh-thunderbolt, ran up toward (him): (the verse Jaim. saṃh. I. 3. 8. 1=ṚS. IX. 101. 1), (and saying its last words:) 'Slay, o Friends, Dīrghajihvī' he slew her.

11. There is the mahāvaiśvāmitra (-sāman)[1] (the great Viśvāmitra chant).

[1] Grām. IX. 1. 22, composed on SV. I. 343, chanted (see § 5) on SV. II. 378–380 as third uktha-laud. On SV. I. 343 are composed two sāmans of this name, see SV. ed. Calcutta, Vol. I, page 700, but see §§ 13, 14.

12. In that they[1], having slain the evil, prospered (*amahīyanta*), therefore the m a h ā vaiśvamitra (-sāman) is called thus.

[1] Probably understand: 'the Gods'.

13. (It has the stobha:) '*hayā i hayā, ohā ohā.*' By means of

this (stobha) they (the Gods) pushed the kine on their own behalf (toward their stables)[1].

[1] *nyauhanta* with a pun on the stobha *ohā ohā*.

14. It has a triple *iḍā*[1]: for sustaining the three-day period[2].

[1] $\overset{3}{\textit{ho}}$ *'4* $\overset{5}{\textit{iḍā}}$ | $\overset{3}{\textit{ho}}$ *'4* $\overset{5}{\textit{iḍā}}$ | $\overset{7}{\textit{ho}}$ *'2345 i-iḍā.*

[2] The second three-day period, the fifth day of which is the middle one.

15. They undertake ('chant') the last *iḍā* as a 'running' one[1], for connecting the sixth day.

[1] See note on XII. 5. 25.

16. Thrice-ninefold (or twenty-seven-versed) is the stoma, for gaining a firm support, for gaining prosperity; for it (the triṇava-stoma) is a big (and prospering) trivṛt[1].

[1] Cp. X. 1. 13, 14.

(Sixth day.)

XIII. 7.

(Out-of-doors-laud of the sixth day.)

1. (The tristich beginning:) 'The lustre of sacrifice is being clarified, the sweet, the welcome'[1] is the opening (tristich) of the sixth day.

[1] SV. II. 381–188=ṚS. IX. 86. 10–12 (var. r).

2. The gāyatrī is the l u s t r e of the metres[1], the revatī (-verses) are the l u s t r e of the sāmans, the thirty-three-fold stoma is the l u s t r e of the stomas[2]. He thus completely unites the lustre and also the son of his son will be possessed of lustre.

[1] Because it is connected with Agni, see VI. 1. 6.

[2] The trayastriṃśa is III. 2. 2 called the highest of the stomas.

3. 'The sweet, the welcome': the revatī (-verse)s, are the cattle, (*i.e.*) the sweet, the welcome[1]; this he thereby addresses.

[1] Milk, the product of the cows, being sweet and welcome.

4. 'The intoxicating, gladdening juice, pertaining to Indra[1]: strength is vigour (*indriyam*), cattle are juice[2]; this he thereby addresses.

1 SV. II. 381*d*.

2 See note 1 on § 3.

5. (The tristich beginning:) 'The swift ones have been let forth [1]' (*asṛkṣata*) is the anurūpa (-tristich).

1 SV. I. 482=ṚS. IX 64. 4-6=SV. II. 384-386.

6. For now these days are let forth (*sṛṣṭāni*), as it were.

7. And, and moreover, after the former characteristic he thereby speaks the latter characteristic; that he speaks after the former characteristic the latter characteristic, that is the reason why the corresponding tristich is called *anurūpa*. A son resembling to him he gets, who knows this. The stotriya and the anurūpa are tristichs, for retaining the breaths [1].

1 This § is identical with XI. 6. 4-6.

8. There are two (hymns) of ten verses [1]: ten-syllabic is the virāj, food is virāj-like [2]: to obtain food.

1 SV. II. 387-396=ṚS. IX. 2. 1-8, 10, 9 (=IX. 2),—SV. II. 397-406=ṚS. IX. 4—These daśarcas are indicated by their words in the Jaim. br. III. 137-138.

2 Cp. IV. 8.4.

9. The second dekastich has (in each verse) the same closing words [1]: in order that valour, strength (and) pith may not flow away.

1 *athā no vasyasas kṛdhi.*

10. Where the Gods saw valour, strength (and) pith, they pushed it down (immediately) afterwards [1].

1 ? *anunyatudan.* Perhaps the valour and strength of the adversaries of the Gods is meant, but cp. Jaim. br. I. 217: *yatra yatra vai devāś chandasāṃ rasam anvavindaṃs tat punar nitunnam akurvaṃs, tat punar abhyāghnan.* Perhaps, this compound has the same or nearly the same meaning as *anutud* 'to repeat', thus Sāyaṇa: *pratyṛcam abhyasyan* (*r. abhyāsyan*).

11. There is a tetrastich [1], for gaining firm footing.

1 SV. II. 500=ṚS. IX. 58=SV. II. 407-410.

12. Dhvasrā and Puruṣantī [1] wished to give a thousand (cows) to Taranta and Purumīḍha, the son of Vidadaśva. These (latter mentioned) two thought: 'How may this (gift) be taken (and) not received, by us?' They accepted (it) with (the words, occurring in the tetrastich): 'Of Dhvasrā and Puruṣantī we take a thousand: hastening, he rushes

on, the gladdening one'[2]. Thereupon this (gift) was taken, not received by them[3].

[1] On these names cp. Vedic Index of names and subjects, Vol. I, page 407. The gift of the two was probably unfit for acceptance, as they were female Asuras, and therefore Taranta and Purumīḍha felt (according to the Jaim. br. III. 139, see Journal of the Amer. Oriental Society, Vol. XVIII, page 39) as if they had swallowed poison, just as was the case with Uśanas, as he had accepted the gift of the Asuras.

[2] SV. II. 409.

[3] The stress must be laid on *ā dadmahe* 'we take' which is not the same as *pratigṛhṇīmaḥ*. In this manner the tale becomes clear, not by the translation of Oertel: 'how may what we have taken become unreceived' and 'from the two Puruṣantis we receive a hundred'.

13. He who knows this, (for him) a (gift bestowed on him) becomes taken, not received.

14. It (this tetrastich) is nārāśaṃsa-less[1], for obtaining both kinds of food, human and divine.

[1] This expression is similarly not clear to me as *vinārāśaṃsā* in X. 6.6. Sāyana is of no help. The connection with the following words is thereby not apparent. Similarly the Jaim. br. III. 138: *vinārāśamsam iva bhavaty ubhayoḥ kāmayor upāptyai yac ca divo yac ca mānuṣaḥ* (read *yaś ca divyo yaś ca ?*).

15. A tristich is the last[1]. With which breath they start, in view of that they finish (the laud)[2].

[1] SV. II. 411–413=ṚS. IX. 62. 22–24. The Jaim. brāhmana mentions the beginning words of this tristich.

[2] See XI. 6. 9.

16. The stoma is the thirty-three-fold one, for obtaining a firm standing[1]; amongst the deities, forsooth, he has firmly been established)[2].

[1] Cp. III. 1. 3.

[2] Because there are thirty-three deities, cp. Jaim. br. III. 139: *trayastriṃśad vai sarvā devatāḥ, sarvāsv evaitad devatāsu pratitiṣṭhanto yanti.*

XIII. 8.

(Ājya-lauds of the sixth day.)

1*a*. (The tristich beginning:) 'To Jātavedas who deserves this our praise[1]' is the ājya(-laud) addressed to Agni, having in each verse) the same closing words[2], in order that valour, strength (and) pith may not flow away[3].

[1] SV. II. 414-416=ṚS. I. 94. 1, 4, 3.

[2] *mā riṣāmā vayaṃ tava.*

[3] Cp. XIII. 7. 9.

1*b*. Where the Gods saw valour, strength (and) pith, they pushed it down (immediately) afterwards[1].

[1] Cp. XIII. 7. 10.

2. (The tristich beginning): 'Towards ye, the sun having risen'[1] (is the ājya-laud) combined with 'sun', addressed to Mitra and Varuṇa.

[1] SV. II. 417-419=ṚS. VII. 66. 7-9.

3. The sun is the end, and this sixth day is the end of the days[1]; at the end even they thereby chant the end: in order to obtain firm footing.

[1] The six-day period being considered as a whole.

4*a*. (The tristich beginning): 'Drive away all hostilities'[1], is (the ājya-laud) destined for Indra, having (in each verse) the same closing words[2], in order that valour, strength, (and) sap may not flow away[3].

[1] SV. II. 420-422=ṚS. VIII. 45. 40, 42, 41 (varr. r.).

[2] *vasu spārhaṃ tad ābhara.*

[3] Cp. § 1. *a*

4*b*. Where the Gods saw valour, strength, (and) pith, they pushed it down (immediately) afterwards[1].

[1] Cp. § 1. b.

5. (The tristich beginning): 'For ye both are the priests of the sacrifice'[1] is the (ājya-laud) addressed to Indra and Agni, having (in each verse) the same closing words[2], in order that valour, strength, (and) pith may not flow away. Where the Gods saw valour, strength, (and) pith, they pushed it down (immediately) afterwards.—The stoma (is given)[3].

[1] SV. II. 423-425=ṚS. VIII. 38. 1-3.

[2] *indrāgnī tasya bodhatam.*

[3] See XIII. 7. 16.

XIII 9.

(The midday-pavamāna-laud of the sixth day.)

1. (The verses beginning): 'For Indra, accompanied by the Maruts, o Soma'[1] are gāyatrīs in which the Maruts are invoked.

[1] SV. I. 472=ṚS. IX. 64. 22–24 (var. r.)=SV. II. 426–428.

2. For accompanied by the Maruts is the midday-service[1].

[1] To the first pṛṣṭhastotra runs parallel the marutvatīya-śastra.

3. (The verses beginning): 'Cleansing thyself, o handy one'[1], are characteristic of the simās (of śakvarī-verses)[2].

[1] SV. I. 517=ṚS. IX. 107. 21–22 (var. r.)=SV. II. 429–430.

[2] Because of the word 'cows' in SV. II. 430. d, the śakvarīs being cattle.

4. The characteristic feature of the simās and the revatī(-verse)s is the same, for from the simās the revatīs spring forth[1].

[1] From VII. 8. 133 it appears, at least, that the revatīs came into existence immediately after the śakvarīs.—The first pṛṣṭhastotra of this day is on the revatī-verses, XIII. 10. 4.

5. (The tristich-verses beginning): 'This one the ten fingers'[1] are āditya(-verses); the young ones (the progeny) are the Ādityas (the children of Aditi)[2]; in the midst of them he is firmly established.

[1] SV. II. 431–433=ṚS. IX. 61. 7–9.

[2] The motherhood is an essential trait of Aditi, see Macdonell, Vedic Mythology, § 41.

6. Being gāyatrī (-verse)s (they are) by their characteristic feature triṣṭubhs[1]; therefore, they are applied at the place of the triṣṭubhs.

[1] Because Indra is mentioned in them and this God is connected with the triṣṭubh, see VI. 1. 8. Ordinarily, the last sāman of the midday-pavamāna is chanted on triṣṭubhs, cp. Ārṣeyakalpa, Einl., page XXIV.

7. There is the gāyatra (-sāman). The brāhmaṇa of the gāyatra is the same[1].

[1] Cp. VII. 1. 1 sqq.

8. There is the iṣovṛdhīya (-sāman)[1].

[1] Grām. XIII. 1. 13, composed on SV. I. 472, chanted on SV. II. 426–428.

9. The iṣovṛdhīya is cattle; (it is applied) for retaining the cattle. The fifth day (is practised) in view of vitality (*iṣe*)[1], the sixth day in view of prospering (*vṛdhe*)[1]. For they (the Gods?) prospered at that moment. By means of this (sāman) they make prosper the Sacrificer.

[1] The nidhana of this sāman (see SV. ed. Calcutta, vol. II, page 20) is
21r 2
iṣo vṛdhe I.

10. There is the krauñca (-sāman)[1] (the chant of Kruñc).

[1] Grām. V. 1. 11, composed on SV. I. 165, chanted on SV. II. 426–428. There are more krauñcas, but this is the only one on a gāyatrī verse; moreover, it agrees with the sāman prescribed by the Jaiminīyas, who designate it also as sauparṇa, see Jaim. ārṣeya brāhmaṇa page 8, *krauñcaṃ sauparṇaṃ vā*. It must be an *aiḍam sāma*, as is t h i s one.

11. Kruñc[1] found the day that was to be sought; to be sought, as it were, is the sixth day. They find the day by means of this (sāman).

[1] A fantastical ṛṣi name abstracted from the name of the sāman. Cp. note 1 on XI. 10. 19

12. There are the vājadāvarī(-verse)s[1] ('the strength giving ones').

[1] Sometimes, as in *revatīs śakvarīs*, the name of the verses is used to indicate a sāman. The sāman is Grām. IV. 2. 14, composed on SV. I. 153, chanted on SV. II. 426–428.

13. Strength (*vāja*) is food; (this sāman, then, is applied) to obtain food. For when there is food, cow, horse and man are strong.

14. There are the revatī(-verse)s, ('the rich or beautiful ones')

[1] Aranyegeyagāna II. 1. 17, composed on SV. I. 153, chanted on SV. II. 426–428. The first of the two sāmans of this name, see SV. ed. Calcutta, vol. II, page 324.

15. It is of six nidhanas[1], to prop the six-day period.

2r 1 1 2 1r 3 2 2 5
[1] According to Sāyana: *tīrnāḥ, ihā, sadhamādā, hā 31, uvā 23, ī 34 ḍā*

16. The revatī (verses, *i.e.*, the raivata-sāman) are the waters. If they made of them the pṛṣṭha (*i.e.*, if they chanted the first pṛṣṭha-laud on them), the Sacrificer would be without cattle: they (these verses, this chant) would destroy (lit. 'burn down') his cattle. Where the water falls down in different directions, there the herbs grow up, but where it remains standing, there they rot away[1]. Therefore they apply them (the revatīs, the raivata-sāman) at the (midday-)pava-

māna(-laud), for the pavamāna (-laud) is chanted thitherward (*i.e.*, without returning, without repetition, right off)[2].

[1] Böhtlingk-Roth propose to read *nirmretuka* instead of *nirmṛtuka*, but the last form is equally possible, cp. the present tense *mṛtyati* of the Kāṇvīya-Śbr. as against *mrityati* of the Mādhyandina recension, see my edition of the Kāṇvīya-ŚBr. introduction page 42.

[2] We expect the *raivataṃ sāma* for the first pṛṣṭha-laud (cp. VII. 8. 13 in connection with the preceding §§, and Ait. br. V. 12. 1 : *raivataṃ sāma*, as compared with IV. 27. 1 : *rathantaraṃ sāma*, IV. 31. 1 : *bṛhat sāma*, V. 1. 1 : *vairūpaṃ sāma* ; V. 4. 1 : *vairājam sāma*, V. 6. 1 : *śākvaram sāma*), but in the praxis it forms part of the midday-pavamāna ; this is explained by the comparison of the revatīs with the water : water flowing away in different directions, is harmless, so are the revatīs if chanted at the pavamāna, where no repetition is practised and in a sense, they flow away ; but, the pṛṣṭhastotra being performed by repetition of the verses, the revatīs are, in a sense, s t a n d i n g and thus would harm the cattle of the Sacrificer. The Jaim. br. (III. 145) argues : 'The revatī-verses are the water, and the raivata-sāman is the water ; if they chanted the raivata-sāman as pṛṣṭhastotra on the revatī-verses, they would sink into a bottomless (pit) and gain no firm standing'.

17. The iṣovṛdhīya (-sāman), forsooth, is the post (at which, before the milking, the cow is fastened), the krauñca is the rope, the vājadāvarī (-sāman) is the calf, the revatīs are the mother-cows : by applying these sāmans in t h i s way, he milks (the cow) whose milk has been caused to flow[1].

[1] On *pratta* cp. Vienna Oriental Journal (W.Z.K.M.), Vol. XXVI, page 121. The word does not mean 'given away', but is equivalent to *prasnuta*. The milking for ceremonial purposes is performed in the following manner : The milch cow and her calf are bound with a rope to the milking-post (*upadohanī methī*), and the calf is permitted to suck the mother-cow (*upasṛṣṭā gauḥ*) ; the calf takes the udder of the cow (*gauḥ prasnutā, prattā*), so that the milk begins to flow, and then the milker himself continues the work, cp. for example Jaim. br. I. 19 1 *vatsena vai mātaram prattāṃ duhre*.

18. There are the two aukṣṇorandhra (-sāmans)[1].

[1] Grām. XV. 1. 6 (*svāram*), composed on SV. I. 517, chanted on SV. II. 419–420 ; Grām. XV. 1. 12 (*aiḍam*), on the same verses.

19. Ukṣṇorandhra, the son of Kavi, beheld, by means of these two (sāmans), straightway the world of heaven. (So these sāmans serve) for beholding the world of heaven. He who in lauding has applied (them), does not fall from the world of heaven[1].

[1] According to the Jaim. br. (III. 150) it is Ukṣṇa Randhra, the Kāvya, who saw the sāman, who wished to reach by water upstreams the world of heaven, and to behold in the water, on the summit (*vartmani ?*) a vehicle (*niyānam*). He went along the Yamunā upstreams and reached the world of heaven. He is the same as Raumanvata, the same as Uśanas Kāvya; cp. Jaim. br. III. 231.

20. There is the vājajit (-sāman) [1], for attaining all, for getting all. They, forsooth, who undertake the sixth day (who perform the rite of the sixth-day) get all strength (*vājaṃ jayanti*).

[1] Grām. XV. 1. 13, composed on SV. I. 517, chanted on SV. II. 429–430.

21. Strength is food: to obtain food [1].

[1] See XIII. 9. 13. a.

22. There is the varuṇasāman [1].

[1] Grām. VII. 1. 18, composed on SV. I. 255, chanted on SV. II. 429–430. There are three sāmans of this name, see SV. ed. Calcutta, vol. I, page 447; the last of the three is *svūram*.

23. By means of this (sāman) Varuṇa attained the reign, the supremacy. He who, in lauding, has applied the varuṇasāman, attains the reign, the supremacy [1].

[1] How Varuna obtained the supremacy is set forth in the Jaim. br. (III. 152): "King Varuna was (originally) the equal of the other deities. He desired: 'May I be consecrated as king over all the Gods.' He dwelled a hundred years with Prajāpati as his pupil. He (Prajāpati) imparted this chant to him (saying): 'Accept this royalty, this characteristic of mine; the Gods will make thee their king'. He (Varuna) went to the Gods. The Gods seeing him approaching, got up in honour of him. He said to them: 'Do not ye get up in honour of me; ye are forsooth, my brothers, I am your equal'. 'No' they said, 'we see on thee the characteristic of our father Prajāpati', and they g o t up in honour of him. They put down for him the kings-seat, and, whilst he was seated on it, the Vasus consecrated him to royalty, the Rudras consecrated him to kingship, the Ādityas consecrated him to supremacy, the All-gods consecrated him to sovereignty, the Maruts consecrated him to all-mightiness, the Sādhyas and Āptyas consecrated him to overlordship". See the text in das Jaim. br. in Auswahl, No. 188.

24. There is the aṅgirasāṃ goṣṭha(-sāman) [1] ('the cow-pen of the Angirases').

[1] Grām. XIV. 2. 14. b (omitted in SV. ed. Calcutta, vol. II, page 82, but registered in the Grantha edition, page 142), composed on SV. I. 512, chanted on SV. II. 429–430.

25. The revatī (-verse)s, forsooth, are the cattle; they thus erect a cow-pen for the cattle, and drive it within, in order that it may not slip away [1].

[1] Almost identical with XIII. 4. 13.

26. There is the vāmadevya (sāman) with (the word) *iha* ('here') [1].

[1] Grām. I. 2. 6, composed on SV. I. 22, chanted on SV. II. 431-433. SV. ed. Calcutta, vol. I, page 130 (*svāram*), contains thrice the stobha *ihā*.

27. By means of this (sāman), Vāmadeva came to the chaplain's office of food: the chaplain's office is the Brahman's food; (so it serves) for obtaining food [1].

[1] The reasoning is somewhat inverted: the position of the Brahman as purohita is his living, his food; so, if one gets an office as purohita, he gets an office of food.

28. They chant (it) on gāyatrī(-verse)s, for the sake of getting a firm support, for (the obtainment of) priestly lustre. With which breath they start, in that they finish (the laud) [1].

[1] See XII. 9. 23.

29. They are gāyatrī(-verse)s containing the word 'Indra' [1]; thereby, they do not depart from the characteristic feature of the triṣṭubh [2].—The stoma (is given) [3].

[1] SV. II. 432: *sam indreṇota vāyunā.*

[2] Indra is connected with the tristubh, cp. VI. 1. 8

[3] See XIII. 7. 2

XIII. 10.

(The pṛṣṭha-lauds of the sixth-day.)

1. Of exhausted strength are the other metres, of unexhausted strength is the gāyatrī(-verse) [1]. Therefore, they chant (the first pṛṣṭha-laud) on gāyatrī(-verse)s [2].

[1] This probably refers only to the metre of the verses, on which the first pṛṣṭhastotra of the first five days is chanted, amongst which the gāyatrī does not occur.

[2] SV. I. 153=ṚS. I. 30. 13-15 (varr. rr.)=SV. II. 434-436, cp. below, § 4.

2. (The verses beginning:) 'The doer of fair deeds to our aid' [1] are, by their repetition [2], of six verse-quarters: characteristic of the sixth day [3]. Thereby, they begin the sixth day, for the sake of connection [4].

1 SV. I. 160=ṚS. I. 4. 1–3=SV. II. 437–439.

2 In the sāman (Araṇyegeyagāna I. 2. 19, cp. below, § 10) the first pada is chanted thrice (3), the second once (4), the third once (5) and the last half verse-quarter is then chanted twice (which makes one pada) (6).

3 Merely because it contains s i x padas.

4 For connecting the sixth day with the following one.

3. (The verses beginning): 'That both, heaven and earth'[1] are of six verse-quarters[2]: characteristic of the sixth day. Thereby they begin the sixth day, for connection's sake.

1 SV. I. 379=ṚS. X 134. 1 , 6 , 2 (with varr. rr.)=SV. II. 440–442.

2 They are mahā-pankti-verses, each of six padas.

4. On the revatī (-verse)s the vāravantīya (-sāman)[1] is (chanted) as (first) pṛṣṭha (-laud).

1 Grām. I. 1. 30, composed on I. 17. chanted (see § 1, note 2) on II. 434–436. There are several vāravantīya sāmans, but this is the only one on gāyatrī verses: moreover, cp. § 9.

5. The revatī (-verse)s, forsooth, are the pith of the waters and the vāravantīya(-sāman) is the pith of the revatī (-verse)s. He thus applies the revatī (-verse)s together with their pith.

6. In that they chant the vāravantīya (-sāman) as pṛṣṭha (-laud), the vāravantīya being rich (*revat*) (and) connected with the revatī (-verses) (*raivata*), he gets a rich (*revat*) and wealthy (*raivata*) son[1].

1 I combine the last sentence of § 5 with § 6.

7. Rich and wealthy becomes he who knows this.

8. To Keśin, the son of Dalbha, this sāman showed itself (in human form). It addressed him: 'Unskilled chanters chant me. Let them not chant me.' He said: 'Reverend Sir, how is thy intonation?'[1] 'I must be intoned; let him chant me, intonating, as it were, for obtaining firm support.' Thereupon, he (Keśin) perceived Alamma, the son of Parajānat, lying behind the axle (of the southern havirdhāna-cart) chanting this intonation. To him he said: 'I will make thee my purohita (*i.e.*, my Udgātṛ)'. About him they (the other Brāhmins), said: 'Who, forsooth, is this man? For what is he fit (*alam*)?' 'Fit for me (*alaṃ mahyam*)' he (Keśin) answered. And thence Alamma has its name[2].

[1] Probably *āgā* refers to the strength of tone, or to the pitch of tone in chanting, cp. Jaim. up. br. I. 37, where three kinds of *āgā* are distinguished. The word *āgā* occurs also Ṣaḍviṃśa br. II. 2. 9–13.

[2] Through the wrong readings of Oertel, it has been unknown hitherto that this same story, with some variants, occurs also in the Jaim. up. br. (III. 31); instead of Oertel's: *sai 'vā 'lam masyā 'lam matāyai 'tasya ha 'lam evo 'jjagan,* we ought to read: *saivālammasyālammatā 'thaitasya hālamma evojjagau.* The same Alamma has been mentioned above in our Brāhmaṇa: XIII. 4. 11.

9. He should chant (in this saman, the words:) *ihā*, *ihā* ('here! here!') for obtaining a firm support[1].

[1] By chanting the stobha *ihā* 234 (see the sāman in SV. ed. Calcutta, vol. I, page 121), he gets a support on this world ('here').—During the chant of the vāravantīya-sāman on the revatī-verses, according to the Sūtrakāras Lāṭy. III. 6. 1–6, Drāhy. IX. 2. 1–6 (cp. supra VII. 8. 13 and Baudh. XVI. 5: 251. 6, Āp. XXI. 8. 1–7, Kāty. XII. 3. 12), the following ceremonies must take place: 'At the laud of the vāravantīya they should cause (some) milch-cows to bellow together (with their calves), having brought (the cows) to the south (of the sacrificial ground) and the calves to the north (this agrees with Jaim. br. III. 146: *uttarato vatsāh syur dakṣiṇato mātaraḥ*). Having led them together to the east of the sadas, they drive them behind the āgnidhrīya (-shed) in a northerly direction. Having made the Sacrificer say (the formula, *viz.*, Pañc. br. I. 3. 8), he should address them with the names of the cow: 'o Havyā, o Kāmyā, o Candrā, o Jyotā, o Iḍā, o Rantā, o Justā, o Sunarī, in me may rest your riches; come, o Iḍā, come, o Aditi, o thou delightful one, may I attain thy delight. O you that are invited, may your invitation fall to my part' (cp. TS. I. 6. 3. *e.g.*,) or with the verse (beginning:) 'Together with the bull', (Sāmaveda ārcika-saṃhitā IV. 14), or with both. If they (the Adhvaryus, as prescribed, *e.g.*, Baudh. and Āp.), summon (for the stotra) by means of water, he should pour this (water) out on the āstāva, with the three *āpo-hi-ṣṭha*-verses' (SV. II. 1187–1189).

10. There is the ṛṣabha-raivata (-sāman)[1] ('the b u l l of the rich ones').

[1] Araṇyegeyagāna I. 2. 19, composed on SV. I. 160, chanted (see § 2) on SV. II. 437–439 (as third pṛṣtha-laud).

11. The revatī (-verse)s are the cattle; in his cattle he thereby produces a copulation, in order that it may procreate, for not without a bull does cattle procreate[1].

[1] Nearly identical with XIII. 5. 18.

12. There is the śyena (-sāman)[1] ('the falcon-chant').

[1] Araṇyegeya III. 1. 19, composed on SV. I. 379, chanted (see § 3) as fourth pṛṣṭha-laud.

13. The falcon, forsooth, reaches the birds that precede him in flying; preceding, as it were, are the former days[1]; to reach these the falcon(-sāman) is applied.

[1] Read *pūrvapretānīva* instead of *pūrvapretān iva*.

14. The falcon, forsooth, is able to convey this day, for it is the swiftest of the birds; it (the falcon-chant) is applied in order not to hold off, in order to convey this (day); for the sixth day as well as the seventh day is the end[1].

[1] And the falcon (-sāman) must help to reach this 'end'.

15. The theologians argue: 'The pṛṣṭha (-laud)s having the bṛhat as their support[1], and there being these two gāyatrīs and two jagatīs[2], where then, are the bṛhatīs?'[1]

[1] In the ordinary and normal agniṣṭoma the pṛṣṭhasāmans (with the exception, however, of the second, the maitrāvaruṇasya stotra, which always is on gāyatrī) are always chanted on bṛhatī-verses.

[2] The two gāyatrīs are the verses of the first and the second pṛṣṭha (the usual vāmadevya, on SV. II. 32-34); the two jagatīs are 1. the verses of the third pṛṣṭha, which are each of six verse-quarters (cp. note 2 on XIII. 10. 2), each of eight syllables (=48); 2. the fourth pṛṣṭha consists by its nature of verses of four times eight syllables; so the last two ones are equal to jagatīs.

16. Two verse-quarters of the two jagatīs fall on the gāyatrī, (*i.e.*, are to be transferred to the gāyatrīs); thereby, all become bṛhatīs. He (thereby) supports the pṛṣṭha(-stotra)s on their place and he (himself) comes into the possession of a support[1].

[1] From each of the two jagatīs SV. II. 437-439 (cp. note 2 on preceding §) and SV. II. 440-442, a pada, twelve syllables, are transferred to each of the two gāyatrīs, and in this way the gāyatrīs become of 36 syllables and the jagatīs equally so. This all is mere speculation: *mīmāṃsaiva*! It is of no effect for the practice; the Prayogas, at least, take no notice of these remarks.

17. They hold the laud on verses of s i x verse-quarters[1], for propping the s i x-day period.

[1] This refers only to the last two pṛṣṭhastotras, cp. XIII. 10. 2 and 3.

18. They perform the sacrifice with a verse of s e v e n verse-quarters[1], to connect the s e v e n t h day.—The stoma (is given)[2].

[1] The Hotṛ and his assistants, the Hotrakas, perform at the sixth day the *prasthitahomas* (cp. *e.g.*, C.H. § 146. d, § 188) with verses of seven quarters, *e.g.*, ṚS. I. 139. 6, I. 137. 1, etc., cp. Āśv. VIII. 2.—It has been remarked in X. 6. 6 that the *saptapadā* verse is a characteristic feature of the sixth day.

[2] See XIII. 7. 16.

XIII. 11.

(Ārbhava-pavamāna-laud of the sixth day.)

1. (The verses beginning): 'Around, the soma standing on the mountains, being pressed'[1] are gāyatrīs containing (the word) 'around'[2], for encompassing (*p a r yāpti*) all.

[1] SV. I. 475=ṚS. IX. 18. 1-3 (var. rr.)=SV. II. 443-445.

[2] And these verses are apt for the sixth day: X. 6. 6.

2. (The verses beginning): 'He is being pressed, who of the riches'[1], the riches being cows, (are applied) for retaining cows.

[1] SV. I. 352=ṚS. IX. 108. 13-14=SV. II. 446-447.

3. (The verses beginning:) 'Him, ye friends, for the carouse'[1] are vālakhilya(-verse)s[2].

[1] SV. I. 569=RS. IX. 105. 1-3 (var. rr.)=SV. II. 448-450.

[2] The reason why these verses here, and other ones at XIV. 5. 4, are designated as vālakhilya is not obvious. So much is certain, that at the corresponding śastra the vālakhilya-hymns (ṚS. VIII. 49-59) are recited. On the sāman, treated below XIV. 5. 4, the Jaim. br. III. 170 remarks: *tad āhur: yad vālakhilyā viharanti* (cp. Ait. br. VI. 28), *katham etāsu* (*sc.* on the verses corresponding with Kauth. SV. II. 457-459) *vihṛtāsu stuvata iti. sa brūyād: yad evaitāni (d)vyūnākṣarāṇi vyatiṣaktāni padāni bhavanti, teneti.*

4. These two vālakhilya-tristichs (are applied) not only at the sixth, but also at the seventh day[1].

[1] Cp. XIV. 5. 4.

5. That these two vālakhilya-tristichs are (applied on these two days) is done in order that these two days may be reciprocally connected, that they may not slip away, that they may be tied together.

6. (The verses beginning:) 'The somas, the drops, are being clarified'[1] are anuṣṭubh(-verse)s with their hinderpart directed netherward[2].

[1] SV. I. 548=ṚS. IX. 101. 10, 12 11 (var. r.)=SV. II. 451-453.

[2] The word *nibhasadaḥ* is left unexplained by Sāyana; its exact meaning is not clear.

7. (The verses beginning): 'By the clarification clarify these riches'[1], being triṣṭubhs, are jagatīs by their characteristic[2]. Therefore, they are applied at the place of the jagatīs[3].

[1] SV. I. 541=ṚS. IX. 97. 52–54 (var. r.)=SV. II. 454–456.

[2] According to Sāyana, because in these verses 'riches' are mentioned, and these are connected with the Vaiśya, who in his turn is connected with the jagatī (cp. X. 1. 10).

[3] The last stotra of the ārbhava-pavamāna is normally chanted on jagatī-verses.

8. There is the gāyatra (-sāman). The brāhmaṇa of the gāyatra is the same[1].

[1] Cp. VII. 1. 1. sqq.

9. There are the vaidanvata(-sāmans)[1] (the chants of Vidanvat).

[1] Grām. XIII. 1. 33, 31, and 34, composed on SV. I. 475, chanted on SV. II. 443–445. To SV. I. 475 belong f o u r vaidanvata-sāmans, see SV. ed Calcutta, vol. II, page 26. From a comparison with the ūhagāna, we learn that of these four the three in this sequence (33, 31, 34) are intended. But, even without the comparison of the ūhagāna, we must be able to conclude, that t h i s sequence is intended: in order to avoid *jāmitvam*: Grām. XIII. 1. 33 is *aiḍa*, 31 is *svāra*, 34 is *nidhanavat*, and this is the sequence required for more than one sāman chanted on the same verses.

10. Vidanvat, the son of Bhṛgu (once upon a time) struck at Indra. Remorse came upon him; he performed penance and saw these vaidanvata (-saman)s and by means of them he removed his remorse. He who in lauding has applied the vaidanvata (-sāman)s removes his remorse[1].

[1] For the reason why Vidanvat struck at Indra and for the longer version of this legend see Jaim. br. III. 159, 160 in the Journal of the American Oriental Society, vol. XXVI, page 63 sqq.

11*a*. There is the (saman called) 'the hair of Bharadvāja'[1].

[1] Grām. XVII. 2. 22, composed on SV. I. 582, chanted on SV. II. 446–447; *svāram*, see SV. ed. Calcutta, vol. II, page 233.

11*b*. Hair is cattle; (it is applied) for retaining cattle.

12. This (sāman) they call also 'the long one'[1]: life is long: in order to reach (the normal lease of) life.

[1] It is the only name of this sāman with the Jaiminīyas. Must we understand under the word: 'they': the Jaiminīyas?

13a. There is the kārṇaśravasa (sāman)[1] (the chant of Karṇaśravas).

[1] Grām. XVII. 1. 16, composed on SV. I. 569, chanted on SV. II. 448–450, see SV. ed. Calcutta, vol. II, page 208, must be *aiḍa*, and this is the first of the three sāmans of this name.

13b. They (the Gods) hear him who has lauded (with this saman).

14. Karṇaśravas, the son of Angiras, being desirous of cattle, saw this sāman. By means of it he created a thousand head of cattle. (The reason) that there is this sāman, is for making thrive the cattle[1]

[1] The Jaim. br. III. 163 explains the name differently: 'Indra having hurled his thunderbolt at Vṛtra, thinking that he had not laid him low, was terrified (*sa vyasmayata*) His ears crumpled up *, (so that) he did not hear with them. He wished: 'May I be not-deaf, may I hear with my ears.' He saw this sāman and lauded with it. Thereupon he became not-deaf and heard with his ears. He said: 'I have heard (*aśrauṣam*) with my ears (*karṇa-*).' Hence the name (of the saman) '*kārṇaśravasa*'. In the sequence it is said that this sāman is called also gauloma, because it had been seen by the Angiras Golomas (*golomā āṅgirasaḥ*).

15. There is the gaurīvita (-sāman)[1]. The brāhmaṇa of the gaurīvita is the same[2].

[1] Grām. V. 1. 22, composed on SV. I. 168, chanted on SV. II. 451–453.

[2] See XI. 5. 13 sqq.

16. There is the (sāman) with (the word) *madhuścut* as nidhana[1].

[1] Grām. IX. 2. 17, composed on SV. I. 355, chanted on SV. II. 451–453. The nidhana (see SV. ed. Calcutta, vol. I, page 726) is: *madhuścutā 2345 ḥ* (with the marks 2 1 3 1111 printed above).

17. (It is applied) for obtaining the highest (the best kind of) food, for honey (*madhu*) is the highest food.

18. The (sāman) with (the word) *ghṛtaścut*[1] and the one with (the word) *madhuścut* as nidhana are the breasts of Prajāpati[2]. Prajāpati is the sacrifice; by means of these two (sāmans, *i.e.*, the breasts of Prajāpati-Sacrifice) he milks him (*i.e.*, gets out of him the essence

---

* *tasya karṇau samaiṣitām* (r. *samaiṣatām*); this meaning (to crumple, to hrivel) seems to fit better than 'to stretch', also in TS. and Kāṭh.

of what is desirable). Whatever wish he has, he thereby milks ('gets fulfilled').

[1] Grām. V. 1. 12, composed on SV. I. 165, cp. note 1 on IX. 1. 17.

[2] Cp. Jaim. br. I. 225: 'These two sāmans are the breasts of Prajāpati; by them Indra milked (obtained the fulfilment of) all his desires (out of the sacrifice).'—Prajāpati as a mother-being with female breasts occurs elsewhere, see Śat. br. II. 5. 1 3 (misunderstood by Eggeling!), Maitr. Saṃh. I. 6. 9: 101. 15, 16.

19. There are the two krauñca(-sāman)s[1].

[1] Grām. XVI. 24 and 25, composed on SV. I. 548, chanted on SV. II. 451-453.

20. Kruñc found the day that was to be sought; to be sought, as it were, is the sixth day. They find the day by means of these two (sāmans).

[1] Cp. XIII. 9. 11.—Besides krauñca, these two sāmans are also called udvat and śāmmada by the Jaiminīyas (Br. III. 164). The last name originates in the words of the Gods, who, when the worlds had in fear receded from them, recovered them by this sāman, saying: '*śaṃ vai na ime lokā amādiṣuḥ*.

21. There is the śnauṣṭa(-sāman)[1] (the chant of Śnuṣṭi).

[1] Grām. XVI. 1. 1, composed on SV. I. 541, chanted on SV. II. 454-456. The first of the two sāmans of this name is intended, cp. § 23.

22. Śnuṣṭi, the son of Angiras, beheld, by means of this sāman, straightway the world of heaven. (So this sāman is) for beholding the world of heaven. He who in lauding has applied (it), does not fall from the world of heaven[1].

[1] Cp. XIII. 9. 19.

23. This, forsooth, is the sāman of Agni vaiśvānara. They undertake (chant) as nidhana (the word) *dīdihi*[1] ('light thou strongly'), for Agni vaiśvānara lights strongly, as it were.

[1] The nidhana is (cp. SV. ed. Calcutta, vol. II, page 142) *dīdihī 1* (marked 2 r 3 2). The Jaim. br. (III. 165, see Auswahl, No. 189) gives as origin of the name: 'Agni (originally) was just as the glowing coals; he wished: 'May *śnuṣṭis*, flames be born unto me'. (Hence the name *śnauṣṭa*.)

24. The pavamāna(-laud)s of this day end on a nidhana, for propping the day[1].—The stoma (is given)[2].

[1] Cp. XIII. 5. 28.

[2] Cp. XIII. 7. 2.

XIII. 12.

(The uktha-lauds of the sixth day.)

1. The theologians argue: 'Are the two-quarter-verses[1] to be applied at the beginning or at the closing (of the six-day period)?'

[1] On which the uktha-lauds, described in this khaṇḍa, are to be chanted, *viz.*, SV. II. 457–459=ṚS. V. 24. 1, 2, 4, see note 4 on § 5; SV. II. 460–462=ṚS. X. 157. 1–3 (varr. rr.); SV. II. 463–465, on which see note 1 on XIII. 12. 9. The last two two-verse-quarters here intended are not designated by their beginning words, but in the Jaim. br. they are minutely indicated and treated.

2. They are to be applied at the closing[1]; the two-quarter verses are man: for getting a firm support.

[1] Cp. Āśv. VIII. 2. 1: '(the ritual) for the Hotrakas (is as follows): on two-quarter verses they (the Chanters) here chant the uktha (stotras of the sixth day)', etc.

3. By means of the Voice they perform the whole sacrifice; therefore, man speaks the whole Voice, for in him it is firmly established, when it is wholly chanted (*i.e.*, applied in lauding).

4. There is the gūrda (-sāman)[1].

[1] Grām. XII. 1 12, composed on SV. I. 448, chanted on SV. II. 457–459: *svāram*.

5. The vital principles of the Gaupāyanas when they were performing a sacrificial session, were scattered on the inside of the enclosing-pegs (laid around the āhavanīya) by two crafty Asuras[1] (called) Kirāta and Ākuli[2]. They[3] (the Gaupāyanas) approached the fire with (the verses beginning): 'O Agni, (be ever) nigh unto us'[4]. Thereby, they recovered their vital principles[5]. This, forsooth, they had wished to do at that time. A wish granting sāman is the gūrda; by it he gets (the fulfilment of) his wish.

[1] According to the Jaim. br. (III. 167 in Journal of the American Or. Soc., Vol. XVIII, page 42) these Asuras were so crafty, that they could cook porridge and meat without fire and that (this passage has been obscure to Oertel) they used to go before, sowing, whilst they (the other Asuras) followed them (already) reaping; read the text: *vapantau ha sma purastād ito, lunanto* (or some such participle) *ha sma paścād anuyanti*, cp. Śat. br. I. 6. 1. 2.

[2] The text has *kirātakulyau* instead of *kirātākulyau*. Sāyaṇa's explanation follows the text as printed.

[3] In the other versions of this legend it is only from one of the Gaupāyanas that the vital airs are taken away; this is more logical and comprehensible.

[4] See note 1 on § 1 (SV. II. 457–459).

[5] The version of the Kauthuma-brāhmaṇa gives no explanation of the name *gūrda*, but the Jaim. br. (III. 171) does. According to this text, *gūrda* was a name of a certain food that the Gods took away from the Asuras (*gūrda eva nāma mahad annādyam*). Having obtained it, they *agūrdan* over it.

6. There is the (sāman called) gautamasya bhadram[1].

[1] Aranyegeya III. 1. 21, composed on SV I. 452, chanted on SV. II. 460–462.

7. By means of this (sāman), he (the Chanter) invokes a blessing for him (for the Sacrificer), for the sāman is a true blessing[1].

[1] As is apparent from the words of the verse, especially SV. II. 461: *yajñaṃ ca nas tanvaṃ ca prajūṃ ca … indraḥ siṣadhāhe.*

8. By means of this (sāman), Gotama attained power and greatness. Therefore, those (of this family) who are after and before Gotama, are both termed Gotama-seers[1].

[1] Cp. note 1 on XI. 5. 22. Are we to read *gotamā*? But the two Leyden MSS. read as the printed text.

9. There is the udvaṃśaputra (-sāman)[1].

[1] Grām. XII. 1. 9, composed on SV. I. 446, chanted on SV. II. 463–465. These verses do not occur in the Ṛksaṃhitā, but they are found (with var. r.) in the Ait. āraṇyaka (V. 2. 2) and in the Śāṅkhāyana śrs. (XVIII. 15. 5). The text of the sāman stands nearer to that of Śāṅkh. than to that of Ait.ār. In Ait.ār. and Śāṅkh. these verses are given in the sequence in which they are found in the uttarārcika, but in the pūrvārcika they are found in reversed order (SV. I. 444, 445, 446 corresponding to SV. II. 465, 464, 463). If the rule given by Lāṭy. VI. 3. 2 had force also for the Brāhmaṇa, the starting point may be either Ait. ār. or Śāṅkh. śrs.

10. What the udvaṃśīya[1] is, that is the udvaṃśaputra[2].

[1] Grām. IX. 1. 16, composed on SV. I. 342.

[2] All the peculiarities of the udvaṃśīya (see VIII. 9.6 sqq.) are found also in the udvaṃśaputra. For the udvaṃśīya cp. SV. ed. Calcutta, vol. I, page 695, for the udvaṃśaputra ib. page 895.

11 Both are of a half *iḍā* and have *atisvāra*[1].

[1] Literally: 'it overtunes the half *iḍa*'. Both these sāmans have as half *iḍā* the stobha *up*, which is equivalent to *iṭ* (*i.e. iḍ*: *iḍā* without *ā*). As to the

expression *atisvarati*, I presume that it means the same as *atikrāmati* and *atisvāra* the same as *atikrama* (cp. Simon, Introduction to Puṣpasūtra, page 516): the falling out (passing over) of one or more musical tones, so that the transition is not a regularly gliding one. The udvaṃśīya has after the *ardheḍā*: $\overset{1\ \sqcap}{}$*mā* '*2 iro* '*35* and the udvaṃśaputra: $\overset{1\ \sqcap}{}$*sā* '*2 to*' '*35*. Here the transition from the musical tones *3* to *5*, with omission of note *4*, seems to be the *atisvāra*. Cp. also VIII. 9. 14.

12. Therefore, the jets (of milk) overflow the udder. In *iḍā* (that is), in cattle, he becomes firmly established at the end (of the day).

13. When it (the six-day period) has been settled (brought to end), afterwards the verse and the chant are released[1]; moreover, by means of the tune he bespeaks[2] (addresses) the seventh day, for the sake of connection.

[1] Just as, for instance, after the usual sacrifice, the two spoons are released (Śat. br. I. 8. 3 27, Baudh. I. 19: 29. 18: *srucau vimuñcati*).

[2] *abhisvarati*, a compound as *abhimantrayate*: 'to utter a mantra over (something)'. Cp. Jaim. br. III. 172; *tat* (*i.e.*, the last sāman) *svāraṃ bhavati* (the udvaṃśaputra ends: $\overset{2}{\textit{hāyi}}$, cp. on this ending note 1 on XIII. 5. 28), *abhi saptamam ahaḥ svarati, svareṇa śvo bhūte pratipadyante.*

14. For at this moment, when the sixth day is completed, the Word (the Voice) has fulfilled, as it were, its task of conveying (the sacrifice to the Gods)[1]. He should neither speak much, nor ask another, nor announce to another (answer another ?)[2].

[1] Vāc is here also considered as a drawing-animal that must be yoked at the beginning and unyoked at the end, when it has become exhausted.

[2] Kāty. XII. 3. 17 is based on our Brāhmana.

15. He (the sacrificer) should feed (the officiating priests) with honey or melted butter[1]; this is as if he besmeared the shoulder of the (animal) that has conveyed (its burden to its destination)[2].

[1] Cp. Āp. XXI. 8. 9 and Kāty. XII. 3. 18, who both draw upon our Brāhmaṇa. The Sūtrakāras (Lāṭy. III. 6. 7–10, Drāhy. IX. 2. 7–10) prescribe: 'After the completion of the (ritual of the) sixth day, they should avoid talking much; nor should they study their texts until the commencement of the next day; he should feed the priests with honey and butter or with one of these at ahīna-sacrifices, with butter only at a sattra and then at the third service.' It is known, that a dvādaśāha can be performed as an ahīna or as a sattra.

[2] Which shoulder otherwise would become as if burnt by fire, cp. Śat. br. I. 1. 2. 9.—For the rest, Āp. XXI. 8. 10 draws again on our Brāhmaṇa, when he says, *yathohuṣo vahaṃ pratyañjyāt tādṛk tad iti vijñāyate*. The Jaim. br. has nothing comparable to § 14 and 15.

16. The stoma is the thirty-three-fold one, for gaining a firm support; amidst the deities, forsooth, he has become established.

Fourteenth Chapter.

(Chandoma-days, 7th, 8th, 9th of the twelve-day-rite.)

(Seventh day.)

XIV. 1.

(Out-of-doors-laud of the seventh day.)

1. By the fact that the six-day period arrives at its end, the stomas and metres are used up[1].

[1] Cp. note 1 on III. 9. 3 and Ait. br. V. 16. 10, Kauṣ. br. XXVI. 7, beg.

2. The six-day period being brought to an end, they proceed (with the Chandoma-days), using the metres as stomas[1].

[1] This is explained by the Jaim. br. (III. 173): 'Prajāpati created this thunderbolt, this twelve-day period; through the pṛṣṭhya-six-day period he reached all. He thought: 'How can I put the four days (the last four days of the daśarātra contained in the dvādaśāha) unto it?' He formed out of the gāyatrī the day of twenty-four-versed stotras (the first Chandoma-day), out of the triṣṭubh the day of forty-four-versed stotras (the second Chandoma), out of the jagatī the day of forty-eight-versed stotras (the third Chandoma), and out of the anuṣṭubh the tenth day. Because he formed (*nir-mā*), them out of the metres (*chandas*), therefore, they are called *chandoma*.

3. (There are the verses beginning:) 'Proclaiming himself, as Uśanas, a Kāvya'[1]: with the characteristic feature of the gāyatrī[2] they proceed (begin the first Chandoma-day).

[1] SV. I. 524=ṚS. IX. 97. 7-9 (var. rr.)=SV. II. 466-468.

[2] The praep. *pra*, cp. for instance X. 6. 1, XI. 3. 1.

4. The gāyatrī is the earth: having got a firm standing on the earth, they start (undertake this day).

5. The introductory (verse) is a triṣṭubh [1].

[1] *Viz.*, the introductory tristich is on triṣṭubh verses (II. 466-468), cp. Lāty. VI. 3. 1, Drāhy. XVI. 3. 1.—That the morning service begins with triṣṭubh, not with gāyatrī, as is normal, rests on the fact that here the dvādaśāha with transposed metres is described: *vyūḍhadvādaśāha*.

6. The triṣṭubh is strength and valour [1]; having advanced in strength and valour they proceed.

[1] Being connected with Indra and the Baron.

7. The stotriya is a tristich, for retaining the breathings [1].

[1] See note 2 on VII. 3. 8, note 1 on XI. 6. 6.

8. (The verses of this tristich) contain the word *hari* [1]: in order that the Chandoma-days may not be exhausted [2].

[1] In SV. II. 468. d.

[2] Because the *harivat*-verses bestow energy (cp. XII. 13 7)? The chandoma-days are threatened by exhaustion, because all the metres and stomas have already been applied.

9. There are two complexes of twelve verses [1].

[1] SV. II. 416-477 and II. 478-489. In our Brāhmaṇa they are not indicated by their beginning words, in the Jaim. they are. These twenty-four verses consist of the tristich II. 466-468 (cp. note 1 on § 3), of the sūkta II. 469-477= ṚS IX. 10; of the sūkta II 478-486=ṚS. IX 7 and of the tristich SV. I. 498=ṚS. IX. 67. 28-30 This manner of indicating the verses used for the bahiṣpavamāna is rather confusing; it is, nevertheless, in harmony with the uttarārcika. But this distribution as two dvādarśarcas may finally rest on our Brāhmana, if we start from the surmise (see Introduction, Chapter II) that the author of the Brāhmaṇa draws his verses directly from the Ṛksaṃhitā. More logical and, in one point, interesting is the Jaim. br. (III. 174-176), where, firstly, the *pratipad* answering to Kauth. SV. II. 466-468 is indicated: then, for the *anurūpa* the verses beginning *pra svānāso rathā iva* (SV. II. 469-477), which here are designated as a sūkta (*navarca*), *viz.*, apparently, RS. IX. 10. Thereupon, follows one more *navarca* (answering to SV II. 478-486), thus time not designated as a sūkta, although these verses respond to the sūkta ṚS. IX. 7, and, finally, the *paryāsa*, beginning *ā te dakṣam* (II. 487-489).

10. The year is (equal to) twelve months; he thus counterbalances [1] the year to the preceding six-day period [2], for the sake of equilibrium.

[1] Is this the meaning of *pratyudyacchati*? Cp. XX. 2. 4.

[2] The six-day period being likewise comparable with the year, because the year has the six seasons and the ṣaḍaha, the six pṛṣṭhasāmans.

11. There are twenty-four verses; the year is (equal to) twenty-four half months; he thus counterbalances the year to the preceding six-day period: for the sake of equilibrium.

12. 'O Dṛti, son of Indrota'[1], thus spoke Ābhipratārin, the son of Kakṣasena, 'those who ascend to the top of a big tree, how do they fare afterwards'? 'Those, o King, who have wings, fly forth, those who are wingless, fall down.'

[1] The text has *dṛta aindrota iti*, these points to nom. *dṛtir aindrotiḥ* and so the Jaim. br. has it (Jaim. up. br. III. 40. 2). Dṛti is a Śaunaka and in Jaim. up. br. I. 59. 1 appears as purohita of King Ābhipratārin. He is mentioned also below, XXV. 3. 6.

13. Those who know, have wings, those who are devoid of knowledge, are wingless. Having made the trivṛt (nine-versed) and the fifteen-fold stoma their wings[1], they proceed to the world of heaven.

[1] Now that they have reached the end of the six-day period, the highest point: the top of the sacrificial tree, they can now by the application of two wings proceed further. The thrice-three-fold stoma and the fifteen-fold make together the twenty-four-versed stoma. The same speculation is found Kauṣ. br. XXVI. 7: *athaitau trivṛtpañcadaśau stomau saptamam ahar vahataś caturviṃśaḥ stomo bhūtvā.*

14. The stoma is the twenty-four-versed one: for (getting a) firm support, strength, and priestly lustre.

XIV. 2.

(Ājya-lauds of the seventh day.)

1. (The verses beginning:) 'The crest of heaven, the disposer of the earth'[1] are the ājya (-laud) addressed to Agni.

[1] SV. I. 67=RS. VI. 7. 1, 4, 2 =SV. II. 490-492.

2. The third three-day period, forsooth, is the crest of heaven[1].

[1] The first being comparable with the earth, the second with the intermediate region, cp. Kauṣ. br. XXVI. 10: *ayaṃ lokaḥ prathamaś chandomo 'ntarikṣaloko dvitīyo 'sau loka uttamaḥ.*

3. 'Agni vaiśvānara born in the sacred rite'[1]: vaiśvānara, forsooth, is Agni's favourite resort; by means of his favourite resort he thereby appropriates[2] (Agni) cryptically.

[1] SV. II. 490. b.

[2] *upaśikṣati*, cp. X. 12. 2.

4. (The verses beginning:) 'Chant ye unto Mitra'[1], being addressed to Heaven and Earth[2], (serve for) the ājya (-laud) addressed to Mitra and Varuṇa. Heaven and Earth, forsooth, are the favourite resort of Mitra and Varuṇa; by means of their favourite resort he thus appropriates them cryptically.

[1] SV. II. 493-495=ṚS. V. 68. 1-3.

[2] By the words (in SV. II. 495. a, b) *pārthivasya....divyasya*.

5. (The verses beginning:) 'Come hither, o Indra, thou bright one'[1], being addressed to the Ṛbhus[2], (serve as) the (ājya-laud) addressed to Indra. The Ṛbhus, forsooth, are Indra's favourite resort: by means of his favourite resort he thus appropriates him cryptically.

[1] SV. II. 496-498=ṚS. I. 3. 4-6.

[2] The connection with the Ṛbhus is by no means clear, the verses contain no allusion whatever to them.

6. (The verses beginning:) 'Praise him, who by his light'[1], being 'unexpressed'[2] (serve as) the (ājya-laud) addressed to Indra and Agni: in order not to violate (the dignity of) the deities[3]. In the last half (of the verse) he 'expresses'[4], in order not to cause destruction to the deities[5].—The stoma (is given)[6].

[1] SV. II. 499-501=ṚS. VI. 60. 10-12.

[2] This refers to the fact that these deities, Indra and Agni, are not expressly named in these verses (this is only partly true, as they are named in the last pada of the third verse). According to the Ait. br., the verses, which are taken for the first day of each trirātra, have the names of the deities to which the śastra is addressed, in the first verse-quarter, those of the second day of each trirātra are in the second pada, and those of the third day in the third pada (Ait. br. IV. 29. 3; IV. 31. 3; V. 1. 3, and V. 4. 2; V. 6. 4; V. 12. 2). This seems to be only a theoretical speculation. The corresponding expression of the Kauṣ. br. is: *prathame (dvitīye, tṛtīye) pade sadevam*.

[3] Just as highly placed persons are angered if they are addressed, with omission of the complimentary name (*aupacārikaṃ nāma*), with their own name.

[4] In the third pada of the last verse (*endram agniṃ ca voḍhave*) the names of the deities are expressed.

[5] Because, otherwise, the deities would not be named personally and thus the laud would not reach them.

[6] See XIV. 1. 14.

XIV. 3.

(Midday-pavamāna-laud of the seventh day.)

1. 'Be thou, a bull, clarified by the stream'[1] is the gāyatrī, for supporting the day.

[1] SV. I. 469=ṚS. IX. 65. 10-12=SV. II. 153-155.

2. Containing the word 'bull' they are, by their characteristic, triṣṭubhs, for this day is a triṣṭubh-day.

3. (The verses beginning:) 'Being clarified, o Soma, by the stream'[1] are for propping[2].

[1] SV. I. 511=ṚS. IX. 107. 4-5=SV. II. 25-26.

[2] § § 1-3 are identical with XI. 8. 1-3.

4. (The verses beginning:) 'Forth has the Soma gone to Indra's trysting-place'[1], contain (the word) 'forth' (*pra*), for this day is rather apt to bring forward[2].

[1] SV. I. 557=ṚS. IX. 86. 16-18 (varr. rr.)=SV. II. 502-504.

[2] Just as the first day of the six-day period (cp. XI. 5. 1), so the seventh day is called thus, because it introduces the third trirātra, wherewith they start anew.

5. Being jagatīs, they are triṣṭubhs by their characteristic feature[1]; therefore, they are applied at the place of the triṣṭubhs[2].

[1] Because Indra is mentioned in them, the God connected with the triṣṭubh, cp. VI. 1. 8.

[2] The last sāman in the midday-pavamāna is otherwise chanted on triṣṭubh-verses.

6. There is the gāyatra (-sāman). The brāhmaṇa of the gāyatra is the same[1].

[1] See VII. 1. 1 sqq.

7. There is the santani (-sāman)[1], for connecting the seventh day.

[1] Grām. XVIII. 2. 32, composed on SV. I. 584 and 585, chanted (see § 1) on SV. II. 153-155. -See note 1 on XIII. 5. 9.

23

8. Just as two persons, dwelling away from each other, go their different ways, so these sixth and seventh days go their different ways; as if he were to connect them, having brought them together so he connects these two (days) by means of this (sāman).

9 There is the sauparṇa (-sāman)[1] (the chant of Suparṇa), for reaching the world of heaven.

[1] Grām. III. 2. 24, composed on SV. I. 125, chanted on the same verses' see SV. ed. Calcutta, vol. I, page 307 (*aiḍam*, as expressly stated in Jaim. br.)'

10. The sacrifice went away from the Gods. It went about in the form of suparṇa (the well-winged, the falcon). By means of these sāmans[1] the Gods laid hold on it (on the sacrifice). The chandoma-days, now, are, as it were, a non-sacrifice; this (the chanting of this sāman) is a laying hold on the sacrifice.

[1] Note the plural. Must we infer therefrom that they were optional for the author of the Brāhmana?

11. There is the rohitakūlīya (-saman)[1]: for winning the race.

[1] Grām. IV. 1. 2, composed on SV. I. 129, chanted on the same verses. There are (see SV. ed. Calcutta, vol. I, page 314) two sāmans of this name, but the first is *nidhanavat*.

12. By means of this (sāman), Viśvāmitra, through his two ruddy (*rohita*) ones, won the race at Rohitakūla.

13. Viśvāmitra (once upon a time) went with the cart-train of the Bharatas. He made a wager with (certain) fellows, the Adanti by name: 'Ye shall win from me this wealth, ye shall fill these (carts) for me, if these two ruddy ones shall drive up the bank this (cart) laden with stones'. He (thereupon) saw these two sāmans; by means of these, having yoked them, he drove them forward and won (the wager)[1].

[1] There are many corruptions in the printed text, which should be read: *viśvāmitro bharatānām anasvatyāyāt so 'dantibhir nāma*, etc., and *jayāthemāni mahyaṃ yūyaṃ pūrayātha*..and *aśmācitam* instead of *aśmacitam*. Sāyaṇa explains, in all earnest, the faulty reading *manasvatyā*! The exact meaning of *vasnikā* is uncertain. After the sentence: 'Ye shall win from me this wealth', we must supply: 'if my oxen cannot drive up the bank, but if they can, ye shall fill my carts (with y o u r possessions)'. The corresponding passage of the Jaim. br. (III. 183, see Das J. Br. in Auswahl, no. 192) runs: 'Viśvāmitra in the company of the waggon-train of the Bharatas, encountered the Mahāvṛṣas. Now, there was, either on the Ganges or on the Yamunā, a high, steep bank

(at the opposite side). Said the Mahāvṛṣas: 'Which, forsooth, are now those two draught-oxen, that will be able to drive up such a high, steep bank?' Viśvāmitra answered: 'These two ruddy ones of mine'. He had namely two ruddy draught-oxen. Said the Mahāvṛṣas: 'Let us make a wager: if thy draught-oxen will drive up this (bank), thou shalt fill the carts with wares (?), but if they do not drive up, we shall win thy wares (?)'. He agreed to this and they made the wager They put the two (oxen) to the yoke of a (cart) laden either with barley or with rice. Viśvāmitra wished: 'May I win the race'. He saw these two sāmans and by means of them, going around them, he drove them on. The two (oxen) reached the opposite bank and won. So he won the race; .. And because he had won at the bank (*kūla*) by means of his two ruddy ones (*rohita*), therefore these sāmans are called *rohitakūlīya*'.

14. The twelve-day rite, forsooth, is a race performed; for the winning of this (race serve) these two sāmans.

15. There is the kaṇvarathantara (-saman)[1].

[1] Grām XIV. I. 29, composed on SV. I. 511, chanted (see § 3) on SV. II. 25-26: SV. ed. Calcutta, vol II, page 73. Cp. Kauṣ. br XXVI. 9: *yady u kaṇvarathantaraṃ kuryuḥ*, etc.

16. The kaṇvarathantara is the lustre of the rathantara; he thus applies the rathantara with its pith. by chanting the kaṇvarathantara on the seventh day.

17. 'There is sameness of performance in the twelve-day rite', thus Ugradeva, the son of Rājana[1], used to say, 'the sixth day is a bṛhat-day[2] and the seventh (day) is a bṛhat-day; by the fact that the kaṇvarathantara is applied, the sameness is taken away.'

[1] The same ritualistic authority twice in the Jaim. br., once more in our Brāhmana (XXIII. 16. 11) and in Taitt. ār. V. 4. 12.

[2] The sixth day being a raivata-day (*i.e.*, having the revati-verses as first pṛṣṭha-laud) is a bṛhat-day (cp. Ait. br. V. 16. 22). Thus the kaṇvarathantara (the rathantara, according to the Jaim. br.) separates, as it were. the bṛhat-sāmans of the two days.

18. There is the gauṅgava (-sāman)[1].

[1] Grām. V. 2. 30, composed on SV. I. 247, chanted on the same verses; cp. SV. ed. Calcutta, vol. I, page 511.

19. Agni wished: 'May I be an eater of food'; he performed austerities and saw this gauṅgava (-sāman); through it he became an eater of food. Because, after acquiring the food, he loudly rejoiced and jubilated[1] (*agaṅgūyat*), therefrom the gauṅgava has its name. For gaining food the gauṅgava is applied.

[1] The meaning of *agardat* and *agaṅgūyat* (v. *aguṅgūyat?*) must be guessed. The Jaim. br. (III. 185) derives the name from the noise, *gaṅgaṇi*, which the Gods made after their victory over the Asuras.

20. By a sāman that praises the deities, by that the Sacrificers see their wishes fulfilled[1]. They undertake the sacrificial session hoping that their wishes may be fulfilled, and, indeed, their wishes are fulfilled

[1] Cp. the words of the verse (SV. I. 247): *tvam aṅga praśaṃsiṣo devaḥ śaviṣṭha martyam.*

21. There is the āyāsya (-sāman) with crosswise nidhanas[1], for obtaining firm standing.

[1] Grām. XIV. 1. 30, composed on SV. I. 511, chanted on SV. II. 25-26, see SV. ed. Calcutta, vol. II, page 73; the comm. on Ārṣeyakalpa calls it *dvinidhanam*. The exact meaning of *tiraścīnanidhana* I do not see. The Jaim. br. (III. 187) calls it *madhyenidhanam.*

22. Ayāsya of the Angiras clan, had eaten food of the Ādityas, who had undergone the consecration (dīkṣā)[1]. He (consequently) went amiss. He (then) saw these āyāsya (-sāmans) and, by means of them, redressed himself. Gone amiss, as it were, is the seventh day[2]: in that there is this sāman, he redresses the day by means of it.

[1] Cp. XI. 8. 9 with note 1.

[2] In so far as it comes after the complete six-day period (?).

23. There is the pravad-bhārgava(-sāman)[1]; (the chant of Bhṛgu containing the word 'forth').

[1] Grām. XVI. 2. 16, composed on SV. I. 557, chanted (see § 4) on SV. II. 502-504, cp. SV. ed. Calcutta, vol. II, page 181; it is *nidhanavat.*

24. By means of the (sāman), containing (the word) 'forth' (*pra*), the Gods went forth (*pra*) to the world of heaven, by means of the (sāman), containing (the word) 'up' (*ud*), they went up[1].

[1] This last remark is made for the sake of completeness in anticipation of the eighth-day ritual, cp. XIV. 9. 39.

25. The pavamāna-lauds (of this day) end on a nidhana[1], for propping the day.—The stoma (is given)[2].

[1] The nidhana of the pravadbhārgava, according to Sāyaṇa, is: *mā' 2 nā* (1r) *pathā '3 | u | vā 2345.*—Cp. XIII. 5. 28. (2 … 1111)

[2] See XIV. 1. 14.

XIV. 4.

(The pṛṣṭha-lauds of the seventh day.)

1. (The verses beginning:) 'We with the soma thee'[1] are satobṛhatīs; (in chanting on these) he steps on to a larger metre: in order not to fall down[2].

[1] SV. I. 261=II. 214-216.

[2] Cp. XII. 4. 3.

2. (The verses beginning:) 'No one shall by his deed equal him'[1], being bṛhatī(-verse)s, are, by their repetition, jagatīs[2].

[1] SV. I. 243=ṚS. VIII. 70. 3-4 (var. r.)=SV. II. 505-506.

[2] The verses are bṛhatīs (8+8+12+8), but, by the repetition of 12 syllables (four at the end of the 2nd, 3rd, and 4th padas), they come to be of 48 syllables =jagatī. In this way the verses are construed in the grāmegeya: the vaikhānasa-sāman, see § 6.

3. A slipping down it is, as it were, if, after a larger stoma they apply a smaller one[1]; that these (bṛhatīs) become by repetition jagatīs, is for the sake of counterbalancing[2].

[1] If, after the sixth day of thirty-three-fold stoma, they undertake the twenty-four-versed seventh day.

[2] Cp. Ait. br. V. 16. 23: *tad yad bṛhat pṛṣṭhaṃ bhavati bṛhataiva tad bṛhat pratyuttabhnuvanti.*

4. There is the kaṇva (-sāman) with the word *abhi* ('on to') as finale[1].

[1] Grām. VII. 1. 30, composed on SV. I. 261, chanted on SV. II. 214-216. Its nidhana is: *ā'234 bhi*, see SV. ed. Calcutta, Vol. I, page 541. Apparently *abhi* has here the hostile meaning as in *abhicarati.*

5. By means of the (sāman) with (the word) 'on to' as nidhana, Indra hurled his thunderbolt at Vṛtra and slew him. He who in lauding has applied the (sāman) with (the word) 'on to' as nidhana, slays his rival[1].

[1] According to the Jaim. br. (III. 189), Indra, wishing to slay Vṛtra, called on Kaṇva to assist him (saying: *iha no 'dhi brūhi*), whereupon Kaṇva saw this sāman and Indra slew his foe. Because Kaṇva by means of this sāman had called over the thunderbolt the word *abhi* ('on to!'), therefore it is called the abhinidhana-kāṇva.

6 There is the vaikhānasa(-sāman)[1].

[1] Grām. VI. 2. 20, composed on SV. I. 243, chanted on SV. II. 505-506, cp. SV. ed. Calcutta, Vol. I, page 502.

7. The Vaikhānasas were Seers dear to Indra. These were killed at (a place called) 'Saints' Death' by Rahasyu Devamalimluc ('the God-robber'). The Gods said (to Indra): 'What has become of these Seers?'[1] He went in search of them but did not find them. He (thereupon) clarified these worlds with one single stream[2] and found them at 'Saints' Death' and revived them by means of this sāman. That, forsooth, had been his wish at that moment. The vaikhānasa is a wish-granting sāman. By means of it he gets his wish.—The stoma (is given)[3].

[1] Note the irregular sandhi *kva tarṣayo* instead of *kva ta ṛṣayo*.

[2] It is impossible to say what is the precise meaning of the purifying process by means of one stream Perhaps *ekadhārena* is adjectival, but which substantive is in this case to be supplied? Although agreeing in part, the tale is different in the Jaim. br. (III. 190, see Auswahl no. 193): 'There was a certain kind of Seers, called Vaikhānasa. These Seers were dear to Indra. They were killed by Rahasyu, the son of Malimluc. Indra, searching for them, encountered Rahasyu. He said to him: 'Rahasyu, hast thou happened to have seen those Seers called Vaikhānasa?' He answered: 'It is I who have killed them, o Bhagavan!' Him answered Indra: 'Hey, Rahasyu, the killing of a Brāhmin being difficult to confess, how hast thou confessed (it)?' He answered: 'I have taken on me (the guilt of) falsehood and Brāhmin-killing. Falsehood has gone from me and I have come to truth (?)'. To him said Indra: 'Choose a boon, thou who hast confessed'. He said: 'May a Brāhmin be born in my progeny'. (This was granted to him and his descendants) are those Takṣus, the descendants of Rahasyu....Thereupon, Indra revived them through this sāman, and because this sāman had been seen by Indra Vikhānas, therefore, it is called 'vaikhānasa'.

[3] See XIV. 1 14.

XIV. 5.

(The ārbhava-pavamāna-laud of the seventh day.)

1. (The verse beginning:) 'The intoxication desirable for thee'[1] is the gāyatrī. Intoxicating, rich in sap is the evening-service; he (thereby) puts (in it) intoxication and sap.

[1] SV. I. 470=ṚS. IX. 61. 19-21=SV. II. 165-167.—This § is identical with XI. 10. 1, 2.

2. (The verses beginning:) 'This one, pressed by the stream'[1] being kakubhs, are triṣṭubhs by their repetition[2].

[1] SV. I. 584 and 585=ṚS. IX 108. 5-6. In the uttarārcika the verses answering to pūrvārcika 584 and 585 seem simply to have been forgotten! They ought to have been inserted after vs. 506, where they are actually and correctly given in the Jaim. saṁhitā. But the reason for this irregularity can be guessed: it is the fact that in the pūrvārcika, by way of exception, the two verses are recorded, on which the corresponding sāmans are to be chanted. Thus the irregularity is rather in the pūrvārcika, where we expect only vs. 584, and not also vs. 585, the melody of 585 being apparently the same as that of 584.

[2] The verses serve for the śārkara (§ 14), which, being composed on SV. I. 400 (a kakubh of 8+12+8 syllables), becomes a triṣṭubh (of 44 syllables) by the repetition of the first pada and last eight syllables of the second pada. See the sāman in SV. ed. Calcutta, Vol. 1, page 817.

3 A slipping down it is, as it were, if, after a larger stoma they apply a smaller one: that these (kakubhs) become triṣṭubhs by repetition, is for the sake of counterbalancing[1].

[1] Cp. XIV. 4. 3.

4*a*. (The verses beginning:) 'O Friends, sit ye down'[1] are vālakhilya(verse)s[2].

[1] SV. I. 568=ṚS. IX. 104 1-3=SV. II 507-509.

[2] Cp. note 1 on XIII. 11. 3.

4*b*. These two vālakhilya-tristichs (are applied) not only on the sixth, but also on the seventh day. That those two vālakhilya-tristichs (are applied on the two days), is done in order that they may not slip away, that they may be tied together[1].

[1] Identical with XIII. 11. 4 and 5.

5. (The verse beginning:) 'By fore-conquest, from your plant'[1] is a virāj. The virāj is food, for retaining food[2].

[1] SV. I. 545=ṚS IX. 101. 1-3=SV. II. 47-49.

[2] Cp. VIII. 5. 7 (with note)

6. (The verse beginning:) 'Forward has the swift one flowed'[1] is an akṣarapaṅkti: the source of the stomas[2].

[1] SV. II. 510-512=ṚS. IX. 109. 16-18 (var. r.), do not occur in the pūrvārcika.

[2] The akṣarapankti, or dvipadā virāj of 40 (8×5) syllables, is said to be the source or the strength of the stomas, because all the stomas, from the trivṛt to

the forty-eight-fold, are contained in it. How they are contained in it, is not apparent to me.

7. Moreover, the akṣarapaṅkti-metre is, at this moment, of unexhausted strength[1]; by means of it the Chandoma (-days) are made of unexhausted strength.

1 Not having been used on any of the preceding days.

8. The Theologians argue: 'The stomas and metres at the six-day period having arrived at their end[1], what is the metre of the Chandoma-(days)?' One should answer: 'These akṣarapaṅktis are their metre'.

1 Cp. XIV. 1. 1.

9. (There is the tristich beginning:) 'Which Somas, far away'[1]; far away, as it were, has the sacrifice now gone: this (the sacrifice) they, by means of this (tristich), seek to get

1 SV. II. 513–515=ṚS. IX. 65. 22–24, not in pūrvārcika.

10. Being gāyatrīs, they are jagatīs by their characteristic feature[1] Therefore, they are applied at the place belonging to the jagatīs[2].

1 I see no other feature which these verses have in common with the jagatī than the rain mentioned in SV. II. 515. a, the jagatī being artificially brought forward in connection with the rainy season, cp VI. 1. 10.

2 At the end of the ārbhava-pavamāna.

11. There is the gāyatra (-sāman). The brāhmaṇa of the gāyatra is the same[1].

1 See VII. 1. 1. sqq.

12. There is the (sāman) with (the word) *dakṣa* as nidhana[1].

1 Grām. IV. 1. 24, composed on SV. 1. 141. chanted (see § 1) on SV. II. 165–167. Its nidhana (see SV. ed. Calcutta, Vol. I, page 333) is *dakṣā* 3 *yā 2345* (marks: 1 2 over dakṣā, 1 1111 over yā 2345). The sāman is called also *maukṣam dakṣanidhanam*. The Sūtrakāras (Lāṭy. III. 6. 22-23. Drāhy. IX. 3. 3-4) make regarding this part of the ārbhava-pavamāna the following remarks: 'On the seventh day the agner arka and the somasāman with one and a half *iḍā* (should be applied) on the first two verses of the mauksa, or the maukṣa and the somasāman (should be applied) on the last two verses of the gāyatrī, and the agner arka on the three'. The schema, then is either

yas te mado vareṇya iti

1–3 *gāyatraṃ tisṛṣu*, on SV. II. 165–167.

4 *agner arkaḥ prathamāyāṃ* (ar. g. I. 2. 7, chanted on II. 165).

5 *somasāma dvitīyāyāṃ* (grām. XIII. 1. 6, chanted on II. 166).

6 *maukṣaṃ tṛtīyāyām* (grām. IV. 1. 24, chanted on II. 167).

Or:

yas te mado vareṇya iti

1 *gāyatraṃ prathamāyām* (chanted on 165).

2 *maukṣaṃ dvitīyāyāṃ* (chanted on II. 166).

3 *somasāma tṛtīyāyām* (chanted on II. 167).

4–6 *agner arkas tisṛṣu* (chanted on II. 165–167).

(The ūhagāna, which in the sequence of the sāmans follows closely the Brāhmaṇa, does not give this somasāman at the place where we would expect it, in case its author followed the prescripts of the Sūtrakāras, but in the ūhyagāna the agner arka is given in accordance with the Sūtrakāras). The necessity for this prescript of Lāṭy. and Drāhy. is not obvious: the stoma is the twenty-four-fold one, and the Brāhmaṇa gives for the ārbhava-pavamāna eight sāmans; if each of these were chanted on complete tristichs, the stoma would come all right. The author of the Nidānasūtra (IV. 7) makes the following remarks, of which, although the text is neither sufficiently certain nor wholly clear, an attempt at translation may be given: 'The Paiṅgins read (the Chandoma-days) with the arka (-sāman)s for pṛṣṭha (-laud)s, (*i.e.*, they prescribe for each first pṛṣṭhastotra of the 7th, 8th, and 9th day one of the three arka-sāmans, probably *svāśirām arkaḥ, dīrghatamaso 'rkaḥ* and *agner arkaḥ*: araṇyegeya I. 2. 3, 4, 7); this is the pṛṣṭha-part of the Chandoma (-days); (but) he does not cause them to be visibly present in the pṛṣṭhas, because he fears the bṛhat and the rathantara (to whom by rights belongs the first pṛṣṭhastotra), but applies them before, on the ārbhava (at the beginning of the ārbhava): in this way they are nearest to the pṛṣṭhas (see our Brāhmaṇa XIV. 11. 8 and XV. 3. 34). On the seventh day, it (the arka) is optional, because it is not prescribed by the Brāhmaṇa; it must (however) be applied, according to (our) Teachers, for it is the joining of the Chandoma-days, as not only the Paiṅgins read (it), but also some of the Chandogas.' The text runs: *arkapṛṣṭhān paiṅgino 'dhīyate, saiṣā chandomānāṃ pṛṣṭhavibhaktis; teṣāṃ pṛṣṭhatve tiṣṭhamāno* (?) *na sākṣātkaroti, bṛhadrathantare vā* (?) *nikāmayamānaḥ pūrvā cārbhave* (read perhaps *pūrvāṃs tv ārbhave*) *karoty, evam nedīyasi pṛṣṭhānām; saptame 'hani kṛtākṛto bhavaty abrāhmaṇavihitatvāt; kartavya ity ācāryāś chandomānām cārkasamādhir yathā caitān paiṅgino 'dhīyate chandogāś cāpy enam eke 'dhīyate.* To me it seems probable that the ritual prescripts of the Sūtrakāras, where they order the arka and the somasāman to be chanted on this day, follow the Jaiminīyas (br. III. 191), and the *eke chandogāḥ* of the Nidānasūtra are probably the Jaiminīyas.

13. Prajāpati created (emitted from himself) the creatures; these being created out of him[1], deemed themselves rather weak. By

means of this sāman, (and especially) by (its nidhana) *dakṣāya*[2] ('for energy'), he puts into them strength and valour. That there is this sāman. (thereby) he puts strength and valour into himself.

[1] *asmāt* here seems to be transferred from the occurring expression: *tā asmāt sṛṣṭāḥ....apākrāman*, *e.g.*, VI. 7. 19.

[2] See note 1 on § 12.

14. There is the śārkara(-sāman)[1] (the chant of Śarkara).

[1] Grām. X. 2. 35, composed on SV. I. 400, chanted (see § 2) on SV. I. 584-585: there are two sāmans of this name (see SV. ed. Calcutta, Vol. I, page 817) but the *svāram* is intended.

15. All beings praised Indra. He, meeting Śarkara, a Śiśumāra-(Dolphin) ṛṣi[1], said: 'Praise me'. He, scattering water, said: 'With this much would I praise thee'[2]. From him he (Indra) caused the flow of the water to recede. He thought himself rather left behind (on the dry land) and saw this sāman. By means of it he again attained to the water[3] This, forsooth, he had wished at that time. A wish-granting sāman is the śārkara By means of it he obtains (the fulfilment of) his wish.

[1] Read with the two Leyden MSS. *śiśumāra ṛṣim*, with sandhi as XIII. 12. 8.

[2] *etāvato 'haṃ tvāṁ stuyām*; although the Jaim. br. has precisely the same, I guess, that this stands for *etāvato aham=etāvatā u aham*, as an instrumental is required. Perhaps the meaning is: 'with water only, not with a song I will praise thee'.

[3] Read with the two Leyden MSS. *vegam avejayat* and *sa etat sāmāpaśyat tenāpo 'nusamāśnuta.*—The Jaim. br. (III. 193, see das J. Br. in Auswahl, No. 194) contains the following version of this tale: 'All beings praised Indra. Śarkara the Dolphin did not wish to praise Indra. He said to him: 'Praise me'. He answered: 'I for one will not praise thee; in the ocean, amid the waters, I roam immerging. With this much would I praise thee', and (with these words) he showed him the water. (Thereupon) Parjanya by means of the rains caused him to swim upward, stranded him on the dry land and dried him up through the wind from the north. As he lay there wholly dried up, he knew: 'That I am come to this, has been caused by Indra. Now, then, I will praise him. He, being praised, will make me swim again down to the ocean'. He saw this sacred text and lauded him with it: 'He who repeatedly has formerly brought us good things, him ye must praise, o Friends, him: Indra, for help' (Jaim. saṃh. I. 2. 4. 7=SV. Kauth. I. 400). He said to him (to Indra, or to Parjanya): 'Do they clarify the ocean by rain? Do make me swim again to the ocean'. Him Parjanya caused to swim (again) below (the

surface of the waters)....By means of this same sacred text he (Śarkara) ascended the world of heaven. He is that śarkara (the constellation) that rises yonder....The Chandoma (-days) are an ocean. The dolphin, now, is able to set one over the ocean. That there is the śārkarasāman, is for crossing the ocean.'

16. There is the plava(-sāman)[1] (the boat-chant).

[1] Grâm. XIV. 1. 34, composed on SV. I. 511, chanted (see § 4. a) on SV. II. 507–509. See SV. ed. Calcutta, Vol. II, page 75.

17. 'A sea they cross' they say, 'who enter upon the twelve-day rite.' He, verily, who without a boat crosses the sea, does not come out of it; that there is the plava(-sāman), is for reaching the world of heaven[1].

[1] Cp. V. 8. 5.

18. By (the words of the nidhana of this sāman): 'may we overcome all difficulties', they overcome that which by them is wrongly chanted or recited[1].

[1] Cp. V. 8. 6 with note 1.

19. It has a nidhana of eleven syllables[1]; of eleven syllables is the triṣṭubh[2]. The triṣṭubh is strength and valour; he is (thereby) firmly established in (the possession of) strength and valour.

[1] See note 1 on preceding §.

[2] *i.e.*, of four times eleven syllables.

20. There is the gaurīvita(-sāman)[1]. The brāhmaṇa of the gaurīvita is the same[2].

[1] Cp. XI. 5. 13.

[2] See XI. 5. 14–20.

21. There is the kārtayaśa(-sāman)[1] (the chant of Kṛtayaśa).

[1] Grām. XVI. 1. 9, composed on SV. I. 545, chanted (see § 5) on SV. II. 47–49, cp. SV. ed. Calcutta, Vol. II, page 151.

22. They undertake (chant) as nidhana (the word) *hī*[1] for repelling the evil[2].

[1] Instead of *upā2345* (31111) of the sāman, cp. note 1 on IX. 6. 1.

[2] Because the word *hi* is etymologically connected with the root *han*, (Sāyaṇa).

23. He who in lauding has applied the kārtayaśa(-sāman), repels evil[1].

[1] The name kārtaveśa, which is another one for the same sāman, is explained in the Jaim. br. (III. 196, Auswahl No. 196) in the following manner 'The realm (once) was divided in three parts: (one part rested) with the Bharatas, one third (part) with the Vaitahavyas, one third (part) with the Mitravats. Kṛtaveśa (who probably was king of one of these three parts) desired: 'May these two realms be united (with my part)'. He saw this sāman with double nidhana and lauded with it. Thereby, these two realms were united (with his realm).'

24. There is the sauhaviṣa(-sāman)[1] (the chant of Suhavis).

[1] Grām. XI. 2. 11, composed on SV. I. 427, chanted (see § 6) on SV. II. 510–512. There are more sāmans of this name, see SV. ed. Calcutta, Vol. I. page 848, which are also partly designated as *(indrasya) saṃkrama.* A comparison of the ūhagāna proves that the first (*svāram*) is intended, though we might expect, in view of the next following §, that the sauhaviṣa with the word *svar* as nidhana was meant.

25. Suhavis, of the Angiras clan, by means of this (sāman) straightway beheld the world of heaven, (so it serves) for beholding the world of heaven. He who in lauding has applied (this sāman) does not fall from the world of heaven (he reaches the world of heaven).

26. The Theologians argue: 'The stomas and metres at the six-day period having arrived at their end, what is the metre of the Chandoma(-day)s?"[1] One should answer: 'they have man for their metre'. Man is fivefold[2], and the two-footed verses are man: in order that the Chandomas may not be exhausted.

[1] Cp. XIV. 5. 8, XIV. 1. 1.

[2] This remark is made à propos of the *dvipadā virāj* or *akṣarapaṅkti* (cp XIV. 5. 6, note 2), on which this last mentioned sāman is performed. For the rest, man is fivefold because his 'elements' are flesh, sinew, bones, marrow and semen. For the rest, here and at the parallel passages, *puruṣacchandasaḥ* should be read.

27. There is the Jarābodhīya(-sāman)[1]: for obtaining food.

[1] Grām. I. 1. 26, composed on SV. I. 15, chanted on SV. II. 513–515. The last of the two is intended, because it must be *aiḍam* (see § 31); cp. SV. ed. Calcutta, Vol. I, page 117.

28. The jarābodhīya (-sāman) is food[1], the gāyatrī is the mouth[2], he thus places food in his mouth, he eats food.

[1] Because of the fanciful connection of *jarā* in *jarābodīya* with the root *jṛ* (*jīryate*, 'to digest').

[2] The two are, at least, connected together, cp. VI. 1. 6. For the rest, this last chant is performed on gāyatrī, cp. XIV. 5. 9, 10.—An interesting tale in the Jaim. br. (III. 197, cp. Auswahl, No. 197) explains the origin of the jarābodhīya: 'The Śāktyas, who used to offer meat-cakes, (once) held a sacrificial session. Gaurivīti, one of these Śāktyas, had shot a deer. Tārkṣya Suparna came flying unto him from above. He (Gaurivīti) put (his arrow) on (his bow) and aimed at him. He (Tārkṣya) addressed him: 'Seer, do not shoot at me (cp. XI. 5. 14, note 1). We will help thee to fulfil what desire thou mayest have'. 'And what desire, then, do I have'? he said. 'Thou lovest the daughter of Asita Dhāmnya, to her I will convey thee'. Now, Asita Dhāmnya was jealous; he possessed a palace in the intermediate region (in the air, just as in the story of Uśanas, the Gandharva, who was jealous of his sister, had a palace in the sea). There they guarded his daughter. Having hidden him in the stalk of a leaf, he conveyed him (Gaurivīti) day by day to the maiden, and every morning he (Suparna) awakened him by means of this sāman, saying: 'Awaken, thou lover' (a variation in the beginning words of the sāman: *jarā bodha*). Hence the name jarābodhīya. The maiden became pregnant and a son was born to her. But he was torn asunder and thrown away by the Asuras, who said: 'This, forsooth, is the fruit of a sister (*jāmigarbha*), it is an ogre that has been born here'. He (probably the father) wished: 'May I revive him'. He saw this sāman and revived him with it. He (was) Saṃkṛti, the son of Gaurivīti'. In the pravara-texts a Saṃkṛti occurs as father of Gaurivīti.

29. An eater of food becomes he, who knows this.

30. They chant (it) on gāyatrī(-verse)s, for the sake of getting a firm support, for (the obtainment of) priestly lustre. With which breath they start, in that they finish (the laud)[1].

[1] This § agrees with XIII. 9. 28.

31. The pavamāna-(laud)s (of this day) end on *iḍā*[1]; *iḍā* is cattle and the Chandoma(-day)s are cattle. He, thereby, brings cattle into his cattle.—The stoma (has been given)[2].

[1] The second of the two jarābodhīyas is *aiḍam*.

[2] See XIV. 1. 14.

XIV. 6.

(The uktha-lauds of the seventh day.)

1*a*. (There are the verses beginning :) 'Let the calf draw hither (*ā*) thy mind'[1].

[1] SV. I. 8=ṚS. VIII. 11. 7-9=SV. II. 516-518.

1*b*. That part of the sacrifice, which consists of the uktha (-laud)s, is a cutting, as it were; that it contains (the word) 'hither' is for the sake of congruence[1].

[1] This § agrees with XI. 11. 2.

2. (The verses beginning :) 'Bring thou hither, o Indra, on our behalf'[1] are full kakubhs[2].

[1] SV. I. 405=ṚS. VIII. 98. 10-12 (var. rr.)=SV. II. 519-521.

[2] The expression *pūrṇāḥ kakubhaḥ* is here just as obscure to me as XIII. 6. 3. Sāyaṇa's explanation : *akṣaraikanyūnāḥ*, if it were right, might refer to SV. II. 520 a and b. Otherwise, the first two verses are regular kakubhs and the last is a pura-uṣṇih.

3. A slipping down, as it were, it is, if after a large stoma they undertake (apply) a smaller one[1]: that there are these full kakubhs, is for not slipping down.

[1] Cp. note 1 on XIV 4. 3.

4. (There is the tristich beginning:) 'What prosperity, o wonderful Indra, thou bearer of slingstones, is in fulness given by thee, bring that, o thou who procurest riches, with both hands unto us'[1]; he thereby gains prosperity.

[1] SV. I. 345=ṚS. V. 39. 1-3 (var rr.)=SV. II. 522-524. The first verse of the tristich is quoted in full, because of the word *rādhas*, on which the explanation (*rāddhim*) rests. In the translation I have followed the recension of the Ṛksaṃhitā, the Sāmavedic reading is due simply to the extension of syllables in the gāna : *mā iha nā (ya[4]d i[5]ndra[4] hā i | ci[2]tra ma iha[2] nā 23)* out of Ṛgvedic *mehanā*.

5. There is the vātsa(-sāman)[1] (the chant of Vatsa).

[1] Grām. I. 1. 16, composed on SV. I. 8, chanted on (see § 1. a) SV. II. 516-518. There are two sāmans of this name on SV. I. 8, but the first, being *svāram*, is required.

6. Vatsa and Medhātithi were both sons of Kaṇva. Medhātithi reproached this Vatsa: 'Thou art a non-brāhmin, (thou art) the son of a Śūdra (mother)'. He answered: 'Let us walk according to the rite through fire (to decide) which of us two is the better brāhmin'. With the vātsa(-sāman), Vatsa walked through the fire; with the maidhātitha(-sāman), Medhātithi. Not even a hair of him (of Vatsa) was burned by the fire. That was what he at that time had wished. A wish-granting sāman is the vātsa(-sāman). By means of it he gets (the fulfilment of) his wish[1].

[1] The same interesting tale is recorded more elaborately in the Jaim. br. (III. 234, 235, see 'Auswahl' No. 203). Explaining the name maidhātitha, it treats of Medhātithi and T r i ś o k a, not Vatsa, but in III. 198 it is expressly stated that Vatsa Kāṇva is the same person as Triśoka. The text runs: 'The two sons of Kanva, Medhātithi and Triśoka, contended about the sacred lore (brahman). They said: 'Come, let us cross the flaming fire'. They crossed the flaming fire. Triśoka crossed over it (unharmed), but of the other it scorched the eye-lashes. He (Triśoka) said to him (to Medhātithi): 'I have vanquished thee'. 'No', said he, 't h o u art the son of an Asura-mother; even the deities have not wished to touch thee'. Then, they (said): 'Come, let us cross the water'. They crossed the flowing Rathaspā. Triśoka crossed over it (unharmed), but of the other the rims of his cart were moistened by the water of the Rathaspā (translation uncertain, text corrupted!). He (Triśoka) said to him (to Medhātithi): 'I have vanquished thee'. 'No', said he, 't h o u art the son of an Asura-mother, even the deities have not wished to touch thee'. Then, they (said): 'Come, let us let loose cattle'. Thereupon, Triśoka immediately let loose the hairless and earless cattle. These became heated and out of their urine sprang the '*vrā*', therefore, one who obtains from viands should neither eat the '*vrā*'; others of these fever-stricken animals ran westward and entered the Sindhu, where they were changed into riversalt. Hence it is said: 'Riversalt is (the same as) cows'. Medhātithi, on the other side, desiring cattle, stretched himself out near (the place, whence the cows were to be emitted) during a year, and from this same stone-bedecked hole let loose (*i.e.*, did come forth) the cattle (by means of the verse): 'Thou of the cow-containing hole' (Jaim. Saṁh. III. 48. 17, one of the verses on which the maidhātitha-sāman is chanted, cp. below, XIV. 12. 8)'. From Jaim. br. III. 198, we infer that the sāman used by Triśoka for 'letting out' the cows, was the vātsa-sāman: 'Vatsa, the son of Kaṇva, being desirous of cattle, practised austerities. He saw this sāman and lauded with it. He is (the same as) Triśoka. . .He immediately obtained the hairless and earless cattle'.

7. There is the sauśravasa(-sāman)[1] (the chant of Suśravas).

[1] Gram. IV. 2. 1, composed on SV. I. 145, chanted (see § 2) on SV. II. 519–521. There are two sāmans of this name and both are *nidhanavat*. From

the ūhagāna it appears that the first of the two is intended; with equal right the second might be taken (SV. ed. Calcutta, Vol. I, page 341).

8. Upagu, the son of Suśravas, was the chaplain of Kutsa, the son of Ūru. This Kutsa cursed any one who should offer a sacrifice to Indra. Indra (once) having met Suśravas, said: 'Offer a sacrifice to me, I am hungry'. He offered to him and Indra, having the sacrificial cake in his hands, came up to Kutsa and said: 'They have offered a sacrifice to me, what has become of thy curse?' 'Who has offered a sacrifice to thee?' (he asked). 'Suśravas', he answered. Then this Kutsa, son of Ūru, cut off, by means of the pillar of udumbara-wood, the head of Upagu, the son of Suśravas, as he (Upagu) was chanting the sāman. (Thereupon) Suśravas said to Indra: 'From thy part has this sort of thing happened unto me'. He (Suśravas) by means of this sāman revived him (*viz.*, Upagu). This, forsooth, he had wished at that time. A wish-granting sāman is the (sāman) of Suśravas. By it he gets (the fulfilment of) his wish [1].

[1]. The version of the Jaim. br. (III. 198-201, cp. 'Auswahl' No. 198) runs as follows, 'Kutsa Aurava ('sprung from the thigh') was formed out of Indra's thigh, just as Indra was, so was he: even as one who has been formed out of himself. He made him his charioteer. He (Indra) (once) surprised him (Kutsa) with his (Indra's) spouse, Śacī, the daughter of Puloman, and said to her: 'How hast thou done this'? She answered: 'I have not discerned you both' He said: 'I will make him bald, in this way thou wilt discern (us)'. He made him bald. But he (Kutsa), having covered his head with a turban, approached (her). This is the (origin of the) turban of the charioteer. He (Indra) again surprised him (with his spouse) and said to her: 'How hast thou done this'? She answered: 'I have not discerned you both, he has covered (his head) with a turban and so has approached me'. He (Indra) said: 'Between his shoulders will I strew sand, in this way thou wilt discern (us)'. And he strewed sand between his shoulders. That is the sand that is found between a charioteer's shoulders. But he (Kutsa), having covered it with his upper-garment, approached her. He again suprised him and said to her: 'How hast thou done this'? She answered: 'I have not discerned you both, he has covered himself with his garment and so has approached me'. He (Indra) drove him away, saying: 'Be a Malla'. He said: 'May we, o Indra, not go to ruin; give thou that to us, by which we may live; from thee, forsooth, we are born'. (Indra answered:) Then shake thou off that sand between thy shoulders'. He shook it off and it arose as that great people called the Rajas and Rajīyas. Of them he was the king. His house-chaplain was Upagu, the son of Suśravas. He (Kutsa) said: 'Let no one offer sacrifice. He who in my realm acts as offering-priest, must be deprived

of his possessions. The Gods, forsooth, do not eat if no offering is made. Not even the leaf of a tree must be offered'. Now, Indra went to Upagu, the son of Suśravas, and said: 'I pray thee to offer for me'. He answered: 'They do not offer sacrifice here; he who would offer, him they would deprive of his possessions'. He showed him the world (of heaven ?) saying: 'This world thou wilt gain, if thou offerest sacrifice'. He (Upagu) thought: 'Let them deprive me! Come, I will offer'. (Now, Upagu performs in a simplified manner alone the sacrifice of soma for Indra. This takes place thrice, and each time Upagu is deprived of his possessions. But when Kutsa hears, that again for the third time, Upagu has sacrificed) he rose and smashed him to pieces and scattered him in the water. But his father, Suśravas, the son of Sthūra, learned: 'Kutsa Aurava has smashed thy son to pieces and thrown him in the water'. He came running to him and asked: 'Where hast thou put my son'? 'He lays there smashed to pieces in the water'. He went after him in the water (to fetch his son). From out his mouth Indra in the guise of a rohita (fish) drank the soma. He thought: 'This forsooth, is Indra, him I will praise. He will revive this (son) of mine'. He saw this sāman and lauded him with it' (and then Indra revived his son).

9. There is the vin̄ka(-sāman)[1].

[1] Grām. IX. 1. 31, composed on SV. I. 345, chanted (see § 4) on SV. II. 522–524. There are (see SV. ed. Calcutta, Vol. I, page 705) three sāmans of this name, but the last of these, being *aiḍam*, is required.

10. Cyavana, the son of Dadhyañc, was beloved by the Aśvins. As he became of old age, they, by means of this (*vin̄ka-*) sāman, shook (*vin̄kayati*) him in the water and made him young again. This they had wished at that time. A wish-granting sāman is the vin̄ka. By means of it he gets (the fulfilment of) his wish.

11. The stoma is the twenty-four-versed one, for (obtaining) strength and priestly lustre.

(Eighth (second Chandoma-) day.)

XIV. 7.

(Out-of-doors-laud of the eighth day.)

1. (The tristich beginning:) 'The young one, being born, the beloved one, they wipe,'[1] is the opening one of the eighth day.

[1] ṚS. IX. 96. 17–19 (var. rr.)=SV. II. 525–527.

2. As a young one, forsooth, comes this one[1] into existence through the seventh day, him they wipe off through the eighth day.

[1] It is not certain to whom this pronoun refers, according to Sāyaṇa the stoma is meant.

3. The stotriya is a tristich, for retaining the breaths [1].

[1] See note 1 on XIV. 1. 7.

4. They (the verses mentioned in § 1) contain (the word) *hari*,[1] in order that the Chandoma(-day)s may not be exhausted.

[1] This is forced, the word occurring in SV. II. 525 being *haryatam*. The verses, being *harivatyaḥ*, are apt for the bestowing of energy and strength on the Chandomas (who are in need of this! see XIV. 1. 1 and XIV. 5. 7), cp. XII. 13. 7.

5. There are (complexes) of nine verses [1].

[1] I. SV. II. 528-536=ṚS. IX. 8 (*sūkta*) 1-7, 9, 8; II. SV. II. 537-545=ṚS. IX. 13 (*sūkta*) 1-4, 6, 5, 7-9; III. SV. II. 546-554=ṚS. IX. 12 (*sūkta*) 1-7, 9, 8. None of the verses are indicated in our Brāhmaṇa, the Jaim. br. (III. 206) indicates only the first nine verses, designating them as a *sūkta*, the second group and the third group are likewise called a *navarcaṃ sūktam*.

6. There are nine breaths [1], the Chandoma(-day)s are cattle [2]; he thereby puts the breath into the cattle.

[1] See note 1 on VI. 2. 2.

[2] See note 1 on III. 8. 2.

7. There is a (complex) of five verses [1]; the paṅkti(-metre) is of five feet (of five verse-quarters), fivefold is food [2], (so they serve) to obtain food.

[1] SV. II. 555-559=ṚS. IX. 50 (*sūkta*).

[2] Cp. note 2 on XII. 1. 9.

8. It contains (the word) 'lute' [1]; the lute, forsooth, is the end [2] and this eighth (day) is the end of the days [3]: on the end (on the eighth day) they thereby chant with the end (the lute, *i.e.*, the hymn containing this word): for gaining a firm support.

[1] In SV. II. 555. c.

[2] See note 1 on V. 6. 12.

[3] It is the last (but one!) day of the nine-day period; in the same manner, the mahāvrata day is called the end of the year in V. 6. 12.

9. There are three tristichs [1], for connecting the out- and in-breathings.

1 I. SV. II. 560–562 (=I. 495)=ṚS. IX. 61. 1–3; II. SV. II. 563–565 (=I 510)=ṚS. IX. 61. 25–27; III. SV. II. 566–568 (=I. 493)=ṚS. IX. 63. 7–9.

10. It is the fourty-four versed stoma [1]; in strength and valour he thereby is firmly established: the triṣṭubh is strength and valour [2].

1 According to Kauṣ. br. XXVI. 7, composed of the seventeenfold and the triṇava stomas (17+27=44).

2 Because the out-of-doors-laud here also, as at the seventh day (XIV. 1. 6), begins on triṣṭubh-verses.

XIV. 8.

(The ājya-lauds of the eighth day.)

1. (The tristich beginning:) 'Agni, the God, in accordance with the Agnis,' [1] is the ājya(-laud) addressed to Agni.

1 SV. II. 569–571=ṚS. VII. 3. 1–3.

2. (By the plural) 'with the Agnis,' he kindles the eighth day in view of the preceding days that have been kindled [1].

1 The plural *agnibhiḥ* refers to the preceding days, the singular *agnim* to this eighth day. Is *abhi* to be taken in the sense of 'in view of' or 'together with' ('daarbij', Dutch)?

3. (The tristich beginning:) 'Mitra do we call,' [1] (is destined) for the ājya(-laud) addressed to Mitra and Varuṇa, being connected with the bṛhat [2].

1 SV. II. 143–145, cp. XI. 7. 3.

2 Cp. note 4 on page 33 of the edition of the Ārṣeyakalpa.

4. The Chandoma(-day)s, forsooth, are a ford difficult to cross, as it were. Just as in daily life they enter into a stream, which is difficult to cross, having linked themselves mutually together, so he links thereby [1] the two characteristic features [2] mutually together, in order that the Chandomas may not oscillate.

1 Thereby, *i.e.*, by taking, as first and third ājyastotra, a rathantara-tristich, and by taking, as second and fourth, a bṛhat-tristich.

2 Of the rathantara- and the bṛhat-days, this eighth day being a rathantara-day.

5. (The tristich beginning:) 'This Indra we incite' [1] is (the ājya-laud), addressed to Indra.

1 SV. II. 572–574 (=I. 119)=ṚS. VIII. 93, 7–9 (var. rr.).

6. By means of the eighth day, forsooth, the Gods had incited Indra, by means of the ninth they had repelled evil[1]. The day they thereby incite.

[1] Read *pāpmānam aghnann*.

7. (The tristich beginning:) 'On Indra, on Agni, a loud (*bṛhat*) praise,'[1] is (destined for) the (ājya-laud) addressed to Indra and Agni, being connected with the bṛhat[2].

[1] SV. II. 150-152, cp. XI. 7. 3.

[2] See note 2 on § 3.

8. The Chandoma(-day)s, forsooth, are a ford, difficult to cross, as it were. Just as in daily life they enter into a stream, which is difficult to cross, having linked themselves mutually together, so he links thereby the two characteristic features mutually together, in order that the Chandomas may not oscillate[1].—The stotra (is given)[2].

[1] Cp. § 4.

[2] See XIV. 7. 10.

XIV. 9.

(The midday-pavamāna-laud of the eight day.)

1. (The verse beginning:) 'O Adhvaryu, the (soma) pressed by means of the stones,'[1] is a gāyatrī, for supporting the day[2].

[1] SV. I. 499=ṚS. IX. 51. 1, 3, 2 (var. r.)=SV. II. 575-577.

[2] Because of the word 'stones', which are of hard and durable substance.

2. Being gāyatrīs, they are triṣṭubhs by their characteristic feature[1]; for this day is a triṣṭubh-day.

[1] They mention Indra, who is connected with the triṣṭubh, VI. 1. 8.

3. (There are the verses beginning:) 'The living Somas, unto'[1]. 'Unto' is the characteristic of the rathantara, 'great' of the bṛhat; he applies the characteristic of both together, for this (eighth) day is equal to both these aspects[2].

[1] SV. I. 518=ṚS. IX. 107. 14-16=SV. II. 206-208.

[2] Cp. XII. 3. 4-5.

4. (The tristich beginning:) 'The sustainer of the day is being clarified by the strong juice'[1]—this three-day period being unsustained, as it were—(serves) by (the word) 'the sustainer' for sustaining (it).

[1] SV. I. 558=ṚS. IX. 76. 1-3 (var. r.)=SV. II. 578-580.

5. Being jagatīs, they are triṣṭubhs by their characteristic feature[1]; therefore, they are applied on the place belonging to the triṣṭubhs[1].

[1] Cp. note 1 on § 2.

6. There is the gāyatra(-sāman). The brāhmaṇa of the gāyatra is the same[1].

[1] See VII. 1. 1. sqq.

7. There is the vairūpa(-sāman)[1].

Grām. XIV. 1. 5, composed on SV. I. 499, chanted (see § 1) on SV. II. 575-577. There are (see SV. ed. Calcutta, Vol. II, page 57) two vairūpas on this verse; that the first is intended rests on a comparison of the ūhagāna.

8. The vairūpa is cattle: (so it serves) for obtaining cattle; the year is of different features[1] (*virūpa*) and food is of different features: for obtaining food.

[1] Why this assertion?

9. There is the āśu bhārgava(-sāman)[1] (the swift chant of Bhṛgu).

[1] Grām. XII. 2. 25, composed on SV. I. 469, chanted on SV. II. 575-577. It is *svāram*, see SV. ed. Calcutta, Vol. II, page 11.

10. This day (once upon a time) collapsed; by means of the swift (chant) the gods restored it again; therefore, it is called 'the swift one'.

11. There is the mārgīyava(-sāman)[1], (the chant of the 'hunter').

[1] Grām. III. 2. 1, composed on SV. I. 115, chanted on SV. II. 575-577. There are (see SV. ed. Calcutta, Vol. I, page 289) more than one sāman of this name, but the *nidhanavat* is intended.

12. This God[1], forsooth, they call 'the hunter'. By means of this (sāman) he attained the supremacy over both kinds of animals[2].

He who in lauding has applied the mārgīyava(-sāman), attains the supremacy over both kinds of animals[3].

[1] Ominis causa, the name Rudra is avoided; the mārgīyava-sāmans are also called 'the chants of Rudra'.

[2] That live in the village and that live in the wilds, Jaim. br.

[3] And the God aims not (*nābhimanyate*) at his cattle, Jaim. br. III. 212.

13. There is the saumitra(-sāman)[1], (the chant of Sumitra).

[1] Grām. X. 2. 11, composed on SV. I. 388, chanted on SV. II. 575–577, see SV. ed. Calcutta, Vol. I, page 797 (last of the three).

14. The brāhmaṇa of the saumitra is the same[1].

[1] See XIII. 6. 9-10.

15. There is the aiṭata(-sāman)[1] (the chant of Iṭan).

[1] Grām. III. 2. 6, composed on SV. I. 117, chanted on SV. II. 575–577. The first of the two of this name, SV. ed. Calcutta, Vol. I, page 293. According to the Jaim. br., it is *triṇidhanam*.

16. Iṭan, the son of Kavi, by means of this (sāman) straightway beheld the world of heaven: (it serves) for beholding the world of heaven. He who is lauding has applied (it), falls not from (reaches) the world of heaven.

17*a*. There is the sākamaśva(-sāman)[1].

[1] Grām. V. 2. 19, composed on SV. I. 193, chanted on SV. II. 575–577. It is *aiḍam*, see SV. ed. Calcutta, Vol. I, page 420.

17*b*. The brāhmaṇa of the sākamaśva is the same[1].

[1] See VIII 8. 4-5.

18. This (sāman) they also call 'the chant of the yokes'.[1] The yokes are the breaths[2]: for retaining the breaths (the life).

[1] *dhurāṁ sāma*, this must be the meaning of *dhur*, cp. *dhuroḥ śamyā*.

[2] Sāyana explains as follows: 'for those (breaths), leaving the body of a dying man, injure (*dhūrvanti*), hurt, the surrounding people that stand near.' This explanation seems questionable. The name *dhurāṁ sāma* is given to this sākamaśva to bring in a new commendation, the *dhuraḥ* being equalised with the *prāṇas*, so that *dhurāṁ sama* is equal to *prāṇānāṃ sama*. The *dhuraḥ* support the cart, as the *prāṇas* support the living being. Besides the explanation proffered by our brāhmaṇa, the Jaim. br. (III. 210) gives another one: 'the yokes are the metres: the Chandoma-days have their strength gone, so to say (because the metres are repeated in them); by applying the chant of the

yokes, the Chandoma-days become possessed of yokes, of metres, and of unexhausted strength'.

19. There is the vilambasauparṇa(-saman)[1], (the soaring chant of Suparṇa).

[1] Grām. III. 2. 26, composed on SV. I. 125, chanted on SV. II. 575–577. It is (see SV. ed. Calcutta, Vol. I, page 308) *nidhanavat*; *caturakṣara-nidhanam* according to Jaim. br.

20. That one of the sauparṇa(-sāman)s, which (is applied) on the eighth day, is the trunk, those two (sauparṇasāmans) that (are applied) on the seventh[1] and ninth[2] day, are the wings at the side (of the trunk). Now, the trunk, as it were, soars between (*vilambate*) the two wings. Because the trunk soars between the two wings, therefore, it is (called) the *vilambasauparṇa*(-sāman).

[1] Cp. XIV. 3. 9.

[2] Cp. XV. 5. 18.

21. The sauparṇa(-sāman) (thus) is applied to reach the world of heaven.

22*a*. There is the vāmadevya with double *him*-sound[1].

[1] Grām. XIV. 2. 22, composed on SV. I. 514, chanted on SV. II 206–208. The sāman has (see SV. ed. Calcutta, Vol. II, page 87) twice *hum* [1] *mā 2*. It is *aiḍam*. According to the Ārṣeyabrāhmana, Grām XI. 2. 2 (ed. Calcutta, Vol. I, page 855) is equally called *dvihiṃkāraṃ vāmadevyam*, besides *saṃjaya*. But the grantha-edition of the grām. designates it only as *saṃjaya*, not as *dvihiṃkāraṃ vāmadevyam*.

22*b*. (It serves) for obtaining food[1].

[1] Probably because the vāmadevya is cattle: IV. 8. 15, VII. 9. 9, XI. 4. 8.

23. For the Chandoma(-day)s are this second characteristic feature[1].

[1] The first complex of days is the preceding six-day period, the second is the three-day period, which is constituted by the Chandomas.

24. The vāmadevya is a cattle, the Chandoma (-day)s are cattle: he thus brings cattle into (his) cattle.

25. There is the gāyatrapārśva(-sāman)[1].

[1] Grām. XVII. 2. 31, composed on SV. I. 584, chanted on SV. II. 206–208. It is *nidhanavat*, cp. SV. ed. Calcutta, Vol. II, page 237.

26. This day collapsed; by means of the gāyatrapārśva the Gods connected it: therefore there is the gāyatrapārśva.

27. When the three day period[1] was shattered, they (the Gods) healed it by means of these sāmans: by means of the gāyatrapārśva[2] they propped it, by the santani[3] they connected it, by the saṃkṛti[4] they brought it into good order (*samaskurvan*). The two preceding three-day periods were well established, but t h i s one was not. That t h e s e sāmans are thus applied, is in order that it may be well established.

[1] The third trirātra: the Chandoma-days.

[2] Of the second Chandoma-day.

[3] Of the first Chandoma-day, cp. XIV. 3. 7.

[4] Of the third Chandoma-day, cp. XV. 3. 28. b.

28. There is the pauruhanmana(-sāman)[1] (the chant of Puruhanman).

[1] Grām. VII. 2. 17, composed on SV. I. 273, chanted on SV. II. 206–208. It is *aiḍam*, see SV. ed. Calcutta, Vol. I, page 563.

29. Puruhanman, of the Vikhānas clan, by means of this (sāman) straightway beheld the world of heaven; (so it serves) for beholding the world of heaven. He who in lauding has applied (it) does not fall from (attains) the world of heaven

30. It is provided with 'up-beat'[1], for the Chandoma(-day)s have sāmans with 'up-beat'[2].

[1] *abhyāghātya* (from *abhyāhanti*, 'to strike on, subsequently') denotes a certain way of repetition (the Jaim. br. seems to use here *abhyārambha*). Cp. also note 1 on XIV. 11. 10. The syllables of the verse (SV. I. 273. b) (*bhir a*) *dhriguḥ* become in the chant: (*bhir ā*) *dhr*$\overset{2}{\text{ā}}$*'1 igū'2ḥ—dhr*$\overset{1}{\text{ā}}$*-i gū2ḥ*; the syllables of SV. I. 273. c: *tarutā* become: *t*$\overset{1}{\text{ā}}$*rut*$\overset{2}{\text{ā}}$*'3—t*$\overset{1}{\text{ā}}$*rut*$\overset{2}{\text{ā}}$*'3*, the syllables of SV. I. 273. d: *vṛtrahā gṛṇe* become (*vā*)*—trāh*$\overset{2}{\text{ā}}$ *g*$\overset{3}{\text{ā}}$*'234 rṇ*$\overset{5}{\text{ā}}$ *i—tr*$\overset{4}{\text{a}}$ *hā'5 gṛṇā i*.

[2] The acchidra (§ 35) at least has similar repetitions.

31. There is the dvaigata(-sāman)[1] (the chant of Dvigat).

[1] Grām. VII. 2. 1, composed on SV. I. 264, chanted on SV. II. 206–208, the first of the two: SV. ed. Calcutta, Vol. I, page 546.

32. Dvigat, of the Bhṛgu clan, by means of this (sāman) went twice to the world of heaven, after having arrived, he returned.

The dvaigata(-sāman) is applied for obtaining (the fulfilment of) two wishes [1].

[1] The tale is more comprehensible in its recension of the Jaiminīyas (Jaim. br. III. 216, see 'Auswahl' n° 200): 'The Gods, having seized the whole sacrifice, went up to the world of heaven. The men did not know of the sacrifice, so the continuity was broken (the sacrifice, to be effective, must be acknowledged by both: Gods and men). (In consequence), Gods and men suffered from hunger, for, upon what is given from here (from the earth, *i.e.*, from the men to the Gods), the Gods exist, upon what is given from thence (from heaven) men exist: neither the oblations went upward, nor was the rain poured downward. The Gods said to Ayāsya: 'The men do not know of the sacrifice, so the continuity has been broken. Go and dispose the sacrifice for the men'. This is the sacrifice as disposed (now-a-days) to men. Having dwelt among the men, Ayāsya did not know again the (way to the) world of heaven. He wished: 'May I know the (way to the) world of heaven'. Having lauded with this sāman, he again knew the (way to the) world of heaven... Because Ayāsya from yonder world came to this world and from this world to yonder world and thus visited twice these worlds, hence the sāman has its name: dvaigata'.

33. There is the hārāyaṇa(-sāman) [1] (the energy-chant).

[1] Grām. VII. 1. 11, composed on SV. I. 253, chanted on SV. II. 206–208, see SV. ed. Calcutta, Vol. I, page 423 (*aiḍam*).

34. Indra, being desirous of lustre, of energy (*haras*), practised austerities. He saw this hārāyaṇa(-sāman) and by means of it obtained lustre, energy. Lustrous and full of energy becomes he who in lauding has applied the hārāyaṇa(-sāman).

35. There is the achidra (-sāman) [1] ('the cleftless chant').

[1] Grām. XIV. 2. 1, composed on SV. I. 512, chanted on SV. II. 206–208. According to the Jaim. br. (III. 218), it is *padanidhanam* and *jyāyo'bhyārambham* (cp. note 2 on § 30), see SV. ed. Calcutta, Vol. II, page 77.

36. What cleft there was in this day, that the Gods by means of the cleftless (sāman) covered up. Therefore, it is called the cleftless (sāman).

37. There is the bārhaduktha(-sāman) [1] (the chant of Bṛhaduktha).

[1] Grām. VIII. 1. 17, composed on SV. I. 296, chanted on SV. II. 207 (last pada) and 208, see SV. ed. Calcutta, Vol. I, page 601. There are many sāmans of this name, but it must be *aiḍam*. As the ūhagāna forgets to give this sāman, it is only a Prayoga which has enabled me to identify it.

38. Bṛhaduktha, the son of (the woman) Vāmnī, came by means of this (sāman) to the chaplain-office of food. The chaplain-office is the Brāhman's food; (so the sāman serves) for obtaining food[1].

[1] Cp. XIII. 9. 27.

39. There is the udvat-bhārgava (-sāman)[1], (the chant of Bhṛgu containing the word 'up').

[1] Grām. XVI. 2. 7, composed on SV. I. 555, chanted on SV. II. 578-580. It is *nidhanavat*, see SV. ed. Calcutta, Vol. II, page 174 (the first of the three here called āṅgirasa). According to Jaim. br. (III. 219), it is also called *viśālam*.

40. By means of the (sāman) containing (the word) 'forth', the Gods went forth to the world of heaven; by means of the (sāman) containing (the word) 'up', they went up[1].

[1] This § is found already XVI. 3. 24.

41. The pavamāna(-laud)s (of this day) end on a nidhana[1], for propping the day.—The stoma (has been given)[2].

[1] Cp. note 1 on § 39.

[2] See XIV. 7. 10.

XIV. 10

(The pṛṣṭha-lauds of the eighth day.)

1. (The verses beginning:) 'Who knows him together with the soma' are satobṛhatīs[1].

[1] SV. I. 297=ṚS. VIII. 33. 7-9=SV. II. 1046-1048.

2. A slipping down, as it were, is the fact that on the seventh day there are satobṛhatī(verse)s[1], but (if these would) not (be applied) on the eighth; therefore, they are to be applied on the eighth (day); for not slipping down.

[1] Cp. XIV. 4. 1.

3. On this matter (however) they (the Theologians) say: 'The satobṛhatī metre is loose, as it were[1]; firmly established (on the contrary) is the bṛhatī[2] with its repeated verse-quarters. (The verses beginning:) 'What, o Indra, in front, behind, above'[3] (on which the third pṛṣṭha-laud is to be chanted) are a consideration (contain a consideration) of the regions: to obtain a firm standing'.

[1] In the satobṛhatī, consisting of 12+8+12+8 syllables, the pairs of verse-quarters (12+8) follow on each other uninterruptedly and thus show a certain uniformity, a kind of *jāmitvam*.

[2] The bṛhatī, consisting of 8+8+12+8, has, on the contrary, a repetition of verse-quarters, in so far as here follow two quarters of eight syllables immediately. For the rest, the verses which are rejected (in § 1 and 2) as being satobṛhatīs, as well as those which are commended as being bṛhatīs (in § 3), are both bṛhatīs, but the first is followed by two other bṛhatīs and the second by one satobṛhatī. It is probable that their bṛhatī-and satobṛhatī-being, is made effective by the mode of chanting in the praxis.—The hautra-ritual of the Aitareyins (Āśv. VII. 4. 3) has a different pragātha, (*viz.*, ṚS. VII. 66. 14), but the Kauṣītakins (Śāṅkh. śrs. XII. 4. 4–7) allow the verses mentioned by our brāhmaṇa in § 1 and 2 as well as those mentioned in § 3. Against these, then, our brāhmana apparently polemizes.

[3] SV. I. 279=ṚS. VIII. 4. 1-2=SV. II. 581-582.

4. On these (verses) he should chant, as the Brahman's saman[1], the naipātitha(-sāman)[2] (the chant of Nepātithi).

[1] As third pṛṣṭhastotra, the first and second are the usual ones.

[2] Grām. VII. 2. 27, composed on SV. I. 279, chanted on SV. II. 581-582. The last of the two, being *nidhanavat* (cp. SV. ed. Calcutta, Vol. I, page 573), is required. According to Jaim. br. III. 220, this sāman was seen by the son of Kaṇva, Nepātithi, when, at a sacrificial session of the Kānvāyanas, their cattle ran short.

5. A sāman, being of ṛṣi-descent, is fit for reaching the world of heaven[1]. He who in lauding has applied (it), does not fall from the world of heaven (reaches the world of heaven).

[1] Cp. XI. 5. 22.

6, 7. (The verses beginning:) 'Both let him hear'[1] (serve) for connecting b o t h : the pṛṣṭha(-laud)s and these days[2].

[1] SV. I. 290=ṚS. VIII. 61. 1-2=SV. II. 583-584.

[2] The pṛṣṭhas of the six-day period and these Chandoma-days.

8. On these (verses) the vaiyaśva(-sāman)[1] (must be chanted) (the chant of Vyaśva).

[1] Grām. VIII. 1. 10, composed on SV. I. 290, chanted on SV. II. 583-584; is *aiḍam*, cp. SV. ed. Calcutta, Vol. I, page 593.

9. Vyaśva, of the Angiras clan, by means of this (sāman) straightway beheld the world of heaven[1]. This (sāman) is applied at the

end of the pṛṣṭha(-laud)s (as the last), for beholding the world of heaven.—The stoma (has been given)[2].

[1] The origin of the name Vaiyaśva is explained in the Jaim. br. (III. 221, see 'Auswahl' No. 201) in the following manner: 'About Vyaśva, the son of Śākamaśva, when he was (still) in the womb of his mother, his paternal uncle Gaya knew that he would be born as a seer. When he was born, he (Gaya) gave order to expose him, with the words: 'One has been born, who directly after his birth is gone to ruin'. Him (the exposed infant) the shadow did not leave, and his two thumbs procured him (miraculously) the mother-milk. Of this they informed him (Gaya): 'The boy thou hast ordered to be exposed lives!' He took his club and went near to slay him. He (Vyaśva) wished: 'May I get out of this, may I find deliverance and assistance'. He saw this sāman and chanted it over (him, over Gaya). Thereupon, his (Gaya's) club fell back and split up his head'.

[2] Cp. XIV. 7. 10.

XIV. 11.

(The ārbhavapavamāna-laud of the eighth day.)

1. (The verse beginning:) 'Be clarified, o God, united with long life; unto Indra let thy intoxication go'[1] is the gāyatrī. Intoxicating, rich in sap, is the afternoon-service; he (thereby) puts (in it) intoxication and sap[2].

[1] SV. I. 483=RS. IX. 63. 22-24 (var. r.)=SV. II. 585-587.

[2] Cp. XI. 10. 2.

2. (In the verses beginning:) 'Unto us lustre and great glory'[1], (the word) 'unto' is characteristic of the rathantara, (the word) 'great', of the bṛhat. He applies the characteristics of both together, for this day (has) both these features[2].

[1] SV. I. 579=ṚS. IX. 108. 9-10=SV. II. 361-362

[2] This § is identical with XIII. 5. 2.

3. (The verses beginning:) '*Prāṇā*, the young of the great ones,'[1] contain (the word) 'breath'. He, thereby, puts breath into the Sacrificer.

[1] SV. I. 570=ṚS. IX. 102. 1-3=SV. II. 363-365. Cp. note 1 on XIII. 5. 3.

4. (The verses beginning:) 'Unto (*abhi*) us booty containing riches,'[1] are by the word 'unto' characteristic of the rathantara, for this day is a rathantara-day.

[1] SV. I. 549=ṚS. IX. 98. 1, 5, 3 (var. rr.)=SV. II. 588-590.

5. (The verse beginning:) 'Be clarified, o Soma, as a great ocean,'[1] is an akṣarapaṅkti, the source of the stomas. Moreover, the akṣarapaṅkti-metre is, at this moment, of unexhausted strength; by means of it, the Chandoma(-day)s are made of unexhausted strength. The Theologians argue: 'The stomas and metres at the six-day period having arrived at their end, what is the metre of the Chandoma(-day)s?' One should answer: 'These akṣarapaṅktis are their metre'.

[1] SV. I. 429=ṚS. IX. 109. 4-6=SV. II. 591-593.—The rest of this § is identical with XIV. 5. 6-8.

6. (The verses beginning:) 'The cows urge the running'[1], being gāyatrīs, are, by their characteristic, jagatīs[2]. Therefore, they are applied at the (proper) place of the jagatīs.

[1] SV. II. 254-256=ṚS. IX. 65. 1-3 (cp. XII. 1. 10).

[2] Because they mention (255. b) the Gods and (256. b) the rain, both of which are connected with the jagatī-metre, cp. VI. 1. 10.

7. There is the gāyatra(-sāman); the brāhmaṇa of the gāyatra is the same[1].

[1] See VII. 1. 1. sqq.

8. There is the svāśirām arka(-sāman)[1] ('The praise of the well mixed ones').

[1] Araṇyegeya I. 2. 3, composed on SV. I. 468, chanted on SV. II. 585-587. —Cp. note 1 on XIV. 5. 12. See the sāman in SV. ed. Calcutta, Vol. II, page 404.

9. The hymn of praise (*arka*), forsooth, is food; (so it serves) for obtaining food[1].—The 'well-mixed ones' are the breaths[2], (so it serves) for retaining the breaths (the life).

[1] Cp. Śat. br. XII. 8. 1. 3: 'for the hymn of praise (*arka*) is the food for the Gods'.

[2] Probably the author of our brāhmaṇa combines the word with *sva* ('own') and *śiras* ('head'). Or are the breaths well-mixed, because they are inseparable from each other?

10. There is the surūpa(-sāman),[1] ('the chant of beautiful form').

[1] Grām. XII. 2. 15, composed on SV. I. 468, chanted on SV. II. 585-587. There are on this verse (see SV. ed. Calcutta, Vol. II, page 8) rwo sāmans of this name, both *aiḍa*. A comparison of the ūhagāna proves that the first of

the two is intended, and this is confirmed by the Jaim. br. (III. 223), where it is designated as *punarnitunna: tat punarnitunnam akurvan, tat punar abhyāghnan.* In this last word we have a kind of illustration of *abhyāghātya,* above, XIV. 9. 30.

11. The surūpa (or 'a thing of beauty') is the cattle; (so it serves) for retaining cattle.

12. There is the bhāsa(-sāman),[1] ('the chant of Light'); he who has applied (it), in chanting, shines.

[1] Grām. XIII. 1. 5, composed on SV. I. 470, chanted on SV. II. 585-587. There are two sāmans of this name on the same verse (see SV. ed. Calcutta, Vol. II, page 14 and 16), but the last is intended; this is proved by the Jaim. br. where not the bhāsa- but the mādila-sāman is prescribed. Now, this mādila is in its melodious figuration precisely equal to the s e c o n d bhāsa.

13. It has at each verse-quarter a nidhana[1], (and is) rathantara-like; for this day is a rathantara-day[2].

[1] From the Prayogas consulted by me it appears that of each pada of the ṛc the last two syllables are chanted as nidhana.

[2] The *padanidhana* is characteristic of the (first) rathantara-day, see X. 10. 1.—The text of our Brāhmaṇa should be read: *padanidhanaṃ rāthantaraṃ rāthantaraṁ hy etad ahaḥ.*

14. The dæmoniac Svarbhānu struck the sun with darkness[1], so that it did not shine; by means of the bhāsa ('the Light'), Atri repelled the darkness, so that it (again) shone. Because it (the sun) got this as its light[2], therefore, it (the sāman) is called 'the Light'.

[1] Identical with IV. 6. 13, IV. 5. 2, IV. 6 8.

[2] Uncertain: *yad vai tadbhā abhavat* or *yaddhaitadbhā abhavat.*

15. These Chandoma(-day)s, forsooth, are, as it were, darkness[1]; by means of this sāman he makes the light shine on them.

[1] 'By the manifoldness of their practice,' according to Sāyaṇa.

16. There is the kākṣīvata (-sāman)[1] ('the chant of Kakṣīvat').

[1] Grām. IV. 1. 22, composed on SV. I. 139, chanted on SV. II. 585-587, *svāram*, see SV. ed. Calcutta, Vol I, page 329.

17. Kakṣīvat, the son of Uśij, by means of this (sāman) came into the possession of progeny, of plurality. He who in lauding has applied the kākṣīvata (-sāman) is progenerated and multiplied.

18. **There is the āsita(-sāman)[1] ('the chant of Asita').**

[1] Grām. III. 1. 28, composed on SV. I. 107, chanted on SV. II. 585–587; is *aiḍam*, see SV. ed. Calcutta, Vol. I, page 275.

19. **Asita, the son of Devala, by means of this (sāman), had a glimpse of these three worlds[1]. The āsita(-sāman) is applied for the fulfilment of three wishes.**

[1] Cp. Kāṭh. XXII. 11: 67. 9: 'As to the verses addressed to Yama, by means of these the worlds, as well those that are on this (on the nearer) side as those that are on the other side, became visible to Asita, the son of Devala. To him the worlds that are on this side and those that are on the other side become wholly visible' (*sam asmai bhānti*). Of the interesting parallel of the Jaim. br. (III. 268, 269, see 'Auswahl' No. 209), although it is only partly intelligible, may follow here an attempt at translation: 'The Seers said: 'Come, let us try to obtain that world of heaven which is situated above the Falcon, where (are) those Atharvans'. (These Seers were) Preṇin, the son of Somāhita, Madhucchandas, the son of Viśvāmitra, Asita the son of Devala, and as many others as wished to see its vicinity. Of these (Atharvans), who were a long time engaged in sacrifice, they (the Seers) did not hear during many years. But of those (Seers) they (the Atharvans) heard: 'He (the Āgnīdhra) holds the *śrauṣaṭ*, he (the Hotṛ) holds the *vaṣaṭ*-call'. Now, one of the Atharvans, Udvanta by name, descended to (the Seers) with a cup (of Soma) in his hand. He said to them: 'With what wish do ye perform your sacrificial session?' They answered: 'We wish to obtain that world of heaven, which is situated above the Falcon, where are those Atharvans'. He said: 'Do ye go behind the village?' 'Yes, we do'. For what end?' 'For the path'. 'Just so', he said, 't h a t is not efficacious for you to reach the world of heaven', and, thereupon, he looked down on his cup. Now he said: 'Do ye eat meat?' 'Yes, we do'. 'For what end?' 'For retaining sight and breath'. 'Just so', he said, 'neither is that efficacious for you to reach the world of heaven', and he again looked down on his cup. He said: 'Do ye visit your wives?' 'Yes, we do'. 'For what end?' 'For obtaining progeny's continuation and continuity'. 'Just so', he said, 'neither is that efficacious for you to reach the world of heaven'; and he again looked down on his cup. He said: 'Do ye speak untruth'? 'Yes, we do'. 'For what end?' 'Wishing for women, wishing for a joke, wishing for a friend'. 'Just so', he said, 'arise you and wish your wishes (read perhaps *kāmān icchadhvam*). For you there is no hope that ye should gain yonder world'. Now, Preṇin, the son of Somāhita, was a wicked man; he said: 'Of seven he-goats do I choose the rut; whichever woman I may call unto me, may she desire me'. And Madhucchandas, the son of Viśvāmitra, said: 'I will choose the summit of the Brāhmins'. But Asita, the son of Devala, said: 'Let me look on this cup (of soma)'. He (Udvanta) said: 'He alone chooses what is right (?)'. Having looked down on this (soma-cup), he (Asita) saw this sāman and lauded with it: *rāye agne mahe tvā dānāya samidhīmahi | iḍiṣvā hi mahe vṛṣam*

dyāvā hotrāya pṛthivī (Jaim. Saṃh. I. 1. 10. 3=SV. Kauth. I. 93). Heaven and earth are (equal to) all these worlds. Thereupon, he moved along all these worlds: during the first part of the day he stayed at the meeting of the Gods, at midday, of the meeting of men: of Drūpada Vāddhraviṣṇa, at the afternoon at the meeting of the Fathers'.

20. There is the aiṣira(-sāman)[1]. The aiṣira(sāman)s are a (means of) progeneration. He who in lauding has applied the aiṣira (-sāman) is progenerated and multiplied.

[1] Grām. XI. 1. 10, composed on SV. I. 406, chanted on SV. II. 361-362. There are many aiṣira-sāmans, but the Jaim. br. points also to *vāyor aiṣiram*, the second of the three is intended, which is *svāram*, see SV. ed. Calcutta, Vol. I, page 826.

21. There is the traita(sāman)[1]: for obtaining firm support.

[1] Grām. X. 2. 1, composed on SV. I. 384, chanted on SV. II. 363-365; the first of the four (SV. ed. Calcutta, Vol. I, page 790) is intended, being *nidhanavat*, cp. § 22.

22. It has at each verse-quarter a nidhana (and) is rathantara-like, for this day is a rathantara-day[1].

[1] This § is identical with XIV. 11. 13.

23. It (this sāman) is also assistance bringing[1]; he (thereby) procures himself assistance.—These Chandoma(-day)s, forsooth, procure assistance; by means of them he procures himself assistance.

[1] The reason is found in the Jaim. br. I. 184, see Journ. of the American Oriental Society, Vol. XVIII, page 19.

24. There is the gaurīvita(-sāman)[1]. The brāhmaṇa of the gaurīvita is the same[2].

[1] Grām. V. 1. 22, composed on SV. I. 168, chanted on SV. II. 588-590; it is *svāram*, see SV. ed. Calcutta, Vol. I, page 383.

[2] See XI. 5. 14.

25. There is the kautsa(-sāman)[1] (the chant of Kutsa).

[1] Grām. V. 1. 4, composed on SV. I. 162, chanted on SV. II. 588-590. There are several kautsa-sāmans, but the *aiḍam* one is required, see SV. ed. Calcutta Vol. I, page 370. The Jaiminīyas designate it as pāñcavāja.

26. By means of this (sāman), Kutsa saw 'the separate drinking' of the liquid[1]; he used to ride out to the (to his?) dwelling[2] with a leathern bag with brandy. The kautsa(-sāman) is applied for retaining both kinds of food.

[1] *andhaso vipānam*, cp. Śat. br. XII. 7. 3. 4, where we find *andhasor vipānam*; Eggeling translates: 'the (means of) drinking separately the two liquids'. Although some arguments seem to vouch for the reading *andhaso vipānam* as our text has it (cp. *vipānaṃ śukram andhasaḥ*, Vedic Concordance, *in voce*), the Jaim. recension points distinctly to the dual (Jaim. br. III. 228, cp. 'Auswahl' No. 202): 'Pañcavājas, the son of Kutsa, was able to drink the two liquors separately (*andhasī vyapipīta*); the divine and the human he, by means of this sāman, drank separately. Pañcavājas, the son of Kutsa, desired: 'May I drink separately the two liquors: the divine and the human'. He saw this sāman and, by means of it, he drank separately the two liquors, the divine and the human. Since that time he, having put on (his cart) a leathern bag, used to ride out for the soma'. The purport of this last sentence is here equally far from clear.

[2] *sa ha vai surādṛtinopavasathaṃ dhāvayati.* Are we to divide: *dṛtinā upa vasathaṃ dhāvayati*, and has *vasathaṃ* the same sense as *āvasathaṃ*? Or must we accept, with Sāyaṇa, the word *upavasathaṃ*? But, what, in this case, is the meaning?

27. There is the śuddhāśuddhīya(-sāman)[1].

[1] Grām. IX. 2. 7, composed on SV. I. 350, chanted on SV. II. 588-590, the first of the two, being *nidhanavat*, see SV. ed. Calcutta, Vol. I, page 715.

28. Indra gave the Yatis over to the hyenas; an inauspicious voice reproached him and he thought himself impure (*aśuddha*). He (thereupon) saw this śuddhāśuddhīya(-sāman) and was purified by it. He who in lauding has applied the śuddhāśuddhīya(-sāman), is purified.

29. There is the krauñca(-sāman)[1]; the brāhmaṇa of the krauñca is the same[2].

[1] Grām XVI. 1. 13 composed on SV. I. 546, chanted on SV. II. 588-590. It is, see SV. ed. Calcutta, Vol. II. page 154, the first of the three, being *svāram* and, according to Jaim. br. *madhyesvāram*.

[2] See XI. 10. 19.

30. There is the rayiṣṭha(-sāman)[1].

[1] Grām. XIV. 2. 2, composed on SV. I. 512, chanted on SV. II. 588-590; seems to be *aiḍam* (ending on *ūpā*), see SV. ed. Calcutta, Vol. II, page 78. According to the Jaim. br. it is *madhyenidhanam*.

31. The rayiṣṭha(-sāman) is cattle; (so it is applied) for obtaining cattle[1].

[1] According to Jaim. br. III. 229, it is a *paśavyaṃ sāma*, because by it Prajāpati retained the runaway cattle.

32. There is the audala(-sāman)[1] ('the chant of Udala').

[1] Grām. IV. 2. 36, composed on SV. I. 160, chanted on SV. II. 588-590; it is *svāram*, see SV. ed. Calcutta, Vol. I, page 367.

33. Udala, the son of Viśvāmitra, by means of this (sāman), came into the possession of progeny, of plurality. He who in lauding has applied the audala(-sāman), is progenerated and multiplied.

34 There is the dharman(-sāman)[1], for sustaining the right (*dharma*).

[1] Grām. XI. 2. 20, composed on SV. I. 429, chanted on SV. II. 591-593, grām. l.c. 19 is likewise dharman, and both are *nidhanavat*, see SV. ed. Calcutta, Vol. I, page 873.

35. The Theologians argue: 'The stomas and metres at the six-day-period having been used up, what is the metre of the Chandoma(-day)s? One should answer: 'They have m a n as their metre'. Man is fivefold, man is two-footed: in order that the Chandoma(-day)s may be unexhausted[1].

[1] This brāhmaṇa, identical with XIV. 5. 26 (and cp. XV. 5. 32), should, to all appearances, have been given after XIV. 11. 5, to which it belongs.

36. There is the viśoviśīya(-sāman)[1].

[1] Grām. II. 2 27, composed on SV. I. 87, chanted on SV. II. 254-256. It is (cp. § 39) *aiḍam*, see SV. ed. Calcutta, Vol. I, page 243.

37. Agni desired: 'Of house on house (*viśo viśaḥ*) may I be the guest, of house on house may I obtain the hospitality'. He performed austerities and saw this viśoviśīya(-sāman). By means of it he became of house on house the guest, he obtained of house on house the hospitality. He who in lauding has applied the viśoviśīya (-sāman), becomes the guest of house on house, obtains the hospitality of house on house.

38 They chant (it) on gāyatrī(-verse)s, for the sake of getting a firm support, for (the obtainment of) priestly lustre. With which breath they start in that they finish (the laud)[1].

[1] This § is identical with XIII. 9. 28, XIV. 5. 30.

39. The pavamāna(-laud)s (of this day) finish on *iḍā*; *iḍā* is cattle and the Chandoma(-day)s are cattle. He thereby brings cattle into his cattle[1].—The stoma (has been given)[2].

1 Identical with XIV. 5. 31.

2 See XIV. 7. 10.

XIV. 12.

(The uktha-lauds of the eighth day.)

1. (There are the verses beginning:) 'The guest most beloved to you'[1]; thereby the characteristic feature of hospitality is brought about.

1 SV. I. 5=ṚS. VIII. 84. 1-3 (var. rr.)=SV. II. 594-596.

2. (The verses beginning:) 'Come unto us, o beloved Indra'[1] (are applied) for obtaining valour and strength.

1 SV. I. 393=ṚS. VIII. 98. 4-6=SV. II. 597-599.

3. (The verse:) 'The destroyer of the strongholds, the young, clever Indra of immeasurable strength was born as the supporter of every deed, armed with his thunderbolt, praised by many.'[1] (is applied) for supporting.

1 SV. I. 359=ṚS. I. 11. 4, 5, 8=SV. II. 600-602.

4. There is the auśana(-sāman)[1] (the chant of Uśanas).

1 Grām. I. 1. 9, composed on SV. I. 5, chanted on SV. II. 594-596; it is *svāram*, see SV. ed. Calcutta, Vol. I, page 101.

5. Uśanas, the Kāvya, wished: 'May I obtain as much dominion as the other Kāvyas possess. He practised austerities and saw this auśana(-sāman). By means of it he obtained as much dominion as the other Kāvyas possessed. This at that time he had wished. A wish granting sāman is the auśana. He obtains (the fulfilment of) his wish.

6. There is the sāṃvarta(-sāman)[1].

1 Grām. X. 2. 26, composed on SV. I. 393, chanted on SV. II. 597-599; it is *nidhanavat*, see SV. ed. Calcutta, Vol. I, page 807. According to the Jaim. br. it is *padanidhanam*.

7. The Ogres sought to destroy the sacrifice of the Gods. Indra, by means of this (sāman), repeatedly rolling together (dust and sand?) buried them. Because he buried them, repeatedly rolling together (*saṃvartam*), hence it is called the sāṃvarta(-sāman). This[1] was an evil, forsooth, that pursued them (the Gods); by

means of the sāṃvarta they repelled it. He who in lauding has applied the sāṃvarta, repels the evil.

[1] *pāpmā vāva sa tān asacata*, the same construction XV. 5. 20: *sa* refers to the fact that the Ogres pursued them.

8. There is the māruta(-sāman)[1] ('the chant of the Maruts').

[1] Grām. IX. 2. 21, composed on SV. I. 359, chanted on SV. II. 600-602. It is *aiḍam*, see SV. ed. Calcutta, Vol. I, page 733.

9. The rays are the months, the rays are the Maruts[1]; the Maruts are the most numerous of the Gods[2]. They undertake the sacrificial session, hoping to be most numerous[3]. They (thereby) become even most numerous. Provided with seasons are the preceding (six) days[4], devoid of seasons are the Chandoma(-day)s. In that there is this sāman[5], thereby these days (the Chandomas) become provided with seasons.

[1] Therefore, the Maruts are the months, each of which contain two ṛtus. (This is said to connect the Maruts and the māruta-sāman with the seasons, see the next following words.) For the rest, we may compare Śat. br. IX. 3. 1. 25: *ye te mārutā raśmayas te* (although here the *mārutāḥ* are the *puroḍāśas*).

[2] As consisting of seven groups.

[3] Hoping to be multiplied, to get abundant offspring.

[4] The trivṛt-stoma, etc., are connected successively with spring, summer, raining season, see VI. 1. 6. sqq.

[5] Which, as belonging to the Maruts, these being the rays and the rays being the seasons, contains the seasons!

10. It is the forty-four-versed stoma, in strength and valour he thereby is firmly established: the triṣṭubh is strength and valour[1].

[1] This § is identical with XIV. 7. 10.

FIFTEENTH CHAPTER.

(Ninth (third Chandoma-) day.)

XV. 1.

(Out-of-doors-laud of the ninth day.)

1. (The verse beginning:) 'The ocean has roared on the farthest[1] border'[2] is the opening tristich of the ninth day.

[1] This is the second case, where the Brāhmana deviates from its own Saṃhitā, cp. note 1 on XI. 4. 4. It is remarkable that the Jaim. br. (III. 239), reading equally *parame* instead of *prathame*, also deviates from the Saṃhitā. For a possible explanation, see note 1 on § 2.

[2] SV. I. 529=ṚS. IX. 97. **40, 42, 41** (var. r)=SV. II. 603-605.

2 This day, forsooth, is 'the farthest border'[1]; the ninth day, forsooth, is, as compared with[2] the other days, the farthest border, for it is the highest and the largest[3].

[1] It is not impossible that the word of the Saṃhitā has been intentionally changed by the author of our Brāhmaṇa, because *prathame* would not well fit for the ninth day. Similarly, the Jaim. br. (III. 239): *akrūn samudraḥ parame vidharmann iti... paramaḥ samudraḥ paramam navamam ahah.*

[2] Is this the meaning of the instrumental? Cp. Speyer, Sanskrit Syntax, § 107.

[3] As it has the largest stoma (48).

3. One (of these verses, beginning:) 'Gladden thou Vāyu, for our sacrifice, for our wealth',[1] is addressed to Varuṇa[2]. That part of the sacrifice which is badly performed is seized by Varuṇa, this he thereby disperses by his sacrifice.

[1] SV. II. 604.

[2] It is addressed to Soma pavamāna, but Varuṇa (beside Mitra) is mentioned in it.

4. The stotriya is a tristich, for retaining the breaths[1].

[1] See XIV. 1. 7.

5. There is a complex of ten verses[1]; ten-syllabic is the virāj; food is virāj-like: to obtain food[2].

[1] SV II. 606-615=ṚS. IX. 3 (but in this order: 1, 6, 4, 5, 3, 2, 7, 8, 9, 10). The Jaiminīyas (III. 240): *esa devo amartya iti sūktam anurūpo bhavati.* The Jaiminīyas agree with ṚS.

[2] Cp. XIII. 7. 8.

6*a*. They (these verses) are of the same beginning words, in order that valour, strength (and) pith may not flow away.

6*b*. Where the Gods saw valour, strength (and) pith, they pushed it down (immediately) afterwards[1].

[1] Cp. XIII. 7. 9, 10.

7. There is a complex of eight verses[1].

[1] SV. II. 616-623=ṚS. IX. 15 (but in this order: 1, 2, 7, 3, 5, 4, 6, 8) The Jaiminīyas agree more closely with ṚS. (only one transposition)

8. Eight-hoofed is cattle; hoof by hoof he thereby obtains cattle. Eight-syllabic is the gāyatrī(-verse), strength and priestly lustre is the gāyatrī: strength and priestly lustre he (thereby) obtains.

9. There are complexes of six verses: for propping the (six) seasons.

10. There are four complexes of six verses[1]; the year consists of twenty-four half-months: in the year even he is thus firmly established.

[1] 1. SV. II. 624-629=ṚS. IX. 38 (1, 2, 4, 5, 6, 3).

2. SV. II. 630-635=ṚS. IX. 28 (1-5a; 5. b, c=IX. 27. 5. b, c; 6. a=IX. 27. 5. a, 6. b, c=IX. 26. 4. b, c).

3. SV. II. 636-641=ṚS. IX. 27 (1-4; 6; IX. 28. 6).

4. SV. II. 642-647=ṚS. IX. 37.

11. The complex of six verses, beginning with the word 'he', is the last: for obtaining both (kinds of profit) the remote as well as the near[1].

[1] *sa* (at the beginning of the verses 642-647) expresses something which is remote (*parokṣa*), *eṣa* (occurring at the beginning of the verses 636-641) expresses something which is near (*pratyakṣa*) to the speaker, cp. Jaim. br. III. 241: *yadā vai pratyakṣaṃ bhavaty athaiṣa ity ācakṣate, yadā parokṣam atha sa iti*; and Speyer, Sanskrit Syntax § 271 and the kārikā quoted there.

12. A tristich comes at the end[1]: with which breath they start, in that they finish (the laud).

[1] In the uttarārcika another *ṣaḍṛca* follows after II. 647 (vs. 648-653), of which vs. 648 and 649 answer to ṚS. IX. 67. 30, 31; vs 650-652 to Ṛgveda-khila III. 10. 1-3 (ed. Scheftelowitz, page 95) and vs. 653 to ib. 6. a, b. It is remarkable that these verses are ignored by the commentator on the Ārṣeya-kalpa, who prescribes, as last trca, the same that has been applied on the seventh day (*viz.*, SV. II. 487-489), and cp. the Sūtrakāra (Lāṭy. III. 6. 26-27, Drāhy. IX. 3. 7): 'of the ninth day, the finishing part (the 'Schlussstück') is that of the jyotiṣṭoma, according to some, that of the seventh day' (here *jyotiṣṭoma* is an adjective, just as in the Ārṣeyakalpa, cp. Introd. to this text, page XX). The first view is found represented by the Jaiminīyas, who give (Jaim. Saṃh. III. 53. 6-8) vs. II. 7-9, the ordinary *paryāsa* of the jyotiṣṭoma; the second view is accepted by the commentator of the Ārṣeya-kalpa and by the Anupadasūtra (IV. 4): *navamasyā te dakṣam iti paryāsah saprakṛtitvāt prākṛto vāpratyāmānād, ubhayos tu codanā bhāllavinām* (as do the

Sūtrakāras).—From these facts we may conclude that, at least, the verses SV. II. 648-653 were absent from the uttarārcika at the time of the composition of the Sūtra and perhaps even later, as Dhanvin also seems to ignore them: *kaḥ punar asau tṛca iti na jñāyate tatrādhyayanābhāvāt.*

13 The stoma is the forty-eight-versed one, for getting a firm support[1] and for progeneration.

[1] Cp. III. 12. 3.—The forty-eight-versed stoma is again to be thought as composed from the 21-fold and the 33-fold one, cp. Kauṣ. br. XXVI. 7.

XV. 2.

(The ājya-lauds of the ninth day.)

1. (The verses beginning:) 'We have approached with deep obeisance the ever young one'[1], are the ājya(-laud) addressed to Agni.

[1] SV. II. 654–656=ṚS. VII. 12. 1–3.

2. They approach, as it were, who approach (undertake the rite of) the ninth day.

3. 'Who brightly shines, kindled in his own dwelling'[1], for he shines brightly, as it were, who has chanted the (sāmans of the) nine days[2]; 'well pleased by sacrifices (of clarified butter)'[1], for well pleased by sacrifices is he who is pleased by the (sacrifice of the) nine days; 'him who is turned toward all sides'[1], for turned to all sides is he[3].

[1] Parts of verse 654.

[2] Apparently, the ninth day, though at the moment only begun, is taken into account.

[3] Probably: 'ready for all emergencies'. It is not probable, as Sāyaṇa means, that *eṣa* refers to Agni.

4. One (of these verses, beginning:) 'Thee, o Agni, Varuṇa and Mitra'[1], is addressed to Varuṇa. That part of the sacrifice, which is badly performed, is seized by Varuṇa; this he thereby disperses by his sacrifice[2].

[1] SV. II. 656. a.

[2] Cp. XV. 1. 3.

5. (The tristich beginning:) 'Mitra, of holy might, I call for'[1], is the rathantara-like (ājya-laud) addressed to Mitra and Varuṇa[2].

[1] SV. II. 197–199.

[2] This § is identical with XII. 2. 3.

6. The Chandoma(-day)s, forsooth, are a ford difficult to cross, as it were. Just as in daily life they enter into a stream which is difficult to cross, having linked themselves mutually together, so he links, thereby, the two characteristic features mutually together, in order that the Chandomas may not oscillate[1].

[1] Identical with XIV. 8. 4.

7*a*. (The verses beginning:) 'Great is Indra, who by his might'[1], (serve for) the (ājya-laud) addressed to Indra.

[1] SV II. 657-659=RS. VIII. 6. 1, 3, 2.

7*b*. By means of the eighth day, the Gods had incited Indra, by means of the ninth, they had repelled evil. The day they, thereby, gladden[1].

[1] Nearly identical with XIV. 8. 6.

8. (The tristich beginning:) 'These two I call for, who'[1], is the rathantara-like (ājya-laud) addressed to Indra and Agni[2].

[1] SV. II. 203–205.

[2] Identical with XII. 2. 8.

9. The Chandoma(-day)s, forsooth, are a ford difficult to cross as it were. Just as in daily life they enter into a stream which is difficult to cross, having linked themselves mutually together, so he links thereby the two characteristic features mutually together, in order that the Chandomas may not oscillate[1].—The stoma (has been given)[2].

[1] See § 6.

[2] See XV. 1. 13.

XV. 3.

(The midday-pavamāna-laud of the ninth day.)

1. (The verses beginning:) 'Of the mightily slaying Pavamāna, (*i.e.* soma), the yellow one (*hari*), the bright (drops) have been pro-

duced '[1], are gāyatrīs containing the word 'yellow': in order that the Chandoma(-day)s may not be exhausted[2].

[1] SV. II. 660-662=ṚS. IX. 66. 25-27 (var. r.).

[2] Cp. note 2 on XIV. 1. 8.

2. (The words:) 'Of the mightily slaying Pavamāna' are characteristic of the bṛhat[1]; (the words:) 'of the yellow one, the bright (drops) have been produced' are characteristic of the jagatī[2]. He (thus) practises the characteristics of both together: of the sāman and the metre[3].

[1] Because of the words 'mightily slaying' which are the characteristic of the Baron, he being connected with the brhat, cp. probably X. 6. 2.

[2] This connection is not clear to me.

[3] Of the sāman, because the ninth day is a bṛhat-day.

3. (The verses beginning:) 'Go ye round, pour ye out the pressed (soma)'[1], contain the word 'round' (*pari*); the ninth day is the end[2]. These verses (are applied) for reaching this (day).

[1] SV. I. 512=ṚS. IX. 107. 1-3=SV. II. 663-665.

[2] Strictly speaking, of the third three-day-period only.

4. (The verses beginning:) 'The soma has been pressed, the reddish, the bull, the yellow'[1], being jagatīs, are, by their characteristic, triṣṭubhs[2]; therefore, they are applied at the place proper to the triṣṭubhs[3].

[1] SV. I 562=ṚS. IX 82. 1, 3, 2 (var. r.)=SV. II. 666-668.

[2] By the word 'bull', which is connected with the triṣṭubh, X. 6. 2.

[3] At the end of the midday-pavamāna-laud.

5. There is the gāyatra (-sāman). The brāhmaṇa of the gāyatra is the same[1].

[1] See VII. 1. 1 sqq.

6. There is the adārasṛt of Bharadvāja[1].

[1] Grām. IV. 1. 7, composed on SV. I. 132, chanted on SV. II. 660-662. There are more sāmans of this name, but see Jaim. br. III. 244: *atha gātuvinjnidhanam..tad upariṣṭobhavad bhavati bahirnidhanam..tad v evācakṣate bharadvāasyādārasṛd iti.* The sāman (see SV. ed. Calcutta, vol. I, page 318) ends on a stobha: *asmabhyaṃ gātuvittamam.*

7. Divodāsa, who had Bharadvāja as his house-chaplain, (once upon a time) was hemmed in by various individuals (enemies). He

approached (his chaplain), saying: 'Seer, find me a way out of this ('procure me a refuge')'. For him, by means of this sāman, he found a way out. A refuge procuring one is this sāman. (Because they thought): 'By means of this (sāman), we have not fallen into a pit' (*dāre nāsṛnma*)[1], thence it has its name *adārasṛt*. He who in lauding has practised the adārasṛt, finds a way out of his difficulties and does not run into a pit[2].

1 Instead of the form *asṛnma*, we expect an aorist derived from the root *sṛ* (*asāriṣma*), but the faulty form is obviously due to the desire to connect the word with *-sṛt*, as if this were a verbal root!

2 A highly interesting version of this mythic-historical tale is given in Jaim. br. III. 244 sqq. (cp. Das Jaim. br. in Auswahl, No. 205). It runs as follows: 'Kṣatra, the son of Pratardana, at the battle of the ten kings, was hemmed in at Mānuṣa by the ten kings. His house-chaplain was Bharadvāja. He resorted to him, saying: 'Seer, we resort to thee, find us in this circumstances (a way out)'. Bharadvāja wished: 'May we win the battle'. He saw this sāman and lauded with it. Having lauded, he said: 'Indra will come to our call, we will win the battle'. Now, Kṣatra, the son of Pratardana, had as consort. the handsome Upamā, the daughter of Savedas. Of her they killed a brother. She mourned for him (?). As she was (on a certain day) running about, Indra set his mind on her. Having put on an antelope-hide, he went after her. He had, on a shoulder-yoke, a basket with a cake hanging at one side, and at the other side an *āmikṣā* mixed with butter, and he began to dance in her vicinity. He drew her along with the butter (?). Every time she drove him away, he always danced before her. At evening they went apart. Her husband asked her: 'Hast thou observed here something (particular) during the day?' She answered: 'Nothing beside this: an old man has danced in my vicinity; he had, on a shoulder-yoke, a basket with a cake hanging at one side, and at the other side an *āmikṣā* mixed with butter'. He said: 'Indra, forsooth, has come to our call. We will win this battle. That was Indra! Do not drive him away by hurting him. Make him your friend and say to him: 'Let us win the battle' On the following morning, the two met again, and the same man, with just such a shoulder-yoke, began to dance at some distance. Each time she sought to reach him, the other (danced) farther off. She thought: 'Come, I will address him'. (Then follows a metrical dialogue of the two; the verses, however, are incomprehensible.) Running after him, she said: 'Let us win the battle'. He, shaking his antelope-hide, said: 'Just as these hairs flow in all directions (?), so, ye enemies of Kṣatra, flow asunder from Mānuṣa'. With these words, he scattered the hairs of the black antelope (of the hide he wore). These arose as so many war-chariots and, by means of these, he (Kṣatra) won the battle. Thereupon, said Bharadvāja: 'We have not fallen into the pit, (*na vai dāre 'sṛnma*), and hence the name (of the sāman) *adārasṛt*.'

8. There is the surūpa (-sāman)[1]. The brāhmaṇa of the surūpa is the same[2].

[1] Grām. XIV. 2. 16, composed on SV. I. 468, chanted on SV. II. 660-662. It is *aiḍam*, see SV. ed. Calcutta, vol. II, page 8.

[2] See XIV. 11. 11.

9. There is the (sāman) with (the word) *hariśrī* as nidhana[1].

[1] Grām. V. 2. 21, composed on SV. I. 195, chanted on SV. II. 660-662. Its nidhana (see SV. ed. Calcutta, vol. I, page 423) is *harī 3 śrī 2345*.

10. Cattle (cows) are beautifully yellow (*hariśrī*)[1]; (so it is applied) for obtaining cattle. He who has applied (it) in lauding, comes to beauty and energy[2].

[1] ? cp. *gotraṃ hariśriyam*, ṚS. VIII. 50. 10.

[2] As if the word *hariśrī* contained *haras* instead of *hari*.

11. There is the saindhukṣita (-sāman)[1]; the brāhmaṇa of the saindhukṣita is the same[2].

[1] Grām. I. 2. 3, composed on SV. I. 21, chanted on SV. II. 660-662; a comparison with the ūhagāna proves that the third of the three, which is *aiḍam*, is intended, Jaim. br. III, 248: *tad aiḷaṃ bhavati*; cp. SV. ed. Calcutta, vol. I, page 127.

[2] See XII. 12. 6.

12. There is the sāman of Babhru, the nidhana of which consists of a word derived from (the word) 'to go' (*gam*, *gatanidhana*)[1], for attaining ('for going', *gati*)[2].

[1] There are two bābhravasāmans, Grām. XII. 2, 5 and 6; the second is intended, with the nidhana *gvā 234 bhiḥ*, see SV. ed. Calcutta, vol. II. page 3. The Jaiminīyas designate it as *gvābhirnidhanaṃ*. It is composed on SV. I. 467 and here chanted on SV. II. 660-662.

[2] By a true *tour de force*, the nidhana is derived from the verbal root *gam*, with which it cannot be connected. What *gvābhiḥ* means and what its non-sāman form is, is not to be defined. In the Jaim. br. the *gvābhirnidhanaṃ sāma* is chanted for the obtainment of cattle, *gvābhiḥ* being probably taken as the sāman-form of *gobhiḥ*.

13. Babhru, the son of the Kumbhya, by means of this sāman, straightway beheld the world of heaven; (so it serves) for beholding the world of heaven. He who in lauding has applied (it), does not fall from the world of heaven.

14. There is the (sāman called) 'the flowing together of the *iḍās* (*iḍānām saṃkṣārah*)[1].

1 Grām. III. 2. 13, composed on SV. I. 119, chanted on SV. II. 660–662. It is (see SV. ed. Calcutta, vol. I, page 298) *aiḍam*; its name reposes, apparently, on the repeated word *iḍā* at the end: *iḍā*[1] *23 bhā*[2] *3* | *e*[4]*hī*[5]*ḍā* | *ho*[5] *5 i* | *ḍā*[4]. In the Jaim. br. III. 249, it is said that the Angirases obtained cows from all the regions and, thereupon, exclaimed: 'these *iḷās* have flown for us together': *saṃ vai na imā iḷā akṣāriṣuh*.

15. The *iḍā* is cattle, the Chandoma(-day)s are cattle: he thereby puts cattle into cattle[1].

1 He makes his cows to get abundant calves.

16. There is the ṛṣabha-pāvamāna (-sāman)[1], ('the Soma-bull').

1 Grām. XII. 2. 3, composed on SV. I. 467, chanted on SV. II. 660–662; it is *svāram*, see SV. ed. Calcutta, vol. II, page 3.

17. The Chandoma(-day)s are the cattle; he thereby produces a copulation in his cattle, in order that they may procreate, for not without a bull do cattle (cows) procreate[1].

1 Cp. XIII. 5. 18, XIII. 10. 11.

18. There is the pṛṣṭha(-sāman)[1] ('The back-bone-chant').

1 Gram. VI. 2. 12, composed on SV. I. 239. chanted on SV. II. 663–665; it is (see SV. ed. Calcutta, vol. I, page 495) *aiḍam* (*ūrdhveḷam*, the Jaim. br.).

19. The ninth day, forsooth, is the back-bone of the days: on the back-bone (*i.e*, the ninth day) they chant the back-bone (-sāman): for getting a firm support.

20. There is the kaulmalabarhiṣa(-sāman)[1] ('the chant of Kulmalabarhis').

1 Grām. VI. 2. 15, composed on SV. I. 240, chanted on SV. II. 663–665. There are many more sāmans of this name, but the two (grām. VI. 2. 15 and 16) follow in the gāna immediately after the pṛṣṭha; of these two the first is intended, as a comparison with the ūhagāna proves, although both (VI. 2. 15 and 16) are *svāram* (see SV. ed. Calcutta, vol. I. page 498).

21. Kulmalabarhis, by means of this (sāman), came into the possession of progeniture[1], of plurality. He who is lauding has applied the kaulmalabarhiṣa(-sāman), is progenerated and multiplied.

1 Read *prajātiṃ* instead of *prajāpatiṃ*, cp. XIV. 11. 17.

22. There is the arkapuṣpa(-sāman)[1]. ('The food-flavour chant').

[1] Grām. XVI. 2. 34, composed on SV. I. 565, chanted on SV. II. 663-665, the first of the two sāmans is intended; both are *nidhanavat*, see SV. ed. Calcutta, Vol. II, page 199. Originally, they probably were optional.

23. Food is called '*arka*' by the Gods and its flavour 'flower'. He who in lauding has applied the arkapuṣpa(-sāman), obtains food with flavour.

24. There is the dairghaśravasa(-sāman)[1]. ('The chant of Dīrghaśravas').

[1] Grām. II. 1. 6, composed on SV. I. 44, chanted on SV. II. 663-665. The first of the two, being *svāra* (see SV. ed. Calcutta, Vol. I, page 166), is intended, as appears from the ūhagāna.

25. The knightly seer[1], Dīrghaśravas, being expelled (from his realm by his enemies) wandered about[2] for a long time and became hungry. He saw this dairghaśravasa(-sāman) and, by means of it, obtained food from all the (four) quarters[3]. He who in lauding has practised the dairghaśravasa(-sāman), obtains food from all the quarters.

[1] One of the Leyden MSS. reads *rājanyarṣir*, the other as in the printed text.

[2] On the construction, cp. Oertel, the disjunct use of cases, page 21.

[3] Cp. Jaim. br. III. 256 (Auswahl, page 308-309): 'Dīrghatamas, the son of (the mother) Mamatā, going out to battle, said to his younger brother, Dīrghaśravas: 'Mayest thou be the surveyor of these (cows or mares) of ours that are to be taken care of'. Thereupon, Dīrghaśravas desired: 'May I obtain food, may not these (animals) suffer from hunger'. He saw this sāman and lauded Agni with it, and Agni, being lauded, made all his food sweet as honey'. etc.

26. There is the vaiyaśva(-sāman)[1]; the brāhmaṇa of it is the same[2].

[1] Grām. VII. 2. 9, composed on SV. I. 269, chanted on SV II. 663-665. There are on this verse three vaiyaśvas, all *aiḍam*, see SV. ed. Calcutta, Vol. I, page 555. The ūhagāna designates it as *dvyakṣaravaiyaśva*. It is the śulka of the Jaiminīyas.

[2] See XIV. 10. 9.

27. There is the ābhīśava(-sāman)[1]; its brāhmaṇa is the same[2].

[1] Grām. XIV. 2. 5, composed on SV. I. 512, chanted on SV. II. 663-665. It is (see SV. ed. Calcutta, Vol. II. page 79) *svāram*.

[2] See XII. 9. 15-16.

28*a*. There is the devasthāna(-sāman)[1]. ('The Gods-stand chant'), for obtaining firm support.

[1] Araṇyegeyagāna I. 1. 15, composed on SV. I. 239, chanted on SV. II. 663-665. It is *aiḍam*, see SV. ed. Calcutta, Vol. II, page 396.

28*b*. There is the saṃkṛti(-sāman)[1], for making (the last three-day period) in order.

[1] Ar. gāna III. 1. 17, composed on SV. I. 409, chanted on SV. II. 663-665. It is (see SV. ed. Calcutta, Vol. II, page 452) *nidhanavat*.

29. This day (when its rite for the first time was performed by the Gods) collapsed, but the Gods, standing on the 'Gods-stand' (the devasthāna), made it in order by means of the saṃkṛti and, hence, this sāman has its name. By means of the devasthāna, the Gods obtained a firm standing in the world of heaven; (it is applied) with (the desire) that they (the participants of the sacrificial session) may get a firm standing[1].

[1] Cp. with this passage XIV. 9. 27.

30. The deities (formerly) did not yield the sovereignty to Varuṇa. He saw this 'Gods-stand', and, thereupon, the deities yielded to him the supremacy. His (the Sacrificer's) equals yield him the superiority.

31. He who knows this, to his share falls the lustre of might, (and) he gets a firm standing.

32. Lustrous (*bharga*) becomes he, who in lauding has applied the bharga(-sāman)[1], glorious (*yaśaḥ*) he, (who in lauding has applied) the yaśas(-sāman)[2].

[1] Ar. gāna II. 2. 11, composed on SV. I. 258, chanted on SV. II. 663-665. Its nidhana (see SV. ed. Calcutta, Vol. II, page 441) is $\overset{1}{\textit{bhargā}}$ $\overset{1111}{\textit{2345}}$ *ḥ*.

[2] Ar. gāna II. 2. 12, composed on SV. I. 270; it begins: $\overset{2r}{\textit{hā}}$ *u* | $\overset{2r}{\textit{hā}}$ *u* | $\overset{2r}{\textit{hā}}$ *u* | $\overset{2\,r}{\textit{yaśo}}$ $\overset{r}{\textit{hā}}$ *u*. (ed. Calc. l.c.).

33. There is the vāsiṣṭha(-sāman)[1]; its brāhmaṇa is the same[2].

[1] Grām. VII. 1. 24, composed on SV. I. 259, chanted on SV. II. 663-665 The *aiḍam* is intended, see SV. ed. Calcutta, Vol. 1, page 536.

[2] See XI. 8. 14.

34. There is the arka of Dīrghatamas[1]; *arka* is food: for obtaining food.

[1] Ar. gāna I. 2. 4, composed on SV. I. 558, chanted on SV. II. 666-668 It is (cp. § 37) *nidhanavat*, ending: $\overset{3}{\text{ī}}\ \overset{1111}{2345}$, see SV. ed. Calcutta, Vol. II, page 404.

35. There is the sāmarāja(-sāman)[1]. He who in lauding has applied the sāmarāja, comes to sovereignty, to imperial sway.

[1] Grām. XVI. 2. 9, composed on SV. I. 555, chanted on SV. II. 666-668. This sāman likewise is *nidhanavat*, see SV. ed. Calcutta, Vol. II, page 176.

36. They also call it the saṃvat(-sāman), *i.e.*, the sāman containing the word *sam*. By means of the saṃvat(-sāman), forsooth, the Gods went forth to the world of heaven, by means of the sāman containing the word 'up' (*ud*), they went up[1].

[1] Cp. XIV. 3. 23-24: *pravat*, XIV. 9. 39-40: *udvat*, and here *saṃvat*. Neither the sāman nor the ṛc contains the word *sam*, but the sentence (§ 36) is added for the sake of completeness, because something similar was wanted about the third Chandoma-day! For the rest, the three prepositions *pra*, *ud*, *sam* remind us of the triad: *prāṇa*, *udāna*, *samāna*.

37. The pavamāna(-laud)s (of this day) end on a nidhana: for propping the day[1].—The stoma (has been given)[2].

[1] Cp. XIV. 9. 41.

[2] See XV. 1. 13.—Finally, a remark must be made about this pavamāna-stotra. The author of the Brāhmaṇa prescribes 21 sāmans for this stotra. If these are chanted on tristichs, the total number being 48, we would get too many stotriyas. If the eight sāmans on the gāyatrī (SV. II 660-662) are all chanted on tristichs, we get 24 stotriya-verses, and to complete the required number of 48, only another 24 can be placed, but the Brāhmaṇa gives 13 more sāmans; as it is impossible that these are chanted all on tristichs, the Sūtrakāras (Lāṭy. III. 6. 28-33, Drāhy. IX. 3. 8-13) give the following instruction: 'On its (the ninth day's) bṛhatī-verse, (*i.e.*, SV. 663-665) the sāmans of the araṇyegāna (Pañc. br. § 28, § 32) and the pṛṣṭha (§ 18) (are to be chanted) on tristichs (each sāman on all the three verses); (in this case) the vāsiṣṭha (falls) on the appendix-verse, the vaiyaśva before the bharga, and the ābhiśava before the yaśas (this disposition is followed by Varadarāja, see

Ārṣeyakalpa, pages 214, 215). Another possibility is, to chant (on the bṛhatī) seven sāmans only, each on a tristich, but arranging them so that there is no sameness of performance (*jāmi*). (This refers probably to the last part of each sāman: no *aidaṃ* should follow on an *aiḍam*, no *nidhanavat* on a *nidhanavat*, etc.; in this case, the sāmans that are left over may replace facultatively one of the others). The dīrghatamaso 'rka, or the sāmarāja, is the last (sāman) (of the midday-pavamāna); if the sāmarāja is taken as the last, the dīrghatamaso 'rka and the māṇḍava-sāman, which has *iḍā* as nidhana, (are to be applied) on the last two (verses) of the (tristich on which the) pṛṣtha-sāman (is chanted;) (in this case the pṛṣtha falls on the first verse)'.—The aiḍamāṇḍava is given Grām. XIV. 1. 26, composed on SV. I. 511 (SV. ed. Calcutta, Vol. II, page 72), chanted on SV. II. 664. b and 665, but this does not fit in with the notation of ūhagāna IX. 3. 9 (SV. ed. Calcutta, Vol. V, page 650).

XV. 4.

(The pṛṣtha-lauds of the ninth day.)

1. (The verses beginning:) 'Leaning, as it were on Sūrya'[1], contain (the word) *sūrya*.

[1] SV. I. 267=ṚS. VIII. 99. 1, 3, 4 (var. rr.)=SV. II. 669-670.—The text should run: *śrāyanta iva sūryam iti sūryavatyo bh.*

2. For this day has the sun as its deity[1]; the sun is the end and the ninth day is the end of the days (of the last three-day period): on the end they chant the end, (*i.e.*, the verse containing the word *sūrya*), for getting a firm support.

[1] A three-day period is comparable with the three lokas: earth=agni, antarikṣa=vāyu, dyaus=āditya.

3. (There are the verses beginning): 'What we fear, o Indra, of that make thou fearlessness for us. O bounteous one, give us this help by means of thy aid, smite away haters, away scorners'[1]; having smitten haters and scorners by the ninth day, they arise (finish the ten-day period) with the tenth day.

[1] SV. I. 274=ṚS. VIII. 61. 13-14=SV. II. 671-672.

4. There is the śrāyantīya(-sāman)[1].

[1] See note 1 on VIII. 2. 9.

5. The śrāyantīya(-sāman) is wealth (*śrī*)[1], and the ninth day is wealth[2]; he thus establishes wealth into wealth.

[1] A pun on the name.

[2] Because of the manifoldness and great number of sāmans.

6. There is the samanta(-sāman)[1].

[1] Grām. II. 1. 30, composed on SV. I. 61, chanted on SV. II. 671–672. Must be *aiḍam*, the first of the three, cp. SV. ed. Calcutta, Vol. I, page 192.

7. One who desires (to possess) cattle, should laud with the samanta(-sāman); one who desires (to get) a chaplainship, should laud with the samanta(sāman).

8. The earth is Agni-like and the priest is Agni-like[1]; the heaven is Indra-like and the noble is Indra-like[2]. Through the intermediate region, heaven and earth are adjacent (*samanta*); by means of the samanta(-sāman) he makes him adjacent[3]. He, who knowing this, lauds with the samanta(-sāman) acquires cattle[4] and obtains a chaplainship.—The stoma (has been given)[5].

[1] See VI. 1. 6.

[2] See VI. 1. 8.

[3] So that he, the priest, comes into connection with the noble, as his purohita.

[4] Because cattle is *antarikṣāyatana*, cp. Jaim. br. III. 186: *paśavo vā antarikṣaṃ, paśavaḥ samantam.*

[5] See XV. 1. 13.

XV. 5.

(The ārbhava-pavamāna-laud of the ninth day.)

1. (The verse beginning:) 'Thou, o Soma, art streaming (*dhārayu*)'[1], is a gāyatrī, for propping (*dhṛti*) the day. (The word) 'thou' is the characteristic of the bṛhat, for this day is a bṛhat-day[2].

[1] SV. II. 673–675=ṚS. IX. 67. 1–3. (var. r.).

[2] Cp. XI. 9. 1.

2. (In the verses beginning:) 'Yes, thou, the divine'[1], (the word) 'thou' is the characteristic of the bṛhat, for this day is a bṛhat-day[2].

[1] SV. I. 583 = ṚS. IX. 108. 3–4 = SV. II. 288–289.

[2] The § is identical with XII. 11. 2.

3. (The verses beginning:) 'Become clarified for the delectation of the Gods'[1], are characteristic of the bṛhat; for this day is a bṛhat-day.

[1] SV. I. 571=ṚS. IX. 106. 7–9=SV. II. 676–678.

4. (The verses beginning:) 'This desirable yellow one, on all sides'[1], contain (the words) 'on all sides' (*pari*). The ninth day, forsooth, is the end; these (verses are applied) for reaching (*paryāpti*) this day[2].

[1] SV. I. 552=ṚS. IX. 98. 7, 6, 8=SV. II. 679–681.

[2] Cp. XV. 3. 3.

5. (The verse beginning:) 'Become clarified, o Soma, for great dexterity'[1], is an akṣarapaṅkti: the source of the stomas. Moreover, the akṣarapaṅkti-metre, at this moment, is of unexhausted strength; by means of it, the Chandoma(-day)s are made of unexhausted strength. The Theologians argue: 'The stomas and metres at the six-day-period, having arrived at their end, what is the metre of the Chandoma(-day)s?' One should answer: 'These akṣarapaṅktis are their metre[2].'

[1] SV. I. 430=Ṛs. IX. 109. 10–12 (var. rr.)=SV. II. 682–684.

[2] The rest of this § agrees with XIV. 5. 6–8.

6. (The verses beginning:) 'Unto the born active'[1], being gāyatrīs, are, by their characteristic, jagatīs[2]; therefore, they are applied at the proper place of the jagatīs.

[1] SV. I. 487=ṚS. IX. 61. 13–15=SV. 685–687.

[2] Because (according to Sāyaṇa) of the word *gobhiḥ*, cattle being equal to jagatī.

7. There is the gāyatra(-sāman). The brāhmaṇa of the gāyatra is the same[1].

[1] See VII. 1. 1 sqq.

8. There is the āśvasūkta(-sāman)[1] ('the chant of Āśvasūkti').

[1] Grām. III. 2. 19, composed on SV. I. 122, chanted on SV. II. 673–675. It is (see SV. ed. Calcutta, Vol. I, page 303) *pañcākṣaranidhanam*.

9. To Agni he offers libations during the preceding days[1], but this day has the Sun as deity. (Regarding the words of the nidhana:) 'the Bright one to whom libations are offered', yonder

sun, forsooth, is bright, to him he offers libations by means of this (sāman).

1 This would mean that the ritual of the preceding days is performed in honour of Agni, the instrumental *pūrvair aharbhiḥ* being taken as an instrumental of time. I fail to see what is the precise meaning of these words. The remark
2 1
refers to the words added in the gāna (after the words of the verse): *śukra*
r 2 3 1111
āhutā 2345 ḥ. As compared with the gausūkta (grām. III. 2. 18), which ends: *agnir āhutaḥ*, *śukra* must mean the soma, not the sun. All would be clear if the gausūkta with its nidhana *agnir āhutaḥ* occurred on one of the preceding days; but this is not the case with the Kauthumas; the Jaiminiyas apply it before the āśvasūkta, but equally on the ninth day.—For the rest, the rare compound *ājuhoti* is due to the words of the nidhana.

10. There is the śāmmada(-sāman)[1] ('the chant of Śammad').

1 Grām. XIII. 2. 13, composed on SV. I. 483, chanted on SV. II. 673-675. This, not XIII. 2. 12, is intended, being *svāram*, see SV. ed Calcutta, Vol. II, page 38.

11. Śammad, of the Angiras clan, by means of this sāman straightway beheld the world of heaven; (so it serves) for beholding the world of heaven. He, who in lauding has applied (it), does not fall forth from the world of heaven[1].

1 Nearly identical with XIV. 9. 29. In Jaim. br. III. 164, the name is derived from the words: *śam vai na ime lokā amādiṣuḥ*, spoken by the Gods, after they had made the worlds turn again towards them, when they had receded from them in fear.

12. There is the (sāman) with (the word) *dāvasu* as nidhana[1].

1 Grām. III. 2. 11, composed on SV. I. 119, chanted on SV. II. 673-675.
2 r 1 3 1111
It is *nidhanavat*, ending: *dāvasū 2345*, see SV. ed. Calcutta, Vol. I, page 297.

13. By means of this (sāman) he invokes a blessing for him, for the sāman is a true blessing[1].

1 The word *dāvasu* reminding of *-dāvan* '-giving'. This § is identical with XIII. 12. 7.

14. Dāvasu, of the Angiras clan, being desirous of cattle, saw this sāman. By means of it he created a thousand head of cattle. That there is this sāman, is for making the cattle thrive[1].

1 Cp. the nearly identical passage XIII. 11. 14.

15. There is the kāśīta(-sāman) with hitherward directed *iḍā*[1].

[1] Grām. V. 2. 8, composed on SV. 1. 184, chanted on SV II. 673–675. Its last words (see SV. ed. Calcutta, Vol. I, page 407, and cp. note 3 on X. 12. 5) are: *au* '23 *ho*[4] *vā*[5] | *iḍā*[45], whilst usually the *aiḍa*-sāmans end on *o*[1] '2345 *i* | *ḍā* or *ho*[4] '5 *i* | *ḍā*. These last are called *parācīneḍa*. Jaim. br. III. 265: *tasyo pratīcīm iḍām upayanti, chandomebhyo net parāñco 'tipadyāmahā iti*. The same Brāhmaṇa (l.c.) records that a certain Kaśīti, the son of Subhara, was, during a sattra, afflicted by consumption. He saw this sāman, composed on the verses *vāta ā vātu bheṣajam* (=ṚS. X. 186. 1–3), and was healed by Vāta

16. By means of the other *iḍās*, that are directed thitherward, he continually places the seed (into the womb), but this kāśīta(-sāman), with its *iḍā* hitherward directed, (is applied) for production (for delivery of the young out of the womb). Therefore, the embryos come into existence directed thitherward, but are born hitherward[1]. Therefore also, they (the embryos) do not fall forth from their (receptacle, although) its opening is turned downwards. For by this (sāman with thitherward directed *iḍā*) they are supported

[1] Embryos come into existence with the head turned thitherward, *i.e.*, away from the mouth of the matrix, but are born with the head turned hitherward, cp. Ait. br. III. 10. 1: *parāñco garbhā dhiyante parāñcaḥ sambhavanti, amuto 'rvāñco garbhāḥ prajāyante.*

17. There is the hiviṣkṛta(-sāman)[1], for getting firm support. Its explanation[2] is the same (as given formerly)[3].

[1] Grām. IV. 1. 20, composed on SV. I. 138, chanted on SV. II. 673–675. The first of the two, *nidhanavat*, cp. SV. ed. Calcutta, Vol. I, page 328.

[2] *anuvāda*, a portion of a brāhmaṇa-text, which comments on, illustrates, or explains a *vidhi* or direction previously laid down, and which does not itself contain any direction.

[3] See XI. 10. 9.

18. There is the sauparṇa(-sāman)[1]; the brāhmaṇa of the sauparṇa is the same[2].

[1] Grām. III. 2. 25, composed on SV. I. 125, chanted on SV. II. 288–289; the *svāram* is intended, cp. SV. ed. Calcutta, Vol. I, page 308.

[2] See XIV. 3. 10.

19. There is the vaiśvamanasa(-sāman)[1] ('the chant of Viśvamanas').

[1] Grām. X. 2. 8, composed on SV. I 387, chanted on SV. II. 676–678. It is *nidhanavat* (*ū* $\overset{1111}{2345}$), see SV. ed. Calcutta, Vol. I, page 795.

20. The Seer, Viśvamanas, when he had gone out to study[1], was seized by an Ogre. Of him Indra noted: 'The Seer has been seized by an Ogre', and he addressed him: 'O Seer, who (is) this one (that has seized) thee?' The Ogre said (to Viśvamanas): 'Say, 'it is a trunk''[2], and he (Viśvamanas) said (to Indra): 'A trunk'. 'Hit at him with this', he (Indra) said, handing him over a reed, by way of a thunderbolt. Therewith, he split his skull. This is the reed called *indreṇata*[3]. It was an evil that had seized him; this he repelled by means of the vaiśvamanasa(-sāman). He who in lauding has applied the vaiśvamanasa(-sāman), repels the evil[4].

[1] Probably, he was a participant of a sattra and, during the intervals, went out to study the texts for the subsequent day; cp. note 2 on XII. 11. 10.

[2] With regard to the version of the Jaim. (see note 4), it is not advisable to take *sthāṇu* as a proper noun.

[3] *indreṇatā* may stand haplologically for *indreṇa natā*. It is noteworthy that of the two Leyden MSS. of our Brāhmaṇa, one reads *indraṇatā* and, the other, *indreṇata*. Lāṭy. IV. 1. 7, reads *indreṇatā*, Drāhy. XI. 1 7, 8, *indraṇatā*. According to Drāhy. l. c. 8: *yā svayaṃvakrā sendraṇatā*, a reed is meant which of itself is crooked (*mūlataḥ* seems to belong to the preceding sūtra, cp. Lāṭy. l. c.). Dhanvin explains *indraṇatā* by *daivena natā* (thus reads the MS. G.).

[4] The corresponding passage of the Jaim. br. (III 266, see 'Auswahl' No. 208) runs as follows: 'Viśvamanas, who had gone out to collect fuel (for the sacrifice) in the forest, fell in with an Ogre. He wished: 'May I repel the Ogre'. He saw this sāman and chanted it over (him). Indra saw that Viśvamanas had fallen in with an Ogre and came running on to him. By the snorting of him who came running on, he collapsed (or 'became contorted'?). He (Indra) asked him: 'Viśvamanas, who is this one that has ... thee?' He (the Ogre) said (to Viśvamanas): 'Thou must answer, '(it is) a *sūrmī*, o Maghavan', and he (Viśvamanas) said (to Indra): '(It is) a *sūrmī*, o Maghavan, slay thou only with a stick on her'. He (Indra) said: 'Pull out a blade of grass and throw it gently on (her)'. He, having pulled out a blade of grass gently threw it on (her). Into this same (blade of grass) Indra poured his thunderbolt, and he (Viśvamanas) slew him (the Ogre) then and there'.—The *sūrmī* occurs also above, II. 17. 1. It is not clear to me what is meant by it here. The Pañc. br. has *sthāṇu*. In either case some object is intended which is not very harmful, the object of the Ogre being, apparently, to deceive Indra, by inducing him to believe that Viśvamanas is not seriously harmed.—On *sūrmī*, cp. also Acta Orientalia, Vol. VI, page 141.

21. There is the gaurīvita(-sāman)[1]; the brāhmaṇa of the gaurīvita is the same[2].

[1] Grām. V. 1. 22, composed on SV. I. 168, chanted on SV. II. 679-681. It is *svāram*, see SV. ed. Calcutta, Vol. I, page 383.

[2] See XI. 5. 14.

22. There is the nihava(-sāman)[1], for obtaining food.

[1] Grām. VIII. 1. 36, composed on SV. I. 313, chanted on SV. II. 679-681. See SV. ed. Calcutta, Vol. I, page 629 (*nidhanavat*).

23. With (the word) 'yes' (*hi*), food is given[1]; by (the word) *ī*, Agni eats the food[2].

[1] The particle *hi* is used in consenting answers. The nihavasāman opens with the following stobha: $\overset{1}{\textit{ā}}\ \overset{2}{\textit{ihī}}$ *'3* | $\overset{1}{\textit{ā}}\ \overset{2r}{\textit{ihī}}$ | $\overset{3r\ 2\wedge}{\textit{ehiyā}}$ | $\overset{3}{\textit{0234}}$ *vā* | $\overset{5}{\textit{hā}}\ \overset{2}{\textit{i}}$. Although this *ā ihi* seems to be simply the chanting form of *ehi* ('come'), the author of our Brāhmaṇa sees in it the particle *hi*.

[2] Perhaps *ī* is used to express the hissing sound of butter poured into the fire The nidhana of the nihavasāman is $\overset{3\,1111}{\textit{ī 2345}}$.

24. The Seers (in former times) did not see Indra face to face. Vasiṣṭha desired: 'How may I see Indra face to face?' He saw this nihava(-sāman) and, thereupon, he saw Indra face to face. He (Indra) said to him: 'I will tell thee a brāhmaṇa, so that the Bharatas, having thee as their chaplain, may be multiplied, but do not discover me to the other Seers'. He told him those stomabhāga (-formulas)[1], and, thereupon, the Bharatas, having Vasiṣṭha as their chaplain, were multiplied[2]. This sāman is associated with Indra. That there is this sāman, is in order to be associated with Indra[3].

[1] The formulas given above: I. 9 and 10.

[2] The same legend in TS. III. 5. 2 and Kāṭh. XXXVII. 17, only with *prajāḥ* instead of *bharatāḥ*. The beginning of the Kāṭh. has a slight variant: 'The Ṛṣis did not see Indra face to face. Only Vasiṣṭha saw him face to face. He (Indra) feared: 'He will discover me to the other Ṛṣis'. He said: 'I will tell you a brāhmaṇa', etc.

[3] So that Indra in person may come to the sacrifice.

25. There is the yadvāhiṣṭhīya(-sāman)[1].

[1] Grām. II. 2. 26, composed on SV. I. 86, chanted on SV. II. 679-681. There are two sāmans of this name and both (cp. SV. ed. Calcutta, Vol. I, page 242) are *aiḍam* (*ūrdhveḷam*, Jaim. br.).

26. These sāmans, forsooth, are priestly lustre[1]. Lustrous becomes he who in lauding has applied the yadvāhiṣṭhīya(-sāman).

[1] I fail to see the meaning of the words *ṛcā śrotriyāṇi*. The plural also is strange, as there are only two chants of this name.

27. There is the āsita(-sāman)[1]; the brāhmaṇa of the āsita is the same[2].

[1] Grām. III. 1. 3, composed on SV. I. 93, chanted on SV. II. 679-681: *svāram*, see SV. ed. Calcutta, Vol I, page 252.

[2] See XIV. 11. 19.

28. There is the sādhra(-sāman)[1], for succeeding (*siddhi*).

[1] Grām. VI. 2. 32, composed on SV. I. 248, chanted on SV II. 679-681: the *aiḍam* one is meant: SV. ed. Calcutta, Vol. I, page 513.

29. There is the ākūpāra(-sāman)[1]. ('The chant of Akūpāra').

[1] Grām. IX. 1. 30, composed on SV. I. 345, chanted on SV. II 679-681: it is *svāram*, SV. ed. Calcutta Vol. I, page 706.

30 By means of this (sāman), Akūpāra Kaśyapa attained power and greatness. Power and greatness attains he who in lauding has practised the ākūpāra(sāman)[1].

[1] The name, ākūpāra, is explained in a curious myth or legend in the Jaim. br. (III. 272, see 'Auswahl' No. 210): 'Akūpāra Kaśyapa descended together with the Kalis, into the sea. He sought in it a firm standing. He saw this sāman and lauded with it. Thereupon, he found a firm standing in the sea, *viz.*, this earth. Since that time, the Kalis sit on his back. This sāman is (equal to) a firm standing. A firm standing gets he who knows thus. The Chandoma(-day)s are a sea (because of the great number of their stotriya-verses), and Kaśyapa (the Tortoise) is able to convey (them) across the sea. That there is here this ākūpāra, is for crossing over the sea (of the Chandoma-days)'.

31. There is the vidharman(-sāman)[1], for supporting the right (*dharma*).

[1] Grām. XI 2. 21, composed on SV. I. 430, chanted on SV. II. 682-684; it is *nidhanavat*: *vidharmā* 2345 (1 2 3 1 111). See SV. ed Calcutta, Vol. I, page 874.

32. The Theologians argue: 'The stomas and metres at the six-day period having been used up, what is the metre of the Chandoma(-day)s?' One should answer: 'They have man as their

metre'. Man is fivefold, man is two-footed: in order that the Chandoma(-day)s may be unexhausted[1].

1 This § is identical with XIV. 11. 35. It refers to XV. 5. 15, where the verses are treated on which the vidharman is chanted.

33. There is the śrudhya(-sāman)[1].

1 Grām. III. 1. 15, composed on SV. I. 99, chanted on SV. II. 685-687. The *aiḍam* one is intended: SV. ed. Calcutta, Vol. I, page 264, cp. § 37.

34. The śrudhya is cattle[1]; (it is applied) for obtaining cattle.

1 The śrudhya, with other sāmans, is in IX. 1. 32-33 likewise made equivalent to cattle; cp. the next following §.

35. Prajāpati produced the cows; these being produced, went away from him; by means of this sāman (and especially by its stobha): 'Hear thou! Come thou!'[1], he called after them. They returned to him. That there is this sāman, is in order that the cows may return.

1 *śrūdhiyā 3* | *e 23 hiyā 343.* (2r, 3, 2 above)

36. To him who knows this, the cows turn.

37. They chant (it) on gāyatrī(-verse)s, for the sake of getting a firm support, for (the obtainment of) priestly lustre. With which breath they start, in that they finish (the laud).—The pavamāna (-laud)s (of this day) finish on *iḍā*; *iḍā* is cattle, and the Chandoma (-day)s are cattle. He, thereby, brings cattle into his cattle[1].—The stoma (has been given)[2].

1 Identical with XIV. 5. 30-31.

2 See XV. 1. 13.

XV. 6.

(The uktha-lauds of the ninth day.)

1. On (verses) addressed to Agni, they lead on the uktha (-laud)s of the preceding days, but, on this day, they lead them on on a (verse) addressed to Agni and Indra[1]: in both characteristics he (thereby) is firmly established.

1 SV. I. 133=ṚS. VIII. 45. 1-3=SV. II. 688-690. Although the verses are indicated in this way only, it is clear from § 2 that these are intended, even if we do not take into account the uttarārcika.

2. There is the aidhmavāha(-sāman)[1].

[1] Grām. IV. 1. 11, composed on SV. I. 133, chanted on SV. II. 688-690. The first of the three sāmans of this name, being *svāram* (SV. ed. Calcutta, Vol. I, page 321), is intended.

3. They chant (it) on (verses) addressed to Agni and Indra; he, thereby, brings priesthood and nobility into union: he places the priesthood (Agni) before the nobility (Indra), and makes nobility and peasantry as following after the priesthood[1].

[1] See XI. 11. 8.—The Jaim. br. (III. 274, 275) has the following tale relating to this sāman: 'The Seers, when going to the world of heaven, left Idhmavāha alone behind, who had gone out to the forest to collect fuel for the sacrifice. He wished: 'May I go up after (the others) to the world of heaven, may I be united with my fellow-sattrins.' He thought: 'Come, I will laud my fellow-sattrins; they, being lauded, will cause that I will hear them'. He saw this tristich (see note 1 on XV. 6. 1) and lauded with it: '*ā ghā ye agnim....yeṣām indro yuvā sakhā*'. They, being lauded, caused that he heard them: he heard the swishing of their whips. He saw this sāman and lauded with it (SV. I. 135:) 'Now even I hear them, now that their whips swish in their hands, *ni yāmaṃ citram ṛñjate*'; having lauded them with this sāman, he ascended to the world of heaven; (with the sāman) *ā ghā ye agnim* (now follows the verse SV. I. 133 in its sāman-form), he ascended the world of heaven'.—The text probably is corrupt, as is clear from the repetition. It does not appear why vs. I. 135, on which not an aidhmavāha but an aiṣira is chanted, is cited, but note the mention of the whips.

4. There is the traikakubha(-sāman)[1].

[1] Grām. X. 2. 14, composed on SV. I. 389, chanted on SV. II. 691-693 (=ṚS. I. 84. 7, 9, 8). The sāman must be *nidhanavat*, and on SV. I. 389 there are (see SV. ed. Calcutta, vol. I, page 798–799) two sāmans of this kind. A comparison with the ūhagāna proves that the last is intended. In the Nidāna-sūtra (IV. 7), the question is discussed which of the traikakubhāni is preferable: *traikakubhasya nidhane vivadante: padanidhanānām ity eke* etc.; the conclusion is, that the *bahirṇidhanam* one is the best.

5. He, thereby, is firmly established in strength and valour: the traikakubha(-sāman) is strength and valour[1].

[1] Cp. IV. 2. 10 and VIII. 1. 7.

6. There is the udvaṃśīya(-sāman)[1]. The brāhmaṇa of the udvaṃśīya is the same[2].

[1] Grām. IX. 1. 16, composed on SV. I. 342, chanted on SV. II. 694-696 (=ṚS. I. 10. 1-3). It ought to be *svāram* (SV. ed. Calcutta, vol. I, page 695).

[2] See VIII. 9. 6, sqq.

7. The stoma is the forty eight-versed one: for being firmly established[1], for generating.

1 Cp. III. 12. 3.

(The tenth day.)

XV. 7.

(Out-of-doors-laud of the tenth day.)

1. The seventh day is a gāyatrī-day, the eighth is a triṣṭubh-day, the ninth is a jagatī-day[1], but the tenth is an anuṣṭubh-day.

1 The seventh day is twenty-four-versed and the gāyatrī has 24 syllables: the eighth day is forty-four-versed and the tristubh has 44 syllables; the ninth day is forty-eight-versed and the jagatī has 48 syllables: cp. note 1 on XIV. 1. 2.

2. About this they (the Theologians) remark: 'Were they to bring into practice the anuṣṭubh as stoma-verse[1] in a perceptible way, the Sacrificer would go to the farthest distance and lose his support'[2]. The twenty-four gāyatrīs, now, are (equal to) eighteen anuṣṭubhs[3]; they, thereby, bring into practice (*i.e.*, they chant) the anuṣṭubh as stoma-verse in a cryptical way, for getting a support, (and thus) the Sacrificer is firmly supported[4].

1 *stomyām* (?).

2 Because the anuṣṭubh is the l a s t in the regular sequence of the metres: 1. gāyatrī, 2. triṣṭubh, 3. jagatī, 4. anuṣṭubh.

3 The stoma being twenty-four-versed (see XV. 7. 8), the bahiṣpavamāna requires 24 gāyatrīs, *i.e.*, 576 syllables all together. These, being divided by the number of syllables of the anuṣṭubh (4 x 8): 32 syllables, are equal to 18 anuṣṭubhs. Thus, whilst being visibly chanted on gāyatrīs, this laud can be said, cryptically, to be chanted on anuṣṭubhs.

4 The purport of this §, in accordance with injunctions from elsewhere, is, that on this day no anuṣṭubh is to be chanted or recited (see IV. 8. 9 with note 1), but, by reckoning the gāyatrīs as anuṣṭubhs, the condition stated at end of § 1 is fulfilled, *viz.*, that the tenth day is an anuṣṭubh-day. For the fact that the rite of this day may not contain any anuṣṭubh, cp. note 1 on § 5, below.

3. They offer this day as food to Prajāpati; therefore, no revealing must be made[1]. The blame they utter[2], whilst a person of high rank is being served with food[3], is an impediment. Therefore, no revealing must be made[1]: in order not to impede the food.

Śāṇḍilya, everywhere the verses are to be taken in reversed order and not the tristichs'. See the disposition according to Varadarāja in his description of the daśarātra, ed. of the Ārṣeya-kalpa, page 216.

[2] At the first day, undertaking as it were a journey, they have put in the *śamyās*, which now, at the end, are extracted, cp. Jaim. br. III. 278: *prāyaṇīyenaivāhnā dvādaśāho yujyate, daśamenāhnā mucyate. yena vai yoktreṇāśvam aśvataraṃ yuñjanti, tenaivainaṃ punar vimuñcanti; tad yā amūḥ purastān nava stotrīyās* (sc. of the first day), *tā evaitad upariṣṭāc chamyā udasyanti.*

7 Addressed to Varuṇa is one (verse)[1]; that part of the sacrifice which is performed badly is seized by Varuṇa; this he, thereby, disperses by his sacrifice[2]. One (verse) is addressed to Aditi[3]. Aditi is the earth, on her he is firmly established.

[1] I fail to see to which of the verses SV. II. 105-113 this refers. Sāyana forcibly refers it to vs. 109, because the word *kaviḥ* occurs in it, Mitra and Varuna being called sometimes (in SV. II. 199) *kavi*.

[2] Cp. XV. 1. 3.

[3] Sāyaṇa, equally forcibly, refers this to SV. II. 110.

8. The stoma is the twenty-four-versed one, for (obtaining) strength (and) priestly lustre.

XV. 8.

(The ājya-lauds of the tenth day.)

1. The *āprī*(-verses, beginning:) 'Well kindled, lead thou hither for us'[1], are (the verses on which) the ājya(-laud)s[2] (are chanted).

[1] The Ṛksaṃhitā contains ten *āprīsūktas*, originally intended each for members of a different gotra. They are destined for the prayāja-offerings at an animal-sacrifice (paśubandha), see Schwab, das altindische Thieropfer, page 90, M. Muller, a history of ancient Sanskrit literature, page 463. As there are eleven fore-offerings, each *āprīsūkta* ought to consist (as eight of the ten do) of eleven verses, but the descendants of certain Ṛsis address the second prayāja to Tanūnapāt, of others to Narāśaṃsa, and in some of the *āprīsūktas* these verses are given both, so that they now contain twelve verses, verses 2 and 3 being used according to the Ṛṣi-descent of the performer See, for instance, Baudh. (X. 11: 10. 10 sqq.), who, treating of the *āprī*-verses at a cayana (being TS. IV. 1. 8 a—m, 12 verses), says: 'Of these verses he (the Adhvaryu) leaves out the one addressed to Tanūnapāt (TS. l.c. b) and uses the one addressed to Narāśaṃsa (TS. l.c.c) for descendants of Vasiṣṭha; for the other gotras, he leaves out the verse addressed to Narāśaṃsa and uses the one addressed to Tanūnapāt'. Our Brāhmaṇa prescribes, for the first ājyastotra,

the verses ṚS. I. 13. 1 sqq. (= SV. II. 697–700, four: one too many). Intended are either ṚS. I. 13. 1, 2, 4 (SV. II. 697, 698, 700) or ṚS. I. 13. 1, 3, 4 (= SV. II 697, 699, 700); cp. Lāṭy. VI. 4. 13–16: '(In the verses) 'Well kindled', (they should take) the (verse) addressed to Tanūnapāt for descendants of Atri, Vasiṣṭha, Śunaka, Kaṇva, Saṃkṛti, and Vadhryaśva, the (verse) addressed to Narāśaṃsa for the others. In case (the participants of the sacrificial session) belong to both, (*i.e.*, are Vasiṣṭhas, etc., and not-Vasiṣṭhas) the ritual of the plurality (prevails), or the participants of a sacrificial session follow the (ritual of) the Householder (the *gṛhapati*)'. Nidānasūtra IV. 8: 'For the tenth day we hand down a hotur-ājya(-laud) of four verses; in the middle (of these) are two verses, one addressed to Tanūnapāt, one to Narāśaṃsa. There are two kinds of families; for those who accept the Tanūnapāt-verse, he should apply the chant on the verses with the one addressed to Tanūnapāt; for those who accept the Narāśaṃsa-verse, he should apply the laud on the verses with the one addressed to Narāśaṃsa. The Narāśaṃsa-families are the Vasiṣṭhas, the Śunakas, the Atris, the Vadhryaśvas, the Kanvas, and the Saṃkṛtis. The others are the Tanūnapāt-families. (This is precisely the contrary of what Lāṭyāyana proscribes!) How (is it to be done) in the case of both families coming together? He should follow the plurality (*bhūmno vaśaṃ nayet*): the ritual of the 'Householder', according to some, or he should apply for all of them the Tanūnapāt-verse. This belongs to most (of the families) and, moreover, some hand down this verse (only, leaving out the Narāśaṃsa verse)'. In designating as Nārāśaṃsa's, the Vasiṣṭha, Śunaka, etc., the Anupadasūtra (IV. 6) agrees with the Nidānasūtra, as also does Baudhāyana in his pravarasūtra. According to this authority, the following are Nārāśaṃsas: the Ātreyas, Vādhryaśvas, Vādhūlas, Vasiṣṭhas, Kanvas, Śunakas, Saṃkṛtis, Yaskas, Rājanyas, and Vaiśyas, the others are Tānūnapātas.

2 The plural instead of the singular (for only the first ājya-laud is meant) is caused by the preceding plural *āpriyaḥ*.

2. Prajāpati created the creatures; he thought himself milked out and emptied out; he saw these *āprī*(-verse)s as ājya-(laud)s and, by means of these, he gratified (*aprīṇāt*) himself. Milked out, as it were, and emptied out is he who has lauded with the ten days (who has performed as Chanter the ten-day-rite) In that the *āprī*(-verse)s are these ājya(-laud)s, thereby he gratifies himself.

3*a*. (The verses beginning:) 'That now, the sun having risen'[1], containing the word 'sun', are the ājya(-laud) addressed to Mitra and Varuṇa. The sun is the end and this tenth day is the end: on the end they laud with the end (with the verse containing the word 'sun'), for getting a firm support[2].

1 ṚS. VII. 66. 4–6 = SV II 701–703

2 Cp. XV. 4. 2.

3*b*. (The verses beginning:) 'Let the somas exhilarate (*ut-madantu*) thee'[1], containing the word 'up' (*ut*), are the (ājya-laud) addressed to Indra, being characteristic of the rising (*utthāna*, *i.e.*, the close of the sacrificial session).

[1] SV. I. 194 = ṚS. IX. 64. 1-3 (var. rr.) = SV. II. 704-706.

4. (There are the verses beginning:) 'O Indra and Agni, come hither to the pressed (soma)'[1]: with which characteristic feature they start (*i.e.*, begin the sacrifice), in that they break up (or finish).[2]—The stoma (has been given)[3].

[1] Cp. XI. 2. 3.

[2] This is also the fourth ājyastotra of the first day.

[3] See XV. 7. 8.

XV. 9.

(The midday-pavamāna-laud of the tenth day.)

1. (The verses beginning:) 'On high (*uccā*), born of thy plant'[1], are gāyatrīs, containing the word 'up' (*ut*), being the characteristic feature of the rising (*utthāna*).

[1] See XII. 3. 1 (SV. I. 467 = SV. II. 22-24).

2. (There are the verses beginning:) 'Being clarified, o Soma, by the stream'[1]; they thereby come round to the path[2].

[1] See XI. 8. 3 (SV. I. 511 = SV. II. 25-26).

[2] They come round to the introductory day on which, at the midday-pavamāna-laud, these verses have been already applied.

3. (There are the verses beginning:) 'Unto (*ā*) the sacred rite the vigilant poet of prayers'[1]; if, the rite being finished, they were to apply (verses) containing (the word) 'forth' (*pra*)[2], they would go beyond[3]; that there are (verses) containing (the word) 'unto' or 'hither' (*ā*), is for not going beyond.

[1] ṚS. IX. 97. 36-39 (var. r.) = SV. II. 707-709.

[2] As is done on the first or introductory day, cp. XI. 3. 1.

[3] And they would not rest in the world of heaven, which must be reached through the sacrifice.

4. There is the gāyatra(-sāman). The brāhmaṇa of the gāyatra is the same[1].

[1] See VII. 1. 1 sqq.

5. There is the āmahīyava(-sāman)[1]; it is a making-ready (a fitting-out) and it is food. By means of it, they arise (finish) towards making-ready, towards food.

[1] See note 1 on VII. 5. 1.

6. There is the ājiga(-sāman)[1] ('the race-running chant'): for winning the race.

[1] Grām. XII. 2. 14, composed on SV. I. 468, chanted on SV. II 22-24. This sāman (see SV. ed. Calcutta, Vol. II, page 7) is *aiḍam*. We would rather expect the ājiga of Grām. XII. 2. 1, composed on SV. I. 467 = SV. II. 22-24, (see SV. ed. Calc. l.c. page 2), but then there would be *jāmitvam*, as this sāman is *nidhanavat*, whilst the preceding āmahīyava is also *nidhanavat*.

7. A race, forsooth, is begun through this twelve-day period (this sāman is applied) for winning the race.

8. There is the ābhīka(-sāman)[1], for stepping on (*abhi-krānti*).

[1] Grām. XII. 2. 4, composed on SV. I. 467, chanted on SV. II. 22-24. Probably (see SV. ed. Calcutta, Vol. II, page 3) it is *svāram*.

9. The Angirases, who practised austerities, were overtaken by languor; they saw this sāman and in a moment rain fell on them; thereby, they freed themselves of the languor. Because in a moment (*abhīke*) it rained on them, thence the *ābhīka*(-sāman) has its name. The languor they feel, in consequence of the preceding days, of that they free themselves now by means of this (sāman), before rising (before finishing the sacrificial session).

10. There is the utsedha(-sāman)[1].

[1] Grām. XIV. 2. 23, composed on SV. I. 514, chanted on SV. II. 25-26. It is (see SV. ed. Calcutta, Vol. II, page 87) *nidhanavat*.

11. By means of the utsedha(-sāman), the Gods drove up (*ut*) the cattle; by means of the niṣedha(sāman)[1], they laid hold of it.

[1] Grām. XIV. 2. 24, composed on SV. I. 514, chanted on SV. II. 25-26. It is likewise *nidhanavat*, but cp. § 12.

12. Between the utsedha and the niṣedha, the yajñāyajñīya (-sāman)[1].

[1] Grām. I. 2. 25, composed on SV. I. 35, chanted on SV. II. 25-26. This sāman has as nidhana the word *vā(k)* (see SV. ed. Calcutta, Vol. I, page 150), and, as this kind of sāmans is not considered as *nidhanavat* (see note 1 on XIII. 5. 28), the two, utsedha and niṣedha, which are both *nidhanavat*, are separated by a sāman of different ending, so that there is no *jāmitvam*.

13. The yajñāyajñīya is cattle (and) food; in this manner he lays, by means of the utsedha and niṣedha, hold of cattle (and) food.

14. The Gods, having brought the sacrifice to an end by means of the yajñāyajñīya at the midday-pavamāna(-laud)[1], ascended to the world of heaven. So one, who knows this, ascends to the world of heaven, after he has brought the sacrifice to an end, at the midday-pavamāna(-laud), by means of the yajñāyajñīya.

[1] It is known that the yajñāyajñīya is the chant of the last stotra in the ordinary sacrifice.

15. Moreover, the (tenth) day comes cryptically to be (equal to) an anuṣṭubh[1]; the yajñāyajñīya(-sāman), forsooth, is perceptibly an anuṣṭubh. If they applied the yajñāyajñīya at the afternoon service, they would tend perceptibly towards an anuṣṭubh[2]; therefore, they apply (it) at the midday(-service). They, thereby, undertake (apply) the anuṣṭubh cryptically[3].

[1] As is recommended, XV. 7, 2.

[2] Which is disapproved of, cp. l.c. The yajñāyajñīya has $\overset{111}{\textit{vā345}}$ as nidhana (*i.e.*, *vāk*) and *vāc* is equal to anuṣṭubh, cp. V. 7. 1.

[3] As is recommended. The anuṣṭubh (*i.e.*, yajñāyajñīya) is enclosed between other sāmans and is not chanted at the close of the service, whereby it looses its character as anuṣṭubh.

16. There is the gaurīvita(-sāman)[1].

[1] Grām. V. 1. 22, composed on SV. I. 168, chanted on SV. II. 707-709. It is *svāram*, see SV. ed. Calcutta, Vol. I, page 383.

17. The gaurīvita(-sāman) is (that part) of the sacrifice which has relation to the to-morrow[1], the Sacrificer has the midday-service as his resting place[2]. In that the gaurīvita(-sāman) is applied at the midday-service[3], the Sacrificer brings into himself the to-morrow.—The stoma (has been given[4].)

[1] Because of what has been said at V. 7, 2 and V. 7, 5.

[2] How is this to be understood?

[3] Whilst on the preceding days it falls on the afternoon-service.

[4] See XV. 7. 8.

XV. 10.

(The pṛṣṭha-lauds of the tenth day.)

1. (The verses beginning:) 'By which assistance shall the bright one help us',[1] contain (the word) 'which' (*ka*). Thereby,

they are Prajāpati-like, for Prajāpati is 'who' (*kas*): in order that they may reach Prajāpati[2].

[1] SV. I. 169 = ṚS. IV. 31. 1–3 = SV. II. 32–34.

[2] This § is indentical with XI. 4, 2.

2. (The verses beginning:) 'Do ye not praise anything different'[1], are a rising-up[2], for that they have at this moment as their wish.

[1] SV. I. 242 = ṚS. VIII. 1. 1–2 = SV. II. 710–711.

[2] They point to the end of the sacrificial session: the *utthāna*.

3. (The verses beginning:) 'Up, these very sweet',[1] contain (the word) up (*ut*) and (serve) on the finishing (*u d ayanīya*) day, for that they have at this moment as their wish.

[1] SV. I. 251 = ṚS. VIII. 3. 15–16 (var. r.) = SV. II. 712–713.

4. (There are the verses beginning:) 'By strength (*tarobhiḥ*) your treasure-finding one (*vidadvasu*).'[1] The strength (*taraḥ*) is the stoma, the treasure-finding one is the sacrifice. By the stoma the sacrifice is yoked (brought into action). By saying: 'by strength your treasure-finding one,' he, indeed, yokes the sacrifice.

[1] SV. I. 237 = ṚS. VIII. 66. 1–2 = SV. II. 37–38. For the rest, cp. VIII. 3, 3.

5. On the verses of the vāmadevya(-sāman)[1], the rathantara is (chanted) as (first) pṛṣṭha(-laud). The gāyatrī is the womb of the rathantara[2]. In its own womb he thereby establishes the rathantara.

[1] On the verses mentioned in § 1; these are on gāyatrī-metre.

[2] Cp. VII. 8. 8–9.

6. The gāyatrī is the lustre of the metres[1], the rathantara (is the lustre) of the sāmans, the twenty-four-versed stoma (is the lustre) of the stomas[2]. He unites (all kinds of) lustre together, even his son's son becomes lustrous.

[1] As it sprang, together with Agni, out of the head of Prajāpati, see VI. 1. 6.

[2] As containing as many verses as the gāyatrī has syllables.

7. On eight syllables he holds the prastāva of the first verse; he thereby obtains the eight-hoofed animals (cattle).

8. On two syllables he holds the prastāva of the two next verses; the Sacrificer is two-footed. He thereby establishes the Sacrificer in (the possession of) cattle.

9. The rathantara on gāyatrī-metre is gāyatrī-like. In that the rathantara is (chanted) on gāyatrī-verses, thereby, he thrives amongst his own people[1]. In that the rathantara is (chanted) on gāyatrī-verses, they reach these worlds before rising, the gāyatrī being (equal to) these worlds.

[1] Just as the rathantara, chanted on gāyatrī-verses, is chanted on its own *yoni*.

10. There is the maidhātitha(-sāman)[1] ('the chant of Medhātithi').

[1] Grām. VI. 2. 19, composed on SV I. 242, chanted on SV. II. 710-711. It is *svāram*, see SV. ed. Calcutta, Vol. I, page. 501.

11. By means of this (sāman), Medhātithi, the son of Kaṇva[1], did come forth from Vibhinduka[2] two-uddered cows. For obtaining cattle the maidhātitha(-sāman) is applied[3].

[1] *kāṇvo*, the printed text, *kāṇvyo*, the two Leyden MSS.

[2] Read: *vibhindukād dvyūdhnīr* instead of *°kād vyūdhnīr*. Sāyaṇa, who takes *vibhinduka* as the name of an Asura and reads and interprets *vyūdhnīḥ*, is wrong, cp. note 3.

[3] The Kauthuma-brāhmaṇa contains only an allusion to this story of Medhātithi which is told at length in Jaim. br. (III. 233, 234, cp. 'Auswahl' No. 203): 'The inhabitants of Vibhinduka performed a sacrificial session with Medhātithi as their 'Householder' (*gṛhapati*). Their Udgātṛ was Dṛdhacyut, the son of Agasti, their Prastotṛ was Gaurivīti, their Pratihartṛ was Acyutacyut, their Hotṛ was Vasukṣaya, their two Adhvaryus were Sanaka and Navaka. Medhātithi undertook the sacrifice, wishing to obtain cattle; Sanaka and Navaka, wishing to obtain women; the others, each with his special wish. Formerly, forsooth, they used to perform a sacrificial session, each with his own special wish and, having succeeded in their desires and obtained them, they arose (finished the sattra). Of these (Vibhindukīyas) Indra, having assumed the shape of Medhātithi's ram, repeatedly drank the soma. Each time they drove him away, saying: 'Medhātithi's ram is drinking our soma.' Thereupon, he used to drink their soma, having assumed his own shape (as Indra). Since that time, they invocate him: 'O Ram of Medhātithi!' (This refers to the formula of the Subrahmaṇya, see, *e.g.*, Oertel in Journ. of the American Oriental Soc., Vol. XVIII, pages 35, 37). This Medhātithi, wishing for cattle, saw this sāman and lauded with it: (by its verse) 'The destroyer of the strongholds, the young clever one' (Jaim. Saṃh. I. 2. 3. 5. 8, III. 48. 16 = Kauth. Saṃh. I. 359, II. 600), he split open the hole (where the cows were penned up); (with its verse) 'Thou, o stone-thrower, hast opened the entrance of the cow-containing hole' (Jaim. s. III. 48. 17 = Kauth. s. II. 601), he opened

the hole. Thereupon, the cattle came forth. Those that came forth as the first, are the cattle of nowadays, but after (these) came up golden-horned and double-uddered (cows) and after these came up two Nymphs clad in golden petticoats. On these (last) the Householder set his mind. He said: 'To me belong these two (women), that have been acquired by me under my householdership; to the Householder falls all success.' 'No' said Sanaka and Navaka, 'thou hast performed the sacrificial session, wishing for cattle, to thee belong these cows, but we (have performed the sacrifice), wishing for women, of us two these two are the wives.' As they were still disputing, he (Medhātithi) seized upon one of the two (Nymphs). She repelled him. She became that female (animal) that has what resembles a dewlap (?). The other one was startled. She (became) that little female she-gazelle. Thereupon, these two . . . But these gold-horned double-uddered cows ran away and disappeared in the direction whence they had come up, (thinking:) 'Falsely has the Householder acted, we do not belong to him who acts falsely.' These are even now in the land of Vibhinduka known as those bloody bulls changed into *śāris*.'

12. The Brahman's chant[1] is the abhīvarta(-sāman)[2]; it has one syllable as nidhana[3], for getting a firm support[4].

[1] The sāman on which the third pṛṣṭha-laud, corresponding to the śastra of the Brahman (the Brāhmaṇācchaṃsin) is chanted.

[2] Grām. VI. 1. 34, composed on SV. I. 236, chanted on SV. II. 712-713; see SV. ed. Calcutta, vol. I, page 486.

[3] *hā* 2345 *i*. (3 over hā; 1111 over 2345)

[4] See the next §.

13. 'Voice' ('word') is monosyllabic; having found a firm support in the 'Voice', they finish the sacrificial session[1].

[1] Cp. Jaim. br. III. 293: 'It has one syllable as nidhana; monosyllabic is Voice (*vāk*). The world of heaven is, as it were, a steep bank (to climb) from here (from the earth), for, at this moment, the tenth day is this world of heaven (to which they climb upwards, as it were); as to its having one syllable as nidhana, it is as if he nailed down a strong pole, in order not to fall down.'

14. The Acchāvāka's chant[1] is the kāleya(-sāman)[2].

[1] The chant for the fourth pṛṣṭha-laud, corresponding to the śastra of the Acchāvāka.

[2] Grām. VI. 2. 7, composed on SV. I. 237, chanted on SV. II 37-38; it is *aiḍam*, see SV. ed. Calcutta, vol. I, pages 491-492. On the kāleya, see VIII. 3.

15. Of like places are the kāleya and the rathantara[1]; the rathantara is the earth, the kāleya is the cattle. Having gained a

firm support on the earth and in (the possession of) cattle, they finish the sacrificial session.—The stoma (has been given)[2].

1 Because, according to Sāyaṇa, wherever the rathantara is the first pṛṣṭhastotra, the kāleya is used as fourth.

2 See XV. 7. 8

XV. 11.

(The ārbhava-pavamāna-laud of the tenth day.)

1. (The verse beginning:) 'By the most sweet, the most intoxicating,'[1] is the gāyatrī-(verse). Intoxicating, rich in sap is the afternoon-service; he (thereby) puts (in it) intoxication and sap[2].

1 See note 1 on VIII. 4. 5 (SV. I. 468 = II. 39-41).

2 The second half of this § occurs many times, see XI. 10. 2.

2. There is the gāyatra(-sāman). The brāhmaṇa of the gāyatra is the same[1].

1 See VII. 1. 1 sqq.

3. There is the saṃhita(-sāman) with a nidhana of two syllables[1], for obtaining a firm support. Having got a firm support, they finish the sacrificial session.

1 Grām. XII. 2. 22, composed on SV. I. 468, chanted on SV. II. 39-41; its nidhana is (see SV. ed. Calcutta, Vol. II, page 10) *sū234ṭāh* (with 5 above): cp. XI. 5. 4.

4. There is the sapha(-sāman)[1].

1 Cp. VIII. 5. 60; cp. note 1 on VIII. 5. 1. As no other verses are prescribed, it must be chanted on the same.

5. By means of the sapha(-sāman), the Gods reached these worlds. Because they reached (*samāp-nuvan*) (them), therefore, this sāman is called *sapha*[1]. Having reached these worlds by means of this (sāman), they finish the sacrificial session.

1 A fanciful and impossible etymological connection!

6. There is the rohitakūlīya(-sāman)[1]. The brāhmaṇa of the rohitakūlīya is the same[2].

[1] Grām. IV. 1. 1, composed on SV. I. 129, chanted on SV. II. 44–46. The first of the two (cp. SV. ed. Calcutta, Vol. I, page 314) is intended, being *nidhanavat*.

[2] See XIV. 3. 12–13.

7. There are the śyāvāśva-[1] and the āndhīgava(-sāmans)[2]. 'He (in chanting them) joins together two virājs,[3] for (obtaining) food.

[1] Grām XVI. 1. 11, composed on SV. I. 545, chanted on SV. II. 714–716.

[2] Grām. XVI. 1. 12, composed and chanted on the same verses. The first is *svāram*, the second *aiḍam*, cp. SV. ed. Calcutta, Vol. II, page 152.

[3] The verse-quarter virāj and the syllabic virāj, cp. VIII. 5. 7.

8. They laud with them (*i.e.*, they chant them) on pippīlaka-madhya(-verse)s[1].

[1] These verses are anuṣṭubhs (of 32 syllables), that have the middle of an ant, *i.e.*, verses of which the middle verse-quarter (*pada*) is smaller than the first and the third: of 12+8+12 syllables. They are, as indicated by their beginning words in the Jaim. br. (III. 295): SV. I. 428=ṚS. VIII. 110. 1, 3, 2=SV. II. 714, 715, 716.

9. Indra, having slain Vṛtra and thinking that he had not killed him, went to the farthest distance. He pushed asunder the anuṣṭubh and crept away into its middle part. This, forsooth, is Indra's dwelling[1]. In safety does he offer sacrifice, in safety does he finish the sacrificial session, who, knowing this, chants on these verses[2].

[1] As the good Leyden MS. presents the reading, *indragṛho* instead of *indragṛhe*, I defend this reading, although Oertel (The disjunct use of cases, page 211) polemizes against my emendation and Sāyana interprets *indragṛhe*. The sentences are: *indragṛho vā eṣo*; *'bhaye yajate, 'bhaya uttiṣṭhati ya evaṃ vidvān etāsu stute*. Sentences of this kind require no *eṣa* at the beginning, cp. XV. 4. 8: *vindate paśūn . . . ya evaṃ vidvān samantena stute* (cp. X. 1. 8). Another argument in favour of my emendation is procured by the Jaim. br., see note 2.

[2] Cp. Jaim. br. III. 296: 'Indra, having thrown his thunderbolt on Vṛtra, went to the farthest distance, thinking that he had not killed him. The farthest distance is the anuṣṭubh (thus also Ait. br. III. 15. 1). Into it he entered. Twelve of its syllables he pushed forwards and twelve onward; what were the eight syllables in the middle: the gāyatrī, in that he entered (an ordinary anuṣṭubh consists of 4×8 syllables) . . . These verses are Indra's dwelling (*indragṛho vā etā ṛcaḥ*). They, thereby, after having entered into Indra's dwelling, finish the sacrificial session.'

10. There is the sauhaviṣa(-sāman) with the nidhana of the yajñāyajñīya[1]. Thereby, they do not depart at the afternoon-service from the yajñāyajñīya[2].

[1] Grām. XI. 2. 15, composed on SV. I. 427, chanted on SV II. 717-719: the last of the three sauhaviṣa-sāmans is intended (see SV. ed. Calcutta, Vol. I, page 870) with *vā*, (*i.e.*, *vāk*) as nidhana.

[2] As a rule, the yajñāyajñīya is the agniṣṭomasāman, but on this tenth day it is not (cp. XV. 12. 1). The Jaim. br. (III. 297) remarks: 'They depart from the afternoon-service (they do not regard its rules), who transfer the yajñāyajñīya to the midday-service (and, therefore, it is not advisable to transfer the yajñāyajñīya, which as agniṣṭomasāman on this day is replaced by another chant, to the midday-service). But, by applying the chant with the word *vā(k)* as nidhana, they do not depart from the characteristic mark of the yajñāyajñīya (which has the same nidhana)'.

11. There is the vājajit(-sāman)[1].

[1] Grām. XVI. 2. 5, composed on SV. I. 554, chanted on SV. II. 720-722. That this sāman is required (cp. SV. ed. Calcutta, Vol. II, page 172) appears from § 13.

12. (It is applied) in order to reach the whole, in order to win the whole; for they who undertake the (rite of the) tenth day, win all vigour (*vāja*); vigour is food[1]: in order to obtain food.

[1] Cp. Jaim. br. III. 298: '*vāja* is food, for when cow, horse, or man are well satiated, they become vigorous' (*vājin*).

13. They undertake, (*i.e.*, chant) a nidhana of ten syllables[1], for supporting the ten-day rite, (and, moreover,) the virāj has ten syllables, food is virāj-like: for retaining food.

2r1r 2r1r 2r 1 'r ∧ 3 1111
[1] *vājijigīvā viśvā dhanā 2 nī 2345.*

14. They laud, (*i.e.*, they chant the vājajit-sāman) on (verses) containing (the word) 'sun' (*sūrya*)[1]; the sun (*sūra*) is the end (of the visible creation) and this tenth day is the end of the (ten) days; on the end (the tenth day) they, thereby, laud with the end (the sun): for gaining a firm support.

[1] SV. II. 720, 721, 722=ṚS. IX. 69. 6, 2, 4. In the Jaim. br., these three verses are cited, so that there can be no uncertainty as to which *sūryavatya ṛcaḥ* are meant.

15. They contain (the word) 'near to' (*upa*)[1], for getting a firm support; they contain (the word) 'around' (*pari*)[2], for reaching (*paryāpti*) the whole.

[1] In vs. 720. a.

[2] In vs. 720. c and 721. d.

16. The stoma is the twenty-four versed one, for (obtaining) strength (and) priestly lustre[1].

[1] The same as XV. 7. 8.

XV. 12.

(The agniṣṭoma-laud of the tenth day.)

1. The vāmadevya(-sāman), chanted on virāj(-verse)s[1], is the agniṣṭoma-sāman, for pacifying[2] (and) making good order.

[1] Grām. V. 1. 25, composed on SV. I. 169 (see SV. ed. Calcutta, Vol. I, page 385), chanted on SV. II. 723–725=ṚS. VII. 1. 1-3 (var. rr). As to which virāj-verses are required, the Brāhmaṇa gives no indication, nor does the Jaim br., which only adds that they are addressed to Agni. See also Kauṣ. br. XXVII. 2: *virāṭsu vāmadevyam agniṣṭomasāma bhavati.*

[2] Cp. Jaim. br. III. 300: *stutaśastrayor ha khalu vā eṣa śāntir yad vāmadevyam; yad dha vai kiñca yajñasya mithyolbaṇaṃ kriyate tad etenaiva śamayitvottiṣṭhanti.*

2. The vāmadevya is the pith (*sat*) of the sāmans, the virāj of the metres, the twenty-four-fold stoma of the stomas. Having united the highest of piths, they finish the sacrificial session, and even his son's son reaches pith[1].

[1] With this § compare IV. 8. 10.

3. The Theologians say: 'Have ye risen from a going-on or from a still-standing session?' If they answered: 'from a going-on one', he would say about them (about the participants of the sattra): 'Devoid of firm support and of progeny they will be'. If they answered: 'from a still-standing one', he would say about them: 'Standing (not increasing) will be their fortune, they will not be better off'. They should say: 'From a full one unto a full one we have broken up (finished the sattra)'.

4. Those break up from a full one unto a full one, who, having lauded with the vāmadevya, break up[1].

[1] With § 3, 4 cp. IV. 8. 11–13.

5. The vāmadevya, forsooth, is the intermediate region; by the intermediate region (the atmosphere) all is full.

6. That stoma is full of success, which consists of thirty-three (verses in each laud); in the (verses) of thirty-three syllables[1]; in success they are firmly established.

[1] The virāj-verses, mentioned in § 1; cp. also IV. 8. 14.

7. The (verses) of three verse-quarters (*padas*) are characteristic of all the metres: inasmuch as they are of three verse-quarters, they are gāyatrīs; inasmuch as their verse-quarters are of eleven syllables, they are triṣṭubhs; inasmuch as there is a verse-quarter of twelve syllables[1], they are jagatīs; inasmuch as they are of thirty-three syllables, they are virājs. and also anuṣṭubhs, for one syllable does not make any difference with them[2].

[1] This refers, according to Sāyana, to the first *pada*: *agniṃ naro dīdhitibhir araṇyoḥ* (*i.e.*, *araṇiyoḥ* ?).

[2] *na hy ekasmād akṣarād virādhayanti*; cp. Kauṣ. br. XXVII. 1.: *samānaṃ vā etac chando yad virāṭ cānuṣṭup ca, na hy ekenākṣareṇānyac chando bhavati no dvābhyām iti*, Ait. br. I. 6. 2: *na vā ekenākṣareṇa chandāṃsi viyanti na dvābhyām.*

8. The stoma (of this last laud) is thirty-three-versed: in order to gain a firm support: amongst the deities[1] he gets a firm footing.

[1] Who are thirty-three in number, cp. IV. 8. 14.

SIXTEENTH CHAPTER.

(The ekāhas or one-day rites.)

These sacrifices are described in the four chapters XVI–XIX, cp. Jaim. br. II. 81–234; TBr. II. 7, and Kāṭh. XXXVIII. 1–9 give only the savas. In the sūtras belonging to the Sāmaveda they are described: Ārṣeyakalpa III–V; Lāṭy. VIII. 1–IX. 4; Nidānasūtra VI. 2–VII. 13. In the Bahvṛcasūtras: Āśv. IX. 1–X. 1. 10; Śāṅkh XIV, XV. In the sūtras belonging to the Yajurveda: Baudh. XVIII (and cp. XXII. 30–33); Āp. XXII. 1–13; Kāty. XXII. They occur also in the Mānava śrs., but this text has not been consulted.

XVI. 1.

(The Light-stoma: jyotiṣṭoma.)

1. Prajāpati was here at first (alone), neither day was there nor night. In this thick darkness he moved forward. He wished

(for light). He approached this (Light-stoma). Thereupon, it dawned for him. This (one-day rite) is brought near (is performed) as light. Because there was that light (*jyotis*), therefore, this (rite) is called Light-stoma (*jyotiṣṭoma*)[1].

1 Cp. VI. 3. 6.—This ekāha has been described elaborately in Chapters VI–VIII as *prakṛti* of all.

2. This is the foremost[1] of the sacrifices (of stoma). If one, not having performed this (sacrifice), performs any other (sacrifice), this is a falling into a pit[2]: he either loses his property or dies prematurely.

1 And it must be performed before all other sacrifices of soma, cp. Āp. X. 2. 3.

2 Cp. Kauṣ br. XVI. 9, which passage probably, in corrupted form, has been taken from our Brāhmaṇa. The translation of Keith I consider as inadmissible.

3. Just as here from the fire, when it has been produced (by friction), the other (sacrificial) fires are separately taken, so are from this (sacrifice) taken the other sacrifices[1].

1 The jyotiṣṭoma is the *prakṛti*, the norm of all the other sacrifices of soma.

4 For (and this likewise is a reason why this sacrifice is called the Light-stoma) the nine-versed (stoma), which approaches another sacrifice, burns it (by its light), and likewise do the fifteen-versed, the seventeen-versed and the twenty-one-versed (stomas)[1].

1 The stomas of this jyotis-ekāha are successively trivṛt, pañcadaśa, saptadaśa, and ekaviṃśa.

5. This is the reason why they (the Theologians) say: 'It is one single sacrifice', for all Light-stomas are t h i s[1].

1 The meaning seems to be that a trivṛt-day, a pañcadaśa-day, a saptadaśa-day, and an ekaviṃśa-day (as are successively the first four days of the daśarātra) may likewise be considered as jyotiṣṭomas.

6. This sacrifice is yoked not with one single (bullock or horse, but with two) and (properly) put together, for each of its services is conveyed by two stomas: the morning-service by the nine-versed and fifteen-versed stomas, the midday-service by the fifteen-versed and seventeen-versed, the afternoon-service by the seventeen-versed and twenty-one-versed stomas[1].

[1] Cp. TS. VII. 1. 1. 1. In the prātaḥsavana, the out-of-doors-laud is trivṛt and the four ājyastotras are pañcadaśa; in the mādhyandinasavana, the midday-pavamāna-stotra is pañcadaśa, and the four pṛṣṭhastotras are saptadaśa; in the tṛtīyasavana, the ārbhava-pavamāna-stotra is saptadaśa, the agniṣṭoma is ekaviṃśa.

7. This (rite) must be practised as one, at which a limited number of sacrificial fees (*i.e.*, milch cows) are given. The Light (-stoma) is the earth[1] and the earth is supporting unlimited (goods); this limited fee is able to support this (rite).

[1] Cp. Ait br IV. 15. 1, where the jyotis-, go- and āyus-stoma-days are successively identified with earth, intermediate region, and sky. By this reasoning the sacrifice, although of limited dakṣiṇā (cp. § 11) yields idealiter unlimited result.—Read probably with the Leyden MS. *yā mitadakṣineva.*

8. This (rite) comprises one hundred and ninety stotrīya-(verse)s[1]. Of these the one hundred and eighty are six thirty-syllabic virājs; there are six seasons: through the virāj he[2] is firmly established in the seasons.

[1] Cp. note 1 on VI. 3. 6.

[2] The Sacrificer.

9. The (remaining) ten (verses) are the virāj which refers to the person himself[1]; in this virāj (*i.e.*, in these vital airs) man is here (on earth, during his life-time) firmly established.

[1] Its ten *prāṇas*, see note 1 on II. 7. 8.

10. Cow, horse, mule, ass, goat, sheep, rice, barley, sesamum, and beans, in the (possession of) this virāj (in this number of ten) he becomes firmly established.

11. At this (rite), the sacrificial fee consists of one hundred and twelve (milch cows)[1].

[1] Cp. C. H. § 2 note 3.

12. A man-slayer of the Gods is he who presses out the soma: by the hundred (cows) he propitiates the hatred, the Gods[1]; by the (next following) ten—there being ten vital airs—he extricates (from them) his vital principles (his *prāṇas*), by the (next following) one (the eleventh), himself (or: his body, his trunk), the twelfth (or last) is the sacrificial fee.

[1] Cp. TS. I. 5. 2. 1: *devān eva viraṃ niravadāya.* Our passage is cited (with *niravadayate*), but not *verbatim*, in the Karmāntasūtra of Baudh. (XXV. 4: 232. 3).

13. The dakṣiṇās are the internal fastenings of the sacrifice; a chariot devoid of fastenings is not able to convey. Even as by a (chariot) provided with fastenings one is sure to attain the reaching of a desired object, so he attains through this (sacrifice) provided with dakṣiṇās that which he desires.

14. The dakṣiṇās are the ornament of the sacrifice. In that he performs a sacrifice provided with dakṣiṇās, he brings beauty into it.

XVI. 2.

(The cow-stoma: goṣṭoma.)

1. Now the go(-ṣṭoma).

2. By means of the Cow(-stoma), the Gods drove the Asuras away from these worlds. He who knows this, drives his rival away from these worlds.

3. Because they, the Gods, pushed (*agovayan*) away[1] the Asuras from these worlds, thence its name 'Go'.

[1] Probably the verb *govayati*, which occurs only here, is expressly invented for the pun's sake.

4. He who knows this, pushes away his evil rival.

5. Its out-of-doors-laud is fifteen-versed; the fifteen-versed (stoma) is a thunderbolt[1]; so he puts in front (of it) a thunderbolt and, thereby, vanquishes (his rival).

[1] See II. 4. 2, note 3.

6. This is a stoma (fit) for (obtaining) cattle, for the cow is composed in the same manner: the head is larger, the neck is smaller, at the sides it is broader, at the thighs it is thickest.

7. In that the out-of-doors-laud is fifteen-versed, the ājya(-laud)s are nine-versed, the midday-service is seventeen-versed, and the third service is twenty-one-versed, he provides this (rite) successfully with its characteristic features[1].

[1] The stomas, then, are: 15, 9, 9, 9, 9 | 17, 17, 17, 17, 17 | 21, 21, 21, 21, 21; this agrees with the cow's body.

8. Of all the (verses) taken together, one surpasses the virāj; therefore, behind the cow there is a surplus (the tail)[1].

[1] This proves that the Goṣṭoma is taken as an ukthya, for the total number of verses (see note 1 on § 7) is 241. This number is divisible by ten (the virāj) and one is left over. According to the Ārṣeyakalpa (III. 1. b) it may also be performed as agniṣṭoma.

XVI. 3.

(The Life-stoma: āyuṣṭoma.)

1. Now the āyu(-ṣṭoma)

2. By means of the Life(-stoma), the gods took possession (*āyuvata*) of the Asuras. He who knows this takes possession of his rival (brings his rival into his power).

3. One who desires to reach heaven, should sacrifice with it[1].

[1] See next §.

4. The chants go upward[1]: to prevent a falling down.

[1] They are increasing: 9, 15, 15, 15, 15 | 17, 17, 17, 17, 17 | 21, 21, 21, 21, 21.

5. This (same rite) he may perform for one who is suffering from a lingering disease. (In this case), it is to be performed as an over-night-rite.

6. This (ekāha) amounts to the gāyatrī[1]; the gāyatrī is breath[2], and this (rite) is 'life'; he brings into him life and breath, both together.

[1] The number of verses chanted amounts to gāyatrīs. The whole atirātra comprises 69 verses in the prātaḥsavana, 85 in the mādhyandinasavana, 105 in the tṛtīyasavana, 12×15=180 in the rātriparyāyas and 9 in the sandhistotra, together 448; the gāyatrī has 24 syllables; if we divide 448 by 24, the result is 28 gāyatrīs and two padas.

[2] Cp. note 1 on VII. 1. 9.

7. These (three) stomas (the Light-, Cow- and Life-stoma combined) are conducive to heaven: in that there is the Light(-stoma), he carries light before him; then the Cow(-stoma) which exceeds the virāj by one syllable[1]: that is the hold (the seizing, the approach); then the Life(-stoma), which has one syllable less than the virāj[2]: that is the seat (in heaven). But (these) two (lastly mentioned)

stomas, with their plus and minus forming a pair[3], are conducive also to generation.

[1] Cp. XVI. 2. 8.

[2] If the āyus is performed as ukthya, it comprises 259 verses, one less than a number divisible by ten.

[3] The *atirikta* (penis) is the sign of the male, the *ūna* (vulva) of the female.

8. These (three) stomas (together) are the trikadruka stomas; by them Indra became satisfied in every way.

9. He who knows this is satiated with progeny and cattle[1].

[1] In the Jaim. br. (II. 166 and II. 439) the three are considered as forming a trias. 'Then there are these stomas: the Light, the Cow, the Life. The 'Cow' copulated with the 'Life.' From this (union) the 'Light' was born. 'Life' is this world (the earth), the 'Cow' is yonder world (the sky), the 'Light' is the intermediate region. The two ('Cow' and 'Life') made this 'Light' go in front of them, as (parents do with) their son (and, therefore, the jyotis, although it is the middle one of the three, precedes). This world is upward from here, yonder world is hitherward from there, the 'light' is fixed in front of these two (? *tad idam enayoḥ purastāj jyotiḥ paryūḍham*), by means of it we see. As these two were undertaking a joining (*yogam upaprayantau*), they drew the 'light' to the end (*i.e.* out of their middle), just as the parents follow after their son who goes in front of them. These two stomas copulated, ... the child lies (sleeps) between husband and wife; it is now as when they, going to pair, put the child to the right or the left' (*tad etan mithunî stomā bhavanti yad vijyante* [vaṛ. *yad yuñjyante*] *madhye vai jāyāpatyoḥ putraḥ śete; tau yathā mithunîbhaviṣyantāv itthād vetthād vā putraṃ parihareyātāṃ tādṛk tat*). The passage indicates why the jyotiṣṭoma, which originated from these two, is put in front and comes as the first.

XVI. 4.

(Viśvajit and Abhijit[1].)

1. Prajāpati created the beings. These did not yield him the supremacy. Then he took away the pith of the quarters and of the beings and made (of it) a wreath and fastened it on himself. Thereupon, the beings yielded him the supremacy.

2. To him who knows this his equals yield the supremacy.

[1] Compare Jaim. br. II. 181-192, Lāṭy. VIII. 1. 19-2-, 13, Nidānasūtra VI. 4-6, Kauṣ. br. XXIV. 1-2, XXV. 11-15, Āp. XXII. 1. 6-15, Kāty. XXI. 1. 6-43.

3. He wished that amongst his progeny Indra might be the mightiest and fastened this wreath on him. Thereupon, the beings yielded the supremacy to Indra, as they saw (on him) that work of art that they had seen on their father.

4. Therefore, they look upon those of the sons, who enters upon a (father's) biggest inheritance, as upon one who will have success in the world.

5. Thereupon, Indra conquered all (*viśvam ajayat*), hence the name of this (rite): *viśvajit* ('conquering all').

6. He (Indra) wished: 'What I have not conquered, may I be able to conquer that also' (*abhi*). He saw this Abhijit(-rite) and by means of it conquered all the rest.

7. That there is the Abhijit, is for conquering that which one has not already conquered.

8. These two are Indra's mighty stomas; these stomas, forsooth, were the work of art by name[1].

[1] Cp. § 3, end.

9. He who knows this beholds in his house a work of art.

10. There are (otherwise) no twin-stomas. He who wishes to sacrifice with twin-stomas, should sacrifice with these two (together), for the sake of prosperity[1].

[1] How, in this case, the sacrifice must be effectuated, is explained by the Sūtrakāra (Lāṭy. VIII. 1. 19-26) as follows: 'He who sacrifices with the Viśvajit and the Abhijit as twin-stomas, should, according to Dhānañjayya, sacrifice them one after another; according to Śāṇḍilya, he should sacrifice them together. (In the latter case) the sacrificial ground for the Abhijit should be to the south, that for the Viśvajit to the north (of that for the Abhijit). Near (*i.e.* to the west of) this last ground should be the lady's hall (the *patniśālā* or *prācīnavaṃśā*-shed), one single for the two rites; there must be a different set of officiating priests for each, and different are the acts that take place inside the vedi, but the acts outside the vedi are the same (for both). Each sacrificial act should, firstly, be performed of the Abhijit and, thereupon (immediately afterwards), of the Viśvajit. Each of them requires separately a thousand head of cattle (as sacrificial fee)'.

11. The stomas are applied 'constantly returning'[1], for Indra

had conquered the unconquered by these two (rites), 'constantly returning'[1].

[1] This expression (cp. e.g. VI. 8. 13) is explained in the next following §.

12. Of the Abhijit, three (lauds) are led on by the three-fold (or nine-versed) (stoma), three by the fifteen-versed, three by the seventeen-versed, three by the twenty-one-versed[1]. These make together twelve; the year has twelve months. Prajāpati is the year. He reaches (he becomes equal to) Prajāpati.

[1] This is explained by Maśaka, in his Ārṣeyakalpa (II. 1, end): 'The stomas of this (ekāha), which contains all the stomas (cp. XVI. 5. 2), have three series and four 'leadings-on'. (Kaus. br. XXIV. 1: *sa tryāvṛc caturudayo bhavati*). The stomas, then, are:

9, 15, 17, | 15, 17; 21, | 17, 21, 27, | 21; 27, 33. Each stoma (9, 15, 17, 21) opens one of the series. Cp. also XX. 8. 1. a.

13. Of the Viśvajit, four (lauds) are led on by the three-fold (stoma), four by the fifteen-versed, four by the seventeen-versed[1]. These make together twelve; the year has twelve months. Prajāpati is the year. He reaches Prajāpati.

[1] The stomas, then, are:

9, 15, 17, 21, | 15; 17, 21, 27, | 17, 21: 27, 33. Cp. XX. 9. 1 and Ārṣeyakalpa II. 6 end. According to this same text (III. 1. d, e), these two ekāhas are atirātras, but this is not founded on the Brāhmaṇa, neither has it the Jaim. br.; this text, on the whole, seems to agree with the Pañc. br., as it runs: *tasya (sc. abhijitas) tryuttariṇaḥ stomā bhavanti; trayo vā ime lokā, eṣām lokānām abhijityai; caturāvṛto bhavanti, catasro diśo, diśām evābhijityai*, and: *tasya (sc. viśvajitaś) caturuttariṇaḥ stomā bhavanti*, etc. What follows is confused and incomplete.

XVI. 5.

(The Viśvajit; continued.)

1. (The verse beginning:) 'To thee have gone the sisterly praises'[1], which contains (the word) 'to' (*upa*), is the introductory (verse of the out-of-doors-laud): the characteristic feature of the stoma[2].

[1] SV. I. 13=ṚS. VIII. 102. 13=SV. II. 920; addressed to Vāyu.—It is striking that this verse is, in the Kauthuma recension of the SV., not recorded along with the verses (SV. II. 810 sqq.) destined for the Viśvajit, but later on (II. 920), whereas, in the Saṃhitā of the Jaiminīyas (who likewise begin this

stotra with the *upavatī*-verse) this verse is given as the first of those destined for the Viśvajit (*viz.* IV. 2. 3 4).

[2] According to Sāyana, because a verse with *upa* usually introduces the out-of-doors-laud, cp. VI. 9. 1.

2. 'He who gives away all (his possessions, as dakṣiṇās)', they say, 'and who practises all the stomas and all the pṛṣṭha(-sāman)s, loses his vital principles (his breaths, *prāṇas*)'. The use of the verse addressed to Vāyu (Wind)[1] is for establishing his vital principles.

[1] See note 1 on § 1.

3. The next following (verses) are, one addressed to Sarasvat[1] and one addressed to Sarasvatī[2].

[1] ṚS. VII. 96. 4 = SV. II. 810; instead of this verse the Jaim. have RS. VII. 96. 5.

[2] ṚS. VI. 61. 10 = SV. II. 811.

4. Sarasvat and Sarasvatī are a pair At the beginning of his sacrifice he brings about a pairing: for the sake of obtaining progeny.

5. A (verse) addressed to Savitṛ[1] is the fourth.

[1] ṚS. III. 62. 10 = SV. II. 812.

6. A difficult task is undertaken by him who gives away all (his property). By the verse addressed to Savitṛ he hopes that his (sacrificial) act may be impelled by Savitṛ His acts become impelled by Savitṛ.

7. A (verse) addressed to Brahmaṇaspati[1] is the fifth.

[1] ṚS. I. 18. 1 = SV. II. 813.

8. Brahmaṇaspati is the sacred Word; he puts in, at the beginning of his sacrifice, the sacred Word[1].

[1] Cp. Jaim. br. II. 186: 'The creatures that were created by Prajāpati, devoid of the sacred Word (*brahman*), these perished. He saw that introductory verse, addressed to Brahmanaspati, and by it he created the creatures provided with the sacred Word These did not perish. By the use of this verse, the young ones of the Sacrificer do not perish.'

9 A (verse) addressed to Agni pavamāna[1] is the sixth.

[1] ṚS. IX. 66. 19 = SV. 814: as the verse occurs in the Āranyaka-saṃhita (n°.43), the uttarārcika gives only its *pratīka*.

10. Agni purifies him by heat, Pavamāna cleanses him; purified

and cleansed and (therefore) fit for a sacrifice, he is brought near the pṛṣṭha(-sāman)s[1].

[1] At this rite, all the six pṛṣṭhasāmans (four of them at the pṛṣṭha-lauds) are applied.

11. 'They deviate from the (right) path,' they say, 'who apply (verses) brought together' (from different parts of the Veda, and not forming in the tradition a whole)[1].

[1] On *saṃbhārya* cp. note 1 on XI. 1. 5; at the end the text should be read with the Leyden ms. (and cp. XVIII. 8. 9): *kurvata iti.*

12. The last tristich is addressed to Pavamāna[1]. By it they do not go forth from the (right) path.

[1] ṚS. IX. 66. 10—12 = SV. II. 7–9, the usual last tristich of the out-of-doors-laud; Sāyana is wrong here, as is proved by the Ārṣeyakalpa and the Jaim br. II. 187: *pavamānasya te kava iti paryāso bhavaty, etat punaḥ panthānaṃ paryavayanti.*

13. 'He may be said to laud with the pṛṣṭha(-sāman)s, (even at the out-of-doors-laud)' they say, 'who should yoke them (bring them into action) at the out-of-doors-laud'[1].

[1] This is explained in §§ 14–19.

14. The introductory (verse) begins with (the word) 'to' (*upa*)[1], the rathantara is 'to'[2]; by this (verse) he yokes (prepares) for him the rathantara.

[1] See § 1.

[2] According to Sāyana, because the first day of the abhiplava saḍaha (a rathantara-day) begins equally with a verse beginning with *upa* (*upāsmai gāyatā naraḥ*, see Ārṣeyakalpa I. 2).

15. The (verse) addressed to Sarasvat is the second[1]. Sarasvat is the world of heaven[2], and the bṛhat is the world of heaven[3]; by this verse he yokes the bṛhat for him.

[1] See § 3.

[2] Sarasvat is identified in Maitr. S. I. 4. 15 with the full-moon and the full-moon-sacrifice is conducive to heaven (Sāyana).

[3] Cp. VII. 6. 17.

16. The (verse) addressed to Sarasvatī is the third[1]; Sarasvatī is the voice[2] and the vairūpa(-sāman) is the voice. By this verse he yokes the vairūpa for him.

[1] See § 3.

[2] Cp. VI. 7. 7.

17. The (verse) addressed to Savitṛ is the fourth[1]. Savitṛ is Prajāpati, the vairāja is Prajāpati. By this (verse) he yokes the vairāja for him[2].

[1] See § 5.

[2] Cp. *e.g.* Śat. br. XII. 3. 5. 1.

18. The (verse) addressed to Brahmaṇaspati is the fifth[1]. Brahmaṇaspati is the sacred Word, the śakvarī(-verse)s are the sacred Word. By this (verse) he yokes the śakvarī(-verses and the śākvara-sāman) for him.

[1] See § 7.

19. The (verse) addressed to Agni pavamāna is the sixth[1]. The revatī(-verse)s are the gāyatrī[2] and Agni has the gāyatrī as his metre. By this (verse) he yokes the revatī(-verse)s for him.

[1] See § 9.

[2] SV. II. 434-436, on which the raivata-sāman is chanted, are gāyatrī-verses.

20. Four do not suffice for six[1]; in that they are 'unexpressed', thereby they suffice.

[1] There are only f o u r pṛṣṭhastotras in each soma-rite and there are s i x pṛṣṭha-sāmans (rathantara, bṛhat, vairūpa, vairāja, śakvarīs and revatīs), two too many for these four stotras. But two of them (the rathantara and the bṛhat) are to be chanted n o t e x p r e s s l y as pṛṣṭhastotras: the first is incorporated into the midday-pavamāna-laud, and the last is taken for the agniṣṭoma-laud.

21. All the ājya(-laud)s are (at the end) circumflected[1]; this is a sameness of performance. They laud with verses addressed to various deities, for avoiding the sameness.

[1] As ending on $\overset{2}{\bar{a}}\,\overset{1}{3}\,\overset{1}{4}\,\overset{1}{5}$, which also is considered as *svāra*; see Simon, Puṣpasūtra, page 525, *in voce: svāra*, 2.—For the rest, the observation holds for all the ājyas of each soma-rite!

22. The *āprī*(-verse)s (beginning:) 'Well kindled, lead thou hither for us', are (the verses on which) the ājya(-laud)s (are chanted)[1].

[1] This § is identical with XV. 8. 1, see the notes there. The verses which serve for the last three ājyas are not mentioned, neither here nor in the Jaim. br.

23. Prajāpati created the creatures He thought himself milked out (and) emptied out; he saw these *āprī*(-verse)s as ājya(-laud)s and, by means of them, he gratified himself. Milked out, as it were, (and) emptied out is he, who gives away all (his possessions). In that the *āprī*(-verse)s are the ājya(-laud)s he, thereby, gratifies himself [1].

[1] Nearly the same as XV. 8. 2.

24. 'T h e r e b y occur the pṛṣṭha(-sāman)s at their proper place', they say, 'that first comes the rathantara, last the bṛhat, and in the middle the others' [1].

[1] Cp. note 1 on § 20 and Ārṣeyakalpa II. 6.

25 'A sameness of performance is brought about in the sacrifice', they say, 'if all the chants that have a finale are performed together, (*i.e.* one after another without interruption)'. This sameness is removed by the facts that between (each of these lauds) the soma (-draught)s come on (*i.e.* are brought forward for their offering into the fire), that the recitation (by one of the Hotṛ-priests) takes place, and that they make *vaṣaṭ* (*i.e.* that, after the *vaṣaṭ* has been uttered by the Hotṛ-priest, the Adhvaryu pours a quantity of the soma-draught into the fire).

26 They say the *iḍās* and the *nidhanas*, each time transposing them [1]. Thereby (likewise) the sameness is removed.

[1] 'They say' must mean 'they apply'. The meaning is that the pṛṣṭha-sāmans are not applied in their regular order (see note 1 on § 20), but that they are somewhat transposed, so that the four pṛṣṭha-lauds are chanted on: vairāja, śakvarī-verses, vairūpa and revatī-verses. The corresponding passage of the Jaim. br. (II. 189) runs: *tad āhur: yat samānanidhanāni pṛṣṭhāni kenājāmi kriyata iti vairājaṃ ca mahānāmnyaś ca vairūpaṃ ca revatyaś caitenākhyānenājāmīty; atho vai tani madhyenidhanāni bhavanti, teno eveti.*

27. 'The revatī(-verse)s (*i.e.* the chant performed on them) swerve, thereby, from their proper place', they say, 'in that they deviate from the thirty-three-versed stoma' [1]. In that there are gāyatrī(verse)s, they do not deviate, for each gāyatrī whatsoever is a revatī-verse.

[1] The chant on the revatī-verses belongs (see XIII. 10. 4) to the sixth day of the ten-day-period, which day is *trayastriṃśa* The revatī-verses are gāyatrīs

(SV. II. 434-436). The whole reasoning, especially the sense of the last words, is not clear to me.

XVI. 6.

(The Viśvajit; concluded.)

1. 'He who gives away all (his property)', they say, 'suffers a loss in regard to his cattle'[1]. He puts on (as upper garment) a hide[2]; he is not separated from cattle.

[1] At the Viśvajit are given, as sacrificial fee, all the possessions, with the exception of the ground and the inhabitants (the slaves), so Āp. and Kāty. According to the Jaim. br. (II. 192), he gives either a thousand head of cattle, for that amounts to 'all' (cp. Kauṣ. br. XV. 14, end), or as many cows as there are stotra-verses in the Viśvajit, or all his property. If he retained anything this will be his evil lot.

[2] This and the following curious prescriptions prevail for the twelve days which follow immediately after the Viśvajit. They serve to remove the bad consequences of giving away all the property. For the Jaiminīyas, see Jaim. br. in Auswahl, no. 144.

2. The hide is red, for this is the colour most common to cattle (cows). In that it is red, he obtains (cattle) in bodily form.

3. During three nights (and days) he dwells in the forest; by these he obtains the food of the forest.

4. He dwells (during this period) under a fig-tree; the fig-tree is food; food he thereby retains for himself[1].

[1] Cp. V. 5. 2.

5. He lives (by digging up the eatable roots) by means of a shovel; he (thereby) averts the absence of means of subsistence.

6. It is a spade sharp on the two sides; it (thereby) digs out for him the food on both sides: in this world and in yonder world.

7. The (next following) three days he dwells amongst Niṣādas[1]; these, forsooth, are handed over to the earth[2]. He (thereby) obtains the food (that is found) on the earth.

[1] According to Lāṭy. VIII. 2. 8-9, near a hamlet of Niṣādas, of whom he may consume the wild eatables such as wild rice, panicum frumentaceum and venison.

[2] This means probably that they solely subsist by the earth (by digging roots, etc.).

8. Amongst a foreign people [1] he dwells (the) three (next) days. By these he obtains the food of the foreign people[1].

[1] For this meaning cp. *e.g.* Ṣaḍv. br. I. 7. 3, Maitr. Saṃh. I. 4. 9 : 57. 4. The ancient interpreters were at variance regarding the meaning of *jana*, Lāṭy. VIII. 2. 10–12. The meaning of Śāṇḍilyāyana : *prativeśo janapadaḥ* seems to be the most acceptable.

9. Amongst his own people (he dwells the) three (last days of the twelve-day period). By these he obtains the food of his own people.

10. These make twelve days. The year is (equal to) twelve months, in the course of a year the food (the rice, barley, etc.) grows. Having reached this (food), he obtains it.

11. During a year (after the performance of the Viśvajit) he should not ask (any food). If one eats given (food) on the same day, this is (equal to eating) raw food. The year (of man), forsooth, is for the Gods 'to day' [1].

[1] As the day is equal to a year of the Gods, he should this year (=these twelve days) not eat any begged food, which is raw food, because it is not immediately cooked or has not ripened. Sāyaṇa cites TBr. III. 9. 22. 1 : 'The year (of man) is one single day of the Gods'.

12. But he should not decline (any food) that (voluntarily) is offered to him, for not declining (in future) the food.

13. He wears a turban, for not being deprived (in future) of objects of art.

14. He should not drink out of an earthenware vessel. The mouth of a Brāhmin is an offering (to the Gods)[1], but the earthenware vessel is not up to an offering[2]. By not drinking out of an earthenware (but out of a wooden) vessel, he offers into his own mouth an offering.

[1] Because in his mouth the soma, drunk by him, is, so to say, offered.

[2] Because the sacrificial ladles are made of wood

XVI. 7.

(The Sarvajit.)

1. A twenty-four-versed agniṣṭoma (is the next one-day-rite)[1].

[1] This ekāha, the Sarvajit (see § 2) is in the Brāhmaṇas only recorded here; of the Sūtras only Āp., Hir. and Kāty., who draw regularly upon our Brāhmaṇa, mention it.

2. By means of the Sarvajit, the Gods conquered (*ajayan*) all (*sarvam*); (it serves) for attaining all, for conquering all. Through this (rite) he attains all, he conquers all.

3. Its (first) pṛṣṭha(-laud) is the mahāvrata(-laud)[1].

[1] As described V. 1. 1—2. 9.

4. The arkya-śastra[1] is recited (by the Hotṛ immediately afterwards).

[1] *i.e.* the *mahaduktham*, consisting of a thousand bṛhatī-verses, see Ait. ār. II. 35 sqq. The verses are all given by Friedlander: Der Mahāvrata-Abschnitt des Śāṅkh. Ār., page 75 sqq.

5. There are twenty-four half-months in the year; the year is number twenty-five[1]. The vrata[2] is food; out of the year he by this (rite) obtains food.

[1] And, therefore, it is a twenty-five-versed stoma.

[2] Probably, we have here a pun on the word *vrata*, which is used here (1) as meaning the mahāvratastotra and (2) as the *vrata*-milk drunk by the Sacrificer at a sacrifice of soma.

6. He who knows this becomes an eater of food.

7. By means of this (rite), Go, of the Angiras clan, got over all evil. He who has applied in chanting this stoma, gets over all evil.

XVI. 8[1].

(First Sāhasra-ekāha.)

1. Now that Light(-stoma) (at which a thousand cows are given as dakṣiṇā).

2. Thitherward directed[1] is the three-day rite, hitherward directed[1] is the agniṣṭoma. If one goes amiss at a three-day rite, there is no 'again' in this, but, at an agniṣṭoma, there is a (religious act) to atone for this[2]; for he may sacrifice again with this (same agniṣṭoma), at which he (now) gives twenty-one dakṣiṇās. In whichever sacrifice he goes amiss, this is the atonement therefor.

---

[1] In Khandas 8-11 are described the four Sāhasra-ekāhas, which are peculiar to our Brāhmaṇa; only Āp. and Kāty. mention them.

1 This must mean: 'admitting of no return (no repetition)' and 'admitting of return'; cp. XX. 16. 6.

2 Probably to this refers Kṣudrasūtra II. 3 (no. 55–57).

3. At the upasad(-day)[1] (of this one-day rite) he (*viz.* the Hotṛ) recites as morning litany a thousand (verses); this (thousand) is yonder world. (There are) a thousand dakṣiṇās; this (thousand) is the intermediate region. (There are) those thousand syllables[2]; this (thousand) is this world (the earth). He who knows this, is firmly supported in these worlds.

1 This seems to be irregular, as the *prātaranuvāka* is recited not on the (last) upasad-day, but on the day itself of the sacrifice of soma (*sutye 'hani*).

2 From § 5, we infer that this has regard to the brāhmaṇācchaṃsinaḥ stotra.

4. 'Based on verses is one Sāhasra (a sacrifice of a thousand dakṣiṇās)', they say, 'based on syllables is another'. What is given at a three-day rite[1], is based on verses[2], but what is given at an agniṣṭoma, that is based on syllables[3].

1 At the Garga-three-day-rite (XX. 1. 4) are given a thousand cows as dakṣiṇā.

2 Because this trirātra has 1000 verses.

3 See § 5.

5. (The fact) that the Brahman's chant (*i.e.* the third pṛṣṭha-laud, which corresponds to the śastra of the Brahman, *i.e.* the Brāhmaṇācchaṃsin) is on a thousand syllables[1], is in accordance with the thousand dakṣiṇās.

1 The third pṛṣṭha-laud, the śyaita-sāman, is based on the pankti-verses SV. II. 355–357. Each pankti has 40 syllables, and as the stoma of this stotra is the twenty-five-versed one, this makes for each verse a 1000 syllables.

6. 'The world of heaven is as far removed from this (earthly) world' they say, 'as a thousand cows standing the one above the other'[1]. Therefore, they say: 'He who sacrifices with a sacrifice at which a thousand dakṣiṇās are given, reaches[2] these worlds.

1 This must be the meaning of *uttarādhara*, cp. XXI. 1. 9.

2 The parallel passage (l.c.) has *vyāpnoti*.

7. 'He suffers a loss in regard to his cattle', they say, 'who on one and the same day gives a thousand (cows as dakṣiṇās)'. The

Brahman's chant is (based) on paṅkti-verses; the sacrifice is five-fold [1], cattle in five-fold [2]. He is firmly established in sacrifice, in cattle.

[1] Cp. note 1 on VI. 7. 12.

[2] Cp. note 2 on II. 4. 2.

8. It (this rite) amounts to a nine-fold (nine-versed) stoma, to the virāj-metre [1].

[1] All in all, this ekāha (see Ārṣeyakalpa III. 2, end) comprises 190 stotra-verses, which are equal to twenty trivṛts (20×9=180), whilst the remaining ten syllables (cp. III. 13. 3) represent the virāj.

9. The nine-fold stoma is breath [1], the virāj is food [2]. Breath (alone) without food [3] does not preserve (any being), nor food (alone) without breath. He becomes firmly established in the vital principles (the breaths) and in food.

[1] Cp. note 1 on VI. 2. 2.

[2] Cp. IV. 8. 4.

[3] Read, with the Leyden ms., *na vai* instead of *na vaiva*.

XVI. 9.

(Second Sāhasra-ekāha.)

1. Now that 'All-light(-stoma)' (at which a thousand cows are given as dakṣiṇā). It is the obtaining of all, the gaining of all. By this (rite) he obtains all, he gains all.

2. This is the highest sacrifice: the thousand is the highest (number). He who knows this comes to the highest end.

3. It has two hundred stotra(-verses) [1]; two hundred is the highest goal of the Word and a thousand is the highest goal. So he establishes the highest goal into the highest goal.

[1] It consists of the following stomas: 9, 15, 15, 15, 15 | 17, 17, 17, 17, 25 | 17, 21, together 200 verses.

4. It is a winning-stoma [1]. By it he reaches all, he wins all, for by the *kṛta* [1] all is won.

[1] We here must think (different but far from convincing is Sāyana's explication) of the *kṛta* in playing with dice (with the nuts of the vibhīdaka), of which the number four is characteristic (200 being divisible by four).

5. It (this rite) amounts to a virāj[1]; the virāj is food, he retains food.

[1] The number 200 being divisable by 10.

6. Its agniṣṭoma(-laud) is twenty-one-versed. The twenty-one-versed (stoma) is a firm support[1]; at the end of the sacrifice he is firmly supported.

[1] Cp. note 1 on III. 7. 2.

XVI. 10.

(Third Sāhasra-ekāha.)

1. Now that (third ekāha of a thousand dakṣiṇās, called) 'All-light' (*viśvajyotis*), an ukthya-rite.

2. The uktha(-laud)s are cattle[1], and cattle is (for its possessor) an 'all-light' (a means of getting great dignity). He (thereby) is firmly established in 'all-light', in cattle.

[1] Cp. note 1 on IV. 5. 18.

3. By its days, the three-day rite reaches these (three) worlds, by its services (savanas), (this ekāha reaches the three worlds); of the three-day rite each following day is larger (than the preceding one), and of this (ekāha) each following service is larger (than the preceding one)[1]. Thereby, he reaches the three-day rite. Of these worlds (earth, intermediate region, sky) each subsequent one is larger (than the former)[2]. Thereby, he reaches these worlds.

[1] The Gargatrirātra (XX. 14) comprises: 1. agniṣṭoma, 2. ukthya, 3. atirātra. This Viśvajyotis-ekāha has 69 verses in the morning service, 93 in the midday-service, and 108 in the afternoon-service.

[2] The same view is found elsewhere, below XVIII. 2. 7, cp. TS. II. 4. 11. 5: *uttara uttaro jyāyān bhavaty, evam iva hīme lokāḥ.*

4, 5. This sacrifice is yoked not with one (bullock, but with two) and (properly) put together, for each of its services is conveyed by two stomas, the morning-service by the nine-versed one and the fifteen-versed one, the midday-service by the seventeen-versed and the twenty-five-versed, the afternoon-service by the twenty-four-versed and the twenty-one-versed[1].

[1] Cp. XVI. 1. 6.—The schema is: 9, 15, 15, 15, 15 | 17, 25, 17, 17, 25 | 24, 21, 21, 21, 21, cp. Ārṣeyakalpa III. 3. b, end.

6. What is put on a (cart) that is yoked (and properly) put together, that (load) it (the cart) carries. As if one were to put (a load) on a (cart), which is yoked (and properly) put together, so this (number of) thousand (dakṣiṇās) is put on this (sacrifice).

7. There are both: the rathantara and the bṛhat.

8. The rathantara is the earth, the bṛhat is the sky. From this (the earthly) world he obtains, by lauding[1] (the rathantara), from yonder world (the bṛhat). He gets a firm support in both these worlds.

[1] *āgāyati* 'ersingen, herbeisingen'.

9. On the anuṣṭubh(-part of the ārbhava-pavamāna-laud)[1] the ātharvaṇa(-sāman)[2] is (chanted).

[1] Cp. Einleitung on Ārṣeyakalpa, page XXIV.

[2] Araṇyogeyagāna I. a. 23, composed on SV. I. 33 (see SV. ed. Calcutta, Vol. II, page 400), chanted on SV. II 47–49 (see SV. ed. Calcutta, Vol. V, page 457: ūhyagāna III. 1. 1).

10. The Atharvans[1] are the medicine of the Gods, (it serves) for medicine, for being unhurt.

[1] The Atharvans are those mantras of the Atharvasaṃhitā which deal with white magic; cp. note 1 on XII. 9. 10.

11. The udvaṁśīya(-sāman)[1] is the last of the uktha(-laud)s. This (sāman) is the form of all the pṛṣṭha(-sāmans)[2]. In all forms (of cattle) he is firmly established.

[1] See note 1 on VIII. 9. 6.

[2] See l. c. 9, sqq.

12. It is an ukthya(-rite); the uktha(-laud)s are the cattle[1] and the thousand (dakṣiṇās) are cattle. He, thereby, puts cattle into his cattle (so that this will increase).

[1] Cp. note 1 on IV. 5. 18.

XVI. 11.

(Fourth Sāhasra-ekāha.)

1. He who knows the three-day-rite, as fixed on the agniṣṭoma, should give at an agniṣṭoma a thousand (cows as sacrificial fee), for the thousand has its proper place at the three-day-rite[1].

[1] At the Gargatrirātra, XX. 14.

2. The opening(-verses) (of the out-of-doors-laud) are: 'Sing ye, O men, unto him', 'unto the born active'; 'be clarified as the foremost of speech'.[1] Thereby, he has brought about the three-day-rite.

[1] ṚS. IX. 11. 13=SV. II. 1; ṚS. IX. 61. 13=SV. II. 685; ṚS. IX 62. 25=SV. II. 125. With these verses begins successively each of the three days of the Gargatrirātra, cp. Ārṣeyakalpa VI. 3-5.

3. At the (midday-)pavamāna(-laud) he applies the rathantara, and the vāmadevya as the last of (this) pavamāna(-laud); the bṛhat (he applies) as (first) pṛṣṭha(-laud).

4. The rathantara is this (earthly) world, the vāmadevya is the intermediate region, the bṛhat is the sky. The three-day-rite represents these three worlds. In that he unites these (three) sāmans (on one single day), he joins these worlds and, thereby, reaches the three-day-rite[1].

[1] Of which the 1st pṛṣṭhalaud of the 1st day is the rathantara, of the 2nd day the vāmadevya, of the 3rd day the bṛhat.

5. The kakubh(-verse and the sāmans chanted on it) he shifts to the fore-part[1].

[1] The verses *pavasva madhumattamah* (SV. II. 42-43), the first of which is a kakubh, which has its normal place at the ārbhava-pavamāna-laud (see Arṣeyakalpa, Einleitung, page XXIV), are here shifted to the fore-part, they are applied at the midday-pavamāna, see Ārṣeyakalpa III. 4.

6. For by this (kakubh), when it is shifted to the fore-part, he brings virility into his cattle[1].

[1] The interpretation is uncertain. The printed text has: *puro hy etayā satyā apaśuvīryam karoti*, with an unheard of, neglected sandhi; although Sāyaṇa explains *apaśuḥ: paśurahitaḥ* (pointing to *apaśur vīryam*) *somayāgaḥ*, the reading of the Leyden MS. *puro hy etayā satyā paśuvīryam* must be right. The reason why, by doing so, he *paśuvīryam karoti*, escapes me, but, perhaps VIII. 5. 2 may be compared. Would it be possible to read *paśur vīryaṃ karoti*? Cp. note 1 on VIII. 7. 11.

7. On this (kakubh-verse) the *iḍānāṁ saṃkṣāra*[1] (is chanted). The kakubh is man[2], the *iḍānāṁ saṃkṣāra* is cattle[3]; he, thereby, maintains the cattle in himself.

[1] See note 1 on XV. 3. 14.

[2] See note 1 on VIII. 10. 6.

[3] Because the name of the sāman contains the word *iḍā*, one of the designations for 'cow.'

8. (The verses beginning:) 'The ancient milk of former times,'[1] are satobṛhatī(-verse)s.

[1] ṚS IX. 110. 8, 6, 9=SV. II. 844-846 (var. rr.). The sāmans on these verses follow, according to Ārṣeyakalpa, immediately after the kakubh-part in the midday-pavamāna.

9. By means of the satobṛhatī, the Gods reached successively these worlds (and lastly the world of heaven). By these (verses), he reaches successively these worlds.

10. These (verses) are gāyatrīs in that they are of three verse-quarters; they are jagatīs in that their verse-quarters are of twelve syllables; they are bṛhatīs in that they have thirty-six syllables; (so) they are the characteristic of all the metres, all the forms, to obtain cattle (of all forms and colours).

11. This (rite) is, in a visible way, (equal to) the mahāvrata-(laud); its gāyatra(-sāman) is the head (of the mahāvrata), its rathantara and bṛhat are the wings, its vāmadevya is the trunk, its yaiñāyajñīya is the tail, its hundred sacrificial fees are the arkya-śastra. He, forsooth, who performs this (rite), lauds in a visible way with the mahāvrata[1].

[1] Cp. V. 1. 1—2. 9; on the arkya-śastra XVI. 7. 4.

12. Of this (rite), the (first) pṛṣṭha(-laud) is the bṛhat and the Brahman's chant is (based) on paṅkti(-verse)s[1]. About this they (the Theologians) remark: 'In that the pṛṣṭha(-laud) is the bṛhat and the Brahman's chant is (based) on paṅkti(-verse)s, the metre is rent asunder.'

[1] At the other Sāhasra-ekāhas, the Brahman's sāman is based on paṅkti-verses, see XVI. 8. 7.

13. The śrāyantīya(-sāman)[1] must be applied (as Brahman's chant); thereby, the metre is not rent asunder[2].

[1] See note 1 on VIII. 2. 9.

[2] This sāman is based on sato b ṛ h a t ī-verses, and so is in harmony with the b ṛ h a t.

14. This also is the accordance of the thousand[1].

[1] Although, by the chant on other verses than paṅktis the 1000 syllables (cp. XVI. 8. 5) are not obtained.

15. 'One (sacrifice)', they say, 'is reached (directly) by the thousand syllables[1], another is reached afterwards'[2].

[1] *viz.*, the first three Sāhasras.

[2] Is this the precise meaning of *anvātiṣṭhati*? Cp. *anvāsthāyaḥ* of the next §.

16. He shifts the kakubh to the fore-part[1], and, at the place of the kakubh, he applies that dvipadī(-verse)[2]; this (last fact) is the manner by which to afterwards reach the thousand[3].

[1] Cp. § 5.

[2] *viz.* SV. I. 432=ṚS. IX. 109. 1, 3, 2=SV. II. 717, 718, 719. The Brāhmaṇa does not indicate w h i c h dvipadā verse is intended. But note the pronoun *eṣā*; the cited dvipadā is the only one occurring in the ninth book of the ṚS.

[3] This probably must be regarded in the light of XVI. 8. 5.—Nearly the same sentence recurs below, XVII. 1. 4.

17. It (this rite) amounts to the anuṣṭubh[1]. The anuṣṭubh is the Word[2], the three-day-rite is the Word. Thereby, he reaches the (result of the) three-day-rite.

[1] All the stotra-verses, taken together, amount to 192; this number divided by the number of syllables of the anuṣṭubh, 32, yields 6 (anuṣṭubhs).

[2] Cp. V. 7. 1.

[3] Cp. XX. 15. 2.

XVI. 12.*

(First Sādyaskra-ekāha.)

1. The Ādityas and the Aṅgirases were consecrating themselves (for a sacrifice of soma). They contended for (reaching) the world of heaven (as to which of them would reach the world of heaven,

* The Kauthumas acknowledge four ekāhas of this kind, described in XVI. 12-15; according to some authorities, the Ekatriha (Pañc. br. XVI. 16) and the Śyena (Ṣaḍv. br. III. 8) belong to them, so that there are six Sādyaskras. They are described, Jaim. br. II. 115-124 (four kinds); Ārṣeyakalpa III. 5-8; Lāṭy. VIII. 3-4; Nidānasūtra VI. 9; Baudh. XVIII. 20-23 (four kinds); Āp. XXII. 2. 6—4. 12 (or 4. 29); Kāty. XXII. 2. 9—3. 52; Āśv. IX. 5. 12—7. 21; Śāṅkh. XIV. 40-42 (these two acknowledge three Sādyaskras).

leaving behind the others). The Angirases announced to the Ādityas a sacrifice (at which, after the introductory days, the sacrifice of soma proper should take place) on the next day. The Ādityas then beheld (by divine intuition) this (sacrifice); they bought him (*i.e.* the soma for pressing) on the day (of the sacrifice) itself, appointed Ayāsya as their Udgātṛ, lauded with this (rite) and went to the world of heaven, whilst the Angirases were left behind (on earth).

2, 3. He who has a rival, should perform this sacrifice; he, who knows this, comes to prosperity himself and his rival perishes.

4. To him (to Ayāsya) they (the Ādityas) brought, as a sacrificial fee, yonder sun in the form of a white horse. As soon as he had accepted it, he went amiss[1]; he saw these āyāsya(-sāman)s and, by means of them, he strengthened himself.

1 It is known, from the Black Yajurveda, that to accept a horse is dangerous; see W. Caland, die Wunschopfer (Abhandl. der Kgl. Ak. der W. zu Amsterdam, 1908) no. 24, 166.

5. That there are the āyāsya(-sāman)s[1], is for healing, for taking away bad influence.

1 There are three āyāsya-sāmans: 1, 2: grām. XIV. 1. 18 and 19, composed on SV. I. 509; 3. grām. XIV. 1. 30, composed on SV. I. 511 (see SV. ed. Calcutta, Vol. II, pages 68, 73), one for each of the first three Sādyaskras.

6. One who desires (to reach) the (world of) heaven, should perform (it).

7. It (this rite) amounts to the bṛhatī[1]; by the bṛhatī(-verse), the Gods went to the world of heaven[2]. By means of this (rite), he goes to the world of heaven.

1 This ekāha is a *trivṛd agniṣṭomaḥ*: it comprises twelve lauds, each of nine verses =108; this number, divided by the number of syllables of the bṛhatī (36), yields three bṛhatīs.

2 Cp. note 3 on VII. 4. 2.

8. One who is desirous of (obtaining) cattle should perform (it).

9. The bṛhatī is cattle; he is firmly established in (the possession of) cattle.

XVI. 13.

(Second Sādyaskra-ekāha.)

1. The same (rite), but with the agniṣṭoma(-laud) on twenty-one verses, he should perform for one who is suffering from a lingering disease.

2. The ninefold (stoma) is the vital principle[1], the sun is the vital principle; he, who is suffering from a lingering disease, suffers a loss in regard to his breaths (vital principles); he makes him prosper in regard to his vital principles.

[1] Cp. note 1 on VI. 2. 2.

3. It (this rite) amounts to the virāj[1]. Food goes forth from him who is suffering from a lingering disease (he loses his appetite). The virāj is food; he puts food into him.

[1] The first eleven lauds of this ekāha are nine-versed, the twelfth is twenty-one-versed ($9 \times 11 + 21$); that makes together 120, a number divisible by ten, the number of syllables of the virāj.

4. The agniṣṭoma(-laud) consists of twenty-one verses; without firm support is he who is suffering from a lingering disease; the twenty-one-versed (stoma) is a firm support[1]; he gets a firm support.

[1] Cp. note 1 on VI. 1. 11.

5. The same (rite) should be performed for one who is desirous of food, or for one who desires a firm support; the virāj is food, the twenty-one-versed (stoma) is a support; he eats food and becomes firmly established.

6. The (mahā)vedi (for all these Sādyaskra-rites) is plough-land[1]; that, forsooth, is the most powerful (part) of the earth; through power he makes the sacrifice successful.

[1] Wielding ripened rice or barley, Lāṭy. VIII. 3. 4.

7. The uttaravedi (or high-altar) is the threshing floor (of this field); for here the pith (of the crops) comes together. He makes the sacrifice pithful.

8. The sacrificial post (for fastening the victim, the savana-he-goat) is the post of the threshing-floor (to which at threshing the

oxen are fastened)[1]; for by it they press out (of the stalks) the pith (of the crops).

[1] Lāṭy. VIII. 3. 6 declares that 'threshing-post' is to be taken in the sense of 'pole of the plough', probably because he insists on the proper meaning of the word *utkṛṣanti* in our Brāhmaṇa. It is, however, probable that this *khalevālī* is the post, to which are fastened the oxen, which, by treading on the ripened stalks, press out the corn. That oxen are used for the threshing, is explicitly stated by Baudh, XVIII. 21: 368. 5ff.

9. A three year old, ungelded bull serves for the buying of the soma: in order to associate Indra (with the sacrifice).

10. The soma-herolds, seated on chariots drawn by horses, ride out in all directions.

11. From all directions he obtains the food for him (for the Sacrificer).

12. To the distance of four *koss*, riding on a chariot drawn by four horses in an easterly direction, he (one of the four soma-herolds) announces the sacrifice. In this manner the journeys are measured; they travel as far as is the measure of a journey. To the distance of three *koss*, riding on a chariot drawn by three horses in a northerly direction, (he announces the sacrifice). To the distance of two *koss*, on a chariot drawn by two horses in a westerly direction, (he announces it). To the distance of one *koss*, riding on a chariot drawn by one horse in a southerly direction, (he announces it)[1]. This, forsooth, is the form of the directions. Whatever is the form of the directions, thereby he makes the sacrifice thrive.

[1] Lāṭy. VIII. 3. 12–13 treats of this passage in the following manner: 'To the east, they should convey the Hotṛ; to the north, the Udgātṛ; to the west, the Adhvaryu; to the south, the Brahman. Or they may dwell there (in these directions) previously. Here they should announce the (sacrifice of) soma, having got there by means of the chariots drawn by horses; these, as well as the journeys, are explained in the Brāhmaṇa. According to Śāṇḍilya, the officiating priests should (not be conveyed, but) be occupied (in the usual manner on the ground of the sacrifice), but they should convey other Brāhmins in the manner as has been exposed before, and to these the soma-herolds should announce the (sacrifice of) soma with the words: 'So and so is performing a Sadyaskrī, that I announce to Indra, to all the Gods, to the soma-drinking Brāhmins who are worthy of soma'.—Differently, the Jaim. br. (II. 119): at the first Sadyaskrī, the soma-herold rides out on a chariot drawn by horses to the distance of a *yojana*, with the leathern bag filled with sour milk (cp. Pañc. br. XVI. 13. 13).

The priests have previously been placed, each at a distance of three *koss*, in the different directions and they arrive at early morning to perform the sacrifice. At the second and third Sadyaskrī (the two Anukrīs), the soma-herold rides out on a chariot drawn by mules to the distance of three *koss*, and the priests find themselves at a distance of 1½ *koss*. Differently, again, Baudh. (XVIII. 20, sqq.), who for each Sādyaskra enjoins the four chariots (drawn by four, three, two horses and by one), and provided each with a bag of sour milk. The priests arrive at morning on foot. After the preparation of the prāyaṇīya-iṣṭi, those four chariots start on a race-course: the chariot with four horses to the east, a *yojana* far; the one with three horses to the south, three *koss*; the one with two horses to the west, two *koss*; the one with one horse to the north, one *koss*. To everyone they meet, they announce the sacrifice. According to Āpastamba, Hiraṇyakeśin and Kātyāyana the ritual, in substance, is the same as explained by Lāṭyāyana: the priests are fetched by means of the four chariots.

13. On the chariots are leathern bags filled with fresh milk; the butter obtained by it (*i.e.* by the shuttling on the driven chariot) must be added to the ājya[1] (used at the sacrifice), for the sake of immediateness[2].

[1] Cp. note 1 on § 12.

[2] In order that all may be accomplished on one and the same day.

XVI. 14.

(Third Sādyaskra-ekāha: Anukrī.)

1. Now, the Anukrī[1] of the Angirases.

[1] The name is explained in the next following paragraph.

2. By this (rite), the Angirases reached the Ādityas[1]. He who is left behind, coming behind (inferior), as it were, should perform this (rite). He reaches the advantage of those who precede him, for, by it, the Angirases had reached the Ādityas[2].

[1] Who were gone before them to the world of heaven, cp. XVI. 12. 1.

[2] Hence the name: a (*sadyas*)*k r ī*, which comes behind (*anu*, another).

3. Of this (rite), the (last) two pavamāna(-laud)s are twenty-four-versed.

4. The gāyatrī comprises twenty-four syllables; by means of the gāyatrī, the Gods reached these worlds successively. By this (rite), he reaches successively these worlds.

5. The gāyatrī is strength and priestly lustre[1]; strength and priestly lustre he obtains. The gāyatrī is breath[2] (the vital principle) and a means of procreating: out of the breath, the gāyatrī, he is procreated.

[1] The same is said XV. 1. 8, XIX. 5. 9.

[2] Cp. note 1 on VII. 1. 9.

6. Both kinds of stomas (are applied in this rite): the even and the odd ones[1]. This is a pairing. From this pairing he is procreated.

[1] It is partly nine-versed and partly twenty-one-versed, but the last two pavamānas (see § 3) are even (of 24 verses).

7. It amounts to the virāj[1]; the virāj is food, he comes into the possession of food.

[1] It has nine stotras of nine verses, two of twenty four, one of twenty-one, together 150, a number divisible by ten.

8. The agniṣṭoma(-laud) is twenty-one-versed; the twenty-one-fold (stoma) is a firm support[1]. At the end of the sacrifice, he is firmly supported.

[1] Cp. III. 7. 2.

XVI. 15.

(The Viśvajicchilpa-ekāha.)

1. Now, the Viśvajicchilpa[1].

[1] 'The image (or ornament?) of the Viśvajit'; cp. XVI. 4 sqq. According to the Ārṣeyakalpa III. 6. c, its arrangement is, in the main, that of the Viśvajit. This ekāha (reckoned amongst the Sādyaskras, cp. footnote on page 446) is found only in our Brāhmaṇa.

2. It is the ornament of the stomas. He who knows this, beholds in his house a work of art[1].

[1] Identical with XVI. 4. 9.

3. In this (rite) the (last) two pavamāna(-laud)s are eighteen-versed.

4. This sacrifice is a wheeled one[1]: for (obtaining the fulfilment of) a wish; the wish he hopes to see fulfilled, is reached by it, for where he wishes to go with a wheeled (car), that (place) he reaches.

[1] These two pavamānas of equal verse-number are, in a sense, its wheels.

5. One who is desirous of (reaching the world of) heaven, should perform (it).

6. The pṛṣṭha(-sāman)s are the world of heaven[1]; through this (rite) he reaches the world of heaven.

[1] *viz.* the rathantara, bṛhat, vairāja etc., as at the Viśvajit.—Further cp. VII. 7. 17.

7. The pṛṣṭha(-sāman)s are strength and priestly lustre. In that the pṛṣṭha(-sāman)s are applied together (at one and the same sacrifice), he confers on him strength and lustre together.

8. The pṛṣṭha(-sāman)s are food and cattle. In that the pṛṣṭha(-sāman)s are applied together, he confers on him food and cattle together.

9. About this they say: 'The pṛṣṭha(-sāman)s have different places[1]. In that they are, all of them, applied at one and the same sacrifice, the Sacrificer may lose his firm support.'

[1] They appear normally each on one of the first six days of the ten-day-period.

10 The pṛṣṭha(-laud), (which runs parallel to the śastra) of the Hotṛ, is twenty-one-versed. The twenty-one-fold (stoma) is a firm support[1]. In the middle of the sacrifice he obtains a firm support. The agniṣṭoma(-laud) is twenty-one-versed. The twenty-one-fold (stoma) is a firm support. At the end of the sacrifice he obtains a firm support.

[1] Cp. XVI. 13. 4.

11. These are two twenty-one-fold (stomas); the Sacrificer is two-footed. He firmly establishes the Sacrificer in the sacrifice, in (the possession of) cattle.

XVI. 16.

(The Ekatrika-ekāha.)

1. Now, the Ekatrika[1]: Prajāpati's getting-a-top[2].

[1] For the name see § 4.—According to Lāṭy. (VIII. 3. 2-3), the Śyena (described in Ṣaḍv. br. and likewise in the Ārṣeyakalpa, here immediately after the Viśvajicchilpa) and the Ekatrika are also reckoned as Sādyaskras.—It is striking that the Pañcaviṃśabrāhmaṇa nowhere describes any *abhicāra*-rite, as is *e.g.* the Śyena.

[2] See § 2.—On the Ekatrika cp. Jaim. br. II. 125-127; see 'das Jaim. br. in Auswahl,' No. 138.

2. By this (rite), Prajāpati got a-top of these worlds[1].

[1] Or: broke through them, got the supremacy over them, cp. Āp. śrs. XVIII. 19. 5: *udbhinnaṃ rājñaḥ*, with my note on the German translation.—The genitive is noteworthy.

3. This is a winning stoma, for the *kṛta* has got a-top (of the other *grahas*)[1].

[1] Cp. XVI. 9. 4. Here the term *kṛta*, representative of four, is used because the two kinds of stoma (1+3) together make four. Sāyaṇa's explanation here is equally wrong.

4. That they chant on one single (verse) is because Prajāpati is one; he reaches (becomes equal to) Prajāpati; and that they chant on three (verses) is because these worlds are three in number; he is firmly established in these worlds[1].

[1] At this ekāha, the stotras are alternatively chanted on one and on three verses; hence the name: 'containing one and three.'

5. These amount to four; fourfooted is cattle; he is firmly established in (the possession of) cattle.

6. It (the whole rite) amounts to the gāyatrī[1]; the gāyatrī is strength and priestly lustre; strength and priestly lustre he obtains.

[1] Six stotras on one verse and six on three (6+18) make 24, the number of syllables of the gāyatrī.

7. The gāyatrī is breath (and) a means of procreating; out of the breath, the gāyatrī, he is procreated[1].

[1] See XVI. 14. 5.

8. On (the verse beginning:) 'By this golden light purified,'[1] the ārbhava-pavamāna(-laud) is chanted.

[1] SV. I. 463=ṚS. IX. 111. 1=SV. II. 940.

9. This (aticchandas-verse) is (*i.e.*, contains) the features of all the metres[1]; he (thereby) firmly establishes the ārbhava-laud in all the metres.

[1] Cp. Śat. br. III. 3. 2. 11: *eṣā vai sarvāṇi chandāṃsi yad aticchandāḥ*.

10. On this (verse), the gāyatrapārśva(-sāman)[1] (is chanted). (In doing so) he does not deviate from the gāyatra-sāman nor from the finale[2].

[1] Grām. XVII. 2. 31, composed on SV. I. 584; see SV. ed. Calcutta, vol. II, page 237.

[2] The pavamāna-lauds begin normally with gāyatrī-verses, chanted on the gāyatra-sāman; by the name of this sāman, *g ā y a t r a-pārśva*, this condition is fulfilled, although it is chanted on verses of different metre Sāyaṇa's commentary points to the reading, followed by me: *na gāyatrād eti sāmno na nidhanāt.* Neither do they deviate from the nidhana, as this sāman is *nidhanavat* (ending: $\overset{1}{\text{ā}}$ *ivā* $\overset{1}{2}$ $\overset{1}{3}$ $\overset{1}{4}$ $\overset{1}{\text{ō}}$) and the pavamana stotras ought to finish thus.

SEVENTEENTH CHAPTER.

(The ekāhas or one-day-rites, continued.)

XVII. 1[1].

(First Vrātya-stoma.)

1. The Gods, forsooth, went to the world of heaven; of them the adherents of 'the God'[1] were left behind (on earth), leading a Vrātya-life[2]. They came to the spot whence the Gods were gone to the world of heaven. (But) they[3] found neither that stoma nor that metre by means of which they might reach them. Then the Gods said to the Maruts: 'Deliver ye to these that stoma, that metre, by means of which they may reach us.' To them they (the Maruts) delivered that sixteen-versed stoma, (which) cryptically (is) the anuṣṭubh[4]. Thereupon, they reached them.

[1] This translation of *daiva* is conjectural; the word in itself may mean equally: 'adherent of the Gods' and 'celestial', or 'adherent of a', or 'of the God.' In the latter case, that God must be meant who, in Śat. br, is called

---

[1] Our Brāhmaṇa describes in XVII. 1-4 four kinds of Vrātya-stomas; cp. Lāṭy. VIII. 6; Nidānasūtra VI. 11-12; the Jaim. br. (II. 222-227) acknowledges three Vrātya-stomas; further, cp. Baudh. XVIII. 24-26; Āp. XXII. 5. 4-14; Kāty. XXII. 4. 1-28; Āśv. IX. 8.25; Śāṅkh. XIV. 69-73. The subject of the Vrātyas is now being studied in an extensive work by I. W. Hauer, 'der Vrātya', Stuttgart, 1927, of which only the first volume has so far appeared.

yo 'yaṃ devaḥ paśūnām iṣṭe. The god Rudra is often designated not by his name, but by the words: 'this God (see above, XIV. 9. 12; XXI. 2. 9, note 4; Ait. br. III. 34. 3; Kāṭh. X. 6, XXII. 12, (beg.), XXV. 10, and probably elsewhere). The Jaim. br. (Auswahl no. 146) seems to favour this translation, as it is said there that the Vrātyas did not reach the world of heaven, because they had offended either that God which blows here (the Wind) or the mighty God (*iśānaṃ devaṃ i.e. rudraṃ*). In this respect, then, I agree with J. Charpentier, in his paper 'Bemerkungen über die Vrātyas' (Vienna Oriental Journal, vol. XXV, page 355 sqq.).

[2] The meaning of the expression *vrātyāṃ pravasanti* is unknown. Charpentier renders: 'Wohnten ohne Riten in der Ferne'; Hauer: 'die auf Vrātya-Wanderschaft begriffen waren.' Jaim. br. has throughout *vrātyāṃ dhāvayanti*; Baudh.: *vrātyāṃ caranti.* Perhaps *vrātyāṃ pravasanti* is elliptic for *vrātyāṃ vasatim pravasanti*, 'leading the life of a joined group,' from *vrāta*, § 5 and above VI. 9. 24.

[3] Instead of *tena* (wrongly interpreted by Hauer) read *te na.*

[4] Solely on account of the number, the anuṣṭubh is of twice sixteen syllables: *catvāraḥ ṣoḍaśāḥ dve anuṣṭubhau bhavataḥ*, misinterpreted by Hauer, op. cit. page 61.

2. Those who lead the life of a joined group, are destitute, left behind. For they neither practise the study of the Veda nor do they plough or trade. It is by the sixteen-versed stoma that this can be reached.

3. This is a stoma of the Maruts. The smaller metres belong to the Maruts.

4. He shifts the kakubh(-verse and the sāmans chanted on it) to the fore-part; in that, at the place of the kakubh, this dvipadā(-verse) is applied[1], he, thereby, makes them prosper in regard to their own nature.

[1] Cp. XVI. 11. 5 with note 1 and 16 with notes 1 and 2. The passage is wholly misunderstood by Hauer, op. cit., page 64.

5. (The verses, beginning): 'For, o Indra who lovest the chants'[1], are (of) unequal metre. The joined group is unequal, as it were. He makes them equal (by applying the verses of this metre).

[1] ṚS. VIII. 98. 7—9=SV. II. 60—62 (var. rr.); cp. notes 1—3 on VIII. 8. 26. According to the Sāmaveda, the unequal metres are kakubh, uṣṇih and parauṣṇih.

6. On these (verses) the dyautāna(-sāman)[1] (is chanted as third pṛṣṭha-laud).

[1] Grām. VIII. 2. 22, composed on SV. I. 324; see SV. ed. Calcutta, Vol. I, page 656. A comparison of the ūhagāna points to this chant, though grām. VIII. 2. 23 is likewise dyautāna and has the same ending. Probably they were optional, as the Jaim. br. (II. 224) has: *tayor bṛhato mārutasya sāmanī bhavato dyautāne vā devasāme.*

7. Dyutāna, who belonged to the Maruts[1], was their (of the Vrātyas) 'House holder'[2]. They (the Vrātyas) performed this (Vrātya-) stoma and all of them came to prosperity. That there is this sāman, is for prospering[3].

[1] Cp. § 1, where the Maruts receive the command to give a stoma to the Vrātyas in order to reach heaven.

[2] This expression is here somewhat unexpected, for it is used ordinarily when the sacrifice is a sattra, as, for instance, the one described XXIV. 18.

[3] The last words are again wrongly understood by Hauer, op. cit., page 66.

8. If they were to undertake (*i.e.* to chant) the finale 'expressedly,'[1] only the Gṛhapati would prosper and he would repel the others (from prosperity). By the fact, (however), that they undertake it 'unexpressedly,'[2] he firmly establishes all of them[3] (*i.e.* all the other Vrātyas) in prosperity (and) in welfare.

[1] *niruktam*, in that, in chanting, the name of the deity is distinctly and expressly pronounced. Cp. V. 4. 15.

[2] The Sūtrakāra (Lāty. VIII. 6. 5-6) elucidates this: 'they pronounce as finale of the dyautāna-sāman the word 'Indra'. This is prohibited (by the Brāhmaṇa); they should perform the finale as it has been handed down (in the gāna)' (*i.e.* *au*^{2} *3 ho*^{1} *2345*^{1111}). That in the case of *nirukti* the word *indra* is used as finale, seems to rest solely on the fact that the verse of the dyautāna-sāman is addressed to Indra.

[3] If the name of one single God were taken as nidhana, this would refer only to one single deity (and one single person: the Gṛhapati), but the *anirukta nidhana* refers to all the deities (and all the Vrātyas).

9. Swallowing poison are those, who eat foreign food as Brahman's food[1], who call good words bad[1], who use to strike the guiltless with a stick, who, though being not initiated, speak the speech of the initiated[2]. The guilt of these may be removed by the sixteen-versed stoma. That (in this rite) there are four sixteen-versed (stomas)[3], thereby, they are freed from their guilt.

[1] Translation and precise meaning doubtful.

[2] Cp. Baudh. (XVIII. 24): *atha yad vrātyavādaṃ vadanti dīkṣitavādasya tad rūpam.*

[3] The schema, according to Ārṣeyakalpa III. 9, is: 9, 15, 15, 15, 1 6 | 1 6, 17, 17, 17, 1 6 | 1 6, 21.

10. (The verses, beginning): 'The God who bestoweth wealth,'[1] must be taken for the agniṣṭoma-sāman; he establishes them (the Vrātyas) among the deities.

[1] SV. I. 55=ṚS. VII. 16. 11—12=SV. II 863—864 (var. r). On these verses, then, the yajñāyajñīya-sāman (grām. I. 2. 25, see SV. ed. Calcutta, Vol. I, page 150) is applied.

11. But they (the Theologians) say also: 'It should be applied on the satobṛhatī(-verse)s, (beginning): 'The progress-gaining has shown himself.[1]' A joined group is unequal, as it were; he makes all of them equally elevated (*sato bṛhataḥ*).

[1] SV. I. 47=ṚS. VIII. 103. 1, 2, 3=SV. II. 8 6 5, 8 6 7, 8 6 6 (var. rr.). Properly, the verses are all bṛhatīs. Sāyaṇa's remark, *pragrathanair apekṣaṇa-svabhāvata eva bṛhatīcchandaskāsv ṛkṣu*, does not help us, neither has Hauer explained the difficulty. Cp. note 2 on XII. 4. 3, XII. 4. 22, note 2 on XIV. 10. 3.

12. About this (matter) they (other Theologians) say: 'The metre satobṛhatī is loose, as it were, (and) shaking[1]; it (the agniṣṭoma-laud) must, (therefore, rather) be performed on the verses: 'The god who bestoweth wealth.'

[1] Cp. note 1 on XIV. 10. 3.

13. 'Firmly established (on the contrary) is the bṛhatī with its repeated verse-quarters[1]. In that he begins a verse-quarter anew, therefore, the (suckling) child longs after its mother[2].

[1] Cp. XIV. 10: 3 and note 2 on this passage. The bṛhatī consists of the verse-quarters: 8+8+12+8, the first two have an equal number of syllables.
[2] The meaning of the apodosis of the last sentence is less clear.

14. A turban, a goad, a bow without arrow[1], a board-covered rough vehicle[2], a garment with black fringes, two goats-skins: one white, one black, a silver ornament (worn around the neck), (all) that is (the equipment) of the Gṛhapati.

[1] The meaning of *jyāhroḍa* was unknown even to the Sūtrakāras and their authorities. According to Baudh. the Vrātyas are provided with a bow and three arrows in leathern quivers.

[2] The nature of this kind of vehicle is unknown; probably Baudh. gives a description of it.

15. The other (Vrātyas) have (uppergarments) with red borders[1] and corded fringes[1], with strings at each side; each of them has a pair of shoes and doubly-joined goat's hides.

[1] All is, and was to the ancient exegetes, uncertain

16. This is the possession of the Vrātyas; on him, to whom they bestow (this possession), they transfer (their guilt or unworthiness, so that henceforth they are qualified to take part in the sacrifice of the Āryas).

17. Each of them brings to their Gṛhapati thirty-three (cows)[1]. For thirty-three adherents of 'the God'[2] had come (through this Vrātya-stoma) to prospering. (So this rite serves) for reaching prosperity.

[1] And all these cows must be given to the person who is mentioned in the preceding §.

[2] Cp. note 1 on § 1.

XVII. 2.

(Second Vrātya-stoma.)

1. Now (follows the description of) the (Vrātya-stoma) with six sixteen-versed (stotras). This (rite) should be performed by those who, base (and) censured, lead a Vrātya-life.

2. One after another *they* are seized by bad fortune, who, being base (and) censured, lead a Vrātya-life. In that there are six sixteen-versed stotras, thereby, they are delivered from bad fortune.

3. In that the agniṣṭoma(-laud) is twenty-one versed, the twenty-one versed stoma being a firm support, they are firmly supported even in the middle of the sacrifice.

4 It is an ukthya(-rite); the uktha(-laud)s are cattle; it is the cattle that leads the base to superiority. Through cattle he leads them to superiority[1].

[1] The schema (cp. Ārṣeyakalpa III. 10. a) is: 16, 15, 15, 15, 16 | 16, 17, 17, 17, 16 | 16, 21, 21, 21, 16.

XVII. 3.

(Third Vrātya-stoma.)

1. Now, the (Vrātya-stoma) with two sixteen-versed (stotras). This should be performed by those who, being the youngest, lead a Vrātya-life.

2. Destitute, left behind are those who, being the youngest, lead a Vrātya-life. In that the pavamāna-(laud)s are nine-versed, the nine-versed (stoma) being the mouth (or chief one) of the stomas [1], he (thereby) leads them to [2] the mouth (the chief part) of the sacrifice.

[1] Cp. VI. 1. 6.

[2] *mukhataḥ* must be equivalent to *mukham*. Differently Sāyaṇa, who takes it as a locative and supplies as object to the verb: *brāhmaṇatvam*. For this use of the ablative in *-taḥ*, cp. Indogermanische Fozschungen, vol. XXXI, page 105.

3. In that there are two sixteen-versed (lauds), they, thereby, are delivered from their bad fortune.

4. The agniṣṭoma(-laud) is twenty-one versed. The twenty-one versed stoma is a firm support. They are firmly supported at the end of the sacrifice [1].

[1] The schema is: 9, 15, 15, 15, 16 | 9, 17, 17, 17, 16 | 9, 21.

XVII. 4.

(Fourth Vrātya-stoma.)

1. Now, the stoma for those (Vrātyas) who by old age are precluded from sexual intercourse [1]. This (rite) should be performed by those who, being the oldest, lead a Vrātya-life.

[1] *śama-* in *śamanicameḍhra* is the same *śama-* as in *śamaratha*, 'a quiet, not moving chariot'; see references in the edition of Baudh. śrs., in the index, *in voce* The word, then, means: 'having a not moving, hanging down *meḍhra*.'

2. From the top [1] they ascend to the top. The stomas go upwards (increase in number of verses): in order that they may not fall down [2].

1 Which they have reached already by their old age; for the expression cp. II. 1. 3.

2 The schema (cp. Ārṣeyakalpa III. 11) is: 9, 9, 15, 17, 21 | 24, 44, 48, 27, 33 | 32, 32.

3. This (rite) was (once upon a time) performed by those (Vrātyas), who by old age were precluded from sexual intercourse. Their Gṛhapati was Kuṣītaka, the son of Samaśravas. Luśākapi, the son of Khargala, cursed them, saying: 'They are fallen off[1]: they have applied two smaller lauds'.[2] In consequence thereof, none of the descendants of Kuṣītaka amounts to much, for they have fallen off from the sacrifice[3].

1 Sāyaṇa takes *avākīrṣata* in the sense of *avakīrṇinaḥ . . . abhavan*. But as *avakīrṇin* signifies: 'he who has broken his vow of chastity', this is impossible in view of the old age of the performers.

2 See the schema in note 2 on § 2, where, after the increasing stotras, the last two of the midday-service decrease.

3 In this passage, then, the author of our Brāhmaṇa polemizes against the Kauṣītakins who applied in this sacrifice the stomas is a wrong way. In the Jaim. br. (II. 226), the following remarkable passage is read: 'Now the (Vrātya-stoma) of the Aiṣīkapāvas, who had Kuṣītaka as their Gṛhapati, a sacrifice of which the pavamāna-lauds are sixteen-versed' etc. The schema, according to the Jaiminīyas, is wholly different: 16, 15, 15, 15, 16 | 16, 17, 17, 17, 16 | 16, 21. I now cite an equally remarkable passage of the Nidānasūtra (VI. 11): 'In our tradition, two kinds of verses are handed down for the agniṣṭoma(-laud). There are two kinds of Vrātyas: the Śīrṣādis and the Aiṣīkayāvis. 'For the Śīrṣādis, he should apply (*i.e.* chant) the agniṣṭoma-sāman on satobṛhatī(-verses)' (see our Brāhmaṇa XVII. 1. 10), thus says Dhānañjayya. 'These they call the older ones. For the Aiṣīkayāvis (he should chant it) on pragāthabṛhatī (-verses) (cp. XVII. 1. 11). How can he know (which of them are the older and the younger ones)?' They should say this themselves. (But) the older ones, forsooth, are the Śīrṣādis.' In the next kaṇḍikā (VI. 12) we find the following remarkable but difficult passage: *jyeṣṭhayajñaṃ kṛtsnaṃ cikīrṣann athāpimaṃ dvātriṁśam āśiṁstomaṁ* (perhaps the verse *devo vo draviṇodāḥ* is meant) *sākṣāj jyeṣṭhayajñe 'cakīrṣīt; sa ādīyamānaḥ sarvānt stomān ādāyet; tāṁs tu yad evaṃ prayuṅkta, evam anavakāreṇāroho bhavati* (this *anavakāra* is the noun belonging to the verb *avakirati* in XVI. 4. 3). Further on: *akuśalānuvyāhṛtān kauṣītakīn manya iti dhānañjayya, evaṃ hy evaiṣu satsu roho bhavati*. So Dhānañjayya seems to defend the manner of the Kauṣītakins. The question remains open whether the proper noun in Jaim. br. *aiṣīkapāvānām* should rather be read *aiṣīkayāviṇām*.

XVII. 5.[1]

(First Agniṣṭut.)

1. Indra slew the son of Tvaṣṭṛ with three heads. An inauspicious voice addressed him[1]. He resorted for help to Agni. This (God) saw this Agni-laud[2] and, having assigned it to himself[3], he sacrificed with it on behalf of him (of Indra). By it, he drove away his inauspicious voice[4].

[1] Calling out: 'O Brahman-slayer!'

[2] A sacrifice of soma in which all the grahas, stotras and śastras are destined for Agni alone.

[3] The Jaim. br. has: *ātmana adhi . . . atanuta.*

[4] He, Agni, drove away the voice that pursued him.

2. He who knows this repels from himself the inauspicious voice.

3. He who deems himself to be impure[1], should perform the Agni-laud: Agni removes his evil and bestows, by means of the nine-versed (stoma), strength and priestly lustre on him[2].

[1] Because he has committed a murder, etc.

[2] Agni is connected with the trivṛt-stoma, cp. VI. 1. 6.

4. About this they say: 'In that it is a nine-versed (stoma), he removes the evil from one member of his body: from the head only'[1].

[1] Because the trivṛt is born out of the head of Prajāpati: VI. 1. 6.

5. It should be made a jyotiṣṭoma[1].

[1] The ordinary jyotiṣṭoma containing the four stomas: trivṛt, pañcadaśa, saptadaśa, and ekaviṃśa, cp. C.H. page 503.

6. By the nine-versed (stoma), he drives away the impure (element) from his head; by the fifteen versed, from his breast and arms; by the seventeen-versed, from the middle part of his body; by the twenty-one-versed, from his feet and knees[1].

[1] Cp. VI. 1. 8-11. Jaim. br. II. 135, in 'Auswahl' No. 140.

---

[1] In our Brāhmaṇa (XVII. 5-9) are described four Agniṣṭuts; they are given in the Jaim. br. II. 134-138; Taitt. br. II. 7. 12; Ārṣeyakalpa III. 12-13. c; Lāṭy. VIII. 7. 1; Nidānasūtra VI. 13; Baudh. XVIII. 12-13; Āp. XXII. 6. 5-21 and XXII. 27. 3-12; Kāty. XXII. 4. 29-5. 5; Āśv. IX. 7. 22-25; Śāṅkh. XIV. 51-57.

7. 'He enters into Vaiśvānara',[1] they say, 'who performs the Agni-laud.' The vāravantīya(-sāman)[2] must be applied at the agniṣṭoma(-laud). Agni destroys what is impure of him, and the other one (*viz.* the Sacrificer) comes out clean and pure[3].

[1] Cp. V. 3. 9.

[2] Cp. note 1 on V. 3. 8; from the Ārṣeyakalpa, we infer that grām. I. 1. 30 (see SV. ed. Calcutta, vol. I. page 121) is intended.

[3] This expression rests on the ritual of the purifying bath, see, *e.g.* TS. I. 2. 1. f: *ud ābhyaḥ śucir ā pūta emi.*

XVII. 6.

(First Agniṣṭut, continued.)

1. It[1] (is) a nine-versed agniṣṭoma. The agniṣṭoma-sāman (is chanted) on (verses) addressed to Vāyu[2].

[1] Some authorities hold that in khaṇḍa 5 two Agniṣṭuts are described and, in khaṇḍa 6, a third. This probably is not the intention of the author of the Brāhmaṇa. Nidānasūtra VI. 13: *ta ime pañcānuvākāś* (*sc.* Pañc. br. XVII. 5–9), *catvāraḥ kalpāḥ; sa eṣa* (*viz.* Pañc. br. XVII. 5 and 6) *prathamaḥ sarveṣām eva sārṣṭaḥ syād, api vā prathamasya dvau syātām.*

[2] SV. II. 920–922 (Ārṣeyakalpa III. 12) chanted on the vāravantīya-sāman (XVII. 5. 7).

2. One who is desirous of priestly lustre should perform it.

3. The nine-versed (stoma) is strength (and) priestly lustre; in that the agniṣṭoma-sāman is (chanted) on (verses) addressed to Vāyu, he (the performing priest) thereby blows on him[1].

[1] So that all alien substances are removed from him, just as the blacksmith blows on the metal to cleanse it.

4. The Agniṣṭut purifies him by heat, just as he (the smith) would purify the gold by the heat (of the fire)[1].

[1] Cp. Jaim. br. (II. 136, see 'Auswahl' no. 140): 'He who, though being a learned Brāhmin, does not shine (is not conspicuous), should perform this (Agniṣṭut). A learned person who is not conspicuous, is as a (golden) niṣka that is seized with defilement. They hold him, for whom they perform the Agniṣṭut, in the fire. Just as a niṣka seized with defilement is held in the fire, whereupon he (the smith) removes all its defilements by hammering on it with an iron hammer, so he removes from him all evil and he thereby becomes possessed of *tejas* and priestly lustre.'

XVII. 7.

(Second Agniṣṭut.)

1. For him who is desirous of cattle he should perform the same kind (of Agniṣṭut), but chant, as agniṣṭoma-sāman, the vāravantīya on the revatī(-verse)s [1].

[1] The vāravantīya (note 2 on XVII. 5. 7) applied on the verses SV. I. 153=ṚS. I. 30. 13-15=SV. II. 434-436 (var. r).

2. He who is devoid of cattle is (like unto) old, dry grass; as cattle take no delight in old, dry grass (but avoids it), so in him who is devoid of cattle, the cattle does not rejoice (but leaves him). When fire burns down the old, dry grass, then, rain falls on it and, then, new plants grow forth, and, then, cattle rejoice in it (and in him, who was as dry grass).

3. Cattle rejoice in him (and does not leave him), who knows this [1].

[1] More completely the Jaim. br. (II. 137, 'Auswahl' no. 140, end): 'In whom, being worthy of cattle, cattle does not rejoice (but leaves him), such a one should perform this sacrifice. He is as old, dry grass; its agniṣṭoma-laud is performed on the revatī(-verse)s; the revatī(-verse)s are water; he, for whom they perform the Agniṣṭut, is thrown into fire; as old, dry grass, after it is burnt by fire and then water is poured on it, so that beautiful herbs come forth and cattle rejoice in it, so in him rejoices all cattle.'

4. What of him is adverse to cattle, that is burnt down by Agni. What is burnt down by Agni, that he quenches with water: with the revatī(-verse)s.

XVII. 8.

(Third Agniṣṭut.)

1. A Jyotiṣṭoma should be performed as Agniṣṭut [1] by him who goes amiss in a sacrifice [2].

[1] An agniṣṭoma of the usual kind (as described in C.H), but with all grahas stotras and śastras destined for Agni.

[2] Because he was not able to finish it.

2. Or by him who goes amiss in any part of a sacrifice of soma.

3. Agni devours the offering, destined for the Gods, of him who goes amiss in a sacrifice and he does not convey it to the deities. He at once succeeds in relation to Agni[1].

[1] He wins at once, by the Agniṣṭut, the favour of Agni, so that this God conveys henceforth his offerings also to the other Gods.

4. When (a conveyance) breaks down, they fit up another, (for) with it he goes not there (whither he is journeying), (but) when they fit it up, he goes there. He should sacrifice with the same stomas with the same part of it, in which he had gone amiss; he (then) is firmly established in the same stomas, in the same part of the sacrifice in which he had gone amiss[1].

[1] As the Agniṣṭut here described contains the same stomas as the normal agniṣṭoma, he, whose sacrifice of soma (agniṣṭoma) has gone amiss through too much or too less, performs now an Agniṣṭut, which contains the same stomas as the sacrifice that had gone amiss.

XVII. 9.

(Fourth Agniṣṭut.)

1. One who is desirous of food should perform an Agniṣṭut, of which all the lauds are seventeen-versed.

2. The seventeen-fold stoma is food[1]; Agni is the bestower of food; Agni bestows food on him.

[1] Cp. note 1 on II. 7. 7.

3. An eater of food becomes he who knows this.

4. It (this rite) is throughout seventeen-fold. Prajāpati is the seventeen-fold (stoma)[1]. He reaches (becomes equal to) Prajāpati.

[1] Cp. note 1 on II. 10. 5.

XVII. 10.

(The unprecedented rite of Prajāpati.)[1]

1. A nine-versed agniṣṭoma; its morning-service is unexpressed.[1]

[1] Cp. note 1 on VII. 1. 8.

2. Prajāpati created the beings; as these were created, they went forth from him. He saw this unexpressed morning-service; by it

---

[1] Cp. Jaim. br. II. 177; Lāṭy. VIII. 7. 2-3; Nidānasūtra VII. 1; Āp. XXII. 7. 1-4; Kāty. XXII. 5. 6-10.

he passed into the midst of them[1]; they turned to him and surrounded him on all sides[2].

[1] Because at first through the *aniruktabhāva* they did not perceive him (?).

[2] Read *pary enam aviśan* instead of *āviśan*, see § 3.

3. One who is desirous of (obtaining the chieftainship in) his clan should practise (this rite). In that the morning-service is unexpressed, he passes in the midst of them (of the inhabitants of his community, of his clansfolk); they turn to him and surround him on all sides.

4. This is the unprecedented (rite) of Prajāpati. Unpreceded by any one is he who knows this[1].

[1] This ekāha, called simply *apūrva*, is described in the Jaim. br., but its aim is different; it promises the precedency before others in obtaining numerous progeny. It is called *apūrva* ('having no precedent'), because it is throughout trivṛt, and the trivṛt has no precedent as it is the first of all the stomas.

XVII. 11.

(The Bṛhaspati-sava.)[1]

1. A nine-versed agniṣṭoma.

2. As its morning-service, when the Nārāśaṃsa-cups have been deposited, he assigns eleven (cows) as sacrificial fee; at the midday-service (when the Nārāśaṃsa-cups have been deposited) (he assigns eleven) (cows) with a horse as twelfth. Both these groups (of eleven and twelve) he separates (from all the dakṣiṇā-cows that stand together to the south of the sacrificial ground, and he gives them to the officiating priests); at the afternoon-service (he assigns) eleven (cows, when the Nārāśaṃsa-cups have been deposited), and he gives them at the barren cow (*i.e.* when this cow, destined for Mitra and Varuṇa, has been immolated)[1].

[1] The so-called Nārāśaṃsa-cups are deposited five times during the whole rite, see C. H. §§ 147. e, 153 (morning service); 189. b, 197 (midday-service); 230. b (afternoon-service). In our text, the first of each (§ 147. e and 189. b) and the last (230. b) are meant. The last eleven cows are given after the rite described in C. H.

---

[1] Cp. Jaim. br. II. 128-131; Lāṭy. VIII. 7. 4-11; Nidānasūtra VII. 1; Ārṣeyakalpa III. 13. c; Kāṭh. XXXVII. 7; T. Br. II. 7. 1; Śat. br. (Kāṇvīya) V. 7. 5; Baudh. XVIII. 1-2; Āp XXII. 7. 5-16; Kāty. XXII. 5. 11-29; Śāṅkh XV. 4.

§ 256. Usually, the dakṣiṇās are given at the midday service (C. H. § 191). The Jaim. br. ('Auswahl' no. 139) commends other methods of dividing the dakṣiṇās.

3. These make thirty-three dakṣiṇā(-cow)s; there are thirty-three deities[1]; he reaches the deities. The horse is the thirty-fourth of the dakṣiṇās; Prajāpati is the thirty-fourth of the deities[1]; he reaches Prajāpati.

[1] Cp. X. 1. 16.

4. This is the consecration[1] of Bṛhaspati. Bṛhaspati desired to obtain the chaplainship (the office of Purohita) of the Gods. He performed this (sacrifice) and obtained the chaplainship of the Gods.

[1] A sava is an ekāha with which a consecration, an anointing, *abhiṣeka*, is connected.

5. He who knows this obtains a chaplainship.

6. It is the consecration as chief judge[1]. He whom they consecrate for the office of a chief judge should perform this (sacrifice).

[1] The Sthapati was probably a Vaiśya. Some texts (T. Br. and Kāṭh.) describe a sava, which is designated by Baudh. (XVIII. 3) and Āp. (XXII. 25. 2–5) as *vaiśyasava* or *sthapatisava*. Lāṭy. VIII. 7. 10: 'Whom they put at their head, amongst these he should henceforth lead a friendly disposed life (?; differently the commentary, but cp. Lāṭy. VIII. 12. 1. *kṣatravṛttiṃ vartayet*) and they should call him Sthapati.' Nidānasūtra: *purodhākāmayajña uttaraḥ sthapatisavo vā, yaṁ samānāḥ śraiṣṭhye saṃvṛṇīran.*

7. He who knows this gets an office as chief judge.

8. He is sprinkled[1] (*i.e.* inaugurated) (whilst sitting) on a black antelope-hide. This (hide) is visibly the priestly lustre[2]; he is inaugurated on priestly lustre.

[1] On the moment when this sprinkling takes place, see XIX. 13. 8 and cp. note 10 on no. 139 in Jaim. br. in Auswahl.

[2] According to TS. VI. 1. 3. 1, the black antelope-hide is identical, by its white spots, with the Ṛgveda; by its black spots, with the Sāmaveda; according to T. Br. II. 7. 3. 3, it is the form of the Brahman: of ṛc and sāman.

9. He is sprinkled with clarified, liquid butter; the clarified butter is brilliance; he (thus) puts brilliance into himself[1].

[1] Cp. XII. 10. 18.

XVII. 12.

(The Sarvasvāra.)[1]

1. A nine-versed agniṣṭoma; this is throughout circumflected[1]. He who wishes: 'May I go to yonder world not through any disease'[2], should perform this (rite).

1 *sarvasvāraḥ sc. stomaḥ* or *yajñaḥ*: a stoma (a sacrifice of soma) that has the *svāra*, the musical notation 565, throughout on the nidhana of each sāman' cp. R. Simon, Puṣpasūtra *in voce: svāra* (page 525) and *padānusvāra* (page 521): cp. also above, VII. 3. 25.

2 Sāyaṇa supplies to *anāyamatā* the noun *dehena*: 'With a not sick body.' The Jaim. br. runs: 'Śunaskarṇa, the son of Vṛṣṇyaha, was a performer of good, not of wrong deeds. He desired: 'Having done in this world good (only) and not bad, may I go to the world of heaven' (*śunaskarṇo ha vai vārṣṇyahaḥ puṇyakṛd apāpakṛd āsa. sa ha cakame: puṇyam evāsmin loke kṛtvāpāpam kṛtyā* (r. *kṛtvā* ?) *svargaṃ lokaṃ gaccheyam iti.* According to Baudh., it was the king Śunaskarṇa, the son of Śibi, see below, § 6.

2. The nine-versed (trivṛt) stoma is breath[1]; the tone (circumflex) is breath[2]; he brings his breaths (his vital principles) outside him[3]; he dies immediately.

1 Cp. II. 15. 3.

2 Cp. VII. 1. 10, XI. 5. 26, XXIV. 11. 9.

3 The circumflected part of the sāman is outside the verse itself.—On the *ṇ* in *bahir nirādadhāti* (if the reading is correct !) cp. Oertel, Disjunct use of cases, page 311. The Jaim. br. runs: 'They arrange all the sāmans so that they are circumflected; the tone (circumflex) is breath; the Udgātṛ thereby 'tones away' the vital principles of the Sacrificer' (*svārāṇi sarvāṇi sāmāny avakalpayanti, prāṇo vai svaraḥ, prāṇair eva tat prāṇān udgatā yajamānasya ni(ḥ)svarati*).

3. The nine-versed (stoma) is the swiftest of (all) the stomas[1]. That it is a nine-versed (stoma) (is, because he thinks): 'In the swiftest way he shall meet (with his end)'[2]. The tone is endless[3] and yonder world is endless; he makes him go to the endless, to yonder world.

1 Because it is the shortest of all, cp. Śat. br. VIII. 4. 1. 9.

---

1 Cp. Jaim. br. II. 167–169; Lāṭy. VIII. 8. 1–42; Nidānasūtra VII. 2; Ārṣeyakalpa III. 14; Baudh. XVIII. 48; Āp. XXII. 7. 20–25; Kāty. XXII. 5. 31–6. 20; Śāṅkh. XV. 10.

[2] Probably euphonistic for 'he shall die', cp. Lāṭy. VIII. 8. 5: *tad eva saṃgacchate, tad eva mriyata iti.*

[3] *avasānarahitaḥ* (Sāyaṇa).

4. The (verses) contain the (words) 'towards' (*abhi*) and 'forth' (*pra*)[1]; he (thereby) makes him go from this world to the world of heaven.

[1] See the verses in Ārṣeyakalpa III. 14.

5. Whilst the ārbhava-pavamāna(-laud) is being chanted, he (the Sacrificer) lies down, his head being covered by his uppergarment, to the south of the pillar of udumbara-wood[1]. Then, he meets (his end)[2].

[1] He should lie down on his black antelope-hide with his head to the south, according to Lāṭy. VIII. 8. 5; according to the Jaim br., he lies down behind the gārhapatya with his head to the south, whilst the yajñāyajñiya-laud is being performed, or, according to others, as this would cause a drawing asunder of the sacrifice, after the completion of the whole rite.

[2] Lāṭy. VIII. 8. 39-41 provides for the case that the Sacrificer does not die: 'If he lives, he should perform the final iṣṭi of the sacrifice of soma (see C. H. § 259) and, thereupon, seek his death by starving. Dhānañjayya, however, prescribes that he should then eat and abandon his project of dying.'

6. This is the stoma of Śunaskarṇa. This sacrifice was performed by Śunaskarṇa, the son of Baṣkiha[1]; hence it is called Śunaskarṇa's stoma.

[1] Cp. note 2 on § 1.

XVII. 13.

(The Cāturmāsyas as ekāhas.)[1]

1. A nine-versed agniṣṭoma replaces[1] the vaiśvadeva(-cāturmāsya)[2].

[1] Read *loke* instead of *lokaḥ*.

[2] This ekāha must be performed on the day of full-moon in the month Phālguna, Lāṭy. VIII. 8. 43.

---

[1] Cp. Jaim. br. II. 227-234; this description is much more detailed and in many respects different from Pañc. br.: Ārṣeyakalpa IV. 1-5; Lāṭy. VIII. 8. 43-48; Nidānasūtra VII. 3; Baudh. XVII. 55-58; Āp. XXII. 8. 1-9. 6; Kāty. XXII. 7. 1-8. 5; Āśv. IX. 2. 1-25; Śāṅkh. XIV. 7-10.

2. The opening (-verse) is one addressed to Agni; the savana-he-goat is destined for the All-gods, the barren cow (at the end) for Bṛhaspati.

3. They do not erect a sacrificial post, nor do they throw up a high-altar[1].

[1] Cp. Āp. VIII. 1. 8.

4. They fasten the victim to an[1] encircling peg.

[1] Perhaps: to one of the pegs laid around the āhavanīya.

5. The sacrificial fee consists of fifty (milch-cows).

6. Clad in a new garment, he comes out of the lustral bath. During (the then following) four months he abstains from meat and from sexual intercourse.

7. At the end of (these) four months, a (soma-rite) of two days replaces the varuṇapraghāsa(-offering)s.

8–10*a*. The opening (-verse) is one addressed to Varuṇa; the savana-he-goat is destined for the Maruts; (for the second day), a (verse) containing (the word) *ka*[1] (is required) as opening-verse and a he-goat destined for Varuṇa; the barren cow is destined for Mitra and Varuṇa.

[1] See Ārṣeyakalpa IV. 2 and cp. Āp. VIII. 7. 1.

10*b* They erect a sacrificial post, throw up a high-altar[1] and fasten the two victims to the post.

[1] Cp. Āp VIII. 5. 21.

11. The sacrificial fee consists of one hundred (cows).—Clad in a new garment, he comes out of the lustral bath. During four months he abstains from meat and sexual intercourse.

12. At the end of these four months, a (soma-rite) of three days replaces the sākamedha(-offering)s.

13. A (verse) containing the word 'front' is the opening (verse)[1]; the savana-he-goat is destined for Agni; (for the second day), a (verse) addressed to the Maruts[2] is the opening (verse), the victim is destined for Indra and Agni; (for the third day), the opening (verse) is one addressed to Viśvakarman[3], the victims are the set of eleven[4], the barren cow (at the end of the three-day-rite) is destined for Sūrya. They erect a sacrificial post, throw up the high-altar, fasten the

victims to the post. The sacrificial fee consists of one hundred and fifty (cows).

[1] SV. II. 920 (*vāyor anīke asthiran*), cp. Āp. VIII. 9. 2.

[2] Cp. Āp. VIII. 11. 22.

[3] Cp. Āp. VIII. 12. 3 (note 3, end).

[4] Cp. Āp. XIV. 5–7.

14. Clad in a new garment, he comes out of the lustral bath. During four months, he abstains from meat and sexual intercourse.

15. At the end of these four months, an agniṣṭoma-jyotiṣṭoma replaces the śunāsīrya(-offering)s.

16. The opening (verse) contains the (word) *upa* [1]; the savana-he-goat is destined for Vāyu [2], the barren cow for the Aśvins. They erect a sacrificial post, throw up the high-altar, fasten the victim [3] to the post. The sacrificial fee consists of one hundred and twelve (cows).

[1] SV. II. 1.

[2] Cp. Āp. VIII. 20. 4.

[3] Read *paśuṃ* instead of *paśū*.

17. The saṃvatsara [1] is the fire, the parivatsara [1] is the sun, the idāvatsara [1] is the moon, the anuvatsara [1] is the wind. Through the vaiśvadeva, he reaches the fire (and) the saṃvatara; through the varuṇapraghāsa(-offering)s, the sun (and) the parivatsara; through the sākamedha(-offering)s, the moon (and) the idāvatsara; through the śunāsīrya, the wind (and) the anuvatsara.

[1] These are probably four of the five names of the five-years cycle; cp. on these names Vedic Index *in voce: saṃvatsara.*

18. By the (Cāturmāsyas as) sacrifices of rice or barley, the Gods gained this world; by the (Cāturmāsyas), combined with the (immolation of a) victim, (they gained) the intermediate region; by the (Cāturmāsyas as) sacrifices of soma, (they gained) yonder world. He who knows this reaches, thereby, these worlds and is firmly established in them.

XVII. 14.

(The Cāturmāsyas as ekāhas, concluded.)

1, 2. By sacrificing with the agnihotra, he reaches in one day ten 'Houselords' (*i.e.* he becomes equal to, gains the merits of ten H.); by sacrificing with the agnihotra during ten years, he becomes equal to one who (regularly) performs the sacrifices of full- and new-moon; by sacrificing during ten years with the sacrifices of full- and new-moon, he becomes equal to one who performs the sacrifices of soma. By offering ten agniṣṭoma-sacrifices, he becomes equal to one who performs a sacrifice of a thousand cows as sacrificial fee. By offering ten of these, he becomes equal to one who performs a sacrifice with ten thousand dakṣiṇās. By offering ten of these, he becomes equal to one who sacrifices with a sacrifice with a hundred thousand dakṣiṇās. By offering ten of these, he becomes equal to one who sacrifices with a sacrifice of a million dakṣiṇās. By offering ten of these, he becomes equal to one who sacrifices with a sacrifice of 10 millions dakṣiṇās. By offering ten of these, he becomes equal to one who sacrifices with a sacrifice of 100 millions dakṣiṇās. By offering ten of these, he becomes equal to one who sacrifices with a sacrifice of 1,000 millions dakṣiṇās. By offering ten of these, he becomes equal to one who sacrifices with a sacrifice of 10.C00 millions dakṣiṇās. By offering ten of these, he becomes equal to one who sacrifices with a sacrifice of 1,00000 millions dakṣiṇās[1]. By offering ten of these, he becomes the Cow; when he becomes the Cow, then he becomes the Fire; when he becomes the Fire, then he becomes equal to the House-lord of the year[2].

[1] On these numbers, see Vedic Index, vol. I, page 342 in voce *daśan*.

[2] The meaning of the last words is doubtful. Do they equally design high numbers? For the last, cp. perhaps, Ait. br. V. 25. 22.

3. When he becomes the Houselord of the year, he reaches the measure of the vaiśvadeva and, after this, the other (sacrifices) are all of them[1] higher and higher[2].

[1] Read *sarve* instead of *sarvaḥ*.

[2] The translation is doubtful, the purport uncertain. Sāyaṇa cites Śat. br. II. 6. 3. 1: *akṣayyaṃ ha vai sukṛtaṃ cāturmāsyayājino bhavati.*

4. He who knows this reaches these worlds, gains these worlds.

EIGHTEENTH CHAPTER.

(The ekāhas or one-day-rites, continued.)

XVIII. 1.

(The Upahavya.)[1]

1. A seventeen-versed agniṣṭoma.

2. The Gods and the Asuras were the two kinds of sons of Prajāpati. The Asuras were more numerous and stronger, the Gods were less (in number and strength). The Gods resorted to Prajāpati, and he saw this (ekāha called) Upahavya[1].

[1] Cp. Jaim. br. II. 150: 'At the beginning, there were two kinds of descendants of Prajāpati: the Gods and the Asuras. Then the Gods were, so to say, more intent upon doing the will (of Prajāpati), the Asuras were less intent upon it (*abhirādhayattarā iva . . . anabhirādhayattarā iva*). Prajāpati desired: 'May the Gods come to prosperity and the Asuras perish (*devā eva syuḥ parāsurā bhaveyur iti*). He saw this sacrifice, took it unto himself and performed it. At this sacrifice he invited (*upāhvayata*) the Gods, but, by means of a long bamboo-stick, he excluded the Asuras (*dīrghavaṃśenāntaragṛhṇāt*)...He who has an adversary, he who wishes to practise abhicāra, he who contends, should perform this sacrifice. Those officiating priests who are friendly disposed towards him (*pratikāminā iva*) he should invite, the others he should exclude by means of a long bamboo-stick. Along with their not being invited (*teṣām anupahavam anu*), his adversary perishes and he himself reaches prosperity.'

3. He considered: 'If I take (this sacrifice unto me and practise it) 'expressedly', the Asuras will destroy my sacrifice.' So he practised it 'unexpressedly'[1].

[1] On the sense of *aniruktam* here, cp note 1 on XVII. 1. 8. The Sūtrakāra (Lāṭy. VIII. 9. 1-4) prescribes: 'They should pronounce the names of the deities cryptically, if the deities occupy their own place, but explicitly if the deities occupy another place. The word 'God' (and the name of a God) he should everywhere avoid pronouncing, (for instance:) they should replace (the words) *hotā devaḥ* (in the first ājyalaud, see Ārṣeyakalpa IV. 6), by (the words) *hotā yajñe* (read probably *yajñaḥ*), and (the words) *mahi mitrasya* (in the second ājyalaud, SV. II. 948) by (the words): *mahi yajñasya*. Instead of (the word) *soma* they should use (the word) *indu*.' Here all is not clear to me, especially the meaning of *svasthānā devatāḥ* and *asvasthānā devatāḥ*. With this prescript agrees that of

---

[1] Cp. Jaim. br. II. 148-150; Ārṣeyakalpa IV. 6; Lāṭy. VIII. 9. 1-6; Nidānasūtra VII. 4; Baudh. XVIII. 28-29; Āp. XXII. 9. 8-10; Kāty. XXII. 8. 7-9; Āśv. IX. 7. 28; Śāṅkh. XIV. 50.

Baudhāyana, according to whom the names of the deities, in the formulae for drawing and for offering the soma, must be replaced by other names: instead of *indra*, the Adhvaryu must speak *śakra*; instead of *soma*, *indu*; instead of *mitrāvaruṇau*, *ṛtāyuvau*; etc. etc.

4. At the last laud (with the verses beginning:) 'The God who bestoweth wealth'[1], he (Prajāpati, whilst performing this rite.) turned himself to the Gods[2].

[1] See note 1 on XVII. 1. 10.

[2] This seems to imply that now the names of the Gods were pronounced 'expressedly', explicitly. Cp. Baudh.: 'This (unexpressed manner of saying the names of the deities) prevails (only) unto the yajñāyajñīya-laud; at this laud Prajāpati spoke this (verse) openly, because now the Asuras were led astray sufficiently.' Baudh. equally prescribes the verse: *devo vo draviṇodāḥ*.

5. Thereupon, the Gods came to prosperity, but the Asuras perished.

6. He who knows this, comes himself to prosperity, but his adversary perishes.

7. But they (the Theologians) say also: '(The verses beginning:) 'By sacrifice on sacrifice, in honour of Agni'[1] must be applied (at the agniṣṭoma-laud)[2].

[1] Cp. VIII. 6. 1 and 5.

[2] And so does Maśaka, in his Ārṣeyakalpa.

8. Agni is (equal to) all the deities[1]; thereby, he excludes no one of the deities.

[1] Cp. IX. 4. 5.

9. Indra gave the Yatis over to the hyenas; an inauspicious voice reproached him[1]. He resorted to Prajapati who to him gave over this Upahavya. Him (Indra) the All-gods invited[2]. Because they invited (*upāhvayanta*), therefore this rite is called Upahavya.

[1] So far this § is identical with XIV. 11. 28.

[2] Because, when he had practised it, he again was worthy of their society.

10. He should perform it for one who is calumniated.

11. The deities avoid him who is falsely calumniated. He[1] (the officiating priest who performs this rite for him) causes the deities to eat his food (*i.e.* to accept his offerings).

[1] If we may read *ādayati* instead of *ādayanti*.

12. Of him, who (thereby) is purified and made palatable, men eat the food.

13. It should be performed by one who is desirous of (obtaining the chieftainship over) a clan.

14. There is a (verse) addressed to the Maruts[1]. The Maruts are the people (or subjects) of the Gods. He (thus) attaches to him the people. The people will be likely to remain with him.

[1] SV. II. 944, cp. Ārṣeyakalpa IV. 6.

15 It should be performed by one who is desirous of (obtaining) cattle.

16. There is a (verse) addressed to Pūṣan[1]. Pūṣan is the cattle; he obtains cattle.

[1] Must we read *pauṣṇī*, or is *pauṣī* alright: 'connected with thriving'? According to Sāyaṇa, the verse SV. II. 961 is meant, where Pūṣan is not mentioned, but it contains the words: 'cow' and 'horse'.

17. There is a (verse) addressed to the All-gods[1]; the All-gods it was who called him (Indra) to them[2].

[1] SV. II. 945.

[2] Cp. § 9.

18. It has the bṛhat as (first) pṛṣṭha-laud.

19. For Prajāpati had given it (this rite) to Indra[1].

[1] The causal connection between these two § § is far from clear.

20. A dark-brown horse is the sacrificial fee.

21 For this (*viz.* the horse) is 'unexpressed'[1].

[1] Because Prajāpati, as Ka, is *anirukta*, and the horse sprang from Prajāpati, cp. XXI. 4. 2.

22. It must be given (as an extra-fee) to the Brahman.

23. Amongst the officiating priests, the Brahman is 'unexpressed'[1]; through his own characteristic feature he, thereby, makes him prosper.

[1] Probably because the Brahman has no Veda proper as he must take his formulæ from the other Vedas.

24. In him, who knows this, there is not even so much guilt as in a newly born child.

XVIII. 2.

(The Ṛtapeya.)

1. A seventeen-versed agniṣṭoma.

2. At this (rite) there are twelve dīkṣās and upasads [1].

[1] This prescript, being rather vague, is explained by Lāṭy.: nine dīkṣā- and three upasad-days. The Jaiminīyas seem to prescribe equally nine dīkṣā- and three upasad-days. Baudh. allows either nine or twenty-seven dīkṣā-days and three upasads.

3. One who is desirous of (reaching) heaven should perform it.

4. The year is (equal to) twelve months; the world of heaven is the year; he reaches, by this (rite), the world of heaven [1].

[1] This is to be connected with the preceding §, where the twelve days are mentioned.

5. He subsists (during the days of upasad) on clarified butter [1].

[1] Cp. § 7.—The usual *vrata*-food is milk.

6. Clarified butter is the fasting-food of the Gods. Through the fasting-food of the Gods, he approaches the deities.

7. Each time with a subsequent (or 'higher') section (of the fingers), he undertakes, (during the days of upasad, the observance of drinking the fasting-food) [1]: each of these worlds in their successive order is larger (than the preceding one) [2]; (he does so) in order to reach the world of heaven.

[1] The sūtra gives three explanations of this prescript in the Brāhmaṇa. The first is as follows: 'According to Dhānañjayya, he should, during the days of upasad, separately drink (the liquified butter) with three sections of the finger in inverted order.' (*viz.*, he dips, on the first day, the whole of his first finger, *i.e.*, the three sections of it, into the clarified butter and drinks or sips this quantity; the second day, he drinks as much as adheres to the two finger-sections; the third, as much as adheres to the point of the finger: its last section). The second explanation is the following: 'According to Śaucivṛkṣi, there should be (three wooden quadrangular) vessels, having in all directions each the measure of the different joints of the finger (read *aṅgulyāḥ* instead of *aṅgulyā*); out of these (he should partake of the clarified butter) in

---

[1] Cp. Jaim. br. II. 158-161 (Auswahl No. 143); Ārṣeyakalpa IV. 7. a; Lāṭy. VIII. 9. 7-18; Nidānasūtra VII. 4; Baudh. XVIII. 31-34; Āp. XXII. 9. 11-18; Kāty. XXII. 8. 10-25; Āśv. IX. 7. 35-38; Śāṅkh. XIV. 16.

natural order.' The second manner, then, is that three *camasas* are made, one having the height and breadth of one finger-joint, a second having the measures of two, a third having the measures of three finger-joints. The first day, he partakes of so much butter as is contained in the firstly mentioned *camasa*; the second day, out of the secondly mentioned one: the third, out of the thirdly mentioned one. The third explanation is as follows: 'According to Śāṇḍilya, (he drinks) from them in reversed order.' In this last manner the quantity of butter is each day less than that of the preceding day. The view of Śāṇḍilya is apparently based on the fact that ordinarily the quantity of vrata-food is diminished during the days of upasad. Baudh. admits the view of Dhānañjayya; Kāty. seems to accept the view of Śāṇḍilya. The Jaim. br. and Śāṅkh. admit for each day an equal quantity.

[2] Cp. note 2 on XVI. 10. 3.

8. This (rite) has (for its first pṛṣṭha-laud) the bṛhat(-sāman). By means of the bṛhat, the Gods went to the world of heaven[1]. He, thereby, reaches the world of heaven.

[1] That the bṛhat is at least, equalled to yonder world, is seen from VII. 6. 17.

9. Having spoken a (divine) truth[1], they betake themselves into the sadas (where the rest of the libation of soma is going to be consumed by them)[2].

[1] About the meaning of the Brāhmaṇa, the later generations were at variance. In Lāṭy. we read: "When they are about to enter the sadas in order to partake of the soma, they should utter the divine truths: 'Here is the Earth, yonder is the Sun'. According to Śāṇḍilya, they should modify the formulae that contain (the words): 'drunk by that and that God', to whom a part of the soma-draught has been sacrificed'." Such a formula contains, *e.g.*, the words: *indrapītasya madhumata upahūtasyopahūto bhakṣayāmi*. But we are not able to infer from the sūtra in which way the modification of the mantra is to be made.—Other instances of *ṛta* are given by Āśv. and Śāṅkh., cp. the Jaim. br.

[2] Cp. C.H. § 142.—This rite either is invented to account for the name of this ekāha: *ṛtapeya*, or the name rests on this part of the ritual.

10. A wooden, quadrangular cup (a *camasa*) filled with soma is the sacrificial fee; through the deity even he comes to the deities.

11. It is made of udumbara(-wood); the udumbara is strength and food; he obtains strengthening food.

12. It must be given as sacrificial fee to the Brahman(-priest) who belongs to the same gotra (as the Sacrificer), in order that the soma-drunk may not be wrongly milked out (used up)[1].

[1] The Sūtra remarks on this *somacamasa*: "It should be filled with the extracted soma-juice (not with ordinary soma that is not destined for the sacrifice), for to this points the use of the word *camasa*. They should fill this vessel at the midday-service, together with the cups, before the beginning of the offering (see C.H. § 187), and pour a small quantity of it (into the fire). For a brāhmana says: 'it should be given after it has been offered' (this is the Jaiminīya-Brāhmaṇa, not the Tāṇḍya, cp. Jaim. br. in Auswahl No. 143, page 175, below) When the moment has come for bringing near the sacrificial fees, they should bring it around to the east of the āhavanīya(-fire), but not outside the (mahā-) vedi, to the south of havirdhâna and sadas, into the sadas through its eastern door. When the sacrifice has been brought to an end, they should give something to the (other) priests."

13. It is throughout seventeenfold[1].

[1] All the lauds consist of seventeen verses.

14. There are twelve months and five seasons: these are the year. The world of heaven is the year; he reaches, by this (seventeenfold rite), the world of heaven.

XVIII. 3.

(The Dūṇāśa.)[1]

1. A seventeen-versed agniṣṭoma.

2. He gives, at the dīkṣaṇīya-isti, (a piece of) gold weighing 12 mānas; at the prāyaṇīya-iṣṭi, (a piece of) gold of 24 mānas; at the guest-iṣṭi, two (pieces) of 24 mānas; at the first upasad at morning, four pieces of 24 mānas, and, at afternoon, 8; at the middle upasad at morning, 16, and, at afternoon, 32; at the last upasad at morning, 64 and, at afternoon, 128. At the offering of the omentum of the he-goat destined for Agni and Soma, he gives two pieces of 128 mānas; at the offering of the omentum of the

[1] Cp. Jaim. br. II. 98, 99 (Auswahl No. 132), Ārṣeyakalpa IV. 7. b; Lāṭy. VIII. 10. 1-4; Nidānasūtra VII. 4; Baudh. XVIII. 37, 38; Āp. XXII. 9. 19-20. 1; Kāty. XXII. 8. 26-9. 6; Āśv. IX. 8. 1-4; Śāṅkh. XIV. 32., This ekāha, to which no name is given in the Pañc. br., is called also *durāśa*, *bahuhiraṇya*, and *atimūrti*.

savana-he-goat at morning (of the soma-day itself), four pieces of 128 mānas; at the morning service, when the Nārāśaṃsa-cups have been deposited, eight pieces of 128 mānas; at the same occasion in the midday-service, 16 pieces of 128 mānas and (as now has come the usual moment for distributing the dakṣiṇās proper) a hundred oxen, and, to the Hotṛ(-priest), a golden plate (as ornament to be worn round the neck), and, to the Udgātṛ, a (golden) wreath. When the Nārāśaṃsa-cups have been deposited at the afternoon-service, he gives 32 pieces of 128 mānas; at the udayanīya-iṣṭi, 64 pieces of 128 mānas, and, at the offering of the omentum of the barren cow, 128 pieces of 128 mānas[1].

[1] The occasions are successively those described in C.H. §15, 28, 44, 52, 57, 62, 68, 73, 76, 106.f, 141.e, 147.c, 189.b, 191.c, 230.b, 255, 256.—We get the impression that at this time certain pieces of gold, weighing respectively 12, 24, and 128 units (*kṛṣṇalas?*), perhaps in the form of *niṣkas*, were current.

3. He who knows this reaches the world of the Ox[1].

[1] Perhaps Āditya, the sun, is meant.

4. He who, knowing thus, performs this (rite), gains the luminous, lucky world.

XVIII. 4.

(The Vaiśyastoma.)[1]

1. A seventeen-versed agniṣṭoma.

2. At this (rite) he mixes the soma(-draughts) at the morning-service with fresh milk; at the midday-service, with boiled (milk); at the afternoon-service, with sour coagulated milk.

3. One who is desirous of (obtaining) cattle should perform (this rite).

4. In that all the pressings (*i.e.*, the soma-draughts drawn at all the pressings) are mixed with milk, he makes him thrive in regard to cattle, in accordance with each pressing; but his young ones (his children and calves) shrink as it were[1], for he mixes with milk (also the draughts of soma at) the two pressings, which (otherwise) consist of pure soma[2].

---

[1] Cp. Ārṣeyakalpa IV. 7. c; Lāṭy. VIII. 10. 5-6; Āp. XXII. 10. 4-5; Kāty. XXII. 8. 7-14.

[1] Cp. VII. 9. 21.

[2] Cp. TS. VI. 1. 6. 4: *tasmād dve savane śukravatī : prātaḥsavanaṃ ca mādhyandinaṃ ca.* Is the reason why, in doing thus, the young ones shrink, simply that, at the third pressing, the sour milk is adhibited?

5. He should perform (this rite) for a Vaiśya.

6. Cattle is the welfare of the Vaiśya; he makes him thrive with regard to cattle.

7 Its (first) pṛṣṭha(-laud) is the kaṇvarathantara(-sāman)[1].

[1] Grām. XVI. 1. 29, composed on SV. I. 511, here chanted on the usual verses of the pṛṣṭha (SV. II. 30-31).

8. The sadoviśīya(-sāman)[1] is the Brahman's chant (serves for the third pṛṣṭha-laud).

[1] Grām. XVI. 1. 31, composed on SV. I. 511, chanted on SV. II. 842-843.

9. The kaṇvarathantara is cattle, the sadoviśīya is cattle: successive (kinds of) cattle he puts into him (he brings into his possession).

10. It is throughout seventeen-versed.

11. Twelve months, five seasons, these are (equal to) the year. In the course of the year cattle procreate; having reached the cattle, he obtains it[1].

[1] Read *āptvāvarunddhe.*

XVIII. 5.

(The Tīvrasut or Tīvrasoma.)[1]

1. A seventeen-versed ukthya(-day).

2. Indra had slain Vṛtra. His strength went asunder in every direction[1]. The Gods sought for him a (means of) expiation[2], but nothing did satisfy him; it was only the strong soma (*tīvrasoma*) that satisfied (and restored) him.

---

[1] Cp. Jaim. br. II. 151-157 (See Auswahl No. 142 and Oertel in Transactions of the Connecticut Ac. of Arts and Sciences, Vol. XV, page 180 sqq.); Ārṣeyakalpa IV. 7. d; Lāṭy. VIII. 10. 7-14; Nidānasūtra VII. 4; Baudh. XVIII. 29-30; Āp. XXII. 10. 6-18; Kāty. XXII. 9. 15-10. 6; Āśv. IX. 7. 31; Śāṅkh. XIV. 21.

[1] *sa viṣvaṅ vīryeṇa vyārchat*, litt.: 'he went asunder in regard to his strength in every direction'.

[2] That is: a means to repair the evil that had befallen Indra.

3. He should perform (this rite) for one, through whom the soma has flown[1].

[1] For one in whom the use of soma has caused diarrhœa. The exegetes of olden times are at variance as to the precise meaning. According to Śāṇḍilya he is meant who, after performing a sacrifice, becomes worse; according to Dhānañjayya, he is meant who, after drinking the soma, either vomits or suffers from diarrhœa.

4. Pierced, so to say, is he through whom flows the soma. The sacrifice of the 'sharp' soma serves to cover up (the hole), to remove the hole (the defect).

5. He should perform (it) for a king (a Baron) who is being held out of his realm.

6. It is the peasantry (the people) that flows through him (that departs from him) through whom flows the soma. The sacrifice of the 'sharp' soma serves to cover up, to remove the defect.

7. It should be performed by one who desires (to obtain the chieftainship over his) clan.

8. It is the clan that flows through him (that departs from him) who, being qualified to (obtain the chieftainship over) a clan, does not obtain it. The sacrifice of the 'sharp' soma serves to cover up, to remove the defect.

9 It should be performed by one who is desirous of (obtaining) progeny; it is the progeny that departs from him who, being qualified to (obtain) progeny, gets no progeny. The sacrifice of the 'sharp' soma serves to cover up, to remove the defect.

10. It should be performed by one who is desirous of (obtaining) cattle. It is the cattle that departs from him who, being qualified to (obtain) cattle, does not obtain it. The sacrifice of the 'sharp' soma serves to cover up, to remove the defect.

11. He should perform (it) for one who is suffering from a lingering disease. They are the vital principles that depart from him, who

is suffering from disease. The sacrifice of the 'sharp' soma serves to cover up, to remove the defect.

12. They milk a hundred (cows) to get the milk for mixing with the soma[1]. They, thereby[2], sharpen him (the soma, or Indra).

[1] According to Lāṭy. (who here probably follows the Jaim. br. II. 157. 7), this milk is divided into three parts and used for mixing the soma in the manner of the Vaiśyastoma: XVIII. 4. 2.

[2] The word *tat*, at the beginning of § § 13, 15, and 16, is to be combined with the preceding §.

13. These same (cows) serve as sacrificial fee.

14*a*. They constantly fill the soma-cups[1], thinking: 'The 'sharp' soma will satisfy him (Indra)'.

[1] Up to the fourth ājya-laud, the participants should not partake (as usual), after each stotra-śastra, of the soma that has been left over in each *camasa* (when a part of it has been poured out into the fire); but they should only smell at it, with the formula destined for partaking of the soma (Lāṭy. VIII. 10. 10 should be read: *bhakṣāvṛtā camasān avajighreyuḥ*). Into each (not emptied) *camasa*, after each subsequent stotra-śastra, must be poured the rest of each corresponding soma-draught (*graha*); *abhi* denotes: 'hinzu'.

14*b*. Both the Adhvaryu (and) all the Camasādhvaryus make the response to the Acchāvāka[1]; they, thereby, sharpen him (the soma).

[1] See note 3 on Jaim. br. II. 152 (Auswahl, page 173). Usually it is the Pratiprasthātṛ alone who makes the response (C. H. § 170).

15. Not partaking of the soma-draughts, the officiating Priests smell (only) at the (soma in the) vessels. Thereby, they sharpen him. They partake of (the soma in) those (vessels) at the stotra of the Acchāvāka[1]; thereby, they sharpen him (the soma).

[1] *Viz.*, after the (stotra and) śastra of the Acchāvāka, at the moment indicated in C. H. § 171.

16. If they were to partake (of the soma-draughts) during the different services, prosperity would be likely to abandon the Sacrificer. Once, at the end of each service, they partake of the soma[1], in order that the (three) services may not be rent asunder[2].

[1] The procedure, as indicated above in § 14 and 15, prevails for the three savanas; cp. Lāṭy. VIII 10. 11. This probably is not the view of the Jaim. br. where this procedure seems to be restricted to the morning-service.

[2] This would be the case if at the morning-service only the soma-draughts were smelt at, but now they are all made equal.

17. The sāman (of the first pṛṣṭha-laud) is the rathantara.

18. The rathantara is the earth[1]; it is on the earth that he is not firmly established who lacks a firm support; he makes him firmly established on the earth.

[1] Cp. note 2 on VI. 8. 18.

19. The Brahman's chant[1] is the śrāyantiya(-sāman)[2]; he strengthens (*śrīṇāti*) this in him[3].

[1] The third pṛṣṭha-laud.

[2] Grām. VII. 2. 5, composed on SV. I. 267 (*śrāyanta iva sūryam*).

[3] Cp. VIII. 2. 11. What is meant by 'this' (*etad eva*) is not clear, perhaps the vigour which he had lost through vomiting the soma.

20. The yajñāyajñīya(-sāman)[1] is applied on the anuṣṭubh (-part).

[1] Grām. I. 2. 25, composed on SV. I. 35, but here chanted on the anuṣṭubh-part of the ārbhava-pavamāna-laud.

21. The anuṣṭubh is the voice[1]; the yajñāyajñīya is the pith of the voice[2]; he brings the pith into his voice.

[1] Cp. V. 7. 1.

[2] Cp. VIII. 6. 1.

22. For the agniṣṭoma-sāman the viśoviśīya[1] is to be taken; all this he firmly establishes in him[2].

[1] See note 1 on XIV. 11. 36, but here chanted on the verses on which the yajñāyajñīya is composed (cp. § 20).

[2] Cp. note 3 on § 19.

23. The udvaṁśīya(-sāman)[1] is applied at the end of the uktha (-laud)s, (*i.e.*, as the last uktha-laud). This (sāman) is the characteristic feature of all the pṛṣṭha(-sāmans)[2]; in all the forms he is firmly established.

[1] Cp. note 2 on VIII. 9. 6.

[2] Cp. VII. 9. 6.

24. It is an ukthya(-rite): the uktha(-laud)s are (equal to) cattle; in cattle he is firmly established.

[1] Cp. note 1 on IV. 5. 18.

XVIII. 6.

(The Vājapeya.)[1]

1. A seventeen-versed ukthya(-rite) combined with a sixteenth laud, to which is added a seventeenth laud.

2. So big as Prajāpati is vertically, so big is he horizontally[1].

[1] This is why not only all the lauds consist of seventeen verses but their number is likewise seventeen.

3. So big as these worlds are vertically, so big are they horizontally.

4. He, forsooth, who performs the Vājapeya, reaches (*i.e.*, becomes equal to) Prajāpati.

5. In that there are seventeen lauds, thereby, he reaches the vertical (Prajāpati); in that the rite is throughout seventeen-versed, thereby, the horizontal.

6. The services of this (rite) are of different power.

7. The morning-service is 'unexpressed'[1]; the midday-service contains (the word) 'strength' (*vāja*)[2]; the afternoon-service contains (the word) 'wondrous' (*citra*)[3].

[1] This regards the out-of-doors-laud and the ājya-lauds. On *anirukta* cp. note 1 on VII. 1.8.

[2] The rathantara (first pṛṣṭha-laud) is chanted on SV. II. 30-31: *aśvāyanto maghavann indra vājinaḥ.*

[3] The agniṣṭoma-sāman (afternoon-service) is chanted on SV. II. 973-974: *tvaṃ naś citra ūtyā.*

8. In that the morning-service is 'unexpressed', he reaches Prajāpati, this God being 'unexpressed'[1]. That the midday-service contains (the word) 'strength', food being strength, (this serves) for obtaining food. That the afternoon-service contains (the word) 'wondrous', (this serves) for reaching the world of heaven[2].

[1] Prajāpati is *anirukta* as he is addressed mystically as *ka.*

---

[1] Cp. Jaim. br. II. 193-196; Ārṣeyakalpa IV. 7. e, Lāṭy. VIII. 11. 1-12. 15; Nidānasūtra VII. 4; Baudh. XI; Āp. XVIII. 1-7; Āśv. IX. 9; Śāṅkh. XV. 1-3; Śat br. V. 1-2; Kāty. XIV.

[2] The world of heaven hereby is qualified as something wondrous.—With § 7, 8 may be compared Maitr. Saṃh. I. 11. 9 : 171. 3-8 and Kāṭh. XIV. 10 : 209. 1-5.

9. 'The Vājapeya,' they say, 'being sprung from Prājapati, is in disharmony with its place of origin, as it has sāmans that are 'expressedly' chanted (*viz*, in the midday- and afternoon-service). In that its morning-service is 'unexpressed' (as is Prajāpati), it is in harmony with its origin[1].

[1] I read with a Leyden MS. *prājāpatyas san niruktasāmeti*. The Kāṭhaka (XIV. 10 : 209. 1) runs: *víyonir vái vājapéyó 'niruktas sán prájāpatyó 'nirukta-sāmā téna víyonir yád ániruktāḥ prātassavās téna sáyoniḥ*. 'The Vājapeya being 'unexpressed' and sprung from Prajāpati, has 'unexpressed' sāmans. Thereby, it is in disharmony with its origin; (but) in that its morning service (the plural is striking, perhaps the different lauds of it are meant) is 'unexpressed', thereby, it is in harmony with its origin'. The corresponding passage of Maitr. Saṃh. I. 11. 9 : 171. 3 *víyonir vái vājapéyaḥ prājāpatyáḥ sá níruktasāmā yád ániruktaḥ prātaḥsavis téna sáyoniḥ* agrees almost verbally with Pañc. br. (in Maitr. S. I would read equally *sán* instead of *sá*). From the wording of the passage in Pañc. br. (note *ity āhuḥ* !), we may infer that its author was acquainted with the Maitr. S.

10. There is the rathantara-sāman (as first pṛṣṭha-laud) for gaining more quickly the victory[1].

[1] There is not the least doubt that not *ujjhityai* but *ujjityai* is the correct reading (Böhtlingk, in the St Petersburgh Dict. in kürzerer Fassung, registers *ujjhiti*: 'das Verlassen dieser Welt'); *ujjityai* is the reading of the Leyden MS. and, moreover, the two parallel passages, Maitr. Saṃh. I. 11. 9: 171. 5, Kāṭh. XIV. 10: 208. 23, present the same. We must equally infer from this passage that the Pañc. br. has taken this phrase from the MS. (or from the Kāth.), because in this text the Vājapeya has the aim to gain supremacy (*svārājyam*) over the earth.

11. The rathantara is the earth; (sitting) on this (earth), he is consecrated (inaugurated)[1].

[1] To the Vājapeya is joined the *abhiṣeka* : (royal) consecration; see *e.g.* Śat. br. V. 2. 2. 13-15.—The wording of § 11 is exactly that of the Kāṭh. (XIV. 10 : 208. 23), not that of the Maitr. Saṃhitā.

12. 'Therefore, one who has performed the Vājapeya, does not descend (from his seat) to meet (any one) (they say)[1].

[1] Cp. T. Br. I. 3. 9. 2 : *tasmād vājapeyayājī na kaṃ cana pratyavarohati.*

13. For, it is on this (earth) that he is consecrated.

14. The abhīvarta(-sāman)[1] is the Brahman's chant[2]; it is the bull[3] of the Brahman (of Vedic lore); he makes him (the Sacrificer) reach the status of the bull[4].

[1] Cp. note 1 on IV. 3. 4.

[2] For the third pṛṣṭha-laud.

[3] Cp. IV. 3. 8.

[4] *Viz.* chieftainship.

15. The yajñāyajñīya(-sāman) is (applied) on the anuṣṭubh (-part of the ārbhava-pavamāna laud)[1]. The anuṣṭubh is the voice; the yajñāyajñīya is the pith of the voice: into his voice he brings pith.

[1] Cp. XVIII. 5. 20 and 21.

16. The vāravantīya(-sāman)[1] is the agniṣṭoma-chant, in order to encompass valour (and) strength[2].

[1] Grām. 1. 1. 30, composed on SV. I. 17, chanted here, according to Ārṣeyakalpa IV. 7. e, on SV. II. 973-974.

[2] Cp. note 3 on IX. 5. 9.

17. The udvaṃśīya(-sāman) is (applied) at the end of the uktha-(laud)s, (in the last of the ukthas); this (sāman) is the characteristic feature of all the pṛṣṭha(-sāmans); in all the forms he is firmly established[1].

[1] Cp. XVIII. 5. 23.—The Maitr. S. and the Kāṭh. record, for the last ukthastotra, the āṣṭādaṃṣṭra (on SV. I. 343).

18. The gaurīvita(-sāman)[1] is the chant for the ṣoḍaśin (*i.e.*, for the sixteenth laud).

[1] Cp. note 1 on XI. 5. 13.

19. The gaurīvita is excessive (litt. 'left over'); the ṣoḍaśin is excessive: he puts the excessive into the excessive[1].

[1] Cp. XII. 13. 20.

20. About this they say: 'A sameness of performance[1] is brought about by the fact that immediately after the udvaṃśīya they chant the gaurīvita: a circumflected chant after a circumflected chant[2].

[1] On this sameness, cp. note 2 on VII. 2. 5.

[2] Cp. note 1 on XIII. 5. 28.—The udvaṃśīya ends: $\overset{1}{\textit{mā}}$' 2 *iro* 35 $\overset{2}{\textit{hā}}$*-i* and thus is *hā-i-kāra*; the gaurīvita ends $\overset{4}{\textit{pā}}$ 5 *to* 6 $\overset{5}{\textit{hā}}$*-i* and thus is *padānusvāra*.

21. There is no sameness, (for) the service is at an end[1].

[1] The afternoon service closes with the gaurīvita, the last uktha-laud, and the ṣoḍaśin, so to say, introduces a new part of the rite, cp. § 23.

22. The uktha[1] is being recited, the *vaṣaṭ*-call (comes) between; therefore, there is no sameness[2].

[1] The uktha-śastra is h e l d.

[2] And this is another refutation of the objection that there is sameness: when the uktha-laud has been chanted and the uktha-śastra has been recited, the libation of the soma is poured out with the *yājyā*-verse closing with *vau3ṣaṭ*. By this *vaṣaṭ*-call, *i.e.*, this *āhuti*, then, this stotra-śastra is separated from the next following one.

23. That part of the sacrifice which consists of the ṣoḍaśin is a cutting, as it were (it is a separate piece)[1]; therefore, there is no sameness.

[1] Cp. XI. 11. 2.

24. 'In the desert of sacrifice it (the Vājapeya) is completed', they say, 'it goes beyond the uktha(-laud)s, it goes beyond the ṣoḍaśin, (but) does not attain the night' (*i.e.*, the night-rite, the atirātra)[1].

[1] This refers to the extra-stotra (cp. § 25) that, at the Vājapeya, must follow after the sixteenth-laud; cp. *e.g.* Āp. XVIII. 6. 15 sqq.; Baudh. XI. 13: 83. 1 sqq.; TBr. I. 3. 8. 5; Āśv. IX. 9. 10: Śāṅkh. XV. 3. 4.

25. The last (laud) is the bṛhat(-sāman) (chanted) on (verses) addressed to Viṣṇu śipiviṣṭa[1].

[1] Literally: 'on (verses) of Viṣṇu which contain (the word) śipiviṣṭa.' These are: SV. II. 975–977=ṚS. VII. 100. 6 (var. r.), 5 (var. r.) and VII. 99. 7. The Jaim. saṃhitā has the sequence: ṚS. VII. 100. 5, 6 (without var. r.) and 99. 7.

26. Śipiviṣṭa is Prajāpati's manifestation resting on the cattle[1]. The bṛhat is breath; he becomes firmly established in breath (and) in (the possession of) cattle.

[1] Probably this passage is taken from Maitr. S. I. 11. 9: 171. 8: *śipiviṣṭa-vatīṣu stuvata; eṣā vai prajāpateḥ paśuṣṭhās tanūr yañ chipiviṣṭam*, and cp. Kāṭh. XIV. 10: 209. 8, sqq. Both these texts have the older and grammatically more correct form *paśuṣṭhās* with the nominative *s*.—Sāyaṇa cites TBr. I. 3. 8. 5: *yajño vai viṣṇuḥ paśavaḥ śipiḥ, yajña eva paśuṣu pratitiṣṭhati.*

27. They hold the laud on the bṛhat(-sāman)[1]; the bṛhat is equal to reaching yonder world[2]; that (world) he (thereby) reaches.

[1] See note 3 on VII. 6. 11.

[2] The usual phraseology in our Brāhmana is: *asau bṛhat* (*e.g.*, VII. 6. 17) or *svargo loko bṛhat* (XVI. 5. 14). The expression used here is probably taken from Maitr. S. I. 11. 9: 171. 11 or from Kāṭh. XIV. 10.

XVIII 7.

(The Vājapeya, continued and concluded.)

1. Prajāpati desired: 'May I get vigour (*vāja*) (and) the world of heaven.' He saw this Vājapeya. It is, forsooth, a drink of vigour. He (*viz.* the Sacrificer) reaches, by this (rite), vigour and the world of heaven.

2. The (verses), at the morning service, contain (the words) 'bright' (*śukra*) and 'light' (*jyotis*)[1]. By these (verses), he obtains strength (and) priestly lustre.

[1] The word *śukra* occurs in SV. II. 4 (which, according to Ārṣeyakalpa IV. 7. e, cp. Anhang, no. 16, belongs to the bahiṣpavamāna). A verse in which the word *jyotis* occurs in the prātaḥsavana, I am unable to point out. Has the author of the Ārṣeyakalpa taken no notice of this brāhmana?

3. The (verses) containing (the word) *vāja* occur in the midday-service[1]: in order to reach the world of heaven.

[1] See note 3 on XVIII. 6. 7.

4. The verses in the afternoon-service contain (the words) 'food'[1], 'troop'[2] (and) 'cattle'[3]; by these (verses) he obtains fulness (of all these).

[1] Sāyaṇa refers us to SV. II. 47: *purojitī vo andhasaḥ*, where *andhas* should be synonymous with *annam* (*annaṃ vā andhaḥ*, Jaim. br. II. 196).

[2] This refers, according to Sāyaṇa, to the words in the verses of the sākamaśva (1st ukthastotra of the Vājapeya): *ebhir vardhāsa indubhiḥ* (SV. II. 55), of the saubhara (2nd uktha): *bharanto 'vasyavaḥ* (SV. II. 58) and of the vāravantīya (3rd uktha): *gāyanti tvā gāyatriṇaḥ* (SV. II. 694), where the plural should represent the idea of *gaṇa*.

[3] SV. II. 166 (beginning of midday-pavamāna): *gośatir aśvasā asi.*—Some of these explanations seem rather fanciful.

5. It (the Vājapeya) is throughout seventeen-fold (seventeen-versed). Prajāpati is seventeen-fold[1]. He reaches (becomes equal to) Prajāpati.

[1] See note 1 on II. 10. 5.

6. The officiating priests wear golden wreaths; thereby, the characteristic of a festival is brought about.

7. (And he does so) thinking: 'This (gold) will be for me in yonder world a shining-out' (*prakāśa*).

8. Gold is light: he puts light into him.

9. They run a race-course and make the Sacrificer win; thereby, they make him gain the world of heaven.

10. He (the Sacrificer) mounts to the sky[1]; to the world of heaven he thereby ascends.

[1] He mounts by means of a ladder to the top of the sacrificial post, the *yūpa*.

11. He ascends in the region of the dust[1]; they (thereby) separate him from the world of men.

[1] This is rather uncertain, cp. my note in the German Translation of Āpastamba XVIII. 5. 13, who borrows these words from our Brāhmaṇa. They occur likewise in the Vādhūlasūtra; *sarajasa eti*, where the Vyākhyā explains: *sa yajamāno rajaso lokād asmād eti*, but this is impossible. I now reckon that the 'dusted place' (*sarajasa*) is occasioned by the bags of salt that are thrown on the Sacrificer when he has reached the upperpart of the *yūpa*; see, *e.g.*, Śat. br. V. 2. 1. 16 and cp. Agnisvāmin on Lāṭy. X. 19. 15 (where the word *sarajasa* (*iti*) occurs once more): *kusapuṭair* (read *ūṣapuṭair*) *upayanti*. This seems to rest on Anupadasūtra V. 7 (s.f.): *sarajase rohatīty ūṣapuṭair upayanti* (read *arpayanti*, cp. Maitr. S.), *taiḥ sarajasatvam*. The salt-powder covers him so that he is enveloped in a cloud of dust and temporarily invisible. To Sāyana, this sentence is *spaṣṭam*! He might, nevertheless, have offered an explication of it!

12. The Brahman, (seated) on the wheel of a chariot, chants[1] over (those that take part in the race) the 'chant of the vigorous ones'[2]. The world of heaven is vigour (*vāja*). He, thereby, makes him conquer the world of heaven.

[1] A wheel with 17 spokes is fixed horizontally in the ground near the cātvāla; on this wheel the Brahman takes his place and, at the moment when the racers start on their race, he sings the sāman, whilst the wheel is turned round three times sunwise.

[2] The grāmegeyagāna records two sāmans of this name: XV. 2. 24, composed on SV. I. 432 and grām. XI. 2. 30, composed on SV. I. 435. From Jaim. br. II. 194, we infer that the last is intended which contains the words: *ā vājaṃ vājino agman*.

13. On (verses) addressed to Viṣṇu śipiviṣṭa, the bṛhat is (chanted) (as) last (laud)[1]. Having, thereby, ascended to the world of heaven, he bestrides also the height of the ruddy one (the sun)[2].

1 Cp. XVIII. 6. 25-27.

2 Here the *bradhnasya viṣṭapa* seems to be equivalent to Viṣṇu's highest step (*kṣayantam asya rajasaḥ parāke*, SV. II. 976).

XVIII. 8.

(The Rājasūya.)[1]

1. As first (sacrifice), he practises the agniṣṭoma. The agniṣṭoma, forsooth, is the opening of (all) the (other) sacrifices[1]. Taking hold of the opening of the sacrifices, he strides on to the consecration (or inauguration).

1 Cp. VI. 3. 1, XVI. 1. 2.—The Rājasūya comprises seven (partly) unconnected days and so is a conglomerate of diverse Ekāhas. The first day, here mentioned, is the so-called pavitra, or prāyaṇīya or abhyārohaṇīya.—The § agrees almost *verbatim* with TBr. I. 8. 7. 1 and Maitr. S. IV. 4. 10 (beg.).

2. Now follows the day of consecration.

3. Its pavamāna(-laud)s are thirty-two-versed[1]: the anuṣṭubh has thirty-two syllables; the anuṣṭubh is the voice[2]; as far as reaches the voice (*i.e.* by the whole voice), he gets consecrated.

1 Differently the MS., TBr. and Jaim. br.

2 Cp. V. 7. 1.

4. About this they say: 'That the stomas are uneven is, as it were, a breaking down of the metres, (this is) not in the right sequence'[1].

1 The inequality of the three pavamāna-lauds, being all thirty-two-versed, as against the others (of 15, 17 or 21 verses), is qualified as a breaking down; for, the pavamānas are of even, the others of uneven stomas. This sentence is probably taken from MS. or TBr. where we read: *saṁśaro vā eṣa stomānām ayathāpūrvam yad viṣamāḥ stomāḥ*. Here the word *stomānām* seems more justifiable than *chandasām* of the Pañc. br.

---

1 Cp. Jaim. br. II. 197-205; Ārṣeyakalpa IV. 7. f-10. b; Lāṭy. IX. 1-3; Nidānasūtra VII. 5-6; T. Br. I. 6-8; Baudh. XII; Āp. XVIII. 8-22; Śat. br. V. 2, 3-5. 5; Kāty. XV; Maitr. Saṃh. IV. 3-4; Āśv. IX. 3-4; Śāṅkh. XV. 12-27.

5. In that the (three) pavamāna(-laud)s are even, thereby, there is no breaking down; thereby, the right sequence is maintained [1].

[1] More fully the TBr. (I. 8. 7. 2): 'The sacrifice is as great as the pavamāna(-laud)s (these are the essential parts); the rest serves for internally uniting (these chief parts): in that the pavamāna(-laud)s are even, there is no breaking down.'

6. He himself (the Sacrificer) thrives through the agniṣṭoma, he himself gets spiritual merits. (And further) that there are uktha (-laud)s: the ukthas are the cattle and are the people: that there are ukthas is for continuity (is offspring)[1].

[1] More justifiable, again, the M.S and TBr.; these texts agree with Pañc. br. but at the end they have: 'the ukthas are progeny, the ukthas are cattle; that it is an ukthya(-rite), is for continuity.'

7. (The tristich beginning:) 'O Vāyu, the bright (soma) hath been offered unto thee' [1], is the opening (tristich of the out-of-doors-laud)[2], containing the word *vāyu* ('wind'). The wind is the voice; he yokes the voice for him at the beginning of the sacrifice, and by it (*i.e.* by the voice) he is sprinkled (*i.e.* inaugurated). (In the midst) of the whole voice[3] he is consecrated; all voices proclaim him as a king.

[1] ṚS. IV. 47. 1-3= SV. II. 978-980. The Jaiminīyas use the same *pratipad.*

[2] TBr. prescribes as *pratipad* ṚS. VIII. 102. 13= SV. II. 920 (likewise addressed to Vāyu). In the ritual of the Kauthumas, this is the *pratipad* of the Viśvajit (XVI. 5. 1) with which Ekāha the abhiṣecanīya has a narrow contact.

[3] *sarvasyā vācaḥ* must be a genitive, not an ablative. cp. the corresponding passage of TBr. (I. 8. 8. 1): *sarvāsām eva prajānāṁ sūyate.* Probably here the word *madhyataḥ* is to be supplied; cp. note 2 on § 12.

8. There are verses to be brought together (to be collected from different parts of the Veda, which in the tradition do not form a whole)[1]. By means of these, he yokes (*i.e.* brings into action, prepares for action) the pṛṣṭha(-sāmans)[2]. In that they (these verses) are addressed to different deities, thereby, he yokes them. The pṛṣṭha(-sāmans) are strength; (fixed) on strength he is sprinkled (*i.e.* inaugurated).

[1] In the praxis of Ārṣeyakalpa (IV. 8 as compared with II. 6) the verses are:
SV. II. 920=ṚS. VIII. 102. 13 (Agni).
SV. II. 810=ṚS. VII. 96. 4 (Sarasvat).

SV. II. 811=ṚS. VI. 61. 10 (Sarasvatī).
SV. II. 812=ṚS. III. 62. 10 (Savitṛ).
SV. II. 813=ṚS. I. 18. 1 (Brahmaṇaspati).
SV. II. 814=ṚS. IX. 66. 19 (Agni).

From a Ṛgvedistic standpoint, these verses are in truth *saṃbhāryas*; not from the standpoint of the Sāmaveda, where we find them joined together. This is an argument in favour of the thesis (see introduction to this translation, Chapter II) that the uttarārcika was not extant at the time of the composition of our Brāhmana, but that the verses for use were taken directly from the collection of Ṛks. On the *saṃbhāryas*, cp. XI. 1. 5 and XVI. 5. 2–9.

[2] Because of the number s i x of the *saṃbhāryas*; there are s i x pṛṣṭhasāmans: rathantara, bṛhat, vairūpa, vairāja, śākvara, raivata.

9. 'They deviate from the mouth of the sacrifice' (*i.e.* from the regular beginning) 'who apply (verses) brought together (from different parts of the Veda)'[1].

[1] Nearly identical with XVI. 5. 11 and with TBr. 1. 8. 8. 1 (where the older *akran* instead of *kurvate*).

10. In that (they, thereupon, use) the verses (beginning): 'Be strained as the first of speech'[1], they do not deviate from the (regular) opening of the sacrifice[2].

[1] ṚS. IX. 62. 25=SV. II. 125.

[2] Cp. IV. 2. 17. This § closely agrees with TBr. I. 8. 8. 2.

11. (Then follows the tristich beginning:) 'By fiercely brilliant lustre'[1], which is the characteristic of the metres[2]. He yokes, at the beginning of his sacrifice, the metres; by these he gets consecrated.

[1] ṚS. IX. 64. 28-30=SV. II. 4–6.

[2] Cp. VI. 9. 25

12. (The tristich beginning:) 'This one the ten fingers,'[1] are Āditya(-verses). The young ones are the children of Aditi; in the midst of these he gets inaugurated[2].

[1] See XIII. 9. 5 with the notes.

[2] With our text cp. TBr. 1 8. 8. 1: *prajānām evaitena sūyate*, where *madhyataḥ* probably is to be supplied; cp. § 7, note 3.

13. (Then, there are the three verses) containing (the word) 'bull', beginning: 'Be thou, a bull, strained, after being pressed'[1]; they are the characteristic of the triṣṭubh[2]. The triṣṭubh is strength; on strength he gets consecrated.

1 ṚS. IX, 61. 28-30=SV. II. 128-130.

2 Though these verses are gāyatrīs, they are, in a certain sense, triṣṭubhs, because they contain the word 'bull'.

14. (Then, the pentastich beginning:) 'Upward go thy prowesses'[1]; they contain (the word) 'upward'. That which contains the word 'up' is characteristic of the anuṣṭubh[2]. The Noble is anuṣṭubh-like; for this reason there are (verses) containing the word 'up'.

1 ṚS. IX. 50. 1-5=SV. II. 555-559 (var. rr.).

2 Many anuṣṭubhs begin with *ut*.

3 Cp. TBr. I. 8. 8. 2-3: *udvatīr bhavanty, udvad vā anuṣṭubho rūpam, ānuṣṭubho rājanyas, tasmāt udvatīr bhavanti.* Note the older form *udvatīḥ* as against *udvatyaḥ* of Pañc. br.

15. (The then following tristich beginning:) 'Of thee, O wise one, that art being clarified'[1], (is) for arranging (for regulating) the vital principles (the *prāṇas*)[2].

1 ṚS. IX. 66. 10-12=SV. II. 7-9.

2 Because the word in these verses *pavamāna*, signifies also 'wind,' and wind is equal to breath.

16. (Then, the tristich beginning:) "And adorned by the night'[1]. The first (verse) (of the out-of-doors-laud) is an anuṣṭubh[2], the last is an anuṣṭubh. The anuṣṭubh is voice[3]: with the voice they start[4], in the voice they finish.

1 ṚS. IX. 99. 2-4=SV. II. 981-983 (var. r.).

2 Cp. § 7.

3 Cp. V. 7. 1.

4 This must be the meaning of *vācaiva prayanti*; cp. note 1 on VII. 3. 29; cp. TBr. l. c. *vācaiva prayanti vācodyanti*; *pra* is the counterpart of *ud* as in *prāyaṇa* and *udayana*.

17. The single verses[1] are something broken, as it were; that on both sides, (*i.e.* before and after them) these two anuṣṭubh (-tristichs)[2] are (applied), (thereby) he (the inaugurated Noble) has many who go in front (of him) and many who follow (him).

1 The *saṃbhārya* verses (§8) which do not form a continuous whole.

2 The beginning (§7) and the closing (§16) tristich.

18. An anuṣṭubh addressed to Sūrya[1] is the last: for reaching the world of heaven.

[1] See § 16.—Nearly the same in TBr. I. 8. 8. 3 and Maitr. S. l. c.

XVIII. 9.

(The Rājasūya, continued.)

1. Of Varuṇa, after he had been consecrated[1], the lustre (*bharga*) departed. It fell asunder in three parts: one third became (the Seer) Bhṛgu[2]; one third the śrāyantīya(-sāman); one third entered the water.

[1] *Viz.* on the preceding day: the abhiṣecanīya.

[2] And so Bhṛgu often is called Vāruṇi, 'the son of Varuṇa'; see Śat. br. XI. 6. 1. 1, Jaim. br. I 42.—With our passage may be compared Maitr. Saṃh. IV. 3. 9: 49. 4: 'Of Varuṇa, when he was being sprinkled (*i.e.* consecrated as king), the force and strength (*indriyaṃ vīryam*) departed. It fell asunder in three parts: one-third became Bhṛgu; one-third the śrāyantīya; one-third entered the Sarasvatī.' According to the Jaim. br. (II. 202), the sixteen kinds of water with which Varuṇa had been consecrated, drove away his lustre (*bharga*), and this was divided into four parts: Bhṛgu, the Sarasvatī, the Daśapeya and the śrāyantīya.

2. That the Hotṛ belongs to the clan of Bhṛgu, thereby, he (the Sacrificer) reaches and obtains that force and strength[1]. That the śrāyantīya[2] is the Brahman's chant[3], thereby, he reaches and obtains that force and strength. That he puts on a wreath of lotuses, thereby, he reaches and obtains that force and strength.

[1] *indriyaṃ vīryam* is the expression used in the Maitr. S. (see note 2 on § 1). Has the author of the Pañcaviṃśa adapted his text to MS? Otherwise, we would expect *bhargam* instead of these two words.

[2] Grām. VII. 2. 5, chanted on SV. II. 669-670.

[3] The third pṛṣṭha-laud.

3. There is the tenth (deity)[1].

[1] This is wholly uncertain. Sāyaṇa's explanation seems to be unacceptable; he understands: *puṣkarasraj* of the end of the preceding §. The daśapeya is separated from the abhiṣecanīya by ten days, on each of which one of the so-called *saṃsṛp* libations are performed (see *e.g.* Śat. br. V. 4. 5. 2 sqq.), each destined for a different d e i t y. Perhaps these words (of § 3) may be combined, as a paratactical sentence, with the following: '(When) the tenth (deity) of the *saṃsṛp*-libations has come', *i.e.* after the tenth day of these ten libations,

the rite takes place which is described in § 4. Perhaps, though, we have to admit an old corruption of the text and to read simply *daśamo bhavati*, in the sense of Śat. br. V. 4. 5. 3: *daśame 'han prasuto bhavati* ('on the tenth day the sacrifice of soma takes place'; the translation of Eggeling is wrong!); cp. Maitr. Saṃh. IV. 4. 7: 58,11: *tasmād eṣa daśamaḥ*.

4. There are ten (extra) cups and ten (extra) cup-adhvaryus; ten Brāhmins draw near to each cup (to partake of the soma). They enter into (the sadas, where the drinking of the soma must take place,) after each of them has enumerated up to the tenth person (his fore-fathers, as having been entitled to drink the soma); for by the number ten this sacrifice is prosperous[1]. This sacrifice it was, forsooth, that they so had been seeking[1]. He who performs it, into him he (the Udgātṛ) brings that force and strength, having reached these[2].

[1] It is highly probable that these two sentences are taken from the Maitr. Saṃh IV. 4. 7: 58. 13 (in the Pañcaviṃśa text read *etam* instead of *enam*,); for, in the context of this Brāhmaṇa (the Maitr. S.) the words: 'this sacrifice they had been seeking' are intelligible; they refer to the passage: how the Gods sought after this daśapeya sacrifice in the *saṃsṛp*-libations.

[2] For the whole, cp. Āp. XVIII. 21. 1-5 with the notes in the German translation The persons who drink of these extra cups are, according to Lāṭy (IX. 2 3-4), the three Chanters with the Subrahmaṇya and six other Brahmins, who are qualified by their ancestors (read *ṣaṭ cānye* instead of *ṣaṭ vānye*), and, likewise, the other three groups (cp. C. II. § 3), *e.g.* the Hotṛ, Maitrāvaruṇa. Acchāvāka, Grāvastut, with six others. The Sacrificer himself drinks only out of the cup normally destined for him

5. It (the Daśapeya-rite) is throughout seventeen-fold (*i.e.* each laud consists of seventeen verses). Twelve months, five seasons: these are the year. Having got the force and strength out of the year, he obtains (these).

6. Indra slew Vṛtra; of him (of Vṛtra) the Earth obtained the variegated forms; Heaven (obtained the stars). Through the shining (the light) of the stars (and the moon) the lotus springs up. In that he fastens on himself a wreath of lotuses, he fastens on himself that manifestation of Vṛtra: the Baronship[1].

[1] In the interpretation of *avakāśena* I do not follow Sāyaṇa who takes it as: 'the space between heaven and earth'; *avakāśe* occurs in Mān. gṛhs. II. 1. 5 in the sense of *upavyuṣasi* 'at day-break.'—To me there is not the least doubt that this passage of Pañcav. br. (the wreath had already been treated!) rests again on the

Maitr. Saṃh. (IV. 4. 7 : 58. 16 : *indro vai vṛtram ahaṁs; tasyeme rūpāṇy upaitām : citrāṇīyaṃ nakṣatrāṇy asau; nakṣatrāṇāṃ vā avakāśe puṇḍarīkaṃ jāyate, kṣatrasya vā etad rūpaṃ, kṣatrasyaiva rūpaṃ pratimuñcate.* Note the locative *avakāśe* 'under the light of the stars,' *i.e.*, 'at night.' Moreover, in the text of the Pañc. br., a word is missing; the text should run: *tasyeyaṃ citrāṇy upaid rūpāṇy, asau nakṣatrāṇi; nakṣatrāṇāṃ* etc. Further, cp. TS. II. 5. 2. 5, where the earth is said to be *citravihitā*; the sky *nakṣatravihitā*.

7. It is (a wreath) with twelve flowers[1]; twelve months are a year; in the year are contained the past and the future. He makes him prosper in regard to the past and the future.

[1] Cp. Maitr. S. l.c. 18: *dvādaśapuṇḍarīkā bhavati.*

8. A (golden) wreath (should by the Sacrificer be given) to the Udgātṛ; the Udgātṛ is sun-like. It did not dawn upon him[1]. But now (through this golden wreath), he makes it dawn upon him (so that he will see the subsequent dawnings or days).

[1] The imperfect is strange; cp TBr. I. 8. 2. 3: *srag udgātre, vy evāsmai vāsayati*, and Maitr. Saṃh IV. 4. 8 (beg.): *rukmo hotur, āgneyo vai hotā, na vā etasmai vyucchati, vy evāsmai vāsayati.*

9. A golden circular ornament to the Hotṛ; the Hotṛ is fire-like. Besides, he brings unto him yonder sun[1].

[1] Cp. note 1 on the preceding paragraph.

10. Two mirrors to the two Adhvaryus (the Adhvaryu and Pratiprasthātṛ); the two Adhvaryus are as much as twins[1]. Besides, he brings eye-sight into him (into each of them).

[1] And, therefore, they get the same *dakṣiṇā*.

[2] Maitr. S.: *prāvepā adhvaryvor, yamā iva hy adhvaryū* (so to be read!); *prāvepa* must be the same as *prākāśa*.

11. A horse to the Prastotṛ; the horse belongs to Prajāpati[1], and the Prastotṛ is Prajāpati-like. Besides, the horse begins snorting[2], as it were, and the Prastotr begins chanting[3].

[1] As it has sprung from Prajāpati.

[2] *? preva prothati.*

[3] Cp. Maitr. Saṃh. IV. 4. 8: 59. 4: *atho preva hy eṣa prothati preva prastotā.* Apparently, the prastāva is here likened to the loud snorting of the horse. The word *stauti* in Pañc. br. seems to be superfluous as against the text of MS.

12. A milch-cow to the Pratihartṛ; he brings milk into him[1].

[1] Only the first sentence of this § occurs in MS.; the second half differs.

13. A barren cow (*vaśā*) to the Maitrāvaruṇa (as he thinks:) May he bring me to power (*vaśam*)'[1].

[1] Or, perhaps: 'May he subdue me'(?). The same in MS.; TBr. has *rāṣṭram eva vaśy akaḥ*: 'he has subdued the realm'.

14. A bull to the Brāhmaṇācchaṃsin; the bull is strength; he puts strength in him.

15. A garment to the Potṛ, for being purified[1].

[1] Probably the garment is *darbhamaya*, and darbha-blades are used at the *dīkṣā* for the *pavana* 'the purification'.

16. A linen garment[1] to the Neṣṭṛ, for this function of Hotr is dependent, as it were[2].

[1] So Lāṭy.

[2] As he is the last among the Hotrs (C. H. §3 end).

17. A one-horse-cart, loaded with barley, to the Acchāvāka, for this function of Hotr is comparable to a one-horse-cart[1]. Besides, the barley (serves) for delivering from the fetters of Varuṇa. At that time, forsooth, no sacrificial fees reached the Sadasyas. But now these same are gratified and pleased by him[2].

[1] In that the function of the Acchāvāka is, at least during the morning service, isolated from the others; cp. C. H. § 148 with note 1.

[2] Translation and meaning are uncertain. Sāyaṇa is useless, as he seems to take *sadasyān* (which probably should be written *sadasyān*) as standing for *sad* (or *tad*) *asyām* · *tat te*. The passage probably is again taken from MS. (line 9): *na vā asyaitarhi sadasyebhyo dakṣiṇā dīyante, ta evāsyaitenābhiṣṭāḥ prītā bhavanti*.

18. A draught-ox to the Agnīdh: for yoking (bringing into action).

19. A he-goat to the Subrahmaṇya.

20. A heifer to the Unnetr. A not-gelded, three-years old bull to the Grāvastut: for pairing.

21. Twelve pregnant heifers to the Brahman. Twelve months (are equal to) the year; he gets a firm support in the year. As to their being pregnant, the milch-cow is the voice; the embryo is the holy word: he brings the holy word into his voice; he becomes a person that should be consulted. As to the fact that they are about to become milch-cows, they will give twelve sorts of milk,

these he brings into him. Therefore, they say: 'Full of sweet milk is a meritorious king'[1].

[1] This phrase, likewise, must have been taken from the MS.; mark the younger plural form *paṣṭhauhyo garbhiṇyaḥ* as against *hir °ṇīḥ*, and *dhenubhavyā* against *dhenumbhavyā*.

XVIII. 10

(The Rājasūya, continued.)

1. He who deviates from (the rite of the day of) consecration, to his lot the consecration does not fall; he who deviates from the sāmans (of that rite), him bad luck will befall, after he has been consecrated[1].

[1] Agrees literally with Maitr. Saṃh. IV. 4. 10: 61. 18 and TBr. I. 8. 8. 3.

2. There are the *saṃbhārya*(-verse)s; by means of these he yokes the pṛṣṭha(-sāman)s[1].

[1] This § agrees with XVIII. 8. 8 (beg.).

3, 4. The pṛṣṭhas are the sāmans. In that there are the *saṃbhārya*(-verse)s, he does not deviate from the sāmans[1].

[1] This probably refers still to the abhiṣecanīya. Through the *sambhāryas*, then, he deviates not from the sāmans, but our Brahmaṇa says nothing about the question as to how he does not deviate from the *sava*. The Maitr. S. seems to be more complete: 'In that he does not deviate from the God-sāmans, thereby, he does not deviate from the consecration; the pṛṣṭhas are the sāmans, in that they apply the pṛṣṭhas, they do not deviate from the sāmans.'

5. Through the sāmans of the God-kings, he thrives in yonder world; through those of the men-kings, (he thrives) in this world; he thrives in both these worlds: in the world of Gods and of men[1].

[1] To the first kind belong, according to Nidānasūtra VII. 5. the saindhukṣita, the dairghaśravasa. the pārtha, the kākṣīvata; to the second kind, the daivodāsa, vādhryaśva, vaitahavya, trāsadasyava. All these sāmans are applied at the abhiṣecanīya.—The § 5 occurs, almost to the letter, also in MS. IV. 4. 10: 62. 1 and TBr. I. 8. 8. 4 (both with *° rājānām* instead of *° rājñām*).

6. He is inaugurated (anointed as king) at a *sāmatriṣṭubh*[1]; the *sāmatriṣṭubh* is strength; he is inaugurated on strength.

[1] This is unintelligible. What is a *sāmatriṣṭubh*? The inauguration takes place immediately after the drawing of the mahendra-graha (C.H. § 198), and would here coincide probably with the bṛhat-stotra, but this laud is not on triṣṭubh-verses.

7. There are (at the abhiṣecanīya) eleven royal-sāmans[1]; the triṣṭubh is of eleven syllables (in each verse-quarter); the triṣṭubh is vigour and strength; in vigour and strength he is inaugurated.

[1] I am unable to point out which sāmans of this day are intended.

8. If they applied the nine-versed (stoma) on the (rite of) inauguration, they would give over the priesthood[1] to the nobility[2]. In that they take away (*i.e.* do not apply) the nine-versed (stoma), he takes the priesthood away from the nobility. Therefore, the Brāhmins are able to punish in return[3] their supporters (*i.e.* the Barons), for they do not apply the nine-versed (stoma) on the day of inauguration.

[1] The trivṛt is the priesthood, cp II. 16. 4, note 1.

[2] The abhiṣecanīya being a sacrifice for a King or Baron.

[3] As they are not subjected to the Kṣatriyas The word *pratidaṇḍa* occurs only here. The Dictionary of St. Petersburgh renders: 'widerspanstig'—Read *na hi te* instead of *na hi taṃ*.

9. The last stoma of the (day) of inauguration is the twenty-one-versed one; the daśapeya is (throughout) seventeen-versed; the first stoma of the keśavapanīya (the fourth day of the Rājasūya) is the twenty-one-versed one. The twenty-one-fold stoma is nobility[1]; the seventeen-fold is peasantry[2]; he encompasses for him (the king) the peasantry on both sides, the peasantry will not retire from him (but serve him)[3].

[1] Cp. note 2 on II. 16. 4

[2] Cp. VI. 1. 10.

[3] With this passage cp. Maitr. S. IV. 4. 10: 62. 6, TBr. I. 8. 8. 4-5.

10. In that he is consecrated by the Rājasūya, he ascends to the world of heaven. If he did not descend (again) to this world (to the earth), he would either depart to a (region) which lies beyond (all) human beings, or he would go mad. In that there is that sacrifice for shaving the hair (keśavapanīya), with hither wended (reversed) stomas, (this serves) for not leaving this (earthly) world. Just as he would descend (from a tree), catching hold of branch after branch, so he descends by this (rite) to this (earthly) world; (so it serves) for getting a firm support[1].

[1] In the text read *atijanam* (Sāyaṇa is wrong in combining *ati* with *gacchet*; we would then have: *ati vā janaṃ gacchet*; further, read *'rvācīnastomaḥ*. The schema of the keśavapanīya, then, is as follows:

21, 21, 21, 21, 21 | 17, 17, 17, 17, 17 | 15, 15, 15 15, 15 | the rātriparyāyas and the twilight-laud are 9-versed; cp. also Śat. br. V. 5. 3. 3 —With § 10 cp. Maitr. S. IV. 4. 10: 62. 10, TBr. I. 8. 8. 5.

XVIII. 11

(The Rājasūya, concluded.)

1. Indra slew Vṛtra; his strength went amiss in both directions[1]. He saw that śrāyantīya(-sāman), by it he wholly strengthened himself. He who is being consecrated by the Rājasūya suffers a loss in regard to his strength (and) valour, for he slays a foe (*vṛtra*). In that the Brahman's chant is the śrāyantīya(-sāman), he strengthens himself again[2].

[1] Cp. XVIII. 5. 2.

[2] This refers again to the daśapeya, cp. XVIII. 9. 1-2.

2. The yajñāyajñīya(-sāman) is (applied) on the anuṣṭubh(-part of the ārbhava-pavamāna-laud)[1]. He who is being consecrated by the Rājasūya suffers a loss in regard to the voice, for he slays a foe. The anuṣṭubh is the voice; the yajñāyajñīya is the pith of the voice: he brings pith into his voice[2].

[1] Instead of the śyāvāśva on SV. II. 47-49 (cp. Ārṣeyakalpa, Einleitung page XXIV).

[2] Cp. XVIII. 6. 15.

3. The vāravantīya(-sāman) is the agniṣṭoma-sāman. He who is being inaugurated by the Rājasūya suffers a loss in regard to his valour (and) strength, for he slays a foe. That the vāravantīya is the agniṣṭoma-sāman (is) for encompassing valour (and) strength[1].

[1] Cp. XVIII. 6. 16.

4. They (the Gods) strengthened (Indra after the slaying of Vṛtra) by the śrāyantīya (-sāman); they warded off (*avārayanta*) (the bad consequences) by the vāravantīya: this is an encompassing of strength (and) valour.

5. Devoid of firm support is he who is being consecrated by the Rājasūya. When he performs this two-day (-rite), then, there is firm support[1].

[1] Now are treated the last two days but one of the Rājasūya: the *vyuṣṭi-dvirātra*; cp. Ārṣeyakalpa IV. 9. c–10. d.—This rite is a *pratiṣṭhā*, because of its t w o days, man being two-footed.

6. As many days and nights as there are in a year, so many are there stotriya (-verses)[1]: he becomes firmly supported in the year (in time).

[1] The two days together contain 720 stotriya-verses: the first day, 190; the second, 530. Jaim. br. II. 206: *tasya sapta ca śatāni viṁśatiś ca stotriyā bhavanti*. The TBr. has *tāvatīḥ* instead of *tāvatyaḥ*.

7. The first day is an agniṣṭoma-sacrifice; the second an over-night-rite: separately he becomes firmly established in days and nights.

8. The (rite of the) first day (may fall) on the day of new moon; the (rite of the) second on the day when the (new moon) becomes visible[1]: he becomes firmly established separately in the two halves of the month. The first day (may fall) on the day of full moon; the second on the *vyaṣṭakā*[2]: he becomes firmly established separately in two months. About this they say (also): 'It (the two-day-rite) should be performed on two auspicious days in the same half of the month (of increasing moon): for the sake of success.'

[1] *udriṣṭa* must be a false reading for *uddṛṣṭa*, cp. TBr. I. 8. 10. 2 and Āp. XVIII. 22. 15.

[2] According to Lāṭy., the first three days of the dark half of the month are meant. This is far from certain, as an *aṣṭakā* (cp. note 1 on V. 9. 1) is the eighth day after each full moon.

9. 'The two-day (-rite) is not fit for obtaining cattle,' they say, 'there are (only) two metres: the gayatrī-and the triṣṭubh(-day); the jagatī they exclude'[1], and by the fact that they apply (the jagatī) in the after-noon service, it is not applied[2] (on the whole day).

[1] And it is precisely the jagatī that is conducive to cattle: cp. *e.g.* TS. VI. 1. 6. 2 (the jagatī returned with cattle and *dīkṣā*). For the rest, cp. TS. VII. 2. 8. 1–2.

[2] Only on its last part: the ārbhava-laud.

10. When this (jagatī) occupies a day of an ahīna(-rite) or a s e r v i c e o f a o n e - d a y - r i t e, then is the jagatī applied. (Now), the traiśoka(-sāman)[1] is the Brahman's chant of the second day (in this two-day-rite); the vaikhānasa (-sāman)[2] is the Acchāvāka's

chant. In that these are applied on the service of the clear (soma)[3], thereby, the jagatī is applied; thereby, it (this two-day-rite) is conducive to cattle.

1 Cp. XII. 10. 20, chanted on SV. II. 280-282 (jagatī).

2 Cp. XIV. 4. 6, chanted on SV. II. 505-506 (reduced in the praxis to jagatīs).

3 This means: at the pṛṣṭha-lauds, on the midday-service. –The TBr. l.c. agrees, on the whole, but it omits the facts by which the day is made a jagata-day. Does this go so far as to prove that here it is the TBr. that borrows from Pañc. br.?

11. This two-day-rite (is called) 'the dawn'. He makes it dawn (again and again) for him.

Nineteenth Chapter.

(The Ekāhas or one-day-rites, concluded.)

This Chapter comprises the so-called *dvandra*-ekāhas, the pair-ekāhas; they are so arranged that each two of them make a kind of unity, as the Rāj and the Virāj; the Udbhid and Valabhid; the two Apacitis, etc. But, as the Nidānasūtra (VII. 7) remarks, they are not all of them *dvandvas* or pairs; they comprise also those that two by two serve a similar end: *yau yāv eṣām samānam artham upakṛtau tau tau dvandvam bhavataḥ.*

XIX 1

(The Rāj-ekāha.)[1]

1. Now, that (one-day-rite called 'the) king' (*rāj*).

2. He who hoping for a kingdom does not obtain it, should practise this (rite). A king (*i.e.*, this ekāha) makes him a king. He, forsooth, may be called a king, who is made a king by a king; it is a king who makes him a king.

1 In the different texts there is no unity in designing the first pair; Rāj and Virāj they are called in Pañc. br. (XIX. 1, 2) and, as is natural, in Ārṣeyakalpa V. 1. a, b, Lāṭy. IX. 4. 1–2, Nidānasūtra VII. 7, Kātv. XXII. 10. 7–12 (and Āśv. IX. 8. 21–24). The Jaim. br. (II. 85, 86) and Śāṅkh. XIV. 25, 26 know a Virāj and Svarāj. Āp. XXII. 10. 20–21, mentions Rāj, Virāj, and Svarāj, contaminating the two sources.

3. The other sacrifices amount to the metre[1], but this one amounts to the stoma[2]. The stoma is valour; on valour they inaugurate him.

[1] As the Sāhasra-rite, etc.; see, *e.g.* XVI. 11. 17 (Sāyaṇa).

[2] *stoma* means, according to Sayaṇa, the group of metres. Perhaps it is used here for agniṣṭoma (cp. IV. 5. 21), as the Rāj comprises, though in different sequence, the same stomas as the agniṣṭoma. But the proper sense of this § is not clear to me.

4. Taken as a whole, it comprises eight times twenty-one stotra (-verses)[1]. Eight persons of importance sustain together the kingship: the king's brother, the king's son, the house-chaplain, the queen-consort, the equerry (*sūta*), the praefectus urbi (*grāmaṇī*), the chamberlain (*kṣattṛ*) and the charioteer[2]. These are the persons of importance who together sustain the kingship; amongst these they consecrate him.

[1] The three pavamana-lauds, each on 17 verses (=51); the four ājya lauds, each on 9 (=36); the four pṛṣṭha-lauds, each on 15 (=60); the agniṣṭoma on 21 = 51 + 36 + 60 + 21 = 168 = 8 × 21 (for the stomas see Ārṣeyakalpa V. 1. a).

[2] The precise function of these officials is not everywhere certain. They agree partly with the *ratnins*

5. The twenty-one-versed stoma is the nobility[1] and is a firm support[2]. A 'shining-out' among the nobility falls to his share, a firm support gets he who knows this.

[1] Cp. note 2 on II. 6. 4

[2] Cp. note 1 on III 7. 2

XIX. 2.

(The Virāj.)

1. Now, the Virāj[1]. One who is desirous of (obtaining) food, should perform it.

[1] *virāj* means 'splendour' but, besides, it designates a metre of which the verse-quarters consist of t e n syllables (cp. III. 13. 3).

2. The other sacrifices amount to the virāj in a cryptic manner[1], but this (rite) is equal to the virāj in a visible way[2].

[1] The agniṣṭoma, for instance, with its 190 stotra-verses contains cryptically the number 10; see note 1 on VI. 3. 6.

[2] As each stotra consists of ten verses; cp. § 4.

3. In a visible way he who knows this obtains food[1]; he becomes an eater of food.

[1] Because the virāj is food (cp. IV. 8. 4).

4. It consists throughout of tens and tens. Ten-syllabic is the virāj; food is virāj-like, and (so it serves) for obtaining food.

5. Besides, these (stotra-verses) are five and five; five-fold is the sacrifice'[1]; five-fold is cattle; he becomes firmly established in sacrifice (and) in (the possession of) cattle[2].

[1] See note 2 on VI. 7. 12.

[2] Cp. II. 4. 2.

6. One who is desirous of (obtaining) a firm support should perform this same (rite): on ten (toes) man is here firmly supported; he is firmly supported on earth.

XIX. 3.

(The Aupaśada.)[1]

1. Now, the Aupaśada.[1]

[1] The word is derived from the root *śad,* 'to fall'; *upaśad,* 'to increase'; cp. §3.

2. It is the stoma (*i.e.* the sacrifice) of the Gandharvas and the Apsarases. One who is desirous of obtaining progeny should perform (it). The Gandharvas and Apsarases rule over man's possession of progeny and man's want of progeny[1]. These (Gandharvas and Apsarases) have here a share in the soma-draught[2]. These he by their own share gratifies; these, being gratified (and) pleased, grant him progeny.

[1] This statement is found here only.

[2] How they get a share in the soma is detailed by Ap.; see the German translation.

---

[1] It is striking that of the pair śada and aupaśada (or upaśada) our Brāhmaṇa describes only the last.—Cp. Jaim. br. II. 81, 82 (Auswahl No. 129); Ārṣeyakalpa V. 1. c; Lāṭy. IX. 4. 3–4; Nidānasūtra VII. 7; Baudh. XVIII. 44, 45; Āp. XXII. 11. 4–11; Kāty. XXII. 10. 13–15 (aupaśada only); Āśv. IX. 3; Śāṅkh. XIV. 22. 23–26.

3 Each time a stotra(-verse) is added[1] (litt. is engendered, is born)[1]; he (thereby) causes progeny to be born to him.

1 To each stotra of the normal agniṣṭoma one verse is added; so the schema is:

10, 16, 16, 16, 16, | 16, 18, 18, 18, 18 | 18, 22 (all in all 202), see § 9.

4. The kakubh(-verse) he shifts to the fore-part[1]; the kakubh is man[2]; he is placed (conceived) as a foetus in the middle[3],

1 Cp. note 1 on XVI. 11. 5.

2 Cp. note 1 on VIII. 10. 6.

3 The kakubh-verse is shifted from the ārbhava- to the mādhyandina-pavamāna: the middle of the rite, just as the child is conceived in the middle part of the mother.

5. and by applying that two-footed verse[1] at the place of the kakubh, he causes the foetus, that has been conceived, to be born[2].

1 SV. II. 717 (-719).

2 Simply because of the two-footedness.

6. There is the cyāvana(-sāman)[1]. The cyāvana(-sāman) is a (means of) procreation[2] (or: of delivery of the foetus).

1 Grām. XIII. 1. 28, chanted on the kakubh: SV. II. 42-43.

2 Cp. note 1 on XIII. 5. 12.

7. He who knows this is procreated (and) multiplied.

8. There are the two (sāmans called) Vasiṣṭha's janitra[1]. Vasiṣṭha, after his son had been slain[2], saw these two sāmans. He was procreated in children and cattle. That there are these two sāmans, (is) for procreation[3].

1 Grām. VI. 2. 17 and 18, composed on SV. I. 241; the first is applied on the verses of the naudhasa (SV. II. 35-36) as the Brahman's chant, the second on SV. II. 47-49 in the ārbhava-pavamāna-laud; see Ārṣeyakalpa V. 1. c.

2 On *hataputra*, cp. note 1 on IV. 7. 3.

3 On this legend, cp. Journ. of the Amer. Oriental Society, Vol. XVIII, page 47.

9. All the verses being summed up[1], two exceed the virāj[2]: two is the minus of woman[3] for generating; thereby a procreation is brought about; (so this rite serves) for progeneration.

1 Although translated by me as an absolute genitive, the genitive, as partitive genitive, depends on *dve*.

[2] Virāj as the number ten or a plurality of ten; there are, indeed (see § 3, note 1), 202 verses.

[3] The Jaim. br. has: *dve hi te striyā ūne* ('these two redundant verses are the *ūne* of the female'). Sāyaṇa proposes an impossible explanation. I propose the following; usually woman is said to have o n e minus (*ūna*): the vulva, and man one plus (*atirikta*): the penis. Here the dual is used for the sake of argument, but the author probably had in mind the expression *romanvantau bhedau* of RS. IX. 112. 4, which are properly o n e.—There is now a pair: the virāj, *i.e.* man, and the generative organ of woman. See also Journal of the German Oriental Society, Vol. LXXII, page 3.

XIX. 4.

(The Punaḥstoma.)[1]

1. Now, the Punaḥstoma.

2. He who, after having accepted many gifts[1], feels as if he had swallowed poison should perform this (rite).

[1] That ought not to be accepted.

3, 4. The eleventh (verse), taking away what in his y o u t h he accepts (too) much, or what poison he swallows, or what forbidden food he eats, transfers it to the m o r n i n g service; and the twelfth (verse), taking away what in l a t e r a g e he accepts (too) much, or what poison he swallows, or what forbidden food he eats, transfers it to the e v e n i n g service[1].

[1] The stomas are: the nine-versed, for each stotra in the morning- and the afternoon-service: the twelve-versed, for each stotra in the midday-service. The first and the last service have one verse less than the virāj; the midday-service has two more than the virāj. This is because in his middle the Sacrificer has eaten, drunk or swallowed too much; this too much is now removed, as it were (idealiter!), for excesses in youth, by one of the two excessive verses to the morning service (so that this service is now considered as likewise ten-versed): for excesses at old age, by transferring the other of the two verses to the last service. All in all, now, the number of stomas amounts to the virāj (9 + 12 + 9, and, idealiter, 10 + 10 + 10 = 30), so that, now, all is in the most perfect harmony, and the bad

---

[1] All our sources, with the exception of Āśv IX. 3. 1–2 and, as is to be expected, of Ārseyakalpa V. 2. a, Lāṭy. IX. 4. 5–7, and Nidānasūtra VII. 7, give t w o Punahstomas. Jaim. br. II. 83, 84 (Auswahl No. 130); Baudh. XVIII. 46-47; Āp. XXII. 11. 1–8; Kāty. XXII. 10. 16–17; Śāṅkh. XIV. 27–28. The pair of them is probably the older and most natural case.

consequences of the 'too much' are annulled!—Perhaps, a reading *nirharati* would be preferable to *niharati*.

5. Man is virāj-like[1]. He (who has swallowed poison, etc.) is impure in the middle (of his body); from the middle he loosens his bad luck.

[1] Cp. note 1 on II. 7. 8; for the rest, cp. the preceding paragraph.

6. There are the two śuddhāśuddhīya(-sāmans)[1].

[1] Grām. IX. 2. 7, and 8 (composed on SV. I. 350) are both śuddhāśuddhīya; the first, or *padanidhanam*, (SV. ed. Calcutta, vol. I, page 715) is chanted on SV. II. 35-36 (cp. XIV. 11. 27); the second, or *aiḍam*, is chanted on SV. II. 752-754; *svāsu ṛkṣu*, *i.e.* on the verse (and the following) on which it is composed.

7. Indra gave the Yatis over to the hyenas; an inauspicious voice reproached him and he deemed himself impure. He saw these śuddhā-śuddhīya(-sāmans) and was purified by them[1].

[1] Cp. XIV. 11. 28.

8. However many (forbidden) gifts he accepts, what forbidden food he eats, in regard to what he deems himself impure, that is purified by these two (sāmans).

9. There are the gausūkta[1] and the āśvasūkta(-sāmans)[1].

[1] Grām. III. 2. 18, and 19, composed on SV. I. 122, applied on SV. II. 39-41 and SV. II 44-46: cp. Ārṣeyakalpa V. 2. a.

10. Gausūkti and Āśvasūkti, having accepted many (forbidden) gifts, deemed themselves as having swallowed poison[1]. They saw these two sāmans and, by means of them, expelled the poison[1]. However many gifts he accepts, what poison he swallows, what forbidden food he eats, that, by means of these two (sāmans), he expels.

[1] Cp. Jaim. br. III. 250 (see the text in Auswahl, No. 206): 'Gausūkti and Āśvasūkti, the sons of Iṣa, having accepted many gifts, deemed themselves as having swallowed poison. They desired: 'May we expel this swallowed poison'. They saw these two sāmans and applied them in lauding. Then, one of them (of these two Seers) (by the nidhana): *agnir āhutaḥ* expelled, through his sacrifice, (the poison and removed it) to this world: in this world nothing surpasses Agni. The other expelled (and removed it), by (the nidhana): *śukra āhutaḥ*, to yonder world: in yonder world nothing surpasses Āditya (the sun). Thereupon, they expelled the swallowed poison. He who deems himself as having swallowed poison, having received a gift from a person from whom he ought not to accept a gift, having eaten food from one whose food he should not eat, should apply these sāmans in lauding'.

11. There are fifteen lauds[1]; the fifteenfold stoma is vigour (and) strength[2]; having freed him from evil, he makes him prosper in regard to vigour and strength.

[1] This ekāha, as ukthya, has fifteen lauds.

[2] Cp. note 1 on XI. 6. 11.

XIX. 5.

(The first Catusṭoma.)[1]

1. Now, the Catusṭoma.

[1] *catu(ḥ)stoma* is an abbreviation of *caturuttaracatu(ḥ)stoma*; an ekāha with four stomas that increase by four. Its schema is: 4, 8, 8, 8, 8 | 12, 16, 16, 16, 16 | 20, 24.

2. One who is desirous of (obtaining) cattle should perform (it).

3. In that the out-of-doors-laud is (chanted) on four (verses)[1], he obtains the cattle, as cattle is four-footed.

[1] On the instrumental, see Introduction Chapter III, § 8. The Jaim. br. has the normal *tasya catasṛṣu bahiṣpavamānaṃ bhavati.*

4. In that the ājya(-laud)s are (chanted) on eight (verses each), he reaches, cattle (cows) being eight-hoofed, the cattle hoof by hoof.

5. In that the midday-pavamāna(-laud) is twelve-versed, the year being (equal to) twelve months and cattle (cows) being born after the lapse of the year (*i.e.* year after year), he obtains these.

6. In that the pṛṣṭha(-laud)s are sixteen-versed (each), he reaches, cattle consisting of sixteen parts[1], the cattle sixteenth by sixteenth.

[1] According to Sāyaṇa, the sixteen parts are: head, neck, trunk, tail, four feet, eight hoofs; perhaps, though, *kalā* designates a part of the hoof.

7. In that the ārbhava(-pavamāna-laud) is twenty-versed, he reaches the five-fold being of cattle[1].

---

[1] Cp. Jaim. br. II. 176; Ārṣeyakalpa V. 2. b; Lāṭy. IX. 4. 8; Nidānasūtra VII. 7; Baudh. XVIII. 34; Āp. XXII. 11. 16-18; Kāty. XXII. 10. 18-20; Āśv. IX. 5. 14-6. 8; Śāṅkh. XIV. 61. In all our sources (with the exception of Pañc. br., Lāṭy., Nid., Katy. and Āp.) only one single catusṭoma is handed down.

[1] Twenty being divisible by five; on *pāṅkta*, cp. note 1 on II. 4. 2.—He has now reached all the kinds of cattle.

8. In that the agniṣṭoma(-laud) is twenty-five-versed, the gāyatrī being of twenty-four syllables and the gāyatrī being strength (and) priestly lustre, he obtains strength (and) priestly lustre.

9. The gāyatrī is breath (and a means of) procreation: out of the breath: the gāyatrī, he is procreated[1].

[1] With §§ 8, 9, cp XVI. 14. 5.

10. One sāman, many metres[1]: therefore one man thrives in many ways.

[1] This still refers to the agniṣṭoma-laud, which, though being one sāman (the vāravantīya), is chanted on various verses, on verses of various metres; cp. Ārṣeyakalpa V. 2. b.

11*a*. The agniṣṭoma(-laud) is the person (of the Sacrificer) himself, the cattle are the metres[1]; he, thereby, firmly establishes the cattle into himself (into his own possession).

[1] The metres of the verses of which the agniṣṭoma-laud (the vāravantīya-sāman) consists. Now, those metres are those of the verses that usually are applied on the uktha-lauds (sakamaśva, hārivarṇa, tairaścya), and the ukthas are cattle; cp. IV. 5, 18.

11*b*. It (this rite) is neither an ukthya nor an agniṣṭoma, for cattle (cows) is neither living (exclusively) in the village nor living (exclusively) in the wild[1].

[1] This ekāha is not an agniṣṭoma proper, for it contains in its agniṣṭoma-laud the verses of the uktha-lauds (cp. note 1 on §11. a). nor is it an ukthya, for it has no uktha-lauds. The thought is more clearly expressed in the Jaim. br.: 'This (rite) is neither an agniṣṭoma nor an ukthya: it is both, so to say, neither is cattle living (exclusively) in the village nor (exclusively) living in the wild: it is both, so to say. This cattle of both kinds he obtains' (cows live, at day-time, out of the village on the meadows; at night-time, in the village, in the cow-pens or stables).

XIX. 6.

(The second Catuṣṭoma.)

1. Now, that (rite) of which four lauds are chanted on four, four on eight, four on twelve, and four on sixteen verses[1]. That (rite) does not sound beyond the cow[2].

[1] The schema of this catustoma, then, is: 4, 4, 4, 4, 8 | 8, 8, 8, 12, 12 | 12, 12, 16, 16, 16 | 16.

[2] *ativadati* occurs also X. 12. 5.—'It does not sound beyond the cow,' 'it reaches by its chants the cow'; cp. § 2. Sayana refers this, unconvincingly, (not to the cow, but) to the gostoma of XVI 2 (especially § 6), but this is a simple ukthya.

2. Cattle consists of sixteen parts; he reaches the cattle sixteenth by sixteenth[1].

[1] Cp. XIX. 5. 6.

3. It is an ukthya(-day) with a sixteenth (laud). The uktha (-laud)s are the cattle, the soḍaśin is a thunderbolt[1]; by means of the thunderbolt, he encompasses the cattle for him: cattle will not go forth from him. It (this rite) is neither an ukthya nor an over-night-rite, for the cattle is neither (exclusively) living in the village, nor living (exclusively) in the wild.

[1] Cp. XII. 13. 14.

XIX. 7.

(The Udbhid and Valabhid.)[1]

1. The cave belonging to the Asuras was enclosed by darkness (and)[1] (its entrance) was covered with stones. In this (cave) was contained their possession of cows. This (cave) the Gods could not split. They said to Bṛhaspati: 'Free thou this (cattle) for us'. By means of the Udbhid ('who splits up'), he destroyed the cave (and), by means of the Valabhid ('who breaks up the cave'), he broke it up; by means of the utsedha(-sāman), he freed that (cattle) (and), by means of the niṣedha(-sāman), he encompassed it.

[1] Read with Leyden MS. *'śmāpidhāna āsīt.*

2. He, who is desirous of (obtaining) cattle, should perform (it).

3. In that he (the Adhvaryu or the Udgātṛ) performs the Udbhid, he destroys the cave for him; in that he performs the Valabhid, he breaks up the cave for him.

---

[1] Cp. Jaim. br. II. 89-90 (Auswahl no. 131); Ārṣeyakalpa. V. 3. a, b; Lāṭy. IX. 4. 9-12; Nidānasūtra VII. 8; Baudh, XVIII. 31; Āp. XXII. 11. 19-12. 1; Kāty. XXII. 10. 21-22; Āśv. IX. 8. 17-18; Śāṅkh. XIV. 14.

4. The utsedha[1] and the niṣedha[1] are the two Brahman's chants; having driven up the cattle by means of the utsedha, he lays hold of it through the niṣedha.

[1] Grām. XIV. 2. 23 and 24, composed on SV. I. 514 (cp. XV. 9. 10, 11). The utsedha (chanted on SV. II. 771-772) serves for the third pṛṣṭha-laud at the Udbhid; the niṣedha (chanted on the same verses) serves for the same laud at the Valabhid.

5. (The tristich. beginning): 'The sacrifice made Indra increase'[1] (serves in both rites for) the Brahman's (or third) ājya(-laud): it is provided with the characteristic feature[2].

[1] ṚS. VIII. 14. 5, 7, 8 = SV. II. 989-991.

[2] As it contains the words: 'as Indra destroyed the cave (*vala*).'

6. They (the two rites) are (each of them) (alternatively) seven-versed and seventeen-versed. In that they laud on seven verses, there being seven kinds of domestic animals[1], they obtain cattle. The śakvarī(-verse) has seven verse-quarters, the śakvarī is cattle[2]: he obtains cattle. And in that (they laud) on seventeen verses, the seventeen-fold stoma being Prajāpati[3], he reaches (becomes equal to) Prajāpati.

[1] Cp. II. 7. 8.

[2] Cp. XIII. 1. 3, XIII. 4. 13.

[3] Cp. note 1 on II. 10. 5 (the words may also mean: 'Prajāpati is seventeen-fold').

7. It (*i.e.* each of these rites) amounts to the gāyatrī[1]; the gāyatrī is strength (and) priestly lustre; he obtains strength (and) priestly lustre. The gāyatrī is breath, is a (means of) procreation: out of the breath: the gāyatrī, he is procreated[2].

[1] The number of verses in both (read, perhaps, *gāyatrīṁ sampadyete* instead of *sampadyate*) is 144; $\frac{144}{24} = 6$ gāyatrīs.

[2] Cp. XIX. 5. 8-9.—These two rites, according to Lātyāyana, are inseparable: he who has performed the Udbhid should, after the lapse of a half-month, or a month, or a year, perform the Valabhid. In the Jaim. br., the Valabhid comes first, then, the Udbhid (first, the cave was destroyed, then, the cows were set free), and this may have been the original view, the sequence of the elements in the compound *udbhidvalabhidau* being due to the rule that the shorter word precedes the longer one: *alpāctaram* (Pāṇini II. 2. 34).

XIX. 8.

(The first Apaciti.)[1]

1. Now, the Apaciti. He who is desirous of (obtaining) honour (*apaciti*) should perform (it); through honour (*i.e.* through this rite, named *apaciti*) he (the performing priest) acquires honour for him.

2. Two[1] of its pavamāna(-laud)s are twenty-four-versed; the gāyatrī is of twenty-four syllables, the gāyatrī is strength (and) priestly lustre; through strength (and) priestly lustre, he acquires honour for him.

[1] According to the Ārṣeyakalpa, the out-of-doors-laud and the midday-pavamāna-laud.

3 The rathantara and the bṛhat are both (applied)[1]; through both, the rathantara and the bṛhat, he acquires honour for him.

[1] The rathantara on the bṛhatī-part of the midday-pavamāna-laud, the bṛhat as first pṛṣtha laud.

4. The bharga(-sāman) and the yaśas(-sāman)[1] are applied; through the bharga(-sāman), he brings lustre (*bhargas*), through the yaśas(-sāman), fame (*yaśas*) unto him

[1] The bharga is araṇyegeyagāna II. b. 11, composed on SV. I. 258, chanted on the jagatī-part of the ārbhava-pavamāna: SV. II. 47-49; the yaśas is ar. gā. II. b. 12, composed on SV. I. 270, chanted, as third pṛṣtha-laud, on SV. II. 761-762.

5. Both kinds of stomas (are applied), the even and the odd ones[1]. Through both kinds of stomas he acquires honour for him.

[1] The schema is: 24, 9, 15, 9, 15 | 24, 17, 21, 17, 21 | 27, 21.

6. About this, they (the Theologians) remark: 'The stomas violate the proper order; they would be liable to destroy the Sacrificer, for they are applied in an irregular order'[1].

[1] The regular order would be: first comes the nine-fold stoma, whilst here the twenty-four-fold is at the beginning (note 1 on § 5).

---

[1] Cp. Jaim. br. II. 100-103 (Auswahl No. 133); Ārṣeyakalpa V. 3. c, 4a; Lāṭy. IX. 4. 13-17; Nidānasūtra VII. 9; Baudh. XVIII. 38-39; Āp. XXII. 12. 2-9; Kāty. XXII. 10. 28-32; Āśv. IX. 8. 21; Śāṅkh. XIV. 33, 34. Only the Kauthumas and those sources that depend on them have t w o Apacitis.

7. The agniṣṭoma(-laud) is twenty-one-versed, the twenty-one versed stoma is a firm support[1]: at the end of the sacrifice he i firmly supported[2].

[1] *Cp. note 1 on III. 7 2.*

[2] *And so the unfavourable consequences of violating the proper order (§ 6) are annulled.*

XIX. 9.

(The second Apaciti.)

1. Now, the Apaciti which contains all the stomas. He who is desirous of (obtaining) honour should perform (it). Through all the stomas he acquires honour for him.

2. It amounts to the virāj[1]. He is honoured who is an eater of food, the virāj is food[2]; he brings food unto him.

[1] The schema is: 9, 15, 17, 17, 21 | 27, 24, 44, 48, 24 | 33, 21; all in all, 300 stotriya-verses, a number divisible by ten (the virāj of ten syllables).

[2] Cp. IV. 8. 4.

3. The rathantara and the bṛhat are both (applied); the bharga (-sāman) and the yaśas(-sāman) are both (applied)[1], and both kinds of stomas (are applied): those of the Chandomas and those of the pṛṣṭhya-days[2].

[1] Cp. note 1 on XIX. 8. 4.

[2] The 9-, 15-, 17-, 21-, 27- and 33-versed stomas are those of the pṛṣṭhya six-day-period; the 24-, 44- and 48-versed ones are those of the Chandoma-days.

4. The pṛṣṭha(laud)s of this (rite) are those of the Chandoma (-day)s[1]. The Chandomas are cattle[2]; the pṛṣṭha (-laud)s are food[3]; successively, he brings unto him food (and) cattle. In that it (this rite) comprises the Chandomas, he reaches (*i.e.* becomes equal to) one who performs the twelve-day(-rite).

[1] See the schema in note 1 on § 2.

[2] Cp. note 1 on III. 8. 2.

[3] Cp. XVI. 15. 8.

5. About this they remark: 'The stomas (of this rite), those of the Chandoma(-day)s and those of the pṛṣṭhya (six-day-period) have different places[1]. In that they are applied at one and the same sacrifice, the Sacrificer may lose his firm support'[1].

[1] Cp. XVI. 15. 9; *īśvarā* must be a misprint for *īśvaro.*

6. The agniṣṭoma(-laud) is the twenty-one-versed one; the twenty-one-fold stoma is a firm support[1]; they (the different stomas) come[2] to a firm support.

[1] Cp. note 1 on III 7. 2.

[2] Instead of *abhyāyanti*, we expect rather a causative: 'they bring him unto'.

XIX. 10.

(The first stoma of Agni: the winged one.)[1]

1. This (the ekāha that now follows) is a winged stoma[1].

[1] The schema (see § 5) is: 9, 15, 17, 21, 27 | 33, 33, 27, 21, 17 | 15, 9; the increasing and the decreasing numbers of stotra-verses, with the two biggest in the middle, are analogous to the wings of a bird.

2. It is the winged one (the bird)[1] that is here deposited (*i.e.* applied at this rite).

[1] This refers, according to Sāyaṇa, to the sauparṇa sāman, the chant of Suparna, 'the eagle', which (see the Ārṣeyakalpa) is applied on the midday-pavamāna-laud.

3. The wingless one does not reach (is not equal to) the winged one, but in that this winged one is deposited on a winged one[1], therefore, the winged ones (the birds) fly with their wings.

[1] The thought is expressed somewhat unsatisfactorily. Did Sāyaṇa have before him a reading *yad eṣa pakṣy apakṣiṇi nidhīyate?*

4. Winged (and) luminous, he who knows this, frequents the pure world (or regions).

5. On both sides are nine-versed (stomas); the nine-versed (stoma) is strength (and) priestly lustre[1]; he obtains strength (and) priestly lustre.

[1] Cp. VI. 1. 6.

6. Then, two fifteen-versed ones; the fifteen-versed (stoma) is valour[1]; he obtains valour.

[1] Cp. VI. 1. 8.

---

[1] Cp. Ārṣeyakalpa V. 4. b; Lāṭy. IX. 4. 18-19; Nidānasūtra VII. 9; Āp. XXII. 12. 10; Kāty. XXII. 10. 33-11. 2.

7. Then, two seventeen-versed ones; the seventeen-versed (stoma) is cattle[1]; he obtains cattle

[1] Cp. VI. 1. 10

8. Then, two twenty-one-versed ones; the twenty-one-versed (stoma) is firm support[1]; in the middle of the sacrifice he is firmly supported.

[1] Cp. note 1 on III 7. 2.

9. Then, two thrice nine-versed ones: the thrice-nine-versed (stoma) is (equal to) these worlds[1], in these worlds he is firmly established.

[1] Cp. VI. 2. 3.

10. Then, two thirty-three-versed ones; the thirty-three-versed (stoma) is the summit[1].

[1] Cp. III. 3. 2.

11. The highest among his people becomes he who knows this.

12. This (rite), forsooth, is the range of the ruddy one (the sun). In that these two thirty-three-versed (stomas) are brought into connection with each other in the middle, thereby, he ascends the range of the ruddy one[1].

[1] Cp. XXIII. 19. 3.

13. Fire is largest in the middle[1], therefore, these stomas are so applied that the largest ones occupy the middle.

[1] On this sentence probably rests the designation of this ekāha: *agneḥ stomaḥ*.

14. He starts with the nine-versed (stoma) and concludes with the nine-versed (stoma). The nine-versed (stoma) is breath[1]; by breath he begins, in breath he concludes.

[1] The breath is three-fold, cp. III. 6. 3.—Sāyana's interpretation of *praiti* and *udeti* is different here but wrong; it is given rightly at XX. I. 6.

XIX. 11.

(The second stoma of Agni, the 'Light'.)

1. Now (the ekāha designated as) 'the Light'.

2. Its out-of-doors laud is nine-versed; its âjya(-laud)s are

fifteen-versed; its midday-pavamāna(-laud) is twenty-four-versed: its pṛṣṭha(-laud)s are seventeen-versed.

3. The nine-versed (stoma) is the breath, the fifteen-versed is the body[1].

1 The body contains the nine vital airs and the navel (cp. VI. 8. 3), the two hands, the two feet, and the trunk; that makes fifteen.

4. The gāyatrī is the mouth[1], the seventeen-versed (stoma) is food[2]; he, thereby, puts food in his (own) mouth.

1 Cp. VII 3. 7.—This refers to the midday-pavamāna which begins with the gāyatrī and is followed by the pṛṣṭhas on seventeen verses.

2 Cp. II. 7. 7.

5. He who knows this eats food, becomes an eater of food.

6. Through the midday-pavamāna(-laud) the Gods went to the world of heaven[1]. That the midday-pavamāna(-laud) is twenty-four-versed, is for rising to the world of heaven. The gāyatrī[2] is of twenty-four syllables, it is strength (and) priestly lustre, he obtains strength (and) priestly lustre. The gāyatrī is breath, is (a means of) procreation; out of the breath: the gāyatrī, he is procreated.

1 Cp. VII. 4. 1.

2 With which this laud opens.

7. Both kinds of stomas (are applied), the even and the odd ones[1]; this is a copulation; by this copulation he is procreated.

1 The schema, according to Ārṣeyakalpa, is: 9, 15, 9, 15, 15 | 24, 17, 15, 17, 17 | 17, 21. This schema now is not in harmony with § 2, but, as compared with § 10, two stomas are changed. The Nidānasūtra VII. 9 remarks; *trivṛt-pañcadaśāv ājyapṛṣṭheṣu sampadvaśena kurmaḥ* (Sāyana, on § 10, cites this passage with faulty readings!): 'we apply on the ājya- and pṛṣṭha(-laud)s a nine-versed and a fifteen-versed stoma, for the purpose of (getting) the amount,' *i.e.* in order to get the amount as prescribed in § 10.

8. This metre[1] is winged; winged (and) luminous. he who knows this, frequents the pure worlds[2].

1 Is this the meaning of *chandas*? Cp. XIX. 1. 3 note 1.

2 Cp. XIX. 10. 4.

9. Fire is largest in the middle; therefore, these stomas are applied so that the largest ones occupy the middle[1].

[1] Cp. XIX. 10. 13. This statement does not appear to fit in too well here.

10. When all the verses are summed up, one exceeds the virāj[1]: he makes him (the Sacrificer) a sole ruler of food.

[1] Cp. notes 1 and 2 on XIX. 3. 9.--All in all (cp note 1 on § 7), this ekāha comprises 191 verses, one more than a (plurality of the) virāj.

11. This agniṣṭoma[1] is a light. He gains the luminous and pure worlds who, knowing this, sacrifices with it.

[1] The word is used apparently as: laud of Agni.

XIX. 12.

(The Ṛṣabha or 'bull'-ekāha.)[1]

1. Now (the one-day-rite called) 'the bull'.

2. This stoma (sacrifice) is the bull (most excellent) of the stomas. He who knows this comes to excellency.

3 He should perform it for a Noble; the bull is the lord of cattle (cows), the Noble of men. He, forsooth, who is (a bull) becomes the lord.

4. A bull (most excellent) among his equals becomes he who knows this.

5. It (this rite) has the sadoviśīya(-sāman)[1] in the midday-pavamāna(-laud); through both the services he encompasses the peasantry (*viś*) for him (for the Sacrificer)[2]: the peasantry will not leave him.

[1] Grām. XIV. 1. 31, composed on SV. I. 5. 11, chanted on the bṛhatī-part of the midday-pavamāna on this same verse. The ūhagāna does not contain the sadoviśīya on this (SV. II. 26) verse, because perhaps it could be taken unaltered from the grāmegeyagāna (?).

[2] Because the name of the sāman contains the word *viś*, and this sāman, being applied in the middle, is now encompassed by the two other savanas.

---

[1] Cp. Jaim. br. II. 87; Ārṣeyakalpa V. 5. a; Lāṭy. IX. 4. 20-21; Nidānasūtra VII. 10; Baudh. XVIII. 40; Āp. XXII. 12. 11-12; Kāty. XXII. 1. 3-5; Āśv. IX. 7. 30; Śāṅkh. XIV. 23.

6. There is the samanta(-sāman)[1]; he makes the peasantry adjacent (*samanta*) to him: the peasantry will not leave him

1 Grām. II. 1. 30, composed on SV. 1. 61 (SV. ed. Calcutta, vol. I, page 192), chanted immediately after the sadoviśīya on SV. II. 26 (SV. ed. Calcutta, vol. V, page 607).

7. The rathantara and the bṛhat are both (applied)[1]. The rathantara is the earth, the bṛhat is the sky. The bṛhat (*i.e.* the sky) he obtains from t h i s world by chanting, (the earth) from y o n d e r world[2]; in both worlds he obtains a firm standing.

1 The rathantara as first pṛṣṭha-laud, the bṛhat on the anuṣṭubh-part of the ārbhava-laud (§8).

2 The printed text *bṛhad evāsmāl lokād gāyaty evāmusmat* cannot be right; instead of *amusmāt* read *amuṣmāt,* but perhaps something has fallen out. The words, divided are: *bṛhad ā iva asmāt lokāt gāyati, ā iva* etc.

8. The bṛhat is applied on the anuṣṭubh(-part of the ārbhava-pavamāna-laud); the anuṣṭubh is the end of the metres[1], the bṛhat is the end[2] of the sāmans, the Noble is the end[2] of men; in the end he, thereby, establishes the end. Therefore, he of the Nobles who is left behind does not reach again the topmost point[3].

1 Because perhaps it was created from the feet of Prajāpati (VI. 1. 11).

2 The end means 'the highest'.

3 The purport is not clear.—Whilst, according to the Ārṣeyakalpa, the schema for the Kauthumas is: 9, 15, 15, 15, 15 | 17, 17, 17, 17, 17 | 17. 21 (precisely that of the normal agniṣṭoma, with the exception of the midday-pavamāna which, instead of fifteen-versed, is here seventeen-versed), that of the Jaiminīyas: 15, 15, 15, 15, 15 | 21, 15, 15, 15, 15 | 15, 15, is more typical of this ṛṣabha because it shows a highest point in the middle, the hump on the shoulder of the bull. Similarly, Baudh, and Śāṅkh.

XIX. 13.

(The Gosava.)[1]

1. The Vājapeya is (equal to) the Rājasūya and the Rājasūya is the consecration of Varuṇa, but the Gosava is a sacrifice for supremacy[1].

1 Cp. with this § the Kāth, and the TBr.

---

1 Cp. Jaim. br. II. 113 (Auswahl no. 135); Ārṣeyakalpa V. 5. b; Lāṭy. IX. 4. 22-24; Nidānasūtra VII. 10; Kāṭh. XXXVII. 6; TBr. II. 7. 6; Baudh. XVIII. 7; Āp. XXII. 12. 17-13. 4; Kāty. XXII. 11. 6-11; Aśv. IX. 8. 12-14; Śāṅkh. XIV. 15.

2. The supremacy obtains he who knows this.

3. For the supremacy is Prajâpati (and) the supremacy is the most exalted Lord.

4 He who knows this reaches the state of a most exalted Lord.

5. The rathantara and the bṛhat are both (applied); for this (pair) is (equal to) the supremacy[1]. To supremacy comes he who knows this.

[1] Agrees literally with TBr.

6. A myriad (of cows should be given) as sacrificial fee; for that is (equal to) supremacy[1]. To supremacy comes he who knows thus.

[1] Agrees with TBr.

7. They consecrate him by (pouring) fresh milk (over him); for that is (equal to) supremacy[1]. To supremacy comes he who knows this.

[1] Agrees with Kâth.

8. His consecration takes place at the chanting of the bṛhat[1], for that is (equal to) supremacy. To supremacy comes he who knows this.

[1] This is the usual moment destined for a consecration: immediately after the first pṛṣṭha-laud and before the mahendra-graha (C H. § 201)

9. They consecrate him whilst he is sitting to the south of the âhavanîya-fire on a not raised (not thrown up, place); they (thereby) consecrate him on the earth itself, nothing having been interposed[1].

[1] The wording of Kâth. and TBr. differs slightly.

10. It (this rite) is throughout thirty-six-versed. Thereby, it is the Gosava[1].

[1] Because the bṛhatî is of thirty-six syllables and the bṛhatî is cattle (XVI. 12. 9).—The Kâth. runs: *ṣaṭtriṃśah stomo bhavati, paśustomo vā eṣa, tena gosavaḥ.*

XIX. 14.

(The Marutstoma.)[1]

1. Now, the stoma (the sacrifice) of the Maruts. Through this (rite), the Maruts throve illimitably. He who knows this thrives illimitably.

2. In that the stomas (occur) troopwise[1], thereby, it is a stoma of the Maruts; for the Maruts are troopwise.

[1] The schema is: 9, 9, 9, 15, 15 | 15, 17, 17, 17, 21 | 21, 21, see § 4–7. Here are four groups, the Maruts consist of seven groups.

3. This same (rite) he should perform for three persons (as Sacrificers)[1].

[1] Lāṭy.: 'friends or brothers, who wish to come to an agreement, should perform the Marutstoma.'

4. In that there are three nine-versed lauds, they separately are firmly established in priestly lustre

5. In that there are three fifteen-versed (lauds), they separately are firmly established in valour.

6. In that there are three seventeen-versed (lauds), they separately are firmly established in (the possession of) cattle.

7. In that there are three twenty-one-versed (lauds), they separately are firmly established.

8. He who knows this is firmly established.

XIX. 15.

(The indrāgnyoḥ kulāya)[2]

1. Now (the ekāha designated as) 'the case (nest) of Indra and Agni.' It may be performed by one who is desirous of (obtaining) offspring or cattle. 'Nest' is offspring; 'nest' is cattle; 'nest' is dwelling. He becomes a 'nest.'

---

[1] This ekāha is found only in the Kauthuma-text and in those sources that depend on it (Ārṣeyakalpa V. 5. c, Lāṭy. IX. 4. 25–27). It is only the Manustoma of Baudh. XVIII. 42 that has precisely the same schema as this Marutstoma.

[2] Cp. Jaim. br. II. 132, 133; Ārṣeyakalpa V. 5. d; Lāṭy. IX. 4. 28–32; Baudh. XVIII. 35; Āp. XXII. 13. 10–11; Kāty. XXII. 11. 13–22; Āśv. IX. 7. 29; Śāṅkh. XIV. 29.

2. This same rite he may perform for two persons (as Sacrificers).

3. In that there are six nine-versed lauds, these two are separately firmly established in priestly lustre. In that there are two fifteen-versed (lauds), they are separately established in valour. In that there are two seventeen-versed (lauds), they are separately established in cattle. In that there are two twenty-one-versed (lauds), they are separately firmly established[1]. He who knows this is firmly established[2].

[1] The schema, then, is: 9, 9, 9, 9, 9 | 9, 15, 15, 17, 17 | 21, 21.

[2] According to the Jaiminīyas, this ekāha was performed by Indra and Agni together, in order that they might reach the excellency amongst all the other deities that were equal to them. The rite here consists of nine- and fifteen-versed lauds, which are used alternately. Through the trivṛt, Agni reached excellency; through the pañcadaśa, Indra reached it. So it may be performed by a Brāhmin and a Noble together.

XIX. 16.

(The Indrastoma.)[1]

1. Now, the fifteen-versed 'stoma' of Indra; an ukthya-rite.

2. Through this (rite), Indra surpassed the other deities. He who knows this surpasses the other people.

3. It should be performed for a Noble.

4. It is throughout fifteen-versed; the fifteen-versed (stoma) is vigour (and) strength; he makes him thrive through vigour (and) strength.

5. It is performed on (verses) addressed to Indra; he makes him thrive through valour (and) strength.

6. It is an ukthya-rite; the uktha(laud)s are cattle, they are the peasantry; he (thus) attaches to him the peasantry, the cattle. The peasantry will not leave him.

7. There are fifteen fifteen-versed lauds; the fifteen-versed (stoma) is vigour (and) valour; successively. he brings into him vigour (and) valour.

---

[1] Cp. Jaim. br. II. 139, 140; Ārṣeyakalpa V. 6; Lāṭy. IX. 4. 29; Nidānasūtra VII. 10; Baudh. XVIII. 14; Āp. XXII. 10. 3: 13. 8-9; 27. 13-21; Kāty. XXII. 11. 15-17; Āśv. IX. 7. 26-27; Śāṅkh. XIV. 58. This ekāha is equally designated as Indrastut.

XIX. 17.

(The stoma of Indra and Agni.)[1]

1. Now, the 'stoma' of Indra and Agni. Through this rite, Indra and Agni surpassed the other deities. He who knows this surpasses the other people.

2. It is (alternatively) nine- and fifteen-versed.

3. The nine-versed (stoma) is priesthood[1], the fifteen-versed is nobility[1]. He who knows this, becomes a shining-out amongst the priesthood and the nobility.

[1] Cp. VI. 1. 6 and 8.

4. A king and his chaplain should perform this rite.

5. It amounts to the gayatrī and to the jagatī[1].

[1] The schema being: 9, 15, 9, 15, 9 | 15, 9, 15, 9, 15 | 9, 15, there are all in all 54+90=144 verses: $\frac{144}{24}$=6 gāyatrīs, $\frac{144}{48}$=3 jagatīs.

6. Through the gāyatrī, the Brāhmin obtains the priestly lustre; through the jagatī, the king enters the peasantry.

7. One who is desirous of (obtaining) a chaplainship may perform (it).

8. Bṛhaspati desired: 'May I obtain the chaplainship among the Gods.' He performed this (rite); he obtained the chaplainship among the Gods. He who knows this obtains a chaplainship.

XIX 18.

(The first Vighana.)[2]

1. Now, the Vighana.

2. Indra desired: 'May I drive away my evil adversary.'

---

[1] Only given by the Kauthumas and those who follow their authority: Ārṣeya-kalpa V. 7. a; Lāṭy. IX. 4. 30-32; Nidānasūtra VII. 10; Āp. XXII. 13. 10-11; Kāty XXII. 11. 18-22.

[2] Cp. Jaim. br. II. 141. 145 (Auswahl No. 141); Ārṣeyakalpa V. 7. b; Lāṭy. IX. 4.33-35; Nidānasūtra VII. 11; TBr. II. 7. 18; Baudh XVIII. 30; Āp. XXII. 13. 12; Kāty. XXII. 11. 23-26; Āśv. IX. 7. 32-33; Śāṅkh. XIV. 39. 8-10. The Kauthumas only and Kāty. acknowledge two Vighanas, but cp. note on khaṇḍa 19.

He saw this Vighana and drove away his evil adversary. He who knows this, drives away (*vihate*) his evil adversary.

3. In that there is the nine-versed (stoma), he retains his vital principles (his *prāṇas*). In that there is the twelve-versed (stoma), he (obtains) the year. In that there is the fifteen-versed (stoma), (he obtains) strength. In that there is the seventeen-versed (stoma), (he obtains) food. In that there is the twenty-one-versed (stoma), (he obtains) a firm footing. In that there is the nineteen versed (stoma), (he obtains) progeniture. In that there is the twenty-four-versed (stoma), (he obtains) priestly lustre. In that there is the twenty-seven-versed (stoma), he hurls a thunderbolt on his adversary[1].

1 According to the Ārṣeyakalpa, the schema is: 9, 9, 12, 12, 15 | 17, 21 19, 24, 24 | 27, 27. The *navadaśa stoma* occurs nowhere else; it is not even mentioned in Chapter II.

4. One who is desirous of (obtaining) cattle should perform it. It amounts to the bṛhatī[1]. The bṛhatī is cattle[2]: he obtains, cattle.

1 All in all, there are 216 verses, this number, being divided by 36 (the bṛhatī is of 36 syllables), is equal to 6 (bṛhatīs).

2 Cp. XVI. 12. 9.

5. These (verses) amount to six bṛhatīs; the year is (equal to) six seasons; in the course of the year (after the lapse of a year) cattle is born[1]. Having reached it, he obtains it.

1 Cp. XIX. 5. 5.

XIX. 19.

(The second Vighana.)[1]

1. Indra was persecuted by ungodly illusions. He resorted to Prajāpati. He gave him that Vighana; by means of it he (Indra) drove away all his enemies Because he drove them away (*vihan*), hence the name Vighana.

2. He who, knowing this, performs the Vighana, he who performs it for one who knows it drives away all his enemies.

---

1 The text of Pañc. br. contains nothing which would, objectively, give us the right to regard this as a special ekāha. However, all the other Kauthuma-texts and Kāty. admit a second Vighana.

3. One who is desirous of (obtaining) cattle should perform (it) The bṛhatī is cattle[1]: he is firmly established in (the possession of) cattle.

[1] Cp. XIX. 18. 4.

Twentieth Chapter

The Chapters XX, XXI and XXII describe the Ahīnas (comprising likewise the Atirātras, Lāṭy. IX 5. 6) or soma-rites of more than one day and less than thirteen days. The Atirātras, 'over-night-rites,' are treated XX. 1–10

XX. 1.

(The Jyotiṣṭoma-atirātra.)[1]

1. The out-of-doors-laud is nine-versed ; the ājya(-laud)s are fifteen-versed ; the midday-pavamāna(-laud) is fifteen-versed ; the pṛṣṭha(-laud)s are seventeen versed ; the ārbhava(-pavamāna-laud) is seventeen-versed ; the agniṣṭoma(-laud) is twenty-one-versed[1] ; likewise, are the uktha(-laud)s ; the night(rite) is fifteen-versed ; the twilight(-laud) is nine-versed.

[1] This is the normal agniṣṭoma jyotiṣṭoma to which are added the three ukthastotras (cp. Ārṣeyakalpa, Anhang 2), the night-rounds (ib. Anhang 3) and the Sandhistotra (ib.).

2. A jyotiṣṭoma-over-night rite should be performed by him who wishes prosperity This rite is a 'stepping-on' amongst the stomas[1] (the sacrifices of soma) ; (it serves) for stepping-on ; for in the stepping-on (part) of the sacrifice he is prosperous.

[1] Cp. II. 6. 3.

3. This (rite) is an agniṣṭoma[1]; it is an ukthya[2]; it is an over-night-rite. Through the agniṣṭoma, the Gods conquered this (earthly) world : through the ukthas, the intermediate region ; through the night(-rite), yonder world, and through day and night they went near (took possession of these worlds).

[1] By its first twelve lauds.

[2] By its first fifteen lauds.

---

[1] Cp. Ārṣeyakalpa VI. 1. a; Nidānasūtra VIII. 1.

4. Some (dawns) shine forth thitherward, others hitherward[1]. That one shines forth hitherward which shines forth through the āśvina(-śastra)[2]. He makes the dawns shine forth for him hitherward directed.

[1] The thought simply seems to be that for some people the dawn 'shines away,' *viz.*, for those who die, but that it again and again returns for those who do not lose life.

[2] Which is recited at day-break.

5. When all (the stotra-verses) are summed up, two exceed the virāj[1]. This is a virāj with (two) milking breasts. He milks (*i.e.* he gets) out of it (the fulfilling of) what wish he has.

[1] To the number of verses of the normal agnistoma are to be added: of the three uktha-lauds (ad 17): 63 verses, of the twelve night-rounds (rātripa-ryāyas) (ad 15): 180, and of the sandhistotra: 9. In all: 190 + 63 + 180 + 9 = 442; two more than 440, a number divisible by ten (the virāj).

6. He starts with the nine-versed (stoma), he concludes with the nine-versed (stoma). The nine-versed (stoma) is breath; by breath he begins, in breath he concludes[1].

[1] Cp. XIX. 10. 14.

XX. 2.

(The over-night rite with all the stomas.)[1]

1. The out-of-doors-laud is nine-versed; the ājya(-laud)s are fifteen-versed; the midday-pavamāna(-laud) is seventeen-versed; the pṛṣṭha-(laud)s are twenty one-versed; the ārbhava (pavamāna-laud) is twenty-seven-versed; the agniṣṭoma(-laud) is thirty-three-versed; the uktha(-laud)s are descending (in number of verses)[1]: the first is twenty-seven-versed, the (last) two, as also the ṣodaśin (-laud), are twenty-one-versed; the night (-rite) is fifteen-versed; the twilight (-laud) is nine-versed[2].

[1] Whilst, normally, the ukthas are all twenty-one-versed, cp. VIII. 10, 1.

[2] The 9-, 15-, 17-, 21-, 27- and 33-versed stomas are considered as 'all the stomas.'

2. He who wishes to prosper should perform the over-night-rite that contains all the stomas, for reaching a l l, for gaining a l l. By this (rite), he reaches all; he gains all.

---

[1] Cp. Ārṣeyakalpa VI. 1. b, Nidānasūtra VIII. 2; TS. VII. 1. 3.

3. In that the out-of-doors-laud is nine-versed, thereby, he reaches the nine-versed stoma (and) the gāyatrī-metre[1]. In that the ājya(-laud)s are fifteen-versed, thereby, he reaches the fifteen-versed stoma (and) the triṣṭubh-metre[1]. In that the midday-pavamāna(-laud) is seventeen-versed, thereby, he reaches the seventeen-versed stoma (and) the jagatī-metre[1]. In that the pṛṣṭha (-laud)s are twenty-one-versed, thereby, he reaches the twenty-one-versed stoma (and) the anuṣṭubh metre[1]. In that the ārbhava (-pavamāna laud) is twenty-seven versed, thereby, he reaches the twenty-seven-versed stoma (and) the paṅkti-metre. In that the agniṣṭoma(-laud) is thirty-three-versed, thereby, he reaches the thirty-three-versed stoma and the virāj-metre. In that the uṣṇih and kakubh are applied[2], thereby, he reaches the uṣṇih and the kakubh. In that the twilight(-laud) is chanted on bṛhatī(-verse)s[3], thereby, he reaches the bṛhatī. In that the āśvina(-śastra) is recited, thereby, he reaches through this (rite) all, he gains all.

1 Cp. VI. 1. 6, 8, 10. 11.

2 At the uktha-stotras.

3 *Viz.* on SV. II. 99 104 (see IX. 1. 28, note 1).

4. By the thirty-three-versed (stoma), the sacrifice is curved thitherwards[1]. The Adhvaryu counterbalances[2] this is the sequel, through the set of eleven victims[3]; there are eleven ropes (for binding the victims), eleven victims, eleven sacrificial posts. Thereby, he firmly establishes the thirty-three-versed (stoma) in the thirty-three-fold (number).

1 This seems to mean that up to the agniṣṭoma-laud (§1) the stomas increase regularly but, then, a deviation, a curving takes place (schema: 9, 15, 15, 15, 15 | 17, 21, 21, 21, 21 | 27, 33, 27, 21, 21, etc.). This is now counterbalanced through the set of eleven victims, a sacrifice that ideally likewise consists of thirty-three.

2 On *pratyudyacchati* cp. XIV. 1. 10.

3 According to Kāth. XXIX. 10: 180 9 (on which passage Āp. XIV. 7. 19–21 is based), the sacrifice of a peculiar set of eleven victims ought to be combined with an ahīna-rite.

5. By this counterbalanced night(-rite), whatever he wishes, (the fulfilment of) that wish he gets. He who knows this gets (the fulfilment of) whatever wish he has.

XX. 3

(The Aptoryāma.)[1]

1. The out-of-doors-laud is nine-versed; the ājya(-laud)s are fifteen-versed; the midday-pavamāna(-laud) is seventeen-versed; the pṛṣṭha(-laud which runs parallel to the śastra) of the Hotṛ is twenty-one-versed; the other pṛṣṭha(-lauds) are the Chandomas (*viz.* of the 7th–9th day of the ten-day-rite; resp. 24-, 44- and 48-versed); the ārbhava(-pavamāna-laud) is twenty-seven-versed; the agniṣṭoma(-laud) is thirty-three-versed; the uktha (-laud)s are descending: the first is twenty-seven-versed; then, follows a twenty-one versed; then, a seventeen-versed; the ṣoḍaśin(-laud) is twenty-one-versed; the night(-rite) is fifteen-versed; the twilight (-laud) is nine versed; the first extra-laud is nine versed; then, follows a fifteen versed: then, a seventeen-versed, and, then, a twenty-one-versed.

2. Prajāpati created the (domestic) animals (the cattle, the cows). These, being created, left him. Through the agniṣṭoma, he did not reach them, nor through the uktha(-laud)s, nor through the ṣoḍaśin, nor through the night (-rite), nor through the twilight(-laud), nor through the āśvina (-śastra). In regard to them, he said to Agni: 'Try thou to reach these for me'. Agni was not able to reach them through (the first extra-laud:) the nine-versed stoma, the jarābodhīya-(-sāman)[1]. He said about them to Indra: 'Try thou to reach these for me'. Indra was not able to reach them through (the second extra-laud:) the fifteen-versed stoma, the satrāsāhīya (-sāman)[2]. He said about them to the Allgods: 'Try ye to reach these for me'. The Allgods were not able to reach them through (the third extra-laud:) the seventeen versed stoma, the mārgīyava (-sāman)[3]. He said about them to Viṣṇu: 'Try thou to reach these for me'. Viṣṇu reached them, through (the fourth extra laud) the twenty-one-versed stoma, through the vāravantīya (-saman)[4]. he restrained them (from passing away farther, *avārayata*): with the verse: 'Here did Viṣṇu stride'[5], he strode[6].

---

1 Cp. Ārṣeyakalpa VI. 1. c; Lāṭy. IX. 5. 12–24; Nidānasūtra VIII. 2; Kāty. XXIII. 1. 19; Āp. XXII. 13. 19 (and cp. XIV. 4. 12–16). Jaim br. II. 110–112; TBr. II. 7. 14; Baudh. XVIII. 15; Āśv. IX. 11; Śāṅkh. XV. 5–8. Some of these sources reckon the Aptoryāma amongst the ekāhas.

[1] Grām. I. 1. 26, composed on SV. I. 15=SV. II. 1013-1015; it is *idāntam*, see SV. ed. Calcutta, vol. I, page 117.

[2] Grām. V. 1 27, composed on SV. I. 170=SV. II. 992-994; it is *hā-i-kārāntam*, see SV. ed. Calcutta, vol. I, page 387.

[3] Grām. III. 2. 1, composed on SV. I. 115=SV. II. 1016-1018; it is *nidhanavat*, see SV. ed. Calcutta, vol. I, page 289.

[4] Grām. I. 1. 30, composed on SV. I. 17, chanted on SV. II. 1019-1021 (*idam viṣṇur vicakrame*); it is *svāram* (?), see SV. ed. Calcutta vol. I, page 121.

[5] It is striking that the verses on which, according to the Ārṣeyakalpa, the last sāman is chanted (cp. note 4) are afterwards mentioned expressly by the author of the Brāhmana as accompanying an act of Viṣṇu, for which there seemed to be small reason.

[6] The whole passage agrees closely with Taitt. br. II. 7. 14. 1-2, where, however, the sāmans are not mentioned, with the exception of the vāravantīya at the end.—Further, I draw the reader's attention to a highly interesting passage in the Jaiminīya-brāhmana where we find a view attributed to Tāṇḍya (comp. Introduction, Chapter III. b) which in many respects agrees with our passage; see my paper, 'Over en uit het Jaiminīya-brāhmana' in Verslagen en Mededeelingen der Kon. Akad van Wetenschappen te Amsterdam, 4e-reeks, dl. X, page 26. One of the most noteworthy divergences is that whereas in Pañc. br. the Viśve devas with the mārgīyavasāman are mentioned, the Jaim. br. has instead of them *īśānam devam* with the s a m o sāman, and this is the sāman that equally in our text (XIV. 9, 12) is brought into connection with Rudra.

3. He from whom the cattle continually slips away should perform this (rite)[1].

[1] The text agrees with Tbr l.c.

4. When the Gods, by means of this (rite), had conquered (all) that they had to conquer, they obtained (the fulfilment of) whatever wish they fostered. Whatever wish he has, (the fulfilment of) that he reaches by this (rite)[1].

[1] The text agrees again with Tbr.

5. Hence the designation Aptoryāma[1].

[1] The Tbr. has the same. The etymological connection concerns only the first half of the word *aptu* which here is derived from *āpnoti*. The Jaim. br. gives a similar etymon: 'Prajāpati created the animals (the cattle). These, being created, left him. He sought to restrain them (*avivārayiṣata*) through the agniṣṭoma, but they passed beyond it; thereupon, through the ṣoḍaśin, but they passed beyond it also; he stopped them on all sides (*paryâyamat*) through the rounds, hence their name *paryāya*. He encompassed them through the āśvina (-stotra and -śastra, *āśvinena kratunā*). Of them, as they were encompassed, the

small animals escaped, just as the small fishes escape through the meshes of the net (*yathā kṣudrā matsyā akṣy akṣy atiśīyerann evam eva ye kṣudrāḥ paśava āsus te 'tiśeduḥ*; the MS. has *tiśerus*, cp. Baudh XVIII. 15: 360. 1). In regard to them, he wished: 'May I reach them and attach them to myself.' (*ā p t v ainān ātman y a c cheyam*). He saw these four lauds which follow after the night (-rite); he lauded with them, reached them by means of those and attached them to himself; hence the name 'Aptoryāma.' But also because he continued lengthening out the soma drop-wise (*aptuśaḥ*), therefore, it is called 'Aptoryāma.' Similarly, Baudhāyana derives the word from *aptu* and *yāma*; *aptor vā ayam atyareci, tasya ko yāma iti.* On *aptu* cp. also IX. 9 6—About the peculiar rite of *garbhakāra* (*i.e.* chanting the ājya- and pṛṣṭhastotras in such a manner that each of them is enclosed in another sāman) which is known from the Sūtras only, nothing is said in the Brāhmaṇas, but probably some Bahvṛca-brāhmaṇa has mentioned it, cp. Nidānasūtra: *evaṁ hi śaśvad bahvṛcā adhīyate: garbhavanti pṛṣṭhāni bhavanty aptoryāmasya. tāni garbhakāraṁ śaṁset, paśavo vai pṛṣṭhāni, yad garbhavanti bhavanti prajananenaiva paśūnt samardhayantīti.* Maśaka, in his Ārṣeyakalpa VI. 1.e, acknowledges the *garbhakāra*, see Anhang no. 38, 39.

XX. 4.

(The Navasaptadaśa-atirātra.)[1]

1. The out-of-doors-laud is nine-versed: the Hotṛ's ājya (-laud) (*i.e.* the first ājya) is fifteen-versed; (then, follow) nine seventeen-versed lauds; the agniṣṭoma (-laud) and the uktha-lauds are twenty-one-versed; the night (-rite) is fifteen-versed; the twilight-laud is nine-versed[1].

[1] The schema, then, is:

9, 15, 17, 17, 17 | 17, 17, 17, 17, 17 | 17, 21, 21, 21, 21 | 15, 9.

2. The over-night-rite with nine seventeen-versed (lauds) should be performed by one who is desirous of (obtaining) progeny. There are nine vital airs[1]; the seventeen-versed (stoma) is Prajāpati[2]: out of his vital principles, out of Prajāpati, thereby, progeny is born (unto him).

[1] Cp. IV. 5. 21, VII. 7. 6.

[2] Or: 'Prajāpati is seventeen-fold'; cp. II. 10. 6.

3. He shifts the kakubh to the fore-part[1]; the kakubh is man[2]; it is he (man) that, as a foetus, is conceived in the middle[3].

---

[1] Cp. Ārṣeyakalpa VI. 1. d; Nidānasūtra VIII. 2.

[1] Cp. XVI. 11. 5.

[2] Cp. XVII. 11. 7.

[3] Cp. XIX. 3. 4.

4. On this (kakubh-verse) the sākamaśva[1] (is chanted).

[1] Grām. V. 2. 10, composed on SV. I. 193, chanted on SV. II. 42–43. As is proved by the ūhagāna, the *dhurām sākamaśva* is intended: SV. ed. Calcutta, vol. I, page 420.

5. Prajāpati created the creatures; these did not procreate themselves. He saw this sāman; changing himself into a horse, he sniffed at them[1], (then) they procreated themselves. This sāman is a (means of) procreation[2].

[1] A case of the 'sniff kiss'; cp. VII. 10. 15 and Hopkins, in Journal of the Amer. Or. Society, vol. XXVIII, page 120 sqq.

[2] Read *tā na prājāyanta* and *prajananam*.

6. He who knows this procreates himself and is multiplied.

7. At the place of the kakubh he applies the dvipadā-verse[1]; he causes the foetus that was conceived in the middle, to be born.

[1] See note 2 on XVI. 11. 16.

8. It is an over-night rite; young ones (children and calves), forsooth, are born after day and night (each day); after day and night he is procreated in view of progeny and cattle.

XX. 5.

(The Viṣuvat-over-night-rite.)[1]

1. The out-of-doors laud is nine-versed; the ājya(-laud)s are fifteen-versed; the midday pavamāna(-laud) is fifteen-versed; the pṛṣṭha(-laud)s are seventeen-versed; the ārbhava (-pavamāna-laud) is seventeen-versed; the agniṣṭoma (-laud) is twenty-one-versed; the uktha (-laud)s are seventeen-versed; the night(-rite) is fifteen-versed; the twilight(-laud) is nine-versed.

2. A Viṣuvat-over-night-rite he should perform for an eldest son born of an eldest wife. This is amongst the stomas (sacrifices), one that has a middle point. He becomes one who is in the middle[1].

---

[1] Cp. Ārṣeyakalpa VI. 1. e.

[1] The twenty-one-versed stoma is (nearly) in the middle, preceded in increasing numbers by the same stomas and followed in decreasing numbers by the same stomas. So he who practises it will get into the midst of all the others, who will serve him.

3. In that there is one twenty-one-versed (stoma),—the sun, forsooth, is the twenty-first of this (universe): twelve are the months, five the seasons, three the worlds; yonder sun is the twenty-first[1].—he makes him reach the full measure of the sun.

[1] Cp. IV. 6. 3–4.

4. This (sun), forsooth, rises; no other light, forsooth, rises against it.

5. No one amongst his (people) rises against him who knows this.

XX. 6.

(The 'cow'-over-night-rite.)

1*a*. The out-of-doors-laud is fifteen-versed; the ājya (-laud)s are nine-versed; the midday-service is seventeen-versed; the afternoon-service and the uktha(-laud)s are twenty-one-versed[1]; the night (-laud) is fifteen-versed; the twilight(-laud) is nine-versed.

[1] Cp. XVI. 2. 7 (go-ekāha).

1*b*. The goṣṭoma, as over-night rite, should be performed for one who has a rival (whom he wishes to conquer).

1*c*. By means of the go(ṣṭoma), the Gods expelled the Asuras from these worlds[1]; through the night(-rite), they vanquished them for good and all.

[1] Cp. XVI. 2. 2.

1*d*. Having expelled his rival from these worlds, he vanquishes him for good and all by the night(-rite).

XX. 7.

(The 'life'-over-night-rite.)

1*a*. The out-of-doors-laud is nine-versed; the ājya(-laud)s are fifteen-versed; the midday-service is seventeen-versed; the afternoon-service[1] and the uktha(-laud)s are twenty-one-versed; the night (-laud) is fifteen-versed; the twilight (-laud) is nine-versed.

[1] Cp. note 1 on XVI. 3. 4.

1*b*. The āyustoma, as over-night-rite, should be performed by one who is desirous of (reaching) the world of heaven [1].

[1] Cp. XVI. 3. 3.

1*c*. The chants go upward, to prevent a falling down [1].

[1] Cp. ib. 4.

1*d*. In that it is an over-night-rite, he goes to the world of heaven by means of day and night.

XX. 8.

(The Abhijit as over-night-rite.)

1*a*. The out-of-doors-laud is nine-versed; the Hotṛ's (or first) ājya(-laud) is fifteen-versed; the Maitrāvaruṇa's (or second) (ājya-laud) is seventeen-versed; the Brāhmaṇācchaṃsin's (or third) (ājya-laud) is fifteen-versed; the Acchāvāka's (or fourth) (ājya-laud) is seventeen-versed; the midday-pavamāna(-laud) is twenty-one-versed; the Hotṛ's (or first) pṛṣṭha(-laud) is seventeen-versed; the Maitrāvaruṇa's (or second) (pṛṣṭha-laud) is twenty-one-versed; the Brāhmaṇācchaṃsin's (or third) (pṛṣṭha-laud) is twenty-seven-versed; the Acchāvāka's (or fourth) (pṛṣṭha-laud) is twenty-one versed; the ārbhava(-pavamāna-laud) is twenty-seven-versed; the agniṣṭoma(-laud) is thirty-three-versed [1]; the uktha(-laud)s are descending: the first is twenty-seven-versed, the next two, as also the ṣoḍaśin(-laud), are twenty-one-versed each; the night(-laud) is fifteen-versed; the twilight(-laud) is nine-versed.

[1] Cp. XVI. 4. 12 and note 1.

1*b*. The Abhijit, as an over-night-rite, should be performed by one who has a rival (whom he wishes to vanquish).

1*c*. By means of the Abhijit, the Gods took these worlds from the Asuras, and, by means of the night(-rite), they vanquished them for good and all. Having taken from his rival these worlds by means of the Abhijit, he vanquishes him for good and all by the night(-rite).

XX. 9.

(The Viśvajit as over-night-rite.)

1*a*. The out-of-doors-laud is nine-versed; the Hotṛ's ājya(-laud) is fifteen-versed; the Maitrāvaruṇa's (ājya-laud) is seventeen-versed; the Brāhmaṇācchaṃsin's (ājya-laud) is twenty-one-versed; the Acchāvāka's (ājya-laud) is fifteen-versed; the midday-pavamāna(-laud) is seventeen-versed; the Hotṛ's pṛṣṭha(-laud) is twenty-one-versed; the Maitrāvaruṇa's (pṛṣṭha-laud) is twenty-seven-versed; the Brāhmaṇācchaṃsin's (pṛṣṭha-laud) is seventeen versed; the Acchāvāka's (pṛṣṭha-laud) is twenty-one versed; the ārbhava(-pavamāna-laud) is twenty seven-versed; the agniṣṭoma(-laud) is thirty-three-versed[1]; the uktha(-laud)s are descending: the first is twenty-seven-versed, the next two ones and the ṣoḍaśin are twenty-one-versed; the night(-laud) is fifteen-versed; the twilight(-laud) is nine-versed.

1 Cp. XVI. 4. 13, note 1.

1*b*. The Viśvajit, as an over-night-rite, should be performed by one who is desirous of (obtaining) cattle

2 The Nābhānediṣṭha(-hymn) is seed, the Vālakhilya(-verses) are cattle. In that the Nābhānediṣṭha(-hymn) is recited first and, afterwards (are recited) the Vālakhilya(-verses), therefore, cattle is born from seed. He shapes their forms, in that there is the (hymn) of Vṛṣākapi; he gets a firm support in the seasons, in that there is the Evayāmarut(-hymn)[1].

1 Those hymns and verses are the embellishments (*śilpāni*) that are applied at the midday-service of the Viśvajit (see Kauś. br. XXV. 12, beg.). The Nābhānediṣṭha is ṚS. X. 61, 62; the Vālakhilyas are ṚS. VIII. 49–59; the Vṛṣākapi-hymn is ṚS. X. 86; the Evayāmarut is ṚS. V. 87. —For the equations cp. Ait. br. V. 15. 3: *yadi nābhānediṣṭham (antariyāt) reto 'syāntariyād; yadi vālakhilyāh, prāṇān asyāntariyād; yadi vṛṣākapim, ātmānam asyāntariyād; yady evayāmarutam. pratiṣṭhāyā enaṃ cyāvayet.*

XX. 10.

(Four over-night-rites, each of which contains lauds of the same number of verses: Ekastoma's)

1*a*. A nine-versed over-night-rite should be performed by him who is desirous of (obtaining) priestly lustre; the nine-versed (stoma) is splendour (and) priestly lustre; he obtains splendour (and) priestly lustre, he is firmly established in (the possession of) splendour (and) priestly lustre.

1*b*. A fifteen-versed over-night-rite should be performed by him who is desirous of (obtaining) vigour; the fifteen-versed (stoma) is vigour (and) strength; he obtains vigour (and) strength; he is firmly established in vigour (and) strength.

1*c*. A seventeen-versed over-night-rite should be performed by him who is desirous of (obtaining) food[1]; the seventeen-versed (stoma) is food; he obtains food.

[1] Cp. note 1 on II. 7. 7.

1*d*. A twenty-one-versed over-night-rite should be performed by him, who is desirous of (getting) a firm support; the twenty-one-versed (stoma) is a firm support[1]; in that it is an over-night-rite, he is firmly supported in day and night.

[1] Cp. III. 7. 2.

XX. 11.

(First two-day-rite.)[1]

1. The first day is a jyotiṣṭoma-agniṣṭoma, the last an over-night-rite containing all the stomas[1].

[1] Cp. note 2 on XX. 2. 1.

2. Of this (last day), the out-of-doors-laud is twenty-four-versed; the ājya(-laud)s are fifteen-versed; the midday-pavamāna(-laud) is seventeen-versed; the pṛṣṭha(-laud)s are twenty-one-versed; the ārbhava(-pavamāna-laud) is twenty-seven-versed: the agniṣṭoma(-laud) is thirty-three-versed: the uktha(-laud)s are descending: twenty-seven-versed is the first, then, comes a twenty-one-versed, then a seventeen-versed · the ṣoḍaśin(-laud) is twenty-one-versed; the night(-laud) is fifteen-versed; the twilight(-laud) is nine-versed.

3. The Angirases went to the world of heaven. Two of them, the Angirases Haviṣmat and Haviṣkṛt, were left behind[1]. They arrived (at the spot) whence the Angirases had gone to the world of heaven. They practised austerities and saw these two sāmans[2]. By means of these, they accomplished a two-day-rite and, thereby, went to the world of heaven.

[1] Why they were left behind is set forth in the Jaim. br.

[2] The hāvismata-sāman, grām. IV. 1. 19, composed on SV. I. 138, chanted on the second day at the beginning of the midday-pavamāna on SV. II. 39-41

---

[1] Cp Jaim. br. II. 235-237 (Auswahl No 197.*a*); TS VII. 1. 4; Ārṣeyakalpa VI. 2 *d*; Nidānasūtra VIII. 3-4; Baudh. XVI. 24; Āp. XXII. 14. 18-19.

(*svādiṣṭhayā*); it is *nidhanavat*: *haviṣmate* 2 3 4 5, see SV. ed. Calcutta, vol. 1, page 328. The hāviṣkṛta-sāman, grām. IV. 1. 20, composed on SV. I. 138, chanted on the first day at the beginning of the ārbhava-pavamāna on SV. II. 105–107 (*asya pratnām*); it is *nidhanavat*: *haviṣkṛte* 2 3 4 5, see SV. ed. Calcutta, *loc. cit.* Cp. Nidānasūtra VIII. 4: *athaite hāviṣmatahāviṣkṛte; hāviṣkṛtaṃ pūrvasyāhna ārbhavacaraṃ sthānāpannaṃ bhavati dvitīyasthānam ca, hāviṣmatam uttarasya mādhyandine.*

4 He who, (although) being righteous, is left, as it were, behind, should perform this (rite). He reaches the advantage of those who precede him; for those two (who had been left behind) reached the Angirases [1].

[1] Cp. XVI. 14. 2.

5. He who is desirous of (obtaining) progeny should perform (it). For the progeny is that second (day) [1].

[1] Cp. Jaim. br.: *ātmā vai pūrvam ahaḥ prajottaram, ātmānam eva pūrveṇāhnā saṃskurute prajām uttareṇa.*

6*a*. He who is desirous of (reaching the world of) heaven should perform (it), for from the second world the next world (heaven) must be approached.

6*b*. 'Of difficult accomplishing [1] is the two-day-rite', they say: 'if [2] the first day is an agniṣṭoma, they omit the ukthya [3]: if it is an ukthya(-rite), they omit the agniṣṭoma' [4].

[1] *dūrādho* (so a Leyden MS. and the Dict. of St. Petersburgh); the printed text and Sāyana read *durādho*. The parallel-passage of the Jaim. br. runs: *saduṣṣaja* (read perhaps *suduṣṣaja*, 'rather difficult to get ready') *iva ha khalu vā eṣa yajñakratur yad dvirātraḥ.*

[2] Read probably *yady* instead of *yad*.

[3] The ukthya-part of the day (?).

[4] Because then we would have two ukthya-days.

7. In that the first day is a jyoti(ṣṭoma) as ukthya-rite, they do not omit the agniṣṭoma nor the uktha(-laud)s [1].

[1] Cp. XX. 1. 3.

8. About this, they (the Theologians) say: 'The agniṣṭoma is the measure of the sacrifice [1]. In that the first day is an agniṣṭoma, he does not exceed the measure of the sacrifice, and after the uktha(-laud)s

of the next day they undertake the night(-rite), thereby, the uktha (-laud)s are not passed over'[2].

[1] As it is the *prakrti* of all sacrifices of soma.

[2] The conclusion, then, is that the first day may equally well be an agniṣṭoma, and so has it the Ārṣeyakalpa.

9. The out-of-doors-laud of the second day is twenty-four-versed[1]; the gāyatrī is of twenty-four syllables; the gāyatrī is a (means of) procreation[2]. (so this serves) for procreating

[1] Cp. § 2.

[2] Cp XVI. 14. 5.

10. Both kinds of stomas (are applied): the even and the odd ones; this is a pairing: from this pairing he is procreated.

11. It (the second day) is an over-night-rite with all the stomas: for reaching all, for gaining all. He reaches all, he gains all[1].

[1] The TS. treats of this dvirātra in a rather difficult chapter (VII. 1. 4), where it is said: *tāv aitām pūrveṇāhnāgachatām uttareṇābhiplavaḥ pūrvam ahar bhavati gatir uttaram*: 'They (Haviṣmat and Haviṣkrt) went by means of the first day, they came by means of the second, the first is the crossing-over, the second is the going' (there are no sāmans called *abhiplava* and *gati*!) In § 2 we have: *gāyatraṃ pūrve 'hant sāma bhavati..traiṣṭubham uttare*.; *tad āhuḥ: kva jagatī cānuṣṭup ceti; vaikhānasaṃ pūrve 'hant sāma bhavati, tena jagatyai naiti; ṣoḍaśy uttare, tenānuṣṭubhaḥ*. With this cp. Jaim. br. II. 237: *gāyatrīṃ pūrvam ahaḥ sampadyate triṣṭubham uttaram; atha kva jagatī cānuṣṭup cety āhur; gāyatrīṃ caiva pūrvam ahaḥ saṃpādayet triṣṭubhaṃ ca jagatīṃ cānuṣṭubham cottaram;.. uccā te jātam andhasety andhasvatī bhavaty andhasvad vai jagatyai rūpaṃ, tena jagatyai rūpān na yanti; vaikhānasaṃ bhavati jāgatam sāma, tenaiva jagatyai rūpān na yanti.* As we are unacquainted with the exact *kḷpti* of this second day according to the Jaiminīyas, it is difficult to interpret this passage, but it may throw some light on TS. Keith's translation is unsatisfactory.

XX. 12.

(Second or Citraratha's two-day-rite.)[1]

1. Now, the (two-day-rite) the first day of which is a jyoti(ṣṭoma) with uktha(lauds); the second, an āyus (rite) as over-night-rite[1].

[1] As explained in XVI. 3; Ārṣeyakalpa III. l. c. as compared with II. 8.

---

[1] Cp. Jaim. br. II. 238 (Auswahl no. 147. b.); Ārṣeyakalpa VI. 2. e; Nidānasūtra VIII. 4; Āp. XXII. 14. 22-23.

2. Three (verses) of the first day exceed the virāj, by two (verses) the second day is less than the virāj[1]. Conformally to the plus and the minus, the young ones are born[2].

[1] The schema of the first day is:

9, 15, 15, 15, 15, | 15, 17, 17, 17, 17, | 17, 21, 21, 21, 21=253,

of the second day:

9, 15, 15, 15, 15, | 17, 17, 17, 17, 17, | 21, 21, 21, 21, 21, | 180 for the night-rounds and 9 for the twilight-laud=448. The first has three syllables above a number divisible by ten; the last, two less than such a number.

[2] Cp. note 3 on XIX. 3.9 and the Jaim. br. where, however, the *stomakḷpti* must be slightly different.

3. He who knows this is multiplied in children and cattle.

4. When all the (verses) are summed up, one exceeds the virāj; he makes him (the Sacrificer) a sole ruler of food[1].

[1] This § is similar to XIX. 11. 10.—253 of the first day +448 of the second makes 701, one more than a number divisible by ten.

5. This (two-day-rite) was performed by the descendants of Kapi on behalf of Citraratha; him they made a sole ruler of food. Therefore, of the descendants of Citraratha one single lord of the nobility is born, as a dependent one the second[1].

[1] This seems to mean that because of the one syllable that exceeds the virāj (§ 4), only one member of this race has the supremacy, whilst the others, the younger brothers, depend on him.

XX. 13.

(Second, or Kapivana's, two-day-rite.)[1]

1. Now, the (two-day-rite) the first day of which is an agniṣṭoma with (alternately applied) nine-versed and fifteen-versed (lauds), and the last of which is an āyus(-rite) performed as over-night-rite.

2. Through the pairing stomas, they engender the second day; this (day), being engendered, they take hold of at the next morning. These two stomas, the nine-versed and the fifteen-versed, are two

[1] Cp. Jaim. br. II. 239; Ārṣeyakalpa VI. 2.f; Nidānasūtra VIII. 4; Āp. XXII. 14. 20-21.

wheels revolving together. What wish he hopes to see fulfilled, that he reaches by means of this (rite). Wherever he wishes (to go) by means of a (chariot) with wheels, that he reaches.

3. And (as for the second day) that it is an āyus(-day) performed as an over-night-rite, (this serves) for (obtaining) a firm support[1].

[1] Cp. IV. 1. 8.

4. When Kapivana, the son (or descendant) of Bhuva[1], had performed this sacrifice, he was freed from his parchedness[2].

[1] Kapivana Bhauvāyana occurs thrice in the Jaim. br. To account for his 'parchedness', the Nidānasūtra gives the following interesting but difficult passage: 'As to (the passage in the Brāhmaṇa) where it is said that he got parched (the following may be said): 'Kapivana, the son of Bhayajāta (or perhaps: Abhayajāta), undertook the consecration for the four-day-rite of Jamadagni (Pañc. br. XXI. 10), having thrown a Brahmacārin of rightcous family into the water. He (viz. Kapivana) had undertaken the day of nine-versed and fifteen-versed stomas and, then, the other returned, having accomplished that object (Saying): 'Quench ye (finish ye) this day's sacrifice with craft,' he added (to the first day) an āyus-over-night rite. Because he had removed the Brahmacārin and because he had dissolved the sacrifice, he became parched. He who avoids these two faults, shall not become parched'. There is much uncertainty in this passage of which I subjoin the text: *yad etat sa rūkṣo 'bhavad iti. kapivano bhāyajātyaś caturātrāya jāmadagnaye didīkṣe brahmacāriṇam sampannakulīnam apaḥ prahṛtya, tasya trivṛtpañcadaśam ahar upetam babhūvāthetaras tam artham sādhayitvā pratyājagāma samāyam imam aharyāgam niśśamayety āyur atirātram upadadhau; brahmacāriṇaś ca parihāreṇa yajñapratyavahāreṇa ca rūkṣo babhūva; yas tv etau doṣau pariharen na rūkṣaḥ syād iti.*

[2] Probably a kind of disease of the skin.

5. He is freed from parchedness who, knowing this performs this (rite).

XX. 14.

(The three-day-rite of Garga.)[1]

1. The morning service is nine-versed, the midday-service is fifteen-versed, the afternoon-service is seventeen-versed (for the

[1] Gargatrirātra XX. 14-XXI. 2. Cp. Jaim. br. II. 240 sqq. (Auswahl no. 149); Ārṣeyakalpa VI. 3-5; Lāṭy. IX. 6; Nidānasūtra VIII. 5-6; TS. VII. 1. 5-7; Baudh. XVI. 24; Āp. XXII. 15-17; Śat. br. IV. 5. 8; Kāty. XXIII. 2. 8; Āśv. X. 2. 6-9; Śāṅkh. XVI. 21.

first-day). The morning-service is fifteen-versed, the midday-service is seventeen-versed, the afternoon-service, with the uktha(-laud)s, is twenty-one-versed (for the second day). The morning-service is twenty-one-versed, the midday-service is twenty-seven-versed, the ārbhava(-pavamāna-laud) is thirty-three-versed, the agniṣṭoma (-laud) is thirty-four versed, the uktha(-laud)s and the ṣoḍaśin are twenty-one-versed, the first night-sāman is sixteen-versed, the night (-rite further) is fifteen-versed, the twilight(-laud) is nine-versed (for the third day).

2. Prajāpati (at the beginning) was alone this (universe); the Word was his only (possession): the Word was the second (that existed). He thought: 'Let me emit this Word, it will pervade this whole (universe)'. He emitted the Word and it pervaded this whole (universe). It rose upwards as a continuous stream of water. Speaking (the syllable) *a*, he cut off a third part of it; this became the earth. He thought: 'This has come into existence' (*a b h ū t*), hence the name earth (*b h ū m i*). With (the syllable) *ka*, he cut off a (second) part of it, this became the intermediate region. (He thought:) 'This is between', hence it is called the intermediate region. With (the syllable) *ho*, he threw a (third) part upwards; that became the heaven. (He thought:) 'This has shone yonder' (*a d y u t a t*), hence the name of heaven (*dyaus*)[1].

[1] With this passage Jaim. br. II. 244 agrees almost to the letter. The three sounds *a*, *ka*, *ho* are chosen because the vowel *a* is formed in the deepest part of the mouth, the syllable *ka* in the middle and the syllable *ho* at the end with the lips, cp § 3.

3. This (*i.e.* this triad of sounds), forsooth, is perceptibly the Word (the Voice), because by means of the tip of the tongue he (*i.e.* one) speaks that part of the Voice which is *a*; by means of the middle part (of the tongue), that part of the Voice which is *ka*; through the whole (Voice), the pith of the Voice, in speaking *ho*, sounds upwards[1].

[1] Read: *vāco raso 'dhy ūrdhva udvadati*. The Jaim. br. has the same, but adds: *ho iti hi sarvā vāk*. Instead of the t i p of the tongue, we would rather say 'the root of the tongue'.

4. In that these characteristics are revealed day after day[1], they, thereby, let forth (emit) the Voice at the head (*i.e.* at the beginning) of the sacrifice.

[1] The ājya-lauds (which occur at the beginning of the sacrifice as they belong to the morning-service) begin, successively: at the first day, with the verse: *agna ā yāhi*; at the second day, with the verse: *kayā te agne*; at the third day, with the verse: *hotā devaḥ*. Jaim. br.: *yad etāni rūpāny ājyeṣu cāhassu ca niyujyante*, etc.

5. Prajāpati had thus made the Voice (*vāk*), that was one syllabic, three-fold; these (these three parts) had become the worlds, and they were dry[1]: not fit to yield a livelihood. He thought: 'How might these worlds get hair[2], how might they be made fit to yield a livelihood?' He saw this three-day-rite, took it unto himself (and practised it); by means of it, he reached over these worlds[3]; thereupon, they got hair and became fit to yield a livelihood. That (food) which is now (found) on these worlds, is the prosperity of the three-day-rite and its rising upwards[4].

[1] Instead of *rūkṣāḥ*, the Jaim. br. (II. 244) has, much better: *ṛkṣāḥ* 'barren', cp. TS. VII. 4. 3. 1: *ṛkṣā vā iyam alomakāsit*.

[2] *Viz.* herbs and trees, cp. TS. l. c.

[3] Jaim. br (l. c.): *tam* (*sc. etam trirātraṃ yajñam*) *eṣu lokeṣu anvāyātaya* (the MS.: *anvāyatayat*): 'he attached it to these worlds'.

[4] The last sentence, about the translation of which I am uncertain, is precisely so found in the Jaim. br. Among the three worlds here mentioned, the earth seems to occupy the first (and only) place.

6. He who knows this gets abundance of cattle: of two-footed and four-footed[1].

[1] The Jaim. br. agrees literally.

7. Prajāpati emitted the Voice; this (Voice) poured out[1], firstly, (the syllable) *a*; secondly, (the syllable) *kṣa*; thirdly, (the syllable) *ra*. With which characteristic Prajāpati emitted his voice, with that characteristic are the ājya(-laud)s subsequently begun and the (three) days reached[2].

[1] *akṣarat* is used by the author because of the now following word *akṣara* ('word' or 'syllable').

[2] The meaning of our author is not very clear. Sāyaṇa refers to *a*(*yam lokaḥ*), 'this earthly world, (*antari*)*kṣa* 'the intermediate region' and (*dyau*)*r*, where the *r* of the syllable *ra* is found.—Jaim. br. II. 245 has nearly the same.

8. About this, they say: 'Based on syllables is the three-day-rite'; one-syllabic is (the word) *vāk* ('Voice'); three-syllabic is (the word *akṣara* ('syllable'); three-syllabic is (the word) *puruṣa* ('man'). 'He knows it (*viz.* this rite)' they say, 'who knows it as being of equal measure to 'man'[1].

[1] Cp. XVI. 8. 4 (note 1 and 2). The corresponding passage in Jaim. br. (l. c.) runs: *akṣareṣṭhā ha khalu vā eṣa yajño yas trirātro 'kṣaraṃ tryakṣaras trirātro 'kṣaram trirātras; sa ha vā enam veda ya enam puruṣasammitam veda: puruṣas trirātraḥ.*

XX. 15.

(The three-day-rite of Garga, continued.)

1. By means of this (rite), the Gods throve in these worlds; by means of it, they went to the world of heaven.

2*a*. The three-day-rite is the Voice; through the characteristic feature of the Voice, the ājya(-laud)s and the days are divided[1]. Voice (*vāk*) is one-syllabic; (the Word) 'syllable' (*akṣara*) is three-syllabic; they are divided by the characteristic feature of the syllable[2].

[1] Cp. XX. 14. 4.

[2] The trirātra is one as Voice (the word *vāk*), but it is also three, just as *vāk* was divided into three: *a, ka, ha* or *a, kṣa, ra*. The Jaim. br. II. 244 has precisely the same.

2*b*, 3. (There are) three Gandharvas. Their shares are these: to Agni (belongs) the earth, to Vāyu the intermediate region, to Āditya yonder sky. Three lights follow Uṣas: it is Fire that follows Uṣas, it is the Wind that follows Uṣas, it is yonder Sun that follows Uṣas[1].

[1] This Brāhmaṇa gives the impression of being abbreviated from Jaim. br II. 241. *trayo..*(as Pañc. br. XX. 15. 2, b)..*dyaus, tad eṣābhyanūcyate: trayaḥ kṛṇvanti..*(as RS. VII. 33, 7)..*sacante sarvam it tam anu vidur vasiṣṭhā iti* (*sarvam* and *tam* according to the usual sandhi of the Jaim. Saṃh., see 'Die Jaiminīya Saṃhitā', Introduction, page 32); *tad yad iha 'trayaḥ kṛṇvanti bhuvaneṣu reta' ity: agniḥ pṛthivyām retaḥ kṛṇoti, vāyur antarikṣa, ādityo divi; 'tisraḥ prajā āryā jyotiragrā ' iti: vasavo rudrā ādityās, teṣām eti jyotir agram yad asāv ādityas; 'trayo gharmāsa uṣasam sacanta ity': agnir uṣasaṃ sacate, vāyur uṣasam sacata, āditya uṣasaṃ sacate; sarvaṃ it taṃ anu vidur vasiṣṭhā' iti': ye vai brāhmaṇāḥ śuśruvāṃsas te vasiṣṭhās; te hy etat sarvam* (here as accusative neutr.) *anu viduḥ.*

4. These are three pairs [1].

[1] Of masculine beings (Agni, Vāyu, Āditya) paired with one female being (Uṣas). I read instead of *eṣa*, with Jaim br., *eṣu*, and I combine this word with the next sentence.

5. Among these (*i.e.*, of these) two enter into union and what is born in consequence of the pairing, that is the third.

6. Indra raised his thunderbolt against Vṛtra. He (Vṛtra) said: 'Do not smite me. I have here in myself a (thing of) splendour. That I will give up to thee'. (Indra agreed and) he (Vṛtra) gave it up to him; Viṣṇu accepted it. (He raised his thunderbolt) a second time and a third time (and each time) he said: 'Do not smite me, I have here in myself a (thing of) splendour. That I will give up to thee.' He (each time) gave it up to him and Viṣṇu accepted it [1].

[1] For the text of the Jaim., see Auswahl no. 148.

7. In regard to this, now, it is said (by the Seer) [1]: 'Ye have both conquered; ye are not defeated. Neither of them has been defeated. O Viṣṇu and Indra, when ye did strive, then ye did divide in three the thousand' [2].

[1] ṚS. VI. 69. 8.

[2] According to the Jaim. br., Indra claimed the whole of the thousand (delivered up by Vṛtra), but Viṣṇu claimed a third part of it. They went for a decision to Prajāpati, who decided the question by answering with the Ṛk-verse and by assigning to Indra two-thirds and to Viṣṇu one-third. This thousand he, thereby, gave up to them. The thousand are, according to some, the cows taken from the Gods; according to others, they are the Yajus-formulas, the Ṛk-verses, and the Sāmans.

8. This thousand, forsooth, it was that he [1], thereby, gave over to them.

[1] Apparently, Vṛtra, but cp. the Jaim. br. in note 2 on § 7.

9. This (*viz.* these thousand cows destined as sacrificial fee at the three-day-rite) should be divided in the following manner: to a learned (Brāhmin) of pure Ṛṣi-descent must be given on the first day; just as is this (earth) [1] so is he: firmly established is this (earth), firmly established is he (*viz.*, that kind of Brāhmin).

[1] The first day is equal to earth; cp. XX. 14. 2. Jaim. br. has similarly *yo bandhumān anūcānaḥ syāt tasmai prathame 'hani dadyāt.* On the number of cows destined for the persons mentioned in § 9–11, see note 1 on XX. 15. 13.

10. To a learned (Brāhmin) not of pure Ṛṣi-descent must be given on the second day; just as is the intermediate region[1], so is he: they know the intermediate region as standing between (heaven and) earth[2]: they know his (knowledge of) the Veda[3].

[1] The second day is equal to the intermediate region; cp. XX. 14, 2.

[2] *antarikṣa* perhaps is an adjective derived from *antari* (= *antar*) and *kṣāmā*: (being) between the two: earth and sky,' *kṣāmā* taken as an elliptic dual.

[3] The Jaim. br. has: *atho yo'bandhur anūcānaḥ syāt tasmai dvitīye 'hani dadyād; yathā vā idam antarikṣam evam so, 'ntarikṣam iti vā idaṃ vidur, vedaṃ tasya viduḥ.*

11. To a not learned (Brāhmin) of pure Ṛṣi-descent must be given on the third day; just as is the sky[1], so is he; they know the sky as *dyaus*; they know his relation[2].

[1] The third day is equal to the sky; cp. XX., 14. 2.

[2] *Viz.*, his pure Ṛṣi-descent, though he is not learned. The Jaim. br. has: *atha yo bandhumān (an) anūcānaḥ syāt, tasmai tṛtīye 'hani dadyād; yathā vā asau dyaur evaṃ sa; dyaur iti vā amuṃ vidur, bandhu tasya viduḥ.* We meet here with the word *bandhu* as a neuter; the same occurs in a Pitṛbrāhmaṇa of the Kaṭhas: *yadi bandhu nānuvidyāt*, which is the source of Āp Śrs I 9. 6. Here also we ought to read *bandhu*. It is worthy of note that the word *bandhu* in this connection is better justified in the Jaim. br., where everywhere *bandhumān* is used. Has the author of Pañc. br. taken the passage from the Jaim. br.?

12. Hundred (of cows) are given day after day; the hundred is the limit of the sacrifice[1]. This dakṣiṇā (*i.e.*, in this manner the dakṣiṇā) is given undivided. Decades are given day after day; the virāj is ten-syllabic: the sacrifice is virāj-like, this dakṣiṇā is given undivided[2].

[1] At an ordinary sacrifice, 120 cows are given.

[2] The Jaim br. has substantially the same statement. This seems to imply that each day to some officials are given a hundred, to others ten or a plurality of ten.

13. Three hundred and thirty-three must be given on the first day, equally on the second, equally on the third[1].

[1] According to Lāṭy. (IX. 6. 4-13), the division is as follows: 'He should give a hundred to each of the *madhyataḥkārins* (Hotṛ, Brahman, Adhvaryu, Udgātṛ; this makes 400). Fifty to those who are entitled to receive the half

Maitrāvaruṇa, Brāhmaṇācchaṃsin, Pratiprasthātṛ, Prastotṛ; this makes 200) Twenty to the Potṛ and the Neṣṭṛ who belong to those who are entitled to receive a third part. Thirty to the two others of the same order and to the Āgnīdhra of those who are entitled to receive a fourth part (30 to the Acchāvāka, 20 to the Potṛ., 30 to the Āgnīdhra, 20 to the Neṣṭr, 30 to the Pratihartr; this makes 130). Nine to the Unnetr and to the two remaining (*pādins*) (10 to the Grāvastut and the Subrahmaṇya, 9 to the Unnetṛ; this makes 29). Day after day, he should give the same number to the Unnetṛ (*i.e.* 3 on each day). Ten to the Sadasya on the first day, seventy on the second, twenty on the third day (this makes 100). Ten to each of those who are able to claim a Ṛṣi-descendance, who are mentioned in the Brāhmana (see XX. 15. 9-11) (this makes 30). One hundred and ten remain (still to be divided). These he should give (dividing them in equal parts) to the officiating priests and to the *prasarpakas*'. All in all: 400+200+130+29+100 (Sadasya)+30=889; there remain from the 999 cows (for the thousandth cow is treated separately) 110 cows.

14 Now, this (thousandth cow) which belongs to two deities [1] and is three-coloured: (of it) two-third parts (must be given) to the Brahman, one third part to the Agnīdh [2].

[1] According to Sayana, to Indra and Viśvarūpa; perhaps rather Indra and Viṣṇu are meant.

[2] This is specified by Lātyāyana: "On the middle day he should give the thousandth cow to the Brahman and the Āgnidhra. Its colours are: white, black, and red". Cp. Jaim. br. (II. 234, end): *athaiṣā sahasratamī trirūpā dvidevatyā, tasyai dvau bhāgau brahmaṇa, eko 'gnidhaḥ.*—According to Taitt. S. VII. 1. 15. 5, it was for the possession of this thousandth cow that Indra and Viṣṇu contended and agreed that to Indra should belong ⅔, to Viṣṇu ⅓, and, in accordance with this, it is said that she should be given in this proportion to the Brahman, who is Indra-like and to the Āgnīdhra who is Viṣṇu-like.

15. 'Thou art the desirable one, thou art the lovable one, thou art the adorable one; o Iḍā, o Blithesome, o Sarasvatī, o Mighty, o Glorious! These, o Inviolable one, are thy names. Tell thou [1] the Gods of us as doers of good' [2].

[1] Read, with Sāyaṇa and the Leyden MS., *brūtāt* instead of *brūyāḥ*

[2] According to Lāṭy., this formula must be whispered into the right ear of the cow when she is brought forward to be given as dakṣiṇā. But previously this cow must be bought off by another cow and must be joined to the other cows of the Sacrificer. The Jaim. br. (II. 267) runs: *sā yā sahasratamī syāt tasyai karṇam ājaped: iḍe rante mahi viśrute śukre candre havye kāmye 'dite sarasvaty, etāni te 'ghnye nāmāni, deveṣu naḥ sukṛto brūtād iti*, cp. Śat. br. IV. 5. 8 10, TS. VII. 1. 6. 8.

XX. 16.

(The three-day-rite of Garga, continued.)

1. By the first day, he[1] formed what here on this (earth) is firmly rooted; by the second day all living beings that move (on the earth and through the intermediate region); by the third day the rain that falls yonder, the stars and what belongs to yonder world.

[1] According to Śāyaṇa, the subject is the three-day-rite. Perhaps we may take Prajāpati as subject. The Jaim. br. (II. 246) agrees substantially; *prāṇad evaty* is an error of the press for *prāṇad ejaty*.

2. In regard to this (rite), the Theologians say: 'This three-day-rite is the mahāvrata'[1]. The out-of-doors-laud of these (three) days[2] is its head; the two days that are on either side (*viz.*, the first and the third day) are its wings; the middle day is its trunk; the agniṣṭoma-sāmans are its tail.

[1] *Viz.*, the mahāvrata-laud; cp. V. I, 2 (head), 10 (wings), 7 (trunk), 16 (tail). According to Sāyana, this refers to the high-altar built with bricks.

[2] At an ahīna, there is only one single (the first) laud chanted out of doors; cp. Eggeling in Sacred Book of the East, vol. XXIV, page 305, note. The Jaim. br. agrees with our text.

3. That yonder (sun) rises, that is the head; the two days that are on either side are the wings; the middle day is the trunk; the fire is the tail[1].

[1] This (also in Jaim. br.) is not all clear. Perhaps a reference is made to the *citya agni*.

4. That yonder (sun) rises, that is the head; the two days that are on either side are the wings: the middle day is the trunk; that the sun sets, that is the tail[1].

[1] This equally is not clear. Jaim. br. has the same. The three-day-rite seems to be equalized with the sun.

5. So great, forsooth, is the three-day-rite: the gāyatra(-part) is (equal to) the breaths (the vital principles), the triṣṭubh(-part) is the eye-sight; the jagatī(-part) is the ear of sense. He who knows this lives his whole (normal) life.

6. In regard to this, the Theologians say: 'How great is the three-day-rite?' 'So great'[1], should be the answer, for this[1] covers so

great a distance[2]. 'But it is also so great', thus should be the answer, for this[1] also covers so great a distance.—'Is it thitherward directed or hitherward?'[3] they say. The answer should be: 'Thitherward directed,' for thitherward he speaks[4], thitherward he sees, thitherward he breathes out—'Is it one, or two, or three?'[5] they say. The answer should be 'one' for out-breathing, through-breathing (and) in-breathing are one and the same. —Just as in ordinary life a thread strung through a pearl[6], so is this three-day-rite strung through the three worlds. Of him who knows this the face shines (looks beautiful).

[1] It is impossible (Sāyaṇa gives no help) to explain this, as the words of the Brāhmaṇa which are destined to be spoken, not read, must have been accompanied by certain gestures of the hand, indicating what is intended by the speaker.

[2] Read *iyad dhy etad abhi*. Jaim. br. has the same, but without *abhi*.

[3] Cp. note 1 on XVI. 8. 2.

[4] What once has been spoken admits of no return but remains spoken.

[5] Read: *ekā3 dvā3u trayā3 ity*.

[6] Read *maṇau*.

7. What in a three-day-rite is in accordance with the proper course of facts, that in t h i s (three-day-rite) violates the proper course; what of it (*i.e* a three-day-rite in general) violates the proper course, that in this (rite) is in accordance with the proper course of facts. In that this day, which is farther, is applied nearer, he thereby encompasses cattle for the Sacrificer, so as to bring forth young ones, for cattle do not procreate in yonder world[1].

[1] It seems that the three days of this rite are *gāyatra*, *jāgata* and *traiṣṭubha*, whilst the regular order would be *gāyatra* (24), *traiṣṭubha* (44), *jāgata* (48); see X. 5. 9, XXI. 9. 8. The farther day (the *jāgata*) here comes nearer: in the middle, in order to encompass the cattle, which is jagatī-like, b e t w e e n the two days. If the *jāgata*-day were the last day, which is identified with the world of heaven, the Sacrificer would not get cattle, because in yonder world cattle do not procreate. The Jaim. br. (II. 248) has nearly the same: *gāyatraṃ vai trirātrasya* (*i.e.* of a trirātra in general) *prathamam ahas, traiṣṭubhaṃ dvitīyaṃ, jāgataṃ tṛtīyaṃ; yad vā anyasya trirātrasya viloma yad asya saloma tad anyasya viloma; tad yad etat paraṃ sad ahar avaraṃ kriyate, yajamānāyaiva tat paśūn prajanayanti, na hy amuṣmin loke paśavaḥ prajāyante.*

8. The gāyatrī and the triṣṭubh are the strongest among the metres. In that these are on either side and the jagatī is in the middle, thereby, he encompasses the cattle with the strongest of the

metres, so that they may bring forth young ones, for cattle do not procreate in yonder world.

9. The three-day-rite is (equal to) yonder (sun): the first day is as its rising, the second day is as (the sun) at midday, the third day is as its setting. He who knows this attains to union, to sameness of abode with yonder (sun)[1].

[1] The Jaim. br. again nearly agrees: it has equally the rare expression *sāveśya*.

Twenty-first Chapter.

(The ahīnas, continued.)

XXI. 1.

(The three-day-rite of Garga, continued.)

1. Indra took with force a thousand (cows) from the Maruts, his own subjects, having announced this to King Soma. Therefore, they oppress the subjects after having announced it to the king. Yama heard about these two that they had taken with force[1] a thousand (cows) from the Maruts. He came and said: 'Invite me ye both to (have a share in) this thousand'. They invited him. Then Yama saw one cow among these thousand that had as much milk as a thousand, and he said: 'Let this one be mine, take ye both instead of it the thousand'[2]. They answered: 'Just as thou seest this one, so do we see her.'

[1] Read, with the Dictionary of St. Petersburgh and the Leyden MS. and Jaim. br., *ajyāsiṣṭām*.

[2] More precisely the Jaim. br.: 'Let this one be mine, and all the rest of you both'.

2. Then they all said: 'Let us by means of this one divide this thousand'. They made her enter the water. They said: 'Let us draw lots[1] (to decide) for which of us this (cow) will first come out of (the water)'. They drew lots: that of Soma came first, thereupon (in the second place) that of Indra, then (in the third place), that of Yama.

[1] The expression *aṁśān āharante* (*aṃśam apaharante* in the Vādhūla-texts; see ‚Eine vierte Mitteilung über das Vādhūlasūtra', No. 64. a in Acta Orientalia,

Vol. VI, page 176) seems to have the same, or nearly the same meaning as *aṃśaṃ prāsyante* in our Brāhmaṇa, XIV. 3. 13 and XXV. 13. 3—*aṃśān prāsyante* may mean: 'They throw down into a covered receptacle the portions of a stick each marked by a sign so that the thrower may recognise it as his own', whilst *aṃśān āharante* may mean: 'They take out of the receptacle each his own portion of the stick.'

3. They said: 'Come out (of the water) for King Soma with a third part of thyself and a third part of the milk[1] of the thousand'. She came out in the shape of a brown one with red-brown eyes, of one year old, together with a third part of herself and a third part of the milk[1] of the thousand. This, now, is the cow used for buying the soma[2].

[1] I am in doubt whether it would be preferable to translate: 'Come out with a third (part) of thine own (milk) and with a third part of the milk of the thousand', and so each time further on. In the other sources of this legend (TS. JBr.), the word *payasaḥ* ('of the milk'), here and in the sequence, is missing. In TS., the thousandth cow comes up with 333 other cows.

[2] Cp. Śat. br. III. 3. 2, 13, which passage seems to refer to the Brahmaṇa of the Sāmaveda, not of the Black Yajurveda.

4. For a third part of this (cow) self and for a third part of the milk of thousand is the soma bought by him who, knowing this, buys the soma (and) (by him) for whom, whilst he knows this, they buy the soma.

5. They (made her again enter the water and) said: 'Come out for Indra with a third part of thyself and a third part of the milk of the thousand.' She came out in the shape of a spotted heifer together with a third part of herself and a third part of the milk of the thousand. This is the cow that is coveted by Indra[1].

[1] The exact meaning of *indriyeṣyā* is uncertain. Jaim. br., *indreṣyā*. TS. *vārtraghnī*.

6. For a third part of this (cow) self and for a third part of the milk of thousand is the cow, coveted by Indra, given by him, who, knowing this, gives a cow coveted by Indra (and by him) to whom, whilst he knows this, they give such a cow.

7. They (made her again enter the water and) said: 'Come out for Yama with a third part of thyself and a third part of the milk of the thousand'. She came out in the shape of an aged, scurvy[1], hornless (cow), or in the shape of a dusky cow of two years old with shorter fore-legs (then were the hind-legs), together with a third part of herself

and a third part of the milk of the thousand[2]. This is the (cow) used for laying on (a corpse at the cremation)[3].

[1] Instead of *kuṣṭā* the MS. of Leyden reads, as also does the Jaim. br., *kuṣṭhā*: so Böhtlingk guessed also in his Wörterbuch in kurzerer Fassung.

[2] The text should run: '*śṛṅgy udaid dhūmrā vā dityauhirmato hrasīyasī tṛtīyena cātmanas tṛtīyena ca sahasrasya payasaḥ.* If we read in the Jaim. br. (Auswahl No. 149) *jaratī vā* instead of *jarativa*, we have here also the same, alternative, but *vice versa*.

[3] For the *anustaraṇī*-cow, the hide of which is spread out on the corpse on the pyre, cp. W. Caland, die altindischen Toten-und Bestattungsgebräuche, page 20.

8. For a third part of this (cow) self and for a third part of the milk of thousand is the *anustaraṇī*(-cow) applied[1] by him, who, knowing this, applies the *anustaraṇī*(-cow) (and by him) for whom, whilst he knows this, they apply the *anustaraṇī*(-cow)[2]. He may be sure that he has applied her[3].

[1] Read, with the Leyden MS., *kṛtā* instead of *ntatā*.

[2] This is thoughtlessly repeated after the preceding paragraphs, for the dead man cannot know its value.

[3] This is far from certain. Read probably *manyeta*. The Jaim. br. has *no hācakrūr iva manyeta*, for which I proposed to read *hācakrur iva manyeta*: *cakrus*, then, is another example of a part perf. act. with weak form in nomin., as *vidus* in the RS., and cp. Zeitschrift fur vergl. Sprachforschung, vol. XXIX, page 531.—It would, of course, be possible to separate: *na ca ācakrvān manyeta* and *no ha ācakrur iva m.*

9. About this, the Theologians argue: 'He who sacrifices with a thousand (cows) (as dakṣiṇā) is not deprived of space in yonder world. Now, yonder world (the world of heaven) is as far distant from this (earthly) world as is the distance from here of a thousand[1] cows put above one another. He who sacrifices with a thousand pervades these worlds. But the distance (may be) also a thousand *yojanas* (miles), or a thousand-day's journey for a horse (on horseback or on a chariot), or a thousand-day's journey (on foot). That he reaches by each successive cow. These (cows), forsooth, are given in order to tread upon[2] (yonder world).

[1] Cp. XVI. 8. 6; instead of *yāvad itaḥ sahasrasya* (so reads the Leyden MS.) *gaur gavi pratiṣṭhitā*, the Jaim. br. has more clearly: *yāvat sahasraṃ gaur gavy adhi pratiṣṭhitā*.

[2] Read *samākramaṇāya*.

10. As he (Prajāpati) created the thousand (cows) [1], the (garment) of *tṛpā*(-bark) [2] was its place of origin. That they lead them up (in order to give them as dakṣiṇā), after having put over them [3] a *tṛpā*-(garment), is for obtaining the same place of origin [4].

1 This gives the impression as if the reader (or hearer) were acquainted with the legend of Jaim. br. II. 254: *prajāpatir yad agre sahasram asṛjata*, etc.

2 On *tārpya* see the note on Āp. XVIII. 5. 7 of the German translation.

3 Or over the thousandth cow only: see Āp. XXII. 16. 2.

4 This paragraph we expect rather in the context of XXI. 15, before § 15. So the Jaim. brāhmaṇa has it.

XXI. 2.

(The three-day-rite of Garga, continued.)

1. Prajāpati created the creatures. These, being created, went away from him, as they feared that he would devour them. He said: 'Return to me, I will devour you in such a manner that, although being devoured, ye will be procreated more numerous' [1]. 'Swear this (*ṛtam brūhi*) to us,' they said. He swore it to them by means of the (sāman) that has (the word) *ṛta* as nidhana; he consumed them by means of the (sāman) that has (the word) *ī* as nidhana; he caused them to procreate by means of the (saman) with triple nidhana. Through these sāmans, Death here (on earth) devours the creatures and [2] makes them procreate [3].

1 Read *prajaniṣyadhva iti* with the Leyden MS.

2 Read *atti ca pra ca janayati* with the same MS.

3 The three sāmans are the ājyadoha-sāmans, called also *ācidoha* and *ācyādoha*: (cp. § 5); they are composed on SV. 1. 67 and registered araṇyegeyagāna I. b. 16: trinidhana; I. b. 17: īnidhana and I. b. 18 ṛtanidhana. See SV. ed. Calcutta, vol. II, page 409 sqq. The parallel-passage of the Jaim. br. (II. 254) runs: 'As Prajāpati had given over to the Gods the thousand, these, not looking backward, devoured it. As it was being devoured, it vanished from the (eye-sight of) the Gods. They addressed it. It said: 'I fear for consumption.' 'No', they said, 'we will consume thee in such a manner that, although thou art eaten and drunk, thou shalt not diminish for us' (I read the text: *tathā vai tvātsyāmo yathā no 'dyamānam pīyamānam na kṣeṣyasa iti*). 'Swear ye this to me' (*tasmai vai ma ṛtam kuruteti*). They swore it by means of the ṛtanidhana: they consumed it through the īnidhana (*īnidhanenāpāyan*, read probably, as the Pañc. br., *°āvayan*); they did procreate it through the triṇidhana and made it imperishable (*akṣitim cāsmā akurvan*).' It is worthy of note that in the Jaiminiya-araṇya-gāna (II. 4. 1–3), the sequence of the sāmans is: ṛta-, ī- and trinidhana and that on this sequence the legend of Pañc. br. is equally based.

2. Though it[1] is consumed, it increases for him who knows this.

[1] What is the subject to which *adyamānam* belongs as conjunct participle? If we compare the Jaim. br (*l. c.* immediately following after the passage cited in note 3 on § 1): *adyamāna(m a)sya pīyamānam sahasram na kṣīyate ya evaṃ veda*, we might surmise that the author of the Pañc. br. has been acquainted with the Jaim. br., making a variation of the thema there expounded but at the end taking over the chain of thoughts of the Jaim. br. If this is right, the subject is *sahasram*.

3. They are the pre-eminent sāmans[1], the most excellent sāmans, the sāmans of Prajāpati[2].

[1] In the Gobhilagṛhyasūtra (III. 3) we meet with the *jyeṣṭhasāmikavrata* which introduces the study of the ājyadohas.

[2] The Jaim. br. equally calls these sāmans: *prājāpatyāni*.

4. He who knows this gets pre-eminence and excellency.

5. By means of these sāmans, Prajāpati milked out of these worlds (*i.e.* he obtained out of these worlds, as milk out of the cow) (the fulfilment of) all his desires[1]. Because he milked (*adugdha*) them, having bent (*ācya*) (his knee), therefore, these sāmans are called *ācyādoha*.

[1] Read *kāmān adugdha*. The name *ācyādoha* is probably corrupt: *ājidohāni* is the name with the Jaiminīyas: *ime vai lokā ājayo nāma, teṣām ete dohā, duha imān lokān ya evaṃ veda* (II. 255).

6. Out of these worlds he gets (the fulfilment of) all his desires who, knowing this, lauds with these sāmans[1].

[1] In the Jaim. br. there is nothing corresponding with §§ 5, 6.

7. These sāmans are (equal to) these worlds: the one that has *ṛta* as nidhana is the earth; the one with the final *ī* is the intermediate region; the one with triple nidhana is the sky.

8. Just as one who knows the (way through the) fields passes through the fields, so passes he who knows this through these worlds.

9. These sāmans belong to Agni vaiśvānara[1]. Should they laud with these (sāmans) when they are not quelled, then, the God is apt to strike down the young ones. They laud with them (*i.e.* they chant them) after having put down a fire in the vicinity[2]. Having, thereby, paid homage to the presence[3] of the deity (*i.e.* Agni) to which they belong, he chants (them). (In this manner) they laud with the quelled (chants)[4].

[1] The destructive manifestation of Agni: cp. Śat. br. I. 4. 1. 10.

[2] About this, the Sūtrakāra (Lāṭy. IX. 7. 13–16) prescribes that at the first day the fire on the dhiṣṇya of the Hotṛ, which has been brought here during the midday-service (C.H. § 182), should be taken and brought near the spot where during the ārbhava-laud (cp. Ārṣeyakalpa VI. 3) the ṛtanidhana-ājyadoha is chanted, and that at the last two days the fire of the Hotṛ's dhiṣnya is taken, which has been brought here during the morning-service (C.H. § 139), because at the last two days the chanting of the ājyadohas falls on the midday-pavamāna (Ārṣeyakalpa VI. 4 and 5). During these lauds the fire must be set in flame by throwing fresh fuel on it, and over this fire the mantra is spoken: 'Thou art Agni vaiśvānara. Homage to thee! Do not hurt me'. From the Jaim. br. (II. 255) we know that the three ājyadohas are chanted successively on one of the three days (*anvaham*).

[3] On *sāmyekṣya* (thus, with *y* here, also the MS. of Leyden). cp. note 2 on XII. 13. 26.

[4] Whilst, according to our Brāhmaṇa, it is to Agni that these three sāmans belong (see also Ārṣeya-brāhmaṇa, ed. Burnell, page 64: *agner vaiśvānarasya trīṇy ājyadohāni*), the Jaiminīya-text (see Jaiminīya-ārṣeya-brāhmana, ed. Burnell, page 27) calls them *raudrāni*. Now, we read in the Jaim. br. (II. 254): 'As Prajāpati at the beginning created the thousand, he gave this over to the creatures. The Gods addressed the mighty God (*īśānaṃ devam*, *i.e.* Rudra): 'Thou art the most pre-eminent of us; take thou a part for thyself (*tam uddharasva*)'. He carried away these three sāmans, the pith of the thousand: the *rta*-, the i- and the *triṇidhana*. Therefore, these sāmans must be applied at a three-day-rite of a thousand (dakṣiṇās)... These sāmans belong to the mighty God Akhala (on this name, cp. my paper 'Over en uit het Jaiminīya-brāhmaṇa', in Versl. en Meded. der Kon. Akad. van Wetensch., Afd. letterk. IVe. R., dl. X, pages 47, 103); he could covet the cattle of the Sacrificer'. It is probable that this version, according to which these sāmans are *raudra*, is the original one and that when the Pañc. br. attributes them to Agni vaiśvānara, this is a deviation. This is proved, according to my opinion, by the expression used in the Pañc. br.: *tat prajā devo ghātuko bhavati*; *deva* as a designation for Rudra is common (see note 1 on XVII. 1. 1), and the expression *ghātuko bhavati* is in our Brāhmana regularly used of Rudra (see *e.g.* VII. 9 18).

XXI. 3.

(The three-day-rite of Garga, concluded.)[1]

1. The spotted (cow) is the Voice, the three-day-rite is its calf. The three-day-rite (*i.e.* the calf) makes flow her (*i.e.* the cow's) milk [1].

---

[1] On the Śabalī-homa, cp. Lāṭy. IX. 8, Āp. XXII. 7. 10, and Weber in Indische Studien, vol. V, page 437 sqq.

[1] When the Hindoos are going to milk a cow (for ritual purposes), they first let the calf suck (see *e.g.* Āp. I. 12. 10), so that the milk flows, then they remove the calf and continue the milking.

2. Therefore, he who knows this, for him she gives milk after her milk has been set a flowing (by the sucking of the calf)[1].

[1] The correct reading is *prattā*, not, as Sāyaṇa (whom Weber follows) would have it: *aprattā*.

3, 4. He who, though being qualified to obtain food, has no food to eat, should during ten days, wearing a linen garment[1], drinking (only) hot milk, lie (at night) on the bare ground.

[1] Cp. XVIII. 9. 16.

5. At daybreak of the thirteenth day he should perform the sacrifice to Śabalī[1] and, then, before the sounds (the birds) are heard, go to a place (in the wild) where he does not hear the cattle of the village, lay hands on a stalk of darbha-grass and thrice call: 'Śabalī! Śabalī! Śabalī!' If any animal, other than a dog or an ass, by howling or screaming responds to his call, this is lucky.

[1] With the formula of § 7.

6. If no animal responds, he should after a year repeat the (whole Śabalī-rite and the) calling.

7 'O Śabali, thou art the all-expansive ocean, the brahman of the Gods, the first born of Ṛta. Thou art food, thou art light, thou art splendour, thou art immortality. We know thee, o Śabalī, as the shining one. Thy (one) foot is the earth, thy (second) foot the intermediate region, thy (third) foot the sky, thy (fourth) foot the ocean. Thou art quick, o Śabalī. We know thee! Grant us (milk us) strength and food, a stream of wealth, o Śabalī. May I among the creatures go along the mightiest direction—*svāhā*'[1].

[1] Cp note 1 on § 5.—At the end, Pañc. br. has *śaciṣṭhā vratam anugeṣam*; Āp. (who follows our Brahmana): *śaciṣṭhā vrajam anu°* (one MS. has *vratam*). I have followed the Jaim. br. II. 258, where the invocation runs: *śabali samudro 'sy akṣitir brahmadevī prathamajā ṛtasyaikam akṣaraṃ kṣarasi vibhāvary abhīmān lokān amṛtaṃ duhānā tāṃ tvā viduḥ sarame dīdyānām akṣitiṃ devebhyo bhāsā tapantīṃ tejo 'si śukram asy amṛtam asy annam asi mahad asy eṣāsi mahi, tāṃ tvā tathā veda. tasyāṃ tvayy etāṃ dakṣiṇāṃ nidadhe 'kṣitim akṣīyamāṇāṃ śriyaṃ devānāṃ bṛhaj jyotir vasānāṃ priyāṇāṃ śaciṣṭhām āvṛtam anugeṣam iti.* Then, follows a lengthy brāhmaṇa upon this mantra. In the Jaim. br., we find no indication of the aim for which the mantra is intended nor any mention of a Śabalī-homa.

XXI. 4.

(The three-day-rite of the sacrifice of the horse.)[1]

1. A catuṣṭoma-agniṣṭoma[1] (is the first day), a twenty-one-versed ukthya (is the second), an over-night-rite which contains all the stomas[2] (is the third day).

[1] Cp. note 1 on XIX. 5. 1.

[2] Cp. note 2 on IV. 5. 11, 12.

2. The eye of Prajāpati swelled (*aśvayat*); it fell out; it became the horse (*aśva*); hence the horse has its name. By means of the Aśvamedha, the Gods restored it to its place. He who performs the Aśvamedha makes Prajāpati complete[1].

[1] The Jaim. br. (II. 268) has a similar passage. but TS. V. 3. 12. 1 agrees to the letter, and Śat. br. XIII. 3. 1. 1 (first half) agrees closely with our passage.

3. The performer of the Aśvamedha arises bodily for yonder world.

4. A bee tore out (a piece of) the thigh of the horse; this the Gods restored by means of the catuṣṭoma. That there is the catuṣṭoma(-day) is for making the horse whole[1].

[1] Almost equal to TS. l. c. 2. and cp. Śat. br. l. c. 4.

5. In that he transforms the three anuṣṭubh(-verse)s into four gāyatrī-(verse)s[1], thereby, it (the horse) is, whilst standing still, firmly established on three feet, but, whilst running swiftly, puts down all four.

[1] The out-of-doors-laud of the first day is four-versed (cp. § 1); for this stotra are prescribed certain anuṣṭubh-verses, according to the Ārṣeyakalpa VI. 6. a (and this rests, perhaps, on the Brāhmaṇa itself; see note 1 on § 6): SV. II. 366-368=ṚS. IX. 100, 6, 7, 9 (with var. rr.). But for the bahiṣpavamāna not anuṣṭubhs but gāyatrī-verses are required. These three anuṣṭubhs are, in number of syllables, equal to four gāyatrīs ($3 \times 32 = 4 \times 24$) How they are to be divided is seen from the Appendix to Ārṣeyakalpa no. 45. a (page 242). The author of TS. V. 4. 12 must have been acquainted with the Ārṣeyakalpa, as he prescribes equally SV. II. 366 sqq. in the Sāmaveda recension of the Kauthumas. On the other hand, the Jaiminīyas prescribe a different set

---

[1] Cp. Jaim. br. II. 266–274; Ārṣeyakalpa VI. 6: Lāṭy. IX. 9-11: Nidānasūtra VIII. 7, etc. etc.

of anuṣṭubh-verses, *viz.* (cp. Jaim. br. in Auswahl, no. 151) SV. I. 546=SV. II 168-170=ṚS. IX. 101. 7-9. Our Pañc. br. does not indicate explicitly which anuṣṭubhs are to be used, but cp. the next paragraph.

6. The horse is the last (the highest, most perfect) of animals, the anuṣṭubh of metres, Viṣṇu of the Gods[1], the catuṣṭoma of the stomas, the three-day-rite of the sacrifices. In that the opening-verses are anuṣṭubhs addressed to Viṣṇu[1], in that the stoma is the catuṣṭoma and the sacrifice a three-day-rite, thereby, he fixes the last in the last (the most excellent in the most excellent).

[1] This seems to prove that the author of our Brāhmaṇa intended for the *pratipat tṛca* of the first day the verses SV. II. 366-368; see XIII. 5. 4 where these verses are equally designated as addressed to Viṣṇu, for instead of *vaiplavyo* without doubt we ought to read *vaiṣṇavyo*.

7. The day on which the horse is immolated (the second day of this trirātra) is a twenty-one-versed day. The sun (as reckoned) from here, is the twenty-first: (there are) twelve months, five seasons, these (three) worlds; the sun is the twenty-first[1]. He makes him reach the measure of the sun.

[1] Nearly the same in TS. l. c.

8. The mahanāmnī(-verse)s[1] are its (first) pṛṣṭha(-laud).

[1] Cp. XIII. 4. 1, 2.

9. These verses are of different metres; different kinds[1] of animals are (on) this (day) immolated. These verses reach (become equal to) this (three-day-rite). That the mahānāmnī(-verse)s are (taken for) the pṛṣṭha(-laud) is for making the horse whole.

[1] Read *anye 'nya* instead of *anyonya*.

10. The pārthurasma(-sāman) is the Brahman's chant[1].

[1] For the third pṛṣṭha-laud the pārthuraśma is used, on which cp. note 1 on XIII. 4. 18.

11. It (*viz.* the horse), being unrestrained and unretained, is liable to go to the farthest distance. By the rein (*raśmi*) a horse is restrained. That there is the pārthuraśma(-sāman) is for restraining the horse.

[1] §§ 8-11 agree in substance and partly to the letter with TS. V. 5. 12. 2-3.

12. There is (as third day) an over-night-rite, containing all the stomas, to obtain all, to conquer all. He gains and conquers all through this (rite)[1].

[1] Agrees with TS. l. c. 3

13. For the other sacrifices, either one single sacrificial post or the set of eleven victims are (used), but for the Aśvamedha the number of twenty-one (posts is used). The sacrificial post (either the single one or, in case of eleven victims, the middle one) for the other sacrifices is of khadira-, bilva- or palāśa-wood, but for the Aśvamedha it is of nicudāra-wood and it measures twenty-one cubits (in height). Of the blood of the other victims they make no sacrificial portions, but of that of the horse they do make portions. Of the other victims they make portions on the south side, but of the horse at the north side (of the vedi). Of the other victims they make portions on (a mat of) plakṣa-twigs, but of the horse on rattan-twigs. The domestic victims they bind at the sacrificial posts, the wild ones they hold at the open space (between the posts) They immolate the domestic victims, but set free the wild ones[1].

[1] This part agrees almost literally with TBr. III. 8. 19. 1-2: only, there we have *pālāśo* instead of *pārṇo* and the usual *rājjudāla* instead of the unusual *naicudāra*. Instead of the impossible *aśvamedhasya*, the TBr. (and cp. Śat. br. XIII. 5. 3. 8) has the only possible *aśvasya* (read in the text *plakṣa-śākhāsv*). The last sentence should run: *yūpeṣu grāmyān paśūn niyuñjanty, ūrokeṣv āraṇyān dhārayanty: ā grāmyān paśūṁ llabhante, prāraṇyānt sṛjanti.*— This enumeration of bare facts, which, moreover, ought to have been given earlier, as they pertain to the middle day, greatly strengthens the impression that the part has been taken from the TBr.

XXI. 5.

(The three-day-rite of Bida.)[1]

1. Three nine-versed over-night-rites, all combined with a ṣoḍaśin.

2. He who hopes for a kingdom should perform this (rite).

---

[1] Cp. Jaim. br. II. 277-278 (Auswahl no. 152, and cp. the Index under *hiraṇyadat*); Ārṣeyakalpa VI. 7; Lāṭy. IX. 7. 8; Nidānasūtra VIII. 8: Āp. XXII. 18. 4-7; Kāty. XXIII. 2. 9-10; Āśv. X. 2. 10-11.

3. This (nine-versed) stoma is the king of the stomas[1], he brings him into (the possession of) a kingdom.

[1] Because it is the first; cp. VI. 1. 6.

4. That the ākṣāra(-sāmans)[1] fall to the lot of the first day (*i.e.* are applied on the first day)—the Voice being monosyllabic—is for not exceeding the Voice in chanting.

[1] The plural is strange, for only one sāman is intended, the ākṣāra, grām. X. 2. 19 (cp. XI. 5. 7), composed on SV. I. 391, chanted on SV. II. 123; see SV. ed. Calcutta, vol. I, page 803. It has a monosyllabic nidhana. For the expression *anativādāya*, cp. XI. 3. 6. This sāman is chanted at the ārbhava-pavamāna-laud of the first day; see Ārṣeyakalpa VI. 7. a as compared with VI. 3.

5. Now, that there is the ājyadoha(-sāman), with a two-syllabic nidhana[1], (this is) for connecting the last two days. Day after day there are the ājyadohas (one on each day): day after day they make him thrive in regard to cattle.

[1] The ṛtanidhana; cp. XXI. 2, note 3.

6. All (the three days) are combined with a ṣoḍaśin; the ṣoḍaśin is valour (and) strength; he makes him thrive in regard to valour (and) strength.

XXI. 6.

(The Chandoma-pavamāna three-day-rite.)[1]

1. The pavamāna(-laud)s, twenty-four-versed; the ājya (laud)s, nine-versed: the pṛṣṭha(-laud)s, fifteen-versed; the agniṣṭoma (-laud), seventeen-versed (thus the first day).—The pavamāna (-laud)s, forty-four-versed; the ājya(-laud)s, fifteen-versed; the pṛṣṭha(-laud)s, seventeen-versed; the agniṣṭoma(-laud) and the uktha (-laud)s, twenty-one-versed (thus the second day).—The pavamāna (-laud)s, forty-eight-versed; the ājya(-laud)s, twenty-one-versed; the pṛṣṭha(-laud)s, twenty-seven-versed; the agniṣṭoma(-laud), thirty-three versed: the uktha(-laud)s and the ṣoḍaśin, twenty-one-versed; the night-rite, fifteen-versed; the twilight(-laud), nine-versed (thus the third day). (This is) the Chandoma-pavamāna[1].

---

[1] Cp. Ārṣeyakalpa VI. 8; Jaim. br. II. 275, here called govinata-chandoma-pavamāna and described as a variety of the aśvamedhatrirātra, just as in Śat. br. XIII. 5. 4. 20 where the scheme, however, agrees more with Pañc. br.—Āp. XXII. 18. 8.

[1] So called because the pavamāna-lauds agree in their stoma-form with the Chandoma-days (7th, 8th and 9th of the ten-day-rite) which are successively 24-, 44-, 48-versed.

2. It should be performed by one who is desirous of (obtaining) cattle.

3. The Chandoma(-days) are cattle [1]. In that the pavamāna (-laud)s are the Chandomas, he comes into the possession of cattle.

[1] Cp. note 1 on III. 8. 2.

4. Both kinds of stomas are applied, the even and the odd ones; this is a pairing: in consequence of this pairing he is procreated.

XXI. 7.

(The Antarvasu three-day-rite.)[1]

1. The morning-service, nine-versed; the midday-service, fifteen-versed; the afternoon-service, seventeen-versed (first day).—The morning-service, twenty-four-versed; the midday-service, forty-four-versed; the afternoon-service and the uktha(-laud)s, forty-eight-versed (second day).—The morning-service, twenty-one-versed; the midday-service, twenty-seven-versed; the afternoon-service and the uktha(-laud)s, thirty-three versed: the ṣoḍaśin, twenty-one-versed; the night-rite, fifteen-versed; the twilight(-laud), nine-versed (third day). (This is) the Antarvasu [1].

[1] So called because the middle day contains the stomas of the three Chandoma-days which are equal to cattle (§ 5). So this three-day-rite encloses the riches (*vasu*): the cattle

2. The three-day-rite is (equal to) these (three) worlds.

3. This (earthly) world exists, as it were, (visibly); yonder world (the sky) exists, as it were (visibly), but the intermediate region is a void, so to speak.

4. The first day of the three-day-rite exists, as it were; the last day exists, at it were; in the middle there is a void, so to speak.

5. The Chandoma(-day)s are the cattle; that the (stomas of the) Chandoma(-day)s are in the middle (*i.e.*, on the middle-day), is for covering, for removing the void.

---

[1] Cp. Ārṣeyakalpa VI. 9. a, b; Jaim. br. II. 279-280 (Auswahl no. 153).

XXI. 8.

(The Parāka three-day-rite.)[1]

1. The morning-service, nine-versed; the midday-service, fifteen-versed; the afternoon-service, seventeen-versed (first day).—The morning-service, twenty-one-versed; the midday-service, twenty-seven-versed; the afternoon-service with the uktha(-laud)s, thirty-three-versed (second day).—The morning-service, twenty-four-versed; the midday-service, forty-four-versed; the afternoon-service with the uktha(-laud)s, forty-eight-versed; the ṣoḍaśin, twenty-one versed; the night(-rite), fifteen-versed; the twilight(-laud), nine-versed. (This is) the Parāka [1].

[1] So called because *parāñcy eva stotrāṇi bhavanti, parāñci śastrāṇi, parāñci pṛṣṭhāni, parācir viṣṭutayaḥ ; parāṅ eva sarvo bhavati* (Jaim. br.).

2. By means of the Parāka, the Gods went to the world of heaven. It may be performed by one who is desirous of (reaching) the world of heaven. Turning away (from the earth) [1], he, by means of this (rite), treads on the world of heaven.

[1] And not returning, just as the stomas do not return but successively increase.

3. The suffering that was his lot, that becomes (by the performance of this rite) wended away (*parāk*) Hence the name '*parāka*'.

4. For him, when he has gone there, all suffering has ceased.

5. He who knows this, for him there is no suffering.

6. But it (this rite) is unfit for (procuring) progeny, for thitherward directed he treads through it on the world of heaven. (But) in that the ṣoḍaśin(-laud) is twenty-one-versed, the night(-rite) fifteen-versed and the twilight(-laud) nine-versed, thereby, he becomes firmly established in this world [1].

[1] Because these last stomas are, so to say, *pratyañc*, 'returning'. So he will not go directly to the world of heaven, but first get that which is expressed in §§ 3, 4.

---

[1] Cp. Ārṣeyakalpa VI. 9. c–e; Jaim. br. II. 280.

XXI. 9

(The four-day-rite of Atri.)[1]

1. The pavamāna(-laud)s, twenty-four-versed; the ājya(-laud)s, nine-versed; the pṛṣṭha(-laud)s, fifteen-versed; the agniṣṭoma(-laud), seventeen-versed (first day).—The pavamāna(-laud)s, twenty-four-versed; the ājya(-laud)s, fifteen-versed; the pṛṣṭha(-laud)s, seventeen-versed; the agniṣṭoma(-laud) and the uktha(-laud)s, twenty-one-versed (second day).—The pavamāna(-laud)s, twenty-four-versed; the ājya(-laud)s, seventeen-versed; the pṛṣṭha(-laud)s, twenty-one-versed; the agniṣṭoma(-laud) and the uktha(-laud)s, twenty-seven-versed (third day).—The pavamāna(-laud)s, twenty-four-versed; the ājya(-laud)s, twenty-one-versed; the pṛṣṭha(-laud)s, twenty-seven-versed; the agniṣṭoma(-laud), thirty-three-versed; the uktha(-laud)s and the ṣoḍaśin, twenty-one-versed; the night(-rite), fifteen-versed, the twilight(-laud), nine-versed (fourth day)[1].

[1] So the schema is:
24, 9, 9, 9, 9 | 24, 15, 15, 15, 15 | 24, 17 | (1st day).
24, 15, 15, 15, 15 | 24, 17, 17, 17, 17 | 24, 21, 21, 21, 21 | (2nd day).
24, 17, 17, 17, 17 | 24, 21, 21, 21, 21 | 24, 27, 27, 27, 27 | (3rd day).
24, 21, 21, 21, 21 | 24, 27, 27, 27, 27 | 24, 33, 21, 21, 21 | 21, 15, 9 | (4th day).

2. Atri desired: 'May four excellent sons be born to me'. He saw this (rite and practised it). To him four excellent sons were born. Four excellent sons are born to him who knows this.

3. Dismissing one stoma, he begins one stoma[1]. The stoma is a (means of) engendering excellent sons. He, thereby, makes him engender excellent sons.

[1] This is not expressed very clearly. The Jaim. br. has: *ahno 'hna stomam utsṛjamānā yanty, ahno 'hnaḥ stomam abhyupāharante, vīro vā eṣa yat stomo, 'hno 'hna eva tad vīraṃ prajanayanto yanti.* Possibly the meaning is that he ought normally to begin the first day with the nine-versed stoma, the second day with the fifteen-versed, the third day with the seventeen-versed and the last day with the twenty-one-versed stoma; but this first stoma is dismissed and replaced on each day by the twenty-four-versed one (with which he each time begins the day). Sāyaṇa gives no help.

---

[1] Cp. Jaim. br. II. 281-284; Ārṣeyakalpa VII. 1-4; Nidānasūtra VIII. 9; TS. VII. 1. 8; Baudh. XVI. 28; Āp. XXII. 18. 12-15.

4. The pavamāna(-laud)s are twenty-four-versed, the gāyatrī is of twenty-four syllables, the gāyatrī is a (means of) procreation [1]; (so this serves) for procreation.

[1] Cp. XVI. 14. 5, XIX. 5. 9.

5. Both kinds of stomas are applied, the odd and the even ones; this is a pairing; in consequence of this pairing he is procreated.

6. The first day is an agniṣṭoma; the second, an ukthya; the third, a ṣoḍaśin(-day); the fourth is an over-night-rite [1], for obtaining different kinds of strength (of manly vigour in his descendants).

[1] This is the statement of Jaim. br. II. 284: *agniṣṭomo vai prathamam ahar, ukthyo dvitīyaṃ, ṣoḍaśimāṃs* (*sc. ukthyaḥ*) *tṛtīyam, atirātraś caturthaṃ, nānāvīryāṇy ahāni bhavanti, vīrāṇām eva nānāvīryatāyai,* but it collides with our Brāhmaṇa, according to which the third day is an ukthya, cp. § 9.

7. They make the days of different strength.

8. The first day is of gāyatrī-nature; the second, of triṣṭubh-nature; the third, of jagatī-nature; the fourth, of anuṣṭubh-nature [1].

[1] This is not easy to explain, because the total number of verses of each day is not divisible by the number of syllables of gāyatrī, triṣṭubh, jagatī and anuṣṭubh. Cp. XX. 16.7. I subjoin the parallel passage from the Jaim. br. (II. 283), which, however, I am unable to explain: *gāyatryāyātayāmnyā tṛtīyam ahas tāyate, kas tam indra tvāvasav iti maitrāvaruṇasāma; tāsām ihākṣarāṇi sampadyante; yā gāyatryo gāyatryas tā, yāḥ kakubhaḥ kakubhas tā, yā bṛhatyo bṛhatyas tā; yathāyatanaṃ chandāṃsi yujyante; gāyatryā vai prathamam ahas tāyate, triṣṭubhā dvitīyaṃ, jagatyā tṛtīyam, anuṣṭubhā caturtham,* etc.

9. About this, they (the Theologians) argue: 'If they applied the ṣoḍaśin(-laud) on the third day, they would reach through the third day the anuṣṭubh and the fourth day would be deprived of its (appointed) metre, for the ṣoḍaśin(-laud) is anuṣṭubh-like [1].

[1] This argumentation should prove that not the reckoning of § 6 (that of the Jaiminīyas, probably) is right, but rather that which has been explained in § 1. It seems that here the Pañcaviṃśabrāhmaṇa polemizes against the Jaiminīyas.

10. The ṣoḍaśin(-laud) should be applied on the fourth day: (so) it is applied in its proper place [1].

[1] *sva āyatane.*

11. He (thus) makes the days of different strength.

12. The Brahman's chant (or third pṛṣṭha-laud) of the first day is the naudhasa[1]; of the second day, the śyaita[2]; of the third day, the śrāyantīya[3]; of the fourth day, the traiśoka.[4]

[1] Cp. note 2 on VII. 10. 2.

[2] Cp. note 1 on VII. 10. 2.

[3] Cp. note 1 on VIII. 2. 9.

[4] Cp. note 1 on XII. 10. 20.

13. Here they say: 'It is a slipping down, as it were, if, after a larger metre, he applies a smaller one'[1].

[1] Read: *yaj jyāyasaś chandaso 'dhi kanīyaś chanda upaititi.* The third day being jāgata (see § 8) (of 48 syllables); the fourth, ānuṣṭubha (of 36 syllables).

14. That on the fourth day that excessive jagatī is applied[1], (serves) for not slipping down.

[1] The traiśoka of the fourth day (see § 12) is chanted on atijagatī-verses: cp. XII 10. 21.—With § 13 and 14 agrees XII. 10. 3.

15. The Acchāvāka's chant (or fourth pṛṣṭha-laud) of the first day is the kāleya[1]; of the second, the mādhucchandasa[2]; of the third day, the raurava[3]; of the fourth day, the samanta[4]: for bringing about different strength.

[1] Cp. note 2 on VIII. 2. 11.

[2] Cp. note 2 on IX. 2. 17.

[3] Cp. note 2 on VII. 5. 11.

[4] Cp. note 1 on XV. 4. 6.

16. (On the verses beginning:) 'Unto the soma, thee, o Bull'[1] is chanted the rathantara of the first day. (On the verses beginning:) 'Who, o Indra, him that has thee as wealth'[2], the vāmadevya (of the same day). (On the verses beginning:) 'When thou wast born, o unequalled one'[3], the bṛhat of the fourth day. (On the verses beginning:) 'Pour out the intoxicating (draught) of the sweet herb'[4], the vāmadevya (of the same day): for making the metres of different strength[5]. He (in this manner) makes the days of different strength.

[1] SV. I. 161=ṚS. VIII. 45. 22-24 (var. r.)=SV. II. 81-83.

[2] SV. I. 280=ṚS. VII. 32. 14-15 (var. r.)=SV. II. 1032-1033.

[3] SV. āraṇyaka-saṃhitā II. 7=ṚS. VIII. 89. 5-7=SV. II. 779-781.

[4] SV. I. 385=ṚS. VIII. 24. 16-18 (var. rr.)=SV. II. 1034-1036.

[5] The verses are in gāyatrī-, bṛhatī-, anuṣṭubh-, and uṣṇih-metre.

XXI. 10.

(The four-day-rite of Jamadagni.)[1]

1. The first day is an agniṣṭoma, with (alternately) nine-versed and fifteen-versed (lauds)[1].

[1] The schema, then, is as follows:

9, 15, 9, 15, 9, | 15, 9, 15, 9, 15 | 9, 15 (=54+90=144).

2. Of the next day, the out-of-doors-laud is twenty-four-versed; the (first) three ājya(-laud)s are fifteen-versed: that of the Acchāvāka (the fourth ājya-laud) is seventeen-versed; the midday-pavamāna(-laud) is twenty-one-versed; the first two pṛṣṭha(-laud)s are seventeen-versed; the last two are twenty-one-versed; the afternoon-service and the uktha(-laud)s are twenty-one-versed[1]

[1] In the text after *dve pṛṣṭhe* the words *ekaviṁśe dve* have fallen out. The schema, then, is as follows:

24, 15, 15, 15, 17 | 21, 17, 17, 21, 21 | 21, 21, 21, 21, 21 | (=288).

3. Of the third day, the out-of-doors-laud and the (first) three ājya(-laud)s are twenty-one-versed; that of the Acchāvāka is fifteen-versed; the midday-pavamāna(-laud) is twenty-four-versed; the pṛṣṭha(-laud)s are twenty-one-versed; the afternoon-service and the (first) two uktha(-laud)s are twenty-seven-versed; that of the Acchāvāka is twenty-one-versed[1].

[1] The schema, then, is as follows:

21, 21, 21, 21, 15 | 24, 21, 21, 21, 21 | 27, 27, 27, 27, 21 | (=336).

4. Of the fourth day, the pavamāna(-laud)s are twenty-four-versed; the Hotṛ's ājya(-laud) (the first) is fifteen-versed; the (next) three are seventeen-versed; the pṛṣṭha(-laud)s are twenty-one-versed; the agniṣṭoma(-laud) is thirty-three-versed; the uktha(-laud)s and the ṣoḍaśin are twenty-one-versed; the night(-laud) is fifteen-versed; the twilight(-laud) nine-versed[1].

[1] So the schema is:

24, 15, 17, 17, 17 | 24, 21, 21, 21, 21 | 24, 33, 21, 21, 21 | 21, 180, 9 | (=528).

---

[1] Cp. Jaim. br. II. 285–287 (Auswahl no. 154); Ārṣeyakalpa VII. 5; Lāty IX. 12. 1–7; TS. VII. 1. 9; Baudh. XVI. 28; Āp. XXII. 18. 16—19. 2; Kāty. XXIII. 2. 14–3. 2.

5, 6. Jamadagni, being desirous of thriving, grasped this (rite) He got that thriving (*i.e*, so much thriving) that they now say: 'No grey-haired descendants of Ūrva[1] know each other'[2].

[1] Read *aurvau* instead of *ūrau*; probably the Leyden MS. has such, and cp. Jaim. br. l. c. (Auswahl no. 154).

[2] The descendants of Ūrva, *i.e.*, the Jāmadagnyas, are so numerous, that, when they are grown aged, they do not know each other. The passage has been misunderstood by Keith (Translation of Taitt. S., page 565) and by Hopkins, who (in 'Gods and Saints of the Great Brāhmaṇa' page 54) translates: 'The two sons of Ūrva are not recognised as grey-haired men'.

7. So through this (rite) he thrives in all respects.

8. The metre (of this rite) is equal to the jagatī[1].

[1] I read, with the Leyden MS.: *jagatīm chando 'bhisampadyate*, cp. Jaim. br. II. 286: *atha yad evaitāni stotrāṇi saṃstutāni jagatīm abhi sampadyante, teno eva jāgata iti.* The meaning is that each day comprises a number of verses which is reducible to a certain number of jagatīs of 48 syllables. The 144 verses of the first day are equal to 3 jagatīs; the second day comprises 288 verses or 6 jagatīs; the third day comprises 336 verses or 7 jagatīs; the last day has 528 verses or 11 jagatīs.

9. Among the metres it is the jagatī that has reached the highest thriving; he reaches by this (rite) the highest thriving.

10. On the upasad-days, sacrificial cakes (of rice or barley) are offered[1]. The sacrificial cakes are the cattle. He is firmly established in (the possession of) cattle.

[1] TS. has precisely the same; the Jaim. br. II. 287 has: *tasyaitāḥ puroḍāśinīr upasado bhavanti; yonir vai puroḍāśo reta ājyam, tad yat puroḍāśaṃ hutvājyenābhijuhoti, yonyām evaitad retaḥ pratiṣṭhāpayanty, anuṣṭhyāsya retas siktam prajanayate ya evaṃ veda.* Note the Vedic nominative *puroḍāśinīḥ* as against the younger form °*nyaḥ* of Pañc. br. and TS.—According to Lāṭy., the four-day-rite is preceded by twelve upasad-days. On each of these days at morning and evening a puroḍāśa or rice-cake is offered, for which the mantras re given in the Brāhmaṇa, below, §§ 11-22, and the number of kapālas in § 23. Moreover, Lāṭy. ordains that, after the completion of this four-day-rite, these same offerings should be performed during twelve days, but now in reversed order. Kātyāyana, who must have been acquainted with the Sūtra of Lāṭy. (or Drāhyāyana), makes the same statement; cp. Āp. XVII. 18. 17—19. 2.

11. 'O Agni! Take thou upon thyself the office of Hotṛ, take upon thyself the sacrifice. Bring near[1] for help the father Vaiśvānara.

Pour ye out into the fire the sacrificial substance for Indra, for the Gods. *svāhā* !'

[1] *kur* is a misprint for *kar*.

12. 'O Aśvins! Ye two Gods! mix ye to-day through your whip of sweetness this offering for the Sacrificer. Pour out this sacrificial substance for Indra, for the Gods. *svāhā* !'

13. 'O God Viṣṇu! To-day at this sacrifice make thy wide step for the Sacrificer. Pour out the sacrificial substance for Indra, for the Gods. *svāhā* !'

14. 'O God Soma! Be thou to-day a seed-placer at this sacrifice for the Sacrificer. Pour out the sacrificial substance for Indra, for the Gods. *svāhā* !'

15. 'O God Savitṛ! Send to-day at this sacrifice thy good Savitṛ-being for the Sacrificer. Pour out the sacrificial substance for Indra, for the Gods. *svāhā* !'

16. 'O God Dhātṛ! Be thou to-day at this sacrifice a good Dhātṛ. Pour out the sacrificial substance for Indra, for the Gods. *svāhā* !'

17. 'O divine Pressing-stones! Let to-day at this sacrifice loudly resound your voice, full of sweetness. Pour out the sacrificial substance for Indra, for the Gods. *svāhā* !'

18. 'O Goddess Anumati! Allow to-day this sacrifice to the Sacrificer. Pour out the sacrificial substance for Indra, for the Gods. *svāhā* !'

19. 'O Goddess Aditi! Send to-day at this sacrifice your good Aditi-being. Pour out the sacrificial substance for Indra, for the Gods. *svāhā* !'

20. 'O divine Waters! Yield yourselves to-day at this sacrifice to the Sacrificer. Pour out the sacrificial substance for Indra, for the Gods. *svāhā* !'

21. 'Enjoying in each seat, provided with progeny (is) the Ṛbhu. Pour out the sacrificial substance for Indra, for the Gods. *svāhā* !'

22. 'O God Tvaṣṭṛ! Be thou a good seed-placer to-day at this sacrifice for the Sacrificer. Pour out the sacrificial substance for Indra, for the Gods. *svāhā* !'

23. (These offerings are successively) a cake of one kapāla for Agni; a cake of two kapālas for the Aśvins; a cake of three kapālas for Viṣṇu; a cake of four kapālas for Soma; a cake of five kapālas for Savitṛ; a cake of six kapālas for Dhātṛ; a cake of seven kapālas for the Maruts; a cake of eight kapālas for Bṛhaspati; a cake of nine kapālas for Mitra; a cake of ten kapālas for Varuṇa; a cake of eleven kapālas for Indra; a cake of twelve kapālas for the All-gods.

XXI. 11.

(The four-day-rite of Vasiṣṭha.)[1]

1. The morning-service is nine-versed; the midday-service, fifteen-versed; the afternoon-service, seventeen-versed (first day). The morning-service is fifteen-versed; the midday-service, seventeen-versed; the afternoon-service and the uktha(-laud)s are twenty-one-versed (second day). The morning-service is seventeen-versed; the midday-service, twenty-one-versed; the afternoon-service and the uktha-(laud)s are twenty-seven-versed (third day). The morning-service is twenty-one-versed; the midday-service, twenty-seven-versed; the afternoon-service, thirty-three-versed; the uktha(-laud)s are descending[1]: the first is twenty-seven-versed; the second and the third are twenty-one-versed, as is also the ṣoḍaśin; the night(-service) is fifteen-versed; the twilight(-laud) is nine-versed (fourth day)[2].

[1] Cp. note 1 on XX. 2. 1.

[2] The same is expressed more briefly in Jaim. br.: *tasya trayas trayo yuktā ahar vahanti.*

2. After his son had been slain[1], Vasiṣtha thought himself bereft (or 'left behind'). He saw this (rite, practised it), and reached superiority. He who thinks himself bereft, should perform this (rite).

[1] Cp. note 1 on IV. 7. 3.

3*a*. In that he steps on from one stoma to another (subsequent) stoma, he ascends from the top to the top[1].

[1] Cp. note 1 on II. 1. 3.

---

[1] Cp. Jaim. br. II. 289 (called *vasiṣṭhasya saṃsarpa*); Ārṣeyakalpa VII. 6; Lāṭy. IX. 12. 8-9; Nidānasūtra VIII. 10; Āp. XXII. 20. 1-2.

3b. There are the two janitra(-saman)s[1] for obtaining progeny[2].

[1] Cp. note 1 on VI. 9. 5.

[2] It is, and has been to the Sūtrakāra, uncertain, where in this four-day-rite these sāmans ought to be applied, as, strangely enough, Maśaka in his Ārṣeyakalpa does not record them here. According to Lāṭyāyana, they are either to be applied on the fourth day, one of them on the bṛhatī-part (cp. Ārṣeyakalpa, Introduction, page XXIV), the other on the anuṣṭubh-part, because the f o u r t h day is the place for these sāmans (cp. *e.g.*, Ārṣeyakalpa I. 9. a); or these sāmans are to be regarded as optional, because they are not prescribed in the Ārṣeyakalpa.

4. The uktha(-laud)s of the last day are descending: for (gaining) a firm support.

XXI. 12.

(The four-day-rite of Viśvāmitra.)[1]

1. A nine-versed agniṣṭoma; a fifteen-versed ukthya; a seventeen-versed ukthya; a twenty-one-versed over-night-rite. (This is the four-day-rite called) 'Viśvāmitra's victory'.

2. The Jahnus and Vṛcīvats quarrelled for the (possession of the) kingdom. Viśvāmitra, the king of the Jahnus, saw this (rite and practised it). He got the kingdom; the others (the Vṛcīvats) were deprived of it.

3. One who has a rival should perform (it).

4. He who knows this succeeds himself, his rival is defeated.

5. This (rite) is an expanded 'Light'(-stoma)[1].

[1] The jyotiṣṭoma, as agniṣṭoma, comprises on one single day the four stomas that here are distributed over the four days (9-, 15-, 17- and 21-versed).

6. He who knows this becomes a 'light' among his subjects[1].

[1] Cp. note 1 on VI. 3. 7.

7. This (rite) comprises the four stomas (par excellence); four-footed is cattle; he is firmly established in (the possession of) cattle.

8. The stomas (of this rite) do not exceed the twenty-one-versed one; the twenty-one-versed stoma is a firm support[1]; at the end of the sacrifice he is firmly supported.

[1] Cp. VI. 1. 11.

---

[1] Cp. Ārṣeyakalpa VII. 7; Āp. XXII. 20. 2.

XXI. 13.

(The Abhyāsangya or the five-day-rite of the Gods.)[1]

1. The (first) two services nine-versed, one (the third) fifteen-versed (first day). The (first) two services fifteen-versed, one seventeen-versed (second day). The (first) two services seventeen-versed, one twenty-one-versed (third day). The (first) two services twenty-one versed, one twenty-seven-versed (fourth day). The (first) two services twenty-seven-versed, one (the third service) thirty-three-versed; the uktha(-laud)s descending: twenty-seven-versed, the first: (the last) two and the ṣoḍaśin, twenty-one-versed; the night(-laud), fifteen-versed; the twilight(-laud), nine-versed.

2. The Gods and the Asuras strove together but could not gain a definite victory. They said: 'Let us gain the definite victory by a pairing of the word. Those of us (of Gods and Asuras) who do not find a counterpart in the pairing of the Word, those shall be defeated.' The Gods (then) said. 'One' (*ekaḥ*, m a s c .); the Asuras, from their side, found as counterpart in the pairing of the Word: 'One' (*ekā*, f e m .). The Gods said: 'Two' (*dvau*, m a s c .); the Asuras found as counterpart 'Two' (*dve*, f e m .). The Gods said: 'Three' (*trayaḥ*, m a s c .); the Asuras found as counterpart 'Three' (*tisraḥ*, f e m .). The Gods said: 'Four' (*catvāraḥ*, m a s c .), the Asuras found as counterpart 'Four' (*catasraḥ*, f e m .). The Gods said: 'Five' (*pañca*); the Asuras found no counterpart (as the word *pañca* has no separate form for the femininum). Thereupon, the Gods had gained the victory and the Asuras were defeated[1].

[1] This quasi-legend is given here in abbreviated form; see the Jaim. br where (under Auswahl 155) the other recensions are given.

3. He who knows this thrives himself, his rival is defeated.

4. It was the year[1]: the strength (and) the food, that they (the Gods), thereby, took away from them (from the Asuras).

[1] In the Kānvīya-recension of the Śat. br. and in the Jaim. br., it is the f i v e ṛtus (*i.e.*, the year) that by the last unanswered challenge the Gods won from the Asuras.

---

[1] Cp. Jaim. br. II. 291–293 (Auswahl No. 155); Ārṣeyakalpa VII. 8–10; Nidānasūtra VIII. 10; Āp. XXII. 20. 5–8.

5. He who knows this takes away from this rival the year: the strength (and) the food.

6. It is a five-day-rite; man is five-fold[1], cattle is five-fold[1]: thereby, he reaches (comes into the possession of) man and cattle.

[1] Cp. notes 1 and 2 on II. 4. 2.

7. This sacrifice is yoked not with one single (bullock or horse, but with two,) and it is (properly) put together (or 'continuous')[1], for each day is brought into action (or 'begun') by two stomas[2]. Whatever desire he wishes to see fulfilled, that he thereby reaches.

[1] This part of the § is the same as the beginning of XVI. 1. 6. The continuity is explained in § 9.

[2] The first t w o services of each day are in the same stoma.

8. For, whichever goal he hopes to reach by a (cart) drawn not by one single (bullock, but by two bullocks), that he reaches.

9. It is an internally attached five-day-rite[1], for the sake of continuity.

[1] Because each next day begins with the same stoma that ends the preceding day; cp. note 3 on page 96 of the edition of the Ārṣeyakalpa.

10. The uktha(-laud)s of the last day are descending, for obtaining a firm support (on the earth).

XXI. 14.

(The Pañcaśāradīya five-day-rite.)[1]

1. A nine-versed agniṣṭoma; a fifteen-versed ukthya; a seventeen-versed ukthya; a fifteen-versed ukthya; a seventeen-versed over-night-rite: (this is) the Pañcaśāradīya[1] (or) the stoma (*i.e.*, the sacrifice) of the Maruts.

[1] On the name ('rite of five autumns') cp. § 8.

---

[1] Cp. Ārṣeyakalpa VIII. 11. a, b; Lāṭy. IX. 12. 10–14; Jaim. br. II. 178–180; TBr. II. 7. 10–12; Baudh. XVIII. 11; Āp. XXII. 20. 9—21. 11; Kāty. XXIII. 4. 3–27; Āśv. X. 2. 29-30; Śāṅkh. XIV. 62. Amongst these sources, it is only the Jaim. br. that regards this rite as an ekāha; it is striking that TBr. and Baudh., although they consider the Pañcaśāradīya as a five-day-rite, treat of it in the description of the ekāhas.

2. He who desires to see himself multiplied (by progeny of children, and cattle) should perform this (rite).

3. The Maruts are the most numerous among the Gods; he becomes numerous ('multiplied').

4. The stomas (of this day) do not exceed the seventeen-versed one; Prajāpati is seventeen-fold [1]: he reaches (*i.e.*, he becomes equal to) Prajāpati.

[1] Cp. note 1 on II. 10. 5.

5. Agastya consecrated, by sprinkling, the bulls (he was going to immolate), (destining them) for the Maruts [1], (but) he fastened them at the sacrificial posts, (destining them) for Indra [1]. They (the Maruts) took up a thunderbolt and assailed (him) [2]. He saw that [3] kayāśubhīya (-hymn) [4] and, thereby, appeased (them) [5].

[1] So he had said: *marudbhyo vo juṣṭam prokṣāmi* and, *indrāya vo juṣṭam ālabhe.*

[2] According to TBr., Indra took away the victims destined for the Maruts and it was Indra whom they assailed.

[3] Read the text: *te vajram ādāyābhyāpatant sa etat*, etc.

[4] ṚS. I. 165, beginning *kayā śubhā.*

[5] For this legend, cp. also the Author's: Altindische Zauberei, die Wunsch-opfer, no. 56.

6. That the kayāśubhīya(-hymn) is recited [1], is for appeasing.

[1] No Hotṛ-sūtra prescribes this śastra

7, 8. (They bring) [1] seventeen spotted bulls, five years old, and seventeen three years old (cows), that have not been approached (by a bull); on (all) these the ritual of paryagnikaraṇa and of sprinkling is performed [2]; whereupon, they immolate the cows, but set free (*i.e.*, do not immolate) the bulls. After the lapse of a year, they bring (seventeen three years old) reddish-brown (cows), with spots of the colour of fresh butter, and those same (seventeen) bulls; on all these the ritual of paryagnikaraṇa and of sprinkling is performed: whereupon, they immolate the cows, but set free the bulls. After the lapse of a year, they bring (seventeen three years old) striped (cows) and those same bulls; on all these the paryagnikaraṇa and the sprinkling is performed; whereupon, they immolate the cows, but set free the bulls. After the lapse of a year, they bring (seventeen) tawny coloured (three years old cows) and those same bulls; on all these the paryagnikaraṇa and the sprinkling is performed; whereupon, they immolate the cows, but set free the bulls. After the lapse of a year, they bring (seventeen) variegated (three years old cows) and those same bulls; on all these the paryagnikaraṇa and the sprinkling is performed; whereupon, they immolate the cows, but set free the bulls.

1 Has *ānayanti* fallen out, or is the word to be supplied ?

2 To which deities they are consecrated by sprinkling and to which deities they are immolated, will appear from § 12. Because each time the paśubandha takes place during five years in autumn, hence its name *pañcaśāradīya*.

9. After the lapse of a year, the sacrifices of soma (*i.e.*, the five-day-rite) take place.

10. They immolate, day after day, three (of those bulls) (during the first four days of the five-day-rite and) five on the last (day).

11. The (victim to be sacrificed on the day immediately before the soma-days proper is a) he-goat, destined for Agni and Soma[1].

1 This is the usual rite.

12. The bulls are destined for Indra and the Maruts[1], the cows for the Maruts (alone).

1 They replace the savana-he-goat, according to TBr.

13. If (during those five years) Rudra covets (one of those bulls, so that it dies by fever), he should sacrifice a rice-cake to Agni accompanied by Rudra, and immolate another (bull).

14. If (one of them) is destroyed (by falling into a pit), he should sacrifice a rice-cake, prepared on one kapāla, to Earth, and immolate another one.

15. If (one of them) sinks down, he should sacrifice a mess of boiled rice to Nirṛti, and immolate another one.

If (one of them) is drowned, he should sacrifice a mess of rice to Apāṃ napāt, and immolate another (bull).

If (one of them) becomes blind, he should sacrifice a mess of rice to Sūrya, and immolate another (bull).

16. If (one of them) becomes lame or loses its horns, he should sacrifice a mess of rice to Bṛhaspati, and immolate another (bull).

17. If one of them escapes, he should sacrifice a mess of rice to Vāyu, and immolate another (bull).

18. If (one of them) is vanquished [1] by force, he should sacrifice a rice-cake, prepared on eleven kapālas, to Indra Prasahvan, and immolate another (bull).

[1] Āp., who follows our Brāhmaṇa, has *nayeyur* instead of *jayeyur*; but the Leyden MS. agrees with the printed text.

19. If (one of them) perishes through another kind of death, he should sacrifice a rice-cake, prepared on twelve kapālas, to Prajāpati, and immolate another (bull) [1].

[1] With §§ 13–19 we may compare the similar prescriptions for the horse at the Aśvamedha: TBr. III. 9. 17 (TS. VII. 5. 21); Śat. br. XIII. 3. 8; Āp. XXII. 7. 9—8. 2.

20. When Ekayāvan Gāndama had performed this rite at (the place called) Vetasvat, he got all kinds of welfare [1].

[1] In TBr. II. 7. 11. 2 and Jaim. br. II. 178, he is called Ekayāvan Kāndama.

21. He who knows thus gets all kinds of welfare.

XXI. 15.

(The Antarmahāvrata five-day-rite.)[1]

1. A jyotiṣṭoma-agniṣṭoma [1]; a go(-day) as ukthya [2]; a mahāvrata-(-day) [3]: a go(-day) as ukthya [4]; an āyus(-day) as over-night-rite [5]

[1] See XVI. 1.

[2] See XVI. 2.

[3] See XVI. 7.

[4] See XVI. 2.

[5] See XVI. 3.—The mahāvrata-day is in the midst, hence the name in the later sources: *antarmahāvrata*. According to the Jaim. br. this pañcarātra consists of the three-day-rite jyotis, go, āyus, a twenty-five versed mahāvrata and an overnight-rite with all the stomas, and it is destined for one who desires to get food (*annādyakāma*).

2. The vrata (*i.e.*, the mahāvrata-rite) is the year: its head is the season of spring, its wings are the summer and the rainy season, its middle (its trunk) is the autumn, its tail is the winter.

---

[1] Cp. Jaim. br. II. 294; Ārṣeyakalpa VII. 11. c; Āp. XXII. 21. 12–14.

3. Therefore, at the time of autumn the plants (as rice or barley) bear ripe fruits, for the autumn is the middle part of the year[1].

[1] These two paragraphs seem to imply that this rite is destined for one who is desirous of obtaining food, but the reasoning is not over-clear.

4. An unheard-of deed do they, who undertake the (rite of the) mahāvrata before the (end of the) year[1].

[1] The mahāvrata in the gavām ayana comes in on the last day but one of the year, but here it is applied in the middle of the five-day-rite. Jaim. br. II. 294 : *tad āhur ; na purā saṃvatsarān mahāvratam upetyam iti.*

5. This five-day-rite, forsooth, is a complete (mahā)-vrata, for there are five seasons[1] (as there are here five days).

[1] I suspect that we ought to read *yat pañcarātraḥ* instead of *yat pañcarātre.* If we accept this view, the meaning may be : the mahāvrata, it is true, comes here in the middle, but, as the whole five-day-rite, in a mystical way, is identical with the mahāvrata, this unheard-of deed is annulled.

6 He who knows this lauds with a complete (mahā)vrata and reaches the normal term of (human) life.

Twenty-second Chapter.

(The ahīnas, concluded.)

XXII. 1.

(The pṛṣṭhya-six-day-rite.)[1]

1. A six-day-rite with the pṛṣṭha(-sāman)s[1].

[1] On each day, the first pṛṣṭha-laud is one of the pṛṣṭha-sāmans; rathantara, bṛhat, vairūpa, vairāja, śākvara, raivata.

2. The seasons found no firm support; by this (rite) they found a firm support. He who desires to obtain a firm support, should perform (it). He obtains a firm support.

3. There are six seasons; in the seasons he is firmly established. It is a six-day-rite with the pṛṣṭha(-sāman)s: in order to thrive in a visible way.

---

[1] Cp. Ārṣeyakalpa VII. 12. a, b; Nidānasūtra VIII. 11; Āp. XXII. 22. 4.

4. For by this (rite), the seasons throve in a visible way[1]; (so it serves) for thriving.

[1] The autumn *e.g.* thrives in a visible way.

XXII. 2.

(Second six-day-rite.)[1]

1. A nine-versed agniṣṭoma; a fifteen-versed ukthya; a seventeen-versed ukthya; a jyotis(-day)[1]: a go(-day)[1] and an āyus (-day) as over-night-rite[1].

[1] See XVI. 1, 2 and 3.

2. He who wishes to reach the normal term of (human) life should perform this (rite).

3. In that a three-day-period is at the beginning: three in number are the vital principles: out-breathing, in-breathing, through-breathing—these same are, thereby, put together.

4. And that there is a jyotis(-day), a go(-day) and an āyus-over-night-rite, (that is) for getting firmly supported.

XXII. 3.

(The Pṛṣṭhyāvalamba or Abhyāsanga six-day-rite.)[2]

1. An 'internally attached' five-day-rite[1] and a Viśvajit as over-night-rite[2].

[1] See XXI. 13 (note 1 on § 9 ib).

[2] See XVI. 5.

2. For (the fulfilment of) one wish (serves) a sattra; for (the fulfilment of) another (wish) (serves) a sacrifice[1]. By a sattra he does not get that for which a sacrifice[1] (is undertaken), nor by a sacrifice[1] that for which a sattra (is undertaken)

[1] The word *yajña* is here used in the sense of *ekāha* or *ahīna*.

3. This (rite) is, as it were, a sattra, in that the pṛṣṭha(-saman)s (are applied) in their regular order[1]. In that they are (used) at once[2], he, thereby, puts into him at once strength (and) valour.

[1] Cp. Ārṣeyakalpa VII. 12. c; Nidānasūtra VIII. 12; Āp. XXII. 22. 6-7.

[2] Cp. Ārṣeyakalpa VII. 12. d; Nidānasūtra VIII. 12; Āp. XXII. 22. 8-9.

[1] *Viz.*, during the first six days.

[2] *Viz.*, at the Viśvajit, where all the pṛṣṭhasāmans are applied (on one day). In a sattra they occur on each of the first days of the daśarātra, and so this six-day-rite is, as it were, not only an ahīna but at the same time also a sattra.

4. The pṛṣṭha(-sāman)s are food; he brings food unto him[1].

[1] Cp. XVI. 15. 8 and XIX. 9. 4.

5. The pṛṣṭha(-sāmans) are cattle[1]. He is firmly established in (the possession of) cattle.

[1] Cp. XVI. 15. 8.

6. There is the internally attached five-day-rite: for the sake of continuity[1].

[1] Cp. XXI. 13. 9.

7. There is the Viśvajit as over-night-rite: for conquering all.

XXII. 4.

(The seven-day-rite of the Ṛṣis.)[1]

1. A six-day-rite with the pṛṣṭha(-sāmans)[1], (and) a mahāvrata as overnight-rite[2].

[1] See XXII. 1.

[2] See, probably, XVI. 7.

2. The seven Seers throve through this (rite). Thereby, it is a (cause for) thriving. Therefore, they practise it, for thriving.

3. There are seven kinds of breath in the head[1]; the organs of sense are the breaths; the organs of sense he obtains by this (rite).

[1] Cp. II. 14. 2 with note 2.

4. There are seven kinds of domestic animals; these he obtains by this (rite).

5. The vrata[1] is the (first) pṛṣṭha(-laud) of the seventh day, for this is not reached[2]. The vrata is food[3], he reaches food by this (rite).

---

[1] Cp. Ārṣeyakalpa VII. 13. a; Nidānasūtra VIII. 13: Jaim. br. II. 301-302; Āp. XXII. 22. 13-14.

[1] The mahāvrata as described in IV. 10.

[2] Meaning ?

[3] Cp. IV. 10. 1.

6. There is the six-day-rite with the pṛṣṭha(-saman)s, for thriving in a visible manner.

7. For in a visible manner the Seers throve by this (rite), (so it is) for thriving.

XXII. 5.

(The seven-day-rite of Prajāpati.)[1]

1. A six-day-rite with the pṛṣṭha(-sāmans), (and) a seventeen-versed mahāvrata as over-night-rite.

2. Of this (last day), the head is nine-versed, the wings are fifteen-versed, the trunk is seventeen-versed, the tail is twenty-one-versed [1].

[1] The normal mahāvrata-laud is : head: nine-versed; right wing: fifteen-versed; left wing: seventeen-versed; trunk: twenty-five-versed; tail: twenty-one-versed; see V. 1. 2, 10, 16.

3. By means of this (rite), Prajāpati created the creatures.

4. He who knows this is procreated in children and cattle.

5. Prajāpati is seventeenfold ; in that the vrata (or mahāvrata-day) is seventeen-versed, he reaches (*i.e.*, becomes equal to) Prajāpati.

6. In that the head is nine-versed : there are nine vital principles—in the (retaining of the) vital principles he is firmly established.

7. That the wings are fifteen-versed is for the sake of equilibrium [1].

[1] Cp. V. 1. 11.

8. The trunk is seventeen-versed ; Prajāpati is seventeen-fold, he reaches Prajāpati.

9. The tail is twenty-one-versed, for gaining a firm support [1].

[1] Cp. V. 1. 16, 17.

---

[1] Cp. Ārṣeyakalpa VII. 13. b; Nidānasūtra VIII. 13; Āp. XXII. 22. 15-16.

XXII. 6.

(The Chandoma-pavamāna seven-day-rite.)[1]

1. A six-day-rite with the pṛṣṭha(-sāman)s, (and) a mahāvrata (-day) as over-night-rite, in which the pavamāna-lauds agree with the Chandoma (-day)s [1].

[1] Cp. note 1 on XXI. 6. 1.

2. He who is desirous of (obtaining) cattle should perform (it).

3. The Chandomas are cattle [1].

[1] Cp. X. 1. 21, note 1 on III. 8. 2.

4. In that of the mahāvrata(-rite) the pavamāna(-laud)s are Chandomas, (thereby) he obtains cattle.

5. There are both kinds of stomas, even and odd ones; this is a pairing: in consequence of this pairing he is procreated.

XXII. 7.

(The seven-day-rite of Jamadagni.)[2]

1. An internally attached five-day-rite [1]; a thirty-three-versed (one) day (-rite) of which (however) the agniṣṭoma (-laud) is thirty-four-versed (sixth day); (and) a seventeen-versed mahāvrata as over-night-rite of which the out-of-doors-laud is twenty-four-versed, the head nine-versed, the wings fifteen-versed, the trunk seventeen-versed, the tail twenty-one-versed (seventh day).

[1] Cp. XXI. 13.

2. By this (rite), Jamadagni throve in all respects. By this (rite), he thrives in all respects.

3. That there is at the beginning an internally attached five-day-rite, is for continuity [1].

[1] Cp. XXI. 13. 9.

4. Then (there is) that thirty-three-versed day—there are thirty-three deities; he reaches (becomes equal to) the deities.

[1] Cp. IV. 4. 11.

---

[1] Jaim. br. II. 309; Ārṣeyakalpa VI. 13. c; Āp. XXII. 22. 17-18.

[2] Cp. Ārṣeyakalpa VII. 13. d; Jaim. br. II. 308 is similar, not equal.

5. Of this (day), the agniṣṭoma(-laud) is thirty-four-versed; Prajāpati is the thirty-fourth of the deities[1]; he reaches Prajāpati.

[1] Cp. note on X. 1. 16.

6. The out-of-doors-laud of the mahāvrata(-day) is twenty-four-versed; the gāyatrī is of twenty-four syllables; the gāyatrī is a (means of) procreation; (so this is) for procreation.

7. There are both kinds of stomas, even and odd ones; this is a pairing; in consequence of this pairing he is procreated.

8. In that the head (of the mahāvrata) is nine-versed, there being nine vital principles, he is firmly established in his vital principles. That the wings are fifteen-versed, is for equilibrium. The trunk is seventeen-versed; Prajāpati being seventeen-fold, he reaches Prajāpati. The tail is twenty-one-versed, for getting a firm support.

XXII. 8.

(The seven-day-rite of Indra.)[1]

1. A jyotiṣṭoma as agniṣṭoma (1); a go(-day) as ukthya (2); an āyus(-day) as ukthya (3); an Abhijit as agniṣṭoma (4); a Viśvajit as agniṣṭoma[1] (5); a Sarvajit as agniṣṭoma[2] (6); an over-night-rite with all the stomas[3] (7).

[1] Cp. XVI. 1–5. [2] Cp. XVI. 7. [3] Cp. XX. 2.

2. By means of this (rite), Indra surpassed the other deities. He who knows this surpasses (his) other (fellow-) creatures.

3. In that at the beginning there is the three-day-period: jyotis, go, āyus, he reaches (*i.e.*, practises) the well-known stomas: these worlds[1]. He is firmly supported in these worlds.

[1] *Viz.* earth, intermediate region, sky; cp. IV. 1. 7.

4. Then, the Abhijit: by the Abhijit, the Gods conquered these worlds; through the Viśvajit, they conquered all; through the Sarvajit, they conquered the whole[1].

[1] Cp. XVI. 7. 2.

5. There is the over-night-rite with all the stomas, for reaching all, for conquering all. By this (rite), he reaches and conquers all.

---

[1] Cp. Ārṣeyakalpa VII. 13. e.

XXII. 9.

(The generating seven-day-rite.)[1]

1. Four nine-versed days, the first of which is an agniṣṭoma (the three others being ukthyas); a Viśvajit-day; a mahāvrata-day, (and) a jyotiṣṭoma as over-night-rite.

2. By means of this (rite), Prajāpati created man[1]; he obtained the supremacy over all food.

[1] According to Sāyaṇa, the *puruṣa* here is the *virāj*, the primordial individuum of ṚS. X. 90.

3. He who knows this obtains the supremacy over all food.

4. Of the (individual) who comes into existence, the head first comes into existence[1]; four-fold framed is the head: breath, eye-sight, hearing, voice[2]. The pṛṣṭha(-sāman)s are the trunk[3]. In that he undertakes (or 'applies') the pṛṣṭha(-sāman)s, he puts the trunk together after the head.

[1] The head appears first at birth; cp. Śat. br. VIII. 2. 4. 18.

[2] Therefore, the first four days.

[3] Therefore, the Viśvajit in which all the six pṛṣṭhasāmans are applied.

5. So he had made man; to it (to the first seven-day-period and to man) he adds the food: the (mahā)vrata[1].

[1] Cp. IV. 10. 1.

6. And that there is (at the end) a jyotiṣṭoma as over-night-rite, this is for setting a-right what had not been attained (by the preceding days)[1].

[1] This is the same as XXII. 11. 5.

XXII. 10.

(The pṛṣṭhya-stoma seven-day-rite.)[2]

1. A six-day-rite with (alternately) the (rathantara and bṛhat) pṛṣṭha(-sāmans), (and) a Viśvajit(-day) as over-night-rite.

---

[1] Cp. Ārṣeyakalpa VII. 14; Nidānasūtra IX. 1; Āp. XXII. 23. 5-6; on these sources rests the name *janakasaptarātra*, which might mean also: the seven-day-rite of Janaka (cp. Jaim. br. II. 303).

[2] Cp. Ārṣeyakalpa VII 15. a; Nidānasūtra IX. 1.; Jaim. br. II. 303 differs.

2. For (the fulfilment of) one wish (serves) a sattra, for (the fulfilment of) another wish serves a sacrifice. By a sattra, he does not get that for which a sacrifice (is undertaken), nor by a sacrifice that for which a sattra (is undertaken). This (rite) is, as it were, a sattra, in that the pṛṣṭha(-sāman)s (are applied) in their regular order. In that they are (used) at once, he, thereby, puts into him at once strength and valour. The pṛṣṭha(-sāman)s are food, he brings food unto him. The pṛṣṭha(-sāman)s are cattle; he is firmly established in (the possession of) cattle[1].

[1] This is the same as XXII. 3. 2-5.

3. What presents itself in a visible way to men (presents itself) in a cryptical way to the Gods, and what (presents itself) in a cryptical way to men (presents itself) in a visible way to the Gods.

4. The Viśvajit(-rite) is, in a cryptical way, the (mahā)vrata; in a visible way he, by means of this (rite), obtains food[1].

[1] To men, for whom the *parokṣam* of the Gods is *pratyakṣam*, this Viśvajit means: (mahā)vrata, *i.e.*, food; cp. XXII. 9. 5.

XXII. 11.

(The eight-day-rite.)[1]

1. A six-day-rite with the pṛṣṭha(-sāman)s, a mahāvrata(-day) (and) a jyotiṣṭoma-over-night-rite.

2. By means of this (rite), the Gods reached their state of God.

3. He who knows this reaches the state of a God.

4. The eight-day-rite[1] is a complete[2] (mahā-)vrata(-day), for it amounts to an agniṣṭoma[3].

[1] Reading (cp. XXI. 15. 5) *aṣṭarātro.*

[2] *āpta*; cp. XXI. 15. 5, XXIII. 1. 2; Sāyana supplies: *devaiḥ*.

[3] As the number of the verses in the mahāvrata does not agree with that of a normal agniṣṭoma, perhaps, *sampadyate* signifies here: 'turns out to be', for the mahāvrata is an agniṣṭoma: a soma-sacrifice ending with the agniṣṭoma-laud.

---

[1] Cp. Ārṣeyakalpa VII. 15. b; Nidānasūtra IX. 1.

5. Further, that there is (at the end) a jyotiṣṭoma as over-night-rite, this is for setting a-right what had not been attained (by the preceding days).

6. Through the eight-day-rite, the Gods mastered[1] all.

[1] Here is a pun: *aṣṭa* (eight) and *aṣṭa* participle to *aśnute*.

7. He who knows this masters all.

XXII. 12.

(The nine-day-rite of the Gods.)[1]

1*a*. A six-day-rite with the pṛṣṭha(-sāman)s, a jyotis(-day), a go(-day) (and) an āyus(-day) as over-night-rite.

1*b*. The Gods were afraid of death. They resorted to Prajāpati. He gave them immortality through this nine-day-rite.

2. This is man's immortality, that he reaches the normal term of life (and) that he becomes wealthier.

3. He who knows this reaches the normal term of life (and) becomes wealthier.

4. It is a nine-day-rite: nine are the vital principles[1]; in the (possession of the) vital principles he is firmly established.

[1] Cp. II. 15. 3.

5. There is a six-day-rite, with the pṛṣṭha(-saman)s, for thriving in a visible manner, and that there is a jyotis(-day), a go(-day) (and) an āyus(-day) as overnight-rite, is for getting a firm support.

XXII. 13.

(Second nine-day-rite.)[2]

1*a*. A jyotiṣṭoma as agniṣṭoma[1]; a go(-day) as ukthya[1]; an āyus(-day) as ukthya[1]; an internally attached five-day-rite[2], (and) a Viśvajit as over-night-rite[3].

[1] As XVI. 1-3. [2] As XXII. 3. [3] As XVI. 5.

---

[1] Cp. Ārṣeyakalpa VII. 15. c; Nidānasūtra IX. 1; Āp. XXII. 23. 10.

[2] Cp. Ārṣeyakalpa VII. 15. d; Nidānasūtra IX. 1.

1*b*. One who is desirous of (obtaining) cattle should perform (it).

2. In that at the beginning there is the three-day-period: jyotis, go, āyus, he reaches the well-known stomas: these worlds. He is firmly established in these worlds[1].

[1] Identical with XXII. 8. 3.

3. Further, that an internally attached five-day-rite is in the middle: fivefold is man[1]; fivefold is cattle[1]; thereby, he reaches man and cattle[1].

[1] See notes 1 and 2 on II. 4. 2.

4. There is a Viśvajit as over-night-rite, for conquering all.

XXII. 14.

(The Trikakubh-ten-day-rite.)[1]

1. A nine-versed agniṣṭoma; a fifteen-versed ukthya; a nine-versed agniṣṭoma: a seventeen-versed agniṣṭoma; a twenty-one-versed ukthya; a seventeen-versed agniṣṭoma; a twenty-seven-versed agniṣṭoma; a thirty-three-versed ukthya; a twenty-seven-versed agniṣṭoma; a Viśvajit as over-night-rite.

2. Indra, having slain the Asuras, conceived that he had done an unheard-of deed. For him the gods performed this stoma (*i.e.*, this sacrifice). He (thereby) was freed from his bad lot[1].

[1] *nirdaśa* means: 'more than ten days old' ('out of his teens', but applied to days, not to years). A new born infant and its mother are *nirdaśa* when the first dangerous ten-day-period is passed away. This state is *nairdaśya* which, then, assumes the meaning of 'the state of being out of danger'; the word occurs Āp. XXII. 4. 28, whilst the Jaim. Br. (Auswahl no. 158) presents the form *nirdaśya*.

3. Therefore, one who has been wounded by an arrow or a stick is out of danger on the tenth day.

4. This (rite) is a virāj consisting of tens and tens. The virāj is food. He brings food unto him[1].

---

[1] Cp. Ārṣeyakalpa VIII. 1-8; Nidānasūtra IX. 2-3; Jaim. br. II. 327-331, here called mahātrikakubh; TS. VII. 2. 5; Baudh. XVI. 31; Āp. XXII. 23. 17-18; Śāṅkh. XVI. 29.

[1] Cp. XIX. 2. 4.—The rite is a virāj probably simply in so far as it is a t e n -day-rite: cp. Jaim. br. II. 323: *eṣa ha vāva virājaṃ nātiṣṭauti yo daśabhis stute, daśākṣarā virāḍ, annaṃ virāḍ, ahnaiva virājam avarunddhe, 'hnā virājaṃ; sa daśamenaivāhnā sarvāṃ virājaṃ annādyam avarudhya*, etc.; and cp. TS. VII. 2. 5. 1: *vairājo vā eṣa yajño yad daśarātraḥ.*

5. The Gods, having restrained the Asuras by means of the agniṣṭoma, were by the ukthya(-day)s at the middle procreated in their progeny (and) cattle. Having restrained his adversary by means of the agniṣṭoma, he (the performer of this rite) is procreated by the ukthya (-day)s at the middle in progeny (and) cattle.

6. This sacrifice is one of three eminences[1].

[1] Or 'summits, peaks, humps'. These three are the ukthya-days: 9, 15, 9; 17, 21, 17; 27, 33, 27.

7. An eminency amongst his equals and his progeny (or 'his subjects') becomes he who knows this.

XXII. 15.

(The ten-day-rite of Kusurubinda.)[1]

1. Three nine-versed agniṣṭoma(-day)s; three fifteen-versed ukthya(-day)s; three seventeen-versed ukthya(-day)s (and, as last day,) a twenty-one-versed over-night-rite[1].

[1] Jaim. br. has the same arrangement.

2. He who wishes to become multiplied should perform this (rite).

3. In that the stomas (occur) groupwise[1] (thereby) he becomes multiplied.

[1] This is explained in § 4.

4. Together (are applied) (three) nine-versed stomas, together (three) fifteen-versed, together (three) seventeen-versed stomas.

5. There is (at the end) the twenty-one-versed over-night-rite for being firmly established.

6. This (rite) is an expanded jyoti(-stoma)[1].

[1] See note 1 on XXI. 12. 5.

---

[1] Cp. Ārṣeyakalpa VIII. 9; Nidānasūtra IX. 4; Jaim. br. II. 332–333; Āp. XXII. 24. 6-7.

7. He who knows this becomes a light among his subjects [1].

[1] Equal to l.c. 6.

8. This (rite) comprises the four stomas: four-footed is cattle; he is firmly established in (the possession of) cattle [1].

[1] Equal to l.c. 7.

9. The stomas (of this rite) do not exceed the twenty-one-versed one; the twenty-one-versed stoma is a firm support; he is firmly established [1].

[1] Nearly equal to l.c. 8.

10. Kusurubinda, the son of Uddālaka, having performed this (rite), came to plurality (of progeny).

11. He who knows this comes to plurality (of progeny and cattle).

XXII. 16.

(The ten-day-rite with the Chandomas.) [1]

1*a*. An internally attached five-day-rite [1]; four Chandoma (-day)s [2]; a Viśvajit(-day) as over-night-rite.

[1] Cp. XXI. 13.

[2] Cp. XIV and XV (of 24, 44, 48, 24).

1*b*. He who is desirous of (obtaining) cattle should perform (it).

2. In that it begins with an internally attached five-day-rite, man being five-fold and cattle being five-fold, he, thereby, reaches man and cattle [1].

[1] Cp. XXI. 13. 6.

3. The Chandoma(-day)s are in the middle; the Chandomas are cattle [1]; (so this rite serves) for obtaining cattle.

[1] Note 1 on III. 8. 2.

4. There is a Viśvajit as over-night-rite, for conquering all.

---

[1] Cp. Ārṣeyakalpa VIII. 10; Nidānasūtra IX. 5-6; Āp. XXII. 24. 3-4.

XXII. 17.

(The ten-day-rite called 'stronghold of the Gods'.)[1]

1. An agniṣṭoma with three stomas[1] (1): a jyotis(-day) as ukthya (2): an agniṣṭoma with three stomas (3); a go(-day) as ukthya (4); an Abhijit as agniṣṭoma (5); a go(-day) as ukthya (6); a Viśvajit as agniṣṭoma (7); an āyus(-day) as ukthya (8); a Viśvajit as agniṣṭoma[2] (9); an over-night-rite with all the stomas (10).

[1] Either the morning-service of 9, the midday-service of 15, the afternoon-service of 17-versed stotras, or resp. four stotras of 9, four of 15, four of 17; see note 7 on page 120 of the edition of the Ārṣeyakalpa.

[2] Read *viśvajid agniṣṭomaḥ* instead of *v. agniṣṭomasya.*

2. When the Gods were being slain by the Asuras, they resorted to Prajāpati. He gave them this 'stronghold of the Gods'. This they entered.

3. He should perform (it) for one against whom abhicāra is being practised. He enters this stronghold of the Gods: so as not to be laid low[1].

[1] Read *astṛtyai* instead of *astityai.*

XXII. 18.

(The eleven-day-rite of Pauṇḍarīka.)[2]

1. An internally attached six-day-rite; three Chandoma(-day)s; an agniṣṭoma with the four stomas; a Viśvajit as over-night-rite.

2. This sacrifice is one for getting the supremacy[1].

[1] Read, with the Leyden Ms., *svārājyo,* and cp. XIX. 13. 1.

3. Supremacy obtains he who knows this.

4. For the supremacy is Prajāpati (and) the supremacy is the most exalted Lord[1].

[1] See XIX. 13. 3.

---

[1] Cp. Ārṣeyakalpa VIII. 11. a-g; Nidānasūtra IX. 6; TS. VII. 2. 5. 3. (different!); Āp. XXII. 24. 1-2.

[2] Cp. Ārṣeyakalpa VIII. 11. h; Nidānasūtra IX. 7; Āp. XXII. 24. 8-12; Baudh. XVI. 32.

5. He who knows this reaches the state of a most exalted Lord[1].

[1] See ib. 4.

6*a*. The rathantara and the bṛhat are both (applied), for this is (equal to) supremacy.

6*b*. A myriad (of cows should be given) as sacrificial fee, for this is (equal to) supremacy.

6*c*. There is the thirty-six-versed stoma[1]; for this is (equal to) supremacy.

[1] Instead of *saḍviṁśa stomo*, read, with the Leyden Ms., *ṣaṭtriṁśa stomo*, and cp. Ārṣeyakalpa l.c.

6*d*. There is the catuḥstoma stoma[1], for this is the last[2]. He who knows this reaches the end (the limit) of fortune.

[1] As tenth day; cp. note 1 on XIX. 5. 1.

[2] Cp. XXI. 4. 6.

7*a*. Kṣemadhṛtvan, the son of Puṇḍarīka, having sacrificed with this (rite) at the northern border of the Sudāman, throve in all respects.

7*b*. He who knows this thrives in all ways.

Twenty-third Chapter.

The Chapters XXIII–XXV describe the sattras, the sacrificial 'sessions', soma-rites of more than twelve days, where there is no Yajamāna but a Gṛhapati. A sattra must begin and end with an over-night-rite.

XXIII. 1.

(Thirteen-day-rite.)[1]

1. An over-night-rite (1); a six-day-rite with the pṛṣṭha(-sāman)s (2-7); an over-night-rite with all the stomas (8); four Chandoma(-day)s (9-12); an over-night-rite (13).

2. These thirteen-days are a complete twelve-day-rite[1].

---

[1] Cp. Ārṣeyakalpa IX. l.b; Nidānasūtra IX. 9; Lāṭy. X. 3. 12–19; Āp. XXIII. 1. 8-9; T.S. VII. 3. 8.

[1] On *āpta*, cp. XXI. 15. 5, XXII. 11. 4. Sāyana explains *āpta* in the following manner: just as in every-day life one gives, for fear of giving too little, a surplus, in order to give the full measure, so the thirteen-day-rite is a fully reached, fully measured twelve-day-rite.

3*a*. For the introductory day and the concluding day, (being) both over-night-rites, are the same[1].

[1] The wording of the corresponding passage in TS. is: *samānaṁ hy etad ahar yat prāyaṇīyaś codayanīyaś ca.*

3*b*. By these days (*i.e*, by this rite) they get (the fulfilment of) every wish they hope to see fulfilled.

4. But the voice of the Gṛhapati becomes (by this rite) deficient[1]. In that at the middle is the over-night-rite with all the stomas, thereby, the voice of the Gṛhapati becomes not deficient[2].

[1] Perhaps because he deviates from the twelve-day-rite, this rite being equal to the voice (XI. 10. 19, XII. 5. 13).

[2] According to XX. 2. 2, the sarvastoma atirātra serves for gaining all.

5. The (participants of a sacrificial session), who had Aryala[1] as their Gṛhapati (and) Āruṇi as their Hotṛ, used[2] to practise these (days, *i.e.*, this rite) at (or among) the Subhagās[3]. They throve in every respect. They who undertake these (days, who perform this rite) thrive in every respect.

[1] An Aryala Kāhoḍi is mentioned in Jaim. br. III. 177 (the name also in Kāṭh. XXV. 7), who, by a certain rite, had torn asunder the voice or the word.

[2] That *upayanti* cannot be intended as a present tense appears from the following imperfect. Perhaps the particles *ha sma* have fallen out, but cp. Introduction, Chapter III, § 8, b.

[3] About this locality (river or people?), nothing is known.

XXIII. 2.

(Second thirteen-day-rite.)[1]

1. An over-night-rite; the ten days of the twelve-day-period[1]; a mahāvrata-day and an over-night-rite.

[1] As they have been described in Chapters XI–XV.

---

[1] Cp. Ārṣeyakalpa IX. 1.c; Āp. XXIII. 1. 10-11.

2. It is the voice (or the word) that is being continuously stretched out by this twelve-day-rite [1]. This (voice) they would tear asunder [2], if they were to perform an over-night-rite in the middle [3].

[1] Cp. note 1 on XXIII. 1. 4.

[2] Read *vicchindyur yan*, etc.

[3] This remark would seem rather to be applicable to the first thirteen-day-rite (cp. TS. VII. 3. 3. 1-2), where there is an atirātra in the middle. Has the author confused the facts ?

3. In that they undertake the (mahā-)vrata immediately after, they do not tear asunder the voice; they reach the thirteenth month [1].

[1] This is equally unclear. Sāyaṇa's commentary is corrupt and incomprehensible.

4. This is the firmly established thirteen-day-rite. They who perform it are firmly established.

XXIII 3.

(Fourteen-day-rite.)[1]

1. An over-night-rite ; a six-day-rite with the pṛṣṭha(-sāman)s ; a six-day-rite with the pṛṣṭha(-sāman)s, beginning with the thirty-three-versed day [1] (and) an over-night-rite.

[1] The first, normal ṣaḍaha consists of days of 9, 15, 17, 21, 27 and 33 verses ; the second, of days of 33, 27, 21, 17, 15 and 9 verses : in reversed order ; cp. TS. *parācināni pṛṣṭhāni* and *pratīcīnāni pṛṣṭhāni*.

2. These days are (*i.e.*, this fourteen-day-rite is) wish-granting :

3. For the (first) ten are (equal to) the virāj [1] ; the eleventh is the person (of the participant) itself ; the twelfth is progeny ; the thirteenth is cattle ; the fourteenth (serves) for (obtaining) the wish [2].

[1] And the virāj is food.

[2] So they get food ; they retain their own life ; get progeny and cattle and all that they further desire.

4. All their wishes they get fulfilled through these days.

5. These two [1] thirty-three-versed days that in the middle (of the two six-day-rites) are brought into connection with each other, are

---

[1] Cp. Ārṣeyakalpa IX. 1. d ; Nidānasūtra IX. 10 ; TS. VII. 3. 4 ; Baudh. XVI. 33 (beg.) ; Āp. XXIII. 1. 13-14.

(equal to) the range of the ruddy one[2]. Thereby, they mount to the range of the ruddy one.

[1] Read *etau* instead of *etā*.

[2] Cp. XIX. 10. 12.—The days are: atirātra, 9-versed, 15-versed, 17-versed, 21-versed, 27-versed, 33-versed, 33-versed, 27-versed, 21-versed, 17-versed, 15-versed, 9-versed and atirātra.

6. Twice they undertake (perform) the (six-day-rite with the) pṛṣṭha(-sāman)s; they put, in regular order, food[1] into themselves.

[1] Because the pṛṣṭhas are food; cp. XIX. 9. 4.

7. These days are winged[1]; whatever wish they desire to see fulfilled they by these (days) reach.

[1] See note 1 on XIX. 10. 1.

8. For wherever a winged being (a bird) desires to go, all that it reaches.

9. They start with a nine-versed (stoma) and finish with a nine-versed (stoma)[1]. The nine-versed among the stomas are the vital principles (the kinds of breath.) By breath they begin, in breath they are firmly established[2].

[1] This refers only to the two ṣaḍaha-periods.

[2] Cp. XIX. 10. 14.

XXIII. 4.

(Second fourteen-day-rite.)[1]

1. An over-night-rite; a three-day-period: jyotis, go and āyus; a six-day-rite with the pṛṣṭha(-sāman)s; an āyus, a go and a jyotis(-day), and an over-night-rite.

2. These (days, *i.e*, this fourteen-day-rite) should be undertaken by those regarding whom they have doubts as to (admitting them to) bed, water or marriage[1].

[1] The exact meaning of these three words, thus combined, is doubtful; 'bed' and 'marriage' seem to be synonymous. Elsewhere (Kāṭh. XXV. 3) we find: *udake vā pātre vā vivāhe vā*; about *pātra*, cp. note 1 on VI. 5. 9. It is, to me at least, even uncertain that 'water' means 'the pouring out of water for a deceased'. Sāyaṇa: *abhiṣekārtham.*

---

[1] Cp. Ārṣeyakalpa IX. 1.e; Āp. XXIII. 1. 15-16; Baudh. XVI. 33 and cp. TS. VII. 3. 5.

3, 4. In that there is a three-day-period: jyotis, go and āyus, they reach the well-known stomas: these worlds. They are firmly supported in these worlds[1].

[1] Cp. XXII. 8. 3.

5. And as to the six-day-rite in the middle with the pṛṣṭha(-sāman)s, this, forsooth, is the bed of the Gods; they, thereby, mount the bed of the Gods and become worthy of bed[1].

[1] They become worthy of being taken into marriage. Just as *pātriya* (see the quotation from Kāṭh. in note 1 on VI. 5. 9) must mean 'worthy of vessel', 'worthy to take meals together with another,' so *talpya* must signify 'worthy of bed'; cp. above, § 2, and, below, XXV. 1. 10.

6 They reach the bed of a wealthier man[1].

[1] Cp. Kāṭh. XXVII. 2: 139. 14: *pra śreyasaḥ pātram āpnoti.*

7. As to the āyus, go and jyotis(-days) and the over-night-rite, whereby they go hence (from the world), thereby they return (to earth).

XXIII. 5.

(Third fourteen-day-rite.)[1]

1. An over-night-rite; the two days go and āyus; the ten days of the twelve-day-period[1] and an over-night-rite.

[1] Cp. note 1 on XXIII. 2. 1.

2. In that there are the two days go and āyus, they (thereby) undertake (practise) pairing stomas[1]: in order to be procreated.

[1] Cp. XVI. 3. 7 (end), and note 3.

3. Then, the ten days of the twelve-day-period: they, thereby, undertake (practise) the not-broken (not divided) voice[1]: for getting progeny.

[1] The twelve-day-period is the voice: XI. 10. 19.

4. This is the well supported fourteen-day-rite. They who perform it are well supported.

---

[1] Cp. Ārṣeyakalpa IX. 1. f; Āp. XXIII. 1. 17-18.

XXIII. 6.

(Fifteen-day-rite.)[1]

1. An over-night-rite; a six-day-period with the pṛṣṭha(-saman)s; a mahāvrata(-day); a six-day-period with the pṛṣṭha(-saman)s beginning with the thirty-three-versed day[1] (and) an over-night-rite.

[1] Cp. note 1 on XXIII. 3. 1.

2. By means of these days (by means of this fifteen-day-rite) the Gods reached the state of Gods. They who undertake this rite reach the state of a God.

3 This is the sacrificial session of the Gods. Even now the Gods perform (it as) a sattra.

4. The (introductory) over-night-rite is the day of full-moon; the (first) six-day-period, this (is) the (next following) six-day-rite with the pṛṣṭha(-sāman)s; the mahāvrata(-day) (is) the aṣṭakā par excellence; the (second, reversed) six-day-period, this (is) the (next following) six-day-rite with the pṛṣṭha(-sāman)s; the (concluding) over-night-rite (is) the day of new-moon[1].

This means that the first day must fall on the day of full-moon, etc. On *ekāṣṭakā*, cp. note 1 on V. 9. 1. As, however, Āpastamba has *aṣṭamyām*, *ekāṣṭakā* may be used here simply in the sense of eighth day.

5. Therefore, men do not (ordinarily) press (and sacrifice) the soma at that time[1], for it is the time when the Gods press the soma. In a visible way, they by these (days, *i.e.*, by this rite) mount unto the deities.

[1] At that time: during the half of the waning moon.

6. But there is a danger of being repelled (by the Gods); (therefore) they should consecrate themselves (*i.e.*, undergo the ceremony of *dīkṣā*) during the other half of the month: for not to be repelled[1].

[1] About the precise meaning of this sentence, the old commentators, as Dhānañjayya and Gautama, were already at variance. The meaning of the Sūtrakāra himself is that this fifteen-day-rite should be preceded by twelve-dīkṣā-days and twelve upasad-days, so that they begin the dīkṣā during the dark half of the month. Āp. allows to begin the fifteen-day-rite on new-moon and to conclude on full moon.

---

[1] Cp. Ārṣeyakalpa IX. 1. g; Nidānasūtra IX. 10; Lāṭy. X. 1. 7-9; Āp XXIII. 2. 2-4.

XXIII. 7.

(Second fifteen-day-rite.)[1]

1. An over-night-rite; a nine-versed Agni-laud[1] as agniṣṭoma; the three-day-period: jyotis, go, āyus; the six-day-rite with the pṛṣṭha(-sāman)s; an āyus-, a go- and a jyotis-(-day) (and) an over-night-rite.

[1] Cp. XVII. 5. 1.

2. These days (this rite) express (expresses) the nobility[1].

[1] Cp. note 1 on XI. 11. 8.

3. Those who are desirous of (obtaining) priestly lustre should undertake this (rite)[1].

[1] Cp. XVII. 5. 3.

4. In that there is the nine-versed Agni-laud as agniṣṭoma, he, thereby, makes the priesthood reach fame.

5. (For) the nine-versed (stoma) is priesthood[1].

[1] Because (VI. 1. 6) it sprang together with the trivṛt stoma from the head of Prajāpati.

6*a*. In that there is the three-day-period: jyotis, go, and āyus, they reach the well-known stomas: these worlds. They are firmly supported in these worlds[1].

[1] The same as XXIII. 4. 3, 4.

6*b*. In that the six-day-rite with the pṛṣṭha(-sāman)s is (applied) in the middle, the pṛṣṭha(-sāman)s being food, thereby food is brought into the middle (of their body). Therefore, food, being in the middle, satiates.

6*c*. As to the āyus-, go-, and jyotis(-days) (and) the over-night-rite: whereby they go hence, thereby they return[1].

[1] The same as XXIII. 4. 7.

---

[1] Cp. Ārṣeyakalpa IX. 1. h; Nidānasūtra IX. 10; TS. VII. 3. 7; Baudh. XVI. 33 (279 1–4; read *agniṣṭuj jyotir*); Āp. XXIII. 2. 5-6.

XXIII. 8.

(Third fifteen-day-rite.)[1]

1. A nine-versed Agni-laud as agniṣṭoma; the three-day-period: jyotis, go, āyus; the ten days of the twelve-day-rite; an over-night-rite.

2. For (the fulfilment of) one wish (serves) a sattra, for (the fulfilment of) another (wish) (serves) a sacrifice. By a sattra he does not get that for which a sacrifice (is undertaken), nor by a sacrifice that for which a sattra (is undertaken)[1].

[1] The same as XXII. 3. 2.

3. In that an over-night-rite is only at one side[1], thereby it is a sacrifice, and in that there are the ten days of the twelve-day-period, thereby it is a sattra.

[1] Read *anyataro 'tirātras*? A sattra begins and concludes with an atirātra.

4. Both (kinds of) wishes (that connected with an ahīna and that connected with a sattra) they by these (days, *i.e.*, by this rite) reach.

XXIII. 9.

(Fourth fifteen-day-rite.)[2]

1*a*. An over-night-rite; the three-day-period: jyotis, go, āyus; the ten days of the twelve-day-rite (and) an over-night-rite.

1*b*. Those who desire to get progeny should undertake (this rite).

2. By means of these (days, *i.e.*, of this fifteen-day-rite), Prajāpati created the creatures. They who undertake this rite are multiplied in children (and) cattle.

3. In that there is the three-day-period: jyotis, go, āyus, they reach the well-known stomas: these worlds. They are firmly supported in these worlds[1].

[1] The same as XXIII. 4. 3, 4.

---

[1] Cp. Arṣeyakalpa IX. 1. i; Nidānasūtra IX. 10 (end); Āp. XXIII. 2. 7-8.

[2] Baudh. XVI. 33 (278. 17-18); Āp. XXIII. 2. 9-10.

4. Then, the ten days of the twelve-day-rite, they, thereby, undertake (practise) the not-divided voice, for getting progeny [1].

[1] This is the same as XXIII. 5. 3.

5 This is the firmly supported fifteen-day-rite; firmly supported are they who undertake this rite.

XXIII. 10.

(Sixteen-day-rite.)[1]

1. These same days with the mahāvrata(-day) [1].

[1] This day comes in before the concluding atirātra; so Sāyaṇa, and cp. Baudh: 'He inserts the mahāvrata between the tenth day (of the daśarātra) and the (concluding) atirātra.'

2. By means of these (days, of this sixteen-day-rite), Indra gained the supreme victory; by means of these they gain the supreme victory.

3. The thunderbolt is the fifteen-day-rite [1] (contained in this sixteen-day-rite). No one can display any prowess when he has not grasped a (destructive weapon like the) thunderbolt [2]. The sixteenth day is the handle. He displays prowess after he has grasped with this [3] (sixteenth day as handle) the thunderbolt (*i.e.*, the first fifteen days).

[1] Cp. Jaim. br. II. 339: *vajro ha khalu vā eṣa yat pañcadaśarātraḥ*; the pañcadaśa stoma likewise is a thunderbolt: II. 4. 2.

[2] Litt: 'with a non-grasped thunderbolt.'

[3] I take *tadgṛhītena* as a compound.

XXIII. 11.

(Seventeen-day-rite.)[2]

1. An over-night-rite; a five-day-period: jyotis, go, āyus, go, āyus; the ten days of the twelve-day-rite (and) a over-night-rite.

2. By means of these (days: by this seventeen-day-rite), Prajā-

[1] Cp. Āp. XXIII. 2. 11-12; Baudh. XVI. 33: 278. 18–279. 1.

[2] Cp. Ārṣeyakalpa IX. 2*a*; Nidānasūtra IX. 11; TS. VII. 3. 8; Baudh. XVI. 33 (279. 4-5); Āp. XXIII. 2. 13-14.

pati gained endless bliss, endless, verily, are the (rites) of the kind of the five-day-rite [1].

[1] Why they are to be regarded as endless is, to me, inexplicable.

3. In that there is the five-day-period, (thereby) they are procreated in consequence of the endless.

4. Then, the ten days of the twelve-day-rite, they (thereby) undertake (practise) the not-divided voice, for getting progeny [1].

[1] This is the same as XXIII. 4. 3, 4 and XXIII. 9, 3.

5. This is the firmly established seventeen-day-rite. Firmly established are they who perform it.

XXIII. 12.

(The eighteen-day-rite of the Gods.)[1]

1. An over-night-rite; a six-day abhiplava-period [1]; the ten days of the twelve-day-rite (and) an over-night-rite.

[1] See Ārṣeyakalpa I. 2-7: jyotis, go, āyus, go, āyus, jyotis.

2. The Gods were afraid of death; they resorted to Prajāpati. He gave them the immortality through this eighteen-day-rite.

3. This is man's immortality that he reaches the normal term of life (and) that he becomes wealthier [1].

[1] This is the same as XXII. 12. 2.

4. They reach the whole term of life (and) become wealthier, who practise this (rite).

5. These days are twice nine; nine are the vital principles [1], in regular order they bring the vital principles into themselves.

[1] Cp. note 2 on VIII. 7. 6.

XXIII. 13.

(Nineteen-day-rite.)[2]

1. These same days with the mahāvrata(-day) [1].

[1] See note 1 on XXIII. 10. 1.

---

[1] Cp. Ārṣeyakalpa IX. 2. b; Āp. XXIII. 2. 15-16.

[2] Cp. Ārṣeyakalpa IX. 2. b; Āp. XXIII. 2. 17-18.

2. By means of these days (*i.e.*, through this rite), Vāyu gained the sovereignty over the animals of the wild. They who practise this rite reach the sovereignty over both kinds of animals (domestic and wild).

3. This is the sacrificial session for (obtaining) deer.

4. Through these days (through this rite) the wild animals, although they are not fostered[1], are procreated.

[1] The exact meaning of *anūkṛta* is uncertain.

5. Unfostered[1] (progeny) is born to those who perform these days (who perform this sattra).

[1] Likewise uncertain. Sāyana explains 'without effort'.

XXIII. 14.

(Twenty-day-rite.)[1]

1. An over-night-rite; a six-day-abhiplava-period[1]; the two days Abhijit and Viśvajit[2]; the ten days of the twelve-day-rite (and) an over-night-rite.

[1] Cp. note 1 on XXIII. 12. 1.

[2] Cp. XVI. 4 and 5.

2. They who are desirous of (obtaining) men[1] should undertake these days (should perform this rite); by means of these (days), Prajāpati created man.

[1] Of servants, or of male children (?)

3. He obtained the supremacy over all food. They who perform this (rite) obtain the supremacy over all food.

4. This is a sacrificial session for (obtaining) men.

5. Twenty-fold is man, for he has ten fingers, ten toes.

6. In that there are these twenty days, they firmly establish by these man in these worlds.

7. This is the firmly established twenty-day-rite. Firmly established are they who undertake it.

---

[1] Cp. Ārṣeyakalpa IX. 3. a; Nidānasūtra IX. 11; TS. VII. 3. 9; Baudh. XVI. 33 (379. 6–8, agrees more with TS.); Āp XXIII. 2 19-20.

XXIII. 15.

(First twenty-one-day-rite.)[1]

1*a*. An over-night-rite; a six-day-abhiplava-period; an over-night-rite: a six-day-abhiplava-period (and) an overnight-rite.

1*b*. They who are desirous of (obtaining) cattle should perform (it).

2 By means of these days (of this rite), the Ādityas produced the seven kinds of domestic animals[1]. They produce the cattle by these (days).

[1] Cp. note 2 on II. 7. 8.

3. They (these days) are thrice seven: seven are the Ādityas[1].

[1] Eight, according to XXIV. 12. 4.

4. The Ādityas are (equal to) the cattle[1].

[1] This equation rests solely on the number seven.

5, 6. The Ādityas (were) thriving in this world and in yonder world, as the cattle in t h i s (and) the seasons in y o n d e r world[1].

[1] This is not over-clear.

7. In both worlds, in that of the Gods and in that of men, they thrive who undertake these (days, who perform this rite).

XXIII. 16.

(Second twenty-one-day-rite.)[2]

1*a*. An over-night-rite; a six-day-period with the pṛṣṭha(-sāman)s; the (three) svarasāman(-days)[1]; the divākīrtya(-day)[2]; the (three) svarasāman(-days)[3]; a six-day-period with the pṛṣṭha(-sāman)s beginning with the thirty-three-versed (day)[4] and an over-night-rite.

[1]. Cp. IV. 5.

[2] The viṣuvat-day.

[3] Cp. IV. 6.

[4] Cp. note 1 on XXIII. 3. 1.

1*b*. Those who are desirous of (obtaining) priestly lustre should undertake (these days, perform this rite).

---

[1] Ārṣeyakalpa IX. 3. b; Nidānasūtra IX. 12; Āp. XXIII. 3. 2-3.

[2] Cp. Ārṣeyakalpa IX. 3. e; Nidānasūtra IX. 12; Jaim. br. II. 342; TS. VII. 3. 10; Baudh. XVI. 33 (end); Āp. XXIII. 3. 4-9.

2. The demoniac Svarbhānu struck the sun with darkness[1]. For him (for the sun) the Gods sought a means of restoration. They found these days (*i.e.*, this twenty-one-day-rite). By means of these, they drove away from him the darkness.

1 Cp. IV. 5. 2.

3. They who perform this sattra repel the darkness from themselves[1].

1 And obtain priestly lustre.

4. They should, after (the normal he-goat), immolate[1] a victim destined for Soma and Pūṣan[2].

1 Probably on the middle day; cp. Schol. on Kāty. XXIV. 2. 9.

2 According to the Jaim. br., the victim is destined for Vāyu: *vāyur vai śāntiḥ, śāntyā evānirdāhāya* (in view of which, is said below, § 8).

5. The Brāhmin is Soma[1], Pūṣan is the cattle[2]. Their own deity they (the participants of the sattra) thereby strengthen through cattle, and they make a skin for themselves[3].

1 This means: Soma is the deity of the Brāhmin.

2 Cp. XVIII. 1 16.

3 Because by the measure to provide themselves with brahmavarcasa, too much of the *mala* on their body might be removed; cp. § 10, and Kāṭh. XI. 5: 150. 6: *svām eva devatāṃ baṁhayate, tvacam eva kurute.*

6. The verses of Manu are used as kindling-verses[2].

1 Either Maitr. S. IV. 11. 2: 164. 11—165. 16 or TS I. 8. 22. l, m, n. Cp. Kāṭh. l.c.: *manor ṛcas sāmidhenīṣu apy anubrūyāt.*

7. All that Manu did say, that is medicine[1]; (so this is) for healing.

1 Cp. Kāṭh. l.c.: *manur vai yat kiñcāvadat tad bheṣajam āsīt.*

8. They should undertake (this rite) in summer[1].

1 Cp. Jaim. br.: *tā haitā rātrīr naidāghīye māsy upeyuḥ .. tasmād eṣa naidāghīye māsi baliṣṭhaṃ tapaty, api dviguṇā chāyā upasarpanti.* According to the Yajus-texts: on full-moon of Taiṣya.

9. For at that time this (sun) gives most heat[1].

1 And this is in accordance with the nature of brahmavarcasa.

10. But there is a fear of leprosy. For it (the sun) removes too much from them (*i.e.*, from their body) [1].

[1] Cp. Maitr. S II. 1. 5 : 7. 9 : *kilāsatvād vā etasya bhayam, ati hy apahanti.*

11. These days (*i.e.*, this rite) forsooth, were undertaken by Ugradeva, the son of Rājana [1]. He got leprosy.

[1] Cp. XIV. 3. 17.

12. Free from leprosy becomes he who, knowing this, undertakes (this) rite [1].

[1] Cp. Jaim. br. : 'Ugradeva Rājani, longing for priestly lustre, undertook these days (this rite of twenty-one days). Him a Brāhmin addressed : *yāvad brahmavarcasam avāruddhāhi* (so, corrupt, the ms., read, perhaps, *avaroddhāsi*) *śveto bhaviṣyasīti*. And he became (white) as a white horse' (*sa yathāśvaḥ śveta evam āsa*), which seems to indicate that be became leprous.—On this whole khaṇḍa, we remark that the bulk of its contents has been borrowed from the Black Yajurveda, especially from the Kāṭhaka (XI. 5) and the Maitr. Saṃh. (II. 1. 5), where an iṣṭi is described for obtaining *brahmavarcasa*. That these texts form the basis of khaṇḍa 16, is proved by the words : *svarbhānur vā āsuraḥ sūryaṃ tamasāvidhyat*, whereas formerly (IV. 5. 2) our author used *ādityaṃ* instead of *sūryaṃ*. The sequence of the wording is nearly the same as in the Kāṭh. and the Maitr. Saṃh. In the description of a sattra there is no room for mentioning the sāmidhenī verses, which belong to the domain of the iṣṭis. Moreover, the context is broken by the mention of the he-goat to be sacrificed to Soma and Pūṣan, for this sacrifice is intended to guard from *kilāsatva* !—On the whole iṣṭi, cp. the author's paper : Altindische Zauberei (Wunschopfer), no. 40 and 41.

XXIII. 17.

(Twenty-two-day-rite.)[1]

1*a*. An over-night-rite ; a three-day-period : jyotis, go, āyus : a six-day-abhiplava-period ; the ten days of the twelve-day-rite ; a mahāvrata(-day) and an over-night-rite.

1*b*. Those who desire to (obtain) food should perform (this rite).

2. The five seasons, the twelve months, these three worlds, yonder sun as twenty-first, food on the twenty-second place : from these worlds, from the year, from yonder sun is obtained food by those who undertake these days [1] (this twenty-two-day-rite).

[1] The logic is not very strict !

---

[1] Cp. Āp. XXIII. 3. 10-11.

XXIII. 18.

(Twenty-three-day-rite.)[1]

1*a*. An over-night-rite; a five-day-period: jyotis, go, āyus, go, āyus; an abhiplava-six-day-period; the ten days of the twelve-day-rite (and) an over-night-rite.

1*b*. Those who desire (to obtain) a firm support should perform (this rite).

2. By means of these days, Prajāpati was firmly supported in these worlds.

3. In that there are those twenty-three days: three are these worlds; in these worlds, by means of these days, they are firmly supported.

4. This is the firmly supported twenty-three-day-rite. They who perform it are firmly supported.

XXIII. 19.

(Twenty-four-day-rite.)[2]

1. An over-night-rite (1); a six-day-rite with the pṛṣṭha(-sāman)s (2–7); a thirty-three-versed (day), 'unexpressed', arranged in the manner of the Upahavya[1], but with the kaṇvarathantara(-sāman) in the midday-service (8); then, a thirty-three-versed (day), (but now) 'expressed' (9)[2]; a twenty-seven-versed (day) (10); two twenty-one versed (days) (11-12); a twenty-seven-versed (day) (13); a thirty-three-versed day, 'unexpressed' (14); a thirty-three-versed day (but now) 'expressed' (15); a six-day-period with the pṛṣṭha(-sāman)s in reversed order (16–21); a nine-versed day, 'unexpressed' (22); a jyotiṣṭoma as agniṣṭoma (23) (and) an over-night-rite (24).

[1] See XVIII. 1.

[2] So here three thirty-three-versed days (for the last day of the pṛṣṭhyaṣaḍaha is equally 33-versed) follow directly after each other. In order to avoid sameness (*jāmitva*), the middle one is 'unexpressed'; see TS. VII. 4. 2. 3.—On *anirukta*, cp. note 1 on XVIII. 1. 3.

---

[1] Cp. Āp. XXIII. 3. 12-13.

[2] Cp. Ārṣeyakalpa IX. 3. e—6. g.; Nidānasūtra IX. 12; Jaim. br. II. 350 sqq.; TS. VII. 4. 2; Āp. XXIII. 4. 1-2; Baudh. XVI. 34-35 (279. 14–280. 12).

2. By means of these (days, *i.e.*, of this rite), the Gods united themselves in the world of heaven. (So) these days (serve for fulfilling the wish of their performers:) 'May we be united in the world of heaven'[1].

[1] The last sentence is somewhat elliptic; understand probably: *ity etā upayanti*; cp. TS. l. c. 1. From this sentence the rite has its name: *devānāṃ saṃsad* or *saṃsadām ayanam*.

3. These (days, this rite), forsooth, are the range of the ruddy one (the sun). In that the thirty-three-versed (days) are brought into connection in the middle, thereby they ascend the range of the ruddy one[1].

[1] Cp. XIX. 10. 12.

4. In that the six-day-rite with the pṛṣṭha(-sāman)s is (applied) in the middle, the pṛṣṭha(-sāman)s being food, thereby food is brought into the middle. Therefore food, being in the middle, satiates[1].

[1] This is the same as XXIII. 7. 6*b*.

5. These are seven-day-periods[1].

[1] This cannot be taken literally.

6. Hence[1] the young ones are born.

[1] Out of these seven-day-periods, probably because the seven-day-rite is connected with the getting of progeny: XXII. 5, 3.

7. They who perform this rite are procreated in children and cattle.

8. Not conducive to cattle, forsooth, is that sacrificial session where the Chandoma(-day)s are lacking[1]. In that there are seven-day-periods, thereby this (rite) is provided with the Chandomas[2]; thereby, they (*i e.*, these days, this rite) are conducive to cattle.

[1] Because the Chandomas are cattle: note 1 on III. 8. 2.

[2] How are these seven-day-periods to be understood as Chandomas? Sāyaṇa is of no help. A similar difficulty, XXIV. 3. 2.

9, 10. A thirty-three-versed (stoma) comes (immediately) after a thirty-three-versed one[1], a nine-versed after a nine-versed[2]. They mount from the top to the top[3] by (the fact) that the thirty-three-versed (stoma) comes (immediately) after the thirty-three-versed; from[4] the vital principle they are firmly supported in the vital principles by (the fact) that the nine-versed (stoma) comes (immediately) after the nine-versed one.

[1] The last day of the first pṛṣṭhya-ṣaḍaha is 33-versed, this is followed by a 33-versed day; cp. § 1.

[2] The last day of the reversed pṛṣṭhya-ṣaḍaha is nine-versed (the 21st day), and after this comes a nine-versed day.

[3] They reach the highest top: heaven or *bradhnasya viṣṭapam.*

[4] If the ablative *prāṇāt* is right, it is due solely to the parallelism with the preceding *agrād agraṃ rohanti.* At any rate, § 9 and § 10 form one single sentence.

11. These days violate the proper order[1]: that the day of rising from the sacrificial session[2] is a jyotiṣṭoma-agniṣṭoma, is for arranging the unarranged.

[1] It has been already noted by Sāyaṇa that the masc. *vilomānaḥ* (*sc. rātrayaḥ*) is a grammatical irregularity.—The proper order is violated by the 27-versed day (which comes after a 33-versed one), the two 21-versed days and the 27-versed day (the 10th–13th days).

[2] This is the last but one day, here the 23th: cp. Eggeling, in Sacred Books of the East, vol. XXVI. page 447, note 2.

XXIII. 20.

(Second twenty-four-day-rite.)[1]

1*a*. An over-night-rite; two abhiplava-six-day-periods; the ten days of the twelve-day-rite (and) an over-night-rite.

1*b*. Those who are desirous of (obtaining) either progeny or cattle should undertake (these days: should perform this rite).

2 Out of a normal womb children and cattle are born. In that the two six-day-periods are performed normally[1], they are procreated in children and cattle born from a normal womb.

[1] They are normal (well-arranged) as they occur in their regular order, and not the second (as often is the case) in reversed order.

3. Then the ten days of the twelve-day-rite; they (thereby) undertake (practise) the not-divided voice, for getting progeny[1].

[1] This is the same as XXIII. 4. 3, 4, etc.

---

[1] Cp. Nidānasūtra IX. 12 (*etaṃ viśālapṛṣṭhya ity ācakṣate,* the word occurs also in Āśv. XI. 3. 8 and Kāty. XXIV. 2. 16); Āp. XXIII. 3. 15-16.

4. This is the firmly established twenty-four-day-rite Firmly established are they who perform it.

XXIII. 21.

(Twenty-five-day-rite.)[1]

1. These same (days) with the mahāvrata(-day)[1].

[1] Cp. note 1 on XXIII. 10. 1.

2. By these days, Prajāpati obtained all food.

3. The year contains twenty-four half-months; the year is the twenty-fifth; the vrata is food[1]. Out of the year through these (days) the food is obtained by those who perform this (rite).

[1] Cp. note 1 on IV. 10. 1.

XXIII. 22.

(Twenty-six-day-rite.)[2]

1. An over-night-rite; the two days: go, and āyus; two abhiplava-six-day-periods; the ten days of the twelve-day-period (and) an over-night-rite.

2. The seasons lacked a firm support; they got it by these (days). Those who are desirous of (obtaining) a firm support should perform (this rite). They get a firm support.

3. Six (in number) are the seasons; in the seasons they by these (days) get a firm support.

4. In that there are those two days: go, and āyus, they (thereby) undertake (practise) pairing stomas[1], in order to be procreated.

[1] Cp. note 3 on XVI. 3. 7.

5 That the two six-day-periods are performed normally, is for obtaining accomplishment[1].

[1] Cp. XXIII. 20. 2.

---

[1] Cp. Āp. XXIII. 4. 3-4; Baudh. XVI. 34: 279. 12-13: *sa uvevābrāhmanaḥ*, 'this is the (twenty-five-day-rite) that is not described in our (*viz.*, the TS.) brāhmaṇa.'

[2] Cp. Āp. XXIII. 4. 5-6.

6. Then, the ten days of the twelve day-rite, they (thereby) undertake (practise) the not-divided voice, for getting progeny.

[1] This is the same as XXIII. 4. 3, 4, etc.

7. This is the well-supported twenty-six-day-rite. Firmly supported are they who perform it.

XXIII. 23.

(Twenty-seven-day-rite.)[1]

1*a*. An over-night-rite ; a three-day-period : jyotis, go, āyus ; two abhiplava-six-day-periods ; the ten days of the twelve-day-period (and) an over-night-rite

1*b*. Those who are desirous of thriving should perform (this rite).

2. By means of these (days) the moon-stations throve in all respects. They who undertake them thrive in all respects.

3. That there are twenty-seven days : there are twenty-seven moon-stations, these days are commensurable with the moon-stations : they get the thriving of the moon-stations.

XXIII. 24.

(Twenty-eight-day-rite.)[2]

1*a*. These same days with the mahāvrata(-day) [1].

[1] Cp. note 1 on XXIII. 10. 1.

1*b*. Those who are desirous of (obtaining) cattle should undertake (these days, should perform this rite).

1*c*. In that there are these twenty-e i g h t days ; cattle is e i g h t-hoofed, they obtain through them the cattle hoof by hoof [1].

[1] Cp. XV. 1. 8, XIX. 5. 4.

XXIII. 25.

(Twenty-nine-day-rite.)[3]

1. An over-night-rite ; the five-day-period : jyotis, go, āyus, go, āyus ; two abhiplava-six-day-periods ; the ten days of the twelve-day-period (and) an over-night-rite.

---

[1] Cp. Āp. XXIII. 4. 7-8.

[2] Cp. Āp. XXIII. 4. 9-10.

[3] Cp. Āp. XXIII. 4. 11-12.

2. By means of these (days) Prajāpati gained endless bliss.

3. Endless, forsooth, are these twenty-nine (days)[1]; (the word) 'not' is the endless (part) of speech[2].

1 Cp. XXIII. 11. 2.

2 *neti vai vāco 'nantam* (occurs also XXIV. 9. 2); the word *na* is contained in the designation of the number *ekayā na triṃśat* ('thirty days minus one'). This word, according to the interpretation of Sāyaṇa, is 'endless', because it is so often used in rejecting a request for money or help.

4. In that there are those twenty-nine days, through these they gain endless bliss.

XXIII. 26.

(Thirty-day-rite.)[1]

1*a*. An over-night-rite; three abhiplava-six-day-periods; the ten days of the twelve-day-period (and) an over-night-rite.

1*b*. Those who are desirous of (obtaining) food should perform (it).

2. Other sacrificial sessions amount cryptically to the virāj, (but) these (days, this thirty-day-rite,) amount visibly to the virāj[1].

1 Because the virāj is of thirty syllables: X. 3. 12.

3. Visibly (directly), by these days, they who undertake them obtain food[1].

1 Because the virāj is food: IV. 8. 4.

XXIII. 27.

(Thirty-one-day-rite.)[2]

1*a*. These same days with the mahāvrata(-day)[1].

1 Cp. note 1 on XXIII. 10. 1.

1*b*. By means of these days, Prajāpati successively obtained food.

---

1 Cp. Āp. XXIII. 4. 13-14.
2 Cp. Āp. XXIII. 5. 1-2.

2. The virāj is food[1], the vrata is food[2].

[1] Cp. IV. 8. 4.

[2] Cp. IV. 10. 1.—So, in the first place, the first thirty days are food; in the second place, the mahāvrata is food.

3. Successively, they by these days (by this rite) obtain food.

XXIII. 28.

(Thirty-two-day-rite.)[1]

1*a*. An over-night-rite; the two days: go (and) āyus; three abhiplava-six-day-periods; the ten days of the twelve-day-period; an over-night-rite.

1*b*. They who are desirous of (obtaining) cattle should undertake (it).

2. These days are (*i.e.*, this thirty-two-day-rite is) an anuṣṭubh.

3. The anuṣṭubh is of thirty-two syllables.

4. The anuṣṭubh is the voice[1].

[1] Cp. V. 7. 1.

5. Four-footed[1] are animals (cattle).

[1] As is the anuṣṭubh with its four verse-quarters.

6, 7. Through the voice, (*i.e.*,) through these days, he supports[1] cattle.

[1] On the perfect, cp Delbrück, Altind. Syntax, page 297.

8. Therefore, they (the domestic animals, the cows) approach when they are reached by the voice, when they are summoned by the voice[1].

[1] Cp. X. 3. 13.

---

[1] Cp. Ap. XXIII. 5. 3-4.

TWENTY-FOURTH CHAPTER.

(The sattras, continued.)

XXIV. 1.

(Thirty-three-day-rite.)[1]

1. An over-night-rite; three five-day-periods[1]; a Viśvajit as over-night-rite[2]; one five-day-rite[3]; the ten days of the twelve-day-period (and) an over-night-rite.

[1] A jyotis-, go-, āyus-, go- and āyus-day.

[2] Cp. XVI. 5.

[3] In reversed order, according to the Ārṣeyakalpa.

2. Prajāpati created the creatures; these found no firm support; by means of these (days, by means of this rite,) they got a firm support. These worlds found no firm support; by means of these (days) they got a firm support. They who desire (to obtain) a firm support should undertake them: they get a firm support.

3. Through that which is formless, these (days) are provided with form; through that which is formless, the creatures are provided with form; through that which is formless, these worlds are provided with form. In that the bṛhat(-sāman) takes the place of the rathantara (and) the rathantara (that) of the bṛhat, they (*viz.*, the Chanters) engender for them (*viz.*, for the performers of the sattra) that which is provided with form through that which is formless[1].

[1] This seems to mean that, just as the creatures receive their form through the soul, because they only come into existence when they are provided with a soul, and just as the worlds become visible because Prajāpati created them, so these days, in which (during the second and the fourth five-day-period, according to the Ārṣeyakalpa,) the rathantara and the bṛhat change their places (the first day having as first pṛṣṭhastotra, not, as is usual, the rathantara, but the bṛhat, the second day having the rathantara instead of the usual bṛhat), are devoid of form in that their usual first pṛṣṭhastotra is removed, but then again are provided with form, in that this void is filled up with the other chant. I am not sure whether I have rightly interpreted this passage. How the rathantara and the bṛhat change their places is seen from Ārṣeyakalpa IX. 7.

---

[1] Cp. Ārṣeyakalpa IX. 7. a-d; Nidānasūtra IX. 13; Jaim. br. II. 355-358 (slightly different); Āp. XXIII. 5. 6-7.

4. By the fact that they undertake periods of five days, the sixth day is lost[1] (and) the (six) seasons do not arrive in their regular order (because the sixth season would fail). In that, (however,) there is a six-day-period with the pṛṣṭha(-sāman)s[2], thereby the sixth day is not lost, thereby the seasons arrive in their regular order.

1 Usually a six-day-period is adhibited.

2 This is not clear, as there is no *pṛṣṭhyaḥ ṣaḍahaḥ*; but perhaps this term serves here to denote the Viśvajit (which comes immediately after the last five-day-period) in which all the pṛṣṭha-sāmans occur. The Jaiminīya-brāhmaṇa defends the five-day-period as representing properly the seasons: 'Now, the Kāpeyas used to say: 'The six-day-period is founded on what is not-season (*anṛtau*); it is the five-day-period that is founded on the season'. Spring is the first of the seasons, summer is the second, the rains are the third, the autumn is the fourth, the winter is the fifth, the cool time (*śiśira*) is the sixth. The most excellent of the seasons is winter, when cows and men grow fat (*sa eṣa śreṣṭha ṛtūnāṃ yad dhemantaḥ pīvaguḥ pīvapuruṣaḥ*). In accordance with this season (which is the fifth), the five-day-period is well-founded, but the *śiśira* is blamable when cows and men grow meagre; in accordance with this season, the six-day-period is well-founded[1]. They undertake the five-day-period, thinking: 'may we be well established in accordance with winter which is the most excellent of seasons'

5. And in that there are the ten days of the twelve-day-period, thereby they do not deviate from the five-day-periods[1].

1 Thereby, the continuity of the five-day-periods (because a ten-day-period is equal to two five-day-periods) is maintained.

6. The intermediate region is the udder (of a she-goat), on (its) both sides are the two nipples[1]; by means of this[2] nipple, this (rite)[3] yields milk for the Gods; by means of yonder[4] (nipple), for the creatures.

1 Sky and earth that are on both sides of the intermediate region.

2 The earth, see § 7.

3 This rite, thought of as a she-goat.

4 The sky. From the sky comes the rain, from the earth comes the sacrifice, by which the Gods exist.

---

1 This seems to be contradictory; read, perhaps: *tam anu ṣaḍaho 'pratiṣṭhitaḥ*.

7. The interstice between (the two nipples) is this[1] intermediate region; the two nipples on either side are these two (worlds: sky and earth).

[1] Read with the Leyden Ms., *idaṃ* instead of *iyaṃ*.

8. With regard to this, a (verse) occurs (in the sacred texts):

9. 'The Gods, who three and thirty (in number) seated themselves on the sacrificial grass, went asunder in two parts'[1].

[1] This verse; *triṁśati trayaḥ paro ye devā barhir āsata | vyann aha dvitā tanā* is corrupt from ṚS. VIII. 28. 1: *ye triṃśati trayas paro devāso barhir āsadan | vidann aha dvitāsanan.* In view of the precedent (§ 7) word *viyat*, I presume that the author of our Brāhmaṇa takes *vyan* as imperfect of *vyeti.* The meaning *dvitā* here is uncertain, nor it is apparent how this verse should prove the words of § 7.

10. The over-night-rite in the middle is the udder, at either side (are) the nipples (the three preceding and the three following five-day-rites).

11. If this (rite) were without an over-night-rite (in the middle), he would curb the udder.

12. Therefore, the over-night-rite (in the middle) must be performed to avoid curbing the udder.

13. The thirty-three deities throve through this (rite). Thereby it is a (cause for) thriving. Therefore, they should sacrifice with the (rite of) these (days): for thriving.

14. They apply different Brahman's chants[1] for obtaining different kinds of strength. They obtain different kinds of strength.

[1] This difference in the third pṛṣṭha-lauds is applied, according to the Ārṣeyakalpa, only at the four five-day-periods; the chants are given IX. 7. a and c.

XXIV. 2.

(Second thirty-three-day-rite.)[1]

1. An over-night-rite (1); an abhiplava-six-day-period (2–7); an over-night-rite (8); an abhiplava-six-day-rite (9–14); an over-night-rite (15); an abhiplava-six-day-period (16–21); the ten days of the twelve-day-period (22–31); a mahāvrata(-day) (32) and an over-night-rite (33).

2. The Ādityas and the Angirases combined this sacrificial session

[1] Cp. Ārṣeyakalpa IX. 7. e; Nidānasūtra l.c.; Āp. XXIII. 5. 8–9.

(*i.e.*, performed it together): of the Ādityas was the twenty-one-day-rite[1]; of the Angirases, the twelve-day-rite[2]. The Ādityas came to thriving in this and yonder world; the Angirases (came to thriving) in this and yonder world. It is a double sacrificial session. As much welfare as they (the participants) get by a double sattra, so great is the welfare reached by these (days, through this rite).

[1] Up to the third abhiplava.

[2] From the ten days of the daśarātra on.

XXIV. 3.

(Third thirty-three-day-rite.)[1]

1. An over-night-rite; three five-day periods; a Viśvajit as over-night-rite; three five-day-periods; an over-night-rite.

2. Not conducive to cattle is that sacrificial session where the Chandomas are lacking[1]. In that at the Viśvajit they apply the Chandomas[2], thereby they (*i.e.*, these days are, this sattra is) provided with the Chandomas and conducive to cattle.

[1] See note 1 on XXIII. 19. 8; where the ten days of the twelve-day-rite are applied, there are the Chandomas, the 7th, 8th and 9th day.

[2] How is this to be understood? Sāyaṇa, by adding the different stomas of the Viśvajit, succeeds in getting the number of the stomas of the Chandomas (9+15=24, first Chandoma; 17+27=44, second Ch.; 15+33=48, third Ch.), but this seems to be too artificial to be well founded.

3. These days are winged; whatever wish they desire to see fulfilled, that they, by these (days), reach. For wherever a winged being (a bird) desires to go, all that it reaches[1].

[1] This is the same as XXIII 3. 7, 8.—The Viśvajit in the middle is the trunk, the three five-day-rites on either side are the wings.

4. They start with a nine-versed (stoma), they finish with a nine-versed (stoma)[1]. The nine-versed among the stomas are the vital principles. By breath they begin, in breath they are firmly established[2].

[1] Because, according to the Nidānasūtra, they begin with three and end with three five-day-periods: *trivṛtā prayanti trivṛtodyantīti: trayaḥ pañcāhāḥ purastāt traya upariṣṭād iti.*

[2] This is the same as XXIII. 3. 9.

---

[1] Cp. Ārṣeyakalpa IX. 7. f; Nidānasūtra X. 1; Āp. XXIII. 5. 10-11.

39

XXIV. 4.

(Thirty-four-day-rite.)[1]

1*a*. An over-night-rite; a three-day period: jyotis, go, āyus; three abhiplava-six-day-periods; the ten days of the twelve-day-period; a mahāvrata(-day) and an over-night-rite.

1*b*. They who are desirous of thriving should undertake (them).

2. Through these days (this thirty-four-day-rite), Prajāpati reached all kinds of prosperity. They who undertake them reach all kinds of prosperity.

3. In that there are those thirty-three days, the deities being thirty-three in number and Prajāpati being the thirty-fourth of the deities, they get the prosperity of Prajāpati.

XXIV. 5.

(Thirty-five-day-rite.)[2]

1*a*. An over-night-rite; a five-day-period: jyotis, go, āyus, go, āyus; three abhiplava-six-day-periods; the ten days of the twelve-day-period (and) an over-night-rite.

1*b*. They who are desirous of (obtaining) cattle should undertake (them).

2. In that there are those thirty-five days, cattle being fivefold[1], they by these (days) obtain cattle.

[1] Cp. note 2 on II. 4. 2.

XXIV. 6.

(Thirty-six-day-rite.)[3]

1*a*. An over-night-rite; four abhiplava-six-day-periods; the ten days of the twelve-day-period (and) an over-night-rite.

1*b*. They who are desirous of (obtaining) cattle should undertake (them).

---

[1] Cp. Āp. XXIII. 5. 12-13.

[2] Cp. Āp. XXIII. 6. 1-2.

[3] Cp. TS. VII. 4. 6; Āp. XXIII. 6. 3-4; Baudh. XVI. 36 (beg.).

2. By means of these (days), the Gods propped the sun (so that it did not fall down on the earth). They who undertake these (days) conquer the world of the sun.

3. These days are (equal to) the bṛhatī[1], the bṛhatī is the rulership among the metres[2]. He who gets a plurality of cattle comes to rulership. They who undertake these (days) reach rulership.

[1] The bṛhatī being of 36 syllables.

[2] Cp. X. 3. 8 and VII. 4. 5.

XXIV. 7.

(Thirty-seven-day-rite.)[1]

1. These same days with a mahāvrata(-day) (as last but one).

2. By these (days), Prajāpati reached the fulfilment of both wishes: the (mahā-)vrata is food[1], the bṛhatī[2] is cattle. Both wishes they obtain by these (days).

[1] Cp. IV. 10. 1.

[2] The 36 days without the mahāvrata.

XXIV. 8.

(Thirty-eight-day-rite.)[2]

1*a*. An over-night-rite; the two days: go and āyus; four abhiplava-six-day-periods; the ten days of the twelve-day-period (and) an over-night-rite.

1*b*. They who are desirous of (obtaining) cattle should undertake (them).

2. In that there are thirty-e i g h t days, cattle being eight-hoofed, he obtains the cattle hoof by hoof.

XXIV. 9.

(Thirty-nine-day-rite.)[3]

1. An over-night-rite; the three days: jyotis, go, āyus; four abhiplava-six-day-periods; the ten days of the twelve-day-period (and) an over-night-rite.

---

[1] Cp. Āp. XXIII. 6. 5-6, Baudh. XVI. 36: 281. 5-6.

[2] Cp. Āp. XXIII. 6. 7-8.

[3] Cp. Āp. XXIII. 6. 9-10.

2. By these days, Prajāpati gained endless bliss. Endless are these thirty-nine days. The word 'not' is the endless (part) of voice (or 'speech')[1].

[1] Cp. notes 1 and 2 on XXIII. 25. 3.

3. In that there are thirty-nine days they gain by them endless bliss.

XXIV. 10.

(Forty-day-rite.)[1]

1. These same days with the mahāvrata(-day) (as last but one).

2. These days, taken together, make virāj's[1]: the first is the ten-syllabic, the second is the twenty-syllabic, the third is the thirty-syllabic. The forty days are the highest virāj. The paṅkti, forsooth, is the highest virāj.

[1] Cp. note 1 on II. 7. 8.

[2] A paṅkti is equal to forty syllables; cp. Kauṣ. br. XVII. 3.

3. They are firmly established in the highest virāj[1].

[1] Cp. XVI. 1. 9-10.

XXIV. 11.

(Forty-nine-day-rite.)[2]

1. An over-night-rite (1); three-nine-versed days, of which the first is an agniṣṭoma (and the two others ukthyas) (2–4); an over-night-rite (5); ten fifteen-versed ukthyas, of which the tenth is combined with a ṣoḍaśin (6–15); an over-night-rite (16); twelve seventeen-versed ukthyas (17–28); an over-night-rite (29); a six-day-period with the pṛṣṭha(-sāman)s (30–35); an over-night-rite (36); twelve twenty-one-versed ukthyas (37–48) (and) an over-night-rite (49).

2. Prajāpati created the creatures; these, not being kept apart (and) not agreeing together, devoured each other. This pained Prajāpati. He saw these days (*i.e.*, this forty-nine-day-rite). Thereupon, this became separated (*i.e.*, all the kinds of beings kept apart): cows

---

[1] Cp. Āp. XXIII. 6. 11-12.

[2] Cp. Ārṣeyakalpa IX. 8-9; Nidānasūtra X. 2; Jaim. br. II. 365-367; TS. VII. 4. 7; Baudh. XVI. 36: 281. 7-11; Āp. XXIII. 7. 2-3.

(became) cows; horses (became) horses; men (became) men; deer (became) deer[1].

[1] This seems to imply that now the various kinds of creatures no longer devoured each other, but kept separated and then were procreated.

3. They who undertake these (days, *i.e.*, this forty-nine-day-rite) are separated from bad lot.

4. That the (four) over-night-rites (occur) between (the other days, and not only at the beginning and the end, as is usual), is for keeping apart[1]. Therefrom it results that no kind (of beings) brings its semen into (females of) other kind.

[1] The name of these days (of this sattra) is, in accordance with this statement *vidhṛtayaḥ*: 'the separatings'.

5. In that the pṛṣṭhyastomas are united together[1], therefore, of the cattle goats and sheep walk together; therefore, also, the ass brings its semen into the mare[2].

[1] At the six-day-period with the pṛṣṭha-sāmans.

[2] This last consequence is not very apparent.

6. Not conducive to cattle is the sacrificial session where the Chandomas are lacking[1]; in that they undertake (*i.e.*, apply) the (different principal) metres on the sāmans of the twilight-rites[2], thereby, they (these days) are (this rite is) provided with the Chandomas; thereby, (they are) conducive to cattle.

[1] Cp. note 1 on XXIV. 3. 2.

[2] See next §.—The Chandomas are here outweighed by the *chandas*.

7. On gāyatrī(-verse)s, the jarābodhīya(-saman) (is chanted as twilight-sāman); on uṣṇih(-verse)s, the srudhya(-saman); on anuṣṭubh(-verse)s, the nānada(-sāman); on bṛhatī(-verse)s, the rathantara(-sāman); on pankti(-verse)s, the rāyovājīya(-sāman); on triṣṭubh(-verses), the auśana(-sāman); on jagatī(-verse)s, the kāva(-sāman)[1].

[1] As the sandhi-stotra occurs only (as final laud) at an over-night-rite, and this sattra comprises (see § 1) six atirātras, we expect not seven but six sandhi-sāmans, but for the sake of the completeness of the metres, the nānada of the ṣoḍaśin-day (the 15th day) is taken into the account (this stotra which falls together with sunset, may, in a sense, be regarded as a sandhi-stotra). See Ārṣeyakalpa IX. 8. a (end), IX. 8. c (end), IX. 8. d (end), IX. 8. e (end), (here the rathantara comes in, on which at an ordinary atirātra the sandhi is

chanted; ed. of Ārṣ. k. page 204, below), IX. 8. 9 (end), IX. 9. b (end), IX. 9. d (end). The sāmans are:

jarābodhīya, grām. I. 1. 26, composed on SV. I. 15, chanted on SV. II. 1075–1080.

śrudhya, grām. III. 1. 15, comp. on SV. I. 99, chanted on SV. II. 1081–1086.

nānada, grām. IX. 2. 13, comp. on SV. I. 352, chanted on SV. II. 790–793.

rathantara, ar. g. II. a. 31, comp. on SV. I. 233, chanted on SV. II. 99–104.

rāyovājīya, ar. g. III. a. 16, comp. on SV. I. 409, chanted on SV. II. 1087–1095.

auśana, grām. XV. 1. 32, comp. on SV. I. 543, chanted on SV. II. 1096–1104.

kāva, grām. XVI. 2. 6, comp. on SV. I. 554, chanted on SV. II. 257–259 and 1105–1110.

8. They undertake (apply) the metres tending upward[1] to avoid falling down.

[1] The number of syllables of the verses, on which the sandhistotras are chanted, increase by four: 24, 28, 32, 36, 40, 44, 48.

9. The tone (circumflex) is the vital air[1]; in that two circumflexes are at the end[2], therefore, two vital airs (two *prāṇas*) are at the end[3].

[1] Cp. VII. 1. 10, XI. 5. 26. XVII. 12. 2.

[2] The auśana is *svāra*, ending (see SV. ed. Calcutta, Vol. II, page 108, and Vol. V, page 255: ūhagāna): *tā656i*; similarly the kāva is *svāra*, ending (see SV. ed. Calcutta, Vol. II, page 173, Vol. V, page 503) *ṇā656ḥ*.

[3] Regarding the meaning of this, I am not certain. What Sāyaṇa says: 'Therefore, in ordinary life at the time of death the two breaths: out-breathing and in-breathing, are intense' seems to be worthless. Perhaps it refers to the fact that usually in the head are localized seven *prāṇas* (cp. note 3 on II. 15. 3); thus, the two ears may be meant; cp. XXIV. 14. 5.

XXIV. 12.

(Second forty-nine-day-rite.)[1]

1. An over-night-rite (1); two abhiplava-six-day-periods (2–13); a go- and an āyus(-day) as over-night-rites (14, 15); two abhiplava-six-day-periods (16–27); an Abhijit and a Viśvajit as over-night-

[1] Cp. Ārṣeyakalpa IX. 10. a; Āp. XXIII. 7. 4–6; Kāty. XXIV. 3. 6–9.

rites (28, 29); one abhiplava-six-day-period (30–35); a one-day-rite with all the stomas[1] (36); a one-day-rite containing alternately nine- and seventeen-versed lauds[2] (37)—these last two as over-night-rites—the ten days of the twelve-day-rite (38–47); a mahāvrata(-day) (48) and an over-night-rite (49).

[1] As XIX. 9.

[2] As XX. 4.

2. (These are) the-twin-(*yama*)-over-night-rites of the Ādityas

3. They who undertake these (days: they who perform this rite) get double (*yama*) bliss.

4. Through these (days), the Ādityas throve pairwise: Mitra and Varuṇa, Dhātṛ and Aryaman, Aṃśa and Bhaga, Indra and Vivasvat. They who perform this (rite) get the thriving of these deities.

5. With regard to this, a (verse) occurs (in the sacred texts):

6. 'The eight sons that were born out of the person of Aditi, with seven (of these) she went to the Gods, (but) Mārtaṇḍa she threw away'[1].

[1] The verse is (partly corrupt: *tanvaṃ pari* instead of *tanvas pari* and *mārtaṇḍa* instead of *mārtāṇḍa*) ṚS. X. 72. 8. It is cited to prove the number eight of the Ādityas.

7. The Ādityas throve (by this rite) in this world; they throve in yonder (world). In both these worlds, in that of Gods and in that of man, thrive they who perform this rite.

XXIV. 13.

(Third forty-nine-day-rite.)[1]

1. An over-night-rite (1); four abhiplava-six-day-periods (2–25); an over-night-rite with all the stomas (26); two abhiplava-six-day-periods (27–38); the ten days of the twelve-day-period (39–48) (and) an over-night-rite (49).

2. Prajāpati created the creatures; he got parched up; they

[1] Cp. Ārṣeyakalpa IX. 10. b; Nidānasūtra X. 3; Lāṭy. X. 4. 10–16; Kāty. XXIV. 3. 10–16; Āp. XXIII. 7. 7–10.

did not know him as he was parched up; he anointed his eyes and his limbs.

3. They who do not notice themselves (*i.e.*, each other) should undertake these (days: should perform this forty-nine-rite). When they anoint their eyes and their limbs, they bring handsomeness on themselves; they (the others) notice them.

4. With (salve) mixed with bdellion[1] (they should anoint themselves) at the morning-service; with (salve) mixed with the (extract) from fragrant reed-grass, at the midday service; with (salve) mixed with (resin) of the pine-tree, at the afternoon-service.

[1] Read *gaulgu°* here, and in § 5 *gulgu°*.

5. As Agni was about to enter upon the office of Hotṛ for the Gods, he shook himself[1]: what was his flesh, became the bdellion; what were his muscles, became the fragrant reed-grass; what were his bones, became the pine-wood[2]. These, forsooth, are the perfumes of the Gods; they, thereby, anoint themselves with the perfumes of the Gods[3].

[1] The ms. of Leydon has *adhunuta* not *adhūnuta*.

[2] Cp. Śat br. III. 5. 2. 15–17.

[3] According to Lāty., they should, during the upasad-days, skim the liquid butter, boiling it over the gārhapatya, and mix this skimmed butter with the three substances mentioned in the Brāhmaṇa. During the days on which the sacrifices of soma take place, the participants of the sattra, seated before the havirdhāna-shed, should anoint their eyes and limbs at the moment when the different services are begun. According to Gautama, they should anoint themselves after the close of a service, when they have partaken of food in the āgnīdhra-shed. According to some authorities, this anointing takes place day after day, or it is restricted either to the sarvastoma-day (the 26th) or to the six-day-period with the pṛṣṭhasāmans (but in this sattra there is no pṛṣṭhyaṣaḍaha!).

XXIV. 14.

(Fourth forty-nine-day-rite.)[1]

1*a*. An over-night-rite (1); a twenty-four-versed proceeding day[1] (2); three abhiplava-six-day-periods (3–20); an Abhijit (21); the three

[1] Cp, Ārṣeyakalpa IX. 10. c; Nidānasūtra X. 2-3; Lāṭy. X. 5. 1–7; Baudh. XVI. 36: 281. 11–16; Āp. XXIII. 7. 11–13; Kāty. XXIV. 3. 17–20.

svarasāman(-day)s (22–24); the divākīrtya(-day) (25); the three svarasāman(-day)s (in reversed order) (26–28); a Viśvajit (29); one abhiplava-six-day-period (30–35); the two days āyus and go (36-37); the ten days of the twelve-day-period (38–47); a mahāvrata(-day) (48) and an over-night-rite (49).

[1] Read *caturviṁśam* instead of ° *viṁśaḥ*.

1*b*. The (days of this sattra) are commensurable with the (sattra of a) year [1]. The thriving which is joined to the (sattra of) the year, this thriving is connected with these days (with this rite).

[1] The schema agrees, in a way, with that of the gavām ayana or year's sattra; cp. the Introduction to the Ārṣeyakalpa, page XXIV, sq.

2. In regard to this, they say: 'If they were to make the proceeding day twenty-four-versed, they would, after having undertaken the (sacrificial session of the) year, not be able to finish it' [1]. It [2] must be made ninefold (*i.e.*, nine-versed, *trivṛt*); the ninefold stoma is (equal to) the vital principle [3]; they do not (in making it ninefold) depart from the vital principle (but retain it) [4].

[1] It is not clear why not! Perhaps, simply because (see the next sentence) they would then be separated from breath, from life.

[2] Some authorities assert, that the sentence *trivṛd eva kāryam* refers not to the proceeding day or opening day of the whole sattra, but to the first day of the ten-day-period (the 38th), this day likewise being a *prāyaṇīyam ahar*.

[3] See note 3 on II. 15. 3.

[4] Read the text: *prāṇo vai trivṛt prāṇān naivāpayanti*.

3. But they also say: 'It must be made a twenty-one-versed (day), for (reaching) 'success'.

4. As to those svarasāman(-day)s: the divākīrtya (or viṣuvat, or middle day) is the head, the (three) svarasāman(-day)s are the vital principles: that the svarasāman(-day)s are on either side of the divākīrtya(-day), thereby, the vital principles are placed in the head.

5. Further, the Viśvajit and the Abhijit are the two vital airs at the end [1], and as to the āyus and go(-days), they (by these) undertake a pairing stoma [2]: for procreation.

[1] Cp. XXIV. 11. 9; perhaps here also the two ears are meant.

[2] Cp. IV. 8. 3.

6. As to the ten days of the twelve-day-period: they, thereby, undertake (practise) the not divided voice: for getting progeny [1].

[1] This is the same as XXIII. 5. 3.

7. As to the (mahā)vrata(-day): (the) vrata is food, food satiates nowhere but in the mouth. In that after (the ten days) they undertake the vrata, thereby, food is placed into the mouth. Therefore, food, placed in the mouth satiates.

8. As to the two over-night-rites, the proceeding and the closing days: with what vital air they begin in that they finish.

XXIV. 15.

(Fifth forty-nine-day-rite.)[1]

1. An over-night-rite (1); nine nine-versed days (2–10), *viz.*, a six-day-period beginning with an agniṣṭoma [1] and then three days: an ukthya in the middle and an agniṣṭoma on either side of it; nine fifteen-versed days (11–19), *viz.*, a six-day-period beginning with an agniṣṭoma [1] and then three days: an ukthya in the middle and an agniṣṭoma on either side of it; nine seventeen-versed days (20–28), *viz.*, a six-day-period beginning with an agniṣṭoma [1] and then three days: an ukthya in the middle and an agniṣṭoma on either side of it; nine twenty-one-versed days (29–37), *viz.*, a six-day-period beginning with an agniṣṭoma [1] and then three days: an ukthya in the middle and an agniṣṭoma on either side of it; the ten days of the twelve-day-period (38–47); a mahāvrata(-day) (48) and an over-night-rite (49).

[1] The five remaining days of these nine days are ukthyas, according to Sāyaṇa, and so also Kātyāyana.

2. By these days, Savitṛ came into the (state of) setting in motion the whole (universe).

3. They who perform this rite come into the (state of) setting in motion the whole (universe) [1].

[1] This seems to be rather thoughtlessly expressed after the model of § 2.

4. In that the stomas, many (in number), occur troopwise: the nine-versed together, the fifteen-versed together, the seventeen-versed

---

[1] Cp. Ārṣeyakalpa IX. 10. d; Nidānasūtra X. 4; Āp. XXIII. 8. 1–3; Kāty. XXIV. 3. 23–25.

together, the twenty-one-versed together, (thereby) these (days) are Savitṛ's highest places.

5. They who perform this (rite) become the highest among their equals and their subjects.

XXIV. 16.

(Sixth forty-nine-day-rite.)[1]

1. An over-night-rite; four abhiplava-six-day-periods; a mahāvrata(-day); two abhiplava-six-day-periods; the ten days of the twelve-day-period (and) an over-night-rite.

2. The seasons found no firm support; by means of these (days) they got a firm support. They who are desirous of (getting) a firm support should perform this (rite). They get a firm support.

3. Six in number are the seasons; in the seasons they by these (days) get a firm support. That the (four) six-day-periods are performed normally, is for (obtaining) accomplishment[1].

[1] For § 2-3, cp. XXIII. 12. 2, 3 and 5.

4. As to the (mahā)vrata(-day): (the) vrata is food, food satiates nowhere but in the middle (of the body); in that they undertake the (mahā)vrata (rite) in the middle, thereby, food is placed in the middle. Therefore, food, when placed in the middle, satiates.

5. That the (last) two six-day-periods are performed normally, is for (obtaining) accomplishment.

6. As to the ten days of the twelve-day-period: they, thereby, undertake (practise) the not-divided voice: for getting progeny. As to the two over-night-rites: the proceeding and the closing day: with what vital air they begin in that they finish[1].

[1] This § is the same as XXIV. 14, 6 and 8.

XXIV. 17.

(Seventh forty-nine-day-rite.)[2]

1. An over-night-rite; six abhiplava-six-day-periods; the ten days of the twelve-day-rite; a mahāvrata(-day) and an over-night-rite.

---

[1] Cp. Ārṣeyakalpa IX. 10. e; Nidānasūtra X. 4; Āp. XXIII. 8. 4-5; Kā ty. XXIV. 3. 26-27.

[2] Ārṣeyakalpa IX. 10. e; Nidānasūtra X. 4; Āp. XXIII. 8. 6-7; Kāty. XXIV. 3. 26–28.

2. By means of these (days, through this rite) Indra and Agni surpassed the other deities. They who perform it surpass the other creatures.

3. Indra and Agni are the most powerful amongst the Gods. They who perform this (rite) become the most powerful.

4. That they undertake the six-day-periods normally arranged, is for (obtaining) accomplishment. As to the ten days of the twelve-day-period, they, thereby, practise the non-divided voice: for progeny. As for the vrata[1]. As for the two overnight-rites: the proceeding and the closing one: by which breath they start, in that same breath they finish.

[1] This is abbreviated; cp. XXIV. 16. 4.

XXIV. 18.

(Sixty-one-day-rite.)[1]

1*a*. An over-night-rite (1); a twenty-four-versed proceeding day (2); three abhiplava-six-day-periods (3–20); a six-day-period with the pṛṣṭha(-sāman)s (21–26); an Abhijit (27); the three svarasāman(-day)s (28–30); the viṣuvat-day (31): the three svarasāman(-day)s (but now in reversed order) (32–34); a Viśvajit (35); a six-day-period with the pṛṣṭha(-sāman)s, beginning with the thirty-three-versed day[1] (36–41): one abhiplava-six-day-period (42–47), the two days āyus and go (48, 49); the ten days of the twelve-day-period (50–59); the mahāvrata(-day) (60) and an over-night-rite (61).

[1] Cp. note 1 on XXIII. 3. 1; this is misunderstood by Hauer in his book 'Der Vrātya,' page 85.

1*b*. This is the sixty-one-day-rite of the Vrātyas, the adherents of 'the God'[1].

[1] On this (uncertain) translation, see note 1 on XVII. 1. 1.

2. The Vrātyas, the adherents of 'the God,' held a sacrificial session with Budha as their Sthapati[1]. They consecrated themselves without having previously begged of King Varuṇa a place for divine worship[2]. King Varuṇa cursed them: 'I preclude you from a share

---

[1] Cp. Nidānasūtra X. 4; Baudh. XVI. 36: 281. 16-17; Āp. XXIII. 8. 8–10; Kāty. XXIV. 3. 21-22.

in the sacrifice. Ye shall not know the path leading to the Gods'. Therefore, they (the others, other priests) do not take sacrificial substance (rice, barley, etc.,) nor (a draught of) soma for them (to sacrifice it on their behalf).

[1] Cp. note 1 on XVII. 11. 6; here the Sthapati seems to occupy the place of the gṛhapati in a sattra.

[2] Which is the usual practice; cp. Ṣaḍv. br. II. 10. 4–10, Baudh. śrs. II. 2 and, especially, Āp. X. 2. 9.—The Vrātyas were not willing to beg a devayajana of Varuṇa, precisely because they were adherents of 'Deva' and not of the usual Gods.

3. Now, at that time there was neither juice in the herbs nor butter in the milk nor fat in the flesh nor hair on the skin nor leaves on the trees, but since the Vrātyas, the adherents of the God, performed this sixty-one-day-rite, since that time all these (*viz.*, herbs, milk, flesh, etc.) were united with these potencies and were full of lustre, full of juice.

4. With regard to this the following verse [1] is handed down.

[1] These ślokas are not recorded in any other source known to us.

5–7. 'As ye often asked (your) sons, the (adherents) of the God: 'What have ye done?' (they answered): 'Mighty was the *dīkṣā* of Budha: it was he who brought the butter into the milk.

'As Budha, the son of Soma, undertook the mighty *dīkṣā*, (then) he did reach the delighted universe, on my flesh did he put the fat'.

'Poor was the cattle, being meagre (and) boneless, (but) at the *dīkṣā* of the son of Soma it was provided with fat' [1].

[1] The verses are not clear throughout and the metre is defective: read, perhaps, in the second: *mahīṃ dīkṣāṃ saumāyano budho yad udayacchata tad ānandat sarvam āpnon manmāṃse medho 'dhād iti.* In the second verse, read *sa kṣīre* instead of *sakṣīre*.

8. So they who are going to undertake this sixty-one-day-rite should, after they have settled down on the place of divine worship, offer a libation in the gārhapatya(-fire) with (the formula): 'God Varuṇa, give us a place of divine worship, *svāhā*!' They (thereby) perform the sacred rite on a given [1] place of worship.

[1] Read (and cp. Sāyaṇa) with the Leyden MS.: *te datte devayajane yajante.*

9. They (the Vrātyas) throve in all ways. They who undertake these (days)[1] (who perform this rite), thrive in all ways.

[1] Read *ya etā upayanti.*

XXIV. 19.

(The hundred-day-rite.)[1]

1. An over-night-rite; the three days: jyotis, go and āyus; fourteen abhiplava-six-day-periods; the ten days of the twelve-day-period; a mahāvrata(-day) and an over-night-rite.

2. The Gods were afraid of death; they resorted to Prajāpati; he gave them, through this (rite) of a hundred days, the immortality. This, forsooth, is man's immortality, that he reaches the normal term of life, that he becomes wealthier. They who undertake this (rite) reach the normal term of life (and) become wealthier[1].

[1] The last sentences are the same as XXII. 12. 2, 3.

3. They press out (the soma and perform the sacrifices of soma of each day) whilst they move forwards each day (to another spot): for the sake of stepping on (their rival); they press out (the soma) on the same spot, for gaining a firm support[1].

[1] This is either an alternative: they may press out the soma and each day settle down on another place of worship, just as at the Sarasvatī-sattras (XXV. 10–12), but without any restriction of place; or they may press out and sacrifice on one and the same devayajana as at the other sattras, without going forth. But there are others who do not regard the words of the Brāhmaṇa as an alternative and who explain them as follows: the havirdhāna-shed and the shed of the sadas should be made so that they stand on wheels and these wheels should be turned around at the end of each soma-day; thereby, both the prescriptions of the Brāhmaṇa are fulfilled: they move forward and they remain! This must be done, according to some authorities, day after day; according to others, during the abhiplava-periods; according to others, on the three days jyotis, go, āyus only (Lāṭy. X. 5. 10–16).

XXIV. 20.

(The sattra of one year.)[2]

1. An over-night-rite; a twenty-four-versed proceeding day. Four abhiplava-six-day-periods; a six-day-period with the pṛṣṭha-

---

[1] Cp. Nidānasūtra X. 5; Lāṭy. X. 5. 9–20; Āp. XXIII. 8. 11–13; Baudh. XVI. 36: 281. 17–282. 2; Kāty. XXIV. 3. 29–35.

[2] This is the ordinary sattra of one year or gavām ayana, described in its

sāmans: this (*viz.*, these five six-day-periods) is a month; in the same manner the second, the third, the fourth and the fifth (month). Three abhiplava-six-day-periods; a six-day-period with the pṛṣṭhasāmans; an Abhijit-day; three svarasāman(day)s; the viṣuvat(day); three svarasāman(-day)s (in reversed order); a Viśvajit(-day); a six-day-period with the pṛṣṭhasāmans beginning with the thirty-three-versed (day)[1]; three abhiplava-six-day-periods. A six-day-period with the pṛṣṭhasāmans beginning with the thirty-three-versed day; four abhiplava-six-day-periods; this (*viz.*, these five six-day-periods) is a month (*viz.*, in the second half of the year); in the same manner the second, the third and the fourth (month). Three abhiplava-six-day-periods; the two days: āyus and go; the ten days of the twelve-day-period; a mahāvrata(-day) and an over-night rite.

[1] Cp. note 1 on XXIII. 3. 1.

2. The brāhmaṇa is that of the year[1] (*i.e.*, of the one-year's sacrificial session).

[1] As given in Chapters IV and V.

Twenty-fifth Chapter.

(The sattras, concluded.)

XXV. 1.

(The 'course' of the Ādityas.)[1]

1. An over-night-rite; a twenty-four-versed proceeding day. Two abhiplava-six-day-periods, consisting alternately of nine- and fifteen-versed days; a six-day-period with the pṛṣṭhasāmans; two (abhiplava-) six-day-periods, consisting alternately of nine- and fifteen-versed days. This is a month (*viz.*, these five six-day-periods constitute a month). In the same manner the second, third, fourth, and fifth month. Three (abhiplava-) six-day-periods, consisting alter-

details in Chapters IV and V; see Ārṣeyakalpa, Einleitung, pages XXIV, XXV (line 9 read: *4 abhiplavāḥ* instead of *3 abhiplavāḥ*) and Eggeling in Sacred Books of the East, Vol. XXVI, page 427.

[1] Cp. Ārṣeyakalpa X; Nidānasūtra X. 6-7; Āp. XXIII. 9. 1-9; Kāty. XXIV. 4. 3-10.

nately of nine- and fifteen-versed days; a six-day-period with the pṛṣṭhasāmans; a nine-versed Bṛhaspatistoma[1]; the three svarasāman (-day)s; the viṣuvat-day; the three svarasāman(-day)s (in reversed order); a fifteen-versed Indrastoma[2] as ukthya. A six-day-period with the pṛṣṭha-sāmans beginning with the thirty-three-versed day[3]; one (abhiplava-)six-day-period, consisting alternately of fifteen- and nine-versed days; the ten days of the twelve-day-period to be performed as independent nine-versed agniṣṭoma-rites; the two days Udbhid and Valabhid[4]. Two (abhiplava-) six-day-periods, consisting alternately of fifteen- and nine-versed days; a six-day-period with the pṛṣṭha-sāmans; two (abhiplava-) six-day-periods, consisting alternately of fifteen- and nine-versed days. This is a month (these five six-day-periods constitute a month in the second half of the year). In the same manner the second, third, and fourth month. An (abhiplava-) six-day-period, consisting alternately of fifteen- and nine-versed days; a six-day-period with the pṛṣṭha-sāmans; six alternately fifteen- and nine-versed days; the two days go and āyus; the Chandoma-ten-day-period, of which the first day in 48-versed, the second 44-versed, the third 40-versed, the fourth 36-versed, the fifth 32-versed, the sixth 30-versed, the seventh and eighth 28-versed, the ninth 25-versed, the tenth 24-versed. Then a mahāvrata (-day) and an over-night-rite[5].

1 Cp. XVII. 11.

2 Cp. XIX. 16.

3 Cp. note 1 on XXIII. 3. 1.

4 Cp. XIX. 7.

5 This year's sattra differs in some respects from the *prakṛti* as described XXIV. 20. 1: the six-day-periods are arranged so that in each month the pṛṣṭhya-six-day-period is enclosed between two abhiplava-six-day-periods, whence this sattra is called *madhyepṛṣṭhya* ('having the pṛṣṭhya-ṣaḍahas in the middle'); cp. § 2. A second point of difference is that the Abhijit and Viśvajit are replaced by Bṛhaspati- and Indra-stoma. A third difference is that the ten days of the dvādaśāha occur in the middle, while they are replaced (at the end) by the *chandomadaśāha*, which, as far as I see, occurs here only.—Cp. Ārṣeyakalpa, page 139, note 9.

2. This is the (sacrificial session) of the Ādityas with the pṛṣṭhya-ṣaḍaha in the middle[1].

1 Cp. note 5 on § 1.

3. By means of the (rite) with the pṛṣṭhya-ṣaḍaha in the middle, the Ādityas occupied the world of heaven. That they undertake (apply) the pṛṣṭhas in the middle is for occupying the world of heaven.

4. The pṛṣṭhas are food; food is, thereby, placed in the middle: therefore, food being brought into the middle (of the body) satiates.

5. The pṛṣṭhas are cattle: they are firmly established in (the possession of) cattle.

6 The two stomas, the nine-versed and the fifteen-versed, are two wheels revolving together. What wish they hope to see fulfilled, that they obtain by this (rite). For wherever he (*i.e.*, one) wishes to go by means of a (car) with wheels, that he reaches[1].

[1] Cp. XX. 13. 2.

7. As to that nine-versed Bṛhaspatistoma, by means of this Bṛhaspati obtained the chaplain-ship of the Gods. They who are desirous of (obtaining) a chaplain-ship should undertake this (rite): they get a chaplain-ship; they make them their chaplains.

8. As for these svarasāman(-day)s, the viṣuvat(-day) is the head, the svarasāman(-day)s are the vital principles; in that the svarasāman(-day)s are on either side of the viṣuvat(-day), thereby, the vital principles are placed in the head.

9. As for the fifteen-versed Indrastoma as ukthya(-rite), by means of this (stoma) Indra surpassed the other deities. They who undertake (apply) it surpass the other creatures.

10. As for these ten days of the twelve-day-period, to be performed as independent nine-versed agniṣṭomas in the middle (of the whole sattra), by these they are freed from evil. These, forsooth are the bed of the Gods. They, thereby, mount the bed of the Gods and become worthy of bed; they reach the bed of a wealthier man[1].

[1] Cp. XXIII. 4. 5, 6, with notes.

11. As for the Udbhid and Valabhid, by means of these Bṛhaspati let loose the cattle for the Gods. By these, they let loose[1] the cattle.

[1] Read *utsṛjante* instead of *utsṛjantaḥ*.

12. As for the go and āyus (day)s, they (thereby) undertake pairing stomas[1]: for progeneration.

[1] Cp. IV. 8. 3.

13. As for the Chandoma-ten-day-period[1], this is a milking of the metres. They apply the metres hitherward[2]; therefore, cows and goats stand near, hitherward turned, whilst they benefit[3].

[1] The days on which the stomas agree with the number of syllables of the metres.

[2] Beginning with the highest and ending with the lowest numbers.

[3] Whilst they are milked. I am not sure that this is the meaning of *bhuñjantaḥ*.

14. As for the (mahā)vrata(day), (the) vrata is food; food satiates nowhere but in the mouth. In that they undertake (apply) the vrata after (the Chandomas), thereby, food is placed into the mouth. Therefore, food, being in the mouth, satiates[1].

[1] This is the same as XXIV. 17. 4.

15. As for the two over-night-rites, the proceeding and the closing day: with what vital air they begin in that they finish[1].

[1] This is the same as *e.g.*, XXIV. 14. 8.

XXV. 2.

(The 'course' of the Angirases.)[1]

1*a*. An over-night-rite; a twenty-four-versed proceeding day. A six-day-period with the pṛṣṭha-sāmans; four nine-versed abhiplava-six-day-periods; this (*viz.*, these five six-day-periods) is a month. In the same manner the second, third, fourth, and fifth month. Three nine-versed abhiplava-six-day-periods; a six-day-period with the pṛṣṭha-sāmans; a nine-versed Bṛhaspatistoma; the three svarasāman(-day)s; the viṣuvat(-day); the three svarasāman(-day)s (in reversed order); a fifteen-versed Indrastoma as ukthya. A six-day-period with the pṛṣṭha(saman)s beginning with the thirty-three-versed day; one nine-versed abhiplava-six-day-period; the ten days of the twelve-day-period to be performed as independent nine-versed agniṣṭomas; the two days

[1] Cp. Ārṣeyakalpa XI. 1–6; Nidānasutra X. 7; Āp. XXIII. 9. 10–16; Kāty. XXIV. 4. 11–15.

Udbhid and Valabhid. Four nine-versed abhiplava-six-day-periods; a six-day-period with the pṛṣṭhasāmans. This (*viz.*, these five six-day-periods) is a month (in the second half of the year). In the same manner the second, third and fourth (month in the second half). Two nine-versed abhiplava-six-day-periods ; a six-day-period with the pṛṣṭhasāmans ; the two days āyus and go ; the Chandoma-ten-day-period, of which the first is 24-versed, the second and third are 28-versed, the fourth is 30-versed, the fifth 32-versed, the sixth 36-versed, the seventh 40-versed, the eighth 44-versed, the ninth 48-versed, the tenth 24-versed. A mahāvrata (-day) and an over-night-rite [1].

[1] Cp. note 2 on page 156 of the edition of the Ārṣeyakalpa.—In contrast to the preceding sattra, where the pṛṣṭhya-ṣaḍahas occur in the middle of the abhiplavas, h e r e the pṛṣṭhyas precede the abhiplavas in the first half of the year whilst they come after the abhiplavas in the second half

1*b*. This is the (sacrificial session) of the Angirases with the (six-day-period with the) pṛṣṭha(sāman)s in front [1].

[1] Cp. note 1 on § 1. a.

2. By means of the (session) with the pṛṣṭhya-periods in front, the Angirases occupied the world of heaven. That they undertake (apply) the pṛṣṭhas in front is for occupying the world of heaven [1].

[1] Cp. XXV. 1. 3.

3. The pṛṣṭha(sāman)s are food ; food, thereby, is placed in the mouth (or : at the beginning) ; therefore, food, being in the mouth, satiates. The pṛṣṭhas are cattle ; they are firmly established in (the possession of) cattle [1].

[1] Cp. XXV. 1. 4, 5.

4. With the exception of (the brāhmaṇa) : 'these two stomas, the nine-versed and the fifteen-versed, are two wheels revolving together' [1] (all is) the same (as previously explained), up to the (brāhmaṇa on the) Chandoma-ten-day-period [2].

[1] See XXV. 1. 6. For this brāhmaṇa here there is no place, as the six-day-periods here are not alternately 9- and 15-versed but all 9-versed.

[2] This refers to XXV. 1. 7–12 (incl.).

5*a*. As for the Chandoma-ten-day period, this is a milking of the metres. They apply the metres tending upward [1]: to avoid falling down. This, forsooth, is the path leading to the Gods. They who perform this (rite) reach the path leading to the Gods.

[1] In contrast to the preceding sattra (XXV. 1. 13); cp. § 1 of this khaṇḍa.

5b. As for the vrata[1].

[1] Cp. note 1 on XXIV. 17. 4.

6. As for the two over-night-rites, the proceeding one and the closing one, with which breath they start in that they finish.

[1] An oft-recurring sentence.

XXV. 3.

(The year's sacrifice of Dṛti and Vātavat.)[1]

1. An over-night-rite: one month with nine-versed days[1], one with fifteen-versed, one with seventeen-versed, one with twenty-one-versed, one with twenty-seven-versed, one with thirty-three-versed: the mahāvrata (day, instead of the viṣuvat): one month with thirty-three-versed days, one with twenty-seven-versed, one with twenty-one-versed, one with seventeen-versed, one with fifteen-versed, one with nine-versed (days); an over night-rite[2].

[1] The construction is elliptic for *trivṛtā māsaṃ yanti*; cp. introductory remark on IV. 1. 1.

[2] The Sūtrakāra, who has noted that this sattra comprises not 360 but 363 days, decides that in this special case a month does not throughout consist of 30 pressing-days but that two of the months must embrace 29 days (the middle day being always regarded as supranumerous). As to which of the months must be shortened, here the authorities are at variance.

2. The seasons found no firm support; by means of this (sattra), they got a firm support. They who are desirous of (getting) a firm support, should perform (it). They get a firm support. Six in number are the seasons. In the seasons they, by this (sattra), get a firm support[1].

[1] This is nearly the same as XXIV. 16. 2, 3. a.

3. In that the mahāvrata(-rite) is performed in the middle, thereby, food is placed in the middle. Therefore, food, being in the middle (of the body) satiates.

---

[1] Cp. Ārṣeyakalpa XI. 7. q; Nidānasūtra X. 8; Lāṭy. X. 10. 7–20; Āp. XXIII. 10. 1–5; Kāty. XXIV. 4. 16–20; Āśv. XII. 3. 1–8; Śāṅkh. XIII. 23.

4. This sacrificial session [1] is winged [2]; what wish they desire to be fulfilled that they reach by this (sattra), for wherever a winged being (a bird) desires to go all that it reaches.

[1] Properly *sattrāyaṇa* means 'undertaking of a session'; usually the term seems to denote a sattra of more than one year.

[2] Because the two parts, before and after the day in the middle, are precisely paralleled.

5. They start with a nine-versed (stoma), they finish with a nine-versed (stoma). The nine-versed among the stomas are the vital principles. By breath they begin, in breath they are firmly established [1].

[1] This is the same as XXIII. 3. 9, XXIV. 3. 4.

6. This (sacrificial session) was [1] (once upon a time) undertaken by Dṛti [2] and Vātavat in Khāṇḍava [3]. At the viṣuvat (-day) [4], Vātavat broke up the session; Dṛti completed it. Therefore, the descendants of Vātavat are fewer; those of Dṛti are more numerous [5].

[1] The present tense is somewhat striking; see Introduction, Chapter III, § 8. b.

[2] He is called the son of Indrota XVI. 1. 12.

[3] Perhaps the same as the famous Khāṇḍava-forest in the MBh.

[4] *viṣuvat* here must mean 'the middle day', which here is a mahāvrata.

[5] From this we must only infer that it is not considered as commendable to leave a sattra unfinished.

XXV. 4.

(The year's session of the Kuṇḍapāyins.) [1]

1. During a month, they live according to the rules for the consecrated (*dīkṣita*); at the (end of this) month, they (perform the prāyaṇīya-iṣṭi and) buy the soma. For them there are twelve upasad (-day)s. After the performance of the upasads, they tie up the soma (to guard it). Then, during a month, they perform (day after day) the agnihotra. During a (second) month, (on the days of the increasing moon) the sacrifice of full-moon, and, (during the latter half of the month), the sacrifice of new-moon. During a (third) month, (they

[1] Cp. Ārṣeyakalpa XI. 7. b; Nidānasūtra X. 8; Lāṭy. X. 11–12; Āp. XXIII. 10. 6–12; Baudh. XVII. 20, 21, XXVI. 25; Kāty. XXIV. 4. 21–47; Āśv. X. 4; Śāṅkh. XIII. 24.

perform) the vaiśvadeva (-cāturmāsya-sacrifice). During a (fourth) month the varuṇapraghāsa. During a (fifth) month, the sākamedha. During a (sixth) month, the śunāsīrya. During a (seventh) month, (they perform) a nine-versed sacrifice of soma. During an (eighth) month, a fifteen-versed. During a (ninth) month, a seventeen-versed. During a (tenth) month, a twenty-one-versed. During an (eleventh) month, a twenty-seven-versed. During eighteen days (of the twelfth month), a thirty-three-versed sacrifice of soma; during (ten days), the ten-day-period of the twelve-day-rite. Then (comes) a mahāvrata (-day) and an over-night-rite.

2. The Ten-hotṛ-formula is (equal to) the agnihotra; the Four-hotṛ-formula is (equal to) the full and new-moon sacrifice; the Five-hotṛ-formula is (equal to) the cāturmāsya(-offering)s; the Seven-hotṛ-formula is (equal to) the sacrifice of soma [1].

[1] Cp. Baudh. XVII. 21 (end).

3. They who undertake this (sattra), sacrifice with the whole sacrifice; they all reach prosperity [1].

[1] *sarva eva bhavanti* (*bhūti*); cp. V. 3. 3.

4. They should all of them drink (the soma-draughts) out of bowl-shaped vessels without a handle [1].

[1] The absence of the handle is one *kuṇḍa*.

5. He who is Hotṛ (at the same time) is Adhvaryu and Potṛ; he who is Udgātṛ (at the same time) is Neṣṭṛ and Acchāvāka; he who is Maitrāvaruṇa (at the same time) is Brahman and Pratihartṛ; he who is Prastotṛ (at the same time) is Brāhmaṇācchaṃsin and Grāvastut; he who is Pratiprasthātṛ (at the same time) is Agnīdh and Unnetṛ. The Gṛhapati is (only) Gṛhapati, the Subrahmaṇya (only) Subrahmaṇya [1].

[1] So each of the officiating priests must be acquainted with three Vedas. This, according to Baudhāyana, is another *kuṇḍa*.

XXV. 5.

(The years-session of the Tapaścits.)[1]

1. During a year, they live according to the rules for the consecrated. During a year, they perform the upasads. During a year, they perform sacrifices of soma.

---

[1] Cp. Ārṣeyakalpa XI. 7. c; Nidānasūtra X. 8; Lāṭy. X. 13; Āp. XXIII. 11. 1-7; Kāty. XXIV. 5. 1-5; Āśv. XII. 5. 11-12; Śāṅkh. XIII. 26.

2. In that they are dīkṣitas during a year, thereby, they bring about the tapas (ascetism); in that they perform the upasads during a year, thereby, they purify themselves; in that they perform the sacrifices of soma during a year, thereby, they go to the world of the Gods.

3. By means of this (sattra), the Gods, gathering ascetism (*tapaścit*), reached all kinds of welfare. They who undertake this (sattra) reach all kinds of welfare.

XXV. 6.

(Twelve-years sattra.)[1]

1. Three years consisting of nine-versed-days; three years of fifteen-versed, three years of seventeen-versed, three years of twenty-one-versed days. (This is) the twelve-years-rite of Prajāpati.

2. By means of this (sattra), Prajapati came into the state of setting in motion the whole (universe). They who perform this (sattra) come into the (state of) setting in motion the whole (universe)[1].

[1] Cp. XXIV. 15. 3, with note.

3. In that three years are nine-versed, the nine-versed (stoma) being splendour and priestly lustre, they obtain splendour and priestly lustre. In that three years are fifteen-versed, the fifteen-versed (stoma) being might and strength, they obtain might and strength. In that three years are seventeen-versed, the seventeen-versed (stoma) being food, they obtain food. In that three years are twenty-one-versed, the twenty-one-versed (stoma) being a firm support, they obtain, at the end of the sacrifice, a firm support.

4. By means of this (sattra), the inhabitants of Naimiśa[1] throve in all possible ways. They who undertake this rite thrive in all possible ways.

[1] The Jaim. br. throughout likewise has it with *ś*, not with *s*.

5. They broke off the sattra, after the seventeen-versed years. They said: 'He who among our progeny will thrive he shall finish

[1] Cp. Ārṣeyakalpa XI. 7. a; Nidānasūtra X. 8; Lāṭy. X. 13; Āp. XXIII. 11. 8-10; Kāty. XXIV. 5. 19; Āśv. XII. 5. 15-16; Śāṅkh. XIII. 28. 5.

this sattra'[1]. Therefore, the Brāhmins perform this sattra, wishing to finish it.

[1] The text should run: *yo naḥ prajāyām ṛdhyātai.*

XXV. 7.

(Thirty-six-years-sacrificial session.)[1]

1. Nine nine-versed years; nine fifteen-versed, nine seventeen-versed, nine twenty-one-versed years. (This is) the thirty-six-years (sattra) of the descendants of Śakti.

2. By means of this (sattra), Gaurīviti, the descendant of Śakti, using meat (not rice or barley) for the sacrificial cakes, reached, at (the bank of) the Yavyāvatī[1], all (kinds of) welfare. They who undertake this (sattra) reach all (kinds of) welfare.

[1] The name occurs once more: ṚS. VI. 27. 6.—On the beginning words, cp. note 1 on XI. 5. 14.

3. This sacrificial session[1] is (equal to) the bṛhatī[2]. The bṛhatī is the rulership among the metres[3]. They who undertake this (rite) reach rulership.

[1] On *sattrāyaṇa*, cp. note 1 on XXV. 3. 4.

[2] The bṛhatī is of 36 syllables and this sattra is of 36 years.

[3] Cp. note 2 on XXIV. 6. 3.

4. This is the (rite) of the descendants of Śakti, which promises ten strong sons. To them, who undertake it, ten strong sons are born[1].

[1] Read, with the Leyden ms.: *aiṣāṃ daśa vīrā jāyante* (*i.e*, *ā eṣāṃ..jāyante*).

XXV. 8.

(Hundred-years' sacrificial session.)[2]

1. Twenty-five three-versed years; twenty-five fifteen-versed; twenty five seventeen-versed; twenty-five twenty-one-versed. This is the sattra of a hundred years of the Sādhyas.

---

[1] Cp. Ārṣeyakalpa XI. 7. d; Nidānasūtra X. 9; Lāṭy. X. 14; Āp. XXIII. 11. 11–14; Kāty. XXIV. 5. 20–22; Āśv. XII. 5. 16–17; Śāṅkh. XIII. 28. 6, cp. also Jaim br. III. 18 under note 1 on XI. 5. 14.

[2] Cp. Ārṣeyakalpa XI. 7. d; Nidānasūtra X. 9; Lāṭy. X. 14; Āp. XXIII. 11. 15–12. 1; Kāty. XXIV. 5. 23; Āśv. XII. 5. 18; Śāṅkh. XIII. 28. 7.

2. Before the (time of the present) Gods, there were (certain) Gods called Sādhyas. These undertook this sacrificial session; through it they throve. Together with their cattle and their people, they all went together to the world of heaven. In the same manner, forsooth, those who undertake this (sattra) go all together to the world of heaven.

3. This sacrificial session is (equal in duration to) the normal life (of man). Man reaches a hundred years. As long as is life that they (the performers of this rite) reach. For no sacrificial session is longer than (the duration of) life[1].

[1] The adjective *atyāyuṣa* is not registered in the Dict. of St. Petersburgh nor by R. Schmidt in his 'Nachträge.'

4. With regard to this, a (verse) occurs (in the sacred texts): 'Those days were numerous that in the east (have risen) at sunrise whence Dawn, approaching, as it were, her lover (the sun), has shown herself as not returning'[1].

[1] This is RS. VII. 76. 3, but cited inexactly with *uṣā* (so read, with the Leyden ms., instead of *ūṣā*) *dadṛśe* instead of *uṣo dadṛkṣe.*

5. They go with (*i.e.*, they perform) a jyotiṣṭoma as sattra: they become a light[1].

[1] The jyotiṣṭoma equally comprises 9-, 15-, 17-, and 21-versed stomas.

[2] Cp. note 1 on VI. 3. 7.

6. The twenty-one-versed (stoma) is at the end of the stomas. The twenty-one-versed (stoma) is a firm support. They are firmly supported at the end of the sacrifice.

XXV. 9.

(The thousand-day-sattra.)[1]

1. An over-night-rite; a thousand days, (and) an over-night-rite[1]. (This is) the thousand-pressings-rite of Agni.

[1] According to some authorities, the two atirātras are implied in the thousand days; cp. note 2 on XXV. 3. 1.—About this sattra and the next following ones, the duration of which exceeds human power and life (they are called *mahāsattras*), the

---

[1] Cp. Ārṣeyakalpa XI. 7. e; Nidānasūtra X. 9; Lāṭy. X. 14. 11–13; Āp. XXIII. 12. 2-3; Kāty. XXIV. 5. 10–14; Āśv. XII. 6. 20–22; Śāṅkh. XIII. 27. 7.

Nidānasūtra remarks: 'As to these big sattras, they are (the sattras) of the Gods: 'the Gods are long-lived'. Another view is that they are accomplishable also for men; a great number of people join themselves for the pressing (and sacrificing) of the soma: (with the fathers) the sons, the grand-sons and great-grand-sons'.

2. By means of this (sattra), Agni came into (the state of) setting in motion the whole (universe). They who perform (it), come into (the state of) setting in motion the whole universe [1].

[1] Cp. note 1 on XXIV. 15. 3.

3. To Agni belongs all food; all food comes to those who undertake this (sattra).

4. As to its thousand sacrificial days: the highest virāj is of a thousand syllables. They are established in the highest virāj [1].

[1] Here *virāj* in the sense of 'splendour'.

XXV. 10.

(The first sacrificial session on the Sarasvatī.)[1]

1. They (the participants of the sattra) undertake the consecration at the place (*i.e.*, to the south of the place) where the (river) Sarasvatī is lost (in the sand of the desert).

2. They should maintain the mode of life of the consecrated during twelve days, and perform the upasads during twelve days [1].

[1] As the first day of the whole rite must fall on the day of new moon (cp. § 3 and 4), the dīkṣā must begin on the sixth (according to others on the seventh) day after new moon, in the pūrvapakṣa.

3 On the day when the (proceeding) over-night-rite takes place, on this day they drive the calves away (from the mother-cows, in order to get the milk for the sāṃnāyya-offering of the day of new moon). When the over-night-rite is completed, they perform the sacrifice of the sāṃnāyya [1].

[1] The libation of sweet and sour milk offered to Indra at the sacrifice of new moon.

4. After the libation of the sāṃnāyya, the Adhvaryu throws a yoke-pin (in easterly direction, from the place where the sacrifice has

---

[1] Cp. Ārṣeyakalpa XI. 8. a; Nidānasūtra X. 10; Lāṭy. X. 15-17; Āp. XXIII. 12. 4-13. 6; Kāty. XXIV. 5. 25-6. 4; Āśv. XII. 1. 1-19; Śāṅkh. XIII. 29. 1-22.— Further, cp. Jaim. br. II. 297-299, in Auswahl No. 156, and TS. VII. 2. 1.

been performed): the spot where it falls down is the (place for the) gārhapatya(-fire). From this spot, he makes thirty-six strides [1] (in easterly direction): this is the (place for) the āhavanīya(-fire).

[1] For the usual distance, cp. Āp. V. 4.3—4.—This act must be repeated after each iṣṭi, because this sattra is performed along the bank of the Sarasvatī.

5. The havirdhāna(-shed) and the sadas and the āgnīdhra(-shed) are wheeled; the sacrificial stake is mortar-shaped at the base, removable (along the ground) and put down (on its new place, fastened with sand) [1]; they do not dig the resounding holes [2].

[1] According to the Sūtra, the *śālā prācīnavaṃśā* and the śāmitra-fire should likewise be provided with wheels. From the vedi, the high-altar and the dhiṣṇya-hearths, they should take some sand for each subsequent place of worship.

[2] They are on each place only traced.

6. During this (now following) half of increasing moon, they (day after day) perform the sacrifice of new moon [1].

[1] On the same devayajana, as it seems.

7. On the day of full-moon [1], they perform a goṣṭoma as ukthya with the bṛhat(-sāman as first pṛṣṭha-laud).

[1] On the last day of the pakṣa mentioned in § 6.

8. When the goṣṭoma is brought to an end, they sacrifice with the full-moon offerings. During this (now following) half of the waning moon, they perform (day after day) the sacrifice of full-moon. On the day of new moon (*viz.*, on the day at the end of this half of the moon), they perform an āyuṣṭoma as ukthya with the rathantara(-sāman as first pṛṣṭha-laud) [1].

[1] From the Sūtra, I gather that now they settle down on a new devayajana fixing its spot by throwing the yoke-pin etc. In the manner as described in §§ 4-8, they move along the southern bank of the Sarasvatī in easterly direction.

9. (This is) the 'course' (the sattra) of Mitra and Varuṇa.

10. By means of this (rite), Mitra and Varuṇa obtained these worlds. Mitra and Varuṇa are day and night: Mitra is the day, Varuṇa is the night. Mitra and Varuṇa are the two halves of the month: Mitra is the increasing, Varuṇa the waning half. This Mitra pours his seed into Varuṇa [1].

[1] Read *varuṇa* instead of *varuṇo.* I fail to see the purport of this last sentence.

11. By means of the Sarasvatī, the Gods propped the sun but she could not sustain it and collapsed; hence it (the Sarasvatī) is full of bendings [1], as it were. Then, they propped it (the sun) by means of the bṛhatī [2] and, thereupon, she (the Sarasvatī) sustained it. Therefore the bṛhatī is the strongest of the metres, for they had propped the sun with it.

[1] The correct reading (as the Leyden ms. has it) must be *tasmāt sā kubjimatīva*.

[2] Why this mention of the bṛhatī?

12. They move against the stream, for it is not (possible) to reach (the term going) along the stream [1].

[1] This seems simply to imply that only by going against the stream of the Sarasvatī, which flows from east to west, can they reach the term (Plakṣa prāsravaṇa) which is situated to the east.

13, 14. They move along the eastern part (of the stream), for at this (part) one single (other stream) flows into (it): the Dṛṣadvatī.

15. At the juncture of the Dṛṣadvatī (with the Sarasvatī), they sacrifice a mess of boiled rice to Apāṃnapāt and, then, cross (this river).

16. At a distance of a journey of forty days on horseback from the spot where the Sarasvatī is lost (in the sands of the desert), (is situated) Plakṣa prāsravaṇa. At the same distance from here (from the earth) (is situated) the world of heaven [1]: they go to the world of heaven by a journey commensurate with the Sarasvatī [2].

[1] For other views on the distance between heaven and earth, cp. XVI. 8. 6.

[2] Read *sarasvatisaṃmitenādhvanā*.

17. By means of this (rite), Namin Sāpya [1], the king of Videha, went straightway to the world of heaven, (thinking:) 'We have gone straightway'. This is the reason why they are called: 'those who have gone straightway' [2].

[1] The name occurs in the ṚS.; *e.g.* X. 48. 9.

[2] The translation of the last words is far from certain; the word *añjaskīya* is not registered in the Dictionary of St. Petersburgh. The plural may denote Namin and his co-sacrificers.

18. He descended for the expiatory bath into that pool, which is situated to the north of Sthūlarma: there his hundred cows had become a thousand [1].

[1] And this is the reason (see § 19) why the sattra may be finished. It is to be observed that for none of these sattras at the Sarasvatī is a precise number of sacrificial days prescribed, as various circumstances may be considered as ending them.

19. To a hundred cows they admit a bull [1]. When these hundred become a thousand, then, this is a reason for breaking up (the session, *i.e.*, for terminating the sacrifice).

[1] The performers of the sattra are to take along a hundred cows and a bull. These they must cause to be fed and to be guarded. The young bulls may serve as food for the performers.

20, 21. Other reasons for terminating the sattra are: when they come to be deprived of all their possessions, (or) when the Gṛhapati dies, (or) when they reach Plakṣa prāsravaṇa.

22. When they reach Plakṣa prāsravaṇa, they perform an iṣṭi for Agni Kāma; at this (iṣṭi) they give away two females: a mare and a slave (with their young) [1].

[1] This gift should be bestowed on another man qualified to accept such a gift; no one of the participants in the sattra is qualified to accept dakṣiṇās, since all are ṛtvij's.

23. At Kārapacava, they descend for the lustral bath into the Yamunā.

XXV. 11.

(Second sacrificial session on the Sarasvatī.) [1]

1. An over-night-rite; a nine-versed and a fifteen-versed day as Indra's and Agni's 'course'; a go- and an āyus-day as the two flanks (the belly) of Indra, (and) an over-night-rite [1].

[1] Probably the meaning is that at this sattra the intervals between the days of full and new moon are filled up with nine-versed and fifteen-versed days (alternately), and that the term *indrakukṣī* designates the days of full and new moon during which successively a go- and an āyus-rite find place. That the *kukṣī* of Indra are pūrṇamāsa and amāvāsyā appears from RV. Khila V. 7. 4. k (ed. Scheftelowitz, page 146): *obhā kukṣī pṛṇatām vārtraghnam ca māghonam ca.*—For the rest, all the prescriptions of the first sārasvata sattra prevail also for this rite.

2. Through this (rite), Indra and Agni surpassed the other deities. They, who undertake it, surpass the other creatures.

---

[1] Cp. Ārṣeyakalpa XI. 8. b; Nidānasūtra X. 10; Lāṭy. X. 18. 1-8; Āp. XXIII. 13. 7-8; Kāty. XXIV. l. c.; Āśv. XII. 6. 9-20; Śāṅkh. XIII. 29. 23-24.

3. Indra and Agni are the strongest of the Gods; they who undertake this (rite) become the strongest.

4. That the nine-versed and the fifteen-versed days are Indra's and Agni's 'course', and that the go- and āyus(-rites) are the belly of Indra, is to avoid oscillating.

XXV. 12.

(Third sacrificial session on the Sarasvatī.)[1]

1. An over-night-rite; the three-day period: jyotis, go, āyus; the Viśvajit and Abhijit as Indra's belly; an over-night-rite[1].

[1] This seems to mean that the intervals between the days of full and new moon are filled up with this ever repeated, three-day-period, and that on the days of full and new moon successively the Viśvajit and the Abhijit are performed; see note 1 on XXV. 11. 1.

2. By means of this (rite), Aryaman gained this world[1].

[1] Read *etena vā aryamaitaṃ*, etc.

3. The path called Aryaman's path is the path leading to the Gods.

4. They who undertake this (rite) reach the path leading to the Gods.

5. Therefore, he appears at day-time[1] rather ruddy[2], for the path of Aryaman is rather ruddy.

[1] Is *divaḥ* to be taken as acc plural?

[2] Apparently, Aryaman here is the sun, as *e.g.*, Śat. br. V. 3. 1. 2.

6. That there is the three-day-period: jyotis, go, āyus (and) the Viśvajit and Abhijit are Indra's belly, is to avoid oscillating.

XXV. 13.

(The sacrificial session at the Dṛṣadvatī.)[2]

1. During a year, he should guard the cows of a Brāhmin; during a (second) year, he should, at Vyarṇa Naitadhanva, kindle his fire (for

[1] Cp. Ārṣeyakalpa XI. 8. c; Nidānasūtra X. 10; Lāṭy. X. 8. 9; Āp. XXIII. 13. 9-10; Kāty. XXIV. 6. 29-31; Āśv. XII. 6. 21; Śāṅkh. XIII. 29. 25-26.

[2] Cp. Ārṣeyakalpa XI. 8. d; Nidānasūtra X. 11; Lāṭy. X. 18. 10-19. 15; Āp. XXIII. 13. 11-15; Kāty. XXIV. 6. 32-44; Śāṅkh. XIII. 29. 27-31; cp. also Jaim. br. II. 300.

domestic worship); during a (third) year, he should, at Parīṇah, consecrate (and maintain, by sacrificing into them), his (sacred) fires (for vaidic sacrifices)[1].

[1] The khaṇḍas 13 and 14 describe two *iṣṭyayanas* which properly do not belong to the sattra-kind but consist of a series of iṣṭis performed each day on a different spot.

2. Then, he should move along the southern bank of the Dṛṣadvatī, throwing (day after day) forward a yoke-pin (and, in this manner, fixing the spot for each subsequent iṣṭi on the next day)[1], sacrificing to Agni a (rice-)cake baked on eight kapālas.

[1] Cp. XXV. 10. 4. The words *śamyāparāsiyāt* contain : *śamyāparāsī iyāt*.

3. Indra and Ruśamā made a wager : 'Whichever of us shall first run round the earth shall be the winner'. Indra ran round the earth, Ruśamā ran round Kurukṣetra (only). She said : 'I have conquered thee'. But Indra said : 'It is I that have conquered thee'. They went to the Gods for a decision. The Gods said : 'Kurukṣetra is as great as the vedi of Prajāpati'. So neither of the two won[1].

[1] This quasi-myth is inserted to prove that such a kind of iṣṭi equals the greatest. For the last sentence but one, cp. TS. II. 6. 4 1 : 'the vedi is as great as the earth.' In the description of the six-day-rites, according to Jaim. br. II. 300 (where these rites, as in TS., are combined illogically with the going along the Śarasvatī), we have a remarkable parallel, but the passage seems to be handed down in a mutilated state : *teṣām u teṣāṃ parīṇad iti kurukṣetrasya jaghanārdhe saraskandantan dīkṣāyai* (so the ms. ; Oertel, in Journal of the American Oriental Society, Vol. XVIII, page 17, changes the reading of the ms. in a parallel passage : *saraskandad etad* into *saraḥ. tad etad*, but the original reading must have been different) ; *te prāñco yanti samayā kurukṣetram ; etad vai devānāṃ devayajanaṃ yat (kuru)kṣetraṃ ; devānām eva tad devayajanena yanti ; teṣāṃ yamunāvabhṛtha, eṣa vai svargo loko yad yamunā ; svargam eva tal lokaṃ gacchanti.*

4. He who goes with the rice-cake destined for Agni (and) baked on eight kapālas, along the southern bank of the Dṛṣadvatī, throwing (each day) the yoke-pin[1], descends, at the locality called 'the three fig trees,' into the Yamunā for the lustral bath. There he disappears from the (eyes of) men[2].

[1] ° *parāsyeti* must be dissolved ° *parāsī eti.*

[2] This is differently interpreted by the Sūtrakāras : according to Dhānañjayya, this course of iṣṭis was destined for one who desires to retire from the world (*pravrajiṣyat*) ; he should not return to the community, but ascend the world of heaven ; or, it means that he becomes separated from the other people and fares better.

XXV. 14.

(The Turāyaṇa, the 'course' of Tura.)[1]

1. A rice-cake destined for Agni and baked on eight kapālas, one for Indra on eleven kapālas, and a mess of boiled rice destined for the All-gods[1].

[1] These offerings replace the single cake of the preceding khaṇḍa. The first cake is sacrificed at the time of the morning-service of an agniṣṭoma; the second, at the time of the midday-service; the last, at the time of the afternoon-service (see § 4), but there are different views about these offerings.—For the rest, all is the same as the rite described in khaṇḍa 13.

2. (Although) not being consecrated (for a sacrifice of soma), he puts on the hide of a black antelope. In that, not being consecrated, he puts on this hide, thereby, he gets the welfare that is of men.

3. In that he gives himself over to ascetism, thereby, (he gets) the welfare that is of the Gods.

4. That there is the cake for Agni on eight kapālas, the deities having Agni at their front, thereby, he at the beginning even wins the favour of the deities[1], but he, thereby, reaches also the morning service. That there is the cake for Indra on eleven kapālas, the midday-service belongs to Indra; he, thereby, reaches the midday-service. That there is a mess of rice for the All-gods, the afternoon-service belongs to the All-gods, he, thereby, reaches the afternoon-service.

[1] On the expression *tad devatā evardhnoti*, cp. Oertel, Disjunct use of cases, page 33.

5. Through this (rite) Tura the God-muni obtained all welfare. He who undertakes this (rite) obtains all welfare.

XXV. 15.

(The sacrificial session of the Serpents.)[2]

1. An over-night-rite at the beginning and the end; agniṣṭoma (-rite)s in the middle; the year[1] consists throughout of tens and tens[2],

---

[1] Cp. Ārṣeyakalpa XI. 8. e; Nidānasūtra X. 11; Lāṭy. X. 20. 1-9; Kauṣ. br. IV. 11; Āp. XXIII. 14. 1-7; Kāty. XXIV. 7. 1-10; Āśv. II. 14. 4-6; Śāṅkh. III. 11. 11-16.

[2] Cp. Ārṣeyakalpa XI. 8. f—10. b; Nidānasūtra X. 12-13; Lāṭy. X. 20. 10-12; Āp. XXIII. 14. 8-9; Kāty. XXIV. 4. 48-49; Āśv. XII. 5. 1-6; Śāṅkh. XIII. 23.

only the middle day (the viṣuvat) is twelve-versed: at the middle day the sāmans of the serpents are applied [3].

1 *saṃvatsari* is an error of the press for *saṃvatsaro*.

2 The reason of 'ten' is apparent: it is a pun on *daśa* 'bite'.

3 The atirātras are with ṣoḍaśin; the agniṣṭomas are alternately of different arrangement (to avoid sameness!), as is seen from Ārṣeyakalpa XI. 8. e and XI. 9. a; the second half of the year consists of the same agniṣṭomas, but now reversed: Ārṣ. k. XI. 9. a and XI. 8. e; the sixth and the twelfth month comprise 29 days, so that, together with the two atirātras, this makes up 360 days (the viṣuvat-day, as usually, not being reckoned).—The fact that in § 3 are mentioned the Abhigara and the Upagara, who appear only at the mahāvrata (see V. 5. 13), makes a difficulty for the Sūtrakāra, as there is no mahāvrata in this sattra. They argue that, as the author of the Ārṣeyakalpa likewise prescribes no mahāvrata, the conclusion is that these two officials must appear at the last day but one, the usual day for the mahāvrata. Śāṅkhāyana prescribes instead of the viṣuvat-day the mahāvrata. In the text of our Brāhmaṇa, the mention of these two officials need not point to a mahāvrata, for it is possible that the list was given as completely as possible.—The ten sāmans of the serpents are registered in the araṇyegeyagāna II. a. 1-10 (see SV. ed. Calcutta, Vol. II, page 417-421), of these ten the first three are intended.

2. Through this (rite), the serpents gained a firm support in these worlds. They who undertake it get a firm support in these worlds.

3. Jarvara (was at this sattra) the Gṛhapati; Dhṛtarāṣṭra, the son of Īravat, was the Brahman; Pṛthuśravas, the son of Dūreśravas, was the Udgātṛ; Glāva and Ajagāva were the Prastotṛ and Pratihartṛ; Datta, the son of Tapas, was the Hotṛ; Śitipṛṣṭha was the Maitrāvaruṇa; Takṣaka, the son of Viśāla, was the Brāhmaṇācchaṃsin; Śikha and Anuśikha were the Neṣṭṛ and the Potṛ; Aruṇa, the son of Aṭa, was the Acchāvāka; Timirgha, the son of Dūreśrut, was the Agnīdh; the two sons of Kutasta, Arimejaya and Janamejaya, were the two Adhvaryus; Arbuda was the Grāvastut; Ajira was the Subrahmanya; Cakra and Piśaṅga were the two Unnetṛs; Ṣaṇḍa and Kuṣaṇḍa were the Praiser and the Reviler [1].

1 This remarkable list of officials, of which some are known as belonging to the Nāgas, is found twice in another source, *viz.*, in Baudh. śrs. XVII. 18 and in Baudh. gṛhs. III, adhyāya 10. In Baudhāyana, the last two are missing, but, as Sadasya, is mentioned Uparīti Tārkṣya, and, as Dhruvagopa, Paśuka (Paśuga). So much is certain, that in this *sarpasattra*, this sattra performed by the serpents, we have to see the prototype of the *sarpasattra* (the sattra, where the *sarpas* are sacrificed) of Janamejaya in the Mahābhārata. According to Baudh., they were the kings and princes of the *sarpas* who at Khāṇḍavaprastha, in human form, performed

this sattra, desirous of obtaining poison. 'Because it consists of ten-and ten (*daśa*) (-versed-lauds), therefore, the serpents are biting' (*daṃśuka*).

4. Through this (rite), the serpents vanquished death. They who perform it vanquish death. Therefore, they (the serpents), having left aside their old hide, creep further, for they had vanquished death. The Ādityas are the serpents. They who undertake this (rite), to their share falls the shining out, as it were, of the Ādityas.

XXV. 16.

(Three-years-sacrificial session.)[1]

1. The first year is the 'course' (the year's sattra) of the cows [1]; the second, is the 'course' of the Ādityas [2]; the third, is the 'course' of the Angirases [3].

[1] As described in Chapters IV and V.

[2] Cp. XXV. I.

[3] Cp. XXV. 2.

2. By this (rite), the cows obtained procreation (and) plurality. They who undertake it obtain procreation (and) plurality. By this (rite), the Ādityas got a firm support in these worlds. They who undertake it get a firm support in these worlds. By this (rite), the Angirases went to the world of heaven. They who undertake it go to the world of heaven.

3. Para, the son of Ahṇāra, Trasadasyu, the son of Purukutsa, Vītahavya, the son of Śrayas, (and) Kakṣīvat, the son of Uśij, these, being desirous of (obtaining) progeny, undertook this 'course' of sattras. They prospered in getting each a thousand sons. In the same manner, they who undertake this (rite) prosper in getting each a thousand sons.

XXV. 17.

(Thousand-years-sattra of Prajāpati.)[2]

1. An over-night-rite; a thousand nine-versed years (and) an over-night-rite. (This is) the thousand-years-sacrificial session of Prajāpati.

---

[1] Cp. Ārṣeyakalpa XI. 10. c; Nidānasūtra X. 13; Lāṭy. X. 20. 13-17; Āp. XXIII. 14. 10-11; Kāty. XXIV. 5. 12-14; Āśv. XII. 5. 6-7.

[2] Cp. Ārṣeyakalpa X. 10. d; Nidānasūtra X. 13; Lāṭy. X. 20. 18; Āp. XXIII. 14. 12-13; Śāṅkh. XIII. 29. 22.

2. Through this (rite) Prajāpati came into (the state of) setting in motion the whole (universe). They who undertake it come into (the state of) setting in motion the whole (universe)[1].

1 Cp. note 1 on XXIV. 15. 3.

3. This (rite) was undertaken by Prajāpati as he was stupefied by old age; by it he repelled old age. They who undertake it repel old age.

4. This is the thousand-years(-sattra) of Prajāpati. Through it, Prajāpati prospered in all ways In all ways prosper they who undertake it.

XXV. 18.

(Thousand-years-rite of the Viśvasṛjs.)[1]

1. Five times fifty nine-versed years; five times fifty fifteen-versed years; five times fifty seventeen-versed years; five times fifty twenty-one-versed years. (This is) the thousand-years-rite of the Viśvasṛjs.

2. By means of this (rite), the Viśvasṛjs created (*asṛjata,*) this whole (*viśva*) (universe). Because they had created this whole (universe), they are called Viśvasṛj.

3. After those who undertake this (rite), the whole (universe) comes into existence[1].

1 This means, according to Śāyaṇa, that they become Lords of the whole (world).

4. Tapas (ascetism) was the Gṛhapati; Brahman (the holy word) was the Brahman (-priest); Irā was the mistress of the house; Nektar was the Udgātṛ; Bhūta (the past) was the Prastotṛ; Bhaviṣyat (the future) was the Pratihartṛ; the seasons were the additional chanters (*i.e.*, they who accompany the chant of the Udgātṛ proper); the Ārtavas (sections of the year) were the Sadasyas. Truth was the Hotṛ; Right was the Maitrāvaruṇa; Might was the Brāhmaṇācchaṃsin; Splendour and Honour were the Neṣṭṛ and the Potṛ; Glory was

---

1 Cp. Ārṣeyakalpa XI. 10. e; Nidānasūtra X. 13; TBr. III. 12. 9. 3-8; Āp. XXIII. 14. 14-17; Kāty. XXIV. 5. 24; Baudh. XVII. 19; Āśv. XII. 5. 19; Śāṅkh. XIII. 28. 8.

the Acchāvāka; Fire even was the Agnīdh: Bhaga (fortune) was the Grāvastut; Food was the Unnetṛ; Voice was the Subrahmaṇya; Exhalation was the Adhvaryu; Inhalation was the Pratiprasthātṛ; Command was the Cutter[1] (of the victim); Vigour was the Dhruvagopa[2]; Hope was the Haviṣyeṣin[3]; Night and Day were the two carriers of fuel[4]; Death was the Slaughterer.—These undertook the initiation (dīkṣā).

[1] There must be some difference between *viśāstṛ* and *śamitṛ*.

[2] Read: *dhruvagopa āśā* °.

[3] Reading and meaning uncertain; the Leyden ms. has *haviṣyeśy* °, the printed text *haviṣyeṣy* ° (he who procures the *haviṣya*, the substance fit for offering).

[4] Read: ° *rātrāv idhmavāhau*.—This list differs in some respects from the one given in TBr. and Baudh.

5. About this, there is this verse:

'The Viśvasṛjs were the first to perform a sacrificial session, as they sacrificed during a thousand years the (soma) that was pressed out. Therefrom was born the Guard of the Universe, the golden Bird, whose name was Brahman'[1].

[1] The same verse with *prathamāḥ* (not *prathame*) is found in TBr. and Āp., and, with more variants, in Baudh.

6. They who practise this (rite) attain to identity of world with Brahman, to equality with him, to unity with him.

7. This is the thousand-years (sacrificial session) of the Viśvasṛjs. Through it, the Viśvasṛjs prospered in all respects. They who undertake it prosper in all respects[1].

[1] Read; *etena vai viśvasṛjaḥ sarvām ṛddhim ārdhnuvant, sarvām ṛddhim ṛdhnuvanti*, etc.

INDEX I.

The sāmans mentioned in the Brāhmaṇa.

tairaścya XII. 6. 11 : grām. IX. 2. 2, composed on SV. I. 346.
tauraśravasa IX. 4. 9 : ar. gā. III. 1. 6 and 5, comp. on SV. I. 298.
traikakubha IV. 2. 10; VIII. 1. 3; XV. 6. 4 : grām. X. 2. 14, composed on SV. I. 389.
traita XIV. 11. 21 : grām. X. 2 : 1, composed on SV. I. 384.
traiśoka VIII. 1. 8; XII. 10. 20; XVIII. 11. 10; XXI. 9. 12 : grām. IX. 2. 35, composed on SV. I. 370.
tvāṣṭrīsāman XII 5. 18 : grām. XVI. 1. 16, composed on SV. I. 547.
dakṣanidhana (maukṣa) XIV. 5. 12 : grām. IV. 1. 24, composed on SV. I. 141.
dāvasunidhana XV. 5. 12 : grām. III. 2. 11, composed on SV. I. 119.
dāśaspatya XIII. 5. 26 : grām. XV. 2. 29, composed on SV. I. 540.
divākīrtya IV. 6. 13, comprising several sāmans.
dīrghatamaso 'rka XV. 3. 34 : ar. gā. I. 2. 4, comp. on SV. I. 558.
devasthāna XV. 3. 28. a : ar. gā. I. 1. 15, composed on SV. I. 239.
dairghaśravasa XV. 3. 24 : grām. II. 1. 6, composed on SV. I. 44.
daivātitha IX. 2. 18 : grām. V. 1. 9, composed on SV. I. 164.
daivodāsa IX. 2. 8 : grām. IV. 2. 32, composed on SV. I. 159.
dyautāna IX. 9. 13; XVII. 1. 6 : grām. VIII. 2. 22, composed on SV. I. 324.
dvaigata XIV. 9. 31 : grām. VII. 2. 1, composed on SV. I. 264.
dharman XIV. 11. 34 : grām. XI. 2. 20, composed on SV. I. 429.
navastobha V. 4. 12 : ar. gā. III. 1. 14, composed on SV. I. 437.
nānada XII. 11. 18; XXIV. 11. 7 : grām. IX. 2. 13, composed on SV. I. 352.
nārmedha VIII. 8. 21 : grām. I. 2. 27, composed on SV. I. 36.
nidhanakāma XII. 9. 11 : grām. IV. 2. 13, composed on SV. I. 152.
niṣedha XV. 9. 11 : grām. XIV. 2. 24, composed on SV. I. 514.
nihava V. 8. 2; XV. 5. 22 : grām. VIII. 1. 36, composed on SV. I. 313.
naudhasa VII. 10. 2; XI. 4. 9; XXI. 9. 12 : grām. VI. 1. 37, composed on SV. I. 236.
padastobha XIII. 5. 21 : ar. gā. I. 2. 25, composed on SV. I. 558.
pārtha XIII. 5. 19 : grām. VIII. 2. 6, composed on SV. I. 316.
pārthuraśma XIII. 4. 18; XXI. 4. 10 : ar. gā. III. 1. 18, composed on SV. I. 409.
pāvamāna ṛṣabha XV. 3. 16 : grām. XII. 2. 3, composed on SV. I. 467.
pāṣṭhauha XII. 5. 10 : grām. XIII. 1. 12, composed on SV. I. 471.
pṛṣṭha XV. 3. 18 : grām. VI. 2. 12, composed on SV. I. 239.

yaṇva XIII. 3. 6 : ar. gā. III. 1. 11, composed on SV. I. 198. etc.
yadvāhiṣṭhīya XV. 5. 25 : grām. II. 2. 26, composed on SV. I. 86.
yaśas XIX 8. 4 ; XIX. 9. 3 : ar. gā. II. 2. 12, composed on SV. I. 270.
yāma V. 4. 11 : ar. gā. III. 2. 3, composed on SV. I. 320.
yāma IX. 8. 4 : ar. gā. IV. 1. 13, composed on ar. ārc. III. 4.
yāma XI. 10. 20 : grām. XVI. 2. 18 (?), composed on SV. I. 559.
yauktāśva XI. 8. 7 : grām. XII. 2. 30, composed on SV. I. 469.
yaudhājaya VII. 5. 12 ; XI. 2. 10 : grām. XIV. 1. 36, composed on SV. I. 511.
rathantara IV. 8. 18 ; V. 1. 15 etc. : ar. gā. II. 1. 21, comp. on SV. I. 233.
rayiṣṭha XIV. 11. 30 : grām. XIV. 2. 2, composed on SV. I. 512.
rājana V. 2. 6 : ar. gā. IV. 2. 19, composed on SV. I. 318.
rāyovājīya XII. 4. 16 ; XXIV. 11. 17 : ar. gā. III. 1. 15 (16), composed on SV. I. 409.
raivata V. 8. 12 ; X. 6. 6 ; XIII. 9. 14 ; XVI. 5. 27 : ar. gā. II. 1. 17, composed on SV. I. 153.
rohitakulīya XIV. 3. 11 ; XV. 11. 6 : grām. IV. 1. 1, 2, composed on SV. I. 129.
raurava VII. 5. 11 ; XII. 4. 23 ; XIV. 9. 15 : grām. XIV. 1. 35, composed on SV. I. 511.
varuṇasāman XIII. 9. 22 : grām. VII. 1. 18, composed on SV. I. 255.
vaṣaṭkāranidhana VIII. 1. 1 ; IX. 6. 1 : grām. VII. 1. 19, composed on SV. I. 256.
vasiṣṭhasya janitra VIII. 2. 3 ; XIX. 3. 8 ; XXI. 11. 3 : grām. VI. 2. 17, 18, composed on SV. I. 241.
vasiṣṭhasya nihava V. 4. 5 : grām. VIII. 1. 36, composed on SV. I. 313.
vasiṣṭhasya priya XII. 12. 9 : grām. IX. 1. 27, composed on SV. I. 344.
vācassāman XII. 5. 12 : grām. XVII. 2. 15, composed on SV. I. 580.
vājajit XIII. 9. 20 : grām. XV. I. 13, composed on SV. I. 517.
vājajit XV. 11. 11 : grām. XVI. 2. 5, composed on SV. I. 554.
vājadāvarī XIII. 9. 12 : grām. IV. 2. 14, composed on SV. I. 153.
vātsa XIV. 6. 5 : grām. I. 1. 16, composed on SV. I. 8.
vātsapra XII. 11. 23 : grām. VIII. 2. 11, composed on SV. I. 317.
vāmadevya IV. 8. 13, 15 ; V. 1. 1 ; etc. : grām. V. 1. 25 ; composed on SV. I. 169.

INDEX II.

Names of Ṛṣis etc.

INDEX III.

Names of localities, streams, etc.

INDEX IV.

Sanskrit and grammatical Index.

INDEX V.

General Index.

ADDITIONS AND CORRECTIONS.

On page xxv, second alinea. A similar reading occurs in some sāmans: SV. I. 51: *maymanā* instead of *majmanā*, SV. I. 52: *ymo* instead of *jmo*, see SV. ed. Calcutta, Vol. I, pages 177, 178. But the Grantha-edition has everywhere with *j*.

Page xxv, l. 18, read "Bloomfield."

Page xxvi, l. 9, read "Lāṭyāyana."

Page 65, line 18, read ṚS. X instead of IX.

Page 66, line 9 from bottom, read Āśv. VIII instead of VII.

Page 197, line 5 from bottom, read: there are three uktha(-laud)s.

Page 202, line 23, read ṚS. III. 51.

Page 203, line 18, read ṚS. VIII. 13. 1–3

Page 226, line 13, read *sadaso.*

Page 238, line 14 from bottom, read *pratīcī.*

Page 277, line 10, read ṚS. VIII. 70. 5-6.

Page 306, line 3 from bottom, read SV. II.

Page 307, line 5, read Śāṅkh. śrs. IX. 5.

Page 312, line 5, read ṚS. VI. 60. 7–9.

Page 467, line 7, read *656.*

Page 521, line 5 from bottom, read Jaim. br. II. 141, 142.